A GENEALOGY AND HISTORY

OF THE

CHUTE FAMILY IN AMERICA

WITH SOME ACCOUNT OF THE FAMILY IN

GREAT BRITAIN AND IRELAND

WITH AN ACCOUNT OF FORTY ALLIED FAMILIES GATHERED FROM THE MOST AUTHENTIC SOURCES

BY

WM. E. CHUTE

And my God put it into my heart to gather together the nobles, and the rulers, and the people, that they might bereckoned by genealogy. NEH. VII: 5.

The man who feels no sentiment of veneration for the memory of his forefathers; who has no natural regard for his ancestors or his kindred, is himself unworthy of kindred regard or remembrance.
DANIEL WEBSTER.

SALEM, MASS.
1894

This scarce antiquarian book is included in our special *Legacy Reprint Series*. In the interest of creating a more extensive selection of rare historical book reprints, we have chosen to reproduce this title even though it may possibly have occasional imperfections such as missing and blurred pages, missing text, poor pictures, markings, dark backgrounds and other reproduction issues beyond our control. Because this work is culturally important, we have made it available as a part of our commitment to protecting, preserving and promoting the world's literature. Thank you for your understanding.

To my children, brothers, sisters and cousins, their children and grand-children, this volume is dedicated, hoping and praying that under God a study of the work will be an incentive to greater acts of diligence in this life, a help to that life everlasting in the world to come. W. E. C.

Swampscott, Mass., July 9, 1894.

INTRODUCTION.

The Chute family in America is not a record of one who "came over in the Mayflower and fought in the battle of Bunker Hill," nor the account of "three brothers" that came over, but rather the history and genealogy of a humble school master, who came over early to Massachusetts, whose descendants emigrated to Maine and Nova Scotia, and latterly to the South and to the far West.

As every author assumes his book needed, the author of this book assumes; first, that it is needed to show the origin of the family name; second, to show the lines and lineages; third, to show where the different families branch off; fourth, to show the different generations and degrees of relationship; fifth to settle disputes that arise concerning relationships; and sixth, to preserve the records from the "tooth of Time and rasure of oblivion."

The name Chute is of Norman French origin, and means a descent, as down a slope, a sluice, or down from an elevation as by a parachute. By some the name is said to be derived from the name "Jutes."

One author says that Baron Edouard LeChute commanded a company or regiment of French troops in the battle of Hastings, Oct. 14, 1066, which victory put William the Conqueror on the throne of England, from whom, tradition says, the whole family, bearing the name, have descended. The name is among the first surnames used in England.

But our authentic history commences with Alexander Chute, lord of the manor of Taunton, Somersetshire, England, who died in 1268.

His COAT OF ARMS was: *Gu.* three swords, barwise,[*] points to the dexter, ar. pommels and hilts or, within an orle of mullets of the third; on a canton, per fesse, ar. and vert, a lion of England.

CREST: A gauntlet ppr. holding a broken sword ar. pommel and hilt or.

MOTTO: Fortune de Guerre. (Fortune of War.)

Philip Chute, of Appledore, standard bearer to Henry VIII, obtained a recompense for his gallant services at the seige of Bologne, in 1544, an augmentation to his armorial bearings, gu. semé of mullets or three swords

---

[*] The middle sword should encounter the other two, by being turned contrawise.

barwise ppr. the middlemost encountering the other two; a canton perfesse ar. and vert, theron a lion of England: *Crest* same as Chute of Somerset.

In 1827 another addition was made for Wiggett-Chute: *Arms*; quarterly, 1st and 4th CHUTE, gu. three swords barwise, the points toward the dexter, ppr pommels and hilts or; 2d and 3d WIGGETT, ermine, three mullets, two and one, az. pierced gu. on a chief, waring, sa. a dove, reguardant ppr.

CREST OF CHUTE: A dexter cubit arm, in armor, the hand in a guantlet, grasping a broken sword in hand, sinister, ppr. pommel and hilt or.

CREST OF WIGGETT: A griphon's head, couped, sa. holding in the beak an ear of wheat, ppr. between two wings ar. each charged with a mullet gu.

MOTTO: Fortune de Guerre.

PEDIGREES.

Pedigree of the Chutes in England. No. 1.

1. ALEXANDER, lord of the manor of Taunton, Somersetshire; d. in 1268. Left two sons.
2. i JOHN, 1274, m. Jane, daughter of Sir John Brumfield, Kt. ii *Richard*.
3. CUTHBERT, in time of Edward II, 1308, m. Christian, da. of Sir John Chideake, Knt.
4. i JAMES, m. da. of Richard Grenfield. ii *Philip*, in time of Edward III, 1332, m. da. of Sir John Britton, Kt. iii *Anthony*, m. Anne Treforth.
5. i GEORGE, son of Philip, 1344; m. da. of Theo. Tirrell. ii *Joane*, m. Sir John Carmine, Kt.
6. AMBROSE, m. Anabell, da. of Sir John Chichester, Kt.
7. EDMOND, 1379, m. Dyonice, da. of Henry Stourton. ii *Christian*, m. Ralph Menell.
8. i WILLIAM, m. da. of Archdeckne. ii *Henry*, ab. 1420; m. Joane, da. of Edward Baskerville. iii *Anthony*, m. da. of Sir John Clifton, Kt., and had Christopher of Dorsetshire; m. Amancha, da. of Richard Wellgrove, Esq. iv *Robert* Sergeant at Law, and baron of the Exchequer in time of Henry VI, d. 1435.
9. i ROBERT, ESQ., of Taunton. 1438, son of Henry, m. Alice, da. of Morrice Barkley, Esq. ii *Anne*, m. Sir John Scutley, Kt.
10. CHARLES, 1480; m. da. of Sir John Cheney, Kt.
11. EDMOND, of Sussex, sold the manor of Taunton to Lord Denham, 1502.
12. ROBERT, m. Jane, da. of John Lucas.
13. i OLIVER, m. da. of Redd, of Kent. ii *Charles*, m. da. of John Cripps, of the Isle of Thanet. iii *Lyonell*, m. da. of John Butler. iv *William*, m. da. of John Badlesmere, of Tonbridge.
14. i ANTHONY, of Kent, son of Charles, m. da. of Girling, of Suffolk. ii *Philip*, of Appledore, in Kent, m. Margaret, da. of Alex. Culpepper, of Bedgeberry; m. 2nd Joane, da. of Thomas Dussing, of Winchelsea in Sussex.
15. i CHRISTOPHER. ii *William*. iii *Arthur*, m. Elizabeth, da. of Henry See of Herne in Kent. iv *Lyonell*, m. Susan, da. of Stephen Greene, made his will July 24, 1592, to which Arthur Chute, gent. was a witness, and it was proved Aug. 1, 1592.
16. i LIONEL, JR., b. ab. 1580; m. ab. 1610, Rose, da. of Robert Barker, had two sons and a da. Came to Ipswich, Mass. ab. 1634, taught school there, 1636, and d. 1645. His wife m. in 1646, Matthew Whipple, son of Matthew. ii *George*, m. ——— ———. iii *Sarah*, m. Mr. Greenlawn, three children. iv *Cleave*, m. ——— ———. v *Judith*, m. John Adkinson or Edmondson and had seven children. vi *Grace*.

Pedigree No. 2.

15. GEORGE CHUTE, of Bethersden, Kent, son of Philip of Appledore; m. Elizabeth, da. of —— Gage, of Bentley, in Kent.
16. i SIR GEORGE CHUTE, of Stockwell, Surry, knighted July 11, 1660; m. Ann, da. of Sir Martin Barnham, of Hollingborne, Kent, Kt., and had George, m. Joane, da. of Walter St. John, of Lidyerd, Somerset, Bart and Battersey, and had Joane, m. Sir Peter Soames of Heyden in Essex, Bart. She was living in 1696. Margaret, before George, d. y. Sarah, after, m. Sir Ro. Parker, o Ratton, Sussex, Bart. Le Neve's Pedigrees of Knights, Vol. III, p. 91, edited by George W. Marshall, LL D., 1873. ii *Sir Walter, Kt.* iii *Edward, Esq.* m. Lydia, da. of Tho. Gibbon, of Bethersden.
17. i GEORGE, son of Edward b. 1611; m. Eleanor, da. of Nicholas Toke, of Godinton, and was of Surrenden in Kent. ii *Edward.* iii *Philip.* iv *Elizabeth.* v *Lydia.*
18. EDWARD, Esq., of Bethersden. m. Elizabeth, da. of Sir Basil Dixwell of Brome. Bart, by Dorothy, da. of Sir Tho. Peyton, Bart, of Knowlton.
19. i ELIZABETH, m. Sir Jacob Oxenden, Kt. ii *Eleanor,* d. S. P. iii *George,* m. Cecilia, da. of Ralph Freke of Harrington, Wiltshire, and d. 1675. iv *Eleanor.* m. William Gerard.
20. i SIR GEORGE CHUTE, son of George, b. 1663, created a Baronet 1684; d. S. P., Feb 4, 1721, and devised his estate to Edward Austen Esq., the Chute title being extinct. ii *Cecilia,* b. 1663; d. 1675. Partly from "Extinct and Dormant Baronetcies of England,, Ireland and Scotland," by John Burke Esq., and John Bernhard Burke, Esq. of London, 1844.

Pedigree No. 3.

16. CHARLES CHUTE, barrister of the Middle Temple, son of Arthur and cousin to Lionel jr., who came to America, was a member of Parliament for Thetford in Norfolk, living in 1634; m. Ursula, da. of John Challoner, of Fulham a cousin to Sir Thomas Challoner, who having been tutor to Henry, Prince of Wales, son of James I, for whom Bramhill in Hants, was built, is commemorated by a fine monument in Cheswich church.
17. CHALLONER CHUTE, b. ab. 1595, spent his childhood at Kensington, where hi younger brother Charles was b. in 1600; and his sister Dorothy in 1603; th entries of whose births in the register of the Mary Abbotts, Kensington were in Latin, while those of less dignified persons were in the vulgar tongue He had also a brother Alexander, and sisters Maria and Jane, who married John Bolles, of Osberton, in Nollingham. Challoner was admitted student of the Middle Temple, Nov. 11, 1613, as *Caroli Chewte,* and was called to th bar May 23, 1623. He was appointed to conduct one of the earliest of thos experiments for the registrations of titles and sales of land, which hav never ceased to exercise the ingenuity of law reformers down to the present time. Challoner Chute purchased The Vine—a celebrated country-seat in

Hants Co., between Hampshire and Berkshire, of Lord Sandys, grandson of Sir Walter Sandys. who m. Edith, da. of Sir John Cheney, of Sherland, in the Isle of Sheppy, and was sheriff of Hampshire in 1497, in which year he d. having charged his debts by will on his personal property at Andover and The Vyne—in 1649 to 1653. That beautiful place was settled by the Romans, in the 2d or 3d century, and was held by the family of Sandys from Richard II, to 1650. Challoner Chute, m. Ann, da. of Sir John Skory, of Hertfordshire, Kt., June 14, 1627; and they had Anne, Challoner and Scicilia. The latter m. into the family of Henry Barker, of Chiswick, of whom there is a striking portrait, dated 1615, aged 79, at the Vyne. He m. 2d, Dorothy, da. of Dudley, 3d, Baron North and widow of Richard Lennard, 13th Baron Dacre of Hurstmonceaux. He pled earnestly for the bishops, and the royal cause, and was presented a valuable silver tankard by John, Bishop of Rochester, as a reward for so doing. He was elected treasurer of the Middle Temple in 1655; Knight of the Shire for Middlesex 1656 and 1658; and upon the assembling of Parliament under Richard Cromwell, Jan. 29, 1659, he was unanimously chosen speaker of the House of Commons. The French ambassador, M. de Bordeaux, wrote home in February, that Parliament elected its speaker who is one of the most celebrated lawyers in the nation, and there appeared to be no opposition to his election. He d. Apr. 14, 1659, greatly lamented by all, even in America. His wife Dorothy survived him.

). CHALLONER CHUTE, JR., in 1654, m. Catharine Lennard, da of Lord and Lady Dacre; he was elected to Parliament, member for Devizes, 1656 and later on for the city of Westminister. He d. in 1666, aged 36. They were of the Royalists, and were great, good, pious and honest. Their wisdom and judgment—especially the father—were extraordinary.

). i CHALLONER, d. single 1685. ii *Edward*, 1686, m. Catharine Keck, widow of Ferdinand Tracy. iii *Elizabeth*, m. Sir Charles Cotterell. iv *Thomas*, m. Elizabeth Rivett, da. of Nicholas, of Brandeston, Suffolk, 1687, and the Vyne came into possession of his descendants some time after on account of no male descendants from his elder brothers. Edward was high sheriff of Hampshire, 1699, and d. Apr. 18, 1722.

). i EDWARD JR., d. y. 1722. ii *Challoner*, d. 1705. iii *Anthony*, b. 1691, member of Parliament for Yarmouth, Isle of Wight, 1734, d. 1754. iv *Francis*, a chancery barrister, d. 1745. v *John*, b. 1701, succeeded Anthony at the Vyne, 1754; High Sheriff of Hampshire, 1757; d. May 26, 1776. vi *Mary*, d. single. vii *Catharine*, m. Thomas Lennard Chute, cousin, and d. S. P. viii *Margaret*, d. single. ix *Ann*, d. S. John Chute was made acquainted with Horace Walpole and Thomas Gray, who had completed their studies at Eaton and Cambridge, and were travelling on the Continent. Gray parted with Walpole in 1741, and took as his companion John Chute. That year, Walpole, being in the House of Commons, supported John Chute's brother Francis, as a candidate for Parliament. In 1742, Walpole was introduced to John's other brother, Anthony, and expressed satisfaction at having seen and got acquainted with the three. He described John's temperance habits Aug. 20, 1743, as commendable and better than his Norfolk neighbors, Gray admired John the most of anybody, and held correspondence with him for more than twenty years. In 1762 Gray wrote to Chute about taking the professorship of Modern History at Cambridge, but Gray got it himself in 1768, and Chute Chute speaks of shedding skin after the gout, and lively as an eel a week after. Gray died July 30, 1771, a. 55, and Walpole wrote to Chute soon after deploring the sad news. Walpole d. 1797, a. 80.

20. The children of Thomas and Elizabeth (Rivett) Chute were: i *Thomas Lennard*, m. his cousin Catharine. ii *Devereaux*, d. single in 1724. iii *Elizabeth*, m. Thomas Lobb; he m. 2nd, —— Hare. iv *Ann*, m. P. Elwin, and d. S. P.

21. ELIZABETH CHUTE and Thomas Lobb had: i *Thomas*. ii *Elizabeth*, m. John Ellis. iii *Ann*. iv and v *William* and *Henry*. The son Thomas, b. Sept. 19, 1721, added Chute to his name, and his mother's cousin, John Chute, bequeathed to him the Vine estate, Nov. 4, 1774, Thomas Lobb-Chute, m. Ann Rachel, da. of Wm. Wiggett jr., mayor of Norwich, 1753, and assumed the surname and arms of Chute, of the Vnye, and d. 1790, a. 69, and was buried at Pickenham; as his wife was before him.

22. i THO. WIGGETT CHUTE. ii *Ann Rachel*, m. Sir Wm. Hicks, Bart of Whitcomb Park, Gloucester. iii *Elizabeth*, d. 1805. iv *Challoner*, d. 1790. v *William John*, of the Vine, m. 1793, Elizabeth, da. of Joshua Smith, of Stoke Park, Wilts, and d. S. P., 1824; he was born 1757, educated at Harrow and Clare Hall, Cambridge, succeeded to the Vine, 1790; entered Parliament that year, as a member for Hampshire, and had a park of fox-hounds, with which he went hunting with eleven other persons, including the Duke of Wellington. The Duke wrote to William in 1820, desiring to known when he was going out with the hounds that he might go along. He was a sober, temperate man, and on the death of William Pitt, in 1806, he was unseated; but was re-elected in 1807. vi *Mary*, d. soon. vii *Jane*, d. single. viii *Mary*, m. Wither Bramston, of Oakley Hall, Hauts, and d. S. P., 1832. ix *Catharine*, d. soon. x *Rev. Thomas Vere Chute*, of the Vyne and Pickenham Hall, Rector of South Pickenham and Moulton, St. Michael's, Norfolk. He d. single, 1827, a. 55. Ann Rachel, da. of Ann Rachel (Chute) Hicks — the rightful heir — m. Sir Lambert Cromie, Irish Bart, against the wishes of her uncles, so the estates fell to Wm. Lyde Wiggett, Esq.,[4] (Rev. Thomas Wiggett,[3] James,[2] William[1]), high sheriff 1832, M. P., for Norfolk, A. M., Oxford, Barrister at Law, b. June 16, 1800; M. P., for West Norfolk 1837, as owner of Pickenham Hall; after this he sold his Norfolk estate and resigned his seat in 1847.

23. WILLIAM LYDE WIGGETT CHUTE.—having taken the surname arms and title— became the proprietor of the Vyne; which he enriched and improved with pictures, statuary, furniture, etc., very finely. He m. June 1837, Martha, da. of Theophilus Russell Buckworth, Esq., of Cockley Cley Hall, Norfolk, and lived at the Vine from the death of Elizabeth, w. of Wm. John, 1842, till his death July 6, 1879. His brothers and sisters were: i *Anna Maria*, m. Roger Western. ii *Frances*. iii *Mary Ann*. iv *Emeline*, d. 1831. v *Rev. James Samuel*. vi *Caroline*. vii *W. L. W.*, the name now treated of.

24. i CHALONER WILLIAM, ESQ., b. Aug. 1, 1838, of the Vyne, Basingstoke, Southampton, Co., J. P. M. A. Oxford, Barrister at Law, etc., is a bright scholar, called to the bar at Middle Temple, June 1865; m. Eleanor, da. of Wyndham

Portal, a family of French extraction, Apr. 6, 1875, and have Charles Lennard, b. 1879; John Chaloner b. 1881; Rachel Eleanor. ii *Devereaux Wiggett*, b. Dec. 20, 1839; m. Mary, da. of Capt. Hunter, and have Maud and Norah. iii *Charles Thomas, Lieut. R. N.*, b. Aug. 17, 1841, d. 1867. iv *Edward Russell*, b. July 11, 1846, m. 1874, Nina Mary, da. of F. Firth, Esq., and had Fred Russell, and Edward Lennard. v *Theophilus Dacre*, b. June 10, 1852. vi *Lennard Buckworth*, b. 1855, d. 1872. vii *Arthur John Lyde*, b. 1857. viii *Elizabeth Martha*. ix *Emeline Mary*. x *Georgianna Fanny*. xi *Maria Esther*.

It is necessary here to explain that Lionel Chute, the first to America, brought over with him a parchment roll, containing the Chute lineage and pedigree from Alexander[1] to about 1700, which was deciphered by Dean Dudley and John W. Deane, and published in the Gen. Reg. of 1859; but by age and dampness (being in Lionel's chest, see his will), much of it was very imperfect, so we have followed more closely Wm. Berry's Berkskire and Hampshire Pedigrees. This same roll was copied by Amelia (Parish) Perkins, page 23, and so two or three persons in the family have copies of it.

The first instance of the spelling *Chewte* we find in Challoner W. Chute's History of the Vyne, 1888, when Challoner Chute was admitted student of the Middle Temple, in 1613, as *Caroli Chewte*. But like many other names in America, it has several spellings.

The original Chute Arms have been augmented or empaled with the names of Britton, Sturton, Chichester, Barkley, Lucas, Culpepper, and Baker. The following items are taken from various books published in London.

Sir Wm. Hicks,[8] 7th Bart, b. 1754, (Sir Howe,[7] Howe,[6] Sir Michael,[5] Sir Wm.,[4] Sir Michael,[3] Robert,[2] John,[1] of 1557), m. Ann Rachel, da. of Thomas L. Chute, 1793, and had Ann Rachel, m. Sir Lambert Cromie, Bart, living in 1831.

Baptist Hicks 1627—1634. Sir Baptist Hicks, of Campden, Gloucester, kntd July 3, 1603, a bart, 1620, will proved Nov. 19, 1629, upon his death the title became extinct.
— *Wm. Barry's, Hampshire Pedigrees.*

He beareth Gules, three swords extended barways, their points towards the Dexter part of the escutcheon *argent*, the Hilts and Pomels *Or*, by the name of *Chute*, and is the bearing of *Chaloner Chute* of the *Vine* in Hampshire, Esq., a worthy successor of his father's vertues, who was a gentleman of much eminence and knowledge in his practice of the laws.

Gules, three swords Barways, the middle with its point to the Dexter, the other to the Sinister Argent, Hilts and Pomels *Or*, within an orle of Mullets of the *Third*, on a Canton *per Fess Argent* and Vert a Lyon of *England*, is the coat of Sir George

Choute of Bethersden in the County of *Kent* Baronet. I believe the Canton is an augmentation.
— *John Guillim (1565–1621).*

She beareth two coats impaled: the first Gules, Semy de Mullets, Or, three swords barways proper, the middlemost encountering the other two; a Canton per *Fess*, Argent and Vert, thereon a Lion of *England*, by the name of Chute. The Second Argent, a Cheveron, Gules, between three *Flowers de Lis*, Sable by the name of *Dixwell*; which coats were thus impaled by *Elizabeth*, daughter of Mark Dixwell, of Brome in *Barham* in *Kent* Esq., late wife of *Edward Chute*, of *Surrenden* in *Bethersden*, in the said County Esq.
— *John Guillim's Display of Heraldry, London 1724.*

Elizabeth Smith,[4] (Joshua,[3] John,[2] James,[1] before 1800), m. Wm. Chute of the Vine, Co. Hauts, Esquire, Barry's County Genealogies.

Wither Bramston,[5] (Edward,[4] John,[3] Mondeford,[2] Sir Mondeford,[1] d. 1679), 1753-1832, m. Mary, da. of Thomas L. Chute, 1783.

Margaret Colepeper,[7] (Sir Alex,[6] Sir John,[5] Walter,[4] John,[3] Sir John,[2] Sir John,[1] of Bay-Hall, Kent), wife of Philip Choute.

Sir Walter Waller,[8] (Wm.,[7] Wm.,[6] John,[5] Richard,[4] Richard,[3] John,[2] Thomas,[1] before Henry VI), m. Ann, widow of Philip Choute. Esq.

Lydia Gibbon,[5] (Thomas,[4] Thomas,[3] Thomas,[2] ——[1]), m. Edward, 3d brother of Sir Walter Choute, Kt.

John Taylor, jr., m. Elizabeth, da. of Philip Chute, of Bethersden, Esq., 1st wife.

Sir James Oxenden (Sir Henry), knighted 1671, m. Elizabeth, da. of Edward Chute, Bethersden, Kent, d. S. P.

Thomas Knatchbull,[11] (Sir Norton,[9] Richard,[8] John,[7] d. 1540, Wm.,[6] Richard,[5] Richard,[4] Thomas,[3] Thomas,[2] John,[1] ab. 1400), m. Ann, da. of Edward Chute.

Anne Barham, m. Sir George Chute of Salop, Kt., ab. 1600.

Margaret Hussey,[3] (Thomas,[2] Thomas [1]), m. Lawrence Cole; m. 2nd, George Chute, of Surrey.
— *County Genealogies, by Wm. Berry (1774–1851).*

In Wilts Co., England is the parish of Chute, where the records commence in 1582, of which place Walter Millard was vicar in 1591; also Chute Lodge, Mayhill, Hauts, (1659) Chute Forest, (1663) etc.
— *Collectanœ, Topographica and Genealogica, Vol. VIII, 1843.*

John Cowlfax, of Willingham, Suffolk, in his will of May 20, 1569, mentions a brother Arthur Chute.

John Fry, of Come St. Nicholas, Somerset, gent. Will dated Jan. 2, 1635, proved Nov. 20, 1638, by Dorothy Fry, the relict. My kinsman Robert Chute and Julian his wife.
— *Abstract of Somerset Wills, Rev. Fred Brown, M. A. F. S. A. 1888.*

John Perry of Gerbertson, in West Buckland, Somerset gent., will dated Mar. 3, 1581, proved May 3, '82, by John Perry. My wife Elizabeth £100; to Jane Lancaster, my wife's kinswoman, 100 marks; my sister Agnes' children, Henry and John Chute, Mary Popham, my god-daughter, £10; John Perry of Ninehead Flory 40/. My brother-in-law. Mr. Wm. Lancaster an angel of gold; his children, Thomas Roger, Edward, Thomasine and Mary. My brother John Perry of Halse and Robert his son. To Mr.

COATS OF ARMS.

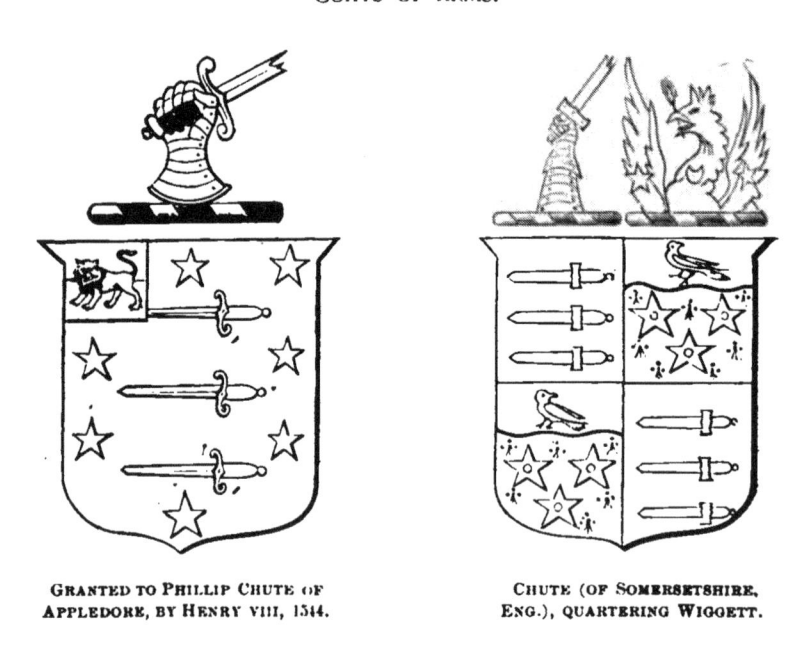

GRANTED TO PHILLIP CHUTE OF
APPLEDORE, BY HENRY VIII, 1544.

CHUTE (OF SOMERSETSHIRE,
ENG.), QUARTERING WIGGETT.

The Coat of Arms of Lionel Chute of Ipswich, N. E., was similar to the first and fourth quarter of the right hand illustration.

John Popham, Attorney general £20. To Mr. Nicholas Wadham, Esq., "one payre of new sylke stockings in grayne." To Mrs. John Francis of Combe Flory "a short gowne furred throughout with callaber." To Mr. Robert Freke Esq., £5. My cousin Mr. John Lancaster, "a new satin doublett." Somersetshire Wills 1887.

Richard Tylden, Esq., purchased the manor and advowson of Milstead, Kent Co., of John Chute, Esq., of Bethersden, Sept. 19, 9th of Charles 1, 1634.

— *Article on the Tilden Arms N. E. Hist. and Geneal. Reg. 1868.*

Certificates from Edward Chute and others, of emigrants in the Hercules, of Sandwich, Mar. 4, 1634, Gen. Reg. Vol. XV.

He probably accompanied Lionel Chute to the ship when he embarked for America.

Anthony Chute published "Beautie Dishonored," 1593, the only copy of which is in the British Museum.

Pedigree of the Chutes of Ireland, No. 4.

1. GEORGE CHUTE, probably a grandson of Philip Chute, of Appledore, stated to have been of the Kentish family, was a military officer, went into Ireland during the rebellion of Desmond, 1578, and obtained grants of land near Dingle, which were soon, however, alienated. He m. Miss Evans, of Cork Co., and had a son.
2. DANIEL CHUTE, who acquired, in marriage with a da. of —— McElliglott, the lands of Tulligaron, since called Chute Hall, which were afterwards, with others since disposed of, confirmed by patent, 1630, under which they are now held. He left (besides a da. m. to —— Crosbie, Esq.), a son and successor.
3. RICHARD CHUTE, ESQ., of Tulligaron, Kerry Co., m. to a da. of —— Crosbie, of Tubrid, and was succeeded by his son.
4. EUSEBIUS CHUTE, ESQ., of Tulligaron; m. Mary, sister of Mr. Justice Bernard, of the Court of Common Pleas, in Ireland, ancestor of the Earls of Bandon, and had: i *Richard*, his heir. ii *Francis*, Collector of Tralee, d. S. P. iii *Pierce*, ancestor of the Chutes of Tralee. iv *Rev. Arthur*, d. single.
5. RICHARD CHUTE, ESQ., of Tulligaron, m. Charity, da. of John Herbert, Esq., of Castle Island, Kerry Co., and had: i *Francis*, his heir. ii *Richard*, of Roxborough, Kerry Co. iii *Margaret*, m. George Rowan, Esq., of Rahtany. iv *Agnes*, m. John Sealy, Esq., of Maglass. v *Catharine*, m. Cornelius McGillicuddy (McGillicuddy of the Reeks).
6. FRANCIS CHUTE, ESQ., of Tulligaron, or Chute Hall, m. 1791, Ruth, da. of Sir Riggs Falkiner, Bart., of Anne Mount, Cork Co., and d. 1782. Ch.: i *Richard*, his heir. ii *Falkiner*, Capt. of 22d Light Dragoons, m. Anne, da. of Capt. Goddard, of Queens Co., and left a da. Catharine, m. Wm. Cooke, Esq., of Retreat, near Athlone. iii *Caleb*, Capt. 69th, Foot, m. Elizabeth, da. of Theophilus Yielding, Esq., of Cahir Anne, Kerry Co. iv *Francis Bernard*, m. Jane, da. of John Rowan, Esq., of Castle Gregory, and had Francis Bernard and Elizabeth. v *Arthur*, m. Frances, da. of John Lindsay, Esq., of Lindville, Cork, and d. Mar. 8, 1863, having had Rev. Francis, d. many years ago: Rev. John, d. Jan. 6, 1871; Frances, d. Sept. 1874; Ruth, d. Sept. 1875, and

GENEALOGIES OF THE CHUTE FAMILY.

Anne. vi *Margaret*, m. Thos. Wm. Saunders, Esq., of Sallowglen, Kerry Co., and is d. vii *Ruth*, m. Thomas Elliot, Esq., of Garrynthenavally, Kerry, and d. Sept. 1875.

7. RICHARD, ESQ., of Chute Hall, b. 1763; High Sheriff, 1786; m. 1785, Agnes, da. of Rowland Bateman, Esq., of Oak Park; she d.; he m. 2d, 1798, Elizabeth, da. of Rev. Wm. Maunsell, D. D., of Limerick. Ch.: i *Francis*, his heir. ii *Rowland, Esq.*, of Lee Brook, near Tralee, Capt. 58th Reg't, m. Frances, da. of James Crosbie, Esq., of Ballyheigue Castle, M. P. for Kerry; 2 sons, 2 das.; he d. Jan 12, 1854; his elder son, Richard Rowland, J. P., succeeded to Lee Brook. iii *Laetitia*, m. Wm. Raymond, Esq., of Dromin, Kerry, and is d. iv *Ruth*, m. Wm. Cooke, Esq., of Reteat, near Athlone, and d. Nov. 20, 1862. v *Agnes*, m. Richard Mason, Esq., of Cappunhame, Limerick, and is d. SECOND FAMILY. vi *Wm. Maunsell*, m. —— da. of Rev. Mr. Nash, of Bally, near Tralee, had children and d. Mar. 15, 1850. vii *Richard, M. D.*, of Tralee, m. Elizabeth Rowan, of Rathtamy, and d. Sept. 14, 1856; leaving Richard, George and Rowena. viii *Elizabeth*, m. Rev. Robert Wade, of Tralee; d. Nov. 10, 1862. ix *Dorothea*, m. Wm. Nelligan, Esq., of Tralee, and is dead. x *Margaret*, d. Sept. 1813.

8. FRANCES CHUTE, ESQ., of Chute Hall, m. Feb. 13, 1810, Mary Anne, da. of Trevor Bomford, Esq., of Dublin; he m. 2d, Arabella, da. of Rev. Maynard Denny, of Churchill, brother of Sir Barry Denny, Bart., of Tralee, M. P. for Kerry; he m. 3d, Penelope, da. of R. T. Herbert, Esq., of Cahirnane, and d. Aug. 12, 1849. Ch.: i *Richard*, his heir. ii *Rowland*, d. Aug. 1851. iii *Sir Trevor, K. C. B.*, b. 1815, m. 1868, Ellen, eldest da. of Samuel Brownrigg, Esq., of Aukland, New Zealand; entered the British army 1832, and now for many years a Major General, and Commander-in-chief of the Australian Colonies, late Col. 70th Foot, Aukland, New Zealand, Army and Navy Club, etc. iv *Mary*, m. Wm. Harnett, Esq. SECOND FAMILY. v *Arthur*. vi *Francis*, Lieut. 70th Regiment. vii *Arabella*. viii *Penelope*, d. Nov. 28, 1863.

9. RICHARD CHUTE, ESQ., of Chute Hall, b. May 22, 1811; m., Oct. 18, 1836, Theodora, da. of Arthur Blenerhassett, Bart., of Blennerville; he m. 2nd, Mar. 3, 1847, Rose, da. of Thomas Townsend Arenberg, Lord Ventry; and d. Sept. 13, 1862. Ch.: i *Francis Blennerhassett*, his heir. ii *Arthur Rowland*, 90th Reg't, b. Dec. 20, 1838; d. Feb. 23, 1858. iii *Melicint Agnes*, m., Apr. 30, 1867, Robert Leslie, Esq., of Tarbet House, Kerry Co., and have ch. iv *Helena Jane*, m. Nov. 30, 1875, Capt. Francis Ogilvie Fuller, of the 101st Regt; and d. Sept. 19, 1876. SECOND FAMILY: v *Thomas Arenberg*, b. Oct. 14, 1853. vi *Richard Trevor*, killed in the battle of Tel el Kebir, July, 1881. vii *Mary Anne*, m., Nov. 1879, M. Thaha, and have ch. viii *Theodora Eliza*. ix *Rosa*. x *Frances Ruth*, d. Aug. 10, 1871. xi *Erneley Arabella*.

10. FRANCIS BLENNERHASSETT CHUTE, ESQ., of Chute Hall, and Blennerville, Kerry Co., b. 1837; m., 1869, Cherry Herbert, eldest da. of Norcott D'Esterre Roberts, Esq., of Dublin. Ch.: i *Richard Arenberg*, b. 1870. Mr. Chute was High Sheriff in 1863, and Lieut. of a Kerry Reg't of Militia.

From Sir Bernard Burke (1815–1892), in his "General Armory" 1878, and "Genealogical and Heraldic History of the Landed Gentry of Great Britain and Ireland," in vo vols. 1886.

OF CHUTES IN AMERICA, NOT OF THE MAIN FAMILY.

Noah Chute is reported of in New Jersey about 1660-70.

Another family is in Athens Co., Ohio. Andrew J. Chute was in the 31st O. V. I., in Sherman's army.

Another family is in Cumberland Co., Me. We well remember two brothers, Freedom and James, in Casco, south of Naples, in 1857. They were two respectable farmers, out of a family of thirteen children of Moses and Ruth (Mosher) Chute; Moses was the son of George and Olive (Brown) Chute; and George was a son of Wm. Shute who m. Hannah Carter in Scarboro 1751. It appears that about the time of the American war, they changed the name from Shute to Chute.

In the Salem Register of October 1806, is recorded the marriage of Jeremiah M. Chute to Betsy Gavet, farther than this we know nothing.

Besides these are some Chutes from Ireland. James Henry is one in South Boston. John J., is one in Neponset, south of Boston. Saw one in New York city in 1880. Another in Chicago in 1870. John Chute was in Rochester, Minn., time of the late war.

Robert and Elizabeth (Higgins) Chute, live in Cleveland, O. They came over fom Ireland to Canada in 1862, lived in Strathroy, Middlesex Co., two years, thence to Pennsylvania, and then to Cleveland, Ohio. He was the son of Isaac and Margaret (Manny) Chute, of Cork, who was the son of Thomas Chute of Tralee, 1770.

Mr. James Chute lives in Utica, N. Y., son of Harry and Nellie (Murphy) Chute, of Grange, Meade Co., Ireland. Harry's children were James, Mary, Bridget, Katharine and Michael. Harry's parents were Patrick Chute and Katie Monohan, and they had Thomas, John, Patrick, Harry and Mary.

Among the British soldiers in America, in the days of George II, was Lieut. Eusebius Chute of the 9th regiment, commission dated July 14, 1759.

Peter Chute, injured by a disaster on the cars of the N. Y. & N. E. R. R., the first of September 1893, died at Hartford, Ct., worth $100,-

000. He left $12,000 to a Mrs. Boyce at Burnley, Lancashire, England; and the balance to a sister, Mrs. Frank Duffey, in Mass., and a brother in New South Wales.

I gratefully acknowledge the kindness of the following named persons who with scores of others have rendered material aid and encouragement.

Dea. Israel Chute; John Hankinson; Frank Aug. Chute; Mrs. Naomi Potter; Judge Savary; Wm. A. Calnek; Mrs. Susan R. Goucher; Mrs. Taylor, the centenarian; Rev. Obed Chute; Charles E. Banks, M. D.; Tristram F. Jordan[6] (Joseph,[5] Rishworth,[4] Samuel,[3] Dominicus,[2] Rev. Robert[1]); Joseph Foster[8] (Joseph,[7] Joseph,[6] Joseph,[5] Jeremiah,[4] John,[3] Reginald,[2] Reginald[1]); James C. Peabody[7] (James,[6] Josiah,[5] Samuel,[4] Francis,[3] Isaac,[2] Francis[1]); Walter Wheelock; Elias Grimes, Esq.; Mrs. Ann S. Woodworth; Fenwick W. Harris; James Gates; Mrs. Eunice M. Bennett; Robert J. Farnsworth; Wm. P. Brechin, M. D.; Edward J. Forster, M. D.[8] (Jacob,[7] Jacob,[6] Jacob,[5] Jacob,[4] Isaac,[3] Reginald,[2] Reginald[1]); Frank E. Woodward[8] (Samuel,[7] James,[6] Samuel,[5] James,[4] Robert,[3] Benjamin,[2] Walter[1]); Joseph C. Foster, D. D.[7] (Moses,[6] Moses,[5] Jonathan,[4] Caleb,[3] Abram,[2] Reginald[1]); Perley Derby; Alfred Poor; Ira J. Patch (1835-1894); Rev. G. M. Bodge[7] (John A.,[6] Thomas,[5] Benjamin,[4] John,[3] Benjamin,[2] Henry[1]); Mrs. Cynthia McConnell; Mrs. Charlotte Baker; A. M Haines; Elder Richard Chute; Moses F. Farnsworth[7] (Reuben,[6] Reuben,[5] Reuben,[4] Reuben,[3] Jonathan,[2] Matthias[1]); Mrs. Clarissa Harris; Mrs. Eliza Felch; Gertie A. Marshall; Arthur Dodge, Esq.; Geo. E. VanBuskirk; Williams Woodworth; Dea. Brown Thurston; S. W. Morse; Rev. Charles L. Woodworth[7] (Charles,[6] Charles,[5] Jonathan,[4] Stephen,[3] Isaac,[2] Walter[1]); Mrs. Susan Easter; Thos. A. Morse; Charles H. Woodworth; Wm. and Hannah Banks; Mrs. Hannah R. Healey; Mrs. Cath. Winchester; Gilbert Roach; Rev. A. P. Chute; Dea. N. VanBuskirk; Henry Watkeys; John B. Newcomb[8] (Obediah,[7] William,[6] Peter,[5] Hezekiah,[4] Simon,[3] Andrew,[2] Andrew.[1]

In seeking the information for making up the volume a few have treated the work with contempt, thus proving that

"Where ignorance is bliss 'tis folly to be wise."
— *Thomas Gray, 1716-1771.*

Another class were afraid of investigation lest they might find some of low repute, illustrating the sentiment

"Be ignorance thy choice where knowledge leads to woe."
— *James Beattie, 1735-1803.*

A third class puffed up with egotism and arrogance have proved that

"By ignorance is pride increased
Those most assume who know the least."
— *John Gay, 1688-1732.*

But while these three classes together make a very small minority, we are proud to say that the masses in general are interested in learning and knowing their origins and history; and we venture the statement that in 1850 not more than 100 volumes of genealogy were published while now there are 2000. And while we express thanks to many for their assistance and patronage, we will say right here that any persons, whose families we have sketched, may use these sketches as foundations to build upon, should they conclude to write up their full family histories.

A FEW EARLY DATES IN AMERICAN HISTORY.

As an aid to a better understanding of the Chute Genealogies a list of early discoveries and settlements in North America are given, chiefly in Massachusetts and the New England States.

America first discovered by Norsemen or Norwegians about the year 1000.

America rediscovered by Christopher Columbus, 1492.

First settlement in the United States, St. Augustine, Fla., 1565, by Spaniards.

Sir Francis Drake visited California, and with his chaplain, Francis Fletcher, priest of the Church of England, held religious service at Drake's Bay, June 24, 1579.

Santa Fe, New Mexico, settled, 1582.

First landing on Arcadia (Nova Scotia), 1583.

Virginia named by Sir Walter Raleigh, 1584.

Potatoes taken to England by Sirs Francis Drake and Walter Raleigh, 1585.

Cape Cod discovered by Bart. Gosnold, 1602.

Capt. DeMonts traversed the coasts, 1603, 1604.

Capt. Champlain named St. John River, N. B., in honor of St. John's Day, June 24, 1604.

Acadia settled by the French, under DeMonts, at Annapolis, first called Port Royal, 1604.

Virginia settled by the English at Jamestown, 1607; resettled by Sir Walter Raleigh (1552–1618), 1616.

Quebec, Canada, settled by the French, 1608.

Hudson River, discovered by Capt. Henry Hudson (1560–1611), 1609.

First settlement in New Brunswick, at the mouth of St. John River, by Edmund Masse, Frenchman, 1611.

Mt. Desert, off the coast of Maine, settled, 1613.

New Amsterdam (New York), settled by Dutch, on Manhattan Island, 1613.

Block Island discovered by Capt. Adrain Block, 1614.

New Jersey settled by Dutch and others, 1614, 1615.

Plymouth, Mass., by English, first settlement in New England, the 101 immortal Pilgrims, over from Leyden, Holland, and Southampton, England, 1620, in the Mayflower.

Acadia changed to Nova Scotia, by Sir Wm. Alexander, a Scotchman, 1621.

Weymouth, Mass., settled, 1622.

Fort Orange (Albany, N. Y.), by Dutch, 1622.
Dr. Richard Vines, Saco River, Me., 1623.
Dover and Portsmouth, N. H., 1623.
Pemaquid Point, Me, 1625.
Barbadoes, West Indies, by English, 1625.
Dutch purchase Manhattan Island, 1626.
Salem, Beverly and Boston, 1626.
Charlestown, Marblehead and Manchester, 1628.
Richmond's Isle, Me., by Walter Bagnall, 1628.
Lynn and Swampscott, 1629.
York, Me., by Gov. Edw. Godfrey (1584-1664), 1629.
Braintree, Cambridge, Dorchester, Medford, Roxbury, Watertown and Nowell; and Biddeford, Me., 1580.
Kittery, Me., and Newton, Mass., 1632.
Portland, Me., by Geo. Cleeve and Richard Tucker, 1632.
Machias, Me., by Dr. Richard Vines, 1633.
Ipswich, Scituate and Hingham, Mass., 1633.
Malden, Mass., Cumberland, R. I., by Wm. Blackstone, and St. Mary's, Md., 1634.
Concord, Dedham, Newbury and Springfield, Mass., 1635.
Hartford, Saybrook, Weathersfield and Windsor, Ct., 1635.
First Public School, Boston, 1635.
Harvard College, Cambridge, by Rev. John Harvard (1605-1638), founded 1636.
Providence, R. l., by Rev. Roger Williams, Lyme, Ct., and Deerfield, Mass., 1636.
Duxbury, and Taunton, Mass., 1637.
Sudbury, and Wayland, Mass., 1638.
Exeter, and Hampton, N. H., 1638.
Milford, and New Haven, Ct., and Newport, R. I., 1638.
Wilmington, Del., by Swedes, 1638.
Aquidneck Island, R. I., by Wm. Coddington, 1638.
Wenham, Salisbury, Rowley, Gloucester, Reading and Barnstable, Mass., 1639.
Fairfield, Guilford and Stratford, Conn., 1639.
Connecticut Constitution, first by the American people, 1639.
First printing press, at Cambridge, 1639.
First American book published, "The Bay Psalm Book," 1640.
Framingham, Marshfield, Woburn, and Haverhill, Mass., 1640.
Farmington, and Greenwich, Ct., 1640.

CONCERNING THE ARRANGEMENT OF THE GENEALOGY.

The Roman numerals tell the number in the generation, and the figures right after tell the number of families thus far traced. See page 27. VI, 10, means the sixth generation, and the tenth family thus far disposed of. The numbers on the left-hand margin are taken up and attended to in their order farther on; so you find 10 on page 20 attended to on page 27. Where a daughter married one of the same name, and had a family, a reference is made to the husband's number, as in two instances on page 32. The same references are in the allied families, and generally are to be found in the "Chute" part of the book.

When surnames are referred to, they speak for themselves.

The following abbreviations have been used: —

a. for aged.
ab. for about.
b. for born.
da. for daughter.
d. for died.
d. y. for died young.
d. s. p. for died without issue.
D. C. for Dartmouth College.
m. for married.
H. C. or H. U., Harvard College, Harvard University.
w. for wife or widow.

In the state or province where the parents lived or settled the children are supposed to have settled also, unless otherwise stated.

WM. E. CHUTE.   MRS. SARAH ANN HARRIS.   MRS. SUSANNA WEBB.

CHUTE GENEALOGIES.

1 Lionel Chute, jun., the emigrant ancestor of the family in America, was born in Dedham, Essex county, England, about 1580; married, about 1610, Rose, daughter of Robert Baker, or Barker.[1]

Children:

2 i JAMES, b.—; bapt. Feb. 2, 1613.
   ii NATHANIEL, b. about 1616; d. in America about 1640.
   iii MARY, bapt. Nov. 23, 1619.

Mr. Chute came over about 1634 and settled at Agawam or Ipswich, in Essex county, province of the Massachusetts Bay, so called. He had received a good education in England and was therefore qualified to teach the grammar school at Ipswich, which he did in 1636, and hence is called the old Ipswich schoolmaster. He bought two parcels of land of William Bartholomew in 1639; 60 acres of upland and 12 acres of meadow were granted him in 1640; made freeman, 1641; made his will in 1644. He died April, 1645.

WILL OF LIONEL CHUTE.

The fourth day of the seventh month Anno Dom: 1644. I Lionell Chute of ye town of Ipswich, in New England, School-master, doe make & ordayne this my last will & testament revoking all former wills by me made.

Item. I give unto Rose, my wife, for terme of her naturall life, all this my dwelling house, with the barne & all the edifices (the two chambers over the house & entry only excepted which I will that James my sonn shall have to his only use for the terme of one yeare next after my decease, with free ingresse egresse & regresse, &c), with the yards gar-

---

[1] Joshua Coffin said, in 1857, that Lionel Chute, jun., married Rose, daughter of Samuel Symonds, Lieutenant-Governor, of Massachusetts, and after the death of Lionel she married Mr. Baker, a merchant; but we find no such personage in the Symonds family, and moreover Samuel Symonds (1595–1678), was only Deputy Governor, 1673–1678.

dens the home lott & planting lott purchased of Mr. Bartholomew, with the commonage & appurtenances thereto belonging: & after my wife's decease I give the said house barne lotts & premises with all the appurtenances unto James Chute my sonne & to his heirs.

Item. I give unto my said sonne James & to his heirs forever all & singular my other lands, lotts, meadow grounds, marshes with all & singular their appurtenances & profit whatsoever immediately after my decease: & I give more unto James Chute my sonne (over & above all things before given him), my heffer that is now at Goodman White's farme, & my young steere.

Item. I give him all my books with all things in my chest, & white boarded deep box with lock & key, one chain four hogsheads two coomsacks two flock bedds two feather pillows one rugg 2 coverletts two blankets my casting nett my silver spoone all my own wearing apparell & that which was his brother Nathaniel's & three pairs of sheets three pillow beeres two table cloths four towells six table napkins & the one half of the brass & pewter & working & five bushels of English wheate.

Item. I give unto my friend Joseph Morse five shillings.

Item. I give unto the poore of the church of Ipswich twenty shillings to be distributed by the deacons.

Item. My meaning is that my wife shall have my chest after that James hath emptied it.

Item. All the rest of my goods household stuff cattell & chattells whatsoever unbequeathed (my debts & legacies being discharged & paid), I will that Rose my wife shall have ye free use of them for terme of her life, but the remainder of them at the time of her decease over & above the value of five pounds sterling I give unto James Chute my sonne & to his heirs & assigns.

Item. I make Rose my wife executrix of this my last will & testament & in witnesse that this is my deed I have hereunto set my hand & seale in the presence of these witnesses hereunder written,

Lionel Chute.

Marke Simonds
Joseph Morse.

The 7th of the 9th month 1645; Affirmed upon oath in Court that this is the last will & testament of Lionell Chute, by Marke Simonds & Joseph Morse.

The Inventory of the goods & chattells of Lionell Chute of Ipswich, deceased: taken this 25th of the 4th month 1645.

	lbs	S	D
Imprimis One cowe	5	0	0
Item one yearling heifer	1	10	0
It one two yearling heifer	3	0	0

ie yearling steere	1	10	0
ie calfe		15	0
gotes	2	5	0
hoggs & piggs	3	10	0
) bushels of wheate	7	6	8
bushels of rie	1	6	0
) bushels of Indian corn	5	15	0
ie casting nett		13	4
pair of boots & 4 pair of shoes	1	10	0
:mp dressed and undressed	1	4	0
bushels of mault		8	0
? sacks & baggs	1	10	0
yards of linsey wolsey		16	8
haulbert		6	8
ro hair lines & 3 sives		4	6
hogsheads		8	0
ie rope		5	0
chests & 3 boxes	1	2	0
ather bed & bolster	3	10	0
feather pillows	1	5	0
ie flock bed & one flock pillow		13	4
ie pair blankets		9	0
ro coverletts & an old rugg	2	0	0
ie old pair of curtains & rodds		10	0
:dstead mat & cord		14	0
flock beds & 2 flock bolsters	1	0	0
ather pillow		5	0
ne pair of blankets & one coverlett	1	0	0
:dstead & line		4	0
yards of yard wide tyking		16	0
? pair of sheets	10	0	0
pillow beers	1	0	0
table cloths	1	10	0
e dozen napkins		12	0
towells & one yard kerchief		10	0
ie short coarse table cloth		1	6
iirts		10	0
s wearing apparell	12	0	0
:oks parchments & other things in a chest	2	0	0
yards of holland		7	0
ne old danakell coverlett		5	0
ewter dishes small & great 14, salts, saucers, poringers 11, chamberpotts 2, one ile pot	2	0	0

It dozen alcany spoons		3 4
It 2 great kettles, 2 smaller kettles, & one brass pan	3	0 0
It 4 skillets, one scumer & ladle		6 0
It two iron potts, old ones		8 0
It frying panns		4 0
It one trevitt, 2 pairs cobirons, tongs & fire pan, 2 trammels 2 pr of pot hooks, one spit	1	12 0
It one silver spoon		6 0
It 2 broad howes & 2 narrow hoes		8 0
It one broad axe, three narrow axes, one hatchet, 2 froes		13 0
It 2 augurs, one gouge, 2 chisels one shave one sickle		5 0
It one beetle & six wedges		10 0
It one spade one mortar & pestle		9 0
It 2 paire of bellows		2 6
It one bible & other books in ye hall	1	0 0
It one great boarded chest		10 0
It 3 chairs and other lumber		6 0
It two pewter candle sticks one pewter bottle		8 0
It one powdering tubb 2 beere vessels one cowle		8 0
It one flock bed, 3 flock bolsters	1	0 0
It one rugg 2 blankets 2 coverlets	1	10 0
It one bedstead matt & cord		10 0
It 3 ladders & pitchforke		5 0
Owing to several persons out of the estate		10 0

Taking out the debts the total sume remaining is eighty-four pounds eleven shillings & four pense,

Mark Symonds, Robert Lord.

II. 2 James Chute (*Lionel*), born in Dedham, Essex county, England, 1613, brought with his parents to this continent, 1634; married, about 1647, Elizabeth, daughter of Daniel Epps and Martha Read.

Child :
3. 1 JAMES.

James Chute, sen., received a good education and was often called upon to sign and witness deeds and other legal documents in Ipswich. His wife was also a good scholar, and she too was called upon to sign her name on several important occasions. In 1645, James Chute was allowed a bill to take a bushel of Indian corn of the constable's for two sheets of parchment for the town's use. He was styled Register of Deeds about that time.

James Chute was a commoner in 1648 and was allowed one shilling town bounty for a fox that year and the same at another time.

Samuel Symonds, jr., made his will Sept. 22, 1653, in which he willed his brother, Harlakinden, his land in Wenham and four of his best bands; to his brother John, £3, 10 s.; to his brother Samuel and to his sisters, Martha, Ruth and Priscilla, and to his nephew, Samuel Epps, 20s. a peece; to his sister, Mary Epps, peece of Holland cloth; to Killignesse Rosse, his chest with the lock and key; to his brother Samuel, all his books; to Rebecca Ward, 5s.; to his brother William (his executor), all his land at Chebacco and Ipswich, etc. In presence of James Chewte   Elisab Chewte.

proved Jan. 28, 1654.

Robert Lord, Cleric.

Thomas Maning of Ipswich sold a small lot to John Woodman, Aug. 13, 1653, witnessed by James Chewte. A similar instrument, same year, is witnessed by James Chewte, and speaks of John Appleton, Reginald Foster and John Woodman. Other similar instruments were witnessed or signed by James Chute, Samuel Symonds and Daniel Denison nearly every year from 1650 to 1660.

Apr. 2, 1656. John Hull of Newbury, yeoman, in consideration of divers legacies, etc., sold to Edward Woodman, jr., of Newbury, yeoman, about 400 acres, with a large stock of horses, cattle and hogs; subscribed, sealed and delivered in the presence of James Chute, Henry Short, Elisab Chute.

James Chute was one of the selectmen in 1654, '61, '64 and '78.

Feb. 28, 1655. Theophilus Wilson sold to Joseph Jewett 32 acres of upland for £16, witnessed by James Chute, John Gage.

Mar. 3, 1658. Samuel Younglove of Ipswich, butcher, sold to Philip Fowler, clothmaker, a six acre lott that he bo't of Geo. Palmer, lying & being within the common field on the north side the river, having ye land of James Chute towards the Northwest & north east, the land of Wm. Averill toward the southeast & other lands of the said Philip toward the southwest.

Mar. 16, 1663. Henry Kingsbury of Rowley, planter, for £4.10, sold to Thomas Harris of Ipswich, fisherman, a portion of the marsh called the hundreds, bounded by the marsh of James Chute towards the north and of John French towards the south, of John Rogers towards the west, towards Plumb Island River, &c. Witnessed by Jer. Belcher, Daniel Hovey, James Chute, Robert Lord, Clerk.

Aug. 29, 1663. John Bishop and wife Rebecca, of Newbury, sold to Peter Cheny for £250, a mill and mill property upon the little river between Nich. Noyes and Capt. Wm. Gerish, a grist mill in Newbury. Witnessed by Anthony Somerby, Hugh Marsh, Samuel Symonds.

Oct. 17, 1663. John Wiate of Ipswich, yeoman, sold to John Edwards, husbandman, for a pair of oxen 5 acres of the great marsh, called the hundreds, bounded on the south side by the lands of Simon Tuttle of Ipswich, on the east side joining to the lands of James Chute, on the northeast side bounded by the land of John Whipple, jr., and on the northwest side by the land of Samuel Younglove.

Feb. 3, 1665. Wm. Bulkly of Ipswich, shoemaker, for eighty pounds, sold to Henry Bridgham of Boston, tanner, 16 acres in Ipswich, within the common field on the north syde the river, the land of Thos. Tredwell toward the south & East, having the marsh of Robert Pearce toward the north, & the land of James Chute toward the west.

1665. James Chute owned a share in Plumb Island, Castle Neck, and Hog Island.

Sept. 13, 1673. James Chute sold to Aron Pengry for £24, two lots —a six acre lott & a three acre lott—in Ipswich within the common field on the north syde the river, bounded by the land of Samuel Bishop & Philip Fowler toward the South & West, the land of Robert Lord & Henry Ossborne toward the north, & Thos. Smith toward the east. James Chute, jr., with the consent of his father in the presence of Robert Lord, sen., & Joseph Lord, Daniel Denison.

Aug., 1675. Samuel Simons died. Inventory taken soon after.

Sept. 23, 1675. James Chute is credited with military service under Capt. Jonathan Poole, to the am't of £1, 10, 10, Narragansett No. 1.

Apr. 21, 1676. Samuel Symonds to Edward Bragg, sold land in Ypswich, in the presence of James Chute and Wm. Smith.

Dec. 11, 1678. The two James Chutes — senior and junior — took oaths of allegiance.

Mar. 20, 1682–3. James Chute sold to Thos. Medcalf, 9 acres of Plumb Island, bounded by marsh of Thos. Clark on ye South & South West, next Plumb Island river fourty five rod in length, Grape Island Cove on ye north east of it thirty six rod: Deacon Knowlton & John Harris & John Staniford & lots of Mr. Francis Wainwright & Nicholas Wallis on ye North West in Rowley Bounds, for certain other lands described, &c. James Chute sen & seal.

John Harris   Samuel Appleton,
Mary × Chute   Assist.
   her mark

The death of Elizabeth Chute is not discovered; but her sister, Mary Epps, married Peter Duncan, 1654, lived in Gloucester, and died there July 21, 1692, leaving several children. He died May 6, 1716, aged 86.

Mr. James Chute died in the spring of 1691, aged about 78 years, when his son James, jun., was granted letters of administration as follows:

Att a Court held at Ipswich, 9, 3, 1691, on adjournment Letters of Administration are granted unto Mr. James Chute of all & singular ye goods & chattels rights & Credits & whole estate of his father Mr. James Chute late of Ipsw^ch deceased & ye s^d James Chute as principle & Mr. John Staniford as Surety owned themselves Bound to ye Treasurer of Essex & parties concerned in ye sum of 140^lb money on condition y^t ye s^d James Chute shall act according to Law In his administration & attend ye Courts order of law, for a settlement of ye said estate of James Chute sen^r deceased taken ye of august 1691, by ye subscribers:—

	lbs	S	D
Imprimis It Cash & 6 silver spoons	3	0	0
It 2 cows	4	0	0
It 6 acres of marsh	12	0	0
It 6 acres of pasture	25	0	0
It half of a homestead	15	0	0
It several peices of holland stuff Linen & wearing apparell & bookes	11	0	0
Sum Total Is	70	0	0

Attests John Staniford
    John Harris jun

This Inventory was presented to ye Court held at Ipswich Nov 3^d 1691 on adjournment by ye administrator James Chute upon oath for a true inventory of ye estate of his father James Chute late of Ipswich deceased to ye best of his knowledge of all ye att present appears as also it more appear to add ye same & give accon^t therof to ye Court, In convenient time as attest

Thos Wade Cler

III. 3 James Chute (*James, Lionel*), born in Ipswich, 1649; seems to have been a man of kind disposition, mild temperament and pious withal. And, judging from his writings, he must have received a good education. He married Mary, daughter of William and Mary

Wood, Nov. 10, 1673; had four children in Ipswich and five in Byfield-Newbury:

Children:

i MARY, b. Sept. 16, 1674; m. March 7, 1693-4, John Cheny.

ii ELISABETH, b. June 22, 1676; m. Andrew (*Amos*,[2] *William*[1]) Stickney; he d. 1720; the widow m., 2nd, Henry Lunt. Children:
1. REBECCA, b. Jan. 16, 1692-3, in Newbury; d. Dec. 29, 1693, in Bradford.
2. REBECCA, b. Dec. 23, 1695.
3. AMOS, b. Apr. 23, 1699; m. Apr. 17, 1722, Hephzibah Wicom.
4. ANDREW, b. Feb. 9, 1701-2; m., 1st, Sarah Brocklebank; 2d, Sarah Lunt.
5. DAVID, b. July 4, 1703; m., 1st, Sarah Atkinson; 2d, Mary Adams.
6. STEPHEN, b. Apr. 4, 1705; m. 1732, Mehitable Goodridge.
7. HANNAH, bapt. July 24, 1708; m. May 6, 1726, Abner Lunt.
8. ANN, bapt. Feb. 17, 1711-12; m. May 16, 1732, Neh. Noyes.
9. MARY, bapt. Apr. 18, 1714.
10. JAMES, bapt. Oct. 9, 1715; m. Jan. 1, 1735, Eleanor Wilson.
11. RUTH, bapt. May 12, 1717; m., York, Me., 1735, Zachariah Beals.

iii ANN, b. Oct. 9, 1679; m., Jan. 5, 1708, Ichabod Cheny; he d. about 1711; she m., 2nd, Dec. 3, 1712, Thomas[4] Brown (*John*,[3] *Francis*,[2] *Thomas*,[1] who came over in the "James," April, 1635; d. 1687, aged 80). Ch.: Francis. Ann, d. young. John. Anne. Daniel and Ruth. Francis, b. 1716; m., 1741, Mercy Lowell, and had Anne. Molly. Thomas. Ruth. Mercy. Benjamin. Francis and John.

4 iv LIONEL, b. 1681.

5 v JAMES, b. 1686.

6 vi THOMAS, 1690.

vii MARTHA, b. Feb. 15, 1693; m. Apr. 15, 1712, Josiah Smith of Newbury. Ch.:
1. SAMUEL, b. June, 1720.
2. JOSIAH, b. 1723.
3. MARTHA, b. Mar. 31, 1728.
4. JAMES, b. Jan. 21, 1732-3.
5. MOSES, b. July 16, 1738.

viii RUTH, b. Nov. 2, 1695; m. Nov. 15, 1718, Wm. Hine of Marblehead. Ch.:
1. WILLIAM, b. Aug. 13, 1722; m., 1758, Elisab. Girdler.
2. THOMAS, b. Nov., 1729.
3. ELISAB., b. March, 1736.

ix HANNAH, b. July 8, 1700; m. Apr. 9, 1723, Timothy Jackman of Rowley; d. June, 1787; he d. in 1787. Ch.:
1. BENJAMIN, b. Sept. 19, 1724; m. Nov. 20, 1745, Elisab. Noyce.
2. HANNAH, b. May 28, 1727; m. ———.
3. TIMOTHY, b. July 13, 1729; m. Oct. 10, 1750, Mary[4] (*Jonathan*,[3] *Daniel*,[2] *Daniel*[1]), Thurston.
4. MARY, b. Aug. 29, 1731.
5. ESTHER, b. Sept. 15, 1734.
6. MARY, b. Feb. 13, 1736-37.
7. RUTH, b. Apr. 12, 1741.

Nov. 20, 1691. James Chute jun. only son & heir & administrator to "ye estate of his father, Mr James Chute deceased," for £36, 1s. in current silver mony, sold to John Wainwright of Ipswich, 20 acres, upon the town hill, bounded south east & southerly by land of Nath. Tredwell, Thos. Newman & Benj. Newman, westerly by Tho. Lowell, northerly by land of John Staniford & Philip Fowler, James Chute & a seale

Jonathan Brown

Mary X Chute & a seale.
her mark

Elizabeth X Rundoll
her mark

Oct. 20, 1692. James Chute to John Staniford for £60, sold 12 acres in Ipswich.
recorded Mar 28, 1717.

James Chute

Mary X Chute.
ye mark

Oct. 7, 1692. James Chute of Ipswich, for £100 in current silver money, sold to John Wainwright, merchant of Ipswich, 3 acres in Ipswich, & 10 acres of marsh land on Plum Island, that he got of Thos. Medcalf, Dec. 20, 1692.

Simon Stacy
John Harris,

James Chute & a seale
Mary Chute
her mark & a seale

James Chute of Ipswich, in ye county of Essex in New England sendeth greeting, sells to Nicholas Wallis six acres of salt marsh, bounded (at ye place called the hundreds in the first division) So west by Mr Tuttle's marsh, Northerly by marsh of Jno Edwards, northerly (easterly?) by Nathan Whipple's marsh, southerly by Francis Young's marsh.

Signed sealed & delivered
in presence of
Simon Stacy
Wm Baker
Richard Smith

James Chute & seale
Mary X Chute & seale
her mark
James Chute & Mary
his wife appeared April
ye 6, 1693, & did acknowledge
this instrum't above written to be
their act & deed before me
Sam^ll Appleton one of ye councell
& Justice of the peace.

Dec. 23, 1696. James Chute sold to Abram Hazeltine of Bradford 7 acres of salt marsh lying in Ipswich division at Plum Island next joining to Rowley, for £25 silver mony, the sixth year of his Majesty's King William defender of the faith.

Witnesses:
Nat Harris
Thomas Nelson
Ephraim ~^{his}~ Nelson
_{mark}

James Chute & a seale
Mary +++^{ye mark of} Chute & a seale.
Mr James Chute & Mary his wife owned this to be their free act & deed Feb ye 17, 1696 '7, before me
Nat Saltonstall Justice of the peace.

May 15, 1695. James Chute of Rowley, for £20, current silver money, sold to Benj. Plumer of Rowley 8 acres of Plum Island.

James Chute & seal
Mary Chute & seal.

Henry Poor, Abig. Poor, Sam'l Hale.

James Chute sen ack this inst to be his act & deed this July 8, 1696, before Dudley Bradford J P.

Apr., 1695. "Mr Jewts wife" joined the 1st church in Rowley, from Ipswich; undoubtedly the wife of James Chute jun.

Aug. 13, 1709. Eldad Cheney, Martha Worcester of Bradford, Ichabod Cheney, Huldah Worcester, Jemima Pettingall, Hannah Chute & Lydia Poor of Rowley, all children of Peter Cheney late of Newbury, for £46, 10, sold to Benj. Pearson, 24 acres in Newbury, south side of Falls River, &c. in the presence of Anthony Morse, Thos. Noyes, jun., Richard Brown Cler. James Chute, John Cheney, Mary ^{ye mark} Cheney, Eldad Cheney, Huldah Worcester & Jemima Pettingall, with the consent of Richard Pettingall her husband, Aug. 10, 1709.

Attest
Joseph Woodbridge, J. P.

Witnesses Ichabod Cheney, Martha Worcester, Anna (Hannah) Chute, with ye consent of Lionel Chute & Lydia Poor with ye consent of Jer. Poor, &c.

The women all made their *marks*.

Mar. 3, 1710. James Chute of Rowley, husbandman, for £20, sold to Andrew Stickney jun 10 acres in Rowley, in a place commonly called "ye new ox pasture," bounded easterly upon ye great swamp lott, southerly side upon Stickney own land westerly end partly upon Stickney's & partly upon James Chute, & northerly side by Chute's meadow, easterly end with a stake & stones & then westerly end from a stake & stones by a dam on a straight to a small white oak tree.

James Chute & seale

Mary ₙₙ *her mark* Chute & seal.

Witnesses, Wm Bennet, James Chute.

Jan. 26, 1720. James Chute to Andrew Stickney jun for £20, 10 acres in Rowley.

June 12, 1724. James Chute of Rowley, to his da Elisabeth, & son in law Henry Lunt of Newbury (successor of Andrew Stickney sen to the wife), a tract of land in Rowley. James Chute & a seal.

Witnessed by And. Stickney, John Pike.

From the name Mary Chute being left off her husband's writings it is inferred that she was dead in 1715; and the above article being the last on record of his, it is inferred that he must have died before 1730. The church records say that Mary Chute and thirteen others founded the church at Rowlberry, alias Byfield, Oct. 13, 1706.

1712-14. Richard Crafft, shoreman, & Elisab. his wife, da of Wm & Mary Wood, lived in Marblehead.

Nov. 28, 1711. Mary wid. of Wm Woods, Marblehead, sold property to Richard Skinner.

IV. 4 Lionel Chute (*James, James, Lionel*), born in Ipswich, April 15, 1681; taken to Byfield-Newbury, with his parents and three older sisters in the summer or fall following, and there doubtless grew up to manhood. He seems to have had a good education and was well beloved and respected by all. He married Dec. 10, 1702, Anna or Hannah, daughter of Peter Cheney, Esq., of Newbury.

Children:

i JEMIMA, bapt. Dec. 19, 1703; m. Mar. 2, 1723, Samuel Jewett.
ii MARY, bapt. about 1706; m. Sept. 24, 1726, Jonathan Core, of Westtown.
iii LYDIA, bapt. Jan. 29, 1709-10.
iv SARAH, bapt. June 27, 1714; m., 1736, Benj. Philbrick of Hampstead, N. H., who was one of three selectmen in 1753, and filled that and other offices for years after. Ch.:
  1. JEMIMA, b. Oct. 20, 1737; m. Nov. 13, 1759, Jer. Kent, and had Mary and John.
  2. JAMES, b. Nov. 29, 1739.
  3. ABIGAIL, b. Feb. 26, 1742.
  4. BETTY, b. Apr. 26, 1744; m. June 11, 1767, Micha Chaplain.
  5. BENJAMIN, b. June 10, 1746.
  6. JOSEPH, b. Aug. 27, 1748.

7. MARY, b. June 23, 1750.
8. MEHITABLE, b. Aug, 24, 1752.
9. SARAH, b. Mar. 10, 1757.

v SAMUEL, bapt. May 25, 1718; d. in childhood.
7 vi JOHN, bapt. June, 1720.
vii SAMUEL, bapt. Aug. 5, 1722; went into the British army in lower Canada, and was probably at the taking of Quebec, under Gen. Wolfe, 1759.
viii HANNAH, bapt. July 12, 1724; m. July 7, 1743, Jonathan⁴ Coburn (*Jonathan*,³ *Thomas*,² *Edward*¹), of Haverhill, b. June, 1720, and had: Lynor, b. June 28, 1744; Jonathan, Oct. 6, 1746; Thomas, Aug. 25, 1751.
ix ELISABETH, bapt. Apr. 10, 1726; m. Feb. 24, 1746, Enoch Noyes.

James Chute to Lionell Chute, recorded Dec. 6, 1714. To all people to whom this present writing shall come. I, James Chute of Rowley in the County of Essex in ye province of the Mafsach Bay in New England America send Greeting & now ye that I yᵉ said James Chute for divers good causes & considerations me thereunto moving, but especially for & in consideration of ye just affection which I bear to my loving dutiful son Lionel Chute of ye town & county aforesaid as alsow for & in consideration of his full satisfaction for his portion of my estate or my fathers by any entail or alienation whatsoever Have given granted Bargained Enfeoffed & Confirmed & do by these presents fully freely Clearly & absolutely give grant bargain Enfeoffe & confirm to him my sᵈ son Lionel Chute a certain piece of land in ye township of Rowley which is part of a farm which I bought of Capt. Jewett of Rowley & is in estimation about thirty acres be ye same more or less as it is bounded on ye North East corner by a black Oake above a foot over near to ye meadow called Billberry, Meadow & running from thence southerly to land of my son Stickney's, & so from thence bounded by sᵈ Stickneys land until it comes to a stake on ye southwest corner of sᵈ Stickneys land & from that stake running pretty near Westerly about 50 rod to a Bass tree by a brook which Tree is about a foot over & from thence running near northerly about 30 rods to a black oak about seven inches over standing on a little Island in a swamp & from thence running Easterly about 30 rods to a rock near to sᵈ Lionell Chutes house running easterly about thirty rodds to ye black Oak first mentioned.

To have & to hold all ye above mentioned lands together with all ye profits & privileges to ye same belonging to him my sᵈ son Lionel Chute his heirs executors administrators & assigns as an estate of Inheritance in fee simple for ever, & I ye sᵈ James Chute for my selfe my heirs executors & adm'rs done Covenant & promise to & with my sd son Lionel

Chute his heirs executors & administrators in manner & form following that I ye s^d James Chute am ye true & Lawful owner of ye above demised premises, & that I have of my selfe full power good right & Lawful authority to make this gift & that my s^d son Lionel Chute his heirs executors & administrators shall by vertue hereof for ever hereafter peaceably & quietly have hold use & occupy possess & enjoy all ye above demised premises without any Lawful let Denial Molestation or interruption of me ye s^d James Chute my heirs executors or administrators or any other person whatsoever. In witness to all above written I ye s^d James Chute have hereunto set my hand & seal this seventeenth Day of January one thousand seven hundred & eight or nine

          James Chute & seale

   signed sealed & delivered by James Chute to Lionel Chute in presence of Peter Cheney, John Cheney, Ichabod Cheney.

          Essex ss.

Mr. James Chute personally appeared before me ye subscriber & acknowledged his hand & seal to ye forewritten deed & said deed to be his voluntary act this thirteenth day of August 1709.

          Jo. Woodbridge J P.

Jan. 26, 1714–5. Lionel Chute to Andrew Belcher, Esq., Addington Davenport, Thos. Hutchinson, John White & Edw Hutchinson, for £55, sold 29 acres in Rowley, bounded easterly & northerly on ye land of James Chute, westerly on land of Maximilian Jewett & southerly by the land of And. Stickney, &c.

signed sealed & delivered   Lionel Chute & seal
in ye presence of us   Annah ◿ Chute her mark & seal
 James Chute
 Josiah Smith.

April 14, 1718. Some thirty persons, including Lionel & Hannah Chute, several Cheneys & Noyeses, being relatives of Rev. Nich. Noyes, signed an article to Messrs. Deacon Cutting Noyes, & Major James Noyes, to enable them, as attorneys, to sell the real estate of the late Rev. Nich. Noyes of Salem.

Feb. 3, 1720–1. Lionel Chute for £30 sold to John Lull jun. 6 acres in Rowley, bounded on the north by my own land & stones set up, on the south by Maximilian Jewett's land, on the west by James

Chewte's & Jona Safford's land that was formerly & stones set up, & on the easterly side or end by land of the Stickneys, there being stones set up.

Lionel Chute & seal
Annah " "

signed sealed and delivered to John Lull by Lionel Chewte in presence of Joseph Pettingall & John Jackson

Dec. 10, 1723. Lionell Chewte of Rowley bo't 10 acres of Ebenezer Stuart & paid £105, in presence of
James Chewte
Edmund Cheney,   Thomas Hale, Justice of ye peace.

Jan. 6, 1724-5. Lionell Chewt, & his wife, sold to Thos Jewett for £5, one acre & 8 rods in Rie plain, Rowley, being the easterly end of house lott, bo't of Eben Stewart (but Lionell had more land left).
Witnesses: Samuel Dickinson, Samuel Dickinson jun.

Aug. 4, 1725. Lionel Chute for £6, sold to Tho Jewett one acre more on the W side of the land above referred to, Lionel & Annah Chute.
Witnessed by Maximilian Jewett, John Lull.

Aug. 31, 1725. Lionel Chute to Aron Plumer for £240, 30 acres in Rowley.   Lionel Chute & seal.
Witnessed by John Cheney, Joseph Plumer.

Essex ss. Aug. 31, 1725. The within named Lionel Chewte & Hannah his wife formerly appeared & acknowledged this instrument to be their free act & deed before me
John Dummer J Peace

Mar. 16, 1729-30. Lionel Chewte of Rowley, yeoman, for £108,8, sold out to Maximilian & Seth Jewett 8 acres in Rowley in ye plaine commonly called Rye plaine being part of a 30 acre lott formerly Capt. Joseph Jewetts of Rowley, dec'd, & bounded the westerly corner by a stake & stones, upon ye easterly corner of a parcell of land Max. Jewett sold to Joseph Pettingall, & from said stake & stones on a line southerly twenty-one rods till it come to ye side of a lott laid out to Shirley's sometimes in ye possession of Samuel Felt now in ye possession of Eben. Stewart & laying southwesterly upon said Shirley's lott till it come to ye southerly corner bound between said land of Thomas Jewett being ye southerly end bounded upon said Thomas Jewett's land the other side & bounded upon Max Jewett's land, all ye above said as it is butted & bounded with all ye houseing orchard fences privileges profitts &c.

Lionel Chewte & seal.

James Chewte, Jonathan Bayley.   Acknowledged Apr. 30, 1730.
before John Dummer J. P.

This is the last notice of Lionel Chute. The Rowley Church Records say Lionell Chute owned the covenant Dec. 19, 1703, and had a child baptized—christened—the same day.

IV. 5 James Chute, brother to the preceding, born in Byfield, Newbury, June 14, 1686. He lived there more than eighty-two years, an honest, pious, sober citizen; more than half of this time deacon of the Congregational church. He married Jan. 26, 1715, Mary^3 (*Daniel^2, Daniel^1*) Thurston, of Newbury.

Children:

   i MARY, b. Nov. 8, 1716; m. 1740, Mark^4 (*Jonathan,^{3} Joseph,^{2} Joseph^1 of Edward in England before* 1600) Jewett, and had twelve children.
   ii RUTH, b. Aug. 27, 1720; m. 1741, Joseph Searls, of Rowley, and had thirteen children.
8 iii DANIEL, b. 1722.
   iv JAMES, b. May 12, 1725; } both d. in childhood.
   v DAVID, b. in 1727;

Feb. 14, 1715–16. James Chute sen. (called sen. here on account of his son James), to his son James, calls him "my loving & dutiful son," & also for £160, conveys to him all his house barne & land & meadow lylying in ye township of Rowley which he formerly bought of Joseph Jewett called "ox pasture," land bounded on ye North side partly by Newbury line & partly by land sold to ye precinct called Byfield, easterly by meadow called Mr. Phillips meadow, southerly partly by land sold to son Andrew Stickney & partly by land which I gave to Lionel Chewte & partly by land of Jonathan Spoffords by a corner stake & incet stones & westerly by Jonathan Wheeler & ye brook to Newbury line, about 90 acres.

James Chewte, seale

signed sealed & delivered by James Chute sen to James Chewte jun in presence of John Cheney.

March 4, 1728-9. Josiah Smith to Joseph Hale & James Chute for £2, sold an acre to go into the Byfield burying yard.

John Dummer J P.

Jan. 6, 1730-1. John Stevens of Rowley for £10, sh. 11, sold to Deacon James Chute 12 acres of upland, being a certain tract he bot of his mother Plumer.

1735. For military service Dea James Chute drew lot No. 15, in township No. 1, Narragansett, on the E side of Saco R. Co of York.

Records of the proprietors of Nar Tp No 1 now the town of Buxton, York Co., Me.

1744. Thos Wilson Jas Chute & others sold a piece of land to Francis Pickard.

Aug. 15, 1760. James Chewte deeded to his son Daniel all his real estate in Rowley near the meeting house in Byfield, about 130 acres.

James Chewte & seal.
John Higginson, Recorder, Jan. 21, 1761.

Mary wife of Dea Jas Chute d Aug 12 1760, about 4 o'clock A.M. of fever & a bloody purging, aged about 67. She was a very useful woman as a midwife; & as she lived desired, so she died much lamented.

(Rowley Records.)

Joseph[3] Pearson (*Capt. John,*[2] *Deacon John*[1]), born Oct. 22, 1677; married Sarah Walker and had Capt. John; and Richard, born 1705. She suicided Sept. 2, 1721, and he married, second, in Newbury, Jan. 1, 1722-3, Sarah Hale and died July 19, 1753; she married, second, Deacon James Chute of Byfield, Mar. 30, 1761, and died May 9, 1762, of dropsy. Deacon James Chute died Jan. 31, 1769, very suddenly of apoplexy, in his eighty-third year.

> The Last Will & Testament of me Sarah Chewte, wife of Deacon James Chewte of Rowley in the County of Essex in New England — in the first place, on this solemn occasion, I do commit my soul into the hands of God, Looking for the mercy of our Lord Jesus Christ unto Eternal Life, & my body I do committ to ye ground in Decent Christian Burial at the direction of my Husband believing the Doctrine of the general Resurrection; as Touching the Worldly Estate which I have or had before my marriage with my present Husband James Chewte & which By an Instrument under his hand duly executed before marriage he obliged himself not to concern himself with but to leave at my Disposal. I give & Dispose of the same in the following manner:—I give & bequeath

unto my husband Deacon James Chewte the use & improvement of my riding chair during his natural life; & then to go & be for the use & property of my son in Law Daniel Chewte & Daughter in Law Ruth Searl, equally between them. I also give to my said Husband the use & improvement of one of my Beds & suitable Furniture therefor & the use & improvement of six chairs & 3 Pewter Dishes During his natural life, then to go to & be for the use & property of my son-in-law Capt John Pearson, & I also give to my Husband James Chewte the sum of four pounds on Consideration of his Charge During my sickness & his giving me a Decent Christian Burial.

em. I give to my niece, Hannah Little, a silver spoon.

em. I give to my cousin John Frazier & Jesia Freazer sons of John Freazer the sum of eight pounds to be equally divided between them.

em. I give to my grand daughter in law Judith Chewte the sum of two pounds.

em. I give to my above-named son in law, Capt. John Pearson, all the rest of my estate not Disposed of by this my Will he paying the above-named Legacies: & I give him all My Just Debts on consideration of his paying what is yet Due for my Riding Chair above mentioned. Finally I do hereby Constitute & appoint my above mentioned son in law Capt. John Pearson sole Executor of this my last Will & Testament in witness whereof I have hereunto set my hand & seal this fourth day of May in the year of our Lord one Thousand seven hundred & sixty two signe sealed Published pronounced & declared by the above named Sarah Chewte as her last will & Testament in presence of us subscribers

her
Sarah ⊥ Chewte
mark

Moses Hale, Lucy Dinsmore, Moses Parsons,

Essex s. s. Ipswich, May 31, 1762, Before the Hon^le John Choate Esq of Probate of wills &c, the Rev'd Mr. Moses Parsons, Moses Hale Personally appeared & mad oath that they were present & saw Sarah Chewte, late of Rowley, Dec^d sign seal & her Publish & Declare that the Within written instrument to be her last will & Testament & when she so did she was of a sound Disposing mind & memory to the best of their discerning & they together with Lucy Dinsmore sett to their hands at the same time in her presence at witnesses

Sworn all^d Danl Appleton Reg'r.

upon which this will is proved appeared & allowed The execut^r appeared & accepted that Trust & to give Bond to pay Debts & Legacies according to the will.

Daniel Appleton Exam'd pr Saml Rogers Reg^r
John Choate Jud Pro.

IV. 6 **Thomas Chute**, the third brother, born Jan. 30, 1690, was a "Jack of all trades," was married Dec. 11, 1712, to Mary Curtice, by Rev. Dr. Cotton Mather, of Boston, and lived there four or five years. He then moved to and settled in Marblehead where he lived some twenty years, a tailor, farmer and innkeeper.

Children:

i. Mary, b. Aug. 25, 1713; d. young.
ii. James, b. Jan. 1, 1715; d. about 1730.
iii. Mary, b. Dec. 30, 1716; d. ——. Boston Records.
iv. Abigail, b. June 7, 1718; m. —— Cobham, in Me. had two or three daughters; she was living in 1799.
v. Thomas, b. July 4, 1720. Marblehead Records.
vi. Edmund, b. June 17, 1722.
vii. Rebecca, b. Jan. 4, 1724; m. Dec. 14, 1743, John² Bodge [Benj.,² Henry¹] of Windham, Me. He was a farmer, d. in 1798, aged 84; she was drowned crossing the Presumpscot river at "Horse Beef" Falls, July 25, 1763. Ch.:
  1. Mary, b. Dec. 29, 1744; m. June 24, 1761, Wm. Stinchfield; lived in New Gloucester, Me.
  2. John, b. Dec. 12, 1747; d. young.
  3. Sarah, b. June 17, 1750; m. Dec. 4, 1774, John Wooster, Poland, Me.
  4. Thomas, b. June 1, 1752; m. Nov. 24, 1775, Abigail Thrasher, Falmouth.
  5. Abigail, b. Feb. 4, 1754; m. Nat⁴ Jordan [Jones,³ Jeremiah,² Jeremiah,¹ Rev. Robert], of Raymond, Me.
  6. Benjamin, b. Jan. 6, 1756; m. 1st, Jan. 1, 1778, Susannah Hunnewell, Windham; 2d, Jan. 30, 1789, Betsy Gammon.
  7. Rebecca, b. 1757; d. single.
viii. Mary, b. Mar. 27, 1726.
9 ix. Curtis, b. Sept. 15, 1728.

Sept. 15, 1722. Thomas Chute, Taylor, of Marblehead sold to Annas & Thomas Trevy a lot in Marblehead for £110.

Oct. 2, 1722. Tho Chute for £100 sold a town lott to Symonds Epps in Marblehead.

Daniel Epes, Margaret Mackie   Thomas Chute & a seal
                                                Daniel Epes J. P.

Aug. 5, 1726. Stephen Dudley of Exeter province of New Hampshire gave to Thomas Chute 250 acres of land, being part of a tract given him by Capt. Peter Penniwett & Abigail his squaw, &c &c.

Aug. 15, 1726. Stephen Dudley of Freetown, N. H., sold to Henry Laine 50 acres, being part of a tract of land given by Capt Peter Peanevit & Abigail his squaw, dated Jan 7, 1718–9, to have & to hold the sd 50 acre right to be laid next to ye right of Thomas Chewte unto him the sd Henry Laine his heirs & assigns forever &c., &c.

Accounts of Thos Chute 1725 to 1733, for shus & hos hire.

Aug. 29, 1727. Isaac Mansfield & Thomas Chute bo't a lot in Marblehead of Nathan Brown.

Jan 5, 1729. Thos Chewte of Marblehead in the county of Essex in New England, Taylor, for £51, sold to Jas Waldron, Mariner, a town lot.

| Samuel Flack | Thos Chute & seal |
| Nathan Brown | Mary Chute & seal. |

1735. Thos. Chute was deputy sheriff of Essex Co., Mass., at Salem. About this time he concluded to move to New Marblehead, or Windham, Me., but we find that he bought property in Marblehead of Thos. Wood in 1737. He moved to Portland that year as per the following:

Received of Thos Chute twenty shillings in part for his fraight of his household goods & family from Newbury to Falmouth.

Received by me, Moses Swett, Oct. 24, 1737.

Received of Thomas Chute twenty two shillings & six pence in fish which I promise to discount with Mr. Joseph Tappin of Newbury in part for sd Chutes fraight of his goods & family from Newbury to Falmouth as witness my hand, John Swett.

Falmouth, now Portland, Feb. 10, 1738.

After that his accounts and correspondence date from Maine. One is dated, "Falmouth April ye 6, 1738," was for Thos Chute to pay Mr Andrew Tuck forty-five shillings & charge it to Phinihas & Stephen Jones.

Thomas Chute was granted land in Windham, Me. (some ten miles north of Portland), in 1735, & sold some again in 1739.

Here is an old account. Falmouth, Nov. 4, 1760: Received of Thos Chute in Cash seventeen pounds in what we call old tenor, it being in full to balance an accompt which Tho. Chutes dafter Abigail Cobham stands charged with in my book. Received by me William Cotton.

New Marblehead & Gorham town gave Thomas Chute power of attorney to plead for them about 1760. Signed by Curtis Chute, Rebecca Bodge, Samuel Conant, Philip Gammon and several more.

Thomas Chute was surveyor of highways 1741–42.

May 19, 1746 to Jan. 19, 1747. Thos. Chute was a member of Capt. Geo. Berry's Company, Falmouth.

John Bodge, Curtis Chute, Wm. and Thos. Mayberry were in the New Marblehead Division, Serg. Thos. Chute in command.

Mary, wife of Thos. Chute (probably daughter of Benj. and Mary Curtis of Scituate), died July 30, 1762, aged seventy or seventy-one.

Thos. Chute bought land in Maine in 1763. He was town clerk of Windham, 1762–65, inclusive, and one of the selectmen 1765–66.

A publishment of marriage between Lonon & Chloe Boeth, negroes of the town of Windham, with the consent of their master, Mr. Wm. Mayberry of said town.

Thomas Chute, Town Clerk, 1763.

After being a church officer some thirty years, being aged and infirm, Mr. Chute desires release from the deaconship in 1770, and died in 1771, in his eighty-second year.

V. 7 John Chute (*Lionel,[4] James,[3] James,[2] Lionel[1]*), born in Rowley, Mass., June, 1720; doubtless grew up to manhood there; about 1740 crossed the Merrimack River, and at Timberlane, since called Hampstead (ten miles north of Haverhill), in Rockingham Co., N. H.; married, Nov. 26, 1745, Judith, daughter of Benjamin and Sarah (Woodward) Foster.

In a petition signed by thirty-three residents of Haverhill district, not to be joined with Kingstown, province of New Hampshire, are John Chute and Benjamin Philbrick, Oct. 16, 1746. (Vol. ix, p. 362, Town Papers.)

John Chuet or Chute was one of eight surveyors of highways in Hampstead, N. H., 1756; and with John Beard "tything men" 1757. In 1759 he moved from there to Granville, Annapolis Co., Nova Scotia, and settled on a farm a mile below Bridgetown, and there for more than thirty years led a life of industry, sobriety and piety, as a farmer, blacksmith, and pioneer Baptist in that province. He died Nov., 1791; his wife died Nov., 1808, in her 83rd year.

Children:

10   i   SAMUEL, b. Feb. 16, 1746–47.
      ii   JOHN, b. Apr. 7, 1748; d. May 7, 1748.
      iii HANNAH, b. Sept. 16, 1749; d. Nov. 1, 1749.
11   iv JOHN, b. Apr. 9, 1752.
12   v   BENJAMIN, b. Sept. 27, 1754.
13   vi THOMAS, b. Mar. 13, 1757.
      vii SARAH, b. Nov. 8, 1758; m., 1777, in Annapolis Co., N. S., Thomas Hicks,[*] who d. Apr. 9, 1826, aged 66; she d. Aug., 1836. Ch.:
           1. PATIENCE, b. April 1, 1778; m. James Chesley,[2] (*Major Samuel[1]*), and had children; d. Oct., 1843; he d. Oct., 1846.

---

[*] John Hicks m. Elizabeth Russell, 1740 and had Hannah, 1743; Ephraim, 1744; Russell, 1745; Seth, 1746; Patience, 1752; John, jun., 1754; Thomas, 1758; Weston, 1760; Hannah, 1763; Ruth, 1765, d. single, 1856.

This family lived in Falmouth, N. S.

2. SARAH, b. Feb. 11, 1780; m. John Rice and lived on Brier Island, Digby Co., N. S.; d. 1814.
3. MARY, b. Feb. 23, 1784; m. Nicholas Hains; lived on Brier Island; he d. about 1817; she d. 1854.
4. ROBY or RUBIA, b. Jan. 26, 1785; m. Asa Foster. See Foster.
5. JOBE, b. Feb. 3, 1786; m. May 4, 1809, Bridget Burrows; lived on Brier Island; d. 1840.
6. SUSAN, b. Apr. 5, 1788; m. John Rice and d. on Brier Island, June, 1872.
7. CHARLES, b. Apr. 7, 1790; m. Bridget Burke, Brier Island.
8. AMELIA, b. June 9, 1793; m. David Welsh, Brier Island, and d. in 1874.
9. GILBERT, b. Feb. 1, 1795; drowned 1834.
10. HARRIET, b. Feb. 7, 1797; m. John Murdock, who d. Nov. 13, 1871, aged 86; d. Oct. 22, 1869.
11. JOSEPH, b. June 10, 1799; m. Lovena Langley, who d. about 1830; he d. 1873, at Bridgetown; m., 2nd, Eliza Fritz, w. of Asa Thomas.
12. HORATIO NELSON, b. July 29, 1801; m. Dec. 14, 1824, Elizabeth (b. May, 1805), daughter of Peter Mongard and had 3 children. He d. May 14, 1872.

viii JAMES, b. Jan. 22, 1762, in Granville, N. S.

ix HANNAH, b. Dec. 25, 1764; m. 1785, Obadiah Morse, who d. Jan. 10, 1817, aged 52; she d. 1841. They lived on the south side of Annapolis river, above Bridgetown. Ch.:
1. SOPHIA, b. Apr. 9, 1786; m. Mar. 29, 1807, Robert Neiley; had eight sons, two daughters; d. Oct. 12, 1849; he d. Jan. 30, 1862, aged 77.
2. PETER, b. Oct., 1788; m. 1811, Mary, daughter of John Wheelock; had four sons, five daughters, and d. Sept., 1868; she d. 1882, near 90.
3. JUDITH, b. Sept. 18, 1791; m. Sept. 30, 1815, Guy, son of Lemuel Newcomb; had four sons, four daughters; d. May 9, 1856; he d. Aug. 24, 1872, aged 81.
4. ALEXANDER, b. 1793; m., 1st, Mar. 11, 1816, Amy Chesley; had six daughters and three sons; she d. July 1, 1860, aged 66; he m., 2nd, Mary Ann Truesdell; d. Oct. 29, 1877; she d. Oct. 22, 1875, aged 67. Margaret Neiley, sister of Robert, children of John, had two husbands, Benjamin Chesley and John Truesdell, and Mr. Morse m. a daughter of each, half-sisters.
5. ABNER, b. July 29, 1795; m, 1st, Feb. 22, 1821, Margaret, daughter of John Hicks, and had three children; she d Mar. 16, 1834, aged 35; m., 2nd, Oct. 16, 1834, Mary, daughter of Jona. Parker, and had eight children; she d. June 27, 1855, aged 50; he m , 3rd, Sept., 1856, Caroline S., daughter of Arche Hicks; had one son; d. Aug. 28, 1858; she m. Dec. 20, 1871, Watson Chipman.
6. LUTHER, b. May 28, 1798; m., 1st, Oct. 12, 1833, Mary, daughter of Fairfield Woodbury; had six children; she d. Jan. 9, 1850, aged 45; m., 2nd, Nov. 6, 1851, Emily Dodge (*Samuel, Stephen, Tristram, etc.*), and d. June 27, 1861.
7. LOVINA, b. Aug. 14, 1801; m. ―――― Taylor. See Taylor.
8. THERESA, b. 1803; m. John Hicks, jun., and had two daughters and one son.
9. HANNAH MARIA, b. Apr. 8, 1806; m. Jan. 20, 1829, Rev. Obed Parker

(*William, Nathaniel, William*); had four daughters and d. Feb. 14, 1836; he m., 2nd, Mary, daughter of Reuben Balcomb; had one daughter and d. July 1, 1890, aged 86.

10. OBADIAH, JUN., b. Dec. 20, 1809; m. Sept. 11, 1834, Minetta, daughter of Asa and Roby (Hicks) Foster, and had Nathan R., b. June 12, 1835; m. Cynthia, daughter of Robert H. Foster and have five children. William T., b. 1837; m. Elizabeth H., daughter of Abner Morse, at Bear river; had one daughter and d. 1862. Obadiah d. Dec. 30, 1837, and his widow m., 2nd, Jacob Foster, 1848; d. Jan. 2, 1890, aged 77.

x SUSAN, b. Dec. 10, 1767; m. Feb. 5, 1788, by Rev. Thomas Handly Chipman, to Amos Randall, a sturdy old farmer, and they lived nearly two miles below Bridgetown in Granville, where he d. Mar. 24, 1837, aged 82. After being blind several years, she d. July 1, 1856. Ch.:

1. ELIZABETH, b. July 1, 1789; m. Benj. Chute, jun. See 32.
2. NATHAN, b. Aug. 15, 1791; m. Harriet Foster. See Foster.
3. JOHN, b. Feb. 1, 1794; m. Ceretha Dexter, 1823.
4. SUSANNA, b. June 3, 1796; d. Aug. 3, 1799.
5. JAMES, b. July 3, 1798; m. Mary Pickup. See Randall.
6. THOMAS, b. July 31, 1800; d. in Antigonish, May 12, 1830.
7. SUSANNA, b. Dec. 16, 1802; m. July 1, 1854, James, son of John Fitz Maurice; d. June 2, 1872; he d. April, 1865, aged 65.
8. POLLY, b. July 21, 1805; d. in Portland, Me., Sept. 9, 1859.
9. THERESA, b. Nov. 9, 1807; m. Joseph Chute. See 34.
10. BENJAMIN, b. May 23, 1810; m. Tamer Foster. See Randall.
11. CHARLOTTE, b. June 8, 1813; m. Sept. 23, 1830, James, son of John Fitz Maurice; had ten children, seven or eight d. in childhood; she d. Nov. 1851.

V. 8 Daniel[5] Chute (*James,[4] James,[3] James,[2] Lionel[1]*), cousin to John, the preceding, born in Byfield-Newbury, Mass., May 6, 1722; became a man of considerable note in his day and generation and was styled "Captain Daniel Chute;" married Apr. 20, 1742, Hannah, daughter of Richard Adams of Newbury.

Children:

i JUDITH, b. Jan. 20, 1743; m. Daniel Thurston. See Thurston.
ii JAMES, b. Jan. 6, 1745; d. Jan. 25, 1749.
iii DAVID, b. Dec. 28, 1747; d. Jan. 25, 1749.

"David & James, sons of Daniel Chute, died Jan. 25, 1749, ye first aged about 2 years, ye other about 4, all of ye throat distemper."

iv SUSANNA, b. Jan., 1749; d. Jan. 20, 1749.
15 v JAMES, b. Feb. 16, 1751.
vi DAVID, b. Jan., 1753; d. May 20, 1756.
vii DANIEL, b. July 25, 1754; d. Aug. 12, 1760.
16 viii DAVID, b. Aug. 19, 1756.
ix RICHARD, b. Aug 4, 1758; d. Aug. 3, 1760.
x DANIEL, b. Sept. 28, 1760; m. 1790, Polly Stimpson of Reading, and d. there Mar., 1843; she d. Oct. 9, 1851, aged 91½ yrs. Nancy, an adopted daughter d. Oct. 1, 1797, aged 3 years.

xi MARY, b. Dec. 8, 1762; m. Deacon Benjamin Coleman and d. 1849; he d. 1846, aged 94.

xii HANNAH, b. April, 1765; m. July 17, 1792, Rev. Ariel Parish, of Lebanon, Conn. (Dartmouth, 1788, ordained 1792), who d. May 20, 1794, aged 30; she d. April 28, 1842. Ch.:
1. PHILOMELA, b. 1793; d. soon after.
2. AMELIA, b. Sept. 18, 1794; m. 1819, Rev. Ebenezer[7] Perkins (*David*,[6] *David*,[5] *Jonathan*,[4] *Timothy*,[3] *Thomas*,[2] *John*[1]), b. July 4, 1794, in Topsfield (Dartmouth, 1814), ordained over the Congregational Church, Royalston, Mass., Feb. 17, 1819; and was there 27 years; she d. June 21, 1859; he d. Nov. 26, 1861. They had seven children: Ariel E. P., Hannah Amelia, Mary Coleman, Daniel Chute, Benjamin Coleman, Joseph Lee, Annette Greenleaf. Hannah A., b. Jan. 10, 1822; m. in Royalston, Nov. 20, 1854, as his 2nd wife, Rev. Charles Louis Woodworth, D.D. (b. May 22, 1820), son of Charles and Lilly (Avery) Woodworth, of Stafford, Conn. He graduated at Amherst, 1845, Hartford Theological Seminary, 1848; ordained over the 2nd Congregational Church in Amherst 1849, and remained there fourteen years; dismissed in 1863, to be chaplain of the 27th Mass. in the war, which he held from Mar., 1862 to June, 1863, when he was appointed secretary of the American Missionary Society, residence Watertown. His son, Charles Louis, b. July 27, 1853; graduated at several colleges, settled a Congregational minister at Wilton, N. H.; m. July 7, 1873, Sarah Emma Tillson (b. Oct. 11, 1853, in Shutesbury), and has two sons and two daughters.

Feb. 21, 1753. Daniel Chewte of Rowley sold to Jeremiah Jewett, blacksmith, for £48, nine acres of land in Rowley, near Byfield meetinghouse, bounded—beginning at the county road, at a stake and stones by land now in possession of the sd Jewett, then running by sd land to a stake and stones by the great swamp so called, then by sd swamp to a stake and stones by Andrew Duty's land, then by said Dute's land to a stake & stones by said road and to the first mentioned bounds.

            · Daniel Chewte & a seal
In presence of   Jos. Gerrish jun J. P. Nov. 10, 1760.
James Chewte, Andrew Duty.

May 31, 1757. "Daniel Chewett was one of a troop of horse under Capt. John Pearson, in Rowley."

From 1762 to 1764, Daniel Noyes, John Pearson and Humphrey Hobson were a committee in Byfield parish; Daniel Chute, Parish Clerk.

In the Byfield parish records, 1764, it is recorded that "Benj. Coleman, Daniel Chewt, and Samuel Northen, was a Committee."

In 1768 "Daniel Chute, Jer. Poor, and Henry Adams was a Committee."

"Byfield, Dec. 14, 1768: at a leagel meeting of the inhabitants of the

Parish of Byfield, at s^d meeting voted to the Rev Mr Moses Parsons for his salary £80.0.0; at the same time voted to give him £4.13.4. to enable him to pirchis his fire Wood this year, at s^d meeting voted to Eliphalet tenny and others their several amounts that have demands on s^d parish, at s^d meeting voted the parish committee shall receive what money is in Mr Joshua Noyeses hands that belongs to said parish to be apropriated to Discharge the parished Debts. at said meeting voted to reconsider the vote for raising the money to defray the Parish Debts (viz) so much of it as the paris Committee shall receive from Mr Joshua Noyes: also voted that the Parish Committee render an account to the parish the next march meeting of what money they receive of the s^d Mr Joseph Noyes. also voted that a number of such as are skilled in musick are desired to assist the Congregation in that part of Divine Worship singing praises to God on the sabbath and other seasons of public worship; voted that a number of such as are skilled in singing are desired to set in the square pew before the pulpit (viz) Jacob Gerrish, Benj. Stickney, Jos. Hale jun., Jos Danford, Jacob Low, Elkanah Lunt, John Coleman, Timothy Jackman, jun., Nat Tenney, Stephen Lunt, Lot Pearson, Joseph Brown, Tim Jackman ye 3rd & Step Gerrish.

Daniel Chute, Parish Clerk."

Daniel Chute, Henry Adams and Jacob Gerrish, Committee for Byfield 1769.

May 27, 1765. Bemsle Plumer of Rowley, in the County of Essex and Province of the Massachusetts Bay in New England, yeoman, for & in consideration of the sum of two hundred & eight pounds eight shillings lawful money to me in hand paid by Daniel Chute of Rowley, &c., sell to David Chute about 50 acres lying by & between the farms of James Chute, Moses Wheeler, Abram Brown, & Timothy Jackman.

July 30, 1768. Daniel Chute of Rowley, yeoman, for £14. 10. 8. sold to Jonathan Wheeler of Rowley, yeoman, the one half of a certain wood lot for quantity & quality, the other half belonging to Moses Wheeler, situate in the town of Newbury. The whole of said lot containing by estimation 12 acres, be it more or less, & is bounded southerly on the falls river, westerly on Longfellow's land, northwardly on the rate lots so called and eastwardly on lands of Moses Wheeler. Daniel Chute & a seal.

In presence of Samuel Wheeler, James Chute.

Nov. 30, 1770. Daniel Chewte of Newbury, for £30, sold to John Searl jun of Rowley 15 acres & 150 rods in Rowley, near Byfield meeting house, bounded westerly & southerly on land of sd John Searl, eastwardly on land of Moses Hale, northwardly on land of sd Hale & Moses Lull & sd Chewte to a locust tree marked & near the road. Northwestwardly on sd road to the westwardly part first mentioned.

Daniel Chewte & a seal

·Jacob Rogers, Wm. Chandler.   Essex p.

May 28, 1790. Nathaniel Perkins of Salem, Rockingham Co., N. H., blacksmith, for £12, sold to Daniel Chute & Daniel Chute jun of Rowley, Essex Co., Mass., 3 acres of saltmarsh in Rowley.

Nat ✗ Perkins & a seal. (his mark)

Bethiah ✗ Perkins & a seal. (her mark)

Evan Jones, Hezek. Jones.   Tim. Ladd, J. P.

Daniel Chute was parish clerk thirty-three years, and also in the parish committees of Byfield, with several others, such as Joseph Hale, Paul Moody, Jos. Poor, Parker Cleaveland, Nat Tenney, Jacob Perley and Thos Pike for several years.

Extracts from Richard Adams' Will, Aug. 3, 1770.

My da Mary to have £4. of my household goods, and the remainder of my household goods to Mary Adams and Hannah Chute to grand son Nat. Adams, son of Enoch, dec'd, £200: to grand-da Hannah, of son Daniel, dec'd, £70, to be paid by sons Moses and Edmund: to son John £267: to sons Moses and Edmund all my homestead in Newbury, with buildings tools utensils cattle sheep horses and other lands meadows &c. Wearing apparel to 4 sons Richard John Moses and Edmund: and to Moses my loom, and to Edmund blacksmithshop and things belonging: and to Richard £100, and him to be my sole executor.

Nov. 21, 1778, the will was delivered to Richard jun. as executor, his father being dead. Inventory taken Nov. 24, £3907.15.7. Capt. Daniel Chute died Jan. 6, 1805; Hannah, his wife, died April 28, 1812, aged ninety years.

Dr. Elijah Parish of Newbury said of Mrs. Hannah (Adams) Chute that "Next to George Washington he knew none more fit to govern this nation than she."—Rev. A. P. Chute.

V. 9 Curtis[5] Chute (*Thomas,[4] James,[3] James,[2] Lionel[1]*), cousin to the two preceding, born in Marblehead, Mass., Sept. 15, 1728; taken to Maine, with his parents and two sisters, 1737, and there grew to manhood, received his education probably from his mother, as she taught the first school in Windham where they settled. He was admitted to communion in the Windham Church 1753; married Miriam Carr, widow of Josiah Worcester[5] (*Timothy*,[4] *Francis*,[3] *Samuel*,[2] *Rev. William*[1]), Mar. 21, 1754, and lived in Windham. He bought land there of Thomas and Bethia Maybery, and Richard and Martha Maybery, sons of William Maybery, deceased, in 1764; was selectman in 1767; killed by lightning, in Portland, June 5, 1767, and was succeeded by Peter Cobb. His widow was admitted to communion in the church that year. She was a very energetic, industrious woman and kept the family together many years. Letters of administration upon her husband's estate were given her, by the Hon. Samuel Waldo, Judge of Probate, June 7, 1768. She kept accounts of debt and credit in the same ledger that her father-in-law had kept in for years, and died Oct. 16, 1799, aged 70.

Children:

 i Ruth, b. Jan. 13, 1755; m. Aug., 1775, Jeremiah[5] Jordan (*James*,[4] *Jeremiah*,[3] *Jeremiah*,[2] *Rev. Robert*[1]), in Windham; she d. Apr. 16, 1803; and he m., 2nd, Mrs. Rebecca Rice, who d.——. See Rice. He d. at Naples, about 1840, aged 87. Ch.:
  1. Mary, b. 1776.
  2. Curtis, b. 1778;? m. Mary Lord, who d. 1871; had two children.
  3. Jeremiah, b. 1780;? m. Roxanna ——; lived in the West.
  4. Dianna, b. 1781; m 1801, Joseph McLellan; had seven children and d. Dec., 1857; he d. June 12, 1841, aged sixty-three, at Webb's Mills.
  5. James, b. May, 1784; m. Eliza Hall; had one son and five daughters and d. about 1830; she d Dec., 1857.
  6. Almira, b. Mar., 1788; m. 1810, George, son of Wm. Babb; had seven children and d. Aug., 1853, at Saccarappa; he d. Nov., 1830, aged 54.
  7. Thomas Chute, b. July 12, 1794; m. Nellie Wood from P. E. I.; had four or five children and d. Apr. 27, 1876; she d. Jan. 30, 1871, aged 69, Naples.
  8. Henry, b. 1799; m. Polly Littlehail; had three or four children; d. Dec., 1861; she d. Jan., 1861, aged 60.
  9. Abigail, b. 1801.
  10. Jotham, b. 1806; killed in the Mexican war.
  11. Ruth, b. Dec. 20, 1808; m. 1827, Caleb Chaplain, and had six daughters and four sons. Mary Jane, b. 1829; m. Newell Nutting Chute. Mr. Chaplain d. Apr. 2, 1886, aged 75; she d. May 14, 1880.
 ii James, b. Apr. 7, 1757; d. in childhood.
17 iii Josiah, b. June 4, 1759.
18 iv Thomas, b. Feb. 19, 1762.
 v James, b. Mar. 17, 1764; d. at sea 1793; he wrote to his brother Josiah from Port au Prince, May 8, 1787, of running on a reef, vessel leaking, etc.
19 vi John, b. Apr. 25, 1767.

SIXTH GENERATION.

I. 10 Samuel Chute[6] (*John,*[5] *Lionel,*[4] *James,*[3] *James,*[2] *Lionel*[1]), n in Hampstead, N. H., Feb. 16, 1746–7, taken to Granville, Annap- Co., N. S., with his parents, 1759; married Sarah, daughter of Na- iiel Barnes, July 11, 1768, and lived in Granville. He was a farmer, lversmith and a good pious man of the Baptist church. In crossing Annapolis River below Bridgetown, to hear Rev. Thomas Handley pman preach, he was drowned Nov. 12, 1786.

1.
 Mysterious are the ways of God,
  And past our comprehension,
 Too much we live on unconcerned
  Without an apprehension.
 When suddenly a scene appears
  Upon the stage of action
 That startles all our grief and fears
  And causes great distraction.

2.
 A christian man was Samuel Chute
  And going o'er the river
 The boat upset and he was drowned
  None coming to deliver.
 His aim to hear the gospel sound
  From Thomas Handley Chipman,
 But oh! alas! he was not spared
  To hear the Heavenly Footman.

3.
 His wife and children did lament
  The loss of a dear father,
 But he had passed the bounds of time
  Into the great hereafter:
 His children all did follow him,
  So far as is recorded,
 In paths of virtue, truth and grace
  And so will be rewarded.

            C. E. W.

Children:

    i   Elizabeth, b. Dec. 31, 1768; m. Joseph Weare. See Weare.
    ii Mary, b. Dec. 24, 1770; m. Eleazer Woodworth. See Woodworth.
20 iii Daniel, b. Oct. 7, 1772; m. Sarah Weare.
21 iv Abraham, b. Feb. 18, 1775; m. Mehitable Foster.
22 v William, b. June 2, 1777; m. Mary Marshall.
    vi Sarah, b. July 9, 1779; d. in Clements, about 1806.
23 vii Samuel, b. Aug. 5, 1781; m. Elizabeth Randall.
    viii Prior, b. Dec 18, 1783; drowned near Liverpool, Eng., 1820.
    ix Rachel. b. Dec. 29, 1785; m. Solomon Marshall, jun., 1803, and lived near the Bay of Fundy, Cornwallis, N. S.; he d. 1840, aged 62; she d. May 5, 1854. Ch.:

        1. Nelson, b. about 1810; m. Catharine Greenham. and had three children who all d. in infancy. Dea. N. Marshall lived in Albany, Annapolis Co., till 1853, when he moved to Marlboro, Mass. and d. there 1875.
        2. James Lynam, b. July 1, 1812; m. Eliza A., dau. of Richard Armstrong, jun., Dec. 3, 1838. They lived in Cornwallis, near Burlington, Bay of Fundy shore, where he d. Nov. 24, 1869. His wife d. Oct 2, 1886, aged 74. Ch.: (1) *Stillman James*, b. Mar. 29, 1841; m. Mina L. Dewolf, Aug. 17, 1865, and had two daus. She d. Feb. 4, 1874, aged 42; he m., 2nd, Alice A. Brown, Dec. 25, 1876. and have three sons, at Nictaux, N. S. (2) *Albert*, b. Sept. 8, 1842; d. Mar. 5, 1847. (3) *Wm. E.*, b. Oct. 13, 1844; now at the Sandwich Islands. (4) *Edward S.*, b. Nov. 13, 1845; m. Jan. 12, 1879, Ruth A. Ogleby. (5) *Cath. A.*, b. Apr. 23, 1848; m. Jan. 28, 1876, Gilbert N. Forbush; four children. (6) *Richard E.*, b. Jan. 15, 1851; m. Mar. 28, 1876, Isabel Howell; four children. (7) *Anna C.*, b. Aug. 1, 1853; m. July 3, 1886, Rev. A. B. Thomas. (8) *Lovenia*, b. Mar. 10, 1857; m. June 30, 1875, John P. Meckins; six children.

Sarah Barnes, widow of Samuel Chute, married, second, Dr. James Lynam, from London, Eng., 1787, and had a son and daughter; the daughter died in infancy, while the son, James, jun., born April 10, 1789, near Paradise, Annapolis Co., grew to manhood, and became a first-class cabinet maker. He was married to Hannah, daughter of John and Hannah (Bancroft) Starratt, by Rev. Tho. Ansley, Dec. 31, 1814. They moved to Canada West, or Ontario, 1845, and lived in London, where he died Jan. 6, 1864. She died July 17, 1880, aged eighty-five. Both were pious members of the Baptist church. Old Dr. Lynam returned to England about 1800. His widow died July, 1799, aged fifty.

Children of James and Hannah:

    i   Leonora, b. Dec. 31, 1815; d. Mar. 30. 1818.
    ii John Starratt, b. Sept 12, 1817; d. June 22. 1819.
    iii Zenas Lyman, b. Aug. 18, 1819; d. Mar. 11, 1820.
    iv James Allen, b. Feb. 2, 1821; m.
    v   Robert Henry, b. Jan. 2, 1823; m.

vi Ann Eliza, b. Dec. 31, 1824; m. Thomas Harrison.
vii David Whitman, b. Oct. 4, 1826; m.
viii Wm. Handley, b. July 8, 1828; m.
ix Sarah Jane, b. July 25, 1830; m. Dea. J. J. Wellstead.
x Eleanor Sophia, b. Jan. 8, 1833; m.
xi John Staurat r, b. Jan. 15, 1835; m.
xii Charles Edwin, b. Nov. 20, 1837; m.
xiii Zenas, b. ———, 1840; m.

VI. 11 John Chute, jun.[6] (*John*,[5] *Lionel*,[4] *James*,[3] *James*,[2] *Lionel*[1]), born in Hampstead, N. H., Apr. 9, 1752; taken to N. S. with his parents, 1759; married Mary, daughter of Capt. Paul Crocker of Lunenburg, Mass. (born Mar. 30, 1751; died Aug. 8, 1829) and had thirteen children. He moved from Granville to Digby-Joggins, Digby Co., in 1799, where he lived a good honest farmer, captain of militia, and pious deacon of the Baptist church; died Mar. 8, 1841, his funeral being attended by Rev. Charles Randall, sermon taken from II Cor. v : 1.
Children :

1 Joanna, b. July 9, 1772; m. 1799, Timothy Brooks, who d. June, 1823, aged 58. His widow m. John Harvey, 1825, went to Lower Canada 1827, and d. 1836. He d. 1837, aged 62.
  1. Mary, b. May 2, 1801; d. 1819.
  2. Timothy, b. Dec. 2, 1802; m. Susan, daughter of John and Ruth Rhodes, 1833, and d. May 7, 1888; she d. Apr. 9, 1884, aged 78. Children: (1) *Israel D.*, b. Dec. 26, 1833; m. Julia A. Steadman (*Charles C.*,[3] *John*,[2] *John*[1]), 1854, and d. 1869; had Susan D., Charles B., Norman, Laura, Florence and Euphemia; she m., 2nd, Wm. Loyte, May 3, 1891, and live in Lynn, Mass. (2) *Mary Ann*, b. July 12, 1835; m. John E. Chute, see No. 136. (3) *Elizabeth E.*, b. Oct. 11, 1837; m. Foster Farnsworth, 1857. (4) *Phebe R.*, b. Sept. 15, 1842; m. John Edward Farnsworth, 1860. (5) *John Fletcher*, b. July 11, 1845; m. Julia, daughter of Seth Brown, Apr. 10, 1874. (6) *Joanna A.*, b. Dec. 3, 1850; m. Geo. Whitman, Mar. 9, 1887. (7) *Lloyd D.*, b. Dec. 16, 1854; m. Mattie, daughter of James, of Sylvanus Snow.
  3. John, b. Jan. 11, 1805; d. 1810.
  4. John, b. Nov. 4, 1808; m. Susan Grimes, Lubec, Me. and d. at 1860.
  5. Thomas, b. Nov. 9, 1812; m. Phœbe Ann, of John and Mary (Chute) Ellis, Dec. 29, 1836, and had twelve children. They moved to Lynn, Mass., 1867, and kept a boarding-house, where he d. Aug. 5, 1891.

24 ii Crocker, b. Jan. 23, 1774.
    iii Elisab. P., b. April 18, 1776; m., 1792, Richard Chandler from Yorkshire, England, and d. Apr., 1813; he d. 1822. Ch. :
      1. Fanny, b. 1793; m. John Lingley, and had Charles, Elizabeth and Frances Ellen. Charles, b. 1829; m. Eliza, daughter of James Miller and d. about 1873. A daughter Elisab. Ann, d. 1873, aged about 20.
      2. Sarah, b. Sept. 27, 1795; m. David M. Chute. See 45.

3. MARY, b. 1797; m. John Harvey and had James Richard, b. about 1820; m., 1st, Mary B., daughter of John Clark and had five children; he m., 2nd, Louise D., daughter of James and Eleanor Miller and had nine children.
4. ELEANOR, b. 1800; m. Dec. 14, 1821, James, son of Michael and Sarah (Farnsworth) Miller and d. 1879; he d. 1876, aged 79. Children: (1) *Eliza*, b. 1822; m. Charles Lingley. (2) *Catherine*, b. 1824; d. 1837. (3) *Ann*, b. 1827; m. Jacob Bogert; 2d, Charles Mills, Lynn, Mass. (4) *James E.*, b. Jan., 1829; m. Horatia D.[4] Steadman (*Charles C*,[3] *John*,[2] *John*[1]), Nov., 1852; had five children. (5) *Weston*, b. 1831; m. Almaretta, daughter of Oliver Saunders; five children. (6) *Lois*, b. 1834; m. David Tucker, Lynn, Mass. (7) *Louise D.*, b. 1836; m. James R. Harvey, Clinton, Mass. (8) *Joseph*, b. 1840; d. 1841.

25 iv GEORGE WASHINGTON, b. Apr. 27, 1778.
    v DANIEL AUSTIN, b. Mar. 16, 1780; d. 1796.
26 vi PAUL, b. 1782.
    vii MARY, b. Apr. 19, 1785; m., 1st, Solomon Farnsworth, 1801; had five children. See Farnsworth. He d. Nov. 19, 1812, aged 74; m , 2nd, John Ellis, Feb. 15, 1813; she d. Nov., 1856. Children:
1. MARGARETTA, b. 1814; m. Robert J. Sherrar.
2. SARAH, b. 1816; d. about 1836.
3. EDWARD, b. 1818; d. about 1834.
4. PHŒBE ANN, b. July 12, 1820; m. Thos. Brooks, 1836, and had twelve children.
5. ABIGAIL, b. Aug. 16, 1822; m. Jacob Bogert.
6. WILLIAM, b. 1824. John Ellis left N. S. in 1829 and took William with him.

    viii LYDIA, b. Apr. 19, 1785; m. Sam Foster. See Foster.
27 ix PETER PRESCOTT, b. May 27, 1787.
    x ELEANOR, b. July 11, 1789; m. James, son of John and Sarah (Foster) Adams, Digby Co., 1808; about 1832, at the age of 52, he left N. S. and lived near Portland, Me.; she d. 1868.
1. JAMES, b. 1809; drowned in the Bay of Fundy, Dec., 1828.
2. MARY A., b. Mar. 10, 1811; m. Thos. O'Connor, Broad Cove, N. S. and d. Dec., 1860; he d. 1880.
3. LYDIA, b. Feb. 22, 1813; m. Edward, son of Wm. Middleton, Dec. 4, 1831; had eleven children. They moved to Elgin Co., Ont., 1850, where he d. June 13, 1872, exactly 72; she d. Aug. 20, 1887.
4. AUSTIN D., b. 1815; m., 1st, Nancy, daughter of Isaac O'Connor, who d. Jan. 15, 1868, aged 63; m., 2nd, Almira A. P. (Densmore) Ham, d. Dec. 16, 1878, aged 42; m., 3rd, Caroline Ward, widow of Wm. Odell and live at Springfield, Elgin Co., Ont. They had three or four children.
5. ROBERT, b. 1818; m. Augusta Campbell, near Digby.
6. MAURICE, b. Sept. 15, 1820; m., 1st, Eliza A. Campbell, Dec. 16, 1842, and had six children; she d. 1855, aged 32; m., 2nd, Eliza Jane, daughter of Charles Pinkney, Nov. 12, 1856, and had five more in Clements.
7. SUSAN, b. Apr. 2, 1822; m. Eleazer Woodworth. See Woodworth.
8. LOVINA, b. 1824; m. William son of Benjamin Cronk, Eastport, Me.; a school teacher.

9. JOHN, b. 1826; m. Mary Ann Morrison.
10. SARAH, b. 1828; m. John Brown.
11. MATILDA, b. 1830; m. John, son of Wm. Middleton, Digby Neck.

xi JOHN, 2nd, jun., b. Oct. 14, 1790.

xii LEAH FOWLER, b. Apr. 7, 1793; m. Robert, son of Jacob and Mary (Chesley) Woodman, 1814, from Durham, N. H.; he d. Mar. 10, 1853, aged 60; Leah d. Mar. 6, 1875. Ch.:
 1. MARY ELISAB., b. Apr. 22, 1815; d. Dec. 21, 1837.
 2. MILES CHESLEY, b. May 26, 1816; m. Caroline, daughter of Samuel Rice, 1840, and had four children.
 3. JAMES EDWARD, b. Sept. 26, 1817; m. Lucy J. Patch, Sept., 1849, and d. Dec., 1884.
 4. JACOB CROCKER, b. May 23, 1819; m. Eliza, daughter of Lewis Cosset, 1850, and had five children.
 5. AGNES JANE, b. Sept. 28, 1820; m., 1st, Benjamin, son of Henry Seely, Nov. 14, 1854; he d. Apr. 8, 1879, aged 73; m., 2nd, Wm. Henry, son of Nathan and Susan (Gates) Randall. See Randall.
 6. SARAH SELINA, b. Apr. 5, 1822; m. John Cosset, 1840; had one son, and d. Aug., 1881; he m., 2nd, Maximilian Armstrong.
 7. ROBERT GEORGE, b. Dec. 20, 1823; d. Dec. 30, 1824.
 8. BETHIA MATILDA, b. Sept. 21, 1825; m. Capt. James T. Hinxman, Christmas, 1854, and live in Danvers, Mass.; she died Jan. 4, 1892.
 9. ROBERT GEORGE, b. May 21, 1827; m. Maria Birstead; was killed at the battle of Cold Harbor, June 3, 1864; she m., 2nd, Joseph Tapley.
 10. CYNTHIA ANNA, b. June 28, 1829; m. John Gabel, 1859; d. June 27, 1888.
 11. JOHN CHUTE. b. May 9, 1831; m. Mary Rice, 1852.
 12. HENRY AUSTIN, b. Apr 10, 1833; went to sea; mate of a ship.
 13. ISRAEL POTTER, b. Mar. 24, 1835; m., 1st, Sarah Jane, daughter of John van Buskirk, 1865; d. Aug. 15, 1867, aged 27; m., 2nd, Sophronia Ann, daughter of Geo. Nichols, 1869, and died Feb. 12, 1875.
 14. VICTORIA SELINDA, b. Apr. 8, 1837; d. Apr. 26, 1855.
 15. MARY AMORET, b. July 9, 1839; d. Dec. 24, 1844.

xiii JOSEPH FOWLER, b. Feb. 21, 1795.

VI. 12 Benj. Chute, born in Hampstead, N. H., Sept. 27, 1754; ken to Granville, N. S., with his parents in 1759; married Martha, ughter of Ezekiel and Mary (Roberts) Foster, 1777, and died Oct. ', 1831; she died Feb. 11, 1816, aged sixty.

i JAMES, b. Apr. 19, 1778.

ii MARY, b. May 21, 1780; m. Jan. 8, 1801, Aquilla, son of John and Patience (Tolman) Langley (Mass. to N. S. about 1760), and d. 1823. He d. 1830, aged about 60. Ch.:
 1. SOPHIA, b. Feb. 4, 1802; d. young.
 2. BENJAMIN, b. July 24, 1805; m. Betsey Clark.
 3. LEVI, b. Sept. 11, 1807; m. Abbie Messenger, 1828, had three sons, three daughters, and d. Oct., 1867.
 4. LOVENA, b. Sept. 2, 1810; m. Joseph. son of Thos. Hicks.
 5. EZEKIEL, b. June 16, 1814; d. young.

6. MARTHA, b. Nov. 9, 1819; m. Wm.² Long (*Peter,² John Henry¹*), and had five children.
31 iii SETH, b. Sept. 15, 1782.
iv HANNAH, b. Dec. 19, 1784; m. Hanly Chute. See 44.
32 v BENJAMIN, b. Apr. 14, 1787.
33 vi EZEKIEL, b. Jan. 6, 1790.
34 vii JOSEPH, b. Dec. 9, 1792.
viii EATON, b. Aug. 25, 1795; d. Sept. 22, 1796.
ix MARTHA, b. Aug. 17, 1799; m. Isaac Woodbury,* jun., Nov. 18, 1823; she d. Jan. 26, 1859; he m., 2nd, Elizabeth Brotha, widow of James Ord, drowned in Spectade Lake, Dalhousie, 1840, leaving six children; and widow of Peter, son of John Henry Long, who d. Jan. 11, 1858, aged 72, leaving five children. Peter Long m., 1st, Martha, daughter of John Langley, jr., 1807, and had: Jacob, Ephraim, John, William, Dexter, Joel, Fletcher, Lydia, Ann, Beulah. Mr. Woodbury d. June 4, 1863, aged 65. His widow d. Jan. 9, 1883, exactly 76. Ch.
1. JOHN G., b. Apr. 9, 1825; m. Naomi, daughter of Deacon John and Bethia (Chipman) Wilson, Feb. 25, 1851, and had three children.

VI. 13 Thomas Chute, born in New Hampshire, Mar. 13, 1757; taken to Nova Scotia with his parents 1759; married Sibyll, daughter of William and Lydia (Willett) Marshall, by Rev. Arsarelah Morse, 1778; lived in Granville till 1801, when he moved to Bear River, in Clements, and there lived thirty-seven years, a good honest farmer, and a pious exemplary deacon in the Baptist church. His wife died Apr. 12, 1829, in her sixty-eighth year and as two of his family married that year, he sought and married Sarah, daughter of Alex. McKenzie, and widow of Joseph Thomas, of Granville, Nov. 29, 1829. He died June 13, 1838; she died Mar. 7, 1846, aged eighty. His funeral was attended by Rev. Ezekiel Masters, the sermon from Psa. 127 : 3, 4 and 5. Children :

i CATHARINE, b. Mar. 1, 1779; m. John Weare. See Weare.
35 ii THOMAS, b. June 14, 1780.
iii PHŒBE, b. Jan. 13, 1782; m. James Chute. See 30.
iv SUSANNAH, b. Mar. 12, 1784; d. Oct. 17, 1797.
v ESTHER, b. Oct. 19, 1785; m. Rev. Gilbert Spurr, July 7, 1809; moved to Wakefield, Carleton Co., N. B., where their family was raised. Besides being a sober, industrious farmer, he was converted and joined the Baptist church about 1808; licensed to preach at the time of the American war; ordained to the gospel ministry 1826, and was an active zealous laborer in the Master's cause, and baptized some dozens of converts. He d. July 30, 1870,

---
* Isaac Woodbury, sen., b. Dec. 8, 1765, Haverhill, Mass.; m. Mary St. Croix (b. July 8, 1763, in New York), and had: 1. Isaac, b. June 8, 1798. 2. Mary, b. Apr 23, 1800; m. James Harris 3. Elisha, b. Apr. 3, 1802; m. Nancy Harris. 4. Edward, a half-brother.

GENEALOGIES OF THE CHUTE FAMILY.

in Nova Scotia aged 83. Esther d. Oct. 25, 1865. In 1853, they had a splendid visit among kindred and friends in Ont. Children:

1. ELIZABETH, b. Nov 24, 1813; m. Oct. 13, 1831, David, brother of Richard, the missionary and son of Thomas Burpee of Sheffield, N. B.; she d. Mar. 9, 1846; he d. Apr. 15, 1842, aged 34. Children: (1) *Julia Ann*, b. Nov. 11, 1832; m. David M., son of George Everett, Apr. 16, 1855, and had four sons and four daughters. (2) *Enoch G.*, b. Aug. 19, 1834; m. Lydia C., daughter of Geo. Everett, Dec. 13, 1855; d. Oct. 18, 1877; and had two sons, and two daughters. A daughter Lily m. Rev. Fred Blackmer. (3) *Syretha J.*, b. Aug. 1, 1836; m. Jonathan Estey, Nov. 12, 1863, had one son and d. Apr. 1, 1868. (4) *Thomas G.*, b. Dec. 10, 1838; m. Alice L. Neal, Dec. 5, 1868, and d. Sept. 10, 1880. (5) *Alfred Judson*, b. Nov. 30, 1840; m. Hepzibah M. Everett, Apr. 2, 1862, and had eight children.

2. MARY, b. Jan. 12, 1816; m. Thomas Chute. See No. 87.

3. ANN, b. Feb. 20, 1818; m. Daniel Chute, jr. See No. 64.

4. JERUSHA, b. Nov. 9, 1820; m. Nathaniel[7] Fletcher (*Daniel*,[6] *David*,[5] *John*,[4] *Samuel*,[3] *Francis*,[2] *Robert*[1] of Concord, Mass., 1630), Oct. 2, 1851, as his 3rd wife. His 1st wife was Mary E. Dingee. 1833; had two sons; d. Oct. 30, 1836, aged 24; 2nd, Mary Ann Tapley, July 31, 1837; had six children; d. Aug. 3, 1850, in Woodstock, aged 33. 3rd wife d. Oct. 26, 1866; he d. in Woodstock, N. B., June 12, 1868. Ch.: (1) *Sarah E.*, b. July 5, 1852; d. 1859. (2) *Gilbert S.*, b. Nov. 14, 1853; artist in Boston. (3 and 4) *Mary Eliza* and *Ella Maria*, b. and d. 1855. (5) *Lewis P. F.*, b. Oct. 28, 1856; m. Ida Jane, daughter of Earl Douglass and Jane M. Brown, May 24, 1882, and have a son Guy Brown, b. Feb. 5, 1884; removed to Brookline, Mass., Oct., 1889, a printer. (6) *Leverett N.*, b. Apr. 16, 1858; m. Ellen, daughter of Benj. and Martha Esty, 1889; a jeweller in Woodstock. (7) *Thomas Havelock*, b. 1860; d. 1862. (8) *Charles Haddon*, b. July 18, 1862. (9) *Alice Gertrude*, b. Feb. 20, 1864; m. Caleb Crawford, Apr. 22, 1885; live in Malden, Mass.

5. HARRIET, b. Sept. 5, 1822; m. Henry, son of Wm. Kitchen, Apr. 11, 1843, who d. 1890, aged 86; she d. June 24, 1866. Ch.: *Caroline*, b. 1843; m. Hughy McGraw, July 23, 1863; d. Sept., 1865, and he m. 2nd, Augusta Estabrooks; m., 3rd, ———. (2) *William*, b. 1845; m. Mary, daughter of Beverly Estey, Mar., 1873; eight children. (3) *Mary A.*, b. 1847; m. Fred, son of Jonathan Estey, June, 1868; six children. (4) *Henry S.*, b. 1848; d. Aug., 1850. (5) *Martha*, b. Aug. 6, 1850; m. Benj., son of Beverly Esty, Dec. 14, 1868, and have four children. (6) *Fanny*, b. Mar. 14, 1853; m. Alfred Smith, 1873, have six children. (7) *Burpee*, b. Feb., 1855; m. Carrie ———, 1885. (8) *Gilbert*, b. July 23, 1857; m. Anna Kinney, and have three children. (9) *Herbert*, b. 1859; d. June, 1877. (10) *Carrie*, b. Dec. 2, 1864; m. ———. (11) *Frank*, b. June 24, 1866; d. Dec., 1867.

6. JANE, b. March 31, 1824; m., 1st, Richard S., son of Elias Clark, Apr. 8, 1841; he d. Nov. 7, 1868, aged 57; she m., 2nd, Charles Bubar (b. Dec. 19, 1812), Dec. 23, 1875, his 3rd wife. Children: (1) *Gertrude*, b. Oct. 24, 1843; m. Elijah Gallup, Apr. 27, 1867; seven children; he d. Dec. 6, 1884, aged 65; she was his 2nd wife. (2) *Martha A.*,

b. June 22, 1845; d. Oct. 25, 1867. (3) *Charles S.*, b. Aug. 7, 1847; d. May 3, 1848. (4) *James T.*, b. Mar. 20, 1850; m. Lo— daughter of Enoch Gallup, June, 1874; had four children; she d. June 24, 1885, aged 30. (5) *Howard P.*, b. Mar. 10, 1852; m. Me— vina Irvin, Oct. 12, 1881. Wakefield, N. B. (6) *Alice Maria*, b. Jan. 18, 1854; m. Jerome Hailey, Oct., 1880; had one child; he d. 1887. (7) *Florence Esther*, b. Jan. 12, 1856; m. Geo. E. Clark, Apr. 1874, and had three children; Bangor, Me. (8) *Susan Ella*, b. Ja. —. 4, 1858; m. Alex. Fleming, Sept., 1882; had one child. (9) *Richard H.*, b. Mar. 17, 1860; m. Emma J. Shaw, Apr. 23, 1883; had one child; Wakefield, N. B. (10) *Mary Eliza*, b. Mar. 19, 1862. (11) *Maggie B.*, b. Aug. 2, 1864; m. Geo. A. Densmore, Sept. 24, 1884; have one son; Upper Brighton, N. B.

7. EMELINE, b. Feb. 17, 1826; m. Rev. Samuel, son of Benj. Burtt, Apr. 3, 1845; lived in Jacksontown, N. B., where he d. the fall of 1887, aged 69. (1) *Albert Herman*, b. Dec. 21, 1845; d. Jan. 14, 1875. (2) *Geo. Roscoe*, b. Jan. 28, 1847; m. Augusta, daughter of Henry Currier, Mar. 3, 1875. (3) *Mary Esther*, b. July 23, 1848; d. Nov. 9, 1869. (4) *Jerusha O.*, b. Dec. 31, 1849; m. Robert, son of William A. Hannah, Jan. 5, 1871; d. 1888. (5) *Albina Maria*, b. Jan. 4, 1852; m. J. D., son of Jacob Jewett, Jan. 24, 1872; d. in 1890. (6) *Cornelius G.*, b. Sept. 14, 1853; m. James P., son of Alex. Watson, Nov. 4, 1881. (7) *Eliza Jane*, b. Feb. 25, 1855; d. Nov. 14, 1878. (8) *Herbert Newton*, b. Dec. 6, 1856; Minneapolis, Minn.

vi SARAH, b. Oct. 30, 1787; m. Dec. 16, 1811, William, son of Isaac Marshall, and lived in Clarence, Annapolis Co., N. S., as an honest, industrious, pious farmer; she d. Dec. 11, 1856; he d. June 29, 1860, aged 83. Children:

1. LUCINDA, b. Feb. 16, 1814; d. Feb. 1, 1851.
2. SIBYL, b. Sept. 6, 1815; m. Gilbert Chute. See 86.
3. SOPHIA, b. Feb. 27, 1817; m., 1st, Jacob, son of Abner Chute, Jan. 9, 1840; he d. Mar. 7, 1843, aged 27; she m., 2nd, Oct. 14, 1845, George C.[7] Banks (*George*,[6] *Joshua*,[5] *Joshua*,[4] *Moses*,[3] *John*,[2] *Richard*[1] *of York, Me.*, 1640), and lived in Clarence; she d. Jan. 6, 1888. They moved from Clarence to Middleton, 1868. Children: (1) *Emma S.*, b. June 13, 1849; d. 1887. (2) *Anna E.*, b. Jan. 7, 1854; m. Wm. L. Jackson, June 8, 1881; she d. 1888. (3) *Howard D.*, b. Dec. 13, 1857, d. 1887. (4) *Alfred M.*, b. Apr. 25, 1860.
4. HIRAM, b. May 17, 1819; m., 1st, Zilphia, daughter of Jeremiah Porter, Dec. 1, 1842, and had two sons: Ritson M., b. 1844; Adelbert E., b. 1850. She d. Apr. 19, 1868, aged 47; he m., 2nd, Adelaide, b. 1835, daughter of John Coleman, Apr. 22, 1869, and after that moved to Lakeville, in Cornwallis, Kings Co., N. S.
5. ROBERT, b. Apr. 30, 1821; m., 1st, Margaret Ann Shaffner, Oct. 14, 1846; had 7 children. She d. Dec. 21, 1856, in her 35th year; he m., 2d, Martha Ann Saunders, Mar. 31, 1857, Clarence, N. S. and had 5 children. Children: (1) *Mary Eliza*, b. 1850; m. Norman Longley; (2) *Gertrude*, b. 1852; m. Edward Leonard. (3) *Annie*, b. ——. (4) *Ella*, of 2nd w.
6. ALFRED, b. Mar. 14, 1823; after travelling several years, teaching school, and taking pictures, m. Harriet C., daughter of James Man-

ning and Leah (Foster) Chute, Dec. 10, 1868. Children: (1) *William Wellington Nelson*, b. Sept. 19, 1869. (2) *Harriet Gertrude Amelia*, b. Apr. 10, 1871. (3) *Edward Manning*, b. Aug. 21, 1872. (4) *Jessie Graham*, b. Apr. 25, 1882.

7. DEACON EDWARD, b. June 10, 1825; m. Salina E. daughter of Caleb Marshall, Nov. 12, 1848, who d. July 25, 1849, aged 21; m., 2nd, Matilda Tomlinson, June 13, 1850, and had 5 daughters, 1 son, besides losing several. The son, Dr. Carey F. Marshall, m. Ida Shaw, and lives at Glenmere, Lynn, Mass. Have three sons.
8. NAOMI, b. Dec. 4, 1827, m. Fred. Banks, brother to Geo. C. B., Nov. 4, 1847, and had a daughter Mary Ellen, that d. aged 6 or 7 years. Naomi d. June 28, 1852; he m., 2nd, Seraph Adelaide, daughter of Ezekiel and Lydia A. (Morse) Chute, June 8, 1854, and had 2 or 3 children.
9. HARRIET, b. Dec. 22, 1829, m. John, son of Isaac and Elizabeth (Patterson) Foster (his 2nd w.), Dec. 22, 1858, and d. Nov. 28, 1872. He d. June, 1871, aged 43.
10. MINETTA, b. Mar. 1, 1833, m. Charles B. Clark, Dec. 1, 1853, and had a son Wm. Stewart, who m. Mary, daughter of Robert Banks. Mr. C. B. Clark d. Feb. 22, 1889, a. 67.

36 vii ANDREW, b. Sept. 15, 1789.
37 viii ABEL, b. Oct. 5, 1791.
 ix ELIZABETH, b. June 30, 1793; d. Dec. 22, 1813; a good singer.
38 x CALVIN, b. Oct. 23, 1795.
39 xi JOHN, b. Sept. 25, 1797.
 xii SUSAN, b. Oct. 22, 1799; m. Abram Chute, No. 59.
40 xiii BINEA, b. June 23, 1801, at Bear River.
 xiv SOPHIA, b. June 26, 1803; m. Boemer Chute, No. 61.
 xv HICKS, b. Aug. 14, 1806; d. Aug. 18, 1806.
41 xvi JAS. EDWARD, b. May 5, 1810.

VI. 14 James, son of John and Judith (Foster) Chute, born in Granville, Annapolis Co., N. S., Jan. 22, 1762; married Elizabeth, daughter of Abner and Anna (Church) Morse, 1783, and had eight children. She died April, 1798, aged thirty-seven; and he married, second, Elizabeth, daughter of John and Sylvia (Harris) Wright, by Parson Milledge, Jan. 28, 1802, and had eight children. He was a farmer and jeweler, and religiously rather skeptical; died April 9, 1829. She died June 19, 1856, aged seventy-six, a good pious woman.

Children:

42 i ABNER, b. Dec. 2, 1783.
 ii JOHN, b. ——, 1785; d. Nov., 1797.
43 iii SILAS, b. June 15, 1787.
 iv JACOB, b. Feb., 1789; drowned Oct. 19, 1817.
44 v HANLEY, b. Dec. 13, 1790.
 vi HELEN, b. ——, 1792; d. Nov., 1797.
45 vii DAVID M., b. Jan. 3, 1795.
 viii ANN, b. ——, 1797; d. soon after.

46 ix DIMOCK, b. Jan. 17, 1803.
    x SIDNEY, b. Oct. 6, 1804; school teacher, drowned June 17, 1826.
    xi CHRISTOPHER HARRIS, b. Jan. 3, 1807; teacher and preacher, d. Aug. 2, 1853.
    xii ANGUS, b. May 14, 1809; teacher in St. Louis, 1860.
    xiii GEORGE, b. Mar. 30, 1812; drowned May 19, 1823.
47 xiv OBED, b. Aug. 8, 1814.
    xv CAROLINE HADASSA, b. Mar. 28, 1819; d. April 3, 1886.
    xvi ELIZABETH CHARLOTTE, b. Aug. 13, 1822; d. Nov. 29, 1843.

VI. 15 James Chute[6] (*Daniel,*[5] *James,*[4] *James,*[3] *James,*[2] *Lionel*[1]), born in Newbury, Mass., Feb. 16, 1751; married June 13, 1775, Mehitable, daughter of Richard Thurston of Rowley, and lived many years a farmer; he was a pious deacon in the Congregational church in Boxford. She died Oct. 18, 1819, aged sixty-six. After that the deacon travelled among his friends and kindred in the West, and died in Madison, Ind., April 28, 1825.

Children:

    i BETSY, b. Dec., 1776; m. Daniel Hale. See Hale.
48 **ii** RICHARD, b. Sept. 3, 1778.
    iii HANNAH, b. Aug. 21, 1780; m. John Poor[5] (*Joseph,*[4] *Samuel,*[3] *Henry,*[2] *John*[1]), 1797, moved to Pittsburg, Pa., the awfully cold summer of 1816, and to Cincinnati, O., the next year, where two of her brothers, James and Daniel, lived; and in 1819, moved to a place forty miles west of Madison, Ind., where Mr. Poor d. Dec. 9, aged 44. She d. Jan. 30, 1872. Children:
      1. AMANDA, b. Oct. 12, 1798; d. Feb. 5, 1799.
      2. WENDELL, b. Dec. 27, 1799; m. Elizabeth Weddell; 2nd, Thirza Guthree.
      3. AMANDA, b. Oct. 15, 1801; m. Moses B. Pearson, jun., 1819.
      4. ALVIN, b. July 31, 1803; m. Julia A. Zaring, 1833.
      5. HANNAH, b. Nov. 17, 1804; m. Jonathan Prosser, 1826, and had 8 children. Son Abram was in Co. H, 2nd Minn. V. I., in Ga., late war.
      6. BETSY CHUTE, b. Jan. 6, 1807; m. Walter Wright, 1826.
      7. MEHITABLE T., b. Nov. 25, 1809; m. Wm. S. Merrill, M.D, 1831.
      8. SUSANNAH, b. Dec. 15, 1811; m. Thos. J. Brooks, 1830.
      9. HARRIET, b. Aug. 27, 1815; m. Wm. H. Houghton, 1836.
      10. JOHN, b. Feb. 1, 1818; away in Cal. and Ore.
      11. AMELIA P., b. Aug. 21, 1820; m. John Dewitt.
    iv MEHITABLE, b. ——, 1782; m. Major Jonathan Elliott[5] (*Jonathan,*[4] *David,*[3] *John,*[2] *Edward,*[1] from England to Salisbury, Mass., 1643), of Concord, N. H. 1800, and d. about 1820. He d. 1812, aged 37. Children:
      1. SOPHRONIA, b. 1800, d. 1812.
      2. CAROLINE, b. ——; d. in infancy.
      3. FIDELIA, b. 1805; m. Joseph Elkins, Nashua.
      4. ELIZABETH HALE, b. 1806, Somerville, Mass.
      5. ANDREW SWETT, b. 1810; d. 1812.
      6. SOPHRONIA, b. 1812; m. Andrew Baldwin, and had Jenny Flora; m., 2nd, John Trow.
    v EUNICE, b. Dec. 1784; m. Joseph Hale. See Hale.

vi MARY, b. Jan. 7, 1786; m. Col. Jeremiah Coleman[4] of Newbury (*John,*[3] *Tobias,*[2] *Thomas*[1] and Joanna Folger; Thomas d. 1682), June 8, 1808, and d. Mar. 4, 1872. He d. Mar. 23, 1866, aged 83. Children:
1. DOROTHY PEARSON, b. Feb. 13, 1810; m. Dea. Wm. Thurston[5] (*David,*[4] *Richard,*[3] *Daniel,*[2] *Daniel*[1]), Oct. 16, 1837, and d. Jan. 4, 1868. He m., 2nd, Caroline E. Greenleaf, and d. Sept. 16, 1882, aged 75.
2. BETSY LITTLE, b. Dec. 21, 1813; d. Dec. 12, 1860.
3. MOSES, b. July 27, 1817; m. Elizabeth Coffin, April 10, 1839, and she d. Feb. 6, 1881; he m., 2nd, Mrs. Isabel L. Buck, Jan. 5, 1884.
4. MEHITABLE T., b. Aug. 28, 1821; d. Sept. 20, 1850.
5. JAMES CHUTE, b. April 28, 1826; m. Sarah E. Withington, Jan. 1, 1857, and live in Newburyport.

49 vii DANIEL, b. June 4, 1787.
50 viii JAMES, b. Nov. 15, 1788.

Mar. 19, 1779. David Jewett, for £900, sold to James Chute all the real estate given by Ezekiel Jewett, late of Boxford, to his 3 sons, Ezekiel, Stephen, & Jonathan, the same being three-fifths of all the lands with the buildings thereon that he, the above Ezek Jewett died seized of, lying in Boxford & Rowley, the aboves'd Chute to come into possession at the decease of the widow Jewett of Boxford & not before.

David Jewett, & seal
In presence of Wm Stickney   Nich. Pike, J. P.
 Daniel Chute.   John Pickering, Reg'r,
            May 20, 1783.

May 18, 1779. Joseph & Joanna Snow, of Wilton, N. H., for £50, sold to James Chute of Rowley one thirtyeth of the lands & salt marsh of the late Ezek. Jewett of Boxford. Jacob Abbot, J. P.

May 19, 1779. Amos Poor of Newbury, to James Chute of Rowley, another thirtyeth part of Ezek. Jewett's estate. Amos Poor 3rd & seal
 Nich Pike, J. P.   Sarah " "

May 19, 1779. Enoch Jewett, of Dunstable, N. H., yeoman, for £200, sold to James Chute of Rowley, yeoman ⅔ of ¼ of all the lands & meadow in the township of Boxford and Rowley with the buildings thereon standing, which Ezek Jewett, late of Boxford, died seized of, to have after the death of the widow Martha Jewett.

Enoch Jewett & seal
Joshua Bailey, J. P., Sept. 21, 1780.

April 18, 1789. Thos Smith of Newbury, cooper, for £15, 6, 6, sold to Daniel Chute jun. of Rowley, 2½ acres, bounded beginning at a white oak bounds tree between sd Smith, Daniel Chute & Richard Little, and running about 20 rods by Little's woodland to a stake and stones, from thence running twenty rods & ten feet southeast to a stake & stones, from thence running about 20 rods S W, to a stake & stones, and from thence by Daniel Chutes land to the first mentioned bounds.

 Daniel Chute   Thos Smith & seal
 Stephen Thurston,   Parker Cleaveland, J. P.

 April 26, 1794. James Chute sold to Thos Perley jun of Boxford, for £336, 2, 6, 42½ acres, also another piece of 17½ acres, also another piece of 6 acres, and his wife Mahitable also joined & signed her right away.   P. Cleaveland, J. P.
                John Pickering, Reg.

 April 17, 1799. Benj. Brown of Andover, yeoman, for $3,078, sold to Daniel Chute of Reading, Middlesex Co., three pieces of land 3 acres, 61 acres, & 107 acres.   Benja Brown & seal
Gideon Foster, Jona Gleason.   Anna Brown & seal
                 Joshua Holt, J. P.

 April 19, 1799. Daniel Chute of Reading, Co. of Middlesex, gentleman, to Benjamin Brown of Andover, Co. of Essex, for $2,276, sold 171 acres of land, explained & described in a very long deed.
                Daniel Chute & seal
 In presence of Peter Brown   Polly Chute & seal
  Jonathan Gleason.
   Received & Receipted June 13, 1799,
      John Pickering, Reg.

VI. 16 David Chute[6] brother to the preceding James, born Aug. 19, 1756; married Ruth Searle, 1793, lived in Newbury, and died Sept., 1843; she died Mar., 1847, aged eighty-one.
Children:

 i SALLY, b. June 23, 1794; m. Enoch Poor[5] (*Jeremiah*,[4] *Jeremiah*,[3] *Henry*,[2] *John*[1]) of Georgetown, Jan. 1833, and d. Oct. 31, 1889. He d. Nov. —, 1855, in his 67th year.
 ii SOPHIA, b. Nov. 23, 1797; d. Dec. 1881.
 iii JUDITH, b. May 25, 1800; m. Jeremiah Clark of Georgetown, Feb. 27, 1834, and had 5 children; 4 d. young, while Geo. Washington, b. Feb. 20, 1839, m. and is living in Lowell, Mass. Mr. Clark d. May 19, 1842, aged 56; his widow d. Feb. 5, 1887.
 iv HANNAH, b. Nov. 5, 1801; m. James, son of Josiah Peabody, April 10, 1827, and d. Feb. 17, 1889; he d. May 29, 1851, aged 52. Children:
  1. JAMES CHUTE, b. Feb. 20, 1828; m. Margaret Pearson, Oct. 20, 1852, lives on the old Chute farm in Newbury, and is an editor in Newburyport.
  2. DAVID, b. Dec. 7, 1833; m. Emily Hills, Dover, N. H., and d. Oct. 4, 1885, leaving one son.

3. LORAINE, b. May 30, 1836.
4. ARIEL, b. Feb. 26, 1838, is on the old farm in Newbury. He was in Co. H, 2nd U. S. Sharpshooters, and in nearly thirty engagements; a prisoner 6 months — 2 months in Andersonville, Ga.— and then exchanged.
5. SARAH L. D., b. July 11, 1845; m. May 30, 1863, W. S. Simonds, and had 3 children. One, Geo. Arthur, m. Nellie Cook.

v MARY, b. April 27, 1809; d. in Nov.
vi DAVID, b. April 27, 1809; d. Jan., 1833.
vii DANIEL, b. Oct. 16, 1812; d. Feb., 1849.

VI. 17 Josiah Chute[6] (*Curtis*,[5] *Thomas*,[4] *James*,[3] *James*,[2] *Lionel*[1]), born in Windham, Cumberland Co., Me., June 4, 1759; was a soldier in the Revolution, in the batles of Hubbardstown, July 7, 1777,— when he was wounded in the shoulder by a musket ball — Monmouth, June 28, 1778, and at Valley Forge in 1779, he was appointed or promoted to the 5th Co. of the 11th Reg. of Mass., Jan. 1, 1778, and honorably discharged Jan. 1, 1779, having been in the service two whole years. He was orderly sergeant, and by many was honored with the title of Colonel. After he returned home in 1781, he was made constable, and collector of taxes. He collected a tax of £370, in 1782, and £421 1 11, in 1783. He bought of Zebulon Noyes for £45, a town lot in Portland, Aug. 7, 1786. He was one of the selectmen in 1788, 1791–6, 1798, 1800, 1802–4, 1806–11, 1814–16. He was town clerk of Windham in 1804, and represented the "District of Maine," in the General Court of Massachusetts, in 1805–12; and again in 1816–20. He married Mary, daughter of David Noyes of Portland, Sept. 11, 1781, and had ten children.

WAR DEPARTMENT.
Invalid pension.

A statement that Josiah Chute, late a sergeant in the Army of the Revolution, was on the 9th day of March 1821, inscribed on the pension list, Roll of Maine Agency, at the rate of five and thirty-three and one-third one hundredths dollars per month; and that his name is now on the roll of the same Agency, at the rate of eight dollars per month, commencing on the 9th day of Jan., 1830. This certificate is issued in lieu of one dated on the ninth of March 1821 (cancelled).

Given at the War Office of the United States this 25th day of Jan. one thousand eight hundred and thirty.

J. L. EDWARDS, Secretary of War.

WAR DEPARTMENT.

Revolutionary Claim.

I certify that in conformity with the laws of the United States of the 7th June 1832, Josiah Chute of the State of Maine, who was a corporal and sergeant in the army of the Revolution is entitled to receive $103.50 per annum, during his natural life, commencing on the 4th of March 1831, and payable semi-annually on the 4th of March, and 4th of September in every year. Given at the War Office of the United States, this 8th day of March 1833.

J. L. EDWARDS, Secretary of War.

Josiah and Mary Chute owned the covenant in the church 1785. Col. Josiah Chute died Oct. 2, 1834; and immediately after, Mary Chute, wife of Josiah, was granted $103.50 per annum as a pension. She died Nov. 19, 1843, aged eighty.

Children:

51 i CURTIS, b. Dec. 15, 1782.
  ii DAVID, b. Dec. 10, 1784; d. at sea, Point Peter Gaudaloupe, Aug. 1, 1810.
  iii MARY, b. Oct. 21, 1786; m. Joseph son of Timothy Noyes, at Portland, Sept. 11, 1803. Joseph Noyes was mate of a ship, under Capt. Joel Prince, sailing to the East Indies, caught yellow fever and was lost at sea, April, 1811, aged 30. The widow m., 2nd, Wm. Abbott, of York, Me., Dec., 1815, and moved from Windham to Westbrook where he remained for 2 or 3 years, then to Gorham 1844, where he d. Oct. 10, 1852, aged 77½ years. She d. in Saco, Oct. 2. 1853. Children:

    1. EDWARD, b. Dec. 2, 1804; m. Rhoda, dau. of John Lunt, Aug. 24, 1827, and d. Feb. 1872. Children: (1) *Rufus M.*, b. Feb. 22, 1829; m. Julia Lane, of Buxton, July, 1853, and d. May 16, 1861. (2) *Philemon B.*, b. Feb. 18. 1831; m. Mary Ford, Feb., 1853; Maria Decosta, 1873; Phebe Carver (3rd husband), 1882. (3) *Lydia R.*, b. June 18. 1833; m. Levi Hamlin, Oct. 6, 1851. (4) *Aurilla B.*, b. June 14, 1836; m. John Parlin, April 21, 1857; m., 2nd, Asher H. Parlin, cousin; a son Wm. E. (5) *Joseph A.*, b. Sept. 15, 1838; m. Sylvina Faunce, Mar. 26, 1859; he was in Co. C, 8th Me., in the late war. (6) *John L.*, b. Aug. 15, 1840; m. Mary, dau. of Jason Harmon, May 16, 1864; 2nd, Mahala (Jacobs) Glines. He was in Co. C, 23rd Me. (7) *Mary A.*, b. June 15, 1842; m. Wright Hammond, Oct. 1, 1864; 2nd, Ariel Carver, both soldiers; she had 6 or 7 children. (8) *James M.*, b. Oct. 3, 1844; m. Sarah, sister to brother Ariel Carver, Dec. 1, 1866; has 5 children; m., 2nd, Maria Martin. (9) *Rhoda L.*, b. April 21, 1846; d. Mar. 3, 1854. (10) *Edward F.*, b. Oct. 12, 1848; d. Mar. 5, 1854.

2. HARRIET, b. June 5, 1807; m. Wm. Lord, 1829, and d. June 9, 1878; he d. Oct. 28, 1873, aged 88½ years.
3. JAMES CHUTE, b. July 28, 1809; m. Mary, dau. of Enoch Hammond, in Woodstock, Oxford Co., Feb. 22, 1833, and lived there till 1846; in Gorham awhile, in Biddeford, 1848, where he was employed in a cottonmill; and in Snow's Falls, 1860. Ch.: (1) *Harriet G.*, b. May 8, 1836; m. Charles Davis, May 19, 1856. He was in Co. H, 13th Me., in the late war, and d. April 17, 1882, exactly 52; m., 2nd, John Briggs, and live at Snow's Falls, Oxford Co., Me. John Briggs, son of Samuel, m., 1st, Marcia C. Todd, and had 2 sons, 1 dau. She d. April 23, 1882, aged 46½ years. (2) *James B.*, b. Oct. 8, 1842; d. Dec. 4, 1848. (3) *Eli M.*, b. Oct. 19, 1845; m. Abba Hyde, Feb. 23, 1863; 2nd, Louise Adams, Oct. 7, 1870, Berlin Falls, N. H.
4. MARY ANN ABBOTT, b. Dec. 15, 1816; m. Lewis Sanborn (*Elisha, Joseph*) Aug. 1, 1841, and had (1) *Charles W.*, b. May 21, 1842; m. Mahala, dau. of Alex. H. Kimball, Oct. 24, 1869, and live in E. Otisfield, Me.; was in Co. H, 17th Me. (2) *Mary S.*, b. Nov. 8, 1854; d. Mar. 13, 1874. Mr. S. d. Jan. 8, 1857, aged 48.
5. SUSAN, b. Oct. 7, 1819; m. Geo. son of Sam'l Kingsbury, Portland, Mar. 7, 1852, and d. April 9, 1889.
6. PRUDENCE, b. Mar. 5, 1822; m. Cyrus, son of David Andrews, Nov. 17, 1854, and d. Aug. 23, 1884, in E. Poland, Me.
7. JOSEPH N., b. April 6, 1824; m. Louisa Chute (see No. 55), May 17, 1846, and lived in Otisfield. She d. June 29, 1890. Ch.: (1) *Alfreda*, b. April 16, 1848; m. James L., son of Abram Green, May 8, 1868, and have 6 ch. He was a soldier in the 25th Me. (2) *William*, b. April 22, 1854; m. Henrietta H. dau. of Danforth Hancock, Dec. 6, 1876, and have one dau. (3) *George R.*, b. July 4, 1856; d. June 17, 1857. (4) *Hattie E.*, b. Nov. 15, 1861; d. Oct. 14, 1863.
8. DORCAS COBB, b. Sept. 4, 1826; m. E. Chute (see No. 161).

iv JOSIAH, JUN., b. Sept. 11, 1789.

v NANCY, b. Oct. 28, 1792; m. Reuben, son of Richard Stubbs, Oct. 27, 1816; lived in Windham, and d. Mar. 26, 1864; he d. May 7, 1868, aged 75. Children:
1. PERCY, b. 1817; m. Mary Turner, and d. at Saco, 1884; she d. 1885, aged 65.
2. ABIGAIL, b. 1819; m. Wm. McDuff, and lived in New Orleans. She d. 1850.
3. HANNAH, b. 1824; m. Isaiah Higgins, Aroostook Co., Me.
4. MARY A., b. 1826; m. Lorenzo D. Todd.
5. JULIETT, b. 1829; m. Fred. Ellis; he d. Fort Fairfield, Me., 1890.
6. CHARLES, b. 1833; d. Sept. 7, 1833.

vi JAMES, b. June 28, 1796; d. Jan. 9, 1798.

vii DORCAS, b. July 8, 1798; m. Isaac, son of Joseph and Sarah (Pike), Cobb, 1816, Windham, Me. He d. July 29, 1865, aged 70. She d. May 28, 1874. Ch:
1. JOSIAH CHUTE, b. July 15, 1817; m. Mary P. dau. of Asa Sawyer, Dec. 25, 1845, she d. Feb. 19, 1875, aged 52; m., 2nd, Julia (dau. of Adam Purvis) Rines, Aug. 19, 1882 (Falmouth, Me.), and d. 1888.

2. ELIZABETH N., b. Oct. 3, 1820; m. Leonard, son of John Baker, Dec. 1, 1844.
3. MERRITT L., b. Sept. 6, 1826; d. Sept. 9, 1827.
4. MARY C., b. Sept. 6, 1831; m. Francis, son of Richard Cobb; he d. 1870, and she m.. 2nd. Adam, son of Wm. Purvis, 1875. N. Gray, Me.
5. GEO. WM., b. Feb. 13, 1834; m. Ameda Thompson, April 4, 1857.

viii SUSAN OSGOOD, b. Nov. 19, 1802; m. Sidney, son of Rev. Amasa Smith,[a] of Belchertown, Mass., 1825, and d. Nov. 4, 1854. He d. April 24, 1843, aged 41. Ch.:
1. JOSIAH CHUTE, b. June 27, 1826; went to sea, not heard from since 1847.
2. SARAH WORTHINGTON, b. Aug. 2, 1827; d. Aug. 5, 1828.
3. SARAH WORTHINGTON, b. Feb. 27, 1830; m. Geo. Conant[7] (Barthol.,[6] Joseph,[5] Joseph,[4] Lot,[3] Lot,[2] Roger[1]), Mar. 12, 1854, and had a son, Charles E., b. Jan. 17, 1855, m. Edith M. Stinchfield, Aug. 28, 1880, lawyer in Minneapolis, Minn. Mr. Geo. Conant, b. in Portland, Dec. 13, 1804; m., 1st, Eliza Ann Thomas, and had 4 sons, 9 daus. She d. Dec. 1851, aged 39.
. GEO. CHUTE, b. April 3, 1832; d., 1888, in Los Angeles, Cal.
5. ALGERNON SIDNEY, b. Jan. 24, 1834; d. 1872; was a soldier.
6. ALMA CAREY, b. Dec. 5, 1835; in a public office, Washington treasury.
7. JOSEPH LYMAN, b. April 28, 1843 (name changed to Ch. L. Patten); m. Emma Busey, and is in Washington, D. C.

ix GEO. WASHINGTON, b. May 4, 1805; d. Nov. 23, 1882, on the old Chute farm, in Windham, inherited from his father and grandfather.

x SARAH, b. Aug. 9, 1807; d. Mar. 6, 1808.

VI. 18 Thomas Chute (*Curtis, Thomas, James, James, Lionel*), born in Windham, Me., Feb. 19, 1762; married Mary, daughter of Richard and Martha Maybery, Jan. 2, 1782, and lived in Windham. He was colonel of militia, war of 1812, and high sheriff of Cumberland Co. In the latter part of his life he was much afflicted with gravel, and was found dead in bed Sept. 4, 1816, in his fifty-fifth year. His wife died Aug. 19, 1839, aged seventy-seven.

Children:

53 i FRANCIS, b. May 15, 1783.
ii SARAH, b. June 5, 1785; m. Robert, son of Capt. Jonathan Leavitt, or Lovett, June 5, 1803, and lived in Gorham, Cumberland Co. She d. Mar. 25, 1844. He d. Sept. 20, 1850, aged 72. (Capt. Jonathan Leavitt d. Mar. 19, 1819, aged 75.) Ch.:
1. DANIEL, b. Aug. 13, 1804; m. Martha W. Morton, Dec. 1827, and d. Sept. 21, 1877; a Baptist deacon, Oshkosh, Wis. She d. 1884, aged 76. A son, Charles W., is in Chicago.

[a] Sidney Smith (b. Sept. 30, 1802; m. Susan O. Chute, Windham, Me., but lived and died at Blanchard, Me.), son of Rev. Amasa Smith (1756-1817), of Belchertown, Mass. Sophia,[6] daughter of Maj. Josiah[5] and Sarah (Worthington), Lyman, b. 1763; m. Rev. Amasa Smith, 1787, and had nine children; d 1844 Gilman, the youngest, b. 1805; m. Joanna Stephens of Portland and went to Yarmouth, N. S. Rev. Amasa S. was son of Dea. Joseph Smith (b. in Hatfield, Mass., 1720), and Eunice Bascom. Maj. Josiah[5] Lyman, of Dea. Aaron Lyman and Eunice[4] Dwight, of Rev. Josiah,[3] Capt. Timothy,[2] John Dwight[1]
Dwight Genealogy.

GENEALOGIES OF THE CHUTE FAMILY.

    2. THOMAS CHUTE, b. July 22, 1809; d. May 20, 1837.
    3. CHARLES, b. June 12, 1811; m. Nancy B. Jackson, Nov. 1842, and d. May 25, 1850, in Windham. She m.. 2nd, John Dawley.
    4. MARGARET, b. Dec. 2, 1818; m. Fred. son of Meshech Purrington, Sept. 10, 1843; had 3 daus. b. at White Rock in Gorham.

iii WM. CARR, b. Feb. 12, 1788.
iv JAMES, b. Mar. 25, 1790; d. July 15, 1791.
v FRANCES, b. May 12, 1792; m. David, son of Ebenezer and Bethia (Mayberry) Proctor, 1813, Windham; moved to Brandy Pond, Naples, where the family was reared. Mrs. Proctor d. July 4, 1866—night of the great fire in Portland; he d. May 1, 1867, aged 75. Ch.:

    1. KEZIA, b. Dec. 8, 1813; m. Benj. A. Goldsmith, and d. Nov. 11, 1875; he is in Cal.
    2. FRANK CHUTE, b. Jan. 3, 1816; m. Anna dau. of Thos. Morton, May 1836; she d. Sept. 22, 1850, aged 37; he m., 2nd, Aug. 1851, Sarah, dau. of Wm. Wentworth, and widow of Sam'l L. Hovey. Wm. Wentworth d. 1869, aged 83. Mehitable, his wife, d. 1862, aged 73.
    3. MIRIAM, b. Mar. 16, 1818; m. N. Penfield Green, Aug. 28, 1835; he d. May 7, 1871, aged 62.
    4. THOMAS, b. July 25, 1820; m. Emily, dau. of Thos. Hall, April, 1847; she d. in May, aged 22; m., 2nd, Lydia Paul, Jan. 21, 1849; she d. Dec. 28, 1882, aged 57 yrs., 7 mos.
    5. LOVETT, b. Dec. 16, 1823.
    6. MARY ELIZABETH, b. May 29, 1827; m. Elijah Varney Jan., 1847.
    7. EBENEZER, b. April 22, 1831; m. Betsy, dau. of Peter Graffham, Esq., Dec., 1854.

vi MARGARET, b. Nov. 21, 1794; d. Oct. 23, 1802.
vii DANIEL, b. Feb. 10, 1797.
viii MARY, b. May 12, 1799; d. Nov. 7, 1802.
ix JAMES, b. Aug. 12, 1801.
x THOMAS, b. Aug. 12, 1803.
xi CURTIS, b. Oct. 2, 1806; d. Oct. 11.

VI. 19 John Chute, (*Curtis, Thomas, James, James, Lionel*), born Windham, April 25, 1767; married Elizabeth Andrew[5] (*John,*[4] *Naaniel,*[3] *Joseph,*[2] *Robert*[1] died in Rowley 1668), of Salem, Mass., Nov. 22, 1793, and lived in Windham till 1816, when he purchased the Inn, or Elm House, at Naples, and occupied it as a Temperance House. It was burnt in 1822, but soon rebuilt, and occupied till burnt again in 1876. John Chute was a sober, industrious, Christian man, deacon of the Congregational church some thirty years; and is recorded a church clerk in Windham in 1827. Mrs. Chute, sister of Jonathan Andrew, father of Gov. John A. (1818–1867), of Mass., died Oct. 22, 1843, aged seventy. He died July 15, 1857, aged ninety years, three months. Children:

  i JOHN, JUN., b. Sept. 22, 1794; d. soon.
  ii BETSY, b. Dec. 22, 1795; d. Feb. 11, 1798.
58 iii ABRAM W., b. Jan. 7, 1797.
  iv JOHN, 2nd, b. Feb. 7, 1798; m. Mary E. D. Kidder, June 29, 1831; lived in Portland, and was cashier of Casco bank there many years; d. Aug. 2, 1862. She d. Aug. 10, 1880, aged 80.
  v ELIZABETH, b. Feb. 9, 1799; m. Wm. B. Winsor, Dec. 7, 1824, and had one dau. Mary Elizabeth, b. Sept. 19, 1825; m. Oliver M. son of Richard and Mary (Mayberry) Cook, Oct. 30, 1859, and had three sons; the first two d. in infancy; the 3rd, Oliver Richmond, b. Jan. 22, 1863, m. Kate F. Stone, Sept. 1, 1885, and live at Freeport; an excellent school teacher. Mr. O. M. Cook d. Jan. 15, 1871, aged 51, and the widow keeps a millinery shop in Bridgton. Mr. Winsor invented and improved many things pertaining to the early cotton mills in Massachusetts, 1814 to 1820; came to Gorham, Me., 1822; to Little Falls; to Naples, 1833. He was town treasurer, 1844, and filled other useful positions; d. Sept. 6, 1875, aged 81 yrs. 8 mo. His w. d. Jan. 15, 1869.
  vi MIRIAM, b. Sept. 25, 1800; m. Nathan Church, jun , Nov. 19, 1829, and lived at or near Naples many years, occupied the large Elm House there, after 1839. (He m., 1st, Mary Fowler, Oct. 14, 1823, who d. Mar. 18, 1828, aged 34, and had (1) *Marshall N.*, b. Feb. 27, 1826, d. Dec. 2, 1832. (2) *Mary*, b. Jan. 31, 1828.). He d. Jan. 27, 1873, aged 80. His 2nd wife d. May 25, 1862. Ch.
    1. AMANDA ELIZAB., b. Sept. 15, 1830; d. May 16, 1863.
    2. MELINDA GAGE, b. Jan. 9, 1833; m. Rev. Thos. T. Merry, and d. April 8, 1873.
    3. LOUISA WINSOR, b. July 25, 1835; d. Dec. 3, 1837.
    4. JOHN MARSHALL, b. Dec. 26, 1837; m. Cordelia, dau. of Nathan Hasty.
    5. ELIZABETH ANDREW, b. Jan. 16, 1840; d. Aug. 29, 1840.
    6. NATHAN ANDREW, b. Mar. 6, 1844; m. Marilla M. Cole, who d. Oct. 7, 1891, aged 45, Malden, Mass., and had (1) *M. Gertrude*, b. about 1868.
  vii JONATHAN ANDREW, b. April 23, 1811, received a good education and became a merchant before he was 20, in Naples. He also became a physician, sold out his store to his brother and brother in law, Abram W. Chute and Wm. B. Winsor, 1834, and left Portland Dec. 18, and went as a missionary among the Ottawa, Chippewa, and Cherokee Indians; d. at Westport, Mo., Oct. 1, 1838.

DEACON JOHN CHUTE.

SEVENTH GENERATION.

VII. 20 Daniel Chute (*Samuel, John, Lionel, James, James, Lionel*), born in Granville, N. S., Oct. 7, 1772; married Sarah, daughter of Elias and Ruth (Banks) Weare, by Rev. T. H. Chipman, Nov., 1795, and lived in Clements, Annapolis Co., seven miles from Digby. He was an energetic, resolute farmer and blacksmith, and a good pious deacon in the Baptist church. He died Jan. 17, 1857. His wife died Jan. 12, 1857, aged eighty.

Children:

59	i	ABRAM, b. Oct. 14, 1796.
60	ii	AARON, b. Aug. 11, 1798.
	iii	SOPHIA, b. Aug. 9, 1800; d. in Sept., 1800.
61	iv	BORMER, b. July 18, 1802.
62	v	JOSEPH, b. May 20, 1805.
63	vi	BENJAMIN, b. May 20, 1805.
64	vii	DANIEL, b. Nov. 12, 1808.
65	viii	DAVID, b. Sept. 29, 1810.
66	ix	ELIAS, b. Apr. 21, 1817.

VII. 21 Abram (*Samuel, John, Lionel, James, Lionel*), born in Granville, Feb. 18, 1775; married Mehitable, daughter of Benjamin and Elizabeth (Richardson) Foster, by Rev. T. H. Chipman, Jan. 6, 1798; and after having eight children moved to Cornwallis, Kings Co., and settled on the Post road, near Berwick, where he died, a good clever old farmer, July 20, 1847. She died Jan. 20, 1864, aged eighty-six.

Children:

i ELIZABETH, b. April 20, 1799; m. Nelson Van Buskirk, by Rev. Thomas Ansley, Feb. 28, 1821, and lived nearly twenty years in Aylesford, Kings Co., a farmer and carpenter. He sold out there in the spring of 1840, and moved to Yarmouth, Elgin Co, Ont., and there settled and followed his trade and profession twenty-five years, when he sold out and moved to Flint, Genesee Co., Mich., and is still living there, 98 years of age. Has been for more than fifty years a good pious deacon in the Baptist church. His wife d. in Flint, Mich., Nov. 23, 1886. Children:

1. MEHITABLE ANN, b. Feb. 12, 1823; m. Sept., 1844, John White, jr.; d. Aug. 2, 1883, in No. Mich. Had 8 children.
2. ELIZA LOVENA, b. June 26, 1825; m. Aug. 31, 1848, John, son of Isaac Webster; d. Sept. 28, 1890, in Mich. Had 8 children.
3. ABRAM GARRETT, b. Jan. 30, 1827; d. July 7, 1832.
4. JOHN ENOS, b. Aug. 9, 1830; m. Aug. 19, 1851, Ann, dau. of Jos. McAlpine. Had 9 children; live in Riley, St. Clair Co., Mich.
5. MARGARET L., b. Sept. 22, 1832; m. Sept., 1854, Andrew Smith. Had 5 children; live at Cora, Pa.
6. WILLIAM HENRY, b. Dec. 27, 1835; m. ——, 1870, Margaret (Richmond) Hopkins; d. Sept. 10, 1888, at Topeka, Kan. Had a pair of twins.
7. JEMIMA, b. Jan. 10, 1837; m. Aug. —, 1855, Samuel Mills. Had 9 children. Live at Flint, Mich.
8. EVERITT CHUTE, b. Nov. 10, 1841, m. ——, 1861, Margaret McGauley; d. Aug. 2, 1873, at Flint. Had 5 children. The widow m., 2nd, Barney McNinny.

67 ii BENJAMIN FOSTER, b. Jan. 31, 1801.
68 iii JOHN NELSON, b. Dec. 8, 1804.
69 iv WILLIAM HENRY, b. Dec. 21, 1806.
   v SUSANNA, b. Apr. 3, 1809; m. Richard Woodworth. See Woodworth.
   vi MARY, b Apr. 20, 1811; m. Dec. 24, 1833, John, son of James, jr., and Elizabeth (Foster) Taylor; d. Dec. 3, 1879. Lived between Morristown and Aylesford. Children:
1. MARIAN PERMELIA, b. Oct. 4, 1834.
2. WM. HENRY, b. June 6, 1837; m. Nov. 8, 1864, Violetta Bowers.
3. THO. ANSLEY, b. Aug. 21, 1839; m. ——, 1865, Rebecca, dau. of Fred Taylor.
4. ALBERT, b. Apr. 18, 1842; m. Feb. 5, 1878, Tenta (Scofield) Brown.
5. JERUSHA TUPPER, b. Jan. 3, 1845; m. Sept. 21, 1881, Elwood, son of John Milberry.
6. SARAH ANN, b. June 1, 1847; d. ——, 1869.
7. MARY ELIZABETH, b. June 19, 1851; m. Sept. 12, 1882, Geo. Akerold.
8. SUSANNA MARIA, b. March 30, 1854.

   vii PHILIP RICHARDSON, b. Dec. 9, 1813; d. Mar. 2, 1826.
70 viii SAMUEL BURTON, b. March 19, 1816.
71 ix THOMAS ANSLEY, b. May 11, 1819.

VII. 22 William (*Samuel, John, Lionel, James, Lionel*), born June 2, 1777; married Jan. 30, 1801, Mary, daughter of Isaac and Mary (Robbins) Marshall. Lived in Clarence and New Albany, N. S., a good Christian couple. He died April 1, 1834. She married, second, Samuel, son of Solomon Marshall, Nov. 24, 1853, and died May 24, 1856, aged eighty.

Children:

   i NANCY, b. Feb. 11, 1802; d. Aug. —, 1803.
72 ii ABRAM, b. Dec. 3, 1804.
   iii MARY, b. Sept. 23, 1807; m. ——, 1823, Fred McDonald. Had 6 children; He d. ——, 1872.

iv PRISCILLA. b. June 23. 1810; m. Nov. 6, 1828. Joseph, son of James Milberry. Lived in Granville and most of the children still live there. He d. Nov. 15, 1877, aged 81. Children:
1. JOSEPH D., b. Oct. 23, 1829; m. Eliza Carson and had 5 daus.
2. JOHN P., b. May 2, 1833; m. Fanny, dau. of James White.
3. WM. W., b. Sept. 6, 1835; m. Oct. 16, 1862, Margaret, dau. of William McKenzie. Had 3 sons. He d. Aug. —, 1883.
4. LOUISE, b. Dec. 26, 1837; m. Wm Murdock. Had 9 children.
5. ANN ELIZA, b. ——, 1839; m. Geo. Snell; d. Mar. —, 1877. Had 5 children.
6. HARRIET S., b. ——, 1841; d. ——, 1852.
7. DELILAH, b. ——, 1843; m. John, son of Edward White. Had 11 children.
8. MARY EMMA, b. ——, 1845; m. Capt. Jas. T. Frisbie, of Boston.

v JAMES LYNAM, b. July 3, 1813.

vi LUCINDA, b. Mar. 11, 1815; m. ——, 1832, Gideon Scofield; d. Jan. 27, 1890. Had 7 children. He d. ——, 1882.

vii SERAPHINA, b. Aug. 1, 1821; m. Jan. 1, 1846, John Milberry. Lived at Port Lorne, but moved to Hampton, April —, 1861, where he d. Oct. 21, 1879, aged 65. Children:
1. CHARLES RUPERT, b. Jan. 26, 1845; d May 14, 1847.
2. CHARLES EDGAR, b. Apr. 15, 1847; m. Aug. 17, 1872, Elizabeth Reynard.
3. TIMOTHY RICE, b. Mar. 23, 1850; m. Dec. —, 1873, Clara Reynard.
4. NORMAN CLARK, b. July 30, 1852; m. ——, 1875, Cynthia, dau. of James Taylor, jr.
5. WM. RUFUS, b. Oct. 25, 1854; d. July 29, 1878.
6. ELWOOD YOUNG, b. July 3, 1857; m. Sept. 21, 1881, Jerusha T. Taylor.
7. JAMES PARKER, b. April 3, 1860.

II. 23 Samuel (*Samuel, John, Lionel, James, Lionel*), born in ville, Aug. 5, 1781; married Feb. 27, 1803, Elizabeth, daughter of nel Randall, by Bishop Charles Ingles and lived several years at the gins," Digby Co. About 1809, they moved to near Harborville shore ie Bay of Fundy, Cornwallis, Kings Co., where he lived an honest, r, pious man, cooper and farmer, and died March 23, 1857. She, od Christian old lady died Oct. —, 1863, aged seventy-nine. iildren:

1 OLIVE, b. Apr. 9, 1805; m. Mar. 1, 1826, Joel Parish, 2d, jun. (b. Dec. 19, 1804); lived in Cornwallis. She d. there Oct. 17, 1873. He d. May 14, 1883, aged 79. Children:
1. ELIZA, b. July 4, 1827; m. Jan. —, 1852, Cyrus West. Had 6 children. m., 1st, ——, 1839, Mary Wood, and had 2 ch., Benj. and Susan Jane.
2. JOEL, b. Feb. 25, 1829; drowned in Cornwallis, June 25, 1849.
3. SAMUEL J., b. Nov. 23, 1830; m. Aug. 7, 1884, Julia, dau. of George Sanford.

4. S. MATILDA, b. Jan. 31, 1834; m. Dec. 3, 1856, Wm. R. Woodworth.
5. M. REBECCA, b. Jan. 17, 1836; m. Mar. —, 1858, Enoch L. Palmer, jr.
6. FOSTER, b. Feb 14, 1838; m. Feb. 10, 1869, Minetta, dau. of Thos. R. Palmer.
7. WM. EDWIN, b. Apr. 18, 1840; m. June 8, 1870, Joanna, dau. of Shepherd and Nancy (Todd) Hoyt.
8. HARDING, b. May 11, 1842; d. Aug. 2, 1871.
9. EZEKIEL, b. Dec. 31, 1845; m. May 8, 1870, Susie, dau. of Church Parker; d. June 18, 1871. She m., 2d, Oscar M. Taylor.
10. ANNA OLIVIA, b. Aug. 14, 1847; m. Sept. 1, 1863, Levi Fox; d. June 27, 1868, aged 31. Mr. Fox m., 1st, Mary A. Dodge, and had 3 sons.
11. CHARLOTTE AMELIA, b. Oct. 9, 1851; m. Dec. 3, 1885, Omer Woodman.
12. SUSAN CORNELIA, b. Oct. 9, 1851; m. May —, 1875, Archibald, son of Church Parker.

74 ii DANIEL, b. Feb. 7, 1807.
iii NAOMI, b. Aug. 21, 1808; d. Sept. 27, 1810.
75 iv THO. HANDLEY, b. May 11, 1810.
v MARIA MATILDA, b. Nov. 7, 1814; m. Dec. 18, 1833, David E. (*Solomon, Joel*), Parish, and lived in Cornwallis till 1845, when they moved to Yarmouth, Ont., where he d. in March, 1854, aged 46. She m., 2d, Wm. Williams, an English weaver, Southwold, Ont., 1856, and d. March 5, 1861. Mr. Williams d. 1882, aged 84, having had two other wives. Children:
1. AARON FOSTER, b. Feb. —, 1836; m. ——, 1856, Eliza, dau. of Wm. Porter; d. Apr. 4, 1861. She m., 2d, Wm. Wadham, Dorchester, Ont.
2. CLARISSA ANN, b. May ——, 1838; d. ——, 1857.
3. ALBERT HILL, m. June 21, 1840; m. Dec. 29, 1863, Polly Ann, dau. of Henry R. Glover, Leonard, Oakland Co., Mich. Had 6 children.
4. ELIZA REBECCA, b. ——, 1844; m.——, 1862, Benjamin Quick. Had 3 children and lived in Fingal, Ont., till 1888, when they moved to Leonard, Mich.
5. JAMES MONROE, b. ——, 1848; m. ——, 1874, Sarah McAlpine, and live in Dunwick, Ont.
6. OLIVE, b. ——, 1842; d. in the fall of 1855.

vi SARAH ANNES, b. May 11, 1816; m. Feb. 15, 1832, Rev. Solomon Bennett Taylor, and lived in New Germany, Lunenburg Co., N. S., where he worked on a farm, besides being an active, energetic minister in the Baptist church. He died worn out in the good cause, March 28, 1870. She, also a hard worker, both spiritually and temporarily, d. Dec. 9, 1872. Children:
1. THOMAS HANDLY, b. Dec. 26, 1832; m. May 19, 1853, Ellen Flint, and live in California.
2. JAMES EDWARD, b. Aug. 30, 1834; m., 1st, Oct. 20, 1858, Mercy, dau. of Isaac Freeman, had 3 sons 2 daus. She d. Dec., 1874. He m., 2d, in 1882, Nellie, dau. of Ezez. Truesdell, and widow of John Simpson and Charles Russell. Live in Somerville, Mass.
3. CHARLES ICHABOD, b. May 17, 1836; m. Aug. 15, 1856, Eleanor Lynch.
4. JEREMIAH TUPPER, b. May 30, 1838; m. June 9, 1859, Sarah, dau. of James Moore. Had 11 children. Live in Charlestown.
5. PHINEAS FOSTER, b. Jan. 12, 1840; d. Nov. 10, 1858.

6. SARAH JANE, b. Dec. 28, 1841; m. Sept. 8, 1870, Jas. Edward, son of Wm. Dunn.
7. ROBERT TWINING, b. Nov. 10, 1843; m. Aug. 26, 1872, Prudence, dau. of Cooper Delong, who d. in 1884. He m., 2d, July —, 1885, Mary, dau. of Nathan Conrad.
8. WM. JOHNSON, b. Sept. 29, 1845; m., 1st, 1867, Jane Abrams; m., 2d, in 1878, Sarah Black. Is an M.D., in Portland, Ore.
9. JOSEPH DIMOCK, b. July 2, 1847; m., 1st, in 1868, Emma Leach (d. in 1869); m., 2d, in 1870, Myra H. Fonda; m , 3d, ———, Capt. J. D. Taylor. Is at Great Falls, Montana.
10. OSCAR MORTIMER, b. Jan 7, 1849; m. Nov. 2, 1874, Susie (Parker) Parish, and had four children. He was a sailor, carpenter, and for several years was president of a Christian Mission in Boston; removed to Argyle, Carleton Co., N. B., 1891.
11. HENRY B. W. NOEL, b. Jan. 22, 1850; m in 1873, Fanny, dau. of John McAuliffe, had three children. Furniture dealer in Charlestown.
12. ELEANOR ELIZABETH, b. Aug. 26, 1852; d. May 16, 1871.
13. AMANDA ANN, b. July 11, 1854; m. May 24, 1874, Thomas H., son of Rev. Silas Viditoe; have three children. Live in Malden, Mass. He is a carpenter.
14. SAMUEL BENNETT, b. Nov. 27, 1856; m. Mar. 22, 1883, Rosa, dau. of Cephas Welton; had five children. They lived in Charlestown a number of years, he as a mechanic and tradesman, but removed to Waterville, Cornwallis, N. S., 1891.
15. MERCY PHILENA, b. Aug. 6, 1858; m. Nov. 22, 1876, Albert C. Morse, 2d, jr., and had two children. He d. Oct. 10, 1880, aged 23. She lives in Charlestown, Mass.
16. REUBEN CLARE, b. May 19, 1862, in Salt Lake City.

vii SAMUEL, 2d, jr., b. Dec. 28, 1818.
viii DAVID PRIOR, b. Dec. 26, 1820.

II. 24 Crocker Chute (*John, John, Lionel, James, James, nel*), born in Granville, N. S., Jan. 23, 1774; married, 1797, in nville, N. S., Cynthia Dodge (probably a descendant of Richard of em, Mass., 1638). Early in the present century he moved to Lunenng, Mass., where his grandparents Crocker lived. He died about 0. His wife died March 16, 1842, aged sixty.

Children:

i SUSAN, b. Oct. 23, 1798; m., 1st, in 1820, Frederick Lloyd, who was accidentally shot April 14, 1823, and d. Oct. 23, aged 25. She m., 2d, 1824, Joseph Dolbear, who d. 1858, aged 58. She d. Dec. 25, 1882, aged 84. Ch. by 1st marriage:
1. SUSAN, b. Dec. 29, 1821; m., 1st, Dec. 29, 1839, John J. Hill of Framingham, who d. Mar. 20, 1842, aged 41; m., 2d, June 28, 1843, Josiah Easter, of Saxonville, from Prince Edward Island. He d. Sept. 2, 1882, aged 69. They had (1) *Fred N.*, b. Feb. 23, 1846; m. Mary E. Ellis; d. Oct. 31, 1890, aged 44; had three ch. (2) *Alice Maud*, b.

Dec. 28, 1848; m. Edgar W. Childs, lived in Everett; d. Nov. 15, 1891; had two ch.

By 2d marriage:
2. JOSEPH W., b. ——; m. ——, of N. Y. City.
3. NANCY J., b. ——; m. Thomas Sloan.
4. EMELINE L., b. ——; m. Benj. P. Green.
5. MARY WADE, b. ——; m. Charles Bradford.
6. MARY CHUTE, b. ——; d. aged 9 yrs.
7. BETSY W., b. ——; m. W. W. Atwood.

ii MARY FALKNER, b. Oct. 12, 1800; m. Nov. 14, 1824, Solomon Augustus, son of Edward Davis; d. Mar. 16, 1855. He d. June 15, 1851, aged 54. Ch.:
1. SOLOMON AUG., b. Dec. 27, 1825; m. Augusta Kilburn, and had three sons; d. Apr. 15, 1888, in Boston.
2. WM. F., b. Sept. 25, 1827; m. Caroline Nason, N. Y.
3. MARY C., b. July 21, 1829; m. Peter Jeffrey; d. Sept. 14, 1876, in N.Y.; he d. June, 1870, aged 46.
4. JOSEPH, b. Feb. 2, 1831; d. Feb. 13, 1831.
5. CYNTHIA A., b. Feb. 17, 1832; m. Dec. 10, 1863, Abram Larkin, jr., Ch.: (1) *Cora Frances*, b. Oct. 6, 1864. Mr. Larkin d. Oct. 24, 1891, aged nearly 65. The widow lives in Charlestown, severely afflicted with rheumatism.
6. JOSEPH W., b. Feb. 1, 1834; m. Hattie Cutten.
7. JANET H., b. Nov. 14, 1835; m. H. L. Hadley; d. Oct. 13, 1888.
8. GEO. W., b. Jan. 18, 1838; m. Lizzie Kimball.
9. ANGELINE A., b. Feb. 29, 1840; d. Dec. 6, 1846.
10. CHARLES S., b. Jan. 17, 1844; d. March 2, 1845.

iii JOHN, b. 1803; lost an arm; d. about 1850, Lunenburg, Mass.

VII. 25 George Washington Chute(*John, John, Lionel, James, James, Lionel*) born in Granville, April 27, 1778; married Anna Bathrick, 1797; lived in Lunenburg, Mass.; died Oct. 23, 1808. She died Aug., 1846, aged seventy.

Children:
i ANNA, b. 1798, in Lunenburg; d. Oct. 30, 1799.
ii JAMES, b. 1800; m. Louisiana Lane, went to N. Y.; d. ——. Had two ch. His wife has been in Canada West since 1840.
iii MARY, b. 1803; m. Reuben Holden, b. 1799; d. 1858. (*Sylvanus*,[5] b. ——, 1766; d. ——, 1843; m. Polly Bathrick who d. ——, 1849; *Philemon*,[4] b. ——, 1725; d. ——, 1810; m. ——, 1751, Lucy Walker; *Stephen*,[3] *Stephen*,[2] *Rickard*[1] (1609-1696) came over in 1634, w. Martha —— d. at Watertown, Dec. 6, 1684.) Ch.:
1. AUGUSTUS, b. 1822; m. 1853, Mrs. Rhoda Maria Reed of Shirley; four ch.
2. ABBY, b. 1826; m. Asahel York; d. 1864.
3. ADELAIDE, b. 1828; m. Harvey Ridout.
4. HANNAH, b. 1830; m. James McGroom.
5. FRANCIS REUBEN, b. 1832.
6. MARTIN FRANCIS, b. 1834; m. Lucinda Scott, Boston.
7. GEORGE, b. 1836; m. 1861, Ellen Reed, Boston.

8. ANNA MARY, b. 1838; m. E. D. Elwell, Boston.
9. WALTER, b. 1839.
10. ELIZABETH, b. 1841; m. Frank Edgecomb; d. 1874.
11. ALONZO, b. 1843; d. 1860.
12. LUCIUS, b. 1845.

Oliver Holden[5] (*Nehemiah*,[4] *John*,[3] *Stephen*,[2] *Richard*[1]), b. in Shirley, Sept. 18, 1765; d. in Boston, Sept. 4, 1844. He was a great musician and author of eight books, one hundred tunes and more than twenty hymns. Wrote Coronation in 1792.

78 iv GEO. W., b. July 4, 1805.
 v JOHN C., b. 1807. School teacher at the South.

VII. 26 Paul Chute (*John, John, Lionel, James, James, Lionel*), born in 1782; married Bethiah, daughter of Dr. Azor and Gloriana Betts of St. John, N. B., Aug. 5, 1804, and lived at the Joggins, Digby Co., N. S.; a farmer and tradesman. He was drowned crossing Annapolis Basin, going to Digby in a boat, February, 1810. His wife went to St. John, N. B., and married Edward Walker and had a daughter Margaret, who married Simon Bazley, and had three children. Mrs. Walker died in 1846. He died in 1847. Dr. Betts died at Digby, N. S., Sept., 1809, aged 72. His wife died at St. John, Mar. 16, 1815, aged 68.

Children:

i JAMES EDWARD, b. Nov. 3, 1805; m. Mary Ann Chapman, Shepherd, N. B.; and had Matilda Jane, b. 1836; lives in San Francisco, Cal. He d. in St. John about 1857; and she went to Ontario.

ii FANNY MATILDA, b. Nov. 10, 1807; m. Capt. William Walker who was drowned off the schooner "Eagle," 1830–31; m., 2nd, Joseph Scammell, Esq. (b. in Wiley, Wiltshire, Eng., Aug. 9, 1806), 1832, who was a merchant and shipper in St. Johns; d. May 7, 1863. She d. Feb. 4, 1881. Ch.:

1. JOHN WALKER, b. Sept. 28, 1833; m. Emma Gilbert Sancton, St. John, N. B. (b. Jan. 5, 1840), 1858. Ch.: (1) *Maude Gertrude*, b. Aug. 19, 1859. (2) *Fanny Matilda*, b. Mar. 2, 1861. (3) *George Byron*, b. July 23, 1862; m. Feb. 16, 1891, Dolly Turpin. (4) *Walter Sancton*, b. Dec. 14, 1863. (5) *James Henderson*, b. Nov. 27, 1873; d. Dec. 3, 1876.

2. ANNIE JILTON, b. May 19, 1835; m. John Byron Cushing, of Carleton, N. B. Ch.: (1) *George Scammell*, b. June 5, 1861. (2) *Wm. Channing*, b. Mar. 18, 1863. (3) *Theophilus*, b. July 19, 1865. (4) *Emma Helen*, b. Dec. 30, 1867. (5) *Edith Jewett*, b. Aug. 28, 1872.

3. JOSEPH HENRY, b. Apr. 10, 1837; m. Louisa Stevens (b. in Maine, Feb. 27, 1842), Oct. 30, 1861. Ch.: (1) *Edward Jewett*, b. July 5, 1863; m. Nov. 25, 1885, Florence Harriet Noble (b. Dec. 3, 1863). (2) *Frank Stevens*, b. Sept. 29, 1864; m. Mar. 29, 1889, Gelette Frances Ally (b. Mar. 31, 1865). (3) *Joseph Henry*, b. Nov. 22, 1870. (4) *John F. Ernest*, b. Feb. 28, 1872. (5) *John Kimball*, b. Sept. 13, 1873. (6) *Sanford Wilder*, b. June 14, 1875.

4. HARRIET MATILDA, b. Aug. 30, 1839; d. May 9, 1847.
5. WM. PEROT, b. July 27, 1841; d. Aug. 5, 1842.
6. EMMA JULIA, b. June 13, 1843.
7. CHARLES EDWARD, b. Mar. 19, 1845; m. Dec. 22, 1868, Annie Maria Sancton (b. Dec. 14, 1846). Ch.: (1) *Annie Cushing*, b. Jan. 19, 1870. (2) *Alice Vaughn*, b. Dec. 25, 1871; d. Jan. 8, 1883. (3) *Georgiana Sancton*, b. Nov. 9, 1873.
8. HARRIET MATILDA, b. Mar. 25, 1847; m. 1870, Joseph Allison (b. July 1, 1840, Hants Co., N. S.). Ch.: (1) *Walter C.*, b. April 22, 1873. (2) *Helen Gertrude*, b. July 15, 1875. (3) *Wm. Scammell*, b. July 29, 1884.
9. FRED. E., b. Jan. 30, 1849; m. 1875, Margaret Amelia McAdam (b. Aug. 21, 1853, St. Stephens, N. B.). Ch.: (1) *John McAdam*, b. July 18, 1876, St. John, N. B. (2) *Fred. Allison*, b. Oct. 23, 1879, Brooklyn, N. Y. (3) *Harold Bernard*, b. Oct. 9, 1885.

iii JANE GLORIANA, b. Sept., 1809; m. Thomas Booth; and lived in New Brunswick. He d. in Frederickton; and she went to the west. Ch.:
1. BETHIAH, b. ———; m. G. D. Jewett.
2. MATILDA, b. ———; m. James Nickerson. Ch.: (1) *Walter*. (2) *Bethiah*. (3) *Margaret*.
3. MARY, b. ———; m. Wm. Armstrong and had six children.

VII. 27 Peter Prescott Chute (*John, John, Lionel, James, James, Lionel*), born May 27, 1787; married Lucy, daughter of Dea. David Randall, by Rev. T. H. Chipman, 1808; and lived in different places in Digby, Annapolis and King counties, N. S. He was a cooper and farmer, and died near Bridgetown, about 1865. She died April 21, 1854, aged sixty-seven.

Children:

79   i   ALEXANDER, b. Feb. 24, 1809.
80   ii   CHARLES, b. Apr. 19, 1811.
     iii   GEORGE, b. Apr. 24, 1814; d. Oct. 11, 1821.
81   iv   GILBERT R., b. Sept. 13, 1817.

VII. 28 John Chute (*John, John, Lionel, James, James, Lionel*), born Oct. 14, 1790; married Abigail, daughter of Stephen Jones, by Rev. Peter Crandall, Dec. 26, 1813, and lived near the Joggin Bridge, Digby Co.; farmer and fisherman. He died Nov. 18, 1865. His wife died Oct. 20, 1871, aged eighty-two.

Children:

  i   STEPHEN JONES, b. Oct. 23, 1814; d. July 28, 1836.
  ii   JAMES HENRY, b. Jan. 20, 1818; d. Aug. 28, 1828.
  iii   ELIZABETH, b. Apr. 8, 1820; m. John Balsor Rice[7] (*Dea. Jonas,[6] Joseph,[5] Beriah,[4] Thomas,[3] Thomas,[2] Dea. Edmund[1]*), of Sudbury, Mass., 1638), Dec., 1837, and lived at or near Smith's Cove. He d. 1852, aged 43. (Dea. Jonas

Rice d. 1861, aged 79. His wife, Dorothy Balsor, d. 1861, aged 79). She m., 2nd, John, son of Silas Rice (his third wife); and he d. June 25, 1877, aged 91. Ch.:

1. AUGUSTA, b. 1840; m. George Cossett; six children.
2. PHEBE ANN, b. 1842; d. 1859 or 60.
3. ELIZA, b. Oct. 1, 1845; m. William, son of David Lee, jr., 1862; eight children, Chelsea, Mass.
4. DOROTHY, b. 1847; m. John Maling.
5. HENRY JONES, b. Sept. 1, 1850; m. Lucy Etta, dau. of Daniel T. Anderson (b. July 2, 1854), 1872, and live in Boston; pious Baptists.
6. JOHN, b. 1851; m. Jessie Chute (*Joseph W., Dea. Aaron*).
7. FITZ, b. 185–; m. Eleanor Devinny.
8. GEORGE, b. 185–; m. Mary Kenny, Boston, Mass.
9. EUDOCIA, b. 185–; m. Edward Morine, son of John.

VII. 29 Joseph F. Chute (*John, John, Lionel, James, James, Lionel*), born in Granville, Feb. 21, 1795; married Susan Harris Pelham July 25, 1816, and lived near Digby, N. S. Cornelius and Anna (Elwood) Harris of Yarmouth, N. S., had five sons and three daughters. Susan born about 1787, married Joseph Pelham, and had a son Joseph and daughter Adaline. Adaline married John Wareham. The father died or was lost at sea about 1812; and the son followed a few years after, leaving a wife and five children. Joseph F. Chute married the widow, as stated above; and they moved from Digby to Lunenburg, Mass., 1827, and died about 1845. She died Feb. 22, 1863.

Children:

82 i JOHN EDWARD, b. Dec. 4, 1816.
    ii ARTHUR WESLEY, b. July 14, 1820; d. at sea, about 1850.
83 iii JOSEPH HOMER, b. Mar. 9, 1822.
    iv SUSAN PELHAM, b. Nov. 26, 1827; m. Oliver, son of Levi Divoll, Sept. 21, 1842, and lived at Lunenburg. He d. May 10, 1888, aged 65. Ch.:
        1. FRANKLIN O., b. June 30, 1843; m. Carrie A. Davis, of Laconia, N. H., Apr. 30, 1868, and had five children.
        2. ARTHUR FITZ G., b. Dec. 21, 1844; m. Lizzie Baldwin, May 1, 1870, and had four children; d. Dec. 22, 1888, in Vicksburg, Miss., of malarial fever.
        3. JOSEPH H., b. Apr. 4, 1846; d. Oct. 9, 1847.
        4. SUSAN F. J., b. Apr. 27, 1850; m. Orren H. Smith, Dec. 25, 1868, and had four children.
    v MARY JOSEPHINE, b. May 29, 1829; d. Jan. 7, 1844.
84 vi CORNELIUS HARRIS, b. Nov. 27, 1832.

VII. 30 James Chute (*Benjamin, John, Lionel, James, James, Lionel*), born in Granville, April 19, 1778; married Phebe, daughter of Dea. Thomas Chute, by Rev. T. H. Chipman, Feb. 5, 1801, and both spent their days in Granville as good Christian people and old-fashioned farmers. He died June 1, 1857. She died Nov. 19, 1868, aged nearly eighty-seven.

Children:

 i NANCY, b. Dec. 10, 1801; m. John Farnsworth, Jan. 14, 1841; d. Jan. 31, 1856.
85 ii EZRA, b. May 9, 1804.
86 iii GILBERT S., b. Aug. 11, 1806.
87 iv THOMAS, b. Sept. 26, 1808.
88 v EVERITT, b. Jan. 8, 1811.
 vi ELIZABETH, b. Jan. 13, 1814; m. John Edmund Brown, Jan. 1, 1833; d. Mar. 17, 1836. Had three daus. (1) *Phebe Ann*, m. John Farquharson.
89 vii ABEL, b. Mar. 5, 1816.
90 viii OLIVER, b. Apr. 26, 1819.
91 ix WILLIAM FOSTER, b. Dec. 26, 1822.
 x PHEBE JANE, b. Mar. 10, 1826; m. Reuben Perkins Rhodes, Oct. 7, 1844; lived in Granville and d. Mar. 3, 1856. He m., 2nd, Phebe Letteney, 1863; had a dau. and d. 1889, aged 70. Ch.:
  1. JAMES, m. Sarah J., dau. of Capt. John Sleith.
  2. ELIZABETH, m. Fred. Morey.
  3. BENJAMIN, d. in infancy.
  4. PHEBE JANE, m. George A., son of Abel Chute. See No. 222.

VII. 31 Seth Chute (*Benjamin, John, Lionel, James, James, Lionel*), born in Granville, Sept. 15, 1782; married Ann, daughter of Caleb Fowler, by Rev. Parson Milledge, Dec. 16, 1805, and lived near Chute's Cove, or Hampton, as farmers. He died Dec. 16, 1829. She died Jan. 15, 1868, aged eighty-three.

Children:

 i MARGARET ANN, b. Oct. 12, 1806; m. Henry Fash, Sept. 18, 1838; d. Apr. 16, 1889. He m., 1st, Ruth Merritt, Jan. 4, 1812; d. Dec. 11, 1837, nearly 46. He d. Oct. 24, 1857, aged 67 yrs. 8 mos. Ch.:
  1. LORENZO DOW, b. Mar. 28, 1839; m. Lavinia, dau. of Hanly Chute. See No. 44.
  2. JOSEPH WILLIAM, b. Feb. 6, 1841; m. Freelove White, Mar. 12, 1885.
  3. JACOB, b. Feb. 9, 1844; m. Janette Work, 1870.
  4. ELIZABETH RUTH, b. Mar. 15, 1848; m. George Byron Brown, Dec. 31, 1872.
  5. CHARLOTTE E., b. Aug. 22, 1851; d. Aug. 12, 1862.
 ii ETHALINDA, b. Dec., 1808; d. Jan. 26, 1810.
 iii ALEXANDER, b. Nov. 2, 1810; d. May 29, 1829.
92 iv GILBERT F., b. Feb. 27, 1813.
 v ELMIRA, b. Feb. 28, 1817; d. Nov. 8, 1887.
 vi EMELINE, b. Apr. 2, 1819; m. Jacob, son of Hanly Chute. See No. 44.

VII. 32 Benjamin Chute (*Benjamin, John, Lionel, James, James, Lionel*), born in Granville, April 14, 1787; married Hepzibah, daughter of Israel and Susanna (Dodge[6]) Fellows, son of Benjamin and Eunice (Dodge[4]) Fellows (*Ebenezer,[3] John,[2] Richard Dodge[1]*) of Salem, 1638, by Rev. Thos. Ansley, Oct., 1808. She died Sept., 1809. He married, second, Elizabeth, daughter of Amos Randall, by Rev. Thomas Ansley, May 16, 1812; lived in Clarence; a farmer; and died Mar. 20, 1854. She died in 1867, aged seventy-eight.

Children:

- **93** i BURTON, b. Apr. 17, 1809.
- **94** ii NATHAN, b. June 10, 1815.
- **95** iii WILLETT, b. Jan. 23, 1820.
-     iv CERETHA, b. Feb. 11, 1822; m. William Clark, Mar. 31, 1867. Mr. Clark m., 1st, Prudence Reagh, and had eleven children. She d. Dec. 28, 1862, aged 46. He d. Apr. 9, 1836, aged 73.
-     v MELVINA, b. Oct. 29, 1824; d. Mar. 13, 1853.
-     vi ALLEN, b. Sept. 18, 1829; m. Mary Ann Savory[6] (*Nathan,[5] Uriah,[4] Thomas,[3] Samuel,[2] Thomas[1]* to Plymouth, Mass., 1634), Apr. 3, 1862, and live at St. Mary's Bay, Digby Co., N. S.
-     vii ISABELLA, b. May 23, 1833; d. Sept. 17, 1862.

VII. 33 Ezekiel Chute (*Benjamin, John, Lionel, James, James, Lionel*), born in Granville, Jan. 6, 1790; married Lydia Ann, daughter of Aaron Morse, by Parson Milledge Mar. 11, 1819, and lived in Granville, one mile below Bridgetown; a farmer; died June 21, 1846. His wife died Mar. 6, 1841, aged forty-three years and three months.

Children:

-     i MINETTA ANN, b. Sept. 2, 1820; m. Dimock Chute. See No. 46.
-     ii ELIZA JANE, b. Dec. 10, 1822; m. Gilbert F. Chute. See No. 92.
- **96** iii AARON M., b. April 10, 1824.
-     iv AMORET S., b. Oct. 30, 1825; m. Edmund P., son of Michael Gilliatt, Oct. 20, 1846; d. Mar. 27, 1865. He m., 2nd, Jerusha Morse, June, 1866. Ch.:
    1. MARY, b. 1847; d. Nov. 9, 1868.
    2. HENRIETTA L., b. Feb. 21, 1849; m. Jarvis Chute. See No. 218.
    3. AARON, b.; d. Apr. 7, 1876.
    4. ADA K., b.; m. James Fox, March, 1881.
    5. BERTHA, b.; m. James Waugh, June 18, 1876.
    6. JAMES M., b.; m. Minetta Ann Chute. See No. 46.
    7. AMORET S., b. Mar., 1865; d. Oct., 1865.
-     v ELLEN, b. 1827; d. an infant.
-     vi MARTHA ADELIA, b. June 10, 1829; m. James M. Gilliatt (b. Feb., 1819), brother to Edmund P. He m., 1st, Susan, dau. of Mich. Spurr. She d. Feb. 4, 1867, aged 64. Martha A. was a good school teacher.
-     vii SERAPH ADELAIDE, b. Sept. 4, 1831; m. Fred Banks[7] (*George,[6] Joshua,[5] Joshua,[4] Moses,[3] John,[2] Richard,[1]* of Mass. before 1640), June 8, 1854, and had two chil-

dren. He d. June 10, 1859, aged 40 yrs. 4 mos. She m., 2nd, Leslie Stone, May 7, 1861; have one child and live in Granville.

viii BENJAMIN, b. Jan. 22, 1833.
ix CHARLES ALLINE, b. Nov. 17, 1834.
x HENRIETTA M., b. Mar. 28, 1838.
xi LYDIA, b. 1840; d. soon.

VII. 34 Joseph Chute (*Benjamin, John, Lionel, James, James, Lionel*), born in Granville, Dec. 9, 1792; married Theresa, daughter of Amos Randall, by Rev. William Elder, Nov. 29, 1831; and lived in Granville, where he died Oct. 29, 1839. She married, second (as his second wife), Paoli, daughter of Samuel Randall, Jan. 5, 1845; and lived in Portland, Me.; grocer and merchant. He died Apr. 12, 1864, aged 73. She died Feb. 17, 1872, aged 65.

Children:

i SUSAN ADELAIDE, b. Oct. 10, 1832; d. Dec. 3, 1842.
ii EMMA THERESA, b. July 22, 1836; m. Charles F., son of Joseph Thrasher. Portsmouth, N. H., June 6, 1857, and was a merchant in Portland till 1873, when he moved to Boston and went into mercantile business again, and since 1875 with Jordan & Marsh. In the great fire of Portland July 4, 1866, he lost about $7000. Ch.:
   1. CHARLES S., b. in Portland, Dec. 5, 1859; policeman in Somerville.
   2. EMMA T., b. in Portland, June 24, 1863.
   3. FRANKLIN J., b. in Portland, Feb. 12, 1867; R. R. postal clerk. He tried to rescue his cousin, Frank Upham, from drowning, at Boothbay Harbor, Me., Aug. 11, 1888, in which he rescued the body but life was gone; and was awarded the largest silver medal provided for such by the Humane Society of Massachusetts.
   4. CLARA DALTON, b. in Portland, Jan. 12, 1870; m. Wm. Parker Bacon. June 9, 1892.
   5. ANNA E., b. in Somerville, Mar. 3, 1878.
   6. EDWARD B., b. in Somerville, July 19, 1880.
iii JOSEPH W. R., b. Feb. 24, 1839; d. Nov. 13, 1842.

VII. 35 Thomas Chute (*Thomas, John, Lionel, James, James, Lionel*), born in Granville, June 14, 1780; married Mary, daughter of John and Eunice (Fellows) Troop, by Rev. James Manning, Oct. 30, 1804; and lived at Bear River in Clements; a sober, upright Christian; farmer, hunter and fisherman. His wife died Nov. 30, 1817, aged thirty-four. He married, second, Jane, daughter of Dea. David Shook of Weymouth, Digby Co., by Rev. Enoch Towner, Dec. 7, 1818. In the spring of 1837, he sold out his farm to Nathan Tupper, Esq., Esq., and moved to the then Upper Canada, called in 1849 Canada West, and in 1867 Ontario; and settled in Malahide, six miles

)f Port Burwell, near Lake Erie, and did well there as a farmer.
spring of 1841, his eldest son being drowned, leaving no heirs
l, he went back to Nova Scotia to get the property, worth about
); but the widow refused to share with him, so he put it into
ry and there "lawed" it seven years, returning in the fall of
with $500.00. After building a fine house and helping build a
t meeting-house, he died Aug. 14, 1850. Aunt Jane, a good,
old lady, died Aug. 28, 1877, aged 85 years, 7 months, after be-
ty years from her native land.
dren:

> HORATIO NELSON, b. Aug. 6, 1805; m. Eliza Ann, dau. of John Crouse, by Rev. Henry Saunders, Jan. 31, 1834; and was a resolute, energetic workman, trader and merchant at Bear River. He was drowned in the Bay of Funday, near St. John, Oct. 11, 1840. His widow m., 2nd, Ezekiel Croscup (of Ludowick from Germany), Jan. 24, 1849. Had four sons.

ON THE DEATH OF NELSON CHUTE.

1.

There was a man of good repute
Known far and wide as Nelson Chute;
His home was in Bear River town,
A place quite famous for renown.
For labor, honor, justice, truth,
He ever was a noted youth;
And as a merchant he did gain
Some wealth by trading on the main.

2.

So, on the Bay of Fundy, he
Had started for St. John, N. B.
On board the Robert laden grand
And James T. Hinxman in command.
When near St. John a strong breeze blew
That called up all the vessel's crew;
When by the gybing of main boom,
Poor Nelson found a watery tomb.

3.

His wife for him did sad lament,
Because her heart was sorely rent,
But he had gone to his reward
T'appear before his blessed Lord;
And there, where all things are arranged
(For God's decrees cannot be changed),
We hope to see him in that land
With all the blest at God's right hand.

C. E. W.

ii IsraEL, b. Oct. 27, 1807; m. Lydia Harris (*George, John*), April 5, 1838, and lived in Hillsburgh, Digby Co., a sturdy farmer. He d. Sept. 25, 1870; his widow m. 2nd, 1872, Dea. Alexander Ross, a school teacher. Mr. Chute had a house burnt Mar. 22, 1842, with Amelia Harris, daughter of George; Naomi Harris, daughter of Stephen; and Statira Yarrigle, daughter of Charles, in it.

97 iii GEORGE, b. March 12, 1810.
98 iv WALTER, b. July 19, 1812
99 v CHARLES, b. Feb. 13, 1815.
   vi MARY, b. Oct. 8, 1817; d. Oct. 13. 1842.
   vii DAVID SHOOK, b. Nov. 23, 1819; killed in Ontario, March 11, 1864, by a limb of a tree falling on him.
   viii ELEANOR, b. April 24, 1822. See McConnell.
   ix CAROLINE, b. July 25, 1824; d. in Ontario, July 22, 1840.
   x SUSAN, b. Apr. 8, 1826; d. in Ontario. July 12, 1840.
   xi ADONIRAM JUDSON, b. May 30, 1828; d. in Ontario, Jan. 21, 1853; a pious young man, and at the time of his death, was W. P. of the Sons of Temperance.
   xii PHEBE JANE, b. Sept. 15, 1830. See McConnell.
   xiii ARMANELLA, b. May 27, 1833; m. Isaac, son of Orlow and Chloe (Hoyt) Smith, Jan. 9, 1862, and had seven children as follows: Terressa Albina, Ida May, Ella, Celesta Jane. Lilly, Orlow and Edward. Mr. Smith moved from Malahide, Ont., to Ordway, S. D., in 1884, where Mrs. Smith d. May 4, 1890. Thence he moved in 1891, to Assa Co., B. C., west of Manitoba.
100 xiv RICHARD LAWRENCE, b. Mar. 31, 1836.

VII. 36 Andrew Chute,[7] (*Thomas,*[6] *John,*[5] *Lionel,*[4] *James,*[3] *James,*[2] *Lionel*[1]), born in Granville, N. S., Sept. 15, 1789; taken 1801, to Bear River by his parents; married, by Rev. Edward Manning in Cornwallis, King's Co., Olive, daughter of Eleazer Woodworth, Feb. 17, 1814, and lived in Clements, a mile and a half from Bear River bridge; one of the most pious, honest, industrious and generous men of the century. His school teacher in youth was William Carr; his singing teacher was Captain Dean, a pupil of William Billings of Boston, studying the books, Worcester Collection, Village Harmony. Northern Harmony and Stephen Humbert's Union Harmony. Thus by persistent effort he became a good singer, leader and teacher, and also composed about forty church tunes. He claimed to "experience religion" under the preaching of Rev. John Saxton, and was baptized by Rev. Enoch Townes in 1810, joining the Baptist church in Clements. He was appointed deacon about 1821, and soon after licensed to preach, which he continued to do off and on till he was seventy years of age. He often preached the gospel to the poor and needy in back settle-

DEACON ANDREW CHUTE AND WIFE, OLIVE CHUTE.

ments, and taught singing during winter evenings. He maintained a constant correspondence with friends and wrote or the religious papers. For several years, between 1850 and 1860, he was involved in controversy with Rev. Israel Rise, on the Millerite doctrine. His wife, too, was a great worker, a weaver and a good Christian woman. He sold his farm in Clements in the spring of 1841, to George Troop, and September 13, left Bear River for Boston on the schooner Wave, Captain Joel McDormand, thence by rail to Providence, R. I., and Stonington, Ct., thence to New York and Albany by steamboat, and through the Erie canal to Buffalo, thence to Port Rowan, Upper Canada, on a schooner commanded by Captain John Redding. From there they moved twenty-five miles in wagons, northwest of Port Buruell into Malahide, and in January, 1842, bought one hundred acres of Captain John McIntyre in the township of Bayham, where he became a prosperous farmer, charitable to the poor. His house was the resort of Christian ministers and pilgrims of all denominations. In the summer of 1851, he went back to Nova Scotia and in the fall brought back with them Mrs. Chute's aged mother and youngest sister. Deacon Chute died at home, happy in the Lord Jesus, Feb. 17, 1862; his wife followed Jan. 18, 1864, in her sixty-eighth year.

Children:

101 i EDMUND, b. Dec. 31, 1815.

ii SARAH ANN, b. May 18, 1818 ; m. by Rev. Edwin Gilpin, Captain Andrew H. Harris, Dec. 27, 1838, and lived at Bear River; a farmer, merchant and vessel owner. He built two vessels, schooner Susanna and brig Matilda, which were run many years across the Bay of Fundy to the West Indies and the states. Captain Harris was a justice, a freemason and a useful member of society. He died at home August 23, 1880, aged 65 years, 8 months. The widow soon after went to Swampscott, Mass., and lived with her eldest daughter, Susanna Webb, including two or three visits in Ontario and Nova Scotia, and in June, 1892, she crossed the "Rockies" to Vancouver where she is stopping with her second daughter, Matilda Short. Children :

1. SUSANNA, b. Mar. 16, 1840; m. Thomas Augustus, son of Thomas Webb, Nov. 18, 1862, and lived at Swampscott, Mass., over twenty years. For the benefit of his health and a change of climate they went to live in St. Thomas, Elgin Co., Ont., where he died Feb. 15, 1886, aged 54 years, 4 months. He was brought home and buried at Swampscott, where his widow still lives.

2. MATILDA, b. Aug. 20, 1842; m. Benjamin J., son of William Short,

Dec. 31, 1863, and lived some eight years at Bear River, N. S., and some years in South Boston and Somerville; in 1882 moved to Moris, Manitoba, and in 1888 to Vancouver, B. C. Children: (1) *Alice Davy*, b. Jan. 1, 1865; m. William Henry (b. in Whitby, Ont., Oct. 16, 1862), son of Alexander Squair, April 12, 1885, and have Edith Matilda, b. Jan. 4, 1886; Frank Benjamin, Sept. 12, 1887; Bertrand Carl, July 25, 1889, and William Alexander, Jan. 20, 1892, live at Vancouver, B. C. (2) *Bertrand Harris*, b. Mar. 4, 1869; m. Maud Kearney, Feb. 23, 1893, and live at Vancouver. (3) *William Andrew*, b. June 29, 1873.

 iii Harriet, b. July 16, 1820; m. Burton Chute. See No. 70.

102 iv ALFRED, b. July 29, 1822.
103 v SIDNEY, b. Nov. 20, 1824.
104 vi EZEKIEL, b. Feb. 20, 1827.
105 vii FREEMAN, b. May 30, 1829.
106 viii WILLIAM E., b. April 24, 1832.
107 ix AARON, b. Aug. 6, 1834.

 x LOVENA, b. Sept. 15, 1836; m. John D. McConnell,[4] (*David*,[3] *Elijah*,[2] *Benjamin*[1]), Feb. 17, 1858, and lived in Bayham, Walsingham, and Malahide, Ont., as farmers. Mrs. McConnell, a hard working Christian woman, weaver like her mother; d. March 16, 1881. Their children were (1) *Rachel*, b. Jan. 21, 1863; m. James Albert Chute, see No. 234. (2) *Irene*, b. Oct. 30, 1865.

 xi CYNTHIA, b. Apr. 7, 1839; m. Elisha, son of Benjamin McConnell jr., by Rev. Martin Shook McConnell, Sept. 6, 1854, in Bayham, Elgin Co., Ont., and lived on his father's old farm in Malahide, a steady, Christian man; d. June 9, 1887, aged 62. The widow still lives on the old place with her three boys. Children:

  1. CAROLINE V., b. Oct. 9, 1855: m. Lewis, son of Allen Stewart McDonald, Feb. 23, 1876, and have eight children as follows: Addison Kent, Hilliard Clyde, Harriet Mabel, Era Maud, Leila Dell, Lewis Earl, Cynthia Pearl and Murray Ellis; live at Castlewood, S. D.
  2. ELISHA KENT, b. Aug. 9, 1857; d. May 28, 1860.
  3. HARRIET A., b. Feb. 27, 1859; m. Roger W. McConnell, Dec. 19, 1883, and have two boys, Lyell Gordon and Harry Ellis; live in Assa Co., N. W. T.
  4. HILLARD LESLIE, b. Aug. 17, 1862; m. Rose Priscilla, daughter of John and Martha Barbara (Moore) Heron, Mar. 2, 1892, and has the old homestead.
  5. BERTHA K., b. Dec. 19, 1864; m. John B. Chute. No. 237.
  6. MINNIE B., b. Jan. 23, 1867; m. Charles P. Blunt, May 10, 1893, Aberdeen, S. D.
  7. JOHN MILTON, b. Jan. 19, 1869; d. Mar. 10.
  8. SARAH ANNA, b. Apr. 10, 1870; m. Will F. Ebinger, Sept. 27, 1890; confectioner, Aberdeen, S. D.
  9. JULIA OLIVIA, b. Nov. 9, 1873; m. Lewis A. Hankinson,[5] (*William*,[4]

*Thomas,*³ *Reuben,*² *Robert*¹), Mar. 2, 1892, and live with his folks on the first concession of Malahide.
10. ELISHA NEWTON, b. June 29, 1877.
11. ALBERT VICTOR, b. Mar. 5, 1882.

108 xii JOHN MILTON, b. in Ontario, July 28, 1843.

VII. 37 Abel Chute, (brother to Andrew), born in Granville, Oct. 5, 1791; married Sophia Potter,⁸ (*Joseph,*⁷ *Joseph,*⁶ *Joseph,*⁵ *Ephraim,*⁴ *Robert,*³ *Robert,*² *Nicholas* ¹), by Rev. James Manning, Dec. 7, 1817, and lived on the "Hessian Line" road, near two miles east of Bear River in Clements. He was a very energetic man in religious or secular pursuits. He was a licentiate preacher in the Baptist church; thirty years a justice of peace; taught singing. He often preached in destitute places among the poor; one place was called the "Back Line" among colored people. One old colored man, Deacon Peter Hawkins, died Feb. 3, 1892, near eighty-four, said he helped Abel Chute nineteen years in haying and harvest. He visited his kindred in Ontario in 1854. He died June 13, 1857; his wife died July 4, 1884, aged eighty-five.

Children:

109 i JAMES MANNING, b. May 16, 1819.
110 ii JOSEPH WARREN, b. March 13, 1821.
111 iii HARRIS HARDING, b. Dec. 27, 1822.
    iv ELIPHAL ANN, b. May 1, 1825; m. Oliver G. Foster,⁷ (*Asa,*⁶ *Isaac,*⁵ *Benjamin,*⁴ *Jacob,*³ *Isaac,*² *Reginald* ¹), Dec. 8, 1843, and lived on his father's place, a mile below Bridgetown, in Granville, farmer and miller. Mrs. Foster d. April 1, 1863; he m. 2nd, Sarah Ann Delap, widow of Capt. William Greenwood, jr., Sept. 2, 1863; (Capt. Greenwood m. Sarah A. Delap, March 29, 1848, had four daughters and a son, d. Feb. 1, 1862; aged 35). Mr. Foster sold the old place in Granville, about 1870, and moved to Ontario; bought the old Benjamin Pritchard farm in Malahide. In December 1875, his wife went to Boston, Mass., and died there the 17th, aged 43. He m. 3d, Mary Ann Lindsay, widow of William Crawford (by whom she had several children), Nov. 11, 1876; and d. Nov. 11, 1881, aged 76. He m. 4th, Eliza A., daughter of David Millard, Feb. 4, 1883. (She m. 1st, Hooks Roy, Mar. 9, 1831; he d. Mar. 5, 1875, aged 67; she m. 2nd, Joel Chamberlain, May 1876; he d. Oct. 19, 1877, aged 72. For a dozen years or more Mr. Foster has lived in Bayham, a few miles north of Vienna, Elgin Co., Ont. Children:
        1. JAMES NORMAN, b. Nov. 19, 1844; m. Hettie Walker, 1870 (both are dead).
        2. S. FREEMAN, b. Mar. 7, 1846; d. Mar. 3, 1865.

3. RHODA ANN, b. Apr. 19, 1848; m. Capt. George Welsh, 1866, and live at Freeport, Digby Co., N. S.
4. HARRIET, b. Jan. 17, 1851; m. George W. McConnell, son of Dea. Moses; four or five children.
5. KATE, b. May 11, 1853; m. Hiram Westover, 1874.
6. ASA H., b. July 19, 1856; m. Ida M. Knapp, 1885; lives in St. Paul, Minn.
7. SERETTA, b. Feb. 3, 1858.
8. JAMES MANNING, b. Aug. 2, 1862; d. Oct. 2.
9. WILLIAM BURPEE, b. Aug. 1, 1864; d. Apr. 1, 1868.
10. ERNEST HAVELOCK, b. Aug. 13, 1866; m. Esther Powell, Christmas, 1884.
11. FREEMAN BURTON, b. Mar. 0, 1869.

v ELIZA, b. May 28, 1827; d. Feb. 27, 1852.

vi CATHARINE B., b. Mar. 17, 1830: m. by Rev. L. P. Smith, Wm. Peet,[7] son of Rev. Orrin H. Tyrrell, Dec. 13, 1843, in Malahide, Elgin Co., Ont., and they lived on his father's farm near Centerville, since called Luton. (*Rev. Orrin H. Tyrrell,*[6] was son of Joel Tyrrell and Mary Hinman — from Connecticut to Bayham, C. W., about 1820 — *Mary Hinman*,[5] or Inman, b. about 1775, was daughter of *Peter*,[4] b. 1742, of *Ebenezer*,[3] b. 1705, of *Capt. Titus*,[2] b. 1656, of *Sergt. Edward Hinman*,[1] from England to America, time of OliverCromwell, about 1650, and settled in Stratford, Ct., with wife Hannah. They had four sons and four daughters. Sergt. E. Hinman died November, 1681 [*]).

Mr. William P. Tyrell sold out in Malahide 1878, and moved to Essex Co., then sold out again and moved to Sanilac Co., Mich., and lived at Cumber, 1882, and also in Huron Co., near Tyre. He died near the latter place April 8, 1891; aged 69. Children:
1. ELISABETH, b. Oct. 1, 1855; d. July 19, 1858.
2. LIONEL POTTER, b. Aug. 23, 1857; d. Jan. 16, 1867.
3. W. HERBERT, b. Mar. 17, 1860.
4. ALBERT EDWARD, b. Jan. 11, 1862.
5. A. MINETTA, b. Oct. 11, 1863; d. Dec. 6, 1864.
6. EDGAR HARDING, b. Aug. 28, 1865.
7. ALVARETTA ELIS, b. April 14, 1867.
8. IDA MAY, b. Oct. 4, 1868; m. William, son of Edward Conner, Oct 26, 1887, and lives in Montana.
9. ULYSSES GRANT, b. Dec. 14, 1872; d. July 22, 1874.

vii MARY JANE, b. Oct. 20, 1833; m. John A. Vroom,[7] (*Henry F.*,[6] *George*,[5] *John*,[4] *Hendrick*,[3] *Hendrick*,[2] *Cornelius Peter*[1], an early settler of New Amsterdam, since called New York. He was from Holland, and died previous to 1657), July 11, 1854, and lived in Clements, a farmer and mason. Children:
1. WILLIAM ELDON, b. May 20, 1855; m. Mary Jane Ditmass (*of Abram, of John*), January 1882; three children, lives in Lynn, a mason.

[*] Royal B. Hinman's Genealogy of the Puritans, New York, 1856.

2. LALIA J., b. April 24, 1857; m. George H. L. Boyce 1880, merchant.
3. M. SOPHIA, b. March 20, 1860; m. Delacy E., son of William Foster, Oct. 31, 1883; two or three children. Lives at Nictaux.
4. EDITH M., b. Oct. 4, 1862,
5. J. AVARD, b. Aug. 20, 1865; m. Melvina Cornish, Feb. 22, 1890, and live in Lynn, Mass.
6. ELLA GERTRUDE, b. Aug. 26, 1868; d. Mar. 3, 1876.
7. CARRIE E., b. Nov. 10, 1772.
8. JESSIE M, b. Feb. 1, 1776.

viii LYDIA SOPHIA, b. May 4, 1835; m. George Albert, son of Richard Ruggles jr., Nov. 29, 1855, and live on a part of her father's old farm. Children:
1. RICHARD HARVEY, b. June 9, 1856; m. Arabel Porter, Apr. 21, 1880.
2. GEORGE MELVILLE, b. Sept. 27, 1858; m. Margaret E. Nichols, June 3, 1885. Three children.
3. ELLA GERTRUDE, b. Sept. 28, 1860; m. Myron M. Ogden, 1892.
4. ERNEST ALBERT, b. Nov. 1, 1866; d. May 27, 1869.
5. ROBENA MAY, b. Dec. 9, 1870; d. Mar. 21, 1876.

ix CAROLINE VICTORIA, b. Aug. 27, 1837; m. Isaac F., son of Dowe Jones, Jan. 25, 1860, and live at Deep Brook, near Clementsport. Children:
1. IDA MAY. b. Feb. 11, 1861; d. Mar. 27, 1863.
2. ALBERTA M., b. May 26, 1863; d. Jan. 2, 1876.
3. CHARLES F., b. Aug. 20, 1865.
4. ASA WARREN, b. Mar. 21, 1868.
5. FRED HERBERT, b. Mar. 3, 1870.
6. AMY LAURA, b. February 19, 1876.
7. ROY MALCOMB, b. May 10, 1878; d. May 21, 1882.

x RHODA ANN, b. Jan. 5, 1840; m. J. Alfred Berry, (*Peter, Thomas*), Oct. 21, 1858, and live on the Hessian Line road, three miles from Bear River. Sober industrious farmers. Children:
1. JANE SOPHIA, b. May 10, 1860; m. Lawrence F. Berry (*James, Henry, Thomas*), May 10, 1876; live in Alston, Mass.
2. ALVIN ELSWORTH, b. Aug. 22, 1862; m. Mary, daughter of Thomas P. Berry, son, of Thomas, April 1886.
3. EDITH EMMA, b. April 12, 1864; m. Capt. Sampson B. Berry, brother to Lawrence, March 20, 1888.
4. HARDING D., b. April 29, 1868.
5. ANNIE V., b. May 24, 1873; d. March 1887.
6. WILLIAM FOSTER, b. Sept. 26, 1875,
7. FRANK HORACE, b. Jan. 23, 1878.

xi OLIVER, b. Jan. 18, 1843; d. Oct. 7.
2 xii WILLIAM OZIAS, b. Aug. 29, 1845.

VII. 38. Calvin Chute, brother of the preceding, born Oct. 23, 95; married Maria, daughter of Joseph and Maria (Burns) Gilliland, Rev. Peter Crandall, Dec. 27, 1819, and lived on the Hessian Line road, opposite his brother Abel; a thrifty farmer. But he unfortunately sold out in 1834 and moved to Prince Edward Island; but not succeeding as he anticipated, returned in 1836. After that the family broke up and scattered some to Massachusetts and others settled in Nova Scotia. The winter of 1851-52, he spent with his brother and other relatives in Ontario. For ten years or more he lived in Salem, Mass. He died at his brother Binea's, Bear River, N. S., March 10, 1864. His wife continued to reside in Salem, till 1880, when her eldest son Isaiah, took her to his home, where she died Aug. 29, 1883, over eighty years of age.

Children:

    i SARAH, b. June 7, 1821; m. Peter Leary, November, 1840, and lived near St. Mary's bay; had three children. He died September, 1846, aged 46. She married 2nd, Morgan Lewis, August, 1849, and had seven more, and died July 27, 1876. Children:
1. EDWARD, b. August, 1842; d. 1843.
2. WILLIAM, b. 1844; moved to Cedar Mt., King Co., Washington, Ter.
3. ELIZA ANN, b. Dec. 18, 1846; m. Amos S. Pinkham of Newburyport, Oct. 12, 1867; lived there nine years, then in Nova Scotia three years, then to Salem, Mass., where he was killed by the cars, Nov. 7, 1883, aged 50 years, 9 months. The widow lives in Salem. He married 1st, Diadama, daughter of George and Caroline (Viditoe) Marshall, June 6, 1855; had three children. She died July 24, 1867, aged 32. 2nd family, Lewis:
1. GEORGE W., b. 1850; m. Maggie McAlpine, twelve children.
2. ANNA MARIA, b. 1852; m. James Haight; eight children and died 1889.
3. LOUISE JANE, b. 1854; d. 1889.
4. HARRIET S., b. 1856; m. Capt. Cann, Yarmouth.
5. CLARENCE L., b. 1859; d. 1860.
6. ANNABELLE, b. 1861; m. Hiram Sabean; four children, Maryville, Snohomish Co., Wash.
7. EDWARD BURTON, b. 1864; m. Mary Everett, North Range, Digby Co., N. S.

113 ii ISAIAH, b. Mar. 22, 1823.

    iii SIBYL, b. Oct. 13, 1824; m. Charles Ansley Armstrong (son of Frank and Mary Barnes widow of Joseph Gilliland), Jan. 5, 1843, and lived over twenty years on Digby Neck. In 1865 they moved to Minnesota and settled in Brown Co., but since 1880 they moved to Mariaville, Rock Co., Neb. Children:
1. WALLACE, b. Oct. 27, 1844; m. Julia Lobdell, Oct. 25, 1869; seven children.
2. HENRIETTA, b. Oct, 25, 1846; m. Stephen Gilliland (son of *George, of George, brother to Joseph*), Jan. 5, 1864, thirteen children.

3. MARY, b. Aug. 2, 1849; m. Edward Foote, Oct. 10, 1869, and had nine children.
4. BURTON, b. May 13, 1851.
5. EDWARD, Sept. 5, 1853; m. Minnie Lobdell, Dec. 1, 1874; seven children.
6. LAVENIA, b. May. 27, 1855; m. John Knowles, Sept. 1, 1873; eight children.
7. HANFORD, b. May 21, 1859; m. Lovinia Prickitt, 1880; five children.
8. ALBERT, b. Oct. 11, 1862; m. Jemima Prickitt, Dec. 10, 1882.
9. IDA, b. Feb. 7, 1865; m. Perry Woolery, Feb. 10, 1881,

4 iv THOMAS, b. Sept. 21, 1826.
5 v ANDREW M., b. June 13, 1828.
   vi ISAAC, b. June 6, 1830; d. in Clements, 1876.
   vii CALVIN, b. Mar. 26, 1832; m. Lydia, daughter of Felix Blackburn, May 24, 1855, Newport, N. S.
   viii HENRY ALLINE, b. Mar. 4, 1834; d. a happy Christian, Jan. 27, 1840.
   ix ISABELLA, b. May 4, 1836; d. at Israel Chute's, Oct. 17, 1854.
   x ELIZA A., b. Nov. 8, 1838; m. David Marshall (*George, Otis, Isaac*), Aug. 1, 1855, and lived at Newburyport, Mass. He departed for "parts unknown" in 1867 (but was heard of afterwards; he died in Trempealeau Co., Wis., spring of 1892, aged 55); she married 2nd, James Marshall of Weymouth, N. S., January, 1869, and lived in Boston. He died early in 1877; she married 3rd, Louis Rouillard, October, 1877, and lived at Littleton, near N. Acton, Mass., and died June 25, 1883; Mr. Rouillard married 1st, Sophia, daughter of John Potter, with whom he lived thirty years; he married 3rd, Ellen Smith, January, 1887. Children: (1) *Adelaide A.*, b. Mar. 9, 1856; m. Oscar A. Moody, Aug. 28, 1873; two children; he died Mar. 15, 1878, aged 29; she m. 2nd, John S. Potter (*Charles, John*), Aug. 8, 1883; seven children; moved from Littleton to Concord, Mass., 1890, (2) *James William*, b. July 17, 1869; lived some years with Robert Sabean at Weymouth, N. S., to Haverhill, Mass., 1883; m. Margaret E., daughter of John G. Durland of Milton, N. S., Jan. 5, 1887, and had Margaret E., b. Jan. 20, 1888; Mrs. M. died Jan. 29, 1888, aged 33; he m. 2nd, Adella A., daughter of Deacon Joseph A. Doty of Weymouth, June 18, 1890, and had Herbert Ansley, b. Apr. 30, 1891, Haverhill, Mass. (3) *Anna Belle*, b. June 1, 1866; m. Edward C. Thurber, Freeport, N. S. (4) *Alice Maria*, b, Nov. 3, 1869; m. ———. (5) *Cora Lewis Rouillard*, b. Mar. 27, 1883.
   xi ABEL, b. Aug. 7, 1841; d. 1846.
   xii GEORGIANA, b. Dec. 24, 1843; d. 1846.
3 xiii WILLIAM HENRY, b. Nov. 20, 1847.

VII. **39 John,**[7] brother of the preceding, born Sept. 25, 1797; married Eliza, daughter of Joseph Potter 2nd jr., by Rev. Thomas Ansley, Sept. 25, 1821, and lived in Clements, east side of Bear River, one mile from the bridge, where he spent his days, a hard working, sober, industrious farmer; died on his birthday exactly 80. His wife, a hard working woman and a weaver; died Nov. 13, 1873; aged 72.

Children:

- 117   i   HIRAM, b. Dec. 21, 1822.
-      ii   WILLETT, b. Oct. 4, 1825; d. Apr. 12, 1826.
-     iii   LOIS HAYDEN, b. Feb. 24, 1827; m. by Rev. Aaron Cogswell, John, son of George Graham, Jan. 6, 1851, and live at Bear River. (He m. 1st, Emeline, daughter of William Benson, 1845, and had (1) *May Sophia*, b. June 24, 1846, m. David, son of Henry Hulseman, July 1863, and had two children, Somerville, Mass., (2) *Emeline A.*, b. Oct. 17, 1849; d. at Digby, Feb. 26, 1867; Mrs. Graham d. May 8, 1850, aged 27); Mr. Graham was a skillful sea-captain, and went many voyages on the ocean. His vessel the Lizzie Chute, was wrecked and all hands lost at Chebeague, near Yarmouth, N. S., Jan. 10, 1868; he was 48, and the widow m. 2nd, John V., son of Joseph and Debby (Woodman) Thomas, as his 2d wife, Jan. 30, 1879, and live at the head of the tide, Bear River. Children:
  1. JESSIE IMOGINE, b. Oct. 17, 1851. See No. 217.
  2. ELIZA JANE, b. Sept. 9, 1853; m. Richard C. Hamilton, Feb. 18, 1885.
  3. JOHN H., b. April 19, 1855; d. Nov. 20, 1861.
  4. GEORGE HOWARD, b. Sept. 9, 1857; m. Jennie Kingsley, 1883.
  5. ANNETTA, b. Sept. 21, 1859; m. Jacob Morgan, 1880.
  6. ROBERT J., b. May 10, 1861; d. July 23, 1864.
  7. MINNIE H., b. Dec. 18, 1863; m. Charles W. C. Trask, March 28, 1886, and live at Milford, N. H.
- 118   iv   JOSEPH BURTON, b. Feb. 7, 1829.
- 119   v   WILLIAM HENRY, b. March 5, 1831.
- 120   vi   ROBERT JOHN, b. March 3, 1833.
-     vii   ELIZA ANN, b. Sept. 14, 1835; m. Gilbert H. Peters (—— Capt. Charles, Maurice), Jan. 26, 1859, and had (1) *Vinah H.*, b. Jan. 15, 1861; d. Feb. 18, 1880; (2), *Ceretha*, b. Jan. 13, 1863; d. Oct. 25, 1865. The mother d. July 1, 1877; and he m. 2nd Emma J. Ames, Aug. 4, 1880; live in Everett, Mass.
-    viii   ISRAEL, b. Nov. 8, 1837; d. Aug. 17, 1844.
- 121   ix   LYMAN W., b. Nov. 8, 1845.

VII. 40 **Binea**,[7] brother of the preceding, born at Bear River, June 23, 1801; married by Rev. William Elder, Louis Jane Foster, Nov. 12, 1829, and lived more than fifty years on his father's old farm, half a mile from Bear River bridge. He was as generous hearted and hospitable a man as any of the name in Nova Scotia; his house was always open for travelers, especially the Christian pilgrims. In 1882 he sold the old farm, that had been the home of his father and mother, to James Manning, son of Robert Rice, and joined his sons in Ontario, locating at Ridgetown, Kent Co., where he died Nov. 12, 1887.

Children:

- **122** i JAMES EDWARD, b. Oct. 18, 1830.
- **123** ii CHARLES PETERS, b. Jan. 1, 1832.
- **124** iii NATHAN, b. June 28, 1833.
- iv SOPHRONIA, b. April 18, 1835; m. James W. Parker,[3] (*Dea. Wilbur, Abednego*). Mar. 31, 1858, as his 3rd wife; m. 1st, Becca Ann daughter of Christopher Benson, and 2nd, her sister, Mary Eliza Benson). Capt. Parker was a skillful navigator. His last trip was on the bark "Tamer E. Marshall," dying at Saigon, India, July, 1892, aged about 65. His widow lives at Bear River.

  Children:
  1. CHARLES HENRY, b. Mar. 25, 1859; m. Sarah E. Hersey, 1881. He is a captain at sea.
  2. BERNARD A., b. Sept. 7, 1861; m. Lilly R., daughter of Alden Harris 1881, and is mate to his brother.
  3. MARY JANET, b. May 31, 1866; m. Arthur E. Wakeling of St. John N. B., June, 1891,
  4. EMMA GERTRUDE, b. Jan. 7, 1869.
  5. JAMES WILBUR, b. June 13, 1873.

- v SARAH MATILDA, b. Feb. 11, 1837; m. Gilbert Morgan,[4] (*Thomas*,[3] *Edward*,[2] *George*,[1] from England), Jan. 1, 1857, and live at Bear River. Children:
  1. ISRAEL, b. July 26, 1859: d. Mar. 22, 1882; a sailor at Bombay.
  2. LOUISE J., b. May 25, 1861; m. John P. Rice, a musician, May 1, 1881; he died May 13, 1886, aged 38 at Sandy Cove. She married 2nd, Dr. Hay.
  3. LIZZIE ANN, b. Oct. 11, 1864; m. Thelbert of David and Melinda Jane (Chute) Rice, May 12, 1881, and d. July 28, 1882; he m. 2nd, Hattie K., adopted daughter of Rev. John J. Woodworth, 1885.
  4. JAMES FLETCHER, b. Aug. 1, 1872; d. Jan. 3, 1876.
  5. WILLIE B., b. Oct. 26, 1876; d. 1888.

- **125** vi GEORGE, b. Oct. 6, 1838.
- **126** vii WILLIAM ALBERT, b. June 2, 1840.
- viii CAROLINE, b. July 5, 1842; m. J. Augustus Purday, Sept, 16, 1862; he d. Feb. 11, 1863, aged 23; m. 2nd, James M. Peake, Oct. 8, 1870; he d. in Boston, Sept. 17, 1870, aged 40. She is a dressmaker in Boston.
- ix BINEA, b. June 28, 1844; d. July 9, 1844.
- x ISRAEL, b. Nov. 12, 1746; m. Mary Elisab Harris (*Elijah, William H. Esq., Capt. Henry*), June 6, 1874; live in Detroit, Mich., he is a first-class carpenter.
- xi MARY ANN, b. April 24, 1848; m. William Setliffe Crouse (*William, John*), Sept. 15, 1877, and live in Hillsburgh, the Digby side of Bear River. Two children.
- xii LOUIS J., b. May 4, 1850; m. J. Fletcher Milberry, son of John, October 1872; live in Hillsburgh, Bear River; have one or two children.

VII. 41 James Edward Chute,[7] the youngest son of Dea. Thomas and Sibyl (Marshall) Chute, born May 5, 1810; married Sara Matilda, daughter of Asa Foster, by Rev. John Chase, Oct. 17, 1839. He was a merchant at Bear River. He sold out there and moved to Salem, Mass., in 1855, and went into the shoe business. At the close of the war they moved to Boston, where his wife died April 11, 1890, aged 71. For more than twenty years, Mr. Chute was an agent, for a manufacturing firm in Boston and travelled extensively in more than twenty of the United States and most of the British Provinces. He lived some with his son-in-law, Foster, in Peterboro, N. H.

Children:

    i RHODA F., b. Aug. 26, 1840; m. Dea. Eben Augustus Burbank, Apr. 7, 1869; lived in Chelsea, Mass., where she died Dec. 8, 1887; he married 1st, Lizzie Archer and had four children.

    ii ELIZA JANE, b. Apr. 6, 1842; m. Samuel W. Foster,[8] (*Samuel B.*,[7] *Isaac P.*,[6] *Moses*,[5] *Jonathan*,[4] *Caleb*,[3] *Abram*,[2] *Reginald*[1]), 6th cousin, 1866, and lived in Boston and Peterboro, N. H. He died Apr. 18, 1889, aged 44; four children; three died in infancy while the fourth, Frank B., b. 1877, is a stout young man.

    iii EMMA MARIA, b. Mar. 18, 1845; m. Stephen R. Davison, Feb., 1870, and died Aug. 9, 1871; he lives in Halifax, N. S.

127 iv JAMES MILLEDGE, b. Oct. 19, 1846.

VII. 42 Abner Chute.[7] (*James*,[6] *John*,[5] *Lionel*,[4] *James*,[3] *James*,[2] *Lionel*[1]), born in Granville, Dec. 2, 1783; married Sophia, daughter of Edward and Lois McBride, Feb. 28, 1807; lived in Upper Granville. He was killed by lightning Aug. 15, 1842; she died Mar. 9, 1864, aged eighty-seven.

Children:

    ROBERT, b. Nov. 6, 1807; d. June 11, 1830.

    ii SOPHIA, b. Oct. 31, 1809; m. Hicks Chesley, (*James, Maj. Samuel*), Jan. 7, 1834, and lived in Clarence, She d. Feb. 16, 1876; he d. Mar. 30, 1881, aged 73. Children:

      1. SALENA, b. 1834; m. Samuel Williams; four children.
      2. MALISSA, b. 1836; m. Wm. A. Kempton, Queen's Co.; two children.
      3. ABNER, b. 1839; was a school teacher, m. Jane Ross, of Colchester, had two sons; d. May 1887.
      4. ADELIA, b. 1841; d. 1883.
      5. PATIENCE, b. 1844; m. Robert Starratt, two children.

    iii TAMER, b. Feb. 15, 1812; m. Sidney Marshall (*Andrew, William*), Feb. 2,

1837, five children; she d. Oct. 6, 1856; he m. 2nd, Helen Banks 1857, two children; he d. Jan. 12, 1862; she m. 2nd, Samuel Moore 1865. Children:
1. MILLEDGE, b. 1838; m. Emma, daughter of William Morse, who died March 1873, five children; m. 2nd, Waity Bogert, two children.
2. ALBERT, b. 1844; m. Belle Edgett, two children; m. 2nd, Bertie Edgett, two children more.
3. AGNES, b. ——; m. James Nichols, six children.
4. SOPHIA, b. ——; died young.
5. EDWARD, b. ——; died young.
6. GEORGE F., b. April 1858; m. Hannah J. Madden; Addie F. Coates.
7. SUSAN, b. 1860; d. 1862.
8. SUSAN AMELIA MOORE, b. Jan. 1868.

iv LOIS, b. May 13, 1814; d. Oct. 25, 1842.
v JACOB, b. Nov. 13, 1816; m. Sophia Marshall, was drowned in a well; she m. 2nd George C. Banks.
vi ABNER, b. Oct. 11, 1821; d. 1822.

VII. 43 Silas Chute,[7] brother of Abner, born in Granville, June , 1788; married by Rev. John Wiswall, Mary Roach[3] (Matthew Pat- k), Nov. 26, 1812, and lived in Upper Clarence. He was a sober, in- strious man, kind and neighborly to all; died June 11, 1833; then the nily moved into or near Aylesford, on the "Post Road," and the dow married 2nd, James Parker, July 1, 1847; he died September , 1848, aged seventy-nine, six months; she died Apr. 5, 1876, aged ;hty-eight.

Children:

8 i JAMES PARKER, b. Sept. 24, 1813.
ii HENRY RICKETSON, b. Apr. 9, 1815; m. Sarah, daughter of Heman Nickerson, 1843; had a son, Israel Lovett, b. 1844; d. 1846. Mrs. Chute d. 1862, aged 40; he m. 2nd, Susan, daughter of Alex Forbes, and is justice of peace near Yarmouth, N. S.
!9 iii ISAAC ROACH, b. Jan. 10, 1817.
;0 iv JOHN MATTHEW, b. Jan. 23, 1819.
v PHEBE, b. Oct. 3, 1820; m. James H. Priestly, 1842, and lived at Melvern Square; had five sons, three daughters; she d. 1887.
vi MARY K., b. Sept. 12, 1822; m. Joseph R. Raymond, (*Jonathan, Daniel*), and lived near Weymouth, Digby Co.; had nine children; she d. Feb. 13, 1872; he m. 2nd, Zilphia Pinkney; b. 1839, daughter of Capt. David S. Kinney (of Nathan Kinney jr., and widow of Daniel Webster Newcomb,[3] (*Daniel Webster,*[7] *Joseph,*[6] *John,*[5] *John,*[4] *Simon,*[3] *Andrew,*[2] *Andrew,*[1] of Boston about 1635), Sept. 20, 1872; he d. at Weymouth, happy in the Lord Jesus, Sept. 24, 1892, aged 69. D. W. Newcomb was a sailor at 14, master at 19 and after that owner of ships. He circumnavigated the globe in 1863, and d. in Weymouth, Digby Co., Jan. 22, 1872, aged 41, leaving three children.

(1) *Robert*, b. 1857. (2) *Edina Agnes*, b. 1862. (3) *Louisa Kinney*, b. 1864.
Raymond's children:
1. IRA ABEL, b. Feb. 8, 1843; m. Nellie Cowper, four children, and died at sea about 1876.
2. ELIZA JANE, b. 1850; m. James Richards, New Haven, Conn.
3. EVALINE A., b. Oct. 5, 1852; m. Dr. J. H. Harris, Beaver River.
4. MARY AGNES, b. Nov. 29, 1855; m. Randolph, son of William Payson, and live at Weymouth.

vii ENOCH, b. Oct. 11, 1824; d. June 30, 1877; he went to sea, and was in California.
131 viii ISRAEL, b. Sept. 22, 1826.
ix ABNER, b. July 25, 1828; to South America, blacksmith.
x HANNAH ANN, b. April 17, 1831; m. James P., son of Dea. Zebina Roach, Jan. 8, 1850, had eight children, and d. 1888; he d. May 1, 1875, aged 48; Dea. Z. Roach; d. June 23, 1860, aged 68.

VII. 44 Handley,[7] brother of the preceding, born Dec. 13, 1790; married Hannah, daughter of Benjamin and Martha (Foster) Chute, by Rev. Thomas Ansley, Jan. 13, 1814, and lived at Chute Cove, since called Hampton, and was a good Christian, citizen, farmer, miller and neighbor. His wife died July 1, 1826, aged forty-two; he married 2nd, Martha Phinney,[7] (*James*,[6] *Zaccheus*,[5] *Benjamin*,[4] *John*[3] *John*,[2] *John*,[1] of Scituate, about 1630), by Rev. William Elder, Oct. 16, 1826; and died Jan. 24, 1857; she received a paralytic stroke of the lower limbs, in 1837, and walked no more for thirty years, but bore it all with Christian fortitude, dying happy in the Lord Jesus, Oct. 10, 1868, aged sixty-four.

Children:

132 i EATON, b. April 12, 1815.
133 ii JACOB, b. Feb. 3, 1817.
iii MARTHA, b. Aug. 1, 1819; m. Harris, son of Samuel Foster, Dec. 24, 1839, and had a son Norman, who d, as 10 years of age; she d. Feb. 2, 1880. See Foster.
iv ELIZA M., b. Aug. 17, 1821; m. Benjamin, son of Isaac Foster, Dec. 24, 1840, and lived in Hampton. He d. Sept. 17, 1856, aged 40; she m. 2nd, James Mitchell 1862, and had (1), *Sarah*, b. 1863; m. Edmund Hall, school teacher Aug. 1, 1882; and d. 1889; (2), *Hallett Ray*, b. 1865; m. Sarah Briggs, Oct. 16, 1889, Mrs. Mitchell; d. June 16, 1877; he marriee 4th, Evalina Sabean, and had a daughter Ina; Mr. Mitchell m. 1st, Rebecca Marshall, and had (1), *Emerson*, m. Catharine, daughter of James Taylor; (2), *Joseph*, m. Martha, daughter of Benjamin Foster; (3), *Albert*, m. Martha, daughter of James Taylor, Mrs. Mitchell d. Nov. 7, 1850, aged 35; he m. 2nd, Athalinda, daughter of John and Mary Brinton, and had (1), *Charles*, m. Amilda, daughter of James Snow; (2), *Anna*, m. Isaiah, son of Robert Elliott, she

d. April 7, 1860, aged 34. He d. June 22, 1884, aged 72. Children of Benjamin and Eliza Foster:
1. HANNAH, b. 1841; d. 1845.
2. ELISABETH, b. 1843; m. Thomas H., son of Samuel Foster, May 12, 1861, had nine children, three dwarfs. One Dudley, b. 1877, twenty-seven inches high.
3. HANLEY, b. June 8, 1845; m. Lizzie, daughter of Geo. Kilpatrick, Sept. 9, 1867, and live in Lynn, Mass.; two children. (1) *Gertrude Lovinia*, b. Mar. 8, 1872. (2) *George Benjamin*, b. Oct. 25, 1875.
4. FRASER, b. 1847; burned to death in John Foster's house, 1861.
5. MARTHA, b. July 7, 1849; m. Capt. Joseph Mitchell, Oct. 23, 1865, and have over a dozen children above Hampton.
6. ADELIA, b. Oct. 29, 1851; m. David, son of Samuel Foster, Dec. 14, 1870; four children.
7. JESSE, b. Dec. 5, 1853; m. Eunice Baxter, 1875.
8. SABRA D., b. Jan. 6, 1856; m. Otis M. Staples, Apr. 29, 1888, and have Mark Johnson, b. July 31, 1889, Lynn, Mass. She had been there seven years.

4   v SETH, b. Dec. 3, 1823.
   vi HANLEY, b. 1825; d. 1825.
5 vii SOLOMON, b. July 15, 1827.
  viii ELIZABETH, b. Nov. 22. 1828; m. Michael Miller (*Harris, Michael and Sarah Farnsworth*), December, 1846, and had
1. MICHAEL, b. 1847; d. 1848. Mr. Miller d. June, 1849, aged 26; she m. 2nd, Charles Hanley Brinton, (*Charles, Charles*), and had
2. ALICE M., b. Sept. 3, 1855; m. George E. Conner, 1878, son of George M., a soldier of the late war, son of Joseph of Newburyport, whose wife was Dorcas Fowler,[7] (*Philip,[6] Joseph,[5] Joseph,[4] Philip,[3] Joseph,[2] Philip,[1]* of 1634), and have eight children.
3. HOWARD C., b. Oct. 4, 1858; m. Nellie Noble, July, 1879.
4. LIZZIE C., b. Oct. 29, 1861; m. George E. Monroe, 1891. Mr. Brinton d. June, 1861, aged 32; she m. 3rd, Samuel M. Gesner, (*Delancy, Abram, John*) and had
5. DELANEY LONGLEY, b. Dec. 13, 1866. Mr. Gesner was a school teacher in Nova Scotia eight years. They moved from St. Croix Cove, N. S., to Lynn, Mass., October, 1870, and since that he is a carpenter.

ix MARY ANN, b. May 21, 1830; m. Capt. Traverse Brinton (*Charles, Charles*), Dec. 1849, and have lived on the shore of the Bay of Fundy, above Hampton, two miles. Children:
1. AVARD B., b. 1850; m. Laleah, daughter of Peter Farnsworth, Jan. 1872, and d. Nov. 5, 1873; she m. 2nd, Elias, son of Jordan Messenger.
2. CHARLES, b. 1855; m. Lucy, daughter of Ingraham Snow, and have six children.
3. ADA, b. 1857; d. 1860.
4. EBER, b. 1860; m. Bessie Charlton.

x HANNAH, b. Jan. 15, 1832; m. Capt. Elias, son of Dea. John Brinton, son of Charles, Jan. 16, 1851, and after sailing twenty-five years, settled down on the bay shore, three miles above Hampton, a farmer, and d. March 1892, aged 67. Children:
   1. MARY M., b. Oct. 10, 1851; m. Joseph Howe Graves, Oct. 19, 1871, five children, Everett, Mass.
   2. HANDLEY J., b. Nov. 6, 1855; m. Amoret, daughter of Thomas, son of Samuel Foster, 1877, three children.
   3. MARTHA, b. July 16, 1861; d. March 4, 1862.
   4. ANSLEY E., b. Jan. 23, 1867; m Rowena Hutchinson, Dec. 1889, Milton, Mass.

136 xi JOHN EBER, b. Oct. 23, 1833.
137 xii ROBERT, b. June 15, 1835.
138 xiii JOSEPH DIMOCK, b. April 26, 1837.
   xiv SELEDA, b. July 15, 1839; d. 1850.
   xv JESSE, b. Jan. 31, 1842; d. 1844.
139 xvi ABNER, b. Dec. 16, 1843.
   xvii LAVINIA, b. Dec. 7, 1845; m. Lorenzo, son of Henry Fash, Mar. 28, 1864, and live a mile below Bridgetown, in Granville. Children:
     1. ZENAS L., b. July 26, 1866; Baptist minister in New York.
     2. FRANK HUBERT, b. Oct. 23, 1870; d. Nov. 10, 1872.
     3. IDA MABEL, b. Aug. 3, 1874.
     4. PERCY LEROY, b. June 23, 1874.

VII. 45 David Morse,[7] youngest son of James and Elizabeth (Morse) Chute, born Jan. 3, 1795; married Sarah, daughter of Richard and Elizabeth Chandler, by Rev. Samson Bushy, Jan. 20, 1818, and lived, a farmer, on the bay shore, a mile below Hampton. They were a Christian couple, formerly Baptists, but latterly Advents. In life they let their light shine and doubtless have gone to their reward. He died Oct. 18, 1864: she died July 14, 1873, aged seventy-eight.

Children:

140 i JOSHUA MARSDEN, b. Oct. 15, 1818.
   ii ZIPPORAH M., b. Feb. 11, 1820; m. Abel Chute. No. 89.
141 iii JOHN WENTWORTH, b. Aug. 20, 1821.
   iv JAMES ALBERT, b. Mar. 14, 1823; d. Apr. 23, 1835.
142 v SIDNEY SMITH, b. Oct. 20, 1824.
   vi ELISABETH CHARLOTTE, b. Jan. 31, 1826; m. John Chute Farnsworth, Sept. 1856, and lived at Hampton. He d. Aug. 6,, 1883. aged 78; she d. in Lynn, Mass., July 1, 1889. Children:
     1. SISSILIA, b. April 28, 1858; m. Rufus M. Benner, Aug. 20, 1879; had one child, live in Lynn, Mass.
     2. ADALINE, b. Jan. 16, 1861; m. Charles Alfred, son of Alfred Cross

REV. OBED CHUTE, AND WIFE MARY JANE CHUTE.

Oct. 20, 1879, a merchant in Lynn, and had (1), *Alfred Burton*, b. May 30, 1880; (2), *Marion Edna*, b. May 30, 1886; and lost one.

 3. MARTHA, b. April 25, 1862; m. Holden Cameron, Aug. 19, 1894; has three children lost two, Lynn, Mass.

 4. JULINA, b. June 19, 1864; m. William Starratt, Oct. 10, 1880; has four sons, Lynn, Mass.

 5. MORTON, b. July 6, 1866; m. ——.

 6. SOLOMON, b. Aug. 20, 1868.

143 vii HANDLEY, b. Sept. 20, 1827.
144 viii TIMOTHY W. B., b. Nov. 11, 1829.
 ix SOPHIA, b. Nov. 11, 1829; m. Capt. John Wm. Reed, 1855; had a daughter, *Eugenia*, m. Harry Timpany, lived at Bridgeport, Conn. Capt. Reed was lost at sea 1856; she m. 2nd Samuel Williston; m. 3d. William H. Hurd, Oct. 1876, and lived in Cambridge, Lynn, Salem, in Maine and Bridgeport, Conn.

 x MARTHA, b. Dec. 1830; d. April 1831.

 xi HELEN ANN, b. Jan. 29, 1832; m. William Locke, May 5, 1855; and d. at Abel Chute's 1868; he d. about 1880.

 xii OBED, b. Oct. 5, 1835; m. Emma White Feb. 20, 1860.

 xiii LYDIA, b. April 5, 1835; m. Zaccheus Dow, Dec. 16, 1855; had two children, and d. April 18, 1865, Newburyport; he m. 2nd, Abbie Burnham.

145 xiv ANGUS, b. Oct. 28, 1836.
 xv URSULA, b. July 27, 1839; d. Aug. 24.
146 xvi DAVID M., b. June 14, 1841.

VII. 46 Dimock,[7] son of James and Elizabeth (Wright) Chute, born in Granville, Jan. 17, 1803; married Minetta Ann, daughter of Ezekiel and Lydia A. (Morse) Chute, Sept. 26, 1850, and lived on his father's old farm, a mile below Bridgetown, in Granville. He was a real "home-body," and only went out of the county once, at Bear River; died May 30, 1869; his wife died May 12, 1854, aged thirty-four. Children:

 i JOSEPH M., b. Aug. 19, 1851; d. in Lynn, Mass., Oct. 10, 1872.

 ii MINETTA ANN, b. Feb. 10, 1853; m. James M. Gilliatt,[4] (*Edmund P.*,[3] *Michael*,[2] *William*[1]), Oct. 31, 1881; have two or three daughters; live in Granville, a mile above the ferry.

VII. 47 Rev. Obed, born Aug. 8, 1815; married Mary Jane,[9] daughter of Charles and Janet (Newcomb) Cox, Mar. 30, 1850; Janet Nesbit Newcomb,[8] (*Abram*,[7] *Abram*,[6] *Capt. Eddy*,[5] *Dea. John*,[4] *Simon*,[3] *Andrew*,[2] *Andrew*[1]), (1800–1867) was 2nd wife of Charles Cox. Mr. Chute early imbibed a taste for study, and after getting what education he could from the common school at home, attended Readfield seminary,

B

Maine, 1835-36; after that he attended Horton academy and Acadia college in Nova Scotia, four years, and was ordained to the Baptist ministry 1850. In 1852 he was sent out by the Baptist association of Nova Scotia, a missionary among the Acadian French in the eastern part of the province, which position he filled six years, till failing health warned him to retire, and since that only preached occasionally. He lives at Upper Stewiacke, Colchester Co.

Children:

    i JAMES RUPERT, b. Feb. 2, 1851.
    ii CHARLES CARSON, b. Feb. 2, 1851; d. Oct. 19, 1864.
147 iii ARTHUR CRAWLY, b. Apr. 10, 1853.
    iv LYMAN HARRIS, b. May 2, 1855; d. Feb. 17, 1893.
    v GEORGE RETTIE, b. July 21, 1861; jeweler.

VII. 48 Richard[7], (*Dea. James*,[6] *Capt. Daniel*,[5] *James*,[4] *James*,[3] *James*,[2] *Lionel*[1]), born in Boxford, Mass., Sept. 3, 1778; married Dorothy, daughter of Benjamin Pearson, Oct. 17, 1805; was a farmer and a man of integrity; lived near the Byfield meetinghouse, Newbury; he was also captain of militia. He died at St. Louis, Mo., Oct. 24, 1820, after which the family moved to Newburyport, where the widow died May 9, 1870, aged eighty-six; nearly fifty years a widow.

Children:

148 i ALEXANDER, b. Sept. 27, 1806.
149 ii ARIEL PARISH, b. May 16, 1809.
    iii BETSY, b. July 7, 1810; d. Oct. 27, 1856.
150 iv ANDREW, b. Apr. 11, 1814.
    v BENJAMIN P., b. May 13, 1816; graduated from Bowdoin college 1836-37, and taught school more than forty years; near home before the war, Huntsville, Ala., after the war, and then for fifteen years in Lincoln and other places in Nebraska, returning home 1885.

VII. 49 Daniel Chute, brother to the preceding, born in Boxford, June 4, 1787; married Rachel, daughter of Thomas McGiffin. Pittsburg, Pa., Dec. 27, 1813, and lived in Cincinnatti, O., about seventeen years; he graduated from Dartmouth college, 1810, and taught school many years; he was also justice of peace, postmaster and an elder in the Presbyterian church. In 1830 he moved to Madison, Ind., and to Evansville, 1836; his wife died Sept. 21, 1840, aged forty-five; he married 2nd, Mrs. Sarah (Waters) Benjamin, Oct. 20, 1842, and died June 20, 1859; his wife died Feb. 4, 1873, aged seventy.

hildren:

1 JAMES MARTIN, b. Nov. 24, 1814.
ii THOMAS MCGIFFIN, b. Aug. 24, 1816; d. Oct. 17, 1816.
iii DANIEL, b. Oct. 29, 1817, to New Orleans, etc.
iv GEORGE HALE, b. Dec. 3, 1819, to St. Louis, etc.
v JOHN McG., b. Nov. 23, 1821; printer, Memphis, Tenn; d. Mar. 4, 1858.
vi ELIZABETH, b. Feb. 14, 1824; m. Samuel T. Jenkins, Sept. 10, 1843; two sons; he d. Apr. 15, 1852.
vii ALANSON W., b. June 10, 1826; m. Anna Paine, Nov. 7, 1848, and had (1) *Mary Jane*, d. in 1866. (2) *Henry.* Mrs. Chute d. May 10, 1868.
viii CHARLES BARTLETT, b. Dec. 10, 1828; reported in Illinois.
ix JANE C., b. Sept. 25, 1830; m. William W. Morgan, Dec. 5, 1850; 3 children.
x CHARLOTTE F., b. Oct. 4, 1833; m. Conrad Baker, Jan. 6, 1858.

Conrad Baker was b. in Franklin Co., Pa., Feb. 12, 1817; educated at Pennsylvania college, Gettysburg, and then studied law in the office of Stevens & Snyder of that city, under Thaddeus Stevens and Judge Daniel M. Snyder. He was admitted to the bar in 1839, and practiced law there two years. He emigrated to Indiana and settled in Evansville, 1841; represented Vanderburg Co. in the General Assembly, 1845; judge of the Court of Common Pleas for the counties of Warwick and Vanderburg, 1852, and resigned 1854. In 1861 he was commissioned colonel of the 1st Cavalry, 28th regiment of Indiana Volunteers, and from August to April, 1863, commanded either his own regiment or a brigade in Missouri, Arkansas or Mississippi. In April, 1863, he was called home to Indianapolis and appointed provost marshal general of Indiana, where he superintended the volunteer recruiting as chief mustering officer, till August, 1864, when his term of service expired and he was mustered out.

In 1865, Gov. Oliver P. Morton convened the General Assembly in special session, and right after delivering his message went to Europe in quest of health, leaving Mr. Baker, the lieutenant governor in charge of the state.

In 1867, Gov. Morton was elected to the United States senate, when Mr. Baker became governor and resided at Indianapolis. In 1868 he was nominated by the Republican convention for governor and elected by a majority of 961, and at the close of his term engaged again in the practice of law in the firm of Baker, Hord & Hendricks, and d. there Apr. 28, 1885, beloved by all.

His character as a lawyer, judge, colonel, general, lieutenant governor and governor, were as firm, kind, honest, generous and merciful as any man could well be, as near perfect probably, as any man that ever lived in the United States. Children:

1. ALICE, b. Dec. 2, 1859.
2. ELIZABETH, b. April 3, 1861; m. Hubert L. Anderson, at Ocala, Fla.
3. NANCY, b. Nov. 11, 1865.
4. CONRAD, b. Dec. 1, 1867; d. June 1, 1868.
5. FLORENCE, b. Aug. 21, 1870.
6. THADDEUS, b. Feb. 14, 1873; at Wabash college.

xi HALLER TRACY, b. Dec. 30, 1843; stove merchant, Evansville, Ind.

VII. 50 James Chute, brother to the preceding, born at Boxford, Nov, 15, 1788; married Martha Hews Clapp[7] (*William Tileston,*[6] *William,*[5] *Ebenezer,*[4] *Ebenezer,*[3] *Nathaniel,*[2] *Nicholas*[1]), of Dorchester, Mass., Oct. 23, 1817, and lived much of his time in the West. He was brought up a farmer, educated in the common school, then in Dummer academy, under Dr. William Allen, and finally graduated from Dartmouth college 1813. On Sept. 10, (day of Perry's victory on Lake Erie), he left his New England home and went to Pittsburg, Pa., where he taught school a few months, and then embarked in trade. Shortly after this he moved to Cincinnati, O., where he continued until 1820, when he resumed teaching again with great success. May 30, 1821, he was elected ruling elder in the First Presbyterian church on Maine street, Rev. J. L. Wilson, D.D., pastor. Under Dr. Wilson he studied for the ministry, and after being licensed to preach he supplied vacant churches in the city and vicinity, keeping up his school until 1828, when he was appointed chaplain to the Ohio state prison, and moved in autumn to Columbus, and shortly after ordained as a gospel minister, at Truro, O. In Sept. 1831, he moved to Fort Wayne, Ind., and became pastor of the First Presbyterian church there. In 1832, he bought twenty-eight acres of land adjoining the town, and mainly with his own hands built for himself a double log house, which was his home the balance of his life, and there his wife died Aug. 18, 1833, aged 38. He married, 2nd, Mary Haven, widow of Rev. Samuel Crane (missionary to Tuscarora Indians near Niagara Falls), at Dayton, O., (with three children, Cornelia, Mary D., and Samuel), Oct. 30, 1834. Rev. James Chute was a man of peace, love, patience, great piety and temperance. In August 1835, he was attacked with bilious fever; convalescing from it, he caught a severe cold, producing a relapse, which terminated his life Dec. 28, 1835. His widow moved to Crawfordsville, Ind., that she might better educate her children, and died there Dec. 22, 1863, aged 60.

Children:

    i James Thurston, b. Sept. 30, 1818; d. Sept. 2, 1819.
152 ii Richard, b. Sept, 23, 1820; d. in Chicago, Aug. 1, 1893.
    iii Sarah C. R., b. Oct. 4, 1823; m. William Chamberlain, June 10, 1843, Fort Wayne, Ind., and had:
      1. James Chute, b. March 8, 1844.
      2. Martha Hews, b. July 26, 1846. Mr. Chamberlain d. April 21, 1847.
153 iv James Thurston, b. Aug. 30, 1827.

GENEALOGIES OF THE CHUTE FAMILY. 77

v SAMUEL HEWS, b. Dec. 6, 1830.
vi ELIZA JANETTE, b. Nov. 7, 1835; m. Alexander Hall Sharp, of New York, at Crawfordsville, Ind., Oct. 13, 1859, and have lived in Brooklyn, N. Y., and West Hoboken, N. J. Children:
  1. MARY CHUTE, b. Jan. 7, 1861, Brooklyn; d. Aug. 25.
  2. GEORGE, b. Nov. 30, 1862, Brooklyn; d. July 30, 1863.
  3. FRANK C., b. July 30, 1866, West Hoboken, N. J.
  4. KATE, b. June 5, 1868; d. Sept. 20.
  5. EDWIN C., b. Jan. 30, 1875.
  6. ARCHE H., b. April 8, 1878.

II. 51 Curtis Chute,⁷ (*Josiah,⁶ Curtis,⁵ Thomas,⁴ James,³ James,² nel¹*), born in Windham, Me., Dec. 15, 1782; married Susan, daughter of Timothy Noyes, 1805, and lived in Cumberland, Me., as farmers. died at Carthage, Franklin Co., Jan. 19, 1858; she died at Rockl, Mass., Dec. 1, 1879, aged ninety-three.

Children:

i JANET G., b. Jan. 5, 1807; m. George W. Drinkwater, Sept. 4, 1823, and lived in Cumberland, east of Portland; he d. Aug. 27, 1865, aged 65 years, 7 months; she m. 2nd, Benjamin Goodnow jr., Aug. 26, 1875. (He m. 1st, Sarah S. Gammond; had twelve children; she d. Nov. 19, 1866, aged 58 years, 8 months; he m. 2nd, Elizabeth Sawyer Rich; she d. Mar. 11, 1872, aged 46); he d. 1888, about 85; she d. Nov. 11, 1889. Children:
  1. ALBERT F., b. 1825; m. Amanda Wilson; eight children.
  2. CATHARINE, b. 1827; m. Eben Rich; five children and d. Feb. 17, 1891.
  3. ELIZA ANN, b. 1829; m. Martin Noyes; four children.
  4. JOSEPH, b. June, 1830.
ii ELIZA S., b. Dec. 24, 1808; m. Daniel, son of Peter and Sarah (Pike) Cobb, Dec., 1829, and lived in Deering, near Portland; she d. May 6, 1877; he d. Aug. 23, 1879, aged 77. Children:
  1. MERRITT C., b. May 24, 1830; d. July 21, 1850.
  2. NELSON B., b. Mar. 6, 1832; d. Nov. 4, 1842.
  3. ANN L., b. Mar. 10, 1834; m. James M. Foster; six children, and d. 1868.
  4. FANNY T., b. Feb. 7, 1837; m. Edward Gilman; eight children, and d. Apr. 6, 1875.
  5. ROSILLA E., b. Mar. 10, 1839; d. June 2, 1859.
  6. ROTHEUS O., b. Oct. 20, 1841; m. Christina B. Herrick.
  7. ANGELINE S., b. Oct. 2, 1843; d. Apr. 51, 1850.
  8. ARABELLA, b. Oct. 15, 1845; d. July 10, 1850.
  9. DANIEL SYLVESTER, b. Aug. 25, 1847; m. Anna M., daughter of Shephel Foster, and had five children.
iii FRANCES NOYES, b. Dec. 28, 1811; m. Edward H., son of David Noyes, jr.,

June 8, 1828, and lived in Portland; some time after the late war they moved to Missouri, and he d. at Union Star, DeKalb Co., Dec. 14, 1884, aged 80; she d. Oct. 20, 1888, and both were buried at St. Joseph, Mo. Children:

1. MARY ANN, b. Sept. 26, 1820; m. Rev. Phineas Libby[7] of the Methodist church, (Abram,[6] Josiah,[5] John,[4] Capt. John,[3] John,[2] John,[1] b. in England 1602; came over 1630; lived at Cape Elizabeth and Scarboro; and d. 1682), b. 1817; m. May 27, 1847; and d. 1882; she d. since. (He m. 1st Mary Ann, daughter of David and Mary (Blake) Waldron, of Portland, a daughter b. and died 1845; she d. Nov. 8, 1846. Windham.) Eleven children by 2nd wife.
2. SARAH E., b. April 22, 1831; m. John H. Karnan, Jan. 11, 1852; and lived near Boston. He died at Medway, June 20, 1888; aged 67. They had (1), *William Henry*, b. Dec. 19, 1849; m. Ida White in Maine, had five children, and d. Aug. 14, 1885; (2), *F. Nellie*, b. Dec. 11, 1854; teacher of oratory in Boston; (3), *Robert Wilson* b. July 2, 1860; m. Henrietta Winchester[8] (*William H.*,[7] *William*,[6] *William*,[5] *Gulliver*,[4] *Stephen*,[3] *Stephen*,[2] *John*,[1] England to Hingham 1632), Sept. 2, 1885; three children, merchant in Somerville. His mother lives with them.
3. OTIS NELSON, b. Jan. 30, 1833; m. Belle Leitch, Jan. 12, 1858; she d. Oct. 17, 1860; aged 21, at Sidney, Iowa; m. 2d, Augusta C. Heaton, Aug. 1, 1881; removed to Union Star, Mo., 1882. He is a druggist.
4. LYDIA M., b. Feb. 22, 1835; m. Joseph B. Jordan, Oct. 14, 1854; and d. July 24, 1856. He d. 1880.
5. WILLIAM HENRY, b. Feb. 22, 1837, m. Carrie Rathburn, May 1, 1867; and d. Dec. 3, 1871.
6. MOSES CHUTE, b. Jan. 23, 1840; m. —— Graves.
7. FRED K., b. Sept. 21, 1843; these two were in the war and in Libby prison.
8. FANNY E., b. Oct. 13, 1845; m. Isaac F. Russell, Aug. 12, 1863.
9. CHARLES H., b. Nov. 7, 1848; d. Aug 30, 1854.
10. GEORGINA, b. Oct. 5, 1853; d. Sept. 3, 1854.

155 iv MOSES STUBBS, b. March 21, 1815.
    v RUTH S., b. June 8, 1817; m. William B. Winchester, May 23, 1833; had two children; and d. Sept. 10, 1836, Portland, Me.
    vi CATHARINE C., b. Oct. 19, 1819; m. the same W. B. Winchester, Nov. 30, 1837; had seven children. He d. Jan. 12, 1877; aged 66.
    vii SYRENA N., b. March 22, 1823; m. Fred Ellis, Nov. 1844; and had a son, Freeman, had three daughters, Aristook, Me.; she d. May 1858; he m. 2nd, Mary Spooner; m. 3rd, Juliette, daughter of Reuben and Nancy (Chute) Stubbs. See No. 17. He d. 1890; aged 73.
    viii JOSIAH, b. March 28, 1825; m. Abba Reynolds, 1849, Providence, R. I. She d. Aug. 1890; aged 65 years, 5 months.
    ix AARON, b. Jan. 1829; d. at sea about 1850.
    x PERSIS, b. March 1833; d. in Cumberland, 1836.

GEORGE WASHINGTON CHUTE.

VII. 52 Josiah Chute jr., born Sept. 11, 1789, Windham, Me., married Catharine, daughter of Joseph and Joanna Clement, Feb. 20, 1820, lived in Portland, a grocer; died Feb. 1, 1837; his widow kept house there three or four years longer, then moved to Windham, kept house for George W. Chute, thirty-five years, and died Dec. 13, 1877, aged seventy-eight years, six months. One son.

156   Joseph Clement, b. Aug. 22, 1823.

VII. 53 Francis Chute (*Thomas, Curtis, Thomas, James, James, Lionel*), born in Windham, May 15, 1783; married Martha, daughter of William and Rebecca (Bodge) Mayberry, June 2, 1805, and moved to Otisfield, 1806. He was a good Christian man, of the old Orthodox church, a lieutenant colonel of militia in the war of 1812, collector and town treasurer 1815 to 1821, selectman 1819, 1823, 1824 and 1835; and died May 29, 1853; his widow died Sept. 1, 1854; aged seventy years and six months.

Children:

  i **Margaret**, b. Mar. 24, 1806; m. Elisha T. Weston, Oct. 1826, and lived in Otisfield, near Meeting-house hill; d. April 10, 1863; he d. Jan. 13, 1875; aged 74. Children:
    1. **Thomas W.**, b. Nov. 25, 1827; m. Serena, daughter of Samuel and Jerusha Knight, Oct. 2, 1855, and died from the kick of a horse in Boston, Nov. 29, 1882, leaving a son Edgar P. W.: b. 1866; d. 1890.
    2. **Abba O.**, b. Dec. 28, 1829.
    3. **Edward F.**, b. Sept. 7, 1833; m. Eunice, daughter of James and Clara Scribner, Aug. 17, 1852; and had two children. He was a soldier in the late war.
    4. **Henry W.**, b. May 24, 1835; m. Lucinda Jane, daughter of Columbus Holden, Sept. 11, 1859; had two sons; m. 2nd, —— ——, and had two daughters.
  ii **Rebecca**, b. Apr. 1808; m. Merrill, son of Johnson Knight, Jan. 29, 1828; and lived in Otisfield. He d. Aug. 18, 1869; aged 65. Children:
    1. **Caroline**, b. Jan. 22, 1829; m. Edward Mead, Jan. 30, 1853, and d. Mar. 31, 1854; he m. 2nd, Sarah Sawyer.
    2. **John N. M.**, b. Nov. 19, 1830; m. Olive, daughter of Hon. William Twombly, Mar. 23, 1856; a daughter Alice T., b. May 7, 1857.
    3. **Harriet H.**, b. March 22, 1833; m. Horace Barrows, Feb. 2, 1856, Portland.
    4. **Mary A. F.**, b. May 17, 1835; m. Rev. W. N. Richardson, Jan. 23, 1861.
    5. **Martha E.**, b. July 7, 1837; m. John A. Upton, Jan. 14, 1865; and d. Mar. 7, 1866; he was killed by the cars July 31, 1866; aged 33.

6. JOSEPH, b. May 3, 1841; m. Mary Kindred, Christmas 1871; he was in the 10th and 29th Maine Volunteer Infantry, in the war and lives in California.

7 LOVISA F., b. July 15, 1843; m. Luther Bradford, Jan. 12, 1868, Clinton, Iowa. He lost an arm in the late war.

157 iii JOHN HOOPER, b. July 29, 1810.

iv SARAH, b. Feb. 15, 1813; m. William, son of Andrew Woodbury, June 10, 1840; and lived in Sweden, Oxford Co., twenty-seven years, Mexico, same Co., five years, then to South Paris, in Dec. 1872; d. May 28, 1888; he d. Jan. 31, 1880; near 69. Children:

1. FRANCIS CHUTE, b Apr. 12. 1841; m. Isabel Heald, Aug. 3, 1865; she d. April 1871, aged 28; he married 2nd, Clara Snell, Nov. 1873, have two sons. He is principal of a high school, or business college, at Los Angeles, Cal.

2. SUSAN, b. Apr. 27, 1843; m. William Wheeler, Feb. 9, 1869; and d. April 16, 1871; he m. 2nd Isabel Bennett, Feb. 1873; she d. Sept 1874, aged 30; he m. 3rd Addie Matthews, June 28, 1876.

3. CLARA M:, b. Sept. 30, 1844; m. Henry Howard, Nov. 26, 1863; one son Charles, b. April 12, 1870. Mr. Howard, a school teacher; d Nov. 22, 1871, aged 34.

4. LOUISE, b. Sept. 4, 1845; m. John H. Jones jr., who was a soldier in Co. I. 30th Me., Aug. 9, 1868; had four children, the eldest, Gertrude L., a school teacher. They live at Amesbury, Mass.

5. WILLIAM M., b. May 11, 1848; d. Apr. 30, 1849.

6. HANNAH E., b. Mar. 29, 1850; m. James S. Wright, a lawyer at Paris Hill, and had two children.

158 v FRANCIS JR., b. Dec. 16, 1816.

VII. 54 William Carr Chute, another brother, born in Windham, Feb. 12, 1788; married Rosannah, daughter of William Mayberry jr., and Rose Waldon, Sept. 10, 1809, and after the opening of the Cumberland canal, about 1832 or 1833, he moved to Naples; he was an honest, industrious citizen and farmer; his wife died Dec. 13, 1831, aged forty-two years, seven months; he married 2nd, Mrs. Nancy Rowe, Dec. 13, 1832, and died Aug. 19, 1864; she died Sept. 19, 1856, aged sixty-nine.

Children:

i MARY, b. Apr. 1, 1810; m. Calvin F. Brown, a blacksmith, 1833, and lived in Bridgeton, Milo, on the Kennebec river, and to Des Moines, Ia., and Carthage, Mo.; she d. Mar. 1884. They had Charles, Edwin, William, Rose and Ellen.

ii THOMAS, b. Jan. 25, 1813; m. Jane Wyer, 1840, and was collector 1850-51. They went to Oshkosh, Wis., 1854, where he d. Sept. 21, 1870; she returned to Portland.

GENEALOGIES OF THE CHUTE FAMILY. 81

    iii CAROLINE, b. Feb. 11, 1815; m. Robert King, 1835; he left for Michigan about 1840, and she went and lived in Peterboro, N. H., eighteen years. Then she married Jonas Kilmer, and went to Council Bluffs, Ia., and had two children; the daughter died in infancy, the son, J. Edward, b. Sept. 6, 1850, grew to manhood. Mr. Kilmer died there before the war; then she married —— Patchin, 1861, and moved to Corpus Christi, Tex., where he died 1869; then she lived with her son at Legato, Live Oak Co., and died 1889.

159 iv JAMES, b. Aug. 30, 1817.
160 v WILLIAM, b. Oct. 22, 1819.
    vi NEWELL NUTTING, b. June 12, 1822; m. Mary Jane, (b. 1828), son of Caleb and Ruth (Jordan) Chaplain, Sept. 13, 1851, and live in Bridgeton on the west side of Long Pond; a watchman in the Pondicherry Woolen mills.
    vii EDWARD, b. Apr. 25, 1824; d. July 20, 1835.
161 viii FRANKLIN A., b. Feb. 25, 1827.

VII. 55 Daniel, another brother, born in Windham, Feb. 10, 1797; married Bathsheba, daughter of William Mayberry jr., Apr. 21, 1816; was a farmer in Otisfield; he was one in Captain Kilburn's company of militia in the American war; he died Apr. 28, 1846; she died Oct. 14, 1859, aged sixty-five.

Children:

162 i EDWIN, b. July 5, 1816.
    ii LOUISA, b. Aug. 19, 1818; m. Joseph Noyes, son of William and Mary (Chute-Noyes) Abbott, May 17, 1846, and lived near Bolster's mills as farmers. They moved from Gorham to Otisfield in 1855; she died June 29, 1890. Children:
      1. ALFREDA, b. Apr. 16, 1848; m. James L., son of Abram Green, a soldier in the 25th Maine, May 3, 1868, and had six children.
      2. WILLIAM, b. April 22, 1854; m. Henrietta W., daughter of Danforth Hancock, Dec. 6, 1876; two or three children.
      3. GEORGE R., b. July 4, 1856; d. June 17, 1857.
      4. HATTIE E., b. Nov. 15, 1861; d. Oct. 14, 1863.
    iii EMILY N., b. Dec. 26, 1820; m. Rev. Alpheus B. Lovewell, of the M. E. church, June 1845; and lived at Bolster's Mills. He d. July 17, 1885, aged 64. Children:
      1. ELLA M., b. April 28, 1854; m. Russell E. Chute, Feb. 27, 1887.
      2. LIZZIE E., b. May 23, 1860; m. Jason B. Scribner, Feb. 27, 1887.
    iv CATHARINE, b. Mar. 12, 1823; m. James, son of Enoch Hanson, Sept. 2, 1845, Harrison, near Bolster's Mills. Children:
      1. CATHARINE S., b. Nov. 30, 1847; m. Fred A. Allen, Apr. 30, 1869.
      2. FRED J., b. April 15, 1850; m. Georgia A. Whitman,[6] (*Jeremiah,[6] Silas,[6] of Round Hill, N. S., Daniel,[5] John,[4] John,[3] Zachariah,[2] Dea. John,[1] of Weymouth, Mass., 1637*), April 13, 1876.
      3. CHARLES W., b. Jan. 22, 1853; m. Annie L. Varney, July 1876.

4. ALPHEUS L., b. Apr. 22, 1855; m. Cassie M. Murray, July 1874.
5. EMMA R., b. May 25, 1858; m. Fred H. Berrick, 1878.
6. MARY LOUISE, b. April 25, 1860; m. Robert D. Libby,[7] (*Dea. Arthur,*[6] *Benjamin M.*,[5] *Capt. Thomas*,[4] *Thomas*,[3] *David*,[2] *John*[1], came over to Cape Elizabeth, Me., 1630), Oct. 20, 1879.
7. EUGENE A., b. Nov. 4, 1862.
8. GEORGE WILLIAM, b. Oct. 3, 1864; d. Sept. 2, 1871.

v SIBYL ANN, b. Sept .12, 1829; m. Mahlon, son of Benjamin Akers, Sept. 12, 1845, and lived in Falmouth and Portland. Children:
1. CHARLES E., b. April 6, 1846; m. Jenny Grey, 1870, Lowell, Mass.
2. EUGENE E., b. April 29, 1888; m. Margaret Ann Brown; she d. May 30, 1872; he m. 2nd, Sarah J. Goodrich.

163 vi ALBION, b. June 29, 1828.
vii ROSILLA, b. Nov. 7, 1830; m. Richard, son of Daniel W. Dole, Nov. 10, 1853; he was killed by cars at Framingham, Mass., Aug. 4, 1864, aged thirty-four years, five months; she m. 2nd, by Rev. George W. Tewksbury, William Stephen Cobb, son of John of Bath, Me., Apr. 5, 1868, and live in South Windham. Mr. Cobb (b. in 1811), m. 1st, Elmira Craig, Nov. 1832; had four children; she d. Feb. 1868, aged sixty-three. Children:
1. JENNIE DOLE, b. June, 1856; d. Aug. 9, 1863.
2. SADIE E., b. Aug. 25, 1860; m. Fred H. Freeman, Nov. 27, 1880.

164 viii DANIEL, b. July 12, 1832.
165 ix WILLIAM WINDSOR, b. Dec. 28, 1834.

VII. 56 James, another brother, born in Windham, Aug. 12, 1801; married Mary Ann Hoyt,[7] (*Phineas*,[6] *Enoch*,[5] *John*,[4] *William*,[3] *John*,[2] *John*,[1] *and Frances* of Salisbury, 1638; died 1687), Oct. 4, 1830, and lived near Naples; a farmer. He was captain of militia and also the light infantry in Otisfield, 1835 to 1850, and was highly respected. In his latter years he became dull of hearing; died July 30, 1884; his widow died 1889, aged seventy-eight.

Children:

i ELIZABETH W., b. Jan. 22, 1832; d. Feb. 7.
ii CATHARINE W., b. June 22, 1833; m. Roscoe M. Mayo, Aug. 1, 1852; ten children.
166 iii WATSON, b. Mar. 20, 1835.
iv CHARLES A., b. Feb. 21, 1837; m. Maria, daughter of Thomas[6] and Nellie (Wood) Jordan, (*Jeremiah*,[5] *James*,[4] *Jeremiah*,[3] *Jeremiah*,[2] *Rev. Robert*[1] of 1640), and live in Lowell, Mass.
v EDWARD P., b. Mar. 11, 1839; was in Co., I, 10th Maine, in the war; suffered from sunstroke, fever, a prisoner in rebeldom, but died at home June 29, 1863.

* Phineas Hoyt was in the war of 1812, and died at Naples, Me., Mar. 11, 1850, aged 64. His wife Ann Andrew, sister to Elizabeth Chute, died Aug. 31, 1845, aged 60; Wm. A. Andrew, a brother, died there Dec. 18, 1846, aged 76.

167 vi ANDREW, b. Jan. 4, 1844.
168 vii ADELBERT C., b. Feb. 4, 1848.
169 viii WARREN B., b. Apr. 10, 1850.
    ix MARY ANN, b. Sept. 20, 1853.

VII. 57 Thomas, another brother, born Aug. 12, 1803; married Mary, daughter of Benjamin Webber, Dec. 10, 1833, Sweden, Me. They lived in Naples till Dec. 1836, moved then to Otisfield, near the foot of Saturday Pond, 1838, and was captain of militia then till 1842. He was town treasurer 1844 to 1846, and was 2nd cashier of Casco bank, Portland, for a while. He moved back to Sweden, Dec. 31, 1840, and died Aug. 15, 1871.

Children:

170 i GEORGE M., b. July 28, 1836.
    ii JOHN WEBBER, b. Dec. 16, 1840; m. Sarah P., daughter of Aaron Woodbury, brother to William, Oct. 23, 1866, and live in Sweden.
    iii SUSANNA, b. May 11, 1843; m. Amos T. White, Dec. 12, 1865; went to Boston that year, and are grocers there. Children:
        1. MARY L., b. Dec. 31, 1866; d. Sept. 28, 1881.
        2. AMOS T., b. Jan. 19, 1874.
        3. FRANK C., b. Sept. 17, 1876.
    iv WELLINGTON, b. Mar. 28, 1848; d. Sept. 21, 1849.

VII. 58 Abram Watson Chute,[7] (*John*,[6] *Curtis*,[5] *Thomas*,[4] *James*,[3] *James*,[2] *Lionel*[1]), born in Windham, Me., Jan. 7, 1797; married Catharine, daughter of Thomas and Esther (Turner) Weston, Feb. 11, 1829, and was an honest, pious, business man in Naples. His brother, John jr., sold him a lot of land in Naples, Oct. 3, 1826; he was paymaster of the 2nd regiment, 1st brigade, 5th division of the militia of the state, Aug. 10, 1827. He was the first postmaster at Naples, then South Otisfield, May 15, 1828. The town of Naples was organized from Otisfield, Casco, Bridgeton and Harrison in 1834, and Mr. Chute was town clerk 1834, 1835, 1841, 1844, 1845. He bought land in Naples of his uncle, Jonathan Andrew, July 24, 1835; bought more of Enoch Gammon, Nov. 8, 1836. The Congregational church was organized there 1834, and Mr. Chute was society clerk, and his brother-in-law, Nathan Church, was collector and treasurer. Mr. Chute was made a member of the missionary society, July 19, 1852. The Cumberland and Oxford canal from Portland up the Presumpscot river to Sebago lake, twenty miles long, with twenty-seven locks, costing $206,-

000, was built 1828 to 1830, and closed about 1870. A. W. Chute was treasurer and paymaster part of the time while it was building. William C. Chute and sons, James, Newell and Franklin, boated on that canal and through the ponds and rivers attached. Mrs. Chute died Oct. 24, 1832, aged thirty; he married 2nd, Margaret Weston, a sister, Jan. 3, 1843, and died Oct. 29, 1874; she died Dec. 4, 1886, aged about eighty.

Children of A. W. Chute:

 i JOHN ANDREW, b. Jan. 12, 1830; d. Nov. 28, 1832.
 ii ISAAC WESTON, b. Sept. 12, 1832; d. Mar. 2, 1833.
 iii MARY ELIZABETH, b. Sept. 30, 1844; d. Apr. 7, 1850.
 iv CATHARINE Weston, b. Aug. 10, 1846; b. Apr. 4, 1850.

EIGHTH GENERATION.

VIII. 59 Abram Chute,[8] (*Daniel,*[7] *Samuel,*[6] *John,*[5] *Lionel,*[4] *James,*[3] *James,*[2] *Lionel*[1]), born in Clements, Annapolis Co., N. S., Oct. 14, 1796; married Susan Chute, his father's cousin, by Rev. Enoch Towner, Jan. 29, 1820, and lived in Clements, about eight miles from Digby. He was a farmer, blacksmith, fisherman and a good pious deacon in the Baptist church; died of asthma June 27, 1859; his widow, a good Christian woman, died Sept. 13, 1880, aged eighty one.

Children:

171   i Robert, b. Dec. 15, 1820.

        ii Lucinda, b. Dec. 16, 1820; m. John Douglass, son of Rev. Israel Potter jr., Jan. 9, 1840, and lived on the east side of Moose River, two miles from Clementsport. He was a farmer and a pious deacon in the Baptist church; d. Oct. 2, 1884, aged 69; she m. 2nd, Anthony, son of Dea. Aaron Potter, 1889; she d. Dec. 24, 1892; he d. July 31, 1890, aged 74. Children:

           1. Sarah, b. and d. 1841.
           2. Catharine Augusta, b. Sept. 26, 1843; m. George W., son of Andrew B. Hardwick, Oct. 2, 1862, and had three children. He m. 1st, Letitia Monroe, and had a son, Alfred B., b. Oct. 27, 1858. Mr. G. W. Hardwick d. Oct. 27, 1881, aged 42, near Annapolis.
           3. Zephaniah Murray, b. Oct. 5, 1845; m. Mary Esther Chute, (See No. 87), June 26, 1869, and had Terissa, b. 1874; Mrs. Potter d. Jan. 9, 1876, aged 37; he m. 2nd, Laura L. Johnson, Mar. 3, 1879, in San Bernardino, Cal.
           4. Abram Chute, b. Oct. 19, 1848; m. Lovina, daughter of Abner Morse,[8] 1874, and had Kizbro F., b. 1874; he d. Sept. 2, 1877; she m. 2nd, Israel Balcomb, son of James, Aug. 1885, in Clements.
    5 and 6. Joseph and Israel, b. June 3, 1850; d. in three weeks.
           7. James W. J., b. July 25, 1851; m. Lillia E. May, March 3, 1879, had three children, and d. Oct. 5, 1890.
           8. Susan Ann, b. April 25, 1853; m. H. Gifford Potter, son of Aaron jr., Sept. 29, 1878, and d. April 9, 1879; he m. 2nd, Adda, daughter of Dea. Jacob Kempton Dec. 1880.
           9. John D., b. April 25, 1853; m. Sabra A., daughter of Reuben D., son of Dea. Aaron Potter, Oct. 1880; three children.
          10. Moses J., b. Nov. 14, 1855; m. Laura M. Chute, April 21, 1886; (see No. 216.)
          11. Obatia E., b. Nov. 5, 1857; d. a happy Christian, Aug. 8, 1881.
          12. Charles T., b. Dec. 21, 1859; d. Feb. 24, 1882.

172 iii WHITEFIELD, b. Mar. 29, 1823.
  iv SOPHIA, b. Dec. 20, 1825; m. Jeremiah, son of Rev. Israel Potter, jr., Feb. 10, 1848, and lives at Clementsvale.
   1. NAOMI ETHALINDA, b. June 24, 1849.
   2. GEORGE WHITEFIELD, b. Jan. 15, 1851; m. Susan Mahling, Mar. 28, 1875; four sons.
   3. H. BRAYMAN, b. Oct. 12, 1852; m. ——.
   4. EDWARD WESLY, b. Sept. 18, 1854; m. Alice Flagg, three children.
   5. SUSAN BERNICE, b. May 28, 1856; m. Fred P. Jones, Aug. 4, 1886; son Edward Vernon, b. 1887.
   6. SOPHIA AMELIA, b. July 10, 1858; d. Jan. 27, 1872.
   7. CHARLES HADDBON, b. Feb. 11, 1861; d. June 21, 1890.
   8. IDELLA B., b. Aug. 16, 1866; d. June 17, 1892.
  v NAOMI, b. March 20, 1828; m. Dea. James Edward Potter, Esq., son of Dea. Aaron Potter, Dec. 22, 1864; and lived on the east side of Moose river, in Clements, a good farmer, and a pious deacon in the Baptist church. He d. Aug. 1, 1890, aged 80. One son.
   1. GEORGE FENWICK, b. Sept. 24, 1865; m. Kate E., daughter of Capt. John Daniels of Freeport, Digby Co., N. S., Aug. 24, 1892, and live in Lynn, Mass. His mother lives with them.
  vi WILLETT MARSHALL, b. Sept. 16, 1830; went to Boston, Mass., 1851, to sea 1852; sailed to the East Indies, to China and other places, fourteen voyages, including four times around the globe; was in the United States Navy 1861; at New Orleans, May 1862, and mustered out 1864; then to sea again. He was shipwrecked twice before the war, and once since, losing all, and dismasted once in the China sea, ship, "Nor Wester," 1200 tons, Aug. 1856. He left the sea in Boston, May 1882, and went to the "Sailor's Snug Harbor," near Quincy, ten miles south of Boston, sustained by bequests and donations, first established by Joshua Bacon (1785–1852), of Boston, Capt. Eph. Doane jr., present commander.
  vii HOWARD DOUGLASS, b. Sept. 10, 1833; went to sea, and d. on the brig. "Tropic Bird," Aug. 19, 1882, and buried at Ounimak Island, Alaska.
  viii SUSAN ANN, b. June 30, 1836; m. Charles T., son of Thomas, son of Dea. Benjamin Potter, of Smith's Cove, Digby Co., Mar. 9, 1864.
   1. JOHN HENRY, b. Nov. 15, 1855; m. Bertha Eldridge, Feb. 21, 1876 He is a farmer and singing teacher. Three children.
   2. LAURA BELL, b. Nov. 24, 1857; m. George B. Thomas; had seven children and d. Nov. 29, 1891, at Smith's Cove.
   3. GEORGE W., b. Mar. 27, 1862; m. ——.
   4. ARTHUR C., b. Feb. 3, 1866; m. in New Zealand.
173 ix AUSTIN SOPHRONIUS, b. Jan. 31, 1839.
  x ABRAM, b. Feb. 28, 1842; went to sea and was lost off the bark "Legal Tender," Falmouth harbor, Alaska, Dec. 13, 1872.

VIII. 60 Aaron Chute, brother to the preceding, born in Clements, Aug. 11, 1798; married by Rev. E. Towner, Eunice Woodworth,

t. 19, 1820, and lived in Clements, about seven miles from Digby; mer, blacksmith, fisherman and a very active, pious, devoted Chrisn in the Baptist church; died March 9, 1884; she died July 7, 91, nearly ninety-three.

Children:

  i SARAH LOVENIA, b. Oct. 3, 1824; m. Edward, son of Stephen, son of Abel Beals, Oct. 10, 1849, and lives on her father's old farm. Children:
1. ROBY JANE, b. Feb. 28, 1850; m. Benjamin, son of Timothy Brooks.
2. EUNICE ANN, b. Sept. 23, 1851; m. Stephen Morine.
3. CHARLES EDWARD, b. Feb. 16, 1854; d. Feb. 6, 1867.
4. PRISCILLA C., b. May 24, 1855; m. Richard C., son of Tim. Brooks.
5. ISAAC F., b. Dec. 7, 1856; m. ——; lives in Halifax.
6. NANCY L., b. June 23, 1858; m. William, son of Jesse[1] Henshaw, Feb. 20, 1879, and d. Dec. 20, 1886.
7. STEPHEN R., b. June 26, 1860; m. Edith, daughter of Michael Spurr, son of James, Mar. 19, 1886.
8. SARAH H., b. Nov. 12, 1862; d. Apr. 18, 1877.
9. MARY ADALINE, b. Oct. 21, 1864; m. William Henshaw; 2nd wife.
10. MARTHA E., b. Jan. 9, 1869; m. Arthur Berry, son of John, son of William, son of Thomas.

  ii MARY ELIZABETH, b. Apr. 17, 1826; m. George, son of John and Eunice (Fellows) Troop, his 2nd wife, July 4, 1867, and d. Mar. 12, 1880; he d. Nov. 9, 1881, aged 83years, 8 months.

4 iii EPHRAIM LARKINS, b. Feb. 27, 1828; d. June, 1893.

5 iv JOSEPH WENTWORTH, b. Dec. 24, 1829.

  v MELINDA JANE, b. Oct. 22, 1831; m. David, son of Allen Rice, Dec. 31, 1856, and still live on the Digby side of Bear River; farmers. Children:
1. THELBERT T., b. May 11, 1858; m. Lizzie Ann, daughter of Gilbert and Matilda (Chute) Morgan, May 12, 1881, and she d. July, 28 1882, aged 18; he m. 2nd, Hattie Kinghorn, adopted daughter of Rev. John Jefferson Woodworth, July, 1885.
2. MELVIN O., b. Jan. 21, 1860; m. Susan E. Spencer, June 27, 1883.
3. ALBERTA L., b. Nov. 26, 1862, } drowned in Annapolis Basin, June
4. ADALINE V., b. Apr. 25, 1865. } 11, 1879.
5. BERNARD J., b. Mar. 24, 1867; m. Jessie, daughter of Isaac Kempton.
6. ORINDA E., b. Jan. 8, 1870.

  vi CHARLOTTE ANN, b. July 14, 1833; m. Joseph Elias, son of Job Weare, by Rev. Aaron Cogswell, Oct. 10, 1855, and lived in Clements, six miles from Digby, till 1888, when they crossed Bear River, and live near Smith's Cove, Digby Co.; farmers and fishers. Children:
1. JOEL ODBER, b. Dec. 13, 1856; d. Aug. 17, 1872.
2. AARON HARVEY, b. Feb. 23, 1858; m. Minnie, daughter of Jesse Odell, Jan. 10, 1883.

3. ISAIAH SPURGEON, b. Nov. 9, 1860; m. Annie L., daughter of Capt. Charles Winchester, April 26, 1886.
4. GEORGE RUPERT, b. Sept. 6, 1862; m. Annie Austin, daughter of Robert.
5. DAVID MINARD, b. March 4, 1864; m. Jessie, daughter of Jesse Odell.
6. SARAH JANE, b. Jan. 14, 1866; d. Aug. 19.
7. JOSEPH BURPEE, b. Aug. 19, 1867; d. Feb. 13, 1877.
8. RICHARD D., b. June 14, 1869; d. April 9, 1892.
9. ISRAEL B., b. April 2, 1871; d. Feb. 2, 1877.
10. HERBERT E., b. Dec. 18, 1973; d. Oct. 6, 1874.
11. CHARLOTTE B., b. Feb. 1, 1876; d. Jan. 22, 1877.

vii MATILDA LOVINA, b. March 30, 1835; m. John Prior, son of Samuel Weare, Sept. 27, 1865, and live in Kempt, Queen's Co., N. S., as farmers. Children:
1. MINNIE GERTRUDE, b. May 17, 1868.
2. EVA JANE. b. Jan. 3, 1870.

176 viii AMOS ALVA, b. May 15, 1837.
177 ix ABNER WOODWORTH, b. July 4, 1840.

x LEONORA SOBRINA, b. May 21, 1842; m. Allen, son of Silas Rice, his 2nd wife, July 12, 1881, and d. July 5, 1890, west side of Bear river, Digby Co. He d. Sept. 1892; aged 80.

xi EUNICE FRANCES ADALINE, b. July 15, 1844; m. Stephen, son of William, son of George Kniffin, Feb. 14, 1864; and d. March 5, 1876; he m. 2nd, Melissa G., daughter of Joseph Copeland, July 28, 1882. Six children.
1. HESTER, b. May 16, 1865; ——, in Malden.
2. HATTIE MARIA. b. Sept. 20, 1866; ——, in Massachusetts.
3. EUNICE ADALINE. b. July 22, 1871.

VIII. 6I Boemer, another brother, born in Clements, July 18, 1802; married by Rev. Israel Potter sr., Sophia Chute, his father's cousin, Nov. 19, 1829, and lived on the "Sissiboo Road," near Bear er, Digby Co., an honest, Christian farmer; died Mar. 28, 1874; she followed Feb. 9, 1876, aged seventy-three.

Children:

1. EMELINE, b. Aug. 1, 1830; m. David Robbins, by Rev. Aaron Cogswell, July 17, 1850, and lived on the "Sissiboo Road," a pious, Christian woman; d. Aug. 16, 1875; he d. at Digby, Dec. 16, 1875, in his 57th year. Children:
1. JOHN HARVEY, b. Apr. 10, 1851; m. Flora McDonald, 1875.
2. JAMES ALBERT, b. Jan. 23, 1853; m. Marietta, daughter of John Berry, 1876.
3. ELEAZER JUDSON, b. June 17, 1855; m. Catharine Louise Jacobs, 1884 of Brooklyn, N. Y., and was killed by cars at Renovo, Clinton Co., Pa.; a Christian.

4. THOMAS ANSLEY, b. Sept. 13, 1857; m. Mary Grace, daughter of Josiah Fisher, Mar. 30, 1880; have three or four children; live at Manchester, Mass.; carpenter.
5. DAVID AMASA, b. 1859; d. 1862.
6. DAVID BRAINARD, b. Aug. 11, 1861; m. A. Evelyn Ripley, Aug. 28, 1887.
7. GEORGE EDWIN, b. Sept. 16, 1863; m. Phebe Lathrop, 1888.

178 ii OBADIAH, b. Jan. 12. 1832.

iii MINETTA, b. Dec. 9, 1833; m. William Sherwin jr., Aug. 6, 1872, Elgin Co., Ont., and d. in Middlesex Co., May 26, 1873.

iv PHEBE Ann, b. Oct. 14, 1835; d. July 13, 1854, a happy Christian.

v SARAH JANE, b. Sept. 19, 1837, d. Aug. 4, 1855.

vi MARY ELIZABETH, b. Sept. 19, 1837; d. Feb. 4, 1856.

vii HARRIET SOPHIA, b. Oct. 18, 1839, living in Aylmer, Ont.

179 viii SIDNEY, b. Nov. 28, 1841.

ix ARMANELLA, b. Sept. 15, 1843; m. William Sherwin, jr., as 2d wife, and lived at Ailsa Craig, Ont., he is a dealer in furniture. They removed to Forest, Lambton Co., where he d. July 10, 1880, aged 44. She d. March, 1881; one son.
1. WILLIAM ROYCE, b. Aug. 13, 1877.

x DAVID MINARD, b. March 6, 1846; cabinet maker and dealer at Port Burwell, Ont., deacon in the Baptist church, singing teacher and composer of music.

xi SUSANNA, b. Oct. 14, 1848; m. George W. Stuart, April 23, 1880, a cooper in Aylmer, Ont., two sons.
1. GEORGE WASHINGTON, b. March 14, 1881.
2. JAMES MINARD, b. June 15, 1885.

VIII. 62 Joseph, another brother, born May 20, 1805; married Mary Ann, daughter of John Newcomb and Charlotte (Woodworth) Sanford, by Rev. Israel Potter jr., Oct. 17, 1839, and lived on his father's old farm, near the "Waldeck Line," in Clements, where she died April 18, 1868; aged forty-seven; he married 2nd Elizabeth (Weare) Christopher-Apt, July 2, 1877, and died April 18, 1886.

Children:—

i JUDSON, b. April 10, 1842; m. Havilah Sophia Chute (see No. 85), Dec. 1866, lived with his father a few years, then in Malden, Mass., a few, and finally settled on the George Troop farm, Bear River, 1887.

ii JEMIMA, b. Aug. 6, 1843; m. John, son of Edward Henshaw, Oct. 6, 1861; had fourteen children in Clements.

iii LOVENIA. b. Sept. 14, 1845; m. Charles, son of Thomas P., son of Thomas Berry, Oct., 1863; have four children; d. Oct. 10, 1870.

iv SATIRA, b. Feb. 1, 1848; m. Eli Jones, son of Abram Brooks and Abigail (Foster) Smith, Mar. 5, 1874; have four sons at Bear River.

C

  v SERETTA, twin sister, m. Charles Berry, Feb. 12, 1872; one son, Ralph, b. 1874.
  vi MARY ELIZABETH, b. Sept. 2, 1850; m. Oliver, son of Daniel W. Milner, have three sons.
  vii JOHN RUSSELL, b. Aug. 16, 1852.
  viii MINETTA JANE, b. Dec. 22, 1854; m. William Earley, 1872; three children.
  ix ISABELLA, b. 1856; d. Nov., 1870.
  x CHARLOTTE MINERVA, b. 1858; m. Frank Phillips, 1877.
  xi MARY ANN, b. Dec., 1861; m. George Reed, 1879.
  xii PRUDENCE, b. Nov. 16, 1863; m. Charles Phillips, 1882.

VIII. 63. Benjamin, twin brother to Joseph, married Susannah Jane, daughter of Nathan and Mary Elizabeth (Cunningham) Rogers, by Rev. Daniel McGregor, Feb, 10, 1833, and lived on the east side of Moose River in Clements; he was a good worker and quite sharp in business as a farmer and trader; she died Feb. 16, 1882, aged seventy-three, and he "still lives" with his children in Clements.

  Children :

    i JERUSHA, b. Nov, 16, 1833; m. R. H. Sanford, as his 2nd wife (see Sanford), and is a merchant at Clementsvale and postmistress.
180 ii DANIEL ROGERS, b. Mar. 22, 1835.
    iii CLARISSA, b. Mar. 11, 1837; m. Dea. Joshua, son of Rev. Israel Potter jr., Oct. 25, 1860; lived at Clementsvale, and d. Aug. 13, 1891. Children:
      1. MINNIE G., b. Sept 28, 1862.
      2. NOBLE S., b. May 26, 1864; d. May 7, 1884.
      3. JENNIE F., b. July 26, 1866.
      4. ABBA V., b. Dec. 23, 1869.
      5. ROSCOE L., b. Apr. 18, 1872.
      6. ROSA B , b. July 24, 1877.
    iv EMILY J , b. Apr. 28, 1839; m. Dea. John G. Lantz, Dec, 19, 1861, and d. Dec. 26, 1883; he m. 2nd, Anna E., daughter of Joseph Potter, Nov. 18, 1884.
    v MELISSA, b. June 25, 1841; m. Hiram M. Chute. See No. 216.
    vi LOUISA A., b, Apr. 22, 1844; m. David Minard jr., Sept. 14, 1865, and lived in Cornwallis, but since 1888, have lived in Boston, Mass. Children:
      1. PERCY J., b. Aug. 29, 1866; m. Mary F. Stewart, Oct. 21, 1891, Boston.
      2. CLARENCE R., b. Apr. 21, 1868; is a Baptist minister.
      3. SERENA A., b. Apr. 24, 1870; d. soon.
      4. SERENA E., b. June 3, 1871.
      5. ADELAIDE M., b. Aug. 25, 1874.
      6. ARCHE E., b. Jan. 18, 1878.
      7. JAMES F., b. Aug. 24, 1881; d. 1886.
    vii AMANDA E., b. May 2, 1846; m. John M., son of R. H. Sanford, by Rev. Mr. Robbins, Sept. 22, 1876, Brooklyn Cornwallis, Kings, Co., N. S. They

moved from Nova Scotia to New Hampshire, in 1879; to Alston, Mass., 1891; and to Linden 1892; farmer and carpenter. Children: (1), *Millient V.*, b. Oct. 14, 1878. (2), *Susan B.*, b. Dec. 22, 1879. (3), *Leroy H.*, b. April 9, 1883. (4), *Otto W.*, b. July 24, 1884. (5), *Ray Milton*, b. Nov. 9, 1886. (6), *Ettie May*, b. Oct. 22, 1889.

1 viii ZENAS E., b. July 4, 1847.

ix SYRENA A., b. Jan. 20, 1850; m. John M. Sanford (first time), Sept. 25, 1873, and d. June 11, 1875.

VIII. 64 Daniel Chute jr., another brother, born Nov. 12, 1808; arried by Rev. Israel Potter, sen., Ann Spurr, Nov. 9, 1837, and ved on a part of his father's old farm near the Waldeck Line; was a rmer and Christian man. In 1875 he sold out in Clements, bought e William Turnbull farm, on the "Back Road," to Digby, and lived ere eight years; died Aug. 1883; and the widow lives with her ildren near Boston, Mass.

12 i EVERETT SPURR, b. May 26, 1838.
13 ii NEHEMIAH, b. 12, 1839.
   iii CERETHA JANE, b. Nov. 11, 1841; d. Dec. 15, 1865.
   iv JULIA ANN, b. Sept. 16, 1843; d. July 16, 1868.
   v ADELIA ESTHER, b. July 12, 1846; m. Charles E., son of Henry Hulseman, (b. in Clements, Nov. 9, 1843), Apr. 30, 1866, and live in Malden, Mass., a happy Christian couple; he a carpenter, etc. Children: (1) *Florence A.*, b. Nov. 1, 1866; m. Charles S. Witham, Apr. 10, 1886. (2) *Ralph R.*, b. Nov. 29, 1868; m. Vesta Witham, Easter, 1889. (3) *Fred E.*, b. Aug. 10, 1870. (4) *Oscar C.*, b. Sept. 23, 1872. (5) *Jennie B.*, b. Feb. 18, 1874. (6) *Arche M.*, b. Nov. 4, 1875. (7) *Lizzie A.*, b. Nov. 11, 1877. (8) *Lorne B.*, b. Apr. 13, 1881. (9) *Frank E.*, b. June 19, 1884. (10) *Joseph L.*, b. May 8, 1887.

4 vi MELBOURN, b. Oct. 15, 1849.
   vii JESSIE ELIZABETH, b. July 24, 1851; m. James W., son of Isaac and Mary (Phillips) Cornwell, May 28, 1874, and live at the "Sea-Wall," on Digby Neck. Children:
      1. ARCHE C., b. Feb. 22, 1875.
      2. EVA GERTRUDE, b. July 20, 1879.
      3. HERBERT, b. ——.
      4. EMDON, b. ——. Mr. Cornwell m. 1st, Sophia, daughter of John Denton, Feb. 27, 1869, and had Della May, b. June 14, 1870. Mrs. Cornwell d. Sept., 1873, aged 26. Mr. Isaac Cornwell d. 1890, aged eighty-six.
   viii SOPHIA A., b. Aug. 5, 1853; d. May, 1859.
15 ix RICHARD SCOTT, b. March 24, 1855.
   x ALICE ELICIA, b. March 7, 1857; m. Jacob, son of Isaac Dakin, July 18, 1883; live at Front Cove, Digby Co., have four children: Lizzie, Alena,

Sadie and Arnold. Mr. Dakin m. 1st, Elizabeth Leighton, and had three children; m. 2nd Amelia Smalley and had six children.

  xi THOMAS ANSLEY, b. April 2, 1859; m. Sarah, daughter of William Pickering of Prince Edward Island, Dec. 25, 1889, and live in South Boston; a car conductor.

VIII. 65 David Chute, another brother, born Sept. 29, 1810; married Sarah Ann Woodworth, by Rev. Edward Manning, Oct. 2, 1834, and lived in Clements, for a few years in Virginia, near Clementsvale, where he died rather suddenly Feb. 2, 1847; the widow, with the two youngest boys (the three older having preceded with their cousin, Ezekiel Chute, the year before), moved to Bayham, Elgin Co., Ont., in Sept. 1851, and there married 2nd by Rev. Alfred Chute, June 24, 1852, Jacob, son of Henry Baumwart and lived near Big Creek, Walsingham, Norfolk Co., where he died Oct. 31, 1854, aged sixty. (He married 1st, Sally, daughter of Isaac and Polly (Colt) Smith, and had several children.) The widow sold out her little property there, and in 1856, moved to Le Sueur, Minn., and there lived with her eldest son. But one William P. F., son of Joseph Cummings, from western New York, a lumberman came in there to board, and married her, by the Rev. Mr. Lagrange, Jan. 7, 1858. In 1860, they sold out there and moved about seventy miles south into Elmore, Faribault Co., near the Iowa line, and in 1867–68, they moved south, across Iowa to Maysville, De Kalb Co., Mo., and there settled on a good piece of rail road land. Mr. Cummings was a farmer and jobber.

Children:

  i LEVI, b. Sept. 11. 1835; went to Ontario, Sept., 1850; to Le Sueur, Minn., 1855; was a soldier in Co. C, 5th Minnesota, and on the frontier fighting the Sioux indians, under Little Crow, in the summer of 1862; m. Julia, daughter of William and Mary Hassel, near Blue Earth city, Jan. 26, 1865; had a son, Edgar, b. Apr. 17, 1867. For twenty years or more Mr. Chute has lived in Missouri.

  ii EZRA, b. Mar. 1, 1837; d. in Bayham, Ont., Oct. 17, 1850.

186 iii ELIAS, b. Feb. 9. 1839.

  iv ZECHARIAH, b. Dec. 1, 1841: was in Co. C, 5th Minnesota in late war; d. on a steamboat on the Mississippi river, Nov. 27, 1863, and buried at Memphis, Tenn.

  v ELEAZER, b. Jan. 5, 1844; d. in Walsingham, Ont., Apr. 15, 1854.

  vi AMANDA, b. Apr. 24, 1846; d. Feb. 14, 1847.

  vii ARMINDA ANN, b. Nov. 6, 1858; m. David, son of David and Harriet (Dyer) Gray, Apr. 25, 1875, and had Ora Alice, b. Feb. 3, 1876, Clarksdale, Mo.

viii ALICE AMANDA, twin sister, m. Fred Strasser, Dec. 18, 1882, and had Edward A., b. Nov. 3, 1883; she d. in Missouri, June 30, 1887; he m. again and is a doctor in Colorado.

VIII. 66 Elias, the eighth and last brother in the family of Daniel and Sarah (Weare) Chute, born Apr. 21, 1817 ; married Martha (b. Feb. 19, 1824), daughter of Abram Bowlby by Rev. Israel Potter jr., Dec. 32, 1842, and lived in the "Virginia" settlement, Clements, N. S.

Children :

i DARIUS, b. Feb. 23, 1844; m. Abba Hobbs, 1871, and live in Worcester, Mass.
ii ALBERT, b. Dec. 14, 1845; drowned in Lake Katy, Sept. 5, 1858.
iii DALINA, b. Oct. 11, 1847; m. Alex. Marriott, July 7, 1864; he m. 1st, A. Rhoda, daughter of Abram Low and had two children; she d. Mar. 28, 1864, aged 18; he d. Oct. 10, 1867, aged 31, and Dalina m. 2nd, Ephraim Chute. See No. 174.
iv PRIOR, b. Feb. 10, 1850; d. Mar. 20.
v MARTHA L., b. Jan. 6, 1851; m. Wallace, son of William Wright, Dec. 30, 1867, and have four children.
vi MARY JANET, twin sister, m. Asa Wright, Dec. 18, 1870; two children.
vii IRENE, b. Nov. 23, 1852; m. Freeman E. Chute. (See 277.)
viii LUCRETIA. b. Oct. 1, 1854; d. Aug. 1865.
ix HIRAM E., b. June 7, 1856; m. Isabel Wyman, June 1881; she d. Apr. 17, 1883, aged 21; m. 2nd, Clara L. Lewis, May 22, 1889. He is head of the firm "Chute & Hall," organ manufacturers, Yarmouth, N. S.
x ARTHUR R., b. Jan. 25, 1858; d. Oct. 20, 1866.
xi A. PERCY, b. Sept. 21, 1860; d. May 30, 1884.
xii ELIAS BURPEE, b. June 18, 1862.
xiii ZEDIVIA, b. Dec. 27, 1864; m. H. William Jack. Nov. 25, 1885, Minneapolis, Minn.

VIII. 67 Benjamin Foster Chute,[8] (*Abram,*[7] *Samuel,*[6] *John,*[5] *Lionel,*[4] *James,*[3] *James,*[2] *Lionel* [1]), born in Granville, Jan. 31, 1801 ; married Hannah Calkins,[8] (*Edmund,*[7] *Ahira,*[6] *Ezekiel,*[5] *John,*[4] *Samuel,*[3] *John,*[2] *Hugh,*[1] of 1600, from Chepston, Monmouthshire, Wales, 1640; died 1690, in Marshfield, Mass., wife Ann. Ezekiel, to Nova Scotia 1760), by Rev. William Chipman, Sept. 24, 1829, and she died May 8, 1832, aged thirty ; Miriam Parker,[4] (*William,*[3] *Major Nathaniel,*[2] *William* [1]), b. in Aylesford, Sept. 21, 1799 ; married William Chase, jr., by Rev. Ezekiel Masters, Nov. 24, 1830 ; he died Oct. 24, 1831, aged twenty-seven ; she married 2nd B. F. Chute, by Rev. E. Masters, Sept.

24, 1833, Cornwallis, Kings Co., N. S. Mr. Chute, a wealthy farmer, died Sept. 24, 1854.

Children :

187 i SILAS PARKER, b. July 23, 1834.
    ii HANNAH MARIA, b. March 17, 1836; m. John H. Barteaux,[5] (William,[4] Charles,[3] William,[2] Phillip,[1] b. about 1720), Nov. 18, 1857, and lived at Nictaux, Annapolis Co., N. S., he d. July 26, 1876; aged 52. She m. 2d, ———. Children:
      1. RUFINA, b. Nov. 8, 1859; m. David M., son of David Jordan, Dec. 21, 1888, lived in Boston, had: Maud R., b. Nov. 29, 1889. Mr. Jordan d. June 19, 1891, aged 42.
      2. JUDSON A., b. Sept. 22, 1862; m. Eloise Gates, Oct. 23, 1889.
      3. ELLA M., b. Sept. 2, 1865. } Dress makers in Boston, Mass.
      4. MARY M., b. Jan. 29, 1870.
    iii SUSAN, b. March 5, 1838; d. Sept. 4, 1841.

VIII. 68 John Nelson, brother to the preceding, born Dec. 3, 1804; married by Rev. William Chipman, Sarah, daughter of Samuel Parker, Sept. 2, 1834, and lived on the "Post Road," near Berwick, King's Co., N. S.; was a sturdy farmer, inn keeper, mill owner, etc.; died Mar. 20, 1882.

Children :

188 i LEANDER, b. July 28, 1835.
    ii ABRAM, b. Dec. 20, 1836.

VIII. 69 William Henry, another brother, born Dec. 21, 1806; married Lovina, daughter of Dea. William Skinner, by Rev. William Chipman, Oct. 28, 1835, and still live in Cornwallis; able farmers; had a "golden wedding," 1885.

Children :

    i LOIS, b. Aug. 14, 1836; d. July 18, 1837.
    ii MARGARET, b. July 9, 1838; m. Isaac, son of Gardner Dodge jr., Mar. 4, 1863; he d. Nov. 26, 1866, aged 30 years and 8 months.
189 iii Richardson, b. Mar. 10, 1840.
    iv MARY, b. May 2, 1842; m. William J. Burgess, Feb. 19, 1879.
190 v JOHN BURTON, b. Aug. 23, 1844.
    vi WAITY, b. Jan. 30, 1847; m. Owen, son of Enoch Palmer, Feb. 18, 1880; have five children.
    vii EUNICE ANN, b. July 20, 1849; m. Charles, son of James Ilsley, Dec. 1, 1875.
    viii LALEAH, b. Feb. 11, 1853.
191 ix HENRY J., b. May 10, 1856.

VIII. 70 Samuel Burton, another brother, born March 19, 1816; married Harriet, daughter of Dea. Andrew and Olive Chute, by Rev. Israel Potter jr., in Clements, Feb. 4, 1841. They moved from Cornwallis, N. S., to Bayham, C. W., or Ontario, in June 1842, lived there and in Malahide (on the farm of Philip Barteaux), seven years; moved to Princeton, Marquett Co., Wis., 1849, moved again to Joe Davies, Faribault Co., Minn., 1859, and they are doing well on a good quarter section (one hundred and sixty acres). During twenty-seven years they visited the old home but once, in 1869.

Children:

    i MELISSA, b. April 26, 1842; m. Josiah Smith son of Aretas and Mercia,[9] (Herrick* Joseph,[8] Joseph H.,[7] Major Israel,[6] Benjamin,[5] Joseph,[4] Joseph,[3] Henry,[2] Sir William[1]), Smith, Dec. 4, 1861, Blue Earth City, Minn., and live near Fairmount, Martin Co., Minn., farmers. Children: (1), Albert A., b. Dec. 11, 1863; m. ——. (2), Ensley J., b. Aug. 26, 1866. (3), Winnifred T., b. June 7, 1886.

    ii ALONZO, b. March 12, 1844; d. in Minnesota, Feb. 8, 1866.

    iii ENSLEY, b. Jan. 13, 1846; d. in Minnesota, Nov. 11, 1864.

192 iv ISAAC N., b. April 5, 1848.

    v TERISSA, b. April 19, 1851; m. Lorenzo J. Green, as his 2nd wife, in Minnesota, Feb. 27, 1868, and had Ernest G., b. Feb. 7, 1869; she d. Feb. 14, 1870; he m. 3d, Mary, daughter of Owen Eagan, May 1872, and d. Nov. 21, 1873; aged 40.

    vi OLIVER CROMWELL, b. Jan. 18, 1853; d. Mar. 5, 1866.

    vii EUGENE. b. Nov. 7, 1854; d. Dec. 1.

    viii LOVINA, b. Dec. 18, 1855; a school teacher.

    ix CYNTHIA, b. Apr. 5, 1858; d. Jan. 1, 1859.

    x GEORGE WILLIAM, b. Nov. 1, 1859.

    xi FRED YOUNG, b. Oct. 14, 1861.

VIII. 71 Thomas Ansley, the youngest son of Abram and Mehitable (Foster) Chute, born in Cornwallis, N. S., May 11, 1819; married Margaret, daughter of Deacon William Skinner, by Rev. William Chipman, Feb. 9, 1843, and lives on his father's old farm (that he bought and settled on in 1817), on the Post Road, two miles from Berwick; farmers. Mrs. Chute died Jan. 17; 1863, in her forty-first year; he married 2nd, Mary Hendry, July 12, 1867; she died Aug. 9, 1885, aged sixty.

* Sir William Heyricke, to London, 1574, changed his name to Herrick, son of John,[6] (Thomas,[7] Robert,[6] Sir William,[5] Robert,[4] John,[3] Henry,[2] Eyricke[1]), 1316 to 1272, descendant of Eric the Forrester.

Children :

193 i Edward Manning, b. Mar. 25, 1844.
ii Lovina, b. Jan. 16, 1845; d. Mar. 9, 1847.
194 iii Joseph Fanshaw, b. Oct. 9, 1846.
195 iv Benjamin Foster, b. Dec. 13, 1848.
v Zephina, b. Dec. 7, 1850; m. A. C. Wade, Oct. 7, 1891.
vi Ermina, b. Dec. 2, 1854; a school teacher.
196 vii James Perry, b. Nov. 22, 1858.
viii Harris Obelin, b. Aug. 12, 1861.

VIII.   72 Abram Chute[8], (*Williaw,*[7] *Samuel,*[6] *John,*[5] *Lionel,*[4] *James,*[3] *James,*[2] *Lionel*[1]), born in Wilmot, N. S., Dec. 3, 1804; went to Frederickton, N. B., in 1818; married Lydia Ann, daughter of Major William Carr, June, 1824; she died in June, 1833, aged forty; he married 2nd, Ann, daughter of William Harris, June 27, 1834, and went to Nova Scotia, but returned to St. John, N. B. in 1840; went to Nova Scotia again and lived in Dalhousie, Annapolis Co., 1842; moved to Taunton, Bristol Co., Mass., 1870, and died there Feb. 10, 1890.

Children :

i William Henry, b. Aug., 1825, near Black Rock, N. S.; d. Sept. 26, 1829.
ii Elijah, b. 1828; d. 1840, Frederickton, N. B.
iii Lydia Ann, b. Sept. 26, 1829; m. Willium, son of John Scofield, Dec. 19, 1852, in Dalhousie.   Children:
   1. Milledge, b. ——; m. ——.
   2. Margaret, b. ——; m. Charles Mailman.
   3. William Henry, b. 1859; d. 1863.
   4. Charles, b. ——; m. Cassie Connell.
iv Priscilla, b. Jan. 7, 1832; m. Stephen Medicraft, Oct. 10, 1852.   Children:
   1. William Albert, b. ——; m. ——
   2. Lydia, b. ——.
   3. Isabella, b. ——.
   4. Abram, b. ——.
   5. Mary Ann, b. ——; m. James Evans.
   6. Alonzo, b. ——; d. aged 4.
   7. Freeman, ——.
   8. Minnie, b. ——.
v Mary, b. Apr. 19, 1837; m. John Medicraft, Aug. 3, 1853; **fourteen children**;
vi Syrena, b. Apr. 3, 1841; m. Richard Booth of Providence, Dec., 1868.
vii Isabella, b. June 20, 1843; m. Charles Spearin, Aug. 23, 1865; **3 children**.
viii Lucinda, b. July 20, 1845; m. Josiah Brown, June 12, 1860; **3 children**
ix Georgiana, b. June 11, 1847; m. Thomas Read, Mar. 16, 1863; **4 children**.
197 x William Albert, b. June 27, 1849.

VIII. 73 James Lynam Chute, brother to the preceding, born in Wilmot, N. S., July 3, 1813; married Lucy, daughter of James Millbury 1837, and lived in Clarence, a good Christian couple; he died Nov. 19, 1851; she died near Providence, R. I., Jan. 4, 1888, aged 76.

Children:

    i SERAPH O., b. Jan. 17, 1838; m. Alfred, son of Nicholas Crowell, Sept. 1, 1866, and lived near Bridgetown; moved to Lynn, Mass., July 1890. Children: (1), *Nicholas Fletcher*, b. Dec. 27, 1867; m. Achsah Mann, Nov. 1887. (2), *Edward Burpee*, b. March 24, 1869. (3), *Minnie May*, b. May 15, 1871. (4), *Andrew Pleaman*, b. June 8, 1873. (5), *Ada Delight*, b. July 16, 1875. (6), *Annie Belle*, b. Oct. 13, 1877.

    ii SUSAN A., b. May 27, 1839; m. James Edward, son of Nicholas Crowell, Sept. 16, 1862; and lived near Bridgetown till Aug. 1891, when they moved to New Milford, N. H. Children: (1) *James Lyman*, b. Aug. 15, 1863; m. Amelia Gillis, Sept. 21, 1888. Two children. (2), *Anna Orlena*, b. Aug. 29, 1865; m. Arche, son of Frank Lowe, Oct. 25, 1882, have seven children, Jamaica Plain, Mass. (3), *Lucy Agnes*, b. Sept. 14, 1867; m. John W. Blanchard, March 1886. (4), *Elizabeth M.*, b. 1869; d. 1874. (5), *Edward W.*, b. Oct. 19, 1872. (6), *Demonford L.*, b. Mar. 1875; d. April 1877. (7), *Mildred May*, b. Sept. 11, 1877; d. the same day. (8), *Harry Lamont*, b. Sept. 4. 1879.

198   iii JAMES WILLIAM, b. July 4, 1841.

    iv MARY ELIZA, b. Aug. 24, 1843; d. 1864.

199   v DAVID FLETCHER, b. Nov. 9, 1845.

    vi LUCINDA, b. Feb. 3, 1817; m. Albert G., son of Christopher H. Waterman, Dec. 24, 1868, and lived in Johnson, R. I.; he was in Co. K, 7th Rhode Island in the late war.

    vii HENRY W., b. Sept. 10, 1850; off to sea; Belfast, Ireland.

VIII. 74 Daniel Dimock Chute,[8] (*Samuel,*[7] *Samuel,*[6] *John,*[5] *Lionel,*[4] *James,*[3] *James,*[2] *Lionel*[1]), born at "Digby Joggins," Digby Co., Feb. 7, 1807; taken to Cornwallis by his parents in infancy; married Elizabeth Rebecca Rand,[8] (*Abishai,*[7] *John,*[6] *Thomas,*[5] *Caleb,*[4] *John,*[3] *Thomas,*[2] *Robert,*[1] over to Charlestown, 1635; died 1639), by Rev. John Prior, Sept. 29, 1831, New Canaan, Cornwallis, and stayed there till March, 1840, (during which time three daughters and a son were born and died in infancy and childhood), when they moved to Frederickton, N. B., and attended the great celebration of the Queen's marriage the first of May, when a whole ox was roasted. He followed shoemaking. To look for more or better work, he left New Brunswick in March, 1849, and lived in Albany and Greenbush, N. Y., and (hearing that his wife was dead or deserted him), married Mary Alice Eliza, daughter of Paoli and Rebecca Randall, and widow of Captain James W. Taylor (lost off the ship Alamance, 1848, aged thirty-three, leaving two sons, James Henry, born 1846, and William George, born 1848), by Rev. George Hall, Apr. 17, 1849, in New York city, and then moved to Mt. Clements, Mich., and drove stage and carried mail till 1852; then he moved to Swan Creek, St. Clair Co., and was a storekeeper and stave merchant through the summer of 1853; then went to California; came back in the fall of 1855, and moved to Eyota, Olmstead Co., Minn., and there "farmed it" on a good quarter section of prairie land till 1863, when he sold out and moved to near Albert Lea, Freeborn Co.; farmer again. In the spring of 1866, he went to California again; came back in the fall, and since that wandered into Western Dakota and settled in the Black Hills, where he died March 26, 1889. As D. D. Chute was reported dead in New Brunswick, his "widow" married Dea. Eli, son of Hosea Taylor of Orient, Me., 1853, and lived in Lower Woodstock and Eel River; had three sons and a daughter, two were twin boys that died in infancy. She died Feb. 28, 1891, about eighty.

Children :

  i EMILY REBECCA. b Nov. 16, 1841; m. Dea. Hezekiah S., son of Joseph Scott. Dec. 4, 1860; moved from Lower Woodstock to Augusta, Me., 1880, and works in the cotton mills. Children:
1. MARY SILVEREIN, b. Dec. 18, 1861; d. Nov. 8, 1864.
2. LUCY AMBROSINE, b. Feb. 18, 1863; m. Lewis M. Currier (James H., William, Amos), Dec. 25, 1882. He is a policeman near Lynn. Two children.
3. LIZZIE FRANCELIA, b. July 2, 1864; m. George S. Jones, Jan. 23, 1887, two or three children.
4. CLARA EMMA, b. May 15, 1866; m. Geo. F. Carson.
5. EDITH MEDORA, b. April 7, 1869.
6. HEZEKIAH E., b. July 25, 1870.
7. MINNIE ESTHER, b. July 4, 1872; m. Charles E. Procter, July 20, 1890, of Waterville.
8. GEORGE SAMUEL, b. Nov. 1, 1873.
9. ETHEL PEARLE, b. Jan. 22, 1880.
10. PAUL LEANDER, b. Jan. 28, 1886.

200 ii JAMES SAMUEL, b. Nov. 30, 1843.
201 iii LAUGHLIN ISADORE, b. Jan. 11, 1846.
  iv CHARLES WILLIAM, b. Jan. 31, 1848; d. May, 1865.

  v Lewis S , b. Apr. 7, 1850; d. Apr. 10, 1852.
  vi Daniel, b. Dec. 23, 1851.
  vii Mary E., b. Oct. 21, 1853.
  viii Leander S., b. June 10, 1856; d. Apr. 25, 1857.
  ix Benjamin Frank, b. Sept. 10, 1859.

VIII. 75 Thomas Handley, brother to the preceding, born in Aylesford, King's Co., N. S., May 11, 1810 ; married Eliza, daughter of William and Amy (Harrice-Balsor) English, July 23, 1838, near Gibbon Harbor, since called Harborville, King's Co., N. S., and there spent his days, a warm-hearted, generous Christian, deacon in the Free Baptist church and a justice of the peace. Mrs. Chute was an invalid several years and died June 12, 1875, aged fifty-six. Deacon Chute married 2nd, Eliza Sophia, daughter of George William Rudolph and widow of James Thomas, son of Daniel and Harriet (Taylor) Gould, Sept. 27, 1876, and died June 1, 1884; she married 3rd, Gilford G. Collins, Dec. 2, 1884, and they live in Boston.

 Children :

202 i David Alfred, b. May 26, 1839.
  ii Amoret R., b. May 13, 1841; m. Benjamin, son of Cyrus West, Apr. 26, 1866; had six children, and d. Dec. 29, 1883.
  iii Bessie Maria, b. June 9, 1843; m. Austin F., son of Hiram M. Balsor, 1874; three children.
  iv Louisa Love, b. Aug. 24, 1845; m. Peter, son of Hiram M. Balsor, Dec. 21, 1866, and live in Aylesford; farmers. Children:
   1. Austin A., b. Sept, 27, 1867; m. ——.
   2. Aubrey F., b. Oct. 27, 1869; m. ——.
   3. Nellie L., b. Sept. 18, 1872; m. Albert McMann, Sept. 20, 1892.
   4. George Washington, b. Mar. 21, 1875.
   5. Thomas P., b. Oct. 7, 1877.
  v Samuel Randall, b. May 16, 1848; m. Jane McGregor, from Prince Edward Island, widow of Perry M. Whitcomb (d. Apr. 5, 1881, aged 47; had five children), Dec. 26, 1883, and live in Massachusetts.
  vi Penelope, b. Nov. 9, 1850; d. May 9, 1854.
  vii Thomas Handley, b. Oct. 29, 1852; m. Anna, daughter of James Foster, Feb. 22, 1882, and live at South Framingham, Mass.
  viii Emma Matilda, b. July 21, 1844; m. James A., son of George William Rudolph, Nov. 20, 1876; and d. March 24, 1885; he d. April 16, 1883; aged 32. Children:
   1. Margaret Elizabeth, b. June 10, 1877.
   2. Bessie Love, b. Jan. 1879.
   3. George Handly, b. 1881; d. in childhood.
   4. Amoret Jane, b. May 11, 1883.

ix CLARA ADELIA, b. May 9, 1857; m. Washington, son of H. M. Balsor, May 8, 1876; six children.

x SARAH, b. Jan. 27, 1861; d. March 15.

xi ALICE JANE, b. Aug 15, 1863; m. Edwin B. Heath, May 8, 1890, Malden, Mass.

xii ADDISON FRANKLIN MILLER, b. Dec. 25, 1880.

VIII. 76 Samuel, another brother, born in Cornwallis, Dec. 28, 1818; married Ruth Ann, daughter of Adam and Sally (Todd) Crane, by Rev. Mr. Busby, March 6, 1843, in York Co., N. B., and lived in Haynesville; farmers, kind, good natured, old fashioned Christians. Mr. Chute cut his right knee badly, Dec. 19, 1867, was laid up seven months, and lame ever after. His brother, Thomas H., visited them from Cornwallis, N. S., in June 1874, and Mr. and Mrs. Chute, with the baby, returned the visit in September, and came home partly on the new railroad, then building up the Keswick River. Mrs. Chute died Aug. 24, 1883, aged fifty-nine.

Children :

 i LYDIA OLIVIA, b. June 4, 1845; m. Isaiah Brewer, July 9, 1863; and live near Zealand Station. Children:
  1. LEBARON C., b. June 15, 1866.
  2. CLARISSA A., b. March 13, 1868; m. James F. Carton.
  3. EDWARD N., b. Oct. 17, 1871.
  4. BESSIE A., b. Nov. 15, 1875.
  5. ORMON H., b. Sept. 22, 1880.

 ii ALMIRA, b. June 20, 1847; m. Zadok Morehouse (b. 1824) Dec. 21, 1865, and live near Zealand Station. Children:
  1. LEANDER, b. Nov. 10, 1866; m. Emma Morehouse.
  2. MAHALA, b. Nov. 19, 1872.
  3. JESSIE, b. Sept. 27, 1880.
  4. EMMA, b. April 15, 1883.

203 iii JAMES WELLINGTON, b. July 15, 1849.

204 iv EDWARD WILLIAM, b. July 3, 1851.

205 v ARTHUR NELSON, b. March 10, 1853.

 vi ARMANELLA JANE, b. Feb. 24, 1855; m. Silas White, May 15, 1878; lived in Haynesville, and d. Aug. 5, 1881. He was drowned April 22, 1886, aged 37. He m. 1st, Mary Elliott; she d. April 17, 1877; aged 25. Children:
  1. NELLIE BERTRESA, b. 1879.
  2. JANET AZUBA, b. 1881.

 vii ABIGAIL O., b. Nov. 20, 1857; m. William, son of John Hill, Sept. 20, 1879.

 viii SARAH ANN, b. April 2, 1860; m. Henry Albert Miller, July 1883.

 ix SAMUEL F., b. Sept. 17, 1863.

 x DAVID HANDLEY, b. Jan. 8, 1867; m. Martha Jane, daughter of John Carton, Nov. 27, 1888.

VIII. 77 David Prior, the youngest brother, born Dec. 26, 1820; married Alice, daughter of Joseph Spicer, Oct. 21, 1846, and lives on his father's old farm, near Harborville.

Children:

- i SAMUEL, b. Oct. 9, 1847; d. Oct. 22.
- ii ROXANA, b. Sept. 18, 1848; m. Joseph H. Frazer, Nov. 22, 1869; lived in Charlestown, Mass., and d. 1887. He m. again, and lives in Boston.
- iii CALVIN C., b. July 28, 1850; d. April 2, 1852.
- iv AMANDA M., b. July 9, 1852; m. Andrew W. Livermore, 1873; m. 2d, James E. Ross, Newton, Mass. Now at New Rochelle, N. Y.
- v MARY JANE, b. July 3, 1854; d. Aug. 30, 1858.
- vi ABBA R., b. July 6, 1856; m. William A. Greenough, Aug. 15, 1873; and live at Newton, Mass. He is a carpenter. Five children.
- vii DAVID PRIOR, b. May 29, 1858; m. Lilly Walton, 1886, and live in California.
- viii ANNA LOVENA, b. May 20, 1859; m. Obed B. Coldwell,[5] (Hiram,[4] John,[3] John,[2] William,[1] b. in England, 1695), May 2, 1876; five children.
- ix THOMAS H., b. Apr. 21, 1862; d. Jan. 27, 1865.
- x ELIZA ANNES, b. Apr. 6, 1864; m. Frank F. Edwards, Nov. 25, 1884.
- xi CAPTAIN JOSEPH N., b. Apr. 26, 1866; m. Rosa Ladner, Feb. 1891.
- xii EDWARD F., b. Mar. 21, 1869; m Ellen, daughter of James Moody, Sept. 18,92.
- xiii OWEN L., b. Feb. 28, 1871.
- xiv JAMES B., b. Aug. 10, 1873; d. Mar. 16, 1874.

VIII. 78 George Washington Chute,[8] (*George W.,*[7] *John,*[6] *John,*[5] *Lionel,*[4] *James,*[3] *James,*[2] *Lionel*[1]), born at Lunenburg, Mass., July 4, 1805; married Maria, daughter of William and Mary (Spaulding) Worcester, July 25, 1831, and lived at Randolph till 1840; then at Canton; to Luenburg, 1843; to Leominster, 1846. Mr. Chute went to sea some, and was a warm-hearted, genial man; died July 13, 1876; she died June 11, 1891, aged eighty years, four months.

Children:

- 206 i WILLIAM GEORGE, b. Oct. 23, 1832.
- ii SARAH A. M., b. Oct. 31, 1834; m. Moses W. Whitcomb jr., May 10, 1855; three children.
- iii ISABELLA CROCKER, b. Mar. 27, 1837; m. Asa L. Putnam, son of Caleb Putnam and Jennie Longley, (daughter of Asa, son of Jonas, 3rd son of Dea. John, the redeemed captive), May 5, 1864; five children, Wilton, N. H.
- 207 iv JOHN WORCESTER, b. May 30, 1839.
- 208 v GEORGE WASHINGTON, b. Apr. 14, 1841.
- vi MARY SPAULDING, b. July 24, 1843; m. Henry P. Durant, Mar. 19, 1867.
- vii CATHARINE T., b. July 26, 1845; d. Mar. 16, 1889.
- viii IZORY M., b. Dec. 19, 1847; m. Charles G. Putney, Feb. 10, 1869; two children.

VIII. 79 Alexander Chute,[8] (*Peter,*[7] *John,*[6] *John,*[5] *Lionel,*[4] *James,*[3] *James,*[2] *Lionel*[1]), born in Aylesford, N. S., Feb. 24, 1809; married Mary, daughter of James Fleet, 1844, and lived in Lower Granville; a singing teacher; died Feb. 26, 1846; his widow married 2nd, John Wright (*Joseph, William*, who fought under General Wolfe at the taking of Quebec in 1759), 1862, and lived in Clements and Bear River. She died Apr. 4, 1878, aged fifty-eight. He died at the head of Bear River tide, 1888, aged ninety. One child.

    1. MARY AMORET, b. June, 1845; m. Capt. William Spicer, July, 1868, and had two sons, one daughter; one son d. in childhood. Capt. Spicer embarked for the West Indies from Bear River on the schooner "Effie Young," in 1884, taking his wife and son along and were never afterwards heard from. Capt. Spicer m. 1st, Louise Wilkins and had a daughter Louise.

VIII. 80 Charles Chute, brother to the preceding, born April 19, 1811; married Abigail, daughter of George Worster, Feb. 7, 1838, and lived in Lower Granville, a singing teacher. Mrs. Chute died May 12. 1869, aged fifty-two; he married 2nd, Emma Fleet (*William, James*), widow of Richard Mott Marshall (*William, Anthony*), 1872; she died 1874, aged about fifty-four; he married 3d, Margaret G., daughter of John Sederquist jr., and widow of Capt. William Mussells, Dec. 7, 1876, and died Aug. 14, 1881. The 3d widow is the eldest of nineteen children, two mothers; Rev. George W. Sederquist, born, 1838, is her half-brother.

Children:

    i ELEANOR, b. 1840; m. John R. Oliver, and had a daughter.
        1. ALICE, b. ——; m. George Johnson. Mrs. Oliver d. Nov. 14, 1884.
    ii JOHN W., b. 1842; off to sea.
    iii SAMUEL, b. 1843; d. young.
    iv SUSAN, b. 1845; m. Edward Slocomb, 1871; two sons James and ——. They live in Lynn.

VIII. 81 Gilbert Randall, another brother born Sept. 13, 1817; married Alice Maria Bowlby (*Jordan, George*), June 16, 1842; (Jordan Bowlby married Eunice, daughter of Thomas Tupper, brother to Rev. Charles Tupper, 1821, had two sons and two daughters; he died 1828, aged thirty-three; she married 2nd, Henry Baker, and lived near Melvern Square.) Mr. Chute lived in Aylesford, a merchant about sixteen years; from there went to Margaretville, on the Bay shore; thence to Lancaster Co., Neb., fifteen miles from Lincoln, April 1868, with his son Charles C. (George Alexander and Jordan being there before), and took a claim under the homestead, the wife and children coming in 1870. They returned in the fall of 1876, and bought the old Cronin farm in Lower Granville. He was in Co. M, 2nd Massachusetts Heavy Artilery, under Capt. Greely in the late war; and George Alexander was in the navy.

Children:

    i GEORGE ALEXANDER, b. May 10, 1843; m. Sarah, daughter of Lieutenant Mayo, 1866, and is reported a minister of the Latter Day Saints in the Southern States.

    ii JORDAN, b. Apr. 18, 1846, is in Iowa.

209 iii CHARLES C., b. June 15, 1848.

    iv EUNICE ELIZABETH, b. Oct. 8, 1850; m. James Kemp, Sept , 1871, and d. 1892.

210 v JOSEPH HOWE, b. May 17, 1854.

211 vi LYCURGUS, b. July 18, 1858.

    vii WILLIAM ROBINSON, b. Feb. 26, 1861; m. Louisa H., daughter of Joseph Lohnas, Nov. 29, 1892; is a merchant at Clementsvale, N. S.

VIII. 82 John Edward Chute,[8] (*Joseph F.,*[7] *John,*[6] *John,*[5] *Lionel,*[4] *James,*[3] *James,*[2] *Lionel*[1]), born near Digby, N. S., Dec. 4, 1816; went to Lunenburg, Mass., with his parents, 1827; married Nancy Amanda, (school teacher), daughter of Sylvester Foster, May 17, 1863; she died July 14, 1864, aged thirty; he married 2nd, Adaline Burgess, Mar. 14, 1865; they lived at Ashburnham; he a carpenter; died there March 10, 1876; she lives at Fitchburg.

Children:

    i EDWARD ABBOT, b. Apr. 12, 1864; m. Effie Whittemore, 1889, and was a railroad hand at Taunton; she d. in 1890.

    ii SUSAN AMANDA, b. Apr. 24, 1867; m. William Baldwin, Apr. 24, 1889; machinist in East Boston.

    iii ARTHUR HARRIS, b. Mar. 28, 1875.

VIII. 83 Joseph Homer, brother to the preceding, born in Nova Scotia, Mar. 9, 1822; married Margaret, daughter of William Wray, Apr. 11, 1859, and lived in or near Leominster; died Jan. 22, 1871, and the widow and family live at North Leominster.

Children:

    i JOSEPH WRAY, b. May 18, 1860.
    ii MARY JOSEPHINE, b. July 29, 1861; m. John A. Richardson, Nov. 20, 1890, South Framingham.
    iii WILLIAM Arthur, b. Aug. 21, 1862.
    iv PAUL CROCKER, b. Sept. 30, 1865; m. Ella McComisky, Aug., 1888.
    v ANNA JANE, b. July 27, 1868.
    vi HOMER HARRIS, b. Feb. 27, 1871.

    On June 5, 1885, Anna Jane, working in the Wheetwright & Page paper mill, North Leominster, picked up, pinned to a bank check, two bills of $1000 and $500 respectively, and when they were discovered as coming from a New York bank, they were returned, and the girl got $300 for her honesty. She had found $10 before that, $10 after, $5 in gold before either, and $2.50 at another time.

VIII. 84 Cornelius Harris, another brother, born at Harvard, Mass., Nov. 27, 1832; married Lydia S. Colburn,[7] (*Ziba,*[6] *William,*[5] *William,*[4] *William,*[3] *Robert,*[2] *Edward*[1]), 1855, lived some time in Lyme, N. H., to Royalston, Wis., next; then to Spencer Brook, Minn., 1857. He was corporal in Co. D, 2nd Minn. Cavalry in the late war. Mrs. Chute died 1875; aged forty; he married 2nd, Mary Jane, an older sister, 1876, and soon after moved to Princeton, Minn.

Children:

212 i ALBERT H., b. Jan. 7, 1856, in New Hampshire.
    ii JEROME A., b. Oct. 20, 1857, in Wisconsin; m. Clara Kelly, 1885.
    iii JOSIE L., b. Dec. 11, 1859, in Minn.; m. Simon Babb, and had Cora, Ever, Charles and Edna.
    iv VIOLA J., b. July 24, 1863; d. Oct. 22, 1865.
    v GEORGE E., b. Feb. 1, 1867.
    vi SABRA M., b. Nov. 10, 1873.

VIII. 85 Ezra Chute,[8] (*James,*[7] *Benjamin,*[6] *John,*[5] *Lionel,*[4] *James,*[3] *James,*[2] *Lionel*[1]), born in Granville, N. S., May 9, 1804; married Frances Steadman,[4] (*James C.,*[3] *John,*[2] *John*[1]), by Rev. William Elder, and lived a mile below Bridgetown, on the old Benjamin Foster farm, a kind Christian couple; died Nov. 2, 1851; she died Sept. 8, 1857; aged fifty years and six months.

Children:

213 i JAMES b. Dec. 15, 1833.
214 ii ENOCH S., b. March 19, 1836.
215 iii WALLACE G., b. March 10, 1839.

iv THOMAS, b. March 10, 1839; d. May 24, 1844; a happy Christian.
v MARY ELIZABETH, b. June 24, 1842; m. John, son of Edward Covert, Dec. 23, 1863, and live in Lower Granville. Children.
1. GRACE E., b. 1865; m. Edward John, three sons.
2. GEORGIA P., b. 1868; m. Calvin Clark, Dec. 25, 1892, and live in Lynn.
3. WALLACE, b. 1874.
4. WALTER STEADMAN, b. 1879.
vi HAVILAH SOPHIA, b. March 13, 1846; m. Judson, son of Joseph Chute, Dec. 1866. See No. 62.
vii MARGERA ANNA, b. Aug. 25, 1849; m. Capt. William Parker jr., Nov. 12, 1875; and had Archie, b. Dec. 1878; Mrs. Parker d. Oct. 16, 1879; he m. 2nd Mary, daughter of Joseph Bent, 1881.

VIII. 86 Gilbert Spurr Chute, brother to the above, born Aug. 11, 1806; married Sibyl Marshall (*William, Isaac*), by Rev. Nathaniel Viditoc, Oct. 24, 1833; and lived in Granville, a mile below Bridgetown, on a part of the old Benjamin Foster farm; a mild, patient Christian man; died Sept. 23, 1882; the widow lived on the place, and with the children, ten years, and in the fall of 1892, went to Lynn, Mass., to live at the age of seventy-seven.

Children:

i SARAH ANN, b. June 15, 1836; d. June 21, 1854.
216 ii HIRAM MARSHALL, b. Oct. 2, 1839.
iii Salina E., b. Mar. 24, 1843; m. A. A. Chute. See No. 176.
iv HARRIET ALICE, b. Apr. 15, 1847; m. James Thomas, son of John, son of Peter Raymond, son of Peter of Freeport, Dec. 9, 1886, and live in Lynn, Mass., (John Raymond was a cousin to Joseph, who m. Mary, daughter of Silas Chute). J. T. Raymond m. 1st, Lydia, daughter of John Haines Esq. of Freeport, and had a daughter, Florence A., b. Aug., 1869; d. Oct. 1886; Mrs. Raymond d. May 9, 1886, aged forty-six.
217 v WILLIAM M., b. Mar. 2, 1850.

VIII. 87 Thomas, another brother, born Sept. 26, 1808; married Mary, daughter of Rev. Gilbert Spurr, Wakefield, N. B., by. Rev. John Chase, Oct. 26, 1837, and lived a steady, sober farmer, two miles northwest of Bridgetown, back of the two preceding brothers. They were a happy, Christian couple; he died Nov. 8, 1875; she followed Aug., 1888, aged seventy-two.

Children:

i MARY ESTHER, b. Dec. 1, 1839; m. Z. M. Potter. See No. 59.
218 ii JERVIS, b. Jan. 31, 1842.
D

219 iii OLIVER, b. Jan. 22, 1844.
    iv ELIAKIM, b. April 10, 1846; d. a happy Christian, Feb. 25, 1878.
    v JESSIE ANN, b. May 15, 1850; d. May 2, 1851.
220 iv THOMAS FLETCHER, b. Nov. 15, 1853.
    vii H. SPURGEON, b. March 29, 1858.

VIII. 88 Everett, another brother, born Jan. 8, 1811, was a mason by trade; traveled considerable in early life; was in New York city time of the great fire in Dec., 1835; in Ontario in 1840; married Abigail,[8] daughter of Isaac,[*] son of John[2] Morehouse from Digby Neck, N. S., in Malahide, Ont., by Rev. M. S. McConnell, July 27. 1851, and lived in Bayham, Elgin Co., near Vienna.

Children:

221 i WILLIAM HANVEY, b. May 19, 1852.
    ii ALZINA W., b. Sept. 30, 1854; school teacher; d. Mar. 2, 1883.
    iii JAMES EVERETT, b. July 23, 1858; m. Mary Ann, daughter of Joseph Carter, Dec. 24, 1889; lives in Boston; a car conductor. He taught school in Ontario before going to Boston.
    iv CHARLES WALTER, b. Feb. 17, 1863; m. Mary, daughter of Francis and Rowena (Taylor) Ash in Boston, Mass.. July 23, 1889; live in Bayham, Ont.; a daughter, Belle, b. 1890.

VIII. 89 Abel Chute, another brother, born Mar. 5, 1816; married Zipporah Chute (See No. 45), Apr. 4, 1849, and lived on his father's place, up under the North Mountain, three miles from Bridgetown, a quiet, peaceable farmer; his wife died June 27, 1870, aged 50; he married 2nd, Eliza, daughter of Samuel Eagleson and widow of Captain Zebadiah Van Blarcom, Feb. 1, 1872; (Captain Van Blarcom was drowned in the Annapolis river, Apr. 5, 1869, aged 33, leaving two children, Samuel and Armina). Mr. Chute died Oct. 25, 1891.

Children:

    i ADONIRAM JUDSON, b. June 13, 1850; lives in Woburn, Mass.
    ii ANZONETTA, b. Mar. 11, 1853; m. William A. Poole, Feb. 29, 1876, and had Herman, b. 1878; she d. June, 1889, in Woburn; he m. 2nd, Mary Flint.
    iii MILLEDGE, b. Sept. 18, 1854; m. Willetta McKin, Nov. 25, 1885, in Woburn; she d. Feb. 24, 1892, aged 24.
    iv ADA J., b. 1856; d. 1857.
222 v GEORGE A.. b. Nov. 1, 1858.

[*] Isaac Morehouse m. Abigail Johnson,[7] daughter of William,[6] (and Hannah Vandyne), from New York to Nova Scotia time of the Revolution, William,[5] Nathaniel,[4] Deacon Samuel,[3] Deacon William,[2] Robert,[1] settled in New Haven Ct., 1637. They are traced back to a general in the army of William the Conqueror, 1066.

REV. MARTIN SHOOK MCCONNELL.

vi ANNIE N., b. Apr. 21, 1868; d. 1869.
vii WILLIAM FREDERICK, b. Sept. 9, 1877.

VIII. 90 Oliver, another brother, born Apr. 26, 1819; married Margaret Ann Chesley (*William Smith, Samuel, Maj. Samuel*), Aug. 24, 1841, and went to Ontario; lived in Bayham, Elgin Co.; Townsend, Norfolk Co., and during the late war in St. Clair Co., Mich.; but since the war in Moore, Lambton Co., Ont.; farmer.

Children:

    i CHARLES, b. July 29, 1842; d. Dec. 5, 1843.
223 ii WILLIAM HENRY, b. Dec. 9, 1843.
    iii EMILY VICTORIA, b. Aug. 26, 1845; m. Columbus H. Fluria, May 8, 1864; three children.
    iv JAMES I., b. Nov. 26, 1847; d. July 28, 1848.
    v MARY HAVILAH, b. Aug. 20, 1850; m. David, son of Joseph Lincoln, Sept. 14, 1869; lived at Alpena, Mich., and d. about 1887; 2 or 3 children.
    vi ISRAEL, b. Dec. 31, 1852; m. Edna, daughter of John Shaw, Sept. 17, 1884.
    vii JOSEPH, b. Dec. 31, 1854; d. Sept. 2, 1855.
    viii JESSIE JANE, b. June 19, 1857; m. John Robinson, July 1, 1879; he d. 1886.
    ix CHARLOTTE A., b. Dec. 16, 1858; m. James, son of William Kimball jr., Dec. 20, 1876; merchant and postmaster at Kimball, Ont.; 3 or 4 children.
    x MARTHA A., b. Mar. 30, 1861; d. Oct. 20, 1874, Moore, Ont.

VIII. 91 William Foster, youngest son of James and Phebe Chute, born Dec. 26, 1822; went to Ontario, a young man; married Margaret, daughter of John M. and Rebecca Glover, by Rev. Jacob Goble, Apr. 2, 1845, Townsend, Norfolk Co.; lived there a while, then moved to Malahide, Elgin Co.; a farmer near Silver Creek; died Aug. 9, 1884; she died in Aylmer, July 12, 1889, aged 69.

Children:

    i PHEBE JANE, b. June 30, 1847; m. Willard E. Mills, Dec. 25, 1869; had nine children; he d. in Aylmer, Dec. 22, 1888, aged 43.
    ii Israel, b. June 26, 1849, in Malahide; d. Sept. 29, 1866.
    iii SARAH REBECCA, b. Aug. 11, 1851; m. James, son of Barnabas Downs, July, 1870, and live in Alymer. Children:
        1. CLARA, b. Dec. 23, 1871; m. Geo. Pickering, Feb. 13, 1889.
        2. WALTER S., b. Jan. 26, 1874.
        3. ARCHIE, b. May 10, 1876.
        4. NINA, b. Oct. 5, 1880.
        5. ALICE, b. Oct. 30, 1882.
        6. MARY MAUD, b. Dec. 31, 1884.
        7. CLAUDIE M. E., b. June 25, 1888; d. Sept. 18, 1889.
        8. MARWOOD A., b. July 13, 1890.

224 iv JOHN HENRY, b. Oct. 17, 1852.
225 v WILLIAM, b. Sept. 24, 1853.
  vi JAMES HAMILTON, b. July 31, 1857.
  vii MADELLA L., b. Sept. 16, 1861; m. George Trim, Sept. 12, 1887.
  viii ELLEN JANE, b. Apr. 12, 1867; m. Sanford Cavalry, Sept. 12, 1887.

VIII. 92 Gilbert Fowler Chute,[8] (*Seth,*[7] *Benjamin,*[6] *John,*[5] *Lionel,*[4] *James,*[3] *James,*[2] *Lionel*[1]), born in Granville, Feb. 27, 1813; married Eliza Jane, daughter of Ezekiel Chute, Oct. 14, 1847; she died Sept. 19, 1848, aged 26; he married 2nd, Helen, daughter of John Starrett, and widow of John Phinney, Nov., 1848, and is a vessel builder and tailor at Hampton, Annapolis Co., N. S. She died 1892, aged eighty.

Children:

  i EZEKIEL, b. Aug. 12, 1848; m. Amelia, daughter of John Allen, July, 1889.
  ii WILLIAM FOWLER, b. Apr. 16, 1850; m. Henrietta, daughter of Henry Alline and Mary Elizabeth (Starrett) Morse, 1879, and live in Lynn, Mass.; he a carpenter, she a dressmaker.

VIII. 93 Burton Chute,[8] (*Benjamin,*[8] *Benjamin,*[6] *John,*[5] *Lionel,*[4] *James,*[3] *James,*[2] *Lionel*[1]), born in Granville, Apr. 17, 1809; married Hannah Banks, Feb. 13, 1837, and lived in Clarence over forty years; tanner and shoemaker; since 1880 they lived near Paradise; he died June, 1893.

Children:

  i LEMUEL, b. Apr. 9, 1838; m. Hannah, daughter of James Brown, July 1, 1879, and had a daughter, Libby B., b. Oct. 30, 1881; they lived in Clarence and he was killed by a log on the side of the mountain, Feb. 4, 1886; she has acted as teacher in the young ladies' seminary, Berwick, King's Co., since.
  ii AMELIA, b. Feb. 20, 1840; d. Aug. 23, 1843.
  iii ELIZABETH, b. July 18, 1844; d. Nov. 22, 1858.
  iv SALINA A., b. May 6, 1849; m. Ritson E., son of Hiram and Zilphia (Porter) Marshall, July 28, 1868, and have a daughter Zilphia Lovena, b. Aug. 20, 1869.

VIII. 94 Nathan Randall Chute, brother to the preceding, born June 10, 1815; married Havilah Steadman,[4] (*James C.,*[3] *John,*[2] *John*[1]), Feb. 20, 1848, and lived at Clarence; she died Mar. 12, 1876, aged about fifty-six; he married 2nd, Lydia, daughter of George Witt and widow of Lyman Potter (1807–1859), and Elliott Ritchie (1816–

1880), Mar. 23, 1882, and lived near Thorn's Cove or Litchfield, near the "Bay Shore." He died Dec. 18, 1891, and the old lady (b. 1808), lives with her children near Boston.

Nathan's children:

    i SUSAN EMMA, b. Oct. 23, 1850; d. 1857.
    ii MARTHA ELIZABETH, b. Oct. 1, 1852; d. Sept. 24, 1892.
    iii CERETHA OLIVIA. b. Aug. 11, 1855.

VIII. 95 Willett, another brother, born Jan. 23, 1820; married Susanna, daughter of Ezekiel and Eliza (Dugan) Foster, Jan. 22, 1853, and lived some in Granville, and some in Lynn, Mass.; died in Nova Scotia, Mar. 31, 1875; she went to Philadelphia, 1876, kept a restaurant through the Centennial and did well. After that she went to Michigan and married A. C. Powell of Berlin, Ottawa Co., and he died from an injury by a fall in a mill at Rockford, Kent Co., 1880; she then took her little family to Petosky in the northern part of the state, and kept a summer boarding house, where she married Alonzo Bonfeoy, but he left in a year or so and went to Dakota. She removed to Grand Rapids, Kent Co., 1883, and had a bakery, grocery, and kept boarders. Because she would not marry him, Charles S. Wernau, a boarder, shot her dead and then himself July 27, 1887, she fifty-six, he forty-four.

Children:

    i WILLETT B., b. 1853; d. 1858.
    ii MINNIE. b. Oct., 1859; m. George Styrnbrough, 1885.
    iii JARED TROOP, b. Jan., 1862; m. ——.
    iv M. ELIZA, b. Oct., 1865; m. Wesley E. Dyer, Sept. 22, 1887.

VIII. 96 Aaron Morse Chute,[8] (*Ezekiel,*[7] *Benjamin,*[6] *John,*[5] *Lionel,*[4] *James,*[3] *James,*[2] *Lionel*[1]), born Apr. 10, 1824; married Mary E., daughter of Enoch, son of Gardiner Dodge, Oct. 23, 1856, and was a merchant in Bridgetown.

Children:

    i ANNA MARIA LYDIA, b. Sept. 22, 1857; m. ——.
    ii WILLIAM TOWNSEND, b. Jan. 16, 1864; m. ——.

VIII. 97 George Chute,[8] (*Thomas,*[7] *Thomas,*[6] *John,*[5] *Lionel,*[4] *James,*[3] *James,*[2] *Lionel*[1]), born in Clements, Mar. 12, 1810; married Cynthia Hersey Levi (and Clarissaa Day) David, by Rev. Peter Crandel, 1830, and lived on Digby Neck a while. Then he lived on his uncle Abel's place 1832 to 1836, when he went off mackerel fishing around by Cape Breton, Prince Edward Island and Bay Cheleur of the then Canada East or Lower Canada. In 1837 they went to Canada West or Ontario, and lived in Malahide seven years, including six months in a volunteer company in London, Ont., 1838–1839; then they lived in Bayham, 1844–1845; to Vienna 1846, grocer and baker; to Acton, Ont., 1855; back to Vienna again 1859; sold out and went to Michigan 1875, and lived near Bay City, Byron and Peck; to Grand Rapids 1882. Religiously, Mr. Chute was converted in the fields 1821 (at which time his uncle Binea and his aunts Olive and Susan, were baptized in Bear River by Rev. Thomas Ansley (1769–1831), and Israel Potter sr., was ordained to the gospel ministry soon after), and was baptized by Rev. Ezekiel Masters at Bear River in June, 1832, with his brother Israel, uncle Edward, Lucinda Chute and Sarah Campbell; Edmund, Sarah A. and Harriet Chute, Betsy Woodworth, Betsy Camplin and others were baptized by Rev. Israel Potter about that time. Mr. Chute was appointed deacon in the Baptist church at Acton, 1856; joined the Adventists at Peck, Mich.; Disciples at Byron; independent since. At certain times in his life Deacon Chute was an ambitious, active, zealous, hard-working farmer, tradesman and Christian.

Children :

    i CHARLES, b. Aug. 18, 1831; m. Lovisa, daughter of Deacon Robert Mercer in Houghton, Norfolk Co., Ont., Jan. 13, 1855, and had a son Linton, b. July 24, 1858; d. Aug. 26, 1878. Mrs. Chute d. Feb. 2, 1878, aged 40 years, 8 months ; Mr. Chute was a sailor, mate and captain on the lakes several years, but finally settled at Grand Rapids, Mich., 1865; a carpenter.

    ii LOUISE JANE, b. Aug. 6, 1834; m. Isaac Beals, (*Stephen, Abel*), Dec. 9, 1857; in Acton, Ont., but moved to Sanilac Co., Mich., about 1870, and live near Peck. Children:

        1. ADDA, b. July 1, 1859; m. George F. Dimond, Sept. 25, 1878, and lives at Maysville, Mich.: four children.

        2. NOLAN A., b. Mar. 11, 1862; d. at Grand Rapids, Feb. 9, 1891.

        3. MINERVA, b. Dec. 22, 1866; m. Robert L. Dewar jr., Feb. 8, 1887, at Grand Rapids; two children.

        4. CARRIE, b. Apr. 28, 1873.

226   iii BINEA, b. June 19, 1838.

227   iv FREEMAN, b. Sept. 26, 1841.

    v SUSAN A., twin sister, m. Walter Glendenning in Acton, Ont., Dec. 25, 1863, but a few years after they removed to Dover, O. Children:

1. ANNA M., b. Dec. 22, 1864; m. Charles Standan, Dec. 31, 1890.
2. FREEMAN, b. Mar. 3, 1868.
3. AMOS, b. Apr. 21, 1872.
4. BELLE, b. June 9, 1874.
5. WILLIAM, b. Sept. 2, 1876.

vi MARY SOPHIA, b. Jan. 14, 1844; m. George L. Wilson, Oct. 27, 1865, and live in Grand Rapids. Children:
   1. JUNIA CHARLES, b. June 8, 1867; m. Minnie, daughter of William Scully, 1888.
   2. FRANK, b. Apr. 7, 1872.
   3. MARY, b. Mar. 17, 1876.
   4. GEORGE, b. Oct. 27, 1879.
   5. MAUD, b. ——; d. young.

vii HATTIE S., b. June 5, 1847; m. Robert J. Dewar, Jan. 4, 1871, and had a son Robert J., b. ——. Mr. Dewar d. 1872, aged 30. Then she m. George W. Wheeler, 1882, a policeman in Grand Rapids; a soldier in the late war.

VIII. 98 Walter Chute, another brother, born July 19, 1812; married Catharine McConnell, June 21, 1843; and live on the 2nd concession of Malahide, Ont. A sturdy farmer.

Children:

228 i HORATIO N., b. Dec. 26, 1847.
    ii THOMAS A., b. Feb. 24, 1855; m. Sarah Louise Mulholland, a school teacher, Feb. 10, 1886, and lives on his father's place with the old folks and have (1), *Morley Cecil*, b. June 16, 1889; (2), *Wilfred Hiram*, b. Aug. 17, 1892.

VIII. 99 Charles, another brother, b. Feb. 13, 1815; after his mother's death in 1818, he was taken and brought up by his uncle and aunt Barteaux, and went with them to Ohio, Grand River, and London, Ont., and finally to the first concession of Malahide, 1838, where they still live. Mr. Chute has been a good and useful man, both civic and religious, farmer, magistrate, etc.

Children:

   i CAROLINE VICTORIA, b. Oct. 31, 1845; m. W. G. Chute. See 215.
   ii ALICE M., b. Feb. 6, 1851; m. Luke H. Parker, Dec. 2, 1874, and d. March 23, 1884.
   iii LAURETTA A., b. Nov. 23, 1855.
   iv JOSEPH B., b. Mar. 21, 1858.
   v ERNEST AUGUSTUS, b. March 24, 1860.

VIII. 100 Richard Lawrence, youngest son of Thomas Chute jr., born in Clements, N. S., March 31, 1836; married Elizabeth,[7] daughter of Benjamin[6] and Caroline (Williams) Tisdale (*Ephraim*,[5]

Ephraim,[4] *John,*[3] *John,*[2] *John*[1]), (to Duxbury, Mass., 1637, killed by Indians, in King Philip's war, 1675), May 3, 1864, and lives on his father's old farm Malahide, Ont.

Children:

    i ARMINTA, b. June 19, 1865.
    ii LAURA A., b. June 30, 1869; d. March 1, 1876.
    iii CLARK H., b. May 26, 1872.
    iv ELGIN L., b. July 31, 1875.

VIII. 101 Edmund Chute,[8] (*Dea. Andrew,*[7] *Dea. Thomas,*[6] *John,*[5] *Lionel,*[4] *James,*[3] *James,*[2] *Lionel*[1]), b. in Clements, N. S., Dec. 31, 1815; married Mary Palmer,[5] (*Enoch Lewis,*[4] *Benjamin,*[3] *Lewis,*[2] *John*[1]), by Rev. William Chipman, in Aylesford, July 15, 1841; went to Ontario, with parents, brothers and sisters in September; lived in Bayham, Elgin Co., two years; in the spring of 1844, he moved to Carradoc, Middlesex Co., settled on the 9th concession, three miles southwest of Strathroy, on a one hundred acre farm given him by his father, and lives there still, one of the neatest farmers in all Canada; known far and wide as a man of integrity, truth and piety; and a deacon in the Baptist church of Strathroy. His wife, too, is known by good works in civic and religious society. In 1863, they went to their native land, Nova Scotia, and had a visit.

Children:

229 i WILLIAM WALLACE, b. Aug. 19, 1842.
    ii OLIVIA (LEAFY), b. Jan. 31, 1844; m. George Saxton,[4] (*Alexander,*[3] *Rev. John,*[2] *William*[1]), June 19, 1866, and lived in Carradoc, near two miles from Strathroy, as farmers, till about 1887, when he sold out and moved to Deckerville, Sanilac Co., Mich. Children:
      1. MINNIE, b. June 17, 1867; m. W. J. Glover, Jan. 31, 1888; have two children.
      2. FREDERICK F., b. Sept. 21, 1868.
      3. LILLIAN, b. Jan. 13, 1870.
      4. FRANCIS, b. July 9, 1873; d. Apr. 6, 1875.
      5. NORA MAY, b. Nov. 29, 1877.
      6. JESSE ALEX, b. Feb. 20, 1881.
    iii XENOPHON, b. Mar. 26, 1846; d. happy, Oct. 26, 1865.
230 iv ELBERT, b. Jan. 13, 1848.
    v CAROLINE, b. Sept. 19, 1849; d. Mar. 14, 1857.
    vi MARGARET, b. July 31, 1851.
    vii EMELINE, b. Aug. 15, 1853; d. Sept. 11, 1855.

viii EMELINE 2nd, b. July 9. 1855; m. Ephraim. son of Ira Doolittle, May 4, 1875, and d. Mar. 9, 1892, in Malahide, Elgin Co.
ix LIONEL James, b. Sept. 7, 1857.
x LEONI, b. Sept. 4, 1859; went to Telugu land, India, fall of 1887.
xi EDMUND JESSE, b. Dec. 5, 1861; is a Baptist minister, to Telugu land.
xii RUFUS, b. Sept. 29, 1866; d. Mar. 16, 1873.

VIII. 102 Alfred, brother to the preceding, born July 29, 1822; married Olivia, daughter of Truman and Elizabeth (Morrison) Miner at Strathroy, Ont., by Rev. William Wilkinson, Nov. 6, 1845, and settled on the east half of the two hundred acre lot given by his father to the two brothers. He was a farmer and carpenter by trade, but, from some cause or other, he sold out in Carradoc and bought again in Adelaide, corner of Lobo and Williams, 1857; sold out again in 1864, and moved to Jo Davies, Faribault Co., Minn., and bought eighty acres; sold out again in 1873, and moved down into Arkansas; moved again across the Mississippi river into Illinois, 1876, where his wife died Jan. 7. 1877, aged fifty-three; he married 2nd, Margaret E. Bridgewater, widow of Thomas Bunfill, April 26, 1877, and have lived at Cooperstown, Brown Co., since. Religiously, he "experienced religion" in June, 1842 in Malahide, Ont.; baptized by Rev. William McDormand; licensed to preach 1848; ordained to the gospel ministy in Lobo, 1851, and has preached most of the time since as a colporteur of the American Baptist Publication Society of Philadelphia, in Canada West, between Strathroy and Toronto; in Bosanquet, Lambton Co., Williams, Adelaide, Lobo and Carradoc, Middlesex Co., and since 1864 in Minnesota, Arkansas and Illinois. He was also a good singer and teacher. But in October, 1891, he received a paralytic stroke and has been confined to his house since.

Children:

i ANGELINA L., b. Sept. 19, 1846; m. James, son of William Ireland, Sept. 21, 1864; they went to Minn., also, and followed farming; he died there Nov. 9, 1875, aged 33 years 6 months. And since that time she has lived in Ontario, at Strathroy and other places, five years; Harrisville, Charlevoix, Advance, Grand Rapids, and Big Rapids, Mich., 1881-82; Cooperstown, Ill., 1883-84; Lone Oak and Rockville, Mo., 1884-85; Rushville, Beardstown and Jacksonville, Ill., 1886-87; Chicago, March to August 1887; Aurora till November; then to Kansas City, August 1888; to Canadian, Texas, November 1888, till January 1889; then to Kansas City again; bought a restaurant Jan. 2, 1890; returned to Illinois, May 1891; to Alton, spring of 1892; and to Quincy in the fall. In most of these places she did well, as tailoress, chief cook, nurse, grocer, etc. Children:—

1. Eva Jane, b. Jan. 24, 1866; m. Emerson L. Steele, Aug. 5, 1885, Strathroy, Ont.
2. Mary E., b. April 23, 1868; d. Dec. 24, 1889.
3. Edith M., b. June 17, 1871; m. George Godden, 1889, near Yale, Mich.
4. Lillie, b. Feb. 26, 1876.

ii Selina E., b. Aug. 3, 1848; m. Henry Straight, May 30, 1869; he departed 1874; she m. 2nd George C. Wilson, Nov. 1875; lived in Illinois. Children: Olivia "Straight;" Clyde C., Fay, Kirk, Porte, and Nellie "Wilson."

231 iii Martin Luther, b. Apr. 29, 1851.

iv Harriet A., b. May 20, 1854; m. George Barclift of Kentucky, in Arkansas, Feb. 11, 1875, and are living in Missouri. Children: (1) *Ethel May*, b. Nov. 15, 1876. (2) *Edith*, b. Jan. 8, 1879; d. July 3, 1881. (3) *John Alfred*, b. Jan. 18, 1881. (4) *Roy Earland*, b. July 28, 1883. (5) *Nellie Olivia*, b. Oct. 4, 1886. (6) *Vivian Maud*, b. Mar. 15, 1889. (7) *Minnie Esther*, b. Feb. 6, 1891.

232 v Andrew Fuller, b. July 17, 1856.

vi Alfred Edward, b. Feb. 10, 1861.

vii Helen Olivia, b. Feb. 28, 1863; m. William, son of Thomas Bunfill, Dec. 4, 1884, Cooperstown, Ill., and have (1) *Maggie Susan*, b. Sept. 20, 1886. (2) *Frank*, b. Sept. 29, 1887. (3) *Grace Olivia*, b. Nov. 21, 1889. (4) *Laura Agnes*, b. Feb. 19, 1892.

viii James H., b. Aug. 16, 1865, in Minnesota; m. Ida Dabb, daughter of Jacob and Margaret (Rush) Snyder, Mar. 31, 1891, and have (1) *Karl Dabb*, b. 1892, Brown Co., Ill.

VIII. 103 Sidney Chute[8] (*Andrew,*[7] *Thomas,*[6] *John,*[5] *Lionel,*[4] *James,*[3] *James,*[2] *Lionel*[1]), born Nov. 20, 1824; married in Bayham Ont., Phebe, daughter of Israel and Betsy Williams, by Rev. Samuel Baker, Apr, 19, 1846, and lived in Bayham, on the west town line, joining Malahide; a farmer; his wife died July 11, 1863, aged thirty-eight; he married 2nd, Harriet Markle (*John Murry, Benjamin*), Mar. 21, 1864. He sold out his farm (one hundred acres) in Bayham, 1873, and bought a lot in St. Thomas, county seat of Elgin Co., built and moved there 1874. Mr· Chute visited his native land in 1869-70.

Children :

8 i Mahlon, b. Feb. 10, 1847.
ii Nancy E., b. Aug. 12, 1848; d. Oct. 1849.
iii Mary O., b. July 27, 1849; d. Oct. 1849.
234 iv James Albert, b. Oct. 3, 1850.
Thur William, b. Mar. 23, 1852.

vi EGERTON R., b. June 4, 1853; m. Kate A. Morse, Dec. 13, 1885, in South Dakota; had Nettie, b. 1886.

236 vii HERBERT M., b. Sept. 12, 1854.

viii MARIETTA M., b. Nov. 13, 1855; m. Isaac, son of Jacob Robenson, Sept. 1873, and lived on the east town line of Bayham. Ch.:
1. JAMES ISAAC, b. Feb. 26, 1875.
2. WILLIAM ARTHUR, b. April 19, 1877.
3. RICHARD EDWIN, b. Aug. 3, 1879.
4. ALBERT LORNE, b. Dec. 31, 1885.
5. MARY PEARL, b. Dec. 24, 1887.

ix ANDREW JUDSON, b. April 2, 1857; drowned in Otter Creek, June 19, 1870.

237 x JOHN BUNYAN, b. July 30, 1859.

xi MARTLAND, b. Dec. 3, 1860; m. Jennie E. Bentley, Oct. 26, 1884; and is a machinist near Chicago.

xii SIDNEY, b. June 1863; d. soon after.

xiii ROBERT SIDNEY, b. Sept. 30, 1867; m. Susanna, da. of John Kinsman, 2nd jr., of Perth Co., Ont. Sept. 6, 1887. Is a machinist in St. Thomas, Ont.

xiv SARAH ANN, b. June 15, 1869; m. Frank Campbell Nov. 13, 1888.

xv ALICE L., b. May 23, 1871; m. Henry Bently, 1890.

xvi LILLIE, b. Jan. 13, 1878.

xvii HATTIE MAY, b. 1880; d. 1882.

xviii FRANK, b. Aug. 24, 1883.

VIII. 104 **Ezekiel Chute,**[8] (*Andrew,*[7] *Thomas,*[6] *John,*[5] *Lionel,*[4] *James,*[3] *James,*[2] *Lionel*[1]), born Feb. 20, 1827; married Eliza McConnell, by Rev. A. Chute, in Malahide, Ont., June 23, 1852; and lived a few years on a part of his father's farm in Bayham; then sold out to his father and bought a small farm west of the "Jubilee Meeting Huose," in Malahide, built on it, then bought out part of the old Jacob Northrup farm, across the road, and there for twenty years lived a good farmer carpenter and mason, also deacon in the Baptist church. About 1880, he bought and located in Ridgetown, Kent Co. But in two or three years he came back, bought and built in Aylmer, Elgin Co., and is there a cabinet maker. He was to Nova Scotia on a visit in 1850, and again with his wife in 1873.

Children:

i JAMES EDWARD, b. Aug. 24, 1853; m. Helen, dau. of Andrew McLeish, Feb. 17, 1875, and he lives on his father's farm in Malahide; one da. Lida Mary, b. May 4, 1882.

ii JULIA, b. Dec. 25, 1855; married Robert A., son of George McConnell, from Ireland, Aug. 4, 1875; Mr. McConnell taught school several years, but being exercised in mind and prompted to preach the gospel, he has been

a preacher in the Baptist church ten years in Mich.; now, winter of 1892-93, at Belding, Ionia Co. Children:
1. LAURA MAY, b. May 10, 1876.
2. NELLIE GRACE, b. Jan. 14, 1878.
3. MINNIE ALBERTA, b. Sept. 24, 1881.

VIII. 105 Freeman Chute,[8] (*Andrew,[7] Thomas,[6] John,[5] Lionel,[4] James,[4] James,[2] Lionel [1]*), born May 30, 1829; after sailing on the lakes and moving barns a few years, he married Elizabeth, daughter of Adam and Anna (Karns) Dodge, descendant of Tristram Dodge of Block Island, R. I., 1660, by Rev. A. Chute, Sept. 16, 1858, and settled on his father's old farm in Bayham, Ont. His wife died Oct. 14, 1861, aged twenty-two years, seven months, thirteen days; he married 2nd, Rhoda Ann, daughter of Asa K. and Clarissa (Waters) Warren (*As Col. Gideon*), by Rev. A Chute, Apr. 30, 1862, near London, Middlesex Co. Mr. Chute, like his father, is much given to hospitality; a farmer, runner of thrashing machines and justice of peace. He visited his native land the winter of 1852–1853 and again in 1873 with his wife.

Children:

238 i EDGAR MILFORD, b. Nov. 29, 1859.
ii WARREN LATIMER, b. Aug. 29, 1863.
iii CLARA MATILDA, b. Sept. 26, 1866; d. Apr. 22, 1875.
iv HARVEY HAVELOCK, b. June 4, 1869; m. Oct. 3, 1869, Lucinda, daughter of George and Catharine Ann McGee.

VIII. 106 William Edward,[8] (*Andrew,[7] Thomas,[6] John,[5] Lionel,[4] James,[3] James,[2] Lionel [1]*), born April 24, 1832; married by Rev. Alfred Chute, at his house in Adelaide, Ont., Mary Ann, daughter of Walter and Phebe (Brown) Hill (*Charles, John*), from Bucks Co., Pa., to Canada, April 24, 1861; drove a covered wagon (prairie schooner), across Wisconsin to Minnesota, July 1862, time of the great outbreak of the Sioux Indians, under Little Crow, their chief: bought out a prairie claim, built a hewed log house, and there settled, two miles west of Blue Earth City, Jo Davies, Faribault Co. In Dec., 1863, the call was so urgent for soldiers in the army, to put down the rebellion, he volunteered at Blue Earth City, Jan. 5, 1864, went to Fort Snelling and St. Paul; mustered into the United States service Feb. 24, into Co. H, 2nd Minn. V. I., (most of the regiment being home on furlough), as a veteran recruit, and went South in March, on sleighs down the Mississippi river, to La Crosse, Wis., then by cars to Chicago, Louisville, Ky., and Nashville, Tenn., then marched (March 23), via. Murfreesboro, Shelbyville, and Tallahoma to Stevenson, Ala., and thence to Chattanooga by rail.

After two days there they marched across the country eighteen miles (camped one night near the Chickamauga battle-ground), to Ringgold, North Georgia, the middle of April. There they rested, drilled and recruited three weeks, and started out on the great campaign under Generals Sherman, Thomas, McPherson, Howard, Palmer, Logan, Dodge, Blair, Slocomb, and others, May 7, about 100,000 strong, and was with the army in their marches, countermarches and bivouacks, to the taking of Marietta, Atlanta, Savannah, etc. He was in the 2nd Brig., 3d Div., 14th army corps. After three weeks in and near Savannah, they marched up the Savannah river twenty-five or thirty miles, crossed over in Jan. 1865, on pontoon bridges into South Carolina, and went through some cold, wet and muddy tramps, crossing the Saluda, Wateree, Great Pedee, Cape Fear and other rivers on pontoon bridges, and arrived at Goldsboro, N. C., the last of March. Being in the left wing of Sherman's army they encountered the rebel, Gen. Wheeler's, cavalry several times. While at Goldsboro the joyful news came of the surrender of Gen. Lee to Gen. Grant; and the dreadful news of the death of President Lincoln! About the twentieth of April, they marched northward through Raleigh, N. C., (when Johnston surrendered to Sherman), and went into camp, south side of James river, near Richmond, Va., May 7, exactly a year from breaking camp in Ringgold, Ga., the year before, and in counting up it was found that they had marched exactly two thousand miles.

They crossed James river on pontoons and marched through Richmond by Libby prison and Castle Thunder, and on to Washington, wading across half a dozen mountain streams and went into camp back of Arlington Heights May 18; then were in the grand review in Washington, May 24 (Gen. Grant's army of the Potomac reviewed the day before), and the last of the month they crossed over the Potomac river and went into camp at Fort Bunker Hill, just back of Washington, in Maryland.

On June 14 they left, and went via. the Baltimore and Ohio railroad across to Parkersburg, West Virginia, thence by steamboat down the Ohio river, calling at Cincinnatti, to Louisville, Ky., and there about three miles out went into camp till July 11; then by railroad to Chicago, Ill., and LaCrosse, Wis., and steamboat to St. Paul; they were returned home, and mustered out at Fort Snelling the twenty-first. Then Mr. Chute returned to his home near Blue Earth City, and there "reconstructed" somewhat, but the severe winters rather "scared him out," so he sold out in 1869, and in 1870 drove a team and moved across Iowa to Maysville, De Kalb Co., Mo., and next year to Island City, Gentry Co., then to Albany, the county seat. In 1872 moved to Guilford, Nodaway Co., and that summer drove across the Missouri river into Kansas; went far as Topeka, and returned again into Missouri, bought a lot, built and settled in Bolckow, Andrew Co. During his sojourn there of five winters he taught about thirty singing classes in five counties, DeKalb, Gentry, Nodaway, Andrew and Clinton. But the grasshoppers came over so thick from Kansas in 1874, threatening a famine, that he sold out there in the spring of 1875, and returned to St. Thomas, Ont., and there for four winters taught singing in Elgin, Middlesex and Lambton counties.

In the fall of 1879 he crossed the St. Clair river into Michigan and there farmed it summers and taught singing ten winters. Mr. Chute received only a common school education, but commenced teaching in 1855, and taught four common schools and nearly two hundred singing schools or classes in thirty different books, in Nova Scotia, Maine, New York, Ontario, Michigan, Minnesota and Missouri. Besides learning to read music and singing in the old-fashioned singing schools, Mr. Chute attended three musical institutes, first at North Reading, Mass., summer of 1857, under Dr. Lowell Mason and George F. Root, using the Hallehujah and Sabbath Bell, and for concert exercises the Haymakers and the Messiah, (and in the fall he went to Portland, Naples and Otisfield, Me., and learned the foundation of the Chutes in America); second at Winona, Minn., Aug., 1868, under George F. Root, P. P. Bliss, T. M. Towne and O. D. Adams in the Triumph, and for concerts Mendelsohn's St. Paul; third at South Bend, Ind., summer of 1870, under G. F. Root, C. M. Wyman, P. P. Bliss, T. M.

Towne and William Mason, using the Palm, and for concerts Haydn's Creation. In all of these he studied harmony and composition, and from time to time has gathered a library of six hundred music and four hundred hymn books.

While on a visit to Nova Scotia in 1855, he commenced teaching singing in the good old American Vocalist, and there commenced gathering the records of the family connections, which are the basis of this volume. In 1885, he steamboated on the lakes all summer and in the fall went down the Erie Canal to New York, thence to Boston, thence to Portland, Me., and forty miles north of there in Otisfield, in Cumberland Co., taught a singing class that winter. In April 1886, he traveled forty miles east across the country to Augusta, visiting friends and relations; then via Waterville and Bangor, took cars to Woodstock, N. B., visiting and gathering records. Then after visiting friends at Eel river, he went down the St. John river on a raft to near Frederickton, and went up the Keswick river to the north, above Zealand Station and visited friends in York Co., then came down to Fredericton, and took a steamer to St. John, where he stopped four nights making calls and seeking out friends and relations. On May 12, he crossed the Bay of Fundy, on the steamer "Secret," to Digby, N. S., and in that province for nearly four months he traveled in four counties, from Weymouth, Digby Co., through Annapolis Co., to Kentville, Kings Co., and over to Caledonia, Queens Co., hunting the "lost tribes" of the family connection. He started at Bear River Sept. 7, on the schooner "Florence Christine." Capt. Norman W. Chute, wood and timber laden, and sailed to Boston; took steamer thence to Portland, Me., and traveled fifty miles north to Snow's Fall's, Oxford Co., calling and hunting family connections. At Portland took cars to Newburyport, Mass., thence across the country to Salem, Lynn and Boston, still searching records and gathering items and statistics.

After spending all of October, chiefly in Massachusetts, he left Boson and went to Taunton November sixth; to Providence, R. I., the eighth and on to New York city the morning of the tenth and went up to Albany on a canal boat, then through the Erie Canal, as a boat hand, to Buffalo, thence through Western Ontario, by cars to Detroit and so on home, arriving Nov. 30; taught singing again four winters; came to Boston in Aug., 1890, to the twenty-fourth annual parade of the Grand Army Republic, and stayed in the state most of the time since, searching, copying and writing up the family history. He went to Washington in Sept., 1892, to the twenty-sixth encampment of the Grand Army Republic.

Children:

  i P HEBE J OSEPHINE, b. Apr. 11, 1862; is in Minnesota.
239 ii A BRAHAM L INCOLN, b. Sept. 22, 1863.
  iii A ARON B ENJAMIN, b. Dec. 22, 1866; m. Mrs. Attie Peery, Dec. 14, 1892, in Lewistown, Mon.
  iv E MMA S ALINA, b. July 23, 1869; d. Sept. 22, 1870.
  v W ILLIAM E DWARD, b. June 4, 1871.
  vi S ARAH A NN, b. Nov. 9, 1873; d. July 28, 1874.
  vii W ALTER A NDREW, b. Aug. 2, 1876.

  Mr. Chute sailed several seasons also, chiefly on the lakes, commencing in 1853, the year the great western railroad was opened through Western Ontario connecting with the Michigan Southern railroad.

VIII. **107 Aaron Chute**[8] (*Andrew,*[7] *Thomas,*[6] *John,*[5] *Lionel,*[4] *James,*[3] *James,*[2] *Lionel*[1]), born Aug. 6, 1834; married in Bayham, Ont., by Rev. M. S. Connell, Sarah Amelia Dakin (*George, Daniel, Abram*), daughter of George and Phebe Ann (Young, daughter of Job and Hannah (Barnes) Young) Dakin, Dec. 24, 1856, and lived on the west side of his father's farm, south side of the second concession, a farmer. As he was appointed one of the executors of his father's will, in order to get funds to pay off legacies, he went to British Columbia, spring of 1862, and did well; but in coming home in the fall he was induced to stop in California and try his hand at gold mining, and somehow in Esmeralda, Mono Co., he contracted some distemper and started for Stockton to a water cure, and was found dead in bed Aug., 1863. His widow married 2nd, James, son of Michael Timmons (b. 1830), July 4, 1866, and live on the same old farm.

DEATH OF AARON CHUTE.

1.

Our father in sixty-two passed away
And left the farm to two of his sons,
Freeman and Aaron, who were to pay
The portion due to the other ones;

DEACON JOHN M. CHUTE, AND WIFE LUCY CHUTE.

  Thinking more quickly to raise his share,
   Than on the farm, he went off West
  To the land of gold, and while out there
   He worked in mines and did his best.

2.

  But overworked his health gave way,
   Doctors prescribed a change of place
  And rest, but our informants say
   He delayed too long, his careworn face
  He turned at last to a milder clime,
   And on the way, was found one morn
  In death's embrace. O! brother mine!
   To think you died so all forlorn!

3.

  'Tis sad to part with those we love,
   And know they'll no more greet us here,
  But if with Christ they reign above,
   We feel our loss much less severe.
  Dear brother Aaron is now at rest,
   His toils on earth are fully done,
  In heaven rejoicing with the blest,
   He'll wear the crown that here he won.

J. M. C.

North Branch, Mich., April, '93.

Children :

240 i GEORGE MAYNARD, b. Sept. 21, 1857.
  ii ADDIE SOPHRONIA, b. Oct. 27, 1859; m. Eugene S. Simpson, Nov. 20, 1878; live in Buffalo, N. Y., with three or four children.
  iii PHEBE ANN, b. Jan. 10, 1862; m. George William Van Velzor (*Raymond, Jacob*), Oct. 28, 1883; have two children, and live on his father's farm, 4th concession, Malahide. Second family—Timmons.
 i ROBERT FREDERICK, b. Feb. 28, 1870.
 ii JAMES EDWARD, b. May 1, 1874.
 iii MARY, b. Dec. 23, 1875.

VIII. 108 John Milton,[8] (*Andrew,*[7] *Thomas,*[6] *John,*[5] *Lionel,*[4] *James,*[3] *James,*[2] *Lionel*[1]), born in Bayham, Ont., July 28, 1843; married by James Cooper, D.D., near London, Lucy, daughter of Asa Kellogg and Clarissa (Waters) Warren, (*Asa, Col. Gideon* of the Revolution), Oct. 8, 1867; Mr. Chute being a mere boy when his father died, was sent to school and received a good education, so that he taught school in Lower Granville, N. S., in the summer of 1862, being there on a visit; then, after being home in Ontario, the next year, he attended Alleghany College, Meadville, Pa., two terms 1864-65, then taught in Port Burwell, Ont., 1866. Near the close of that year, he purchased a scholarship in the Bryant & Stratton chain of Commercial colleges, and went to Chicago, Ill., and attended there graduating in 1867. Soon after he got a situation as bookkeeper with Wisdom & Son, where he remained till July 1871, when he packed up and moved to Gentry Co., Mo., (time of the great fire in Chicago), and there taught a set of singing classes that winter, returning to Chicago again in June 1872; and there engaged as shipping clerk for Hepp & Shoenthaler. In 1873, he became bookkeeper for Smith Bros., but in the fall he moved to London, Ont., and opened a store for the sale of musical instruments, making a speciality of the Mason & Hamlin organ. In 1875, he changed his relations into the subscription book business, which he prosecuted with success till 1879, when he moved to Oakland Co., Mich., and there and in St. Clair Co., he taught music. He moved to Deckerville, Sanilac Co., in the fall of 1880, and there taught the public schools. In December, 1881, he opened a jeweler shop and sold sewing machines; but moved to North Branch, Lapeer Co., in 1885, and has been jeweler and stationer there since; also chorister, superintendent in the Sunday-school, and deacon in the Baptist church. Since 1890 he has acted as Deputy Great Commander of the Knights of the Maccabees, and has organized several tents, thus building up the cause in the state at large. His father-in-law, Asa K. Warren, brother to Dr. Ira Warren (1806-1864), of Boston, claimed near relationship to Gen. Joseph Warren (1741-1775); died near London, Ont., May 3, 1867, aged sixty-nine; Clarissa Waters, his widow died Feb. 27, 1881, aged seventy-nine years.

Children:

   i MINNIE GERTRUDE, b. Sept. 8, 1869, school teacher and music teacher.
   ii MILTON AUGUSTUS, b. Aug. 22, 1872; painter.
   iii ANDREW ELLIS, b. Dec. 7, 1874.
   iv FREDERICK. b. June 5, 1881.

VIII. 109 James Manning Chute,[8] (*Abel,*[7] *Thomas,*[6] *John,*[5] *Lionel,*[4] *James,*[3] *James,*[2] *Lionel*[1]), born in Clements, N. S., May 16, 1819; married Leah, daughter of Asa and Rhoda (Hicks) Foster, by Rev.

Nathaniel Viditoe, June 19, 1840, and lived near his father, two miles east of Bear River, till 1848, when he sold out and moved to Malahide, Ont., in November, lived on his uncle Philip Barteaux's farm two years, then bought a one hundred acre lot, on the 3rd concession, near Silver Creek, built a brick house on it and did well. But about 1873, he sold out and moved to Wheatly, Essex Co., eighty miles west, bought a splendid farm there and accumulated property worth $10,000; a Christian man and a farmer, he died Feb 17, 1878; she died Oct 30, 1891, aged seventy-one years and nine months.

Children;

    i HARRIET CALVERT, b. June 7, 1841; m. William A. Foster, Jan. 2, 1864; he d. Jan. 28, aged 24; she m. 2nd, in Nova Scotia, Alfred Marshall. See No. 13.

241 ii ASA WATSON, b. July 26, 1843.

    iii CATHARINE SOPHIA, b. Dec. 6, 1847; m. William Henry, son of James E. Vail, Jan., 1868; had eight children in Yarmouth, Ont.; moved to a western state.

    iv JANET M., b. Apr. 27, 1853; m. George, son of Russell Fox, Oct. 26, 1872; lived at Lamington, Essex Co., Ont.; had two sons; she d. Mar. 21, 1880; he m. 2nd, —— Chamberlain.

    v ABEL MARSHALL, b. June 7, 1857; m. Emma Snyder, July 1, 1879, and d. May 22, 1880; she m. again.

    vi JAMES MILLEDGE, b. Dec. 26, 1858; m. Phebe, daughter of Russell Fox, 1880, and has the old farm.

242 vii FRANK S., b. Apr. 2, 1861.

    viii MARY LOUISE, b. Apr. 7, 1864; m. George D. Smith, 1889.

VIII. 110 Joseph Warren Chute,[8] (*Abel,*[7] *Thomas,*[6] *John,*[5] *Lionel,*[4] *James,*[3] *James,*[2] *Lionel* [1]), born Mar. 13, 1821; married Eliza F., daughter of Deacon John and Bethia (Chipman) Wilson, by Rev. Harris Harding, Dec. 26, 1847, and lived on the east side of his father's farm in Clements. He went to sea some, to Boston, etc.; died Nov. 20, 1866.

Children:

243 i HANDLEY CHIPMAN, b. Aug. 25, 1850.

    ii JUSTIN R., b. June 25, 1860; d. Mar. 27, 1889.

    iii ABBIE MAY, b. Aug. 18, 1865; m. Charles, son of Jeremiah, son of Charles Van Buskirk, Nov. 1, 1882, and have four children.

VIII. 111 Harris Harding Chute,[8] (*Abel,*[7] *Thomas,*[6] *John,*[5] *Lionel,*[4] *James,*[3] *James,*[2] *Lionel* [1]), born Dec. 27, 1822; married Elizabeth, daughter of David and Mary (Kniffin) Rice, Jan. 25, 1848, and lived at Bear River ; a merchant, vessel owner, mill owner and dealer in real estate. He followed mercantile business till 1880, and then retired, but was elected to the municipal council of Annapolis, 1886 and 1888; in 1887 was warden of the county. In 1890 he was nominated as the colleague of Attorney General James Wilberforce Longley and was elected in May with a large majority. He was also an active and pious deacon in the Baptist church over thirty years; and in the summer of 1890 was elected a member of the Nova Scotia Parliament for Annapolis Co., and died at the Albion hotel, Halifax, Mar. 31, 1892, and buried at his home in Bear River. His property is estimated at over $100,000.

Children :

   i CHARLES HERBERT, b. June 1, 1850; went a trip to the West Indies with Captain John Graham in the schooner "Lizzie Chute,"* in the fall of 1867, which was wrecked and all hands lost seven in number, at Chebogue, near Yarmouth, N. S., Jan. 10, 1868.

   ii MARIETTA, b. May 2, 1854; m. William Wallace Clark, (*Richard, William, Richard*), Dec. 20, 1883, and have two children, merchants at Bear River.

ON THE LOSS OF DEACON H. H. CHUTE'S THREE VESSELS.

1.

From the Isle of Cape Breton, the port of Cow Bay,
A schooner, the "Vivid," had started one day
Coal laden for Halifax, sails were all set,
But failed on the ocean by storms that they met.

2.

Daniel Johnson, the captain, and crew of good men,
A minister and wife and six children, all then
With good cheer and prospects upon the great main,
But alas! they went down, their hopes were in vain.

3.

And then "Lizzie Chute," was another by name,
From West Indies coming with Captain John Graham,
She struck on the rocks on January ten,
And met a sad fate in all seven men.

4.

A young man among them, Charles Herbert, the one,
Only son of the owner, who now felt undone,

---

* Deacon Chute lost two other vessels, one the "Vivid," Capt. Daniel Johnson, coal laden, Dec. 1867, from Cape Breton to Halifax, with six men, a minister, wife and six children; and another the "Heiress," lumber laden, burned at the mouth of Bear River.

> But they went, with the mate, David Pyne and George Vroom,
> And a colored cook too, a very sad doom.
>
> 5.
>
> Another, the "Heiress," at Bear River's mouth,
> Was well lumber laden and off for the South;
> But alas! she was doomed and by fire consumed,
> And so the trip ended as may be presumed.
>
> C. E. W.
>
> June, 1893.

VIII. 112 William Ozias,[8] (*Abel,[7] Thomas,[6] John,[5] Lionel,[4] James,[3] James,[2] Lionel[1]*), born Aug. 29, 1845: married Emma Catharine Berry (*Peter, Thomas*), May 28, 1866, and lived on his father's old farm, a farmer: died of consumption August, 1881.

Children:

    i EDWARD RAYMOND, b. Mar. 22, 1867; m. Annie Frazer, Feb. 29, 1892, in Boston; two children.
    ii ADA BEATRICE, b. Dec. 19, 1868; m. Harding Zwicker, Dec. 29, 1887.
    iii WILLIAM HARDING, b. Dec. 15, 1870; d. Mar. 23, 1876.
    iv ERNEST LIONEL, b. Dec. 20, 1872; d. Feb. 29, 1876.
    v LIZZIE MAUD, b. Aug. 23, 1874; d. Mar. 16, 1876.
    vi LOTTIE OLIVIA, b. Mar. 14, 1876.
    vii HARRY H., b. Feb. 17, 1879.

VIII. 113 Isaiah Chute,[8] (*Calvin,[7] Thomas,[6] John,[5] Lionel,[4] James,[3] James,[2] Lionel[1]*), born in Clements, N. S., Mar. 22, 1823; married Priscilla Purday, Jan. 21, 1847; moved to Salem, Mass., 1851; a pious, industrious carpenter. His wife a smart, Christian woman, died Dec. 2, 1886, aged fifty-five. Mr. Chute had a grand visit to Western Ontario, and Detroit, Mich., in September, 1889, and in August, 1891, was there again, and also to St. Paul, Minneapolis, Sleepy Eye and Blue Earth City, Minn, Mariaville, Neb., and Chicago, Ill. Then to Nova Scotia, 1892. Mr. Chute was also in Co. B, 7th Mass. in the late war.

Children:

    i RUPERT JAMES, b. March 7, 1848; m. Lelia J., dau. of Daniel and Mary Robinson, June 14, 1868; and has reported for several newspapers, in Salem, Lynn and Boston. She d. at Amherest, Mass., Aug. 1891, aged 41.
    ii ALICE M., b. July 29, 1849; m. Charles Warner, June 10, 1874, and live in Peabody.
    iii ANNA MARIA, b. Sept. 4, 1851; m. R. J. Chute. See No. 120.
    iv EBEN POOR, b. Oct. 29, 1853; d. July 24, 1855.

v ELIZA JANE, b. Nov. 14, 1855; d. Sept. 3, 1858.
vi LIZZIE FLORENCE, b. Oct. 15, 1857; m. Robert Milton Hutchinson (*Edward, James*), from Scotland to Richibucto, N. B., time of the Revolution, Nov. 25, 1887, and live in Salem. Children. (1.) *Jesse Milton*, b. 1888. (2.) *Ethel Marguerite*, b. 1889. (3.) *John Lionel*, b. 1891.
vii CHARLES FREEMAN, b. Sept. 20, 1859; d. Jan. 20, 1872.
viii HOWARD E., b. May 22, 1862; d. Sept. 21, 1862.
ix ALBERT PATILLO, b. Feb. 7, 1864; m. Lillian, dau. of Robert John Sewall, April 28, 1887, and went to Buenos Ayres, S. A., and lived at Rosario, Argentine Republic; dau. Gracie Potter, b. Aug. 12, 1889. They returned again to Lynn, Mass., 1890, and now live in Salem. He is a bookkeeper.
x ARTHUR PURDAY, b. May 4, 1866; d. Jan. 12, 1872.

VIII. 114 Thomas Chute,[8] (*Calvin,[7] Thomas,[6] John,[5] Lionel,[4] James,[3] James,[2] Lionel[1]*), born in Clements, N. S., Sept. 21, 1826; married Sarah, daughter of Jesse Kean jr., Mar. 5, 1850, by Rev. E. W. Pray, near Digby; moved to Marblehead, Mass., the same year, and between there and Swampscott for fourteen years, worked several big farms, one the Brookhouse farm, and did well. But in time of the war, 1864, he thought to do better and so moved to South Bend, Blue Earth Co., Minn., bought and located there; but in 1866, he went farther up the Minnesota river, bought half a section of prairie and located near Sleepy Eye, Brown Co., and there they still abide; farmers.

Children :

i HENRY ALLINE, b. June 3, 1851.
ii ANNA MARIA, b. Aug. 5, 1853; m. Theodore G. Wood, 1876; Orie Ella, b. 1878.
244 iii ARTHUR WELLINGTON, b. Apr. 1, 1856.
iv OCIELLA, b. Feb. 17, 1859.

VIII. 115 Andrew Chute,[8] (*Calvin,[7] Thomas,[6] John,[5] Lionel,[4] James,[3] James,[2] Lionel[1]*), born in Clements, N. S., June 13, 1828, came to Salem, Mass., 1850; married Isabella, daughter of Jeremiah Porter of Nova Scotia, Mar. 22, 1852, and located at Swampscott, shoemaker. He went into Co. B, 23rd Mass., in the late war, taken prisoner in Virginia, and died in Andersonville prison in Georgia, 1864.

Children :

245 i THEODORE HARDING PORTER, b. Aug. 26, 1854.
ii EDGAR EUGENE, b. May 11, 1856; passenger and mail carrier, Swampscott.
iii EMMA BELLE, b. Oct. 1, 1858; m. John T. Lowe, Sept. 8, 1881; a gas and steam pipe fitter, Boston.

VIII. 116 William Henry Chute,[8] (*Calvin,*[7] *Thomas,*[6] *John,*[5] *Lionel,*[4] *James,*[3] *James,*[2] *Lionel*[1]), born in Nova Scotia, Nov. 28, 1847, and brought up partly in Nova Scotia and partly in Salem, Mass. He received a tolerably good education, so that he has taught singing, written and composed some hymns and tunes; and has exercised his gifts some as an evangelist among the Adventists. Latterly a painter in Salem and Lynn. He married Fanny Isabel Savory,[7] (*Nathan,*[6] *Nathan,*[5] *Uriah,*[4] *Thomas,*[4] *Samuel,*[2] *Thomas,*[1] England to America 1634,) Nov. 21, 1870, and lived twenty years in Digby Co., N. S., a painter, then came to Salem.

Children :

    i FANNY ELLEN, b. Dec. 16, 1871; m. George M. Morse, Jan. 11, 1893.
    ii MINNIE ADA, b. Nov. 12, 1873.
    iii IRA MOODY, b. Jan. 17, 1876.
    iv LIZZIE MAY, b. Jan. 10, 1878.
    v CHARLES DUNHAM. b. Apr. 7, 1880; d. Mar. 12, 1882.
    vi WILLIAM MAXWELL, b. Dec. 22, 1881.
    vii JAMES KINSMAN, b. Sept. 13, 1884.
    viii RUPERT DYER, b. June 28, 1887.
    ix VERNIE FLORENCE, b. June 28, 1887.

VIII. 117 Hiram Chute,[8] (*John,*[7] *Thomas,*[6] *John,*[5] *Lionel,*[4] *James,*[3] *James,*[2] *Lionel*[1]), born in Clements, N. S., Dec. 21, 1822; married Isabella, daughter of Robert Taylor, by Rev. Joshua B. Cogswell, Aug. 1, 1850, and lived at or near Frederickton, N. B. He early went to sea and advanced step by step till he became captain of the British brig Robert Reed, which sailed to Boston from Matanzas, W. I., with a cargo of molasses in August, 1858; was drowned in the harbor the night of Sept. 1, found the fifth and buried.

Children :

    i ANNETTA, b. June, 1851; m. William Irvine, 1870; had two children.
    ii EUINA M., b. 1854; m. Thomas Earle, 1877, and had five children.

VIII. 118 Joseph Burton,[8] (*John,*[7] *Thomas,*[6] *John,*[5] *Lionel,*[4] *James,*[3] *James,*[2] *Lionel*[1]), born in Clements, Feb. 7, 1829; married Rachel Clark (*Joseph, Richard*), by Rev. Aaron Cogswell, Apr. 22, 1852, and has lived most of the time since at Bear River, and has done some immense business raising and moving buildings, vessels, etc. He lived on a part of his father's farm, but since 1890 has occupied the whole of it.

Children :

246 i WILLIAM ALPHEUS, b. Sept. 9, 1853.
  ii ROBERT WINTHROP, b. Dec. 29, 1856; m. Ada Warden, Jan. 18, 1886, and was a traveling salesman; he settled in Boston and was killed by the cars Oct. 15, 1888; his widow m. 2nd, John Porter.
  iii JOSEPH BERNHARD, b. March 20, 1870; d. Oct. 13.
  iv FLORA ESTELLA, b. Feb. 7, 1876; d. Nov. 1.
  v LAILA MAUD, b. Dec. 26, 1876.

VIII. 119 William Henry,[8] (*John,*[7] *Thomas,*[6] *John,*[5] *Lionel,*[4] *James,*[3] *James,*[2] *Lionel*[1]), born in Clements, March 5, 1831; married Louise, daughter of Dea. James Manning Potter, Esq., by Rev. M. Pickles, Sept. 23, 1856; and occupied his father's farm till 1888, when he moved over to Boston, worked at spar making, but now lives in Everett.

Children:

247 i JAMES POTTER, b. Aug. 4, 1857.
  ii HIRAM FREDERICK, b. July 21, 1861; m. Ada Z., dau. of J. D. Mabee, jr., March 24, 1886, and live at Hampton, N. B. (1.) *Zilla Louise,* b. Dec. 1886.
  iii JOHN HENRY, b. Oct. 7, 1866; m. Jessie, dau. of E. L. Kent, Sept. 28, 1892, Medford.
  iv BERNARD L., b. Fed. 27, 1873; d. Feb. 3, 1878.
  v ARTHUR R., b. April 2, 1882; d. Dec. 27, 1887.

VIII. 120 Robert John,[8] (*John,*[7] *Thomas,*[6] *John,*[5] *Lionel,*[4] *James,*[3] *James,*[2] *Lionel*[1]), born in Clements, Mar, 3, 1833; married Eliza H. Baldwin, of Melrose, Mass., 1862; she died June 16, 1866, aged twenty-nine; he married 2nd, Anna Maria, daughter of Isaiah and Priscilla Chute (see No. 113), Aug. 26, 1869; he was a photographer, in Philadelphia and Boston, twenty years ; and in 1885 went to Buenos Ayres, S. A., and followed the same business at Rosario, Argentine Republic. He died there March 26, 1893.

Children :

  i ELENA ADELAIDE, b. Apr. 1, 1864; d. Aug. 28, 1865.
  ii ELIZA ANN, b. June, 1866.
  iii WILLIAM W., b. May 18, 1874.
  iv CHARLES W., b. Dec. 26, 1879.

VIII. 121 Lyman Wallace Chute,[8] (*John,*[7] *Thomas,*[6] *John,*[5] *Lionel,*[4] *James,*[3] *James,*[2] *Lionel*[1]), born in Clements, Nov. 8, 1845; married Adela, daughter of Admiral Parker of Uruguay, S. A., Sept. 2,

1872, and is an extensive land owner in that part of the world. He has been there now twenty-six years and is reckoned among the wealthy. Lives in Buenos Ayres.

Children:

    i GEORGE ALFREDO, b. 1873.
    ii AMELIA S., b. 1876.
    iii ELENA, b. 1878.

VIII. 122 James Edward,[8] (*Binea,*[7] *Thomas,*[6] *John,*[5] *Lionel,*[4] *James,*[3] *James,*[2] *Lionel* [1]), born in Clements, N. S., Oct. 18, 1830; went to Salem, Mass., 1851; a carpenter; married Sarah, daughter of James and Mary Nichols, and widow of William H. Skinner, Dec. 26, 1853, and till 1877 followed his trade there steadily, when he went to Ontario and worked in Bayham and Malahide; then at Thamesville in Kent Co., and settled in Ridgetown, 1882; sold out there and returned to Salem, Mass., 1889, built a new house on Barr street, and is now well located in North Salem. His wife died in Boston, Nov. 15, 1885, aged fifty-nine. William H. Skinner died Aug. 31, 1851, aged twenty-four; his son, William H. jr., died Oct. 9, 1874, aged twenty-three. Mr. Chute married 2nd, Anna, daughter of Samuel and Lydia (Elliott) Williams, July 10, 1886. Miss Williams, born July 10, 1832; married 1st, Aaron Lane Burnham,* and had George F., born 1853; married Sarah Davis and live in Salem; 2nd, Alice Augusta, born June 17, 1855; married Richard Lander (she died Sept. 18, 1883; he married 2nd, Anna Miller). Mr. Burnham died at sea 1855, aged twenty-four; she married 2nd, Thomas, son of Abner Hall from Liverpool, N. S., Sept. 9, 1863, and had Thomas Henry, born 1865; died 1868. Mr. Hall died 1870, aged forty-one. He married 1st, Lovenia Smith; had four children; she died young and the daughter, Elnora, born 1860; married Raymond Rich, and live in Bangor, Me.

Children:

    i CHARLES E., b. Dec. 4, 1854; a musician; d. in Boston, Nov. 5, 1885.
    ii SARAH LOUISE, b. Apr. 3, 1857; m. George Henry Shepherd, Apr. 3, 1879, and d. July 8.
    iii M. NELLIE, b. 1859; d. 1862.
    iv FLORA SYMONDS, b. Oct. 24, 1863; m. Alfred Ernest, son of Israel and Louise (Cook) Hersey, Oct. 16, 1889, and live at Manchester, Mass.

* A. L. Burnham,[7] Capt. Joseph,[6] 1801-1864, Joseph,[5] Joseph,[4] David,[3] John,[2] Lieut. Thomas[1] of Salem, 1633, over to Ipswich, 1636; m. Mary, daughter of John Tuttle, and d. June, 1694.

v ARNOLD S., b. May 20, 1869; d. Sept. 6, 1891.
vi ADDIE F., b. May 20, 1869; m. Geo. A. Lawrence, Feb. 22, 1890, and lives in Peabody.

VIII. 123 Charles Peter,[8] (*Binea,*[7] *Thomas,*[6] *John,*[5] *Lionel,*[4] *James,*[3] *James,*[2] *Lionel*[1]), born in Clements, Jan. 1, 1832; went to Ontario, 1855, worked with Ezekiel Chute and others as a carpenter, and got means to buy the Alum Marr farm (that he inherited of his father-in-law, Thomas Clarkson) at Vienna, and there lives comfortably. He has held some town offices. He married Helen, daughter of Deacon Kenneth and Christine (McConnell) Hankinson, Jan. 27, 1864.

Children:

i MELVIN, b. Nov. 24, 1864; drowned in Otter Creek, Sept. 4, 1875.
ii ESTELLA, b. Apr. 14, 1868.
iii WILLIAM BINEA, b. Apr. 9, 1870.
iv MARY ANN, b. May 8, 1874.
v CHARLES LINDON, b. Mar. 29, 1876.

VIII. 124 Nathan Chute,[8] (*Binea,*[7] *Thomas,*[6] *John,*[5] *Lionel,*[4] *James,*[3] *James,*[2] *Lionel*[1]), born in Clements, June 28, 1833; married Georgiana, daughter of Deacon Jacob Troop, May 4, 1858, and lived near Bear River till 1882, when he moved to Malahide, Ont.

Children:

i ELLA, b. 1862; m. ——.
ii EDWIN, b. 1872.
iii LAUREN O., b. 1880.

VIII. 125 George,[8] (*Binea,*[7] *Thomas,*[6] *John,*[5] *Lionel,*[4] *James,*[3] *James,*[2] *Lionel*[1]), born in Clements, Oct. 6, 1838; married Sarah Louise, daughter of William Crouse, Oct. 6, 1864; lived with his father a few years longer, and in 1876, moved to Malahide, Ont.

Children:

i WILLIAM OSBORN, b. Oct. 1865.
ii HARRIET MAY, b. Aug. 1867; m. John T. Kipp, Dec. 23, 1886.
iii VERNON, b. Oct. 1878.

VIII. 126 William Albert,[8] (*Binea,*[7] *Thomas,*[6] *John,*[5] *Lionel,*[4] *James,*[3] *James,*[2] *Lionel*[1]), born in Clements, June 2, 1840; married E. Josephine, daughter of John Henry and Lemna (Van Buskirk) Harris, May 28, 1864; worked at Bear River a few years as carpenter, then moved to Vienna, Oct., 1872, worked there and in Aylmer, till 1889, when he moved to Grand Rapids, Mich.

Children :

248 i FRANK AUGUSTUS, b. Aug. 23, 1865.
　　ii CARRIE E., b. July 20, 1869; in Boston.
　　iii LILLIAN B., b. Nov. 18, 1871.
　　iv HARRY, b. June 14, 1875.
　　v EDWARD V. B., b. Oct. 18, 1878.

VIII. 127 James Milledge,[8] (*James Edward,*[7] *Thomas,*[6] *John,*[5] *Lionel,*[4] *James,*[3] *James,*[2] *Lionel*[1]), born in Clements, N. S., Oct. 19, 1846; went to Salem, Mass., with parents and sisters, 1855; to Boston, 1864; married Martha D., daughter of James P. and Catharine (Marshall) Pierce, by Rev. Franklin Johnson, D.D., in Cambridge, Feb. 28, 1878. Mr. Chute has been an active enterprising salesman and grocer, also newspaper reporter. He wrote a valuable history of postal communication etc.

Children :

　　i ARTHUR FOSTER, b. March 22, 1882; d. Aug. 10, 1884.
　　ii PERCY H. MARSHALL, b. May 15, 1886.

VIII. 128 James Parker Chute,[8] (*Silas,*[7] *James,*[6] *John,*[5] *Lionel,*[4] *James,*[3] *James,*[2] *Lionel*[1]), born in Wilmot, Annapolis Co., N. S., Sept. 24, 1813; married Mary E., daughter of Robert King, Oct. 21, 1838, and moved to Yarmouth, that fall, was a farmer; died March 18, 1884; his widow died Sept. 11, 1882, aged seventy-two years and seven months. Her mother, Mary Elizabeth Van Emburg, widow of Robert King, died 1862, aged one hundred and four.

Children :

　　i ALEXANDER SELKIRK, b. June 2, 1840, lost at sea, mate of a vessel, about 1865.
　　ii ELIZABETH ANN, b. Nov. 23, 1841; m. George E. Archer, April 9, 1865; dau. Florence E., b. Oct. 9, 1868. Mr. Archer died Oct. 19, 1870, aged 30; and soon after the widow and daughter went to Boston, Mass.
　　iii MARY JANE, b. June 5, 1843; d. Sept. 4, 1885.
　　iv PHEBE, b. Dec. 26, 1844; m. Joseph Benjamin Crosby,[8] (*Benjamin,*[7] *Benjamin,*[6] *Ebenezer,*[5] *Jonathan,*[4] *John,*[3] *Rev. Thomas,*[2] *Simon*[1]), (the ancestor over from England to Cambridge, 1635; d. 1639, aged 30), May 1, 1865; and live in Brookline, Mass.
　　　　1. GEORGE FRED, b. May 18, 1866, is a fine architect in Brookline.

v CAROLINE M., b. June 27, 1846; m. Patrick Kerrigan, 1870, and are in Boston.
vi JOSEPHINE, b. Oct. 8, 1853; m. William A. Killam 1873, near Yarmouth, N. S.

VIII. 129 Isaac Roach Chute,[8] (*Silas*,[7] *James*,[6] *John*,[5] *Lionel*,[4] *James*,[3] *James*,[2] *Lionel*[1]), born in Wilmot, Jan. 10, 1817; married Sarah Ann, daughter of John Prince, Apr. 21, 1842, and moved to Yarmouth that summer; was a wheelwright and a custom officer for some time. Mrs. Chute died June 8, 1857, aged thirty-four; he married 2nd, Edith, daughter of Thomas Churchill and widow of Amasa Rodney (lost at sea about 1850, leaving a daughter, Alva Jane married Captain George P. Vickery), Feb. 25, 1858, and had four children—three died young. Mr. Chute died Feb. 2, 1875.

Children:

i GEORGE P., b. June 3, 1843; d. July 2, 1850.
ii AZOR D., b. Mar. 15, 1845; d. at sea Mar. 20, 1880.
iii BENJAMIN, b. Feb. 19, 1848; d. Sept. 25, 1849.
iv HARRIET A., b. Sept. 9, 1850; d. Sept. 15, 1852.
v ALBERT, b. Nov. 3, 1852.
vi HARVEY, b. Mar. 25, 1855; d. July 6, 1857.
vii FRANCIS, b. Aug. 3, 1856; d. Jan. 24, 1857.
viii MAY EDITH, b. Mar. 18, 1869; m. Edward F. Cann, and live at Darling's Lake, Yarmouth Co., N. S.

VIII. 130 John Matthew Chute,[8] (*Silas*,[7] *James*,[6] *John*,[5] *Lionel*,[4] *James*,[3] *James*,[2] *Lionel*[1]), born Jan. 23, 1819; married Margaret, daughter of James Whitman, 1841. Mr. Chute was a good school teacher, and taught in Halifax, Aylesford and other places. He died at or near Nictaux, July 15, 1850; she died May 13, 1852, aged thirty.

Children:

i ISRAEL JAMES, b. Apr. 17, 1842; lives at Torbrook.
ii SUSAN MARIA, b. 1843; d. Oct., 1854.
iii MARILLA SOPHIA, b. 1845; d. 1846.
iv MINETTA L., b. 1847; d. Aug. 1850.

VIII. 131 Israel Chute,[8] (*Silas*,[7] *James*,[6] *John*,[5] *Lionel*,[4] *James*,[3] *James*,[2] *Lionel*[1]), born Sept. 22, 1826; married Elizabeth, daughter of Levi Crowell, February, 1849, and lived near Wood's Harbor, Shelburne Co., N. S. Mrs. Chute died April, 1854, aged twenty-eight; he married 2nd, Reliance, daughter of Alfred Nickerson, Jan. 1, 1857; she died June 7, 1885, aged forty-nine. Mr. Chute a good, pious descon in the Baptist church, has worked out in different places, including Boston, Mass., at his trade as carpenter.

Children:

249 i HENRY, b. Nov. 3, 1850.
  ii GEORGE F., b. July 8, 1852; d. Feb. 14, 1854.
250 iii VORUS F., b. Nov. 3, 1857.
  iv EDMUND, b. Jan. 5, 1860; d. May 8, 1879.
  v MARY ADRIA, b. Apr. 24, 1862; a school teacher; m. Stephen Balcomb Sept. 20, 1884.
  vi ALVA MINNA, b. May 20, 1864; d. June 20, 1870.
  vii WINTFRED OLIVE, b. Mar. 23, 1866; d. May, 1891.
  viii MAUD AUDLEY, b. Oct. 23, 1869; m. Capt. Ainsley Perry, Feb. 15, 1890.
  ix EVERETT S., b. Oct. 15, 1871.
  x EFFIE M., b. Sept. 21, 1875.
  xi FLORENCE ESTELLE, b. July 3, 1878.

VIII. 132 Eaton Chute,[8] (*Handley,*[7] *James,*[6] *John,*[5] *Lionel,*[4] *James,*[3] *James,*[2] *Lionel*[1]), born in Granville at Chute's Cove, now Hampton, Apr. 12, 1815; married Sophia Miller (*Harris, Michael*), Dec. 6, 1838; lived near Hampton, and died in Cornwallis, a pious deacon in the Baptist church, 1849.

Children:

  i TERESSA, b. Sept. 16, 1839; m. Capt. Holden Farnsworth, 1860, and had (1) *Norman*, b. August, 1862; m. Edith Templeman. (2) *Bennett C.*, b. 1864; m. ——. Capt. Farnsworth was drowned in the Gulf of Mexico, Nov. 2, 1870; she d. July 12, 1880.
  ii BENNETT, b. July 17, 1841; preacher of the gospel; d. Apr. 11, 1868.
251 iii AARON E., b. Aug. 22, 1843.
  iv MARY EMMA, b. Mar. 6, 1846; m. Capt. Thomas A. R. Fitchett, 1869; he d. Feb. 20, 1875, aged 34; she d. Nov. 14, 1876, leaving two sons.
  v LOVENA, b. Aug. 15, 1848; m. Judson, son of Van Buren Foster, 1868, and had four children.

VIII. 133 Jacob Chute,[8] (*Handley,*[7] *James,*[6] *John,*[5] *Lionel,*[4] *James,*[3] *James,*[2] *Lionel*[1]), born at Hampton, Feb. 3, 1817; married Emeline, daughter of Seth Chute (see No. 31), and was a farmer and justice of peace on the Bay shore, two miles above Hampton. She died Oct. 24, 1887, aged sixty-eight.

Children:

  i EDWIN J., b. Apr. 18, 1845, was a traveler and runner for mercantile firms; m. Mary, daughter of James, son of John Currill, Mar. 26, 1891, and was found dead in a hotel in Buffalo, N. Y., Aug. 13, leaving property worth ten to fifteen thousand dollars.

ii BERTHA, b. Apr. 3, 1847; school teacher; m. Russell Cropley, Jan. 9, 1884, and had *Ethel Beatrice*, b. Nov. 15, and another daughter since. Mr. Cropley m. 1st, Augusta M., daughter of |George W. Troop and had two daughters; she d. Jan. 28, 1883, aged forty-one.

VIII. 134 Seth Chute,[8] (*Handley,[7] James,[6] John,[5] Lionel,[4] James,[3] James,[2] Lionel[1]*), born Dec. 3, 1823; married Lavinia, daughter of Deacon Oliver H. Cogswell, June 10, 1850; and lived near Hampton; died Jan. 8, 1877; she married 2nd, Harris Foster, Esq., March 7, 1880, and died March 27, 1884, aged fifty-four years and three months.

Children :

   i MINARD E., b. Sept. 20, 1852; school teacher and preacher.
   ii OLIVER H., b. Jan. 15, 1854; 'd. from a hotel burning in Milwaukee, Wis. Feb. 15, 1884.
252 iii WILLIAM PRIOR, b. Dec. 10, 1855.
   iv BRAINERD A., b. Sept. 13, 1868.

VIII. 135 Solomon Chute,[8] (*Handley,[7] James,[6] John,[5] Lionel,[4] James,[3] James,[2] Lionel[1]*), son of Handley and Martha (Phinney) Chute, born at Hampton, July 15, 1827; married Charlotte Hall (*James, John, William*), Nov. 7, 1850, and lived a farmer in West Clarence, also a deacon in the Baptist church. His wife died May 9, 1867, aged thirty-eight; he married 2nd, Sophia, his brother Eaton's widow, eight years his senior, May 9, 1868.

Children:

   i WILLIAM AVARD, b. Sept. 23, 1868.
   ii MARY, b. Jan. 8, 1855; m. Frank H. McDonald, Sept. 8, 1885; and d. at Milton, Mass., Feb. 2, 1886.
   iii MARTHA, b. Aug. 23, 1856; m. Wallace I., son of Levi Langley, Dec. 28, 1877; and had *Ralph*, b. Dec. 1, 1878, and another son and daughter.
   iv THERESA, b. May 2, 1858; d. July 2, 1859.
   v NORMAN. b. Nov. 10, 1860; m. Fostinna Messenger, Feb. 26, 1884; and had *Janet*, b. 1888.
   vi FLORA, b. Feb. 6, 1863; m. Scott Tucker, 1892, Milton, Mass.

VIII. 136 John Eber Chute,[8] (*Handley,[7] James,[6] John,[5] Lionel,[4] James,[3] James,[2] Lionel[1]*), born at Hampton, Oct. 20, 1833; married Mary Ann, daughter of Timothy Brooks jr., Sept. 12, 1857, and is a general mechanic and farmer.

Children :

   i JESSE D., b. June 5, 1858; d. Dec. 1864.

GENEALOGIES OF THE CHUTE FAMILY.

ii ALEDIA J., b. Sept. 29, 1859; m. Frederick A. Simms, May 17, 1890, and live in Lynn, Mass. Mr. Simms m. 1st in England, Maggie Berry, and had *Osmon*, b. 1880; *Clara*, b. 1883.

253 iii TRAVERSE BRINTON, b. Feb. 5, 1862.

iv EATON, b. Dec. 2, 1864; m. Emily A., da. of Daniel Hudson, Esq.

v JESSIE A., b. June 29, 1867. See 142 and 260.

vi HENRY DUNN, b. Aug. 1, 1869.

vii IDA MAY, b. Aug. 1, 1869; d. May 1870.

viii HANNAH D., b. April 21, 1871.

ix RHUPURTY, b. Sept. 24, 1874.

x REUBEN PERKINS, b. Apr. 2, 1876.

xi EFFIE, b. May 13, 1878.

VIII. 137 Robert Chute,[8] (*Handley*,[7] *James*,[6] *John*,[5] *Lionel*,[4] *James*,[3] *James*,[2] *Lionel*[1]), born June 15, 1835; married Susan, daughter of Francis Lent, Sept. 26, 1857, at Hampton, N. S. She died Feb. 6, 1867, aged twenty-five; he married 2nd, Emma, daughter of David Eason, May 16, 1869; farmer and miller at Hampton.

Children:

i SELEDA, b. Sept. 6, 1858; d. Oct. 20.

ii FRANCIS, b. Dec. 18, 1859; d. Sept. 28, 1882.

iii IRENE S., b. May 17, 1862; m. Alfred Clark, July, 1884, and live at Center Falls, R. I.

iv LILIAN, b. Dec. 18, 1864; d. Aug. 4, 1867.

v EMMA, b. Mar. 22, 1870; d. Sept. 20.

vi CAREY H., b. Sept. 6, 1873.

vii SUSAN L., b. Mar. 21, 1879.

VIII. 138 Joseph Dimock,[8] (*Handley*,[7] *James*,[6] *John*,[5] *Lionel*,[4] *James*,[3] *James*,[2] *Lionel*[1]), born Apr. 26, 1837; married Elizabeth, daughter of Joseph and Sophia (Viditoe) Hoffman, son of John and Ann (Wheelock) Hoffman, son of Joseph, Feb. 4, 1859. Mr. Chute a first-rate carpenter, went to Boston, 1867, and settled at Milton Lower Mills, where his wife died May 28, 1884; he married 2nd, Carrie Dale, widow of Hezekiah Hall, (*James, John, William*), 1885.

Children:

i MARTHA L., b. Jan. 24, 1861; m. William A. Constable, June 4, 1885, and have *Zilla May* and *Alice*.

254 ii HARVEY F., b. Nov. 12, 1863.

iii FREDDY S., b. Jan. 29, 1871; m. Susan L. Voye, Apr. 20, 1892.

VIII. 139 Abner Chute,[8] (*Handley*,[7] *James*,[6] *John*,[5] *Lionel*,[4] *James*,[3] *James*,[2] *Lionel*[1]), born Dec. 16, 1843; married Diadama, daughter of Nelson Chesley, 1863; moved to Boston, 1868; and located at Milton Lower Mills, carpenter and builder, also deacon of the Baptist church. Mrs. Chute died Dec. 8, 1868, aged twenty-seven; he married 2nd, Louisa Viditoe (*Nelson, John, Jesse*), July 16, 1873.

Children:

    i HATTIE L., b. Dec. 2, 1864; m. Arthur Nichols, Dec. 23, 1885; a son *Leon*, b. 1886.
   ii ALVIN, b. Feb. 27, 1866; m. ——.
  iii BEATRICE, b. July 2, 1880.

VIII. **140 Joshua Marsden Chute,**[8] (*David M.,*[7] *James,*[6] *John,*[5] *Lionel,*[4] *James,*[3] *James,*[2] *Lionel*[1]), born two miles below Hampton, Oct. 15, 1818; married Irene Potter,[5] daughter of Rev. Peter and Anna (Greenlow) Malloch, Apr. 28, 1849, (Anna Greenlow, was the daughter of James Greenlow and Abigail, daughter of Joseph Alline, son of William and Rebecca Alline, from Rhode Island to Horton, N. S., 1756). Mr. Chute lived at Campobello Island, N. B., about thirty years when he moved to Cambridgeport, Mass., but he returned again in a year or two, and she has remained, a hard working, sober, Christian woman.

Children:

      i WILLIAM EVERINGTON, b. March 24, 1852; drowned Jan. 24, 1877.
     ii LORENZO WILSON, b. April 24, 1854; drowned about Feb. 17, 1877.
255 iii DANIEL MARSDEN, b. July 2, 1856.
256 iv MILLARD FILMORE, b. May 24, 1858.
257 v DAVID SAMUEL, b. Apr. 2, 1860.
     vi JAMES LOREN, b. Aug. 27, 1862; m. Ella Howard, daughter of John Howard, 1892, Cambridge, Mass.
    vii IDA MAY, b. Oct. 4, 1865; m. Lewis M. Long[4] (*John Henry,*[3] *Peter,*[2] *John Jacob,*[1] from Prussia), May 16, 1885; have five children and lived in Cambridgeport and Arlington, Mass.
   viii BERTHA, b. May 4, 1873; m. Edward Childs, August, 1891, who was killed in Summerville by a runaway team May, 1892, aged twenty-two.

Irene P., daughter of Rev. Peter Mallock (1794-1877), and Anna Greenlow (1795-1882), was born at Fair Haven, Charlotte Co., N. B., Jan 30, 1830, (the parents were Free Baptists), was a home missionary in New Brunswick, over three years and raised one thousand dollars, with which a meeting house was built on the Isle of Campobello, near the coast of Maine, 1874, for the Free Baptist church, which has flourished ever since.

In Cambridgeport she has been useful in the churches, Christian missions and temperance organizations, and has composed several recitations, lectures and poems, one of which we subjoin:—

DEATH OF JOHN B. GOUGH (1817-1886.)

1.

Our ranks again are broken, a warrior has fled,
From all his earthly troubles, he's numbered with the dead;
But when his sleep is ended, and he's ransomed from the grave,
He then shall meet the army, he tried on earth to save.

2.

I know you all would like it, to know what was his name,
'Tis John B. Gough the warrior, for you have heard the same;
When but a boy in sorrow, he struggled hard for life,
And then got married early and took a loving wife.

3.

But when the ruby cup passed, he couldn't well refrain,
His wife tried to prevent him, but found 'twas all in vain;
But when death came and took her, who was to him so dear,
Then he began to realize, his fearful, wild career.

4.

He signed the temperance pledge then, and there began to preach,
And warn poor drunkards soundly, their doom to them did teach;
And when the church was crowded, he would a story tell,
How he escaped the monster which always pleased them well.

5.

But his career is ended, he lies beneath the sod,
And freed from all earth's trials, his soul is with his God;
But when the last, loud trumpet, shall bid the sleeper rise,
We then shall see the warrior, with unbeclouded eyes.

VIII. 141 John Wentworth Chute,[8] (*David M.,*[7] *James,*[6] *John,*[5] *Lionel,*[4] *James,*[3] *James,*[2] *Lionel*[1]), born near Chute's Cove or Hampton, Aug. 20, 1821; married Elizabeth, daughter of Alexander Spears, Jan. 1, 1847, and moved to near Caledonia, Queen's Co., N. S.; a Christian man, farmer and shoemaker; died July 31, 1884.
Children:

    i SIDNEY, b. Mar 2, 1848; m. Susan Jayne, Dec. 28, 1869, Caledonia, N. S.
    ii MARTHA, b. Dec. 9, 1849; m. Walter Johnson, Sept. 29, 1877, and they live at Caledonia.
    iii CHARLOTTE AMANDA, b. Sept. 21, 1852; m. John K., son of Joseph G. Kent of East Danvers, Apr. 25, 1874; grocer in Lynn, Mass., and have two sons, *Arthur G.*, b. Mar. 2, 1885; *Joseph Frank*, b. May 19, 1887. He was in Company F, 13th Maine, in the late war.
    iv CORDELIA, b. Oct. 2, 1854; m. James B. Griggs, July 31, 1876, and live in Cambridgeport; have two children.

258 v EDWARD ERVIN, b. Feb. 21, 1857.
    vi DAVID ALEXANDER, b. May 2, 1859; m. Flora Peasely, Apr. 21, 1885; live in Cambridgeport.
    vii JAMES BURNHAM, b. May 3, 1860; m. Carrie, daughter of Lieutenant George Glidden of the late war. (1) *Mildred Elizabeth*, b. Jan. 10, 1887. Mr. Chute is a grocer in Lynn.
    viii ROBERT, b. Dec. 22, 1862; m. Lilla Philbrick, Mar. 18, 1883.
    ix HIRAM, b. Mar. 8, 1866.
    x JOHN D'ORSAY, b. May 5, 1870.

VIII. 142 Sidney Smith,[8] (*David M.,*[7] *James*[6] *John,*[5] *Lionel,*[4] *James,*[3] *James,*[2] *Lionel*[1]), born Oct 20, 1824; married Lucretia, daughter of Benjamin Farnsworth, Oct. 31, 1849, and lived in Cambridgeport, a number of years; a pious Adventist, and an exhorter; died May 13, 1885; she married 2nd Priestly Milbury (2nd wife), 1889, and live in Clements, N. S.

  Children:

    i EMMA AUSTIN, b. Nov. 8, 1850; d. Feb. 1851.
259 ii WILLIAM BURKITT FOWLER, b. Dec. 24, 1851.
    iii MARY ELIZABETH, b. 1853; d. 1854.
260 iv FRANK LOWRY, b. Sept. 1855.
    v JOSEPHINE, b. Dec. 24, 1857; d. Nov. 24, 1865.
    vi STEPHEN R. T., b. 1859; d. Nov. 28, 1872.
    vii MARY EMMA, b. June 1861; m. Lester W., son of George Adams, Carthage, Me., July 2, 1879.
    viii JOSEPHINE, b. 1863; d. 1865.
    ix MINNIE WARREN, b. Nov. 29, 1865; m. George B. Young, and are in the far West.
    x GEORGE WASHINGTON, b. April 1868; d. Jan. 4, 1877.
    xi LUELLA, b. Oct. 1875; d. Sept. 11, 1876.

VIII. 143 Handley Chute,[8] (*David M.,*[7] *James,*[6] *John,*[5] *Lionel,*[4] *James,*[3] *James,*[2] *Lionel*[1]), born Sept. 20, 1827; married Naomi, daughter of Frank and Sophia (*Fisher*) Martin, Jan. 2, 1862, and settled near Caledonia, Queens Co., N. S., a farmer; died fall of 1893.

  Children:

    i WILSON, b. Nov. 12, 1863; m. ——.
    ii SOPHIA, b. March 12, 1866; m. Alex. Howie, July 5, 1892.
    iii SELEDA, b. Oct. 12, 1868; m. Charles Spears.
    iv MELVIN, b. Oct. 6, 1870.

VIII. 144 Timothy Willian Brooks,[8] (*David M.,*[7] *James,*[6] *John,*[5] *Lionel,*[4] *James,*[3] *James,*[2] *Lione*[1]), born Nov. 11, 1829; married

Deborah Edwards, May 27, 1856; she died in the fall; he married 2nd, Mary A. Delap, March 24, 1859. He came to Massachusetts in 1850, and was a soldier in Co. A, 48th Massachusetts, in the war; died in Cambridgeport, June 25, 1871.

Children:

    i ANNA L., b. Nov. 29, 1861; m. ——.
    ii CHARLES WILLIAM, b. Feb. 26, 1863; killed by an elevator at Bridgeport, Conn., 1891.

VIII. 145 Angus,[8] (*David M.,*[7] *James,*[6] *John,*[5] *Lionel,*[4] *James,*[3] *James,*[2] *Lionel*[1]), born Oct. 28, 1836; married Nancy Hawley, 1855, had three sons, who all died, wife too, at Key West, Fla., of yellow fever, in 1865. He married 2nd, Emily Anna Wells, July 1, 1871, Lynn, Mass. Mr. Chute was a carpenter, and after living in Cambridge, East Boston, and other places, returned to Florida, and located (1890) at Ocala.

Children:

    i BLANCHE MAY, b. Mar. 4, 1881; d. September, 1889.

VIII. 146 David Melvin,[8] (*David M.,*[7] *James,*[6] *John,*[5] *Lionel,*[4] *James,*[3] *James,*[2] *Lionel*[1]), born June 14, 1841; married Mary White, 1860, who died August, 1866, aged twenty-three. He married 2nd, Fanny A., daughter of Deacon William H. Goudey, (*Stephen, James*), Mar. 28, 1868, and lived in and around Boston over twenty years; a good carpenter and builder. They moved to Lynn in 1891.

Children:

    i ANNA L., b. Sept. 23, 1869; m. Herbert W. Cox, Apr. 5, 1886; have three daughters; live in Lynn.
    ii WILLIAM F., b. Mar. 8, 1873; d. Apr. 16, 1877.
    iii CARRIE M., b. Apr. 4, 1875; m. George C. Merrill, (*Benjamin, James*), Dec. 31, 1891; one son (*Herbert Melvin*), 1892; live in Lynn.
    iv GEORGE M., b. May 17, 1877.
    v HATTIE G., b. Oct. 4, 1880.
    vi LEROY G., b. Feb. 4, 1882.
    vii GRACEY L., b. Oct. 13, 1884.
    viii WILLIAM FREDERICK, b. Dec. 22, 1889.

VIII. 147 Arthur Crawley,[8] (*Rev. Obed,*[7] *James,*[6] *John,*[5] *Lionel,*[4] *James,*[3] *James,*[2] *Lionel*[1]), born at Digby, N. S., Apr. 10, 1853; in his youth a jeweler; pursued a course of study at Horton Academy, and in September, 1877, went into Acadia college at Wolfville, and graduated with the degree of B.A., in June, 1881; he was licensed to preach July, 1880, in Great Village, N. S., and in September, 1881, entered Theological Seminary, Morgan Park, Ill., and graduated B.D., May, 1884, having taken the second year's study at Newton Theological Institution in Massachusetts. He was ordained to the gospel ministry at Stillman Valley, Ill., Dec. 23, 1884. After serving the Baptist church there faithfully nearly five years, came to Austin, near Chicago, in September, 1889, and in the fall of 1892 to Halifax, N. S. He married at Stillman Valley, Ill., Ella Maud, daughter of Rev. Abram Spurr Hunt, (*Elijah, Benjamin*), Aug. 11, 1884.

Children:

    i KATIE JANE, b. July 7. 1886.
    ii ARTHUR HUNT, b. Apr. 17, 1888.

VIII. 148 Alexander Chute,[8] (*Richard,*[7] *James,*[6] *Daniel,*[5] *James,*[4] *James,*[3] *James,*[2] *Lionel*[1]), born in Byfield, Newbury, Mass., Sept. 27, 1806; married Martha F., daughter of Jesse Gould, Malden, Mass., April 18, 1829, and lived in Newburyport; died Oct. 18, 1840; she married 2nd Ellis B. Bramhall, a merchant, Oct. 18, 1848, and moved from Wayland to Plymouth, 1850. He died there January 1865, aged forty-six and the widow (born 1807) still lives in Plymouth.

Children:

    i BETSY JANE, b. 1833; d. Jan. 25, 1837.
    ii BETSY JANE, b. Jan. 17, 1838; m. Benj. O. Strong,[8] (*Ely,*[7] [and Betsey of Elder Benjamin and Eunice Baldwin], *Eleazer,*[6] *Joel,*[5] *Eleazer,*[4] *Jedediah,*[3] *Jedediah,*[2] *Elder John,*[1] born in England 1605; m. 2nd, Abigail Ford, Dec. 1630, [1st wife unknown], and lived together fifty-eight years, had sixteen children, and d. 1699; she d. 1688, aged eighty), Dec. 9, 1855, and lived in Plymouth, and d. Dec. 12, 1889. Children:
        1. CHARLES ALEXANDER, b. June 23, 1858; m. Sarah E., da. of Nathan H. Morton, Nov. 8, 1880, and have two children.
        2. MARTHA JANE, b. Nov. 15, 1873.

VIII. 149 Ariel Parish,[8] (*Richard,*[7] *James,*[6] *Daniel,*[5] *James,*[4] *James,*[3] *James,*[2] *Lionel*[1]), born in Byfield, May 16, 1809; married Sarah Maria Winslow Chandler,[7] (*Peleg,*[6] *Peleg,*[5] *Philip,*[4] *Joseph,*[3] *Joseph,*[2] *Edmund,*[1] and Rebecca Phillips, of Duxbury 1633); Peleg,[6] married Esther Parsons,[5] (*Col. Isaac,*[4] *Dea. Isaac,*[3] *Ebenezer,*[2] *Jeffrey,*[1] of Gloucester, Mass.), Peleg,[5] married Sarah Winslow,[5] (*Barnabas,*[4] *Gilbert,*[3]

REV. ARIEL P. CHUTE.

CAPT. RICHARD H. CHUTE.

DEACON THOMAS H. CHUTE.

JOHN NELSON CHUTE.

Capt. Nathaniel,[2] *Kenelm,*[1] 1599–1672; married Eleanor Newton, 1598–1681, widow of John Adams, over about 1630); of Bangor, Me., April 25, 1836. Mr. Chute fitted for college at Dummer Academy in his native parish, graduated at Bowdoin, Me., 1832; Theological Seminary at Andover 1835; ordained a minister in the Congregational church at Oxford, Me., 1836; held pastorates in Pownal to 1842; Lynnfield, Mass., 1851, to 1857; Ware four years following, including intervals of teaching in Warren Academy, Woburn, 1841 to 1848; the academy at Milton, and the Dummer Academy near his native home. After 1861, he was in the government service in the Boston Custom House, and in the United States Treasury, Boston, retiring with the reputation of a skillful and valuable officer. Since the war he lived a retired life at Sharon, Mass; where he died happy in the Lord Jesus, Dec. 18, 1887. His wife, born in 1805, still lives.

Children :

    i ELLEN MARIA, b. May 23, 1837; m. A. D. Bacon, M.D., Sept. 11, 1865; had a da. He d. Mar. 29, 1881, aged 75; she lives at Attleboro.
    ii FRANCES PEARSON, b. June 2, 1840, at Pownal, Me.
261 iii RICHARD HENRY, b. Mar. 14, 1843.
    iv ESTHER ANDREWS, b. June 22, 1846; m. Edgar M. Hickson, July 13, 1866, and d. Dec 31, he m. 2nd, Mary E. Cromstock, and have four children.
    v SARAH BARNES, b. July 30, 1848, at Harrison, Me.

VIII. 150 Andrew Chute,[8] (*Richard,*[7] *James,*[6] *Daniel,*[5] *James,*[4] *James,*[3] *James,*[2] *Daniel*[1]), born in Byfield, April 11, 1814; married Ann M., daughter of Isaac Perry, Esq., of Orland, Me., Sept. 30, 1836, and was a merchant, and captain of militia in Newburyport, Mass. But he lived in Maine over thirty years, between 1826 and 1859. Had a golden wedding in 1886, and died July 9, 1890; she died Jan. 1, 1888, aged seventy-one.

Children:

    i CHARLES R., b. Aug. 1, 1837; m. Mary Robinson, Aug. 8, 1864, was mate of the ship Quickstep; d. at Queenstown, Ireland, Sept. 1870.
    ii MARTHA ELIZABETH, b. Aug. 1, 1837; d. June 24, 1868; m. Wm. B. Peters,[6] (*Andrew,*[5] *John,*[4] *John,*[3] *Samuel,*[2] *Andrew*[1]), to Boston before 1657, said to be a son of William, brother to Rev. Hugh, b. 1599, to America 1635, preached at Wenham Lake in 1636, from " At Enon near Salem because of much water there," pastor in Salem, successor to Roger Williams; d. in England, Oct. 1660; da. Elizabeth, m. —— Barker, Newport, R. I.

Children:

    1. JOHN ANDREW, b. Aug. 13, 1864; m. ——; is a graduate of Bowdoin college; a lawyer, and lives at Bar Harbor, Me.
    2. CHARLES, b. July 20, 1866; m. ——.
    3. WILLIAM CHUTE, b. June 15, 1868.

262 iii GEORGE ALBERT, b. Mar. 3, 1843.
    iv SARAH BURK, b. Sept. 13, 1846; teacher in Newburyport.
    v KIMBALL P., b. Apr. 28, 1848; d. Sept. 30, 1850.
    vi JAMES ANDREW, b. Nov. 12, 1850; m. Mary S. Van Horn, Oct. 24, 1876, at Salt Lake City, Utah.
263 vii EDWARD LANE, b. Nov. 27, 1853.

VIII. 151 James Martin Chute,[8] (*Daniel*,[7] *James*,[6] *Daniel*, *James*,[4] *James*,[3] *James*,[2] *Lionel*[1]),

born in Cincinnati, O., Nov. 24, 1814; married Abba J. Fairchild, Sept. 9, 1841, and lived in Indiana. Mrs. Chute died December, 1844; he married 2nd, Rachel, widow of Charles Fairchild, June 7, 1846, and died at Thorn Town, Ind., 1886; she died at Evansville, 1852.

Children:

    i RACHEL, b. Nov. 4, 1842; d. in infancy.
264 ii CHARLES HUBBLE, b. Dec. 4, 1843.
    iii WILLIAM FAIRCHILD, b. June 19, 1847; d. 1865.
    iv JANE, b. Aug. 7, 1849 is in Washington.
    v DANIEL, b. Aug. 12, 1852; d. young.

VIII. 152 Richard Chute,[8] (*Rev. James*,[7] *James*,[6] *Daniel*,[5] *James*,[4] *James*,[3] *James*,[2] *Lionel*[1]),

born in Cincinnati, O., Sept. 23, 1820; received a good education, and was a merchant clerk 1832 to 1840 at Fort Wayne, Ind.; he then went into the fur trade till 1854, when he moved to St. Anthony, Minn., which was united to Minneapolis in 1872, and since that has been engaged in real estate business, also a ruling elder in the Presbyterian church; was regent of the university of Minnesota five years; partner in the great water power there, and has given much time to railroads in the state. He married Mary Eliza Young of Indiana, Feb. 28, 1850, and died in Chicago, Aug. 1, 1893, heart disease.

Children:

    i CHARLES RICHARD, b. May 15, 1852; m. Cora M. Moody, Oct. 18, 1871; had Chester B., b. Aug. 24, 1878; d. in Thomasville, Ga., Mar. 14, 1886.
    ii MINNIE OLIVE, b. Mar. 21, 1856; d. on the steamer Dubuque at LeClaire, Ia., Aug. 26, 1876.

iii MARY WELCOME, b. Dec. 4, 1859; d. Apr. 2, 1862.
iv WILLIE YOUNG, b. Sept. 13, 1863.
v GRACE FAIRCHILD, b. Aug. 7, 1865; m. Capt. Joshua W. Jacobs of the United States army, Thomasville, Ga., Mar. 1, 1886.
1. WEST CHUTE, b. Dec. 9, 1886, Atlanta, Ga.

VIII. 153 James Thurston,[8] (*Rev. James,*[7] *James,*[6] *Daniel,*[5] *James,*[4] *James,*[3] *James,*[2] *Lionel*[1]), born at Cincinnati, Aug. 30, 1827, and after he was nine years of age went to Lafayette, Ind., and there engaged in the dry goods, milling and the grain trade. In 1873 he retired, moved to Minneapolis, and is an elder in the Presbyterian church. He married in Lafayette, June 20, 1850, Sarah Jane Peterson; she died Oct. 25, 1852; he married 2nd, Mary Elizabeth McBride, June 27, 1854; she died Apr. 20, 1868; he married 3rd, Leonora T. C. Groendyke, Aug. 21, 1871.

Children:

i JEANNETTE, b. June 2, 1851; d. June 5.
ii MARY LILA, b. May 18, 1852.
iii MARTHA HANNAH, b. May 2, 1855; m. Frank Mann.
iv WINONA PAGE, b. Aug. 30, 1857; m. Charles R. Underwood.
v DAVID MCBRIDE, b. Dec. 19, 1859.
vi JAMES RICHARD, b. Jan. 14, 1864.
vii SAMUEL SHARP, b. Jan. 23, 1866.
viii ROBERT MORRIS, b. Dec. 11, 1873.

VIII. 154 Samuel Hews,[8] (*Rev. James,*[7] *James,*[6] *Daniel,*[5] *James,*[4] *James,*[3] *James,*[2] *Lionel*[1]), born at Columbus, O., Dec. 6, 1830; attended medical college at Cincinnati, and graduated 1852; then from Fort Wayne, Ind., he went to Portland, Ore., and in 1853, to Eureka, Cal.; came back to St. Anthony, Minn., 1857; married Helen E. A. Day, May 5, 1858, and has resided there since, an M.D., and partner with his brother, Richard, in business.

Children:

i CHARLOTTE RACHEL, b. Jan. 30, 1859; d. Jan. 30, 1863.
ii MARY JEANNETTE, b. Aug. 24, 1862.
iii AGNES, b. Sept. 6, 1864.
iv ELIZABETH, b. Oct. 14, 1866.
v LOUIS PRINCE, b. Oct. 17, 1868.
vi FREDERICK, b. Dec. 21, 1872.

VIII. 155 Moses Stubbs Chute,[8] (*Curtis,*[7] *Josiah,*[6] *Curtis,*[5] *Thomas,*[4] *James,*[3] *James,*[2] *Lionel*[1]), born in Cumberland, Me., Mar. 21

1815; married Christiana, daughter of Freeman and Lydia Ellis, Sept. 5, 1843, Carthage, Me.; she died April, 1846, aged twenty; he married 2nd, Violette H., daughter of John and Huldah (Reed) Gray, son of Eliphalet and Mary (Coolidge) Gray (of Sutton, Mass., who went to Jay, Franklin Co., Me.), Oct. 29, 1846, and has followed mercantile business more or less through life. He moved from Carthage, Me. to Rockland, Plymouth Co., Mass., 1872, and there is doing well as a grocer.

Children:

265 i GEORGE CURTIS, b. April 19, 1845.
266 ii CHARLES MOSES, b. July 3, 1849.
267 iii EDWIN ELLIOTT, b. April 8, 1851.
 iv FRANK STANWOOD, b. Nov. 28, 1854; m. Nellie C. Young, April 4, 1886; she d. Oct. 24, 1887, aged thirty.
 v NELLIE SUSAN, b. Feb. 5, 1858; m. Howard M., son of Nathan and Charlotte (Lane) Poole, Jan. 22, 1876.
 vi FLORENCE EMERY, b. Jan. 2, 1860; d. Sept. 29, 1864, Jay, Me.
 vii JAMES H., b. Dec. 27, 1861; d. Oct. 31, 1864, Dixfield, Me.
 viii LIZZIE L., b. Oct. 5, 1865, in Jay, Me.; m. Horatio P., son of Silas Capen, of Norwood, Mass., Nov. 18, 1885; and have *Florence Millon*, b. Jan. 15, 1887; *Harold Norwood*, b. April 28, 1890, Rockland, Mass.
 ix EMMA V. A., b. April 28, 1868.
 x GRACE MABEL, b. Feb. 24, 1875.

VIII. 156 Joseph Clement Chute,[8] (*Josiah,*[7] *Josiah,*[6] *Curtis,*[5] *Thomas,*[4] *James,*[3] *James,*[2] *Lionel*[1]), born in Portland, Me., Aug. 22, 1823; lived there till he was sixteen, then went to sea, and was off several voyages; to Liverpool, London, West Indies, Florida, etc. In 1846, he enlisted in Capt. Bradfute's Co, of Tennessee Volunteers and went into the Mexican war. On his return, while nursing some yellow fever patients in New Orleans, in the hot summer of 1847, he received a sunstroke, which disabled him very much. He got home, however, and lived twelve years with his mother and his uncle George W., in Windham; married Sarah Sylvester Winslow,[7] (*James,*[6] *James,*[5] *Nathan*[4] *James,*[3] *Job,*[2] *Kenelm,*[1] over in 1629), sixth in a family of eight, Oct. 27, 1859; lived five and a half years on the Mark Knight place, which he bought, and in the spring of 1865—having sold his place again—he moved on to his father-in-law's farm, near Windham Center. He was of an amiable disposition, fond of good company, much given to hospitality, and a worthy member of the Masons, and Orthodox Friends. He died Jan. 7, 1886.

Children;

 i GEORGE CLEMENT, b. Oct. 8, 1860; d. July 6, 1863.
 ii EDWARD WINSLOW, b. Feb. 2, 1862.

VIII. 157 John Hooper Chute,[8] *(Col. Francis,*[7] *Col. Thomas,*[6] *Curtis,*[5] *Thomas,*[4] *James,*[3] *James,*[2] *Lionel*[1]*)*, born in Otisfield, Cumberland Co., Me., July 29, 1810; grew up among the natives of that part, a jolly, good-natured soul; married Miriam, daughter of Thaddeus Turner, Nov. 10, 1840, and settled on his father's old farm, near Bolster's Mills. She died Nov. 2, 1852, aged forty-five; he married 2nd, Joanna, daughter of John and Mercy (Jordan) Pike, and widow of Nathaniel, son of Samuel Andrews, Aug. 29, 1854. Mr. Chute was a hard worker over the hills and among the rocks, and in his old age became quite a cripple with rheumatism; died Dec. 11, 1890.

Children;

 i HANNAH, b. Aug. 15, 1842; d. Sept. 4, 1847.
268 ii CURTIS, b. March 29, 1845.
 iii MIRIAM, b. Nov. 1, 1852; d. Jan. 6, 1853.
269 iv ALBERT F., b. Jan. 27, 1856.

VIII. 158 Francis jr.,[8] *(Col. Francis,*[7] *Col. Thomas,*[6] *Curtis,*[5] *Thomas,*[4] *James,*[3] *James,*[2] *Lionel*[1]*)*, born in Otisfield, Dec. 16, 1816; married Maria, daughter of Capt. Wentworth Stuart, Feb. 1844; she died June 9, 1863, aged thirty-nine; he married 2nd, Kaphira A., daughter of Rev. Joseph Wight, May 1, 1865. Mr. Chute has been a blacksmith and merchant at Bolster's Mills, about fifty years. One daughter.

 i MERCY S., b. April 27, 1845; d. March 8, 1865.

VIII. 159 James Chute,[8] *(William C.,*[7] *Col. Thomas,*[6] *Curtis,*[5] *Thomas,*[4] *James,*[3] *James,*[2] *Lionel*[1]*)*, born near Naples, Me., Aug. 30, 1817; married Ellen Jane, daughter of Fisher Mann, March 5, 1843; and lived near Naples; she died Aug. 22, 1868, aged forty four; he married 2nd, Hannah Jane (born Aug. 13, 1833), daughter of David H. and Ruth H. (Eastman) Cole, March 20, 1869. She married 1st, Andrew J. Cole—no relation—Dec. 23, 1850, and had five children. Mr. Cole died June 7, 1864, aged thirty-two. Mr. Chute was a pious, industrious farmer. In doing hard work, as in rolling a log, he was wont to say "canto," and from that he was called "Canto Jim," to distinguish him from others of the name. He was chaplain in the Patrons of Husbandry in 1875; and his wife was Ceres. He was recording steward in the M. E. church in 1879; died June 12, 1884, a prominent Mason and Odd Fellow.

Children:

270   i ALONZO F., b. Nov. 13, 1843.
      ii ELBRIDGE G., b. March 26, 1846; m. Sadie V., da. of Daniel Abbot, of Lawrence, Mass., Nov. 24, 1870, moved to Haverhill, 1880, and is a grocer there
     iii G. H. SHIRLEY, b. June 28, 1847; d. Oct. 31, 1850.
     iv EMMA JANE, b. March 13, 1849; m. Andrew A. Keene,[4] (*Amaziah Almon,[3] Sprague,[2] Sprague[1]*), of Poland, Me., and is foreman in a shoe manufactory, Haverhill, Mass.
          1. GEORGE ALFRED, b. May 14, 1874; jeweler in Haverhill.

271   v HORACE MANN, b. Oct. 7, 1851.
     vi MARY CAROLINE, b. Oct. 12, 1853; m. Frank S. Watkins, November, 1873; had two sons, two daughters, and died Aug. 11, 1880.

272 vii RUSSELL E., b. June 28, 1855.
     viii MELVILLE W., b. Aug. 2, 1857; killed in a paper mill, Fitchburg, Mass., Aug. 11, 1881.
     ix GEORGE AYER, b. July 13, 1865; m. Norah Stone, 1889, living at Big Stone City, S. D.
      x ELLEN S., b. Jan. 30, 1868; m. Fred Hooper, July 3, 1886, and have three sons.
     xi MINNIE A., b. July 11, 1870; m. John, son of Roscoe Mayo, October, 1889; have two children.

VIII. 160 William Chute,[8] (*William C.,[7] Col. Thomas,[6] Curtis,[5] Thomas,[4] James,[3] James,[2] Lionel[1]*), born Oct. 22, 1819; married Emily N., daughter of Joseph Stuart of Harrison, Me., Nov. 21, 1844; was a good and useful man in society; he was a deacon in the Congregational church; a Mason, and treasurer in the Patrons of Husbandry, 1879; died at Harrison, July 15, 1883.

Children:

      i JOSEPH F., b. Mar. 2, 1847; m. Lizzie, daughter of Joseph Dresser of Bridgton, June 4, 1870.
     ii ROSANNAH, b. May 4, 1852; d. Aug. 23.
     iii ROSE, b. Sept. 10, 1855; m. Frank P., son of Henry B. Johnson of Gorham, Jan. 1, 1885.

VIII. 161 Franklin A. Chute,[8] (*William C.,[7] Col. Thomas,[6] Curtis,[5] Thomas,[4] James,[3] James,[2] Lionel[1]*), born Feb. 25, 1827; married Elizabeth J., daughter of Thomas Hall of Naples, Sept. 24, 1853, and moved to Waterford 1863; to Harrison, August, 1877.

Children:

273 i QUINCY MAYBERRY, b. Nov. 30, 1854.
ii CORA BELL, b. Sept. 14, 1863; m. John Witham, Nov. 12, 1881, and have three children at Harrison.

VIII. 162 Edwin Chute,[8] *(Daniel,*[7] *Col. Thomas,*[6] *Curtis,*[5] *Thomas,*[4] *James,*[3] *James,*[2] *Lionel*[1]), born in Otisfield, July 5, 1816; married Dorcas Cobb, daughter of William and Mary (Chute-Noyes) Abbott, Feb. 17, 1844, and lived at Standish in Gorham, south of Sebago Lake, but moved to Otisfield, near Bolster's Mills, 1846; was an industrious farmer; died Feb. 4, 1881.

Children:

i JOSIAH C., b. May 3, 1845; d. May 6, 1849.
ii WILLIAM ADDISON, b. May 2, 1848; was in Company G, 29th Maine and a prisoner; d. at Annapolis, Md., June, 1864.
274 iii JOSIAH C., b. Sept. 18, 1850.
iv EMILY L., b. Sept. 8, 1852; m. Eri, son of Clement Scribner, October, 1867 and have three children.
v MAHLON A., b. Sept. 14, 1854; m. Laura, daughter of Martin Van Buren Jillson, July, 1891.
vi E. WELLINGTON, b. Jan. 29, 1856; d. January, 1859.
vii CLINTON, b. Jan. 29, 1858; d. March, 1861.
viii MARY ABBOT, b. Apr. 11, 1860; d. September, 1861.
ix H. ISABEL, b. Jan. 9, 1863; m. J. Edgar, son of James Dunham, Mar. 1, 1884. (1) *Ellsworth*, b. Dec. 2, 1884.
x IDELLA ROSILLA, b. Mar. 20, 1866.
xi ADELAIDE B., b. July 9, 1869.

VIII. 163 Albion Chute,[8] *(Daniel,*[7] *Col. Thomas,*[6] *Curtis,*[5] *Thomas,*[4] *James,*[3] *James,*[2] *Lionel*[1]), born June 29, 1828; married Dorinda Philbrick[8] *(Joseph,*[7] *Simon,*[6] *James,*[5] *Joseph,*[4] *James,*[3] *James,*[2] *Thomas*[1]), Mar. 15, 1854; she died Oct. 4, 1859, aged twenty-nine; he married 2nd, Merebah D., daughter of Mark Roberts, Jan. 29, 1860, and lived in Ossipee, Carroll Co., N. H.; died Sept. 8, 1892.

Children:

i ALPHONSO B., b. Feb. 16, 1855; m. Annette Fletcher, Mar. 27, 1881; son, *Howard*, b. Jan. 3, 1882.
ii ELLA A., b. July 20, 1862; m. William H. Heath, Sept. 20, 1877.
iii WARREN MARK, b. June 24, 1864.

iv JAMES A., b. Oct. 15, 1866.
v GRACIA A., b. Sept. 8, 1873.
vi WALLACE S., b. Jan. 9, 1877.

VIII. 164 Daniel jr., a brother, born July 12, 1832; married Mary Elizabeth, daughter of Henry Atkins, Portland, Me., 1855; moved to Ebbensburg, Pa.; a wagon maker.

Children:

i ELLA, b. ——.
ii WILLIAM, b. ——.
iii CARRIE, b. ——.
iv SADIE, b. ——.
v DELLA, b.——.

VIII. 165 William Windsor,[8] (*Daniel,*[7] *Col. Thomas,*[6] *Curtis,*[5] *Thomas,*[4] *James,*[3] *James,*[2] *Lionel*[1]), born Dec. 29, 1834; married Lucette Philbrick, sister to Albion's 1st wife, Oct. 21, 1856, and settled in Otisfield, near Crooked River; a farmer. They celebrated their "Silver Wedding" on Oct. 21, 1881. He died May 21, 1892.

Children:

i IDA JANETTE, b. July 31, 1857; m. Charles C. Davis jr., Nov. 11, 1882; a son Harold Windsor, b. 1866; live in East Otisfield.
ii NELLIE F., b. Aug. 7, 1859; m. George Edwards, December, 1881.

SONG, WRITTEN BY SAMUEL LOTEN WESTON, M.D. OF BOLSTER'S MILLS AND SUNG AT THE SILVER WEDDING.

"Of all the faith that wins the highest grace,
Whose indication is a cheerful face,
Of all the works that is the best by half,
That sometimes blossoms in a hearty laugh."

JAMES B. WIGGIN.

1.

Just five and twenty years to-day
Since Windsor to Lucett did say,
"I'll take you for my wedded wife."
Says she "All right, I'm yours for life."

CHORUS.

Then clear the deck, rant, tear and canter,
Clear the deck, rant, tear and canter,
Clear the deck, shake out the bedding,
For we're all here at the Silver Wedding.

2.

At first they lived in humble style
And fortune seemed to frown awhile,
But they laid up some dimes and quarters,
Made pants, raised hens and two fine daughters.
  Then clear the deck, etc.

3.

They bought a farm and built a house,
They kept no cat that caught no mouse,
And what did much to increase their means,
They raised sweet corn and lima beans.
  Then clear the deck, etc.

4.

Now all things lovely went apace,
The daughters grew in gifts and grace,
But when it seemed that they should marry,
They made a most perplexing tarry.
  Then clear the deck, etc.

5.

The parents, since no wedding came
To crown the altar with its flame,
Said "wedded life has had some clover,
We think we'd better marry over."
  Then clear the deck, etc.

6.

So cards and invitations flew,
And brought together a Chutey crew,
Of long Chutes, short Chutes, stout and lean,
A hundred, more or less, I ween.
  Then clear the deck, etc.

7.

Here's Rose, and Belle, and Liz, and Ella,
O what a chance for some good " fella,"
And lots of other charming women
With hideous bangs, fine lace and trimming.
  Then clear the deck, etc.

8.

Here's Albert, 'Siah, Bill and Frank,
And John with many a funny prank,
Can't name them all — we have no quakers,
Excepting uncle Mahlon Akers.
  Then clear the deck, etc.

9.

And how the Chutes with Chutes have chatted,
How some on oyster soup have fatted,
I will refer — I'm such a noodle,
To that old Nincompoup — Dr. Coodle.*
    Then clear the deck, etc.

10.

Kind friends I'm done, my muse is "bust,"
My throat is dry and close I must,
Obliged, lest you some tears be shedding,
To keep the rest for the "Golden Wedding."

CHORUS.

Then clear the deck, etc.,
  Clear the deck, rant, tear and canter,
Clear the deck, shake out the bedding,
  We'll try and be at the "Golden Wedding."

VIII. 166 Watson Chute,[8] (*James,*[7] *Col. Thomas,*[6] *Curtis,*[5] *Thomas,*[4] *James,*[3] *James,*[2] *Lionel*[1]), born in Naples, March 20, 1835; married Harriet (Nelson) Dawes, of Portland, Oct. 31, 1857; lived in Naples, and in later years worked in the Cumberland Mills paper works at Saccarappa, on the Presumpscott river. She died Sept. 16, 1884; aged fifty-five; he died 1888.

Children:

    i CHARLES H., b. May 25, 1861; m. Maria Lord, Dec. 2, 1882.
    ii EMMA C., b. Oct. 18, 1864; m, ——.

VIII. 167 Andrew Chute,[9] (*James,*[8] *Col. Thomas,*[7] *Curtis,*[6] *Curtis,*[5] *Thomas,*[4] *James,*[3] *James,*[2] *Lionel*[1]), born Jan. 4, 1844; married Kate A., daughter of John Donavan, Jan. 4, 1866, and lived at Naples on or near his farther's farm; a farmer; she died Oct. 4, 1892, aged forty-six.

Children:

    i CHARLES EDWARD, b. June 12, 1868; m. ——.
    ii CORA MAY, b. May 10, 1870; m. Clinton, son of Robert Edes, 1888, and have three children.

VIII. 168 Adelbert C., brother to the above, born Feb. 4, 1848; married Lizzie M. Jordan [7] (*Barzillai,*[6] *Winter,*[5] *Jeremiah,*[4] *Jeremiah,*[3]

---

* *Nom de plume* of Capt. James Chute of Naples, and "Nincompoop," a pet name he was in the habit of applying to his friends — called the writer by it at this celebration.

Jeremiah,[2] *Rev. Robert*,[1] of 1640), Jan. 4, 1873; a foreman in the Cumberland mills; also deputy sheriff of Cumberland Co., Portland.

Children:

    i HERBERT E., b. Oct. 11, 1873.

VIII. 169 Warren B. Chute,[8] (*Capt. James*,[7] *Col. Thomas*,[6] *Curtis*,[5] *Thomas*,[4] *James*,[3] *James*,[2] *Lionel*[1]), born in Naples Apr. 10, 1850; married Clara H., daughter of Enoch Gammon jr., Jan. 23, 1875, and live on the east side of Long Pond, in Naples; a farmer.

Children:

    i ERNEST ALFRED, b. Jan. 1, 1877.
    ii FLORA M., b. March 14, 1879.
    iii VIRGINIA E., b. Aug. 22, 1881.
    iv JAMES CLEVELAND, b. June 5, 1884.

VIII. 170 George M. Chute,[8] (*Capt. Thomas*,[7] *Col. Thomas*,[6] *Curtis*,[5] *Thomas*,[4] *James*,[3] *James*,[2] *Lionel*[1]), born in Naples, July 28, 1836; lived in Otisfield, Portland and Sweden; went into Co. A, 18th Mass. and 5th corps in the late war; returned to Brooklyn, N. Y., in October, 1864; Boston, 1867; married Lucy A., daughter of Oliver and Lucinda (Webber) Barnard, Dec. 9, 1868, Sweden, Me.; went and lived in Boston again; then to Clay Co., Minn., 1872, and back to Brooklyn in September; to Brighton, Me., later in the fall; and to Southborough, Mass., April, 1874; to Brighton again 1875; and since 1880, to Harrison, Cumberland Co., Me; burned out in 1885; but doing well again.

Children:

    i FLORENCE L., b. Dec. 29, 1869, in Boston.
    ii EMMA SHAW, b. Jan. 29, 1871, in Boston.
    iii LUCY ALICE, b. Oct. 2, 1872, in Brighton.
    iv MARTHA ELEANOR, b. April 23, 1880, in Brighton.

NINTH GENERATION

IX. 171 Robert Chute,[9] (*Dea. Andrew,*[8] *Dea. Daniel,*[7] *Samuel,*[6] *John,*[5] *Lionel,*[4] *James,*[3] *James,*[2] *Lionel*[1]), born in Clements, Annapolis Co., N. S., Dec. 15, 1820; followed his father and grandfather, in the blacksmith trade; married Elizabeth, daughter of John Everett, of Woodstock, N. B., by Rev. Israel Potter, jr., Feb. 27, 1844; and lived in Clements, moved over to Lower Granville, about 1860, died Sept. 30, 1882. His widow married 2d, Dea. Dowie Ditmars Potter, Dec. 10, 1885.

Children:

275 i RICHARD BURPEE, b. Jan. 2, 1845.

      ii LERAINY JANE, b. July 14, 1849; m. William Henry Bohaker,[4] (*Daniel William,*[3] *Daniel,*[2] *Andreas,*[1] from Germany to New York, before the Revolution; to Nova Scotia 1776), Nov. 15, 1868, lived in Lower Granville; moved to Lynn, Mass., May 1885; he is a carpenter. Children:
1. LALIA, b. July 6, 1870; m. Charles O., son of Hugh Weston, in Lynn by Rev. A. A. Williams, Oct. 21, 1889, a shoe manufacturer, and have a son, *Charles Lester,* b. Oct. 4, 1890; the first and only one in the twelfth generation.
2. ALBERTA, b. Aug. 30, 1872; m. Lamont, son of Trafton Phillips of Wells, Me., May 18, 1892.
3. IRENE, b. Jan. 23, 1875.
4. MARZETTA, b. April 11, 1877.
5. ELWOOD YOUNG, b. March 12, 1882.
6. RICHARD BURPEE, b. July 16, 1883.

      iii ANNABELLE CAROLINE, b. Feb. 6, 1852; m. Stephen H., son of Joseph Robblee, Jan. 29, 1874, and live in Lower Granville, farmers. Children:
1. AVARD MILTON, b. May 24, 1865.
2. OSCAR WILLIAM, b. April 29, 1877.
3. RENA, b. Sept. 29, 1879.
4. HATTIE MAY, b. Dec. 15, 1882.
5. MERTIE W., b. Dec. 31, 1884.
6. WATSON D., b. Feb. 21, 1888.

IX. 172. Whitefield Chute[9] (*Abram,*[8] *Daniel,*[7] *Samuel,*[6] *John,*[5] *Lionel,*[4] *James,*[3] *James,*[2] *Lionel*[1]), born in Clements, N. S., March 29, 1823; married Eliza (exactly the same age), daughter of John, son of

Daniel Felch, March 28, 1852, and lived in Newburyport, Mass., six years; returned to Nova Scotia 1858, and lived near Bridgetown; she died July 26, 1890.

Children:

    i MARY LOUISE, b. Oct. 20, 1356; d. Dec. 30.
    ii NAOMI JANE, b. Nov. 27, 1857; m. Levi H. Milberry (*David F., James, Joseph and Elizabeth (Barnes) Milbery*), Aug. 4, 1886; she was a school teacher, and d. Nov. 23, 1887.

IX. 173 Austin Sophronius,[9] (*Abram*,[8] *Daniel*,[7] *Samuel*,[6] *John*,[5] *Lionel*,[4] *James*,[3] *James*,[2] *Lionel*[1]), born in Clements, Jan. 31, 1839; went to the far west in youth; married Nellie M. Forbes, April 18, 1875, and lives at San Bernardino, Cal., a blacksmith.

Children:

    i BERTHA, b. Mar. 29, 1876; m. Alexander Wixom, Mar. 29, 1893.
    ii ELIZABETH, b. July 8, 1877; m. William Rudell, July 8, 1891.
    iii SUSAN, b. July 15, 1879.
    iv CORA BELL, b. Aug. 9, 1881.
    v NELLIE, b. Oct. 22, 1883.
    vi AUSTIN ABRAM, b. Feb. 10, 1886.
    vii ESSAPHENE, b. Dec. 22, 1888.
    viii WILLIAM ROBERT, b. Nov. 30, 1890.

IX. 174 Ephraim Larkins,[9] (*Dea. Aaron*,[8] *Dea. Daniel*,[7] *Samuel*,[6] *John*,[5] *Lionel*,[4] *James*,[3] *James*,[2] *Lionel*[1]), born in Clements, Feb. 27, 1828; married Ruth E., daughter of William and Sarah (Quereau) Hale, Oct. 10 1849; and lived on a part of his father's old farm, about eight miles from Digby, a farmer; she died Sept. 8, 1868, aged forty; he married 2nd, Dalina (Chute) Marriett, Dec. 18, 1870. See No. 66. Mr. Chute died June 1893.

Children:

276 i NORMAN WILFRED, b. Jan. 6, 1851.
277 ii FREEMAN EZRA, b. Feb. 2, 1853.
    iii ROBERT ODBER, b. Dec. 8, 1855; lost at sea 1881.
    iv WILLIAM EDWIN, b. Dec. 8, 1859; lost off the "Edward Blake" December, 1876.
    v ELMER ELLSWORTH, b. November. 1862; d. of slow fever July, 1867.
    vi LILIA FARRINGTON, b. Apr. 13, 1867; d. of slow fever August, 1867.
    vii MYRON ELLSWORTH, b. Apr. 27, 1872

IX. 175 Joseph Wentworth,[9] (*Aaron*,[8] *Daniel*,[7] *Samuel*,[6] *John*,[5] *Lionel*,[4] *James*,[3] *James*,[2] *Lionel*[1]), born in Clements, Dec. 24, 1829; married Maria Dakin (*Jacob, Abram*), and widow of William A. Southern, Nov. 17, 1851, and lived in Bridgetown, Digby, and in the United States.

Children:

    i IDA E., b. Sept. 1, 1852; m. Ernest A. Stratton 1870, of Boston, and live in Brooklyn, N. Y.; four children.

    ii MEHITABLE, b. Oct. 28, 1853; m. Edwin, son of William and Abba (Simpson) Potter Oct. 29, 1869, Digby, N. S.

278 iii WILLIAM ST. CLAIR, b. Sept. 1, 1855.

    iv DEAN WALKER, b. Aug. 13, 1857; went to sea, and was mate of the United States bark "Mohegan" 1880; m. Agnes, dau. of John and Annie E. Tyler (niece of Pres. John Tyler) Nelson of Orange, N. J., Nov. 13, 1889, and is a first-class plumber in New York city.

    v JESSIE ANN, b. Oct. 3, 1859; m. John Rice jr. 1876, and had a daughter Georgina; m. 2nd, Daniel Vernon, 1884, and live in New York city and Brooklyn.

IX. 176 Amos Alva Chute,[9] (*Aaron,*[8] *Daniel,*[7] *Samuel,*[6] *John,*[5] *Lionel,*[4] *James,*[3] *James,*[2] *Lionel*[1]), born in Clements, N. S., May 15, 1837; married Celina E. Chute (see No. 86), of Granville, Feb. 12, 1862; and lived in Clements; died Jan. 13, 1878; she married 2nd, Almon Moore, October 1884, and lives at Freeport, Digby Co.

Children:

    i ADA J., b. Dec. 25, 1862; m. Charles, son of Israel D. Brooks, Dec. 20, 1880; m. 2nd, James M. Norwood, July 29, 1890; and live in Lynn, Mass.

    ii ENA F., b. July 11, 1866; m. G. Whitefield Moore, 1885, and live at Freeport, N. S.

    iii ELLA G., b. Dec. 9, 1867; m. Fayette Morgan, July 7, 1886, and live at Dickinson, Stark Co., N. D.

    iv MARGURITTA, b. July 9, 1878.

    v BLANCHE MAY MOORE, b. 1885.

IX. 177 Abner Woodworth,[9] *Aaron,*[8] *Daniel,*[7] *Samuel,*[6] *John,*[5] *Lionel,*[4] *James,*[3] *James,*[2] *Lionel*[1]), born in Clements, July 4, 1840; married Mary Ann Kniffin[6] (*Stephen,*[5] *George,*[4] *George,*[3] *George,*[2] *George,*[1] from Rhode Island), Dec. 28, 1865; and lives on a part of his father's old farm.

Children:

    i AVARD, b. Oct. 7, 1866.

    ii WILLIAM, b. Aug. 8, 1868.

    iii CHARLES L., b. June 28, 1870.

    iv AARON I., b. June 10, 1871.
    v EDWARD, b. July 25, 1872.
    vi NORMAN E., b. Aug. 2, 1874; d. Nov. 26. These young men nearly all live in Boston and Lynn.
    vii NELLIE MAY, b. Oct. 25, 1875; d. Feb. 24, 1889.

IX. 178 Obadiah Chute,[9] (*Boemer,*[8] *Daniel,*[7] *Samuel,*[6] *John,*[5] *Lionel,*[4] *James,*[3] *James,*[2] *Lionel* [1]), born in Hillsburgh, Digby Co., Jan. 12, 1832; married Harriet Lovena, (born June 16, 1843), daughter of William Brennan of Round Hill, N. S., Aug. 8, 1865, and lived on the Digby side of Bear River; a farmer and jeweler.

Children:
    i MINETTA SOPHIA, b. May 2, 1866.
    ii WILLIAM MYERS, b. Oct. 17, 1867, jeweler.
    iii FRANK AUGUSTUS, b. June 4, 1870, East Boston.
    iv BERTRAND, b. Jan. 24, 1873.
    v OBADIAH MAXWELL, b. Sept. 17, 1874.

IX. 179 Sidney Chute,[9] (*Boemer,*[8] *Daniel,*[7] *Samuel,*[6] *John,* [5] *Lionel,*[4] *James,*[3] *James,*[2] *Lionel* [1]), born in Hillsburgh, Nov. 28, 1841; married Sophronia Bent, Dec. 31, 1868, and lives on his father's farm on the Sissiboo road; she died July, 1869, aged twenty-two; he married 2nd, Sarah Bell Gilliland (*Jacob Kingsley, Joseph,* from Ireland), Dec. 3, 1873.

Children:
    i IDELLA MAY, b. Dec. 8, 1874; d. Jan. 1, 1876.
    ii CHARLES HERBERT, b. Apr. 22, 1877.
    iii WILLIAM MINARD, b. Jan. 25, 1879.
    iv JANET ELIZABETH, b. Apr. 27, 1881.

IX. 180 Daniel Rogers Chute,[9] (*Benjamin,*[8] *Daniel,*[7] *Samuel,*[6] *John,*[5] *Lionel,*[4] *James,*[3] *James,*[2] *Lionel* [1]), born in Clements, east side of Moose River, March 22, 1835; married Rebecca, born Sept. 6, 1842; daughter of David and Sally (Wear) Minard, Dec. 19, 1865; and lived near Clementsvale, a farmer and lumberman; he was killed by the falling of a tree, Feb. 9, 1881; after that the widow and family lived a few years in New Hampshire; but latterly for a few years in Boston.

Children:
    i EFFIE MAY, b. Nov. 29, 1866; d. Dec. 31, 1882.
    ii FRANK L., b. Sept. 29, 1869; d. Jan. 26, 1892, Boston.
    iii ANNIE LAURIE, b. Jan. 19, 1871; m. Lester Robbins, January 1891.

iv INEZ, b. April 19, 1872, adopted by Dr. Crocker, Cambridgeport.
v SARAH ELIZABETH, b. May 6, 1874.
vi GEORGE OTIS, b. June 14, 1876.
vii NELLIE, b. Sept. 10, 1878; d. June 23, 1883.

IX. 181 Zenas Eliakim, the youngest brother, born July 4, 1847; married Ella S., daughter of Joseph Potter, Dec. 28, 1876, and settled at Colbrook, on "Brooklyn street" Cornwallis, N. S., a farmer.

Children:

i ROLAND ARTHUR, b. Sept. 5, 1877.
ii LENA EVANS, b. June 1, 1879.
iii JOHN MANNING, b. Nov. 9, 1880.
iv HARRY NEWTON, b. Mar. 26, 1882.
v SYRENA AMELIA, b. Aug. 10, 1883.
vi NOBLE BROWN, b. June 12, 1885.
vii ELLA, b ——, 1887.
viii ANNA, b. ——, 1890.

IX. 182 Everett Spurr Chute,[9] (*Daniel,*[8] *Daniel,*[7] *Samuel,*[6] *John,*[5] *Lionel,*[4] *James,*[3] *James,*[2] *Lionel*[1]), born in Clements, May 26, 1838; married Helen, daughter of John Graham of Picton, N. S., in Beverley, Mass., Nov. 26, 1860; lived a few years in Clements, N. S., and about 1865, went to Carleton Co., N. B., and settled in Argyle; being pious and zealous in the Baptist church they made him deacon in 1880.

Children:

279 i SAMUEL GILBERT, b. Feb. 14, 1862.
280 ii JOHN NELSON, b. Mar. 19, 1863.
iii HERBERT N., b. June 26, 1864; m. Olga Sabes, Dec. 25, 1888; live in Chicago.
iv ELIZABETH ANN, b. Jan. 5, 1866; m. Edward D., son of Edward C. Charlton of Cornwallis, N. S., Sept. 1, 1886, and had (1), *Harry H.*, b. May 18, 1887; (2), *Oscar E.*, b. Oct. 6, 1888; (3), *Esther M.*, b. Sept. 21, 1890; d. May, 1891. Mrs. Charlton went to Boston 1880, to Aikin, S. C., 1891, and back again 1892, and d. in New Brunswick, June 29, 1893.
v OTIS EVERETT, b. July 1867; d. in N. B., Aug. 13, 1868.
vi WILLIAM WESLEY, b. Sept. 26, 1868.
vii ELLEN ADELIA, b. Aug. 17, 1872.

IX. 183 Nehemiah,[9] (*Daniel,*[8] *Daniel,*[7] *Samuel,*[6] *John,*[5] *Lionel,*[4] *James,*[3] *James,*[2] *Lionel*[1]), born Nov. 12, 1839; married Melissa Adelia, born July 16, 1843, daughter of Richard and Sarah Ann (Brennan)

GENEALOGIES OF THE CHUTE FAMILY. 157

Harris, by Rev. James Taylor, Jan. 1, 1862, and live on the Sissiboo road, Digby Co., near Bear River, peaceable industrious farmer.
Children:

    i ANNA EUGENIA, b. Feb. 25, 1863; m. Thomas Fletcher Chute (see 220), Aug. 13, 1884.
    ii RICHARD HAVELOCK, b. March 19, 1866; d. Nov. 12, 1875.
    iii ESTHER ALBERTA, b. Mar. 22. 1868; m. Charles Wesley Hardwick, Dec. 29, 1892.
    iv HENRIETTA ORILLA, b. Mar. 22, 1868.
    v WILLIAM OSCAR, b. June 17, 1870.
    vi LORENZO BURPEE, b. Dec. 25, 1872; d. Nov. 25, 1875.
    vii FLORENCE EDITH, b. Jan. 13, 1875.
    viii ARCHE MAXWELL, b. Oct. 6, 1877.
    ix LOTTIE GERTRUDE, b. Mar. 22, 1883.
    x GEORGE ARNOLD, b. Mar. 12, 1886.

IX 184 Melbourn Chute,[9] (*Daniel,*[8] *Daniel,*[7] *Samuel,*[6] *John,*[5] *Lionel,*[4] *James,*[3] *James,*[2] *Lionel*[1]), born in Clements, N. S., Oct. 15, 1849; married by George C. Lorimer, D.D. in Boston, Annie (born May 8, 1852), daughter of Timothy D. Driscoll of Prince Edward Island, June 10, 1874; she died June 12, 1886; he married 2nd, Lucy R. (born 1845), daughter of Richard Picknell and widow of Winslow M. Newcomb,* Aug. 18, 1888; live in Quincy, Mass.
Children:

    i EDWARD ARTHUR, b. May 27, 1875.
    ii EDITH MAY, b. Sept. 1, 1877.
    iii LOIS ELEANOR, b. Feb. 20, 1880.
    iv ERNEST MELBOURN, b. Apr. 27, 1882.
    v JAMES EVERETT, b. May 31, 1885; d. April, 1886.

IX. 185 Richard Scott, brother to the above, born in Clements, Mar. 24, 1855; married Eliza Ann, daughter of Silas Berry, Nov. 7, 1880, and live in Hillsburgh, Digby Co., N. S., on the "Morgan road."
Children:

    i RHODA V., b. August, 1881.
    ii ADA B., b. Sept. 3, 1887.

IX. 186 Elias Chute,[9] (*David,*[8] *Daniel,*[7] *Samuel,*[6] *John,*[5] *Lionel,*[4] *James,*[3] *James,*[2] *Lionel*[1]), born in Clements, Feb. 9, 1839; taken to

---

* Winslow Miller Newcomb[8] (*Jesse P.,*[7] *Bryant,*[6] *Thomas,*[5] *Isaac,*[4] *John,*[3] *John,*[2] *Francis,*[1] came from England, 1635, aged 30, wife Rachel, had 10 children; he d. 1692; signed his name "ffranais nucom"), b. Dec. 20, 1821; m. Mary A., dau. of Ezekiel and Mary Worcester, 1845, had 10 children; lived at Quincy Neck, Mass.; she d. 1863, aged 41; he d. November, Thanksgiving, 1885, aged 63.

Bayham, Ont., October, 1850; learned to be a cabinet maker at Iona; to Michigan 1860; and was in a battery of artillery in Tennessee in the war; went to Blue Earth city, Minn., 1866; to Maysville, Dekalb Co., Mo., 1868; married Sarah A. Hamer (born Feb. 10, 1847), Oct. 8, 1869; was a carpenter and wagon maker there; but since 1880, moved to Lathrop, Clinton Co.

Children:

    i FRANK, b. Oct. 7, 1870; d. Mar. 17, 1890.
    ii MILO L., b. Mar. 19, 1872.
    iii ELLA E., b. Feb. 15, 1874.
    iv JAMES, b. Aug. 8, 1877; d. Nov. 3, 1878.
    v CELESTA A., b. Nov. 3, 1879.
    vi ELBA J., b. June 3, 1881.
    vii HASSEL BLAINE, b. May 24, 1884.

IX. 187 Silas Parker Chute,[9] (*Benj. Foster,*[8] *Abram,*[7] *Samuel,*[6] *John,*[5] *Lionel,*[4] *James,*[3] *James,*[2] *Lionel*[1]), born in Cornwallis, Kings Co., N. S., July 23, 1834; married Mehitable, daughter of Luther Morse, Oct. 29, 1856; she died Feb. 20, 1862, aged twenty-five; he married 2nd, Lucy, daughter of Samuel Balcomb, Aug. 2, 1864; Mr. Chute is a farmer in Cornwallis, also has a sawmill, carding machine, cider-mill, etc.

Children:

    i FOSTER MORSE, b. Sept. 23, 1857; m. Belle, daughter of Samuel Balcomb.
    ii GUILFORD DUDLEY, b. Jan. 31, 1861.
    iii SAMUEL B., b. Apr. 30, 1867; and are in Denver, Colo.
    iv ROSE ELLA, b. Oct. 31, 1868; m. Thomas, son of George Wm. Charlton, Sept. 1889.
    v, vi Twins. } Nameless.

IX. 188 Leander Chute[9] (*John Nelson,*[8] *Abram,*[7] *Samuel,*[6] *John,*[5] *Lionel,*[4] *James,*[3] *James,*[2] *Lionel*[1]), born in Cornwallis, July 28, 1835; married Margaret, daughter of Christopher Rainforth, March 4, 1858, and lived on his father's old farm, on Post Road, near Berwick.

Children:

    i SARAH, b. Oct. 14, 1859; m. Ambrose, son of Thomas R. Palmer,[4] (*Elijah,*[1] *Benjamin,*[2] *Lewis*[1]), Feb. 25, 1882; and live in Somerville, Mass.
    ii ANNA B., b. Oct. 7, 1861; m. George Jones, April 1889.
    iii AUGUSTA, b. Jan. 14, 1864; m. Charles Wm. Trombley, Sept. 17, 1890; a druggist, Lynn, Mass. (*Fred William*), b. July 9, 1891.

GENEALOGIES OF THE CHUTE FAMILY.   159

    iv ELLA BLANCHE, b. Dec. 10, 1865.
    v JOHN NELSON, b. April 23, 1867; m. Alfarata Palmer, wid. of Melbourn Nichols, May 25, 1892.
    vi FREDDY L., b. Sept. 2, 1873; d. Sept. 22, 1875.
    vii MAGGIE I., b. Mar. 2, 1878.

IX. 189 Richardson,[9] (*William H.,*[8] *Abram,*[7] *Samuel,*[6] *John,*[5] *Lionel,*[4] *James,*[3] *James,*[2] *Lionel*[1]), born in Cornwallis, Mar. 10, 1840; married Fanny M., daughter of Dea. Oliver H. Cogswell, Feb. 6, 1862; she died June 21, 1881, aged thirty-eight; he married 2nd, Abba, daughter of William Cox, Dec. 28, 1881; she died Sept. 21, 1890; he married 3rd, Zilpha D. Davidson, Oct. 7, 1891; Mr. Chute is an old-fashioned farmer.

Children:

    i REBECCA LOVINA, b. Dec. 15, 1862.
    ii EDWARD MANNING, b. Mar. 23, 1865.
    iii BRUNELLE D., b. Oct. 6, 1867.
    iv WILLIAM OLIVER, b. Dec. 9, 1869.
    v WALLACE I., b. Feb. 26, 1874.
    vi LENA MAY, b. Jan. 19, 1876; d. June 14, 1877.
    vii BURTON ALDEN, b. Sept. 28, 1879.

IX. 190 John Burton,[9] (*William H.,*[8] *Abram,*[7] *Samuel,*[6] *John,*[5] *Lionel,*[4] *James,*[3] *James,*[2] *Lionel*[1]), born in Cornwallis, Aug. 23, 1844; married Lucy Ilsley, Jan. 4, 1871, and is a merchant in Berwick.

Children:

    i JAMES WINNIFRED, b. Dec. 27, 1872; d. Jan. 24, 1878.
    ii JENNIE MAY, b. Aug. 30, 1874; d. Dec. 1, 1877.
    iii NELLIE ERDINE, b. Apr. 20, 1876; d. Dec. 4, 1877.
    iv FLORA LOVINA, b. Nov. 8, 1877.
    v UNIE MAUD, b. July 7, 1879.
    vi GEORGE KENNETH, b. Feb. 3, 1885.
    vii HOLLIS B., b. Aug. 12, 1889.

IX. 191 Henry J. Chute[9] (*William H.,*[8] *Abram,*[7] *Samuel,*[6] *John,*[5] *Lionel,*[4] *James,*[3] *James,*[2] *Lionel*[1]), born in Cornwallis, May 10, 1855; married Anna, daughter of William Burgess, and is a justice of the peace in Berwick.

Children:

    i ROY, b. ——.
    ii GERTRUDE, b. ——.

  iii WILLIAM HENRY, b. ——.
  iv VERNON E., b. August 1888.
  v —— ——.

IX. 192 Isaac Newton Chute[9] (*Sam Burton*,[8] *Abram*,[7] *Samuel*,[6] *John*,[5] *Lionel*,[4] *James*,[3] *James*,[2] *Lionel*[1]), born in Malahide, Elgin Co., Ont., April 5, 1848; married Florence Green * (born Aug. 30, 1852), Jan. 1871, in Faribault Co., Minn., and live near Fairmount, Martin Co., Minn. Farmer.
 Children:

  i ERNEST NEWTON, b. March 11, 1872.
  ii OLIVER A., b. April 29, 1873; d. June 6, 1877.
  iii

IX. 193 Edward Manning[9] (*T. Ansley*,[8] *Abram*,[7] *Samuel*,[6] *John*,[5] *Lionel*,[4] *James*,[4] *James*,[3] *Lionel*[1]), born in Cornwallis, N. S., Mar. 25, 1844; married Elizabeth, daughter of Enoch L. Cogswell, Nov. 1871, and live on the side of the South Mountain, Cornwallis, a farmer
 Children:

  i ENOLA ETHEL, b. May 2, 1874.
  ii ANSLEY BURNET, b. Nov. 21, 1876.
  iii LAURIE MAGGIE, b. July 8, 1880.
  iv CLYDE CLIFTON, b. Dec. 1, 1884.

IX. 194 Joseph Fanshaw,[9] (*T. Ansley*,[8] *Abram*,[7] *Samuel*,[6] *John*,[5] *Lionel*,[4] *James*,[3] *James*,[2] *Lionel*[1]), born in Cornwallis, Oct. 9, 1846; after traveling in the far west, Minnesota and elsewhere, he returned; married Miriam Louise, daughter of Enoch L. Cogswell, Dec. 18, 1876, and settled down as a farmer, in or near Morristown; died Aug. 13, 1889.
 Children:

  i ESSIE INEZ, b. Nov. 10, 1879.
  ii LOTTIE DEWOLF, b. Jan. 15, 1882.
  iii MAGGIE, b. May 22, 1886.

IX. 195 Benjamin Foster,[9] (*T. Ansley*,[8] *Abram*,[7] *Samuel*,[6] *John*,[5] *Lionel*,[4] *James*,[3] *James*,[2] *Lionel*[1]), born in Cornwallis, Dec. 13, 1848; traveled somewhat in the far West, but returned and married

---

Lorenzo,[7] *Lorenzo*,[6] *Seth*,[5] 1746; *Seth*,[4] 1700 *Henry*,[3] *Henry*,[2] *Thomas*,[1] 1606, Leicester, Eng.; to Massachusetts 1636; to Malden 1650; d. Dec. 19, 1667; had ten children. They are traced back to the royal family of France, about A.D. 1300.

Ermina, daughter of Robert Robinson, July 18, 1888, in Cornwallis.
Children :

    i GRACE, b. July 5, 1889.
    ii ———, b. Aug. 25, 1890.

IX. 196 James Perry, J. P., another brother, born Nov. 22, 1858; married Adelia Foster, in Cornwallis.
Children :

    i FANNY, b. Aug. 7, 1888.
    ii DORA, b. Sept. 1889.
    iii FREDDY, b. Oct., 1890.

IX. 197 William Albert[9] (*Abram*,[8] *William*,[7] *Samuel*,[6] *John*,[5] *Lionel*,[4] *James*,[3] *James*,[2] *Lionel* [1]), born in Dalhousie, Annapolis Co., N. S., June 27, 1849; married in Taunton, Bristol Co., Mass., Jan. 19, 1875, Oliver F., daughter of Allen and Betsey E. (Card) Austin, and is a workman in Taunton.
Children :

    i DANIEL ALDEN, b. Jan. 13, 1884.

IX. 198 James William Chute[9] (*James Lyman*,[8] *William*,[7] *Samuel*,[6] *John*,[5] *Lionel*,[4] *James*,[3] *James*,[2] *Lionel* [1]), born in Clarence, Annapolis Co., N. S., July 4, 1841; married Ellen, daughter of James and Margaret (Moody) Banks, Jan. 13, 1864; lived twenty-five years near Bridgetown, then emigrated to Wilton, N. H.
Children ;

    i SOPHIA. b. Oct. 18, 1864; m. Elias Sabean, June 18, 1882, and had da. Hattie b. Apr. 2, 1884; he was drowned off the Ocean Wave, Nov. 4, 1884, aged twenty-two. She m. 2d, Wm. H. Bent, Feb. 23, 1886; and had *Gordan D. Bent*, b. Dec. 26, 1887; *Elsie*, b. June 10, 1888; and *Lucy*, b. Sept. 8, 1891.
    ii JAMES LYMAN, b. Feb. 9, 1866, m. Cordelia Riley, of Rhode Island, Sept. 15, 1890.
    iii NELSON W., b. Jan. 27, 1868; m. ———.
    iv ANNIE, b. Feb. 26, 1871; m. ———.
    v MARY ETHEL, b. July 28, 1873; m. Wm. F. Potter, of Rhode Island, Jan. 1, 1890.
    vi EDMUND CROWELL, b. Oct. 13, 1874.
    vii MAGGIE MAUD, b. May 2, 1877.

IX. 199 David Fletcher,[9] (*James*,[8] *Lyman*,[7] *William Samuel*,[6] *John*,[5] *Lionel*,[4] *James*,[4] *James*,[2] *Lionel* [1]), born in Clarence, Nov. 9, 1845;

married Anna A. Farris, Feb. 15, 1870; moved to Windsor Depot, N. H., about 1880, and is doing well there as a tradesman.

Children:

    i CHARLES AUGUSTUS, b. Nov. 21, 1870; d. Nov. 2, 1874.
    ii JOHN D., b. Aug. 2, 1872.
    iii MARY E., b. Mar. 21, 1874.
    iv LUCY A., b. Apr. 2, 1876; d. Aug. 8, 1887.
    v CHARLES F., b. Aug. 10, 1877.
    vi RETTA DEAN, b. Sept. 8, 1879.
    vii WILLIAM LAMONT, b. Oct. 19, 1881.
    viii EDITH LILIAN, b. Sept. 25, 1883; d. Aug. 21, 1887.
    ix FLORENCE MABEL, b. Mar. 8, 1885.
    x FREDDY R., b. Aug. 26, 1886.
    xi ARTHUR G., b. Sept. 19, 1887.
    xii HATTIE A., b. Sept. 9, 1889.
    xiii DAVID WESLEY, b. Oct. 6, 1890; d. Dec. 9.

IX. 200 James Samuel,[9] (*Daniel,*[8] *Samuel,*[7] *Samuel,*[6] *John,*[5] *Lionel,*[4] *James,*[3] *James,*[2] *Lionel*[1]), born at Frederickton, N. B., Nov. 30, 1843; went to Orient, Me., in March, 1861, and into Co. I, 7th Maine Volunteers in August, into the war; was wounded at Mechanicsville, was also at Antietam, Pine Run, etc.; was mustered out and came home in March, 1863; reenlisted in 2nd Me. Cav. August, 1863; came home and married by Rev. Mr. Cunningham, Sarah L., daughter of Stillman Stone, Feb. 29, 1864, and was mustered out in March, 1865; lives in Augusta, Me.; keeps a barber shop; had left leg taken off Aug. 16, 1883.

Children:

    i EMMA C., b. Nov. 21, 1864; m. Walter N. Foss, Dec. 31, 1884; live in Augusta.
    ii STILLMAN W., b. May 4, 1869; d. Mar. 5, 1880.
    iii HARRY, b. July 11, 1879; d. March 25, 1883.
    iv FREDDY, b. July 11, 1879; d. Feb. 1880.

IX. 201 Laughlin Isadore Chute[9] (*Daniel,*[8] *Samuel,*[7] *Samuel,*[6] *John,*[5] *Lionel,*[4] *James,*[3] *James,*[2] *Lionel*[1]), born near Frederickton, N. B., Jan. 11, 1846; married Maria E., daughter of Robert and Mary (Taylor) Franklin, Feb. 28, 1868, and lived near Eel River, Lower Woodstock, twenty years; moved to Atkins, Minn., May 1888. Farmer.

Children:

    i CHARLES D., b. Dec. 3, 1868.
    ii EFFIE B., b. Feb. 26, 1871.

iii ROBERT F., b. June 8, 1873.
iv LOUISE M., b. July 17, 1879.
v OLIVE A., b. May 21, 1881.
vi CLARENCE W., b. Mar. 19, 1883.
vii DORA MARIA, b. Nov. 28, 1886.
viii EDWARD HAROLD, Feb. 11, 1891.

IX. 202 David Alfred[9] (*Dea. Thomas H.,*[8] *Samuel,*[7] *Samuel,*[6] *John,*[5] *Lionel,*[4] *James,*[3] *James,*[2] *Lionel* [1]), born in Corwallis, N. S., near Harborville, May 26, 1839; married Mary Ellen, daughter of Michael and Christiana (Bolser) Butler, of Wilmot, N. S., by Rev. Jacob Norton, Jan. 7, 1866, and moved to Charlestown,—now a part of Boston—Mass., in 1867, and has lived there since, an industrious carpenter.

Children:

i THOMAS HANDLEY, b. Nov. 15, 1866; m. Nellie A., dau. of Thomas Wall, Jan. 6, 1893.
ii EDWARD S., b. March 7, 1869; m. ——.
iii NELLIE ELIZA, b. Jan. 11, 2872; m. Charles Sumner Harris, Oct. 18, 1892, Boston.
iv MARY ELLA GOLDIE, b. Sept. 14, 1876.
v MARIAM P., b. May 23 1878.
vi SARAH B., b. Sept. 19, 1880; d. Oct. 18.

IX. 203 James Wellington[9] (*Samuel,*[8] *Samuel,*[7] *Samuel,*[6] *John,*[5] *Lionel,*[4] *James,*[3] *James,*[2] *Lionel* [1]), born in York Co., N. B., July 15, 1849; married Rebecca O., daughter of Henry James Fowler, Dec. 31, 1877, and live in Haynesville, York Co., N. B., farmers.

Children:

i HARLEY EUGENE, b. May 8, 1878.
ii ELLEN, b. July 15, 1879.
iii HAVELOCK, b. Dec. 3, 1882.
iv RAY CECIL, b. Sept. 10, 1884.

IX. 204 Edward William,[9] (*Samuel,*[8] *Samuel,*[7] *Samuel,*[6] *John,*[5] *Lionel,*[4] *James,*[3] *James,*[2] *Lionel* [1]), born in York Co., N. B., July, 3, 1851; married Irene, daughter of Abram Crouse, July 12, 1882, and live in Haynesville, N. B.; farmers.

Children:

i JAMES ABRAM, b. July 28, 1883.
ii HIRAM STILSON, b. Apr. 27, 1885.
iii NELSON, b. May 1, 1887.
iv LEELAND, b. Aug. 1, 1888.
v PERCY H., b. May 22, 1890.

IX. 205 Arthur Nelson,[9] (*Samuel,*[8] *Samuel,*[7] *Samuel,*[6] *John,*[5] *Lionel,*[4] *James,*[3] *James,*[2] *Lionel*[1]), born in York Co., N. B., Mar. 10, 1853; married Susan (born Feb. 29, 1848), daughter of John Elliott, Nov. 26, 1876, and lives in Haynesville; a farmer, and a pious deacon in the Baptist church.

Children:

    i DAVID S , b. Jan. 19, 1878.
    ii ROBERT R., b. Mar. 4, 1879.
    iii RUTH ANN, b. Dec. 11, 1880.
    iv MARY ELLA, b. Aug. 9, 1883.

IX. 206 William George,[9] (*George W.,*[8] *George W.,*[7] *John,*[6] *John,*[5] *Lionel,*[4] *James,*[3] *James,*[2] *Lionel*[1]), born in Boston, Mass., Oct. 23, 1832; married Melvina E., daughter of Calvin Hadley, Jan. 22, 1868. Mrs. Chute died Dec. 4, 1873, aged thirty-four; he runs a shoe shop in North Leominister.

Children :

    i GEORGE W., b. Nov. 7, 1869; d. Aug. 23, 1885.
    ii FREDDY WILBUR, b. Aug. 1, 1873; d. Aug. 3.

IX. 207 John Worcester,[9] (*George W.,*[8] *George W.,*[7] *John,*[6] *John,*[5] *Lionel,*[4] *James,*[3] *James,*[2] *Lionel*[1]), born in Randolph, Mass., May 30, 1839; married Caroline H., daughter of Edward Prevear, Nov. 26, 1869; lived in Boston several years in the shoe business, but since 1888, in North Leominster.

Children :

    i WILLIAM EDWARD, b. Aug. 30, 1872, at Saugus.
    ii WALTER EARL, b. Oct. 27, 1874; d. Mar. 20, 1875.
    iii CHARLES H., b. Apr. 1, 1878, at Marlboro.
    iv CLARA GERTIE, b. Mar. 26, 1880.

IX. 208 George Washington,[9] (*George W.,*[8] *George W.,*[7] *John,*[6] *John,*[5] *Lionel,*[4] *James,*[3] *James,*[2] *Lionel*[1]), born in Canton, Mass., Apr. 14, 1841; married Annie E., daughter of George W. and Sarah (Balch) Wilder of Worcester, Mass., Jan. 8, 1867, and lived some in New York state; moved to Leominster, Mass., 1876.

Children :

    i ETHEL SARAH, b. in Worcester, Jan. 2, 1873.
    ii JOSEPHINE W., b. in Yonkers, N. Y., Mar. 2, 1875.

MRS. IRENE P. CHUTE.

MRS. SUSAN R. GOUCHER.

IX. 209 Charles C.,[9] (*Gilbert R.*,[8] *Peter*,[7] *John*,[6] *John*,[5] *Lionel*,[4] *James*,[3] *James*,[2] *Lionel*[1]), born in Aylesford, N. S., June 15, 1848; married Jennie A. Smith Mar. 12, 1874, and lived at Margaretville, shore of the Bay of Fundy, N. S., about eighteen years; shoemaker, and deacon in the Baptist church. Mrs. Chute died May 1, 1886, aged thirty-eight; he married 2nd, Flora, daughter of Henry L. Baker, 1887, and moved to Melvern Square, 1892.

Children:

    i EFFIE MAY, b. July 18, 1876.
    ii MINNIE ALICE, b. Mar. 4, 1878.
    iii NELLIE E., b. ——, 1879; d. 1880.
    iv JESSIE NORINE, b. Mar. 20, 1881.
    v LAURA, b. 1888.

IX. 210 Joseph Howe,[9] (*Gilbert R.*,[8] *Peter*,[7] *John*,[6] *John*,[5] *Lionel*,[4] *James*,[3] *James*,[2] *Lionel*[1]), born in Aylesford, N. S., May 17, 1854; went to sea several years and was a captain; but since 1880, a merchant at Middleton, Annapolis Co.; married Olivia, daughter of Capt. John Hurst (school teacher John Hurst, and Relief, daughter of Joel Farnsworth), 1874.

Children:

    i CARRIE, b. 1875.
    ii MABEL ANN, b. ——.
    iii ELSIE, b. ——.
    iv HAZEL, b. ——

IX. 211 Lycurgus, another brother, born in or near Aylesford, July 18, 1858; married Annie J. Anderson, April, 1880, and lived in Lower Granville; farmer; she died Sept. 28, 1891, aged thirty-four; he died Jan. 14, 1883.

Children:

    i LIZZIE J., b. Sept., 1881.
    ii CHARLES L., b. Oct., 1882.

IX. 212 Albert H.,[9] (*Cornelius H.*,[8] *Joseph F.*,[7] *John*,[6] *John*,[5] *Lionel*,[4] *James*,[3] *James*,[2] *Lionel*[1]), born at Lyme, N. H., Jan. 7, 1856; taken to Wisconsin and Minnesota by his parents; married in Minneapolis, Mary Hoy, 1885; she died Jan. 27, 1890.

Children:

    i JOSEPH, b. Dec. 27, 1887.
    ii HARRIS, b. Jan. 15, 1890.

IX. 213 James Chute[9] (*Ezra*,[8] *James*,[7] *Benjamin*,[6] *John*,[5] *Lionel*,[4] *James*,[3] *James*,[2] *Lionel*[1]), born in Granville, a mile below Bridgton, Dec. 15, 1833; married Bethia, daughter of Samuel Foster, jr., Feb. 2, 1856; and lives under the North Mountain, back of Bridgton, a farmer.

Children:

    i MARY FANNIE, b. Nov. 19, 1856; m. Whitefield Wilkins, Dec. 31, 1874.
    ii ROBERT MORTON, b. Sept. 21, 1858; m. ——.
    iii HANNAH AZUBA, b. June 20, 1860; m. Wm. Brabzon, July 29, 1878; and d. Oct. 11, 1890. Four children: *Brabzon, Comstock and Ladue*. Is a firm at Marlboro, Mass.
    iv GEORGIANA B., b. Jan. 9, 1862; d. Dec. 4, 1865.
    v EMMA LOVENIA, b. Aug. 29, 1863; m. John P. Lawrence[9]* (*Capt. Samuel C.*,[8] *Joseph S.*,[7] *John G.*,[6] *Abel*,[5] *Jonathan*,[4] *Ebenezer*,[3] *Peleg*,[2] *John*[1], b. in England 1609, to Salem, Mass., 1630, d. July 11, 1667), Oct. 16, 1886; and live in Allston, Mass.; have a son Lester Walter, b. 1888.
    vi GEORGIANA, b. Sept. 28, 1865; m. Herbert J. Banks, Nov. 23, 1884.
    vii ANNA GERTIE, b. Apr. 12, 1867; m. Frank Comstock, Aug. 29, 1890.
    viii CASSIE BELLE, b. May 18, 1869; m. Henry Ladue, Nov. 1889.
    ix WILLIAM JUDSON, b. July 16, 1872.
    x FLORENCE MAY, b. Feb. 16, 1874.
    xi ANGIE SAVILLA, b. Nov. 18, 1875.
    xii WALTER STEADMAN, b. Jan. 22, 1878.

IX. 214 Enoch Steadman[9] (*Ezra*,[8] *James*,[7] *Benjamin*,[6] *John*,[5] *Lionel*,[4] *James*,[3] *James*,[2] *Lionel*[1]), born in Granville, Mar. 19, 1836; married Eliza Ann, daughter of Joseph Gilliatt, Dec. 27, 1865; and lived in Granville; killed by a tree, Jan. 31, 1883; she died Nov. 1, 1878.

Children:

    i JESSIE, b. Oct. 18, 1866; m. Capt. Sidney Berry, 1887.
    ii HOLDEN W., b. July 21, 1872.

IX. 215 Wallace G., another brother, born March 10, 1839; went to Elgin Co., Ont., at about twenty years of age, married Caroline Victoria, daughter of Charles and Tamer (McConnell), Chute (see No. 99), in Malahide, Feb. 25, 1862; lived a few years there; then went to

---

* Ancestral lineage: (1), *Robert Lawrence*, of Lancashire, about 1150, was granted a coat of arms by Richard I, 1191, as Sir Robert Lawrence, of Ashton Hall. (2), *Sir Robert*, son and successor of the Knight of the Crusades. (3), *James*, married Matilda, heiress and daughter of John De Washington. (4), *John*, lived to the 37th year of Henry III. (5), *John*, died in 1260. (6), *Sir Robert*, m. Margaret Holden. (7), *Sir Robert*, married Amphilbis Longford. (8), *Nicholas*. (9), *John*, died 1461. (10), *Thomas*. (11), *John*, married Margery ——, and died 1504. (12), *Robert*. (13), *John*, married Elizabeth ——. (14), *John*, married Agnes ——. (15), *John*, married Johan. (16), *Henry and Mary*, had John, born 1609; and came to America.

Hamilton, at the head of Lake Ontario, a manufacturer of a patent medicine; died Dec. 14, 1875.

Children:

    i MABEL L., b. Aug. 18, 1862; m. Frank W. Crosby, Jan. 5, 1890; live at Ironwood, Wis.

    ii CLARENCE, b. March 1, 1864; m. May (——) Royer, 1886; have two children, in Chicago.

IX. 216 Hiram Marshall Chute[9] (*Gilbert,*[8] *James,*[7] *Benjamin,*[6] *John,*[5] *Lionel,*[4] *James,*[3] *James,*[2] *Lionel*[1]), born in Granville, Oct. 2, 1839; married Melissa, daughter of Benjamin Chute of Clements (see No. 63), Sept. 29, 1864; and lived in Granville till 1872, when they moved to Clements, upon her father's farm, east side of Moose river. Their house was burnt May 25, 1889, and they moved to Lynn, Mass., in the holidays 1891.

Children:

    i CARRIE EULALIA, b. June 29, 1866; came over to Boston about 1888; m. Merritt E. Keith (*Ephraim, Thomas, William?* from north of Ireland, of Scotch origin), of Wavelock, Kings Co., N. B., June 11, 1890, and live in Lynn; son *Edgar Neal*, b. Jan. 6, 1891.

    ii LAURA MELISSA, b. July 9, 1868; m. Joshua Moses, son of Dea. John D. Potter, Apr. 21, 1886; now in Lynn.

    iii JERUSHA MAY, b. Apr. 29, 1870; m. Arthur Kearney, Nov. 29, 1893.

    iv FRED TRUEMAN, b. Apr. 12, 1872.

    v SIBYL BELLE, b. Dec. 2, 1873; m. Donald S. McDonald, May 30, 1893, Lynn.

    vi EMMA JANE, b. Apr. 29, 1875; d. Oct. 3, 1893, Lynn.

    vii LILA GRACE, b. July 31, 1877.

    viii GILBERT ELLISON, b. May 5, 1879.

    ix IDA MERCY, b. Apr. 11, 1881.

IX. 217 William M. Chute,[9] (*Gilbert,*[8] *James,*[7] *Benjamin,*[6] *John,*[5] *Lionel,*[4] *James,*[3] *James,*[2] *Lionel*[1]), born in Granville, Mar. 2, 1850; married Jessie Imorine, daughter of Capt. John and Lois (Chute) Graham, Oct. 22, 1879, and lived with his father till after his death in 1882, and removed to Bear River about 1889.

Children;

    i HARLAND G., b. Apr. 22, 1881; d. soon.

    ii ERNEST GILBERT, b. Dec. 10, 1882.

    iii HOWARD GRAHAM, b. May 1, 1885; d. 1886.

    iv CHARLEY, b. July, 1889.

    v ELLA MAY, b. March, 1892.

IX. 218 Jervis Chute,[9] (*Thomas,*[8] *James,*[7] *Benjamin,*[6] *John,*[5] *Lionel,*[4] *James,*[3] *James,*[2] *Lionel*[1]), born in Granville, Jan. 31, 1842; married Henrietta L., daughter of Edmund P. Gilliatt, Feb. 12, 1867, and lives half a mile below Bridgetown; a farmer.

Children:

- i ARTHUR C., b. Nov. 3, 1867; m. Lilian E., daughter of William Jackson, Sept. 23, 1890.
- ii BURPEE E., b. Mar. 4, 1869; m. Meda, daughter of T. A. Neily, Esq., Feb. 24, 1892 of Middleton
- iii BERNARD A., b. Apr. 25, 1873.
- iv MURRAY, b. Nov, 4, 1874.
- v ARCHIE, b. June 30, 1878.
- vi IDA MAY, b. Oct. 20, 1883; d. Oct. 28.

IX. 219 Oliver, brother to the above, born Jan. 22, 1844; married Mary, daughter of John Milberry, Sept. 11, 1881, and lived on a part of the old home.

Children:

- i ISAIAH, b. Sept. 4, 1883.
- ii ELVIN, b. 1889; d. 1891.

IX. 220 Thomas Fletcher,[9] (*Thomas,*[8] *James,*[7] *Benjamin,*[6] *John,*[5] *Lionel,*[4] *James,*[3] *James,*[2] *Lionel*[1]), born Nov. 15, 1853; married Rubina, daughter of Andrew and Patience Templeman, Dec. 24, 1875, and lived on his father's farm. Mrs. Chute died Sept. 22, 1882, aged twenty-five; he married 2nd, Aug. 13, 1884, Annie E., daughter of Nehemiah Chute, (see 183).

Children:

- i FRANK SEWALL, b. Feb. 26, 1877; d. July 1, 1890.
- ii MARY EDITH, b. Nov. 1, 1879.
- iii ARNOLD VINTON, b. Mar. 13, 1890.

IX. 221 William Hanvey,[9] (*Everitt,*[8] *James,*[7] *Benjamin,*[6] *John,*[5] *Lionel,*[4] *James,*[3] *James,*[2] *Lionel*[1]), born in Bayham, Ont., May 19, 1852; married Eliza Ann, daughter of Jarvis Frazer of Springfield, Ont., Sept. 4, 1876, and lives on a one hundred acre farm in Malahide, that his father bought in 1843.

Children:

- i NINA GRACE, b. July 10, 1878.
- ii EARLE FRAZER, b. May 25, 1882.

GENEALOGIES OF THE CHUTE FAMILY. 169

IX. 222 George Abel Chute,[9] (*Abel,*[8] *James,*[7] *Benjamin,*[6] *John,*[5] *Lionel,*[4] *James,*[3] *James,*[2] *Lionel*[1]), born in Granville, Nov. 1, 1858; married Phebe Ann, daughter of Perkins Rhodes, Dec. 14, 1880, and lived on the old farm of his father and grandfather, near the North Mountain, three miles west of Bridgetown.

Children:

    i PERCY ROSCOE, b. Oct. 29, 1881.
    ii HARRY ALDEN, b. Mar. 15, 1884.
    iii MAUD, b. 1888.
    iv DAUGHTER, b. 1892.

IX. 223 William Henry Chute,[9] (*Oliver,*[8] *James,*[7] *Benjamin,*[6] *John,*[5] *Lionel,*[4] *James,*[3] *James,*[2] *Lionel*[1]), born in Townsend, Norfolk Co., Ont. Dec. 9, 1843; married Alice L., daughter of Jefferson Bowman, by Rev. D. C. Maybin, Nov. 12, 1866, and had two sons, one daughter. The elder son, *Clarence,* born about 1868; died 1888; a smart young man. The family live on Bowman street, St. Clair, Mich.

IX. 224 John Henry,[9] (*William F.,*[8] *James,*[7] *Benjamin,*[6] *John,*[5] *Lionel,*[4] *James,*[3] *James,*[2] *Lionel*[1]), born in Malahide, Ont., Oct. 17, 1852; married by Rev. Walter Brown, Catharine Matilda Wall, Dec. 10, 1873, and live in Malahide; farmers.

Children:

    i EMERY, b. Oct. 22, 1875.
    ii EZRA, b. April 9, 1877.
    iii WILLIAM, b. Mar. 23, 1878.
    iv JAMES EBER, b. Sept. 29, 1879.
    v ROSA MAY, b. May 4, 1881.
    vi JOHN, b. Oct. 14, 1883.
    vii LURINDA M., b. Feb. 20, 1886.
    viii LILLIE JANE, b. Dec. 30, 1887.
    ix GILBERT, b. Oct. 15, 1890.

IX. 225 William Chute[9] (*William F.,*[8] *James,*[7] *Benjamin,*[6] *John, Lionel, James, James, Lionel*[1]), born in Malahide, Sept. 24, 1853; married Elizabeth D. King, Dec. 10, 1873, and live in Aylmer.

Children:

    i MARY, b. Dec. 1, 1874.
    ii CHARLES T., b. June 1, 1879.
    iii EMMA JANE, b. April 27, 1882.
    iv DELILAH LOUISA, b. April 25, 1883.

IX. 226 Binea Chute,[9] (*George,*[8] *Thomas,*[8] *Thomas,*[6] *John,*[5] *Lionel,*[4] *James,*[3] *James,*[2] *Lionel*[1]), born in Malahide, Ont., June 19, 1838; carried mail from Vienna to Simcoe several years; went to Michigan about 1865; married Carrie, daughter of Richard Collins, Aug. 11, 1869, and settled in Mitchie, Bay Co.; farmer and hotel keeper; he has also held town offices.

Children:

    i Cora C., b. Oct. 22, 1872.
    ii Ida M., b. Mar. 20, 1875.

IX. 227 Freeman, brother to the above, born Sept. 26, 1841; was a sailor and traveler several years; captain of a life-saving station at Tawas, Mich., several years; he run a little steamboat at Bay City for some time, where he now lives; he married Emma Collins, September, 1880.

Children:

    i Freeman, b. Dec. 31, 1881.
    ii Palmer, b. Dec. 8, 1883.

IX. 228 Horatio Nelson[9] (*Walter,*[8] *Thomas,*[7] *Dea. Thomas,*[6] *John,*[5] *Lionel,*[4] *James,*[3] *James,*[2] *Lionel*[1]), born in Malahide, Ont., Dec. 26, 1847; received a good education, at the common schools; then entered Woodstock College, Ontario, 1860, and stayed two years; then farmed with his father till 1865; when he taught a district school. In 1866 he took charge of the schools in Aylmer. In 1869, was assistant professor of Latin at Woodstock; resigned in 1870 and entered the University of Michigan, from which he graduated in 1872; as B. A., and since that M. S. Since 1880, he has been a teacher and professor in the Physical Sciences, Ann Arbor, Mich., and has written and published several books. He married Lucretia, daughter of Rev. D. C. Clappison, Aug. 21, 1872.

Children:

    i Flora Evelyn, b. June 9, 1873; d. Sept. 26.
    ii Gertrude May, b. Nov. 15, 1877.

IX. 229 William Wallace,[9] (*Dea. Edmund,*[8] *Dea. Andrew,*[7] *Dea. Thomas,*[6] *John,*[5] *Lionel,*[4] *James,*[3] *James,*[2] *Lionel*[1]), born in Bayham, Ont., Aug. 19, 1842; brought up a farmer; went to Minnesota 1864; then to California; returned about 1867 and went to the Argentine Republic, S. A., for ten years; then he returned, married Catharine, daughter of Thomas Gumb, of Nissouri, Ont., Dec. 25, 1878; lived in Ekfrid, two years; then bought one hundred and fifty acres in Nissouri, and lived there (went on a visit to Florida 1888), but sold out in 1890, and moved to Compton, Los Angeles Co., Cal., spring of 1891; returned to Nissouri, Ont., 1893.

Children:

i THOMAS, b. Dec. 24, 1879.
ii MARY, b. Oct. 12, 1881; d. Apr. 16, 1882.
iii MARY 2D, b. June 19, 1884.
iv CLEVELAND, b. Oct. 18, 1886.

IX. 230 Elbert,[9] (*Dea. Edmund*,[8] *Dea. Andrew*,[7] *Dea. Thomas*,[6] *John*,[5] *Lionel*,[4] *James*,[3] *James*,[2] *Lionel*[1]), born in Carradoc, Middlesex Co., Ont., Jan. 13, 1848; was a convert to Christianity at the age of fourteen; baptized by Rev. George Richardson, and joined the Baptist church at Strathroy; he bought a farm in Carradoc, and worked it a few years, at the same time cultivating his talents as a Christian, and also in the practice of music; he married Sarah Jane, daughter of William Webb of Carradoc, Dec. 25, 1873; built a brick house that year and taught singing. But being impressed with the propriety of preaching the gospel he sold out his farm and attended grammar school in Strathroy, spring of 1875, which he attended for a year and a half; he next attended the Woodstock college or institute two and a half years; then to the Morgan Park school or college near Chicago, where he was ordained to the gospel ministry, and graduated B.D., May, 1882. As a student he was nearly always at the head of his class; he also studied medicine in London, Ont., under Dr. E. G. Edwards; he embarked for India from New York, Aug. 30, 1882; went to Secumderahad, and in 1885 to Palmoor, a missionary and teacher among the Telugus. He has been very successful in winning souls to Christ, having about three hundred members in one church, one third of them converts from the high caste. In 1890 he organized another church fifty miles away. His field is sixty by eighty miles over. In 1887 his sister Leoni, went and joined him in the good work.

Children:

   i Ernest Elbert, b. Oct. 22, 1874.
   ii Ethel Edna, b. Oct. 15, 1876.
   iii Elmer Eirene, b. Aug. 30, 1878.
   iv Mary Lulu, b. Oct. 1, 1879; d. Sept. 18, 1880.
   v Effie Einez, b. Aug. 13, 1881.
   vi Eral Cora, b. July 17, 1884.
   vii Elberta, b. Feb. 23, 1886.
   viii Estella, b. April 14, 1888.
   ix Eulalia Mabel, b. May 14, 1889.

IX. 231 Martin Luther,^{9} (*Rev. Alfred*,^{8} *Dea. Andrew*,^{7} *Dea Thomas*,^{6} *John*,^{5} *Lionel*,^{4} *James*,^{3} *James*,^{2} *Lionel* ^{1}), born in Carradoc, Middlesex Co., Ont., April 29, 1851; lived with his parents in Minnesota and Arkansas, twelve years; married Ella, daughter of William Straight, Dec. 25, 1876, and lived eight or ten years at or near Hillsborough, Vernon Co., Wis., then went to Green Co., Ill. A farmer.

Children :

   i Andrew A., b. Dec. 27, 1877.
   ii A. Edward, b. Oct. 3, 1879.
   iii Martin L., b. July 1, 1882; d. Jan. 18, 1884.
   iv Ernest Elsworth, b. Aug. 7, 1885.
   v Mildred Olivia, b. April, 3, 1888; d. March 18, 1891.

IX. 232 Andrew Fuller,^{9} (*Rev. Alfred*,^{8} *Dea. Andrew*,^{7} *Dea. Thomas*,^{6} *John*,^{5} *Lionel*,^{4} *James*,^{3} *James*,^{2} *Lionel* ^{1}), born in Bosanquet, Lambton Co., Ont., July 17, 1856, was with his parents in Minnesota and Arkansas; married Caroline, daughter of Christian Bouer, March 4, 1878, and lived in Hillsborough, Wis.

Children :

   i Alfred Hervey, b. Sept. 5, 1879.
   ii Hattie, b. June 19, 1881, d. July 3.
   iii Maudie O., b. April 14, 1882.
   iv Adolphus A., b. July 15, 1884.

IX. 233 Mahlon Chute,^{9} (*Sidney*,^{8} *Dea. Andrew*,^{7} *Dea. Thomas*,^{6} *John*,^{5} *Lionel*,^{4} *James*,^{3} *James*,^{2} *Lionel* ^{1}), born in Bayham, Ont. Feb. 10, 1847; married Hannah, daughter of John Murray and Hannah (Showers) Markle, Apr. 24, 1867, in Malahide, Ont., lived in Bayham several years; but since 1880, he brought and occupied the Reuben

Brundage farm, 2nd concession of Mallahide, near Bayham, and is there an industrious prosperous farmer.

Children:

    i ROBERT A. C., b. Nov. 15, 1868; d. Feb. 1875.
    ii ETTA LORINDA, b. Dec. 20, 1870; m. T. M. McConnell. (See McConnell.)
    iii MELVIN, b. June 20, 1873; d. Apr. 1874.
    iv HERMAN S., b. Sept. 4, 1875.
    v JOHN R., b. Jan. 21, 1879.
    vi NELLIE, b. Aug. 23, 1883; d. Jan. 9, 1884.
    vii EDITH M., b. Jan. 6, 1886.

IX. 234 James Albert,[9] (*Sidney*,[8] *Dea. Andrew*,[7] *Dea. Thomas*,[6] *John*,[5] *Lionel*,[4] *James*,[3] *James*,[2] *Lionel*[1]), born in Bayham, Ont., Oct. 3, 1850; married Matilda, daughter of Jacob Robenson, January 1874; and lived in Vienna several years. In 1885 or 1886 he moved to Houghton, Norfolk Co., where his wife died March 27, 1890; aged thirty-nine; he married 2nd Rachael, daughter of John D. and Lovena McConnell, Nov. 9, 1890. Mr. Chute was brought up a farmer, but is also a good blacksmith.

Children:

    i JAMES CLARENCE, b. 1875.
    ii ISAAC MERTON, b. 1879.

IX. 235 Arthur William,[9] (*Sidney*,[8] *Dea. Andrew*,[7] *Dea. Thomas*,[6] *John*,[5] *Lionel*,[4] *James*,[3] *James*,[2] *Lionel*[1]), born in Bayham, Ont., Mar. 23, 1852; married Catharine, daughter of William and Elizabeth (Northcott) Sponemburg, Nov. 24, 1875, and after several years in Ontario, he moved to near Leola, McPherson Co., S. D., 1882.

Children:

    i ILA MAUD, b. 1876.
    ii MARIBELLE, b. 1882.
    iii FREEMAN GUY, b. 1885.

IX. 236 Herbert M., another brother, born Sept. 12, 1854; married Ruth, daughter of William and Martha (Wylie) Conner, Sept. 26, 1877, and lived at Luton, Malahide; a blacksmith; went to McPherson Co., S. D., 1883; and to Yorkton, Assa Co., N. W. T., 1891.

Children:

    i EDGAR, b. Sept. 22, 1880.

  ii Frank, b. May 20, 1882.
  iii Fred, b. May 19, 1884.
  iv Lee, b. May 14, 1886.
  v Stanly, b. July 9, 1890.
  vi ——.

IX. 237 John Bunyan,[9] (*Sidney,*[8] *Dea. Andrew,*[7] *Dea. Thomas,*[6] *John,*[5] *Lionel,*[4] *James,*[3] *James,*[2] *Lionel*[1]), born in Bayham, Ont., July 30, 1859; after learning to be a baker and confectioner under William J. Bond in St. Thomas, he married Bertha Kate, daughter of Elisha and Cynthia McConnell, in Malahide, Oct. 13, 1886, and live in Aberdeen, Brown Co., S. D.

Children:

  i Lloyd Elmore, b. Feb. 16, 1888.
  ii Minnie Ferne, b. June 12, 1890.

IX. 238 Edgar Milford,[9] (*Freeman,*[8] *Dea. Andrew,*[7] *Dea. Thomas,*[6] *John,*[5] *Lionel,*[4] *James,*[3] *James,*[2] *Lionel*[1]), born in Bayham, Ont., Nov. 29, 1859; married Jo Stella, daughter of William Taylor, M.D., of Des Moines, Ia., Dec. 23, 1884, and is a machinist near Chicago.

Children:

  i Howard Lee, b. July 24, 1886; d. Sept. 18, 1891, Pullman, Ill.
  ii Stanley, b. Dec. 3, 1889.
  iii Aloha, b. April 19, 1892.

IX. 239 Abram Lincoln,[9] (*William E.,*[8] *Dea. Andrew,*[7] *Dea. Thomas,*[6] *John,*[5] *Lionel,*[4] *James,*[3] *James,*[2] *Lionel*[1]), born in Jo Davies, Fairbault Co., Minn., Sept. 22, 1863; went with his parents to Missouri and Ontario; learned the blacksmith trade of his cousin, James A. Chute, in Vienna; then went to McPherson Co., S. D., in 1883, and took up a quarter section of prairie, broke up forty or fifty acres and put in crops, but three or four severe drouths following each other induced him to "pull up stakes" and emigrate to near Yorkton, Assa Co., N. W. T., west of Manitoba, in 1891; he married Maggie, daughter of William Conner, Dec. 4, 1888, in South Dakota.

Children:

  i Ray William, b. Jan. 25, 1890.
  ii Victoria, b. Aug. 22, 1891.
  iii —— ——.

GEORGE MAYNARD CHUTE.

IX. 240 George Maynard,[9] *Aaron,*[8] *Dea. Andrew,*[7] *Dea. Thomas,*[6] *John,*[5] *Lionel,*[4] *James,*[3] *James,*[2] *Lionel* [1]), born in Bayham, Ont., Sept. 21, 1857; received a good education in his youth, so he taught school the winter after he was eighteen; in 1881 he went into the employ of the Michigan Southern and Lake Shore R. R., at Buffalo, as clerk in the live stock department, where he remained about ten years. In 1888 he moved to Toledo, O., and became a partner with Hugh Thompson, in a soap manufactory, and in 1892 was elected president and general manager of the firm. He married Grace P., daughter of William H., and Susan (McConnell) Hamilton, Aug. 29, 1889; and have:

   i AARON HAMILTON, b. Oct. 30, 1891.
   ii

IX. 241 Asa Watson,[9] (*James M.,*[8] *Abel,*[7] *Dea. Thomas,*[6] *John,*[5] *Lionel,*[4] *James,*[3] *James,*[2] *Lionel* [1]), born in Clements, N. S., July 26, 1843; taken to Ontario with his parents, 1848; drove stage several years in Essex and Kent Co.'s; married Mary, daughter of John Nichols, of Essex Co., Ont., May 24, 1872; had four children, two died in infancy. Mr. Chute lives at Leamington, Ont.

Children:
   i REUBEN CLARK, b. ——.
   ii JOHN HARDING, b. ——.

IX. 242 Frank S., brother to the above, born in Malahide, Ont., April 2, 1861; married Jane Lonsberry, in Essex Co., Jan. 1886, and lived with his mother in the old home; died of la grippe, Feb. 4, 1890.

Children:
   i SON, b. 1887.
   ii FRANK STANLEY, b. 1890.

IX. 243 Handley Chipman,[9] (*Joseph W.,*[8] *Abel,*[7] *Dea. Thomas,*[6] *John,*[5] *Lionel,*[4] *James,*[3] *James,*[2] *Lionel* [1]), born in Clements, N. S,. Aug. 25, 1850; married Prudence, daughter of Richard H. and Rebecca (Potter) Sanford, Jan. 15, 1874; and lived with his mother on the old farm; died Feb. 16, 1877.

Children:
   i ALDEN C., b. Nov. 25, 1874.
   ii DAISY BLANCHE, b. July 21, 1877; d. a happy Christian, May, 1889.

IX. 244 Arthur Wellington,[9] (*Thomas*,[8] *Calvin*,[7] *Dea. Thomas*,[6] *John*,[5] *Lionel*,[4] *James*,[3] *James*,[2] *Lionel*[1]), born at Marblehead, Mass., Apr. 1, 1856; married in Brown Co., Minn., Alice S. Miner, Sept. 11, 1879, and live there, a prairie farmer.

Children:

    i Carrie Bell, b. July 19, 1880.
    ii Estella S., b. Apr. 22, 1882.
    iii Ella Orie, b. Apr. 6, 1884.
    iv Edgar Eugene, b. Sept. 19, 1886.
    v Roy Edson, b. July 14, 1888.
    vi Alvin Wellington, b. Nov. 15, 1890.

IX. 245 Theodore Harding Porter,[9] (*Andrew*,[8] *Calvin*,[7] *Dea. Thomas*,[6] *John*,[5] *Lionel*,[4] *James*,[3] *James*,[2] *Lionel*[1]), born at Swampscott, Mass., Aug. 26, 1854; is a singer and musician, and since 1890 a piano tuner in Boston; married Clara S., daughter of J. F. Keating, in Boston, June 2, 1886.

Children:

    i Arline Mildred, b. Jan. 25, 1889.
    ii Clarence Lewis, b. Jan. 16, 1892; d. Apr. 4.

IX. 246 William Alpheus,[9] (*Joseph B.*,[8] *John*,[7] *Dea. Thomas*,[6] *John*,[5] *Lionel*,[4] *James*,[3] *James*,[2] *Lionel*[1]), born in Bayham, Ont., Sept. 9, 1853; married Marietta Bishop, Aug. 1, 1882, and live at Bear River, N. S.; he is a great raiser and mover of buildings, vessels, etc.

Children:

    i Lizzie, b. 1883.
    ii Franklin E., b. 1884; d. 1887.
    iii Anna, b. 1887.
    iv Daughter, b. March, 1892.

IX. 247 James Potter,[9] (*W. Henry*,[8] *John*,[7] *Dea. Thomas*,[6] *John*,[5] *Lionel*,[4] *James*,[3] *James*,[2] *Lionel*[1]), born in Clements, N. S., Aug. 4, 1857; married Ella A., daughter of Alexander Simpson, May 28, 1884; lived in East Boston several years, but now in Everett, Mass.; a machinist.

Children:

    i Lida Louise, b. Mar. 23, 1885.
    ii Stanley James, b. Nov. 26, 1889.

IX. 248 Frank Augustus,[9] (*Wm. Albert,*[8] *Binea,*[7] *Dea. Thomas,*[6] *John,*[5] *Lionel,*[4] *James,*[3] *James,*[2] *Lionel*[1]), born in Clements, N. S., Aug. 23, 1865; to Ontario with his parents 1872; to Grand Rapids, Mich., and married Agnes, daughter of Thomas Cameron, and have three or four children.

IX. 249 Henry,[9] (*Dea. Israel,*[8] *Silas,*[7] *James,*[6] *John,*[5] *Lionel,*[4] *James,*[3] *James,*[2] *Lionel*[1]), born at Barrington, Shelburne Co., N. S., Nov. 3, 1850; married Sarah, daughter of John Cook, Feb. 20, 1872; she died Oct. 13, 1874; aged twenty-six; he married 2nd, Martha, daughter of Jacob Hagan, June 6, 1878; she died Feb. 29, 1884; aged thirty. Live at Lockport, Shelburne Co.

Children:

    i HERBERT A., b. Nov. 26, 1879.
    ii MAUD BEATRICE, b. Feb. 10, 1884.

IX. 250 Vorus F., brother to the above, born Nov. 3, 1857; married Ella, daughter of Robert Beveridge, of Brookville, Digby Co., Dec. 24, 1883; and live at Beaver River, Yarmouth Co., N. S.

Children:

    i EUGENIA J., b. Sept. 23, 1884.
    ii RAINSFORD K., b. Feb. 23, 1886.
    iii ADDIE A., b. Nov. 20, 1887.
    iv CHARLOTTE ESTHER, b. Jan. 15, 1890.

IX. 251 Aaron E.,[9] (*Dea. Eaton,*[8] *Handley,*[7] *James,*[6] *John,*[5] *Lionel,*[4] *James,*[3] *James,*[2] *Lionel*[1]), born in Hampton, N. S., Aug. 22, 1843; married Mary Ann, daughter of William Brown (*George, William*, from England before the Revolution), Feb. 11, 1866; he sailed on the Atlantic Ocean, and became a captain; was drowned May 24, 1871; she married 2nd, Harris Foster Esq., Hampton, N. S., Oct. 1884.

Children:

    i HERMAN E., b. Sept. 1, 1867; d. April 11, 1871.
    ii HARRIS MILLER, b. Oct. 2, 1869; m. Eva, dau. of Zebulon Elliott, 1890; one son Boyd, b. 1891.
    iii EMMA S., b. Feb. 2, 1872; d. Jan. 1, 1873.

IX. 252 William Prior,[9] (*Seth,*[8] *Handley,*[7] *James,*[6] *John,*[5] *Lionel,*[4] *James,*[3] *James,*[2] *Lionel*[1]), born near Hampton, N. S., Dec. 10, 1855; went to Woburn, Mass., in 1879, and is doing well in the firm of Cummings & Chute, feed and produce merchants; he married Dec. 3, 1883, Susan Cummings, one of twelve in the family of Ebenezer and Sarah Wilson (Haven) Cummings, of Woburn. Mrs. S. W. Cummings was a daughter of Jonas Haven and Abigail Simonds.

Children:

    i Louis Alfric, b. Dec. 24, 1885.
    ii William Prior, b. May 11, 1887.

IX. 253 Traverse Brinton,[9] (*John Eber,*[8] *Handley,*[7] *James,*[6] *John,*[5] *Lionel,*[4] *James,*[3] *James,*[2] *Lionel*[1]), born at Hampton, N. S., Feb. 5, 1862; married Armina Cook, November 1888, and live on the Bay Shore, near Hampton.

Children:

    i Eaton, b. 1889.
    ii Etta, b. 1891.

IX. 254 Harvey F.,[9] (*Jos. Dimock,*[8] *Handley,*[7] *James,*[6] *John,*[5] *Lionel,*[4] *James,*[3] *James,*[2] *Lionel*[1]), born near Hampton, N. S., Nov. 12, 1863; married Georgiana Hauszer, Sept. 20, 1882, and live at Mattapan, near Milton, a part of Boston; carpenter.

Children:

    i Ethel, b. 1883.
    ii Millie, b. 1885.
    iii Irene, b. 1886.
    iv Louise, b. 1888.

IX. 255 Daniel Marsden,[9] (*Joshua M.,*[8] *David M.,*[7] *James,*[6] *John,*[5] *Lionel,*[4] *James,*[3] *James,*[2] *Lionel*[1]), born on Campobello Island. N. B., July 2, 1856; married Paphena Thurber, 1880.

Children:

    i Seth, b. 1882.
    ii Goldie, b. 1884.
    iii Florence, b. 1886.

IX. 256 Millard Fillmore, brother to the above, born May 24, 1858; married Idella Randolph, 1879.

Children:

    i Blanche, b. 1880; d. aged six months.
    ii Lorenzo, b. 1881.
    iii Levi, b. 1884.
    iv Clarence, b. 1886.
    v Hiram B., b. 1888.

IX. 257 David Samuel, another brother, born Apr. 2, 1860, at Eastport, Me.; went to Boston 1881; married Maria Eliza, daughter of Stathern Bailey, son of Rev. Jacob Bailey (1741-1808), a refugee from Massachusetts to Nova Scotia, Nov. 22, 1882, in Cambridge, Mass.; went to South Boston, 1886; a cooper; to Cambridge again and to Somerville, 1891.

Children:
- i WILLIAM EVERETT, b. June 8, 1883.
- ii STANLEY BAILEY, b. June 8, 1885.
- iii AGNES MYRA, b. May. 21, 1887.
- iv HAFFEZ M. B., b. July 24, 1889.

Mrs. Chute m. 1st, Herbert M., son of Edward Hayes, Windsor, N. S., 1871, and had *Harry Strathern*, b. 1872. Mr. Hayes d. in Nova Scotia, 1873, aged twenty-nine.

IX. 258 Edward Ervin,[9] (*John Wentworth,*[8] *David M.,*[7] *James,*[6] *John,*[5] *Lionel,*[4] *James,*[3] *James,*[2] *Lionel*[1]), born at Caledonia, Queens Co., N. S., Feb. 21, 1857; married Anna, daughter of John H. and Caroline A. (Sprowle) Long, Mar. 16, 1879, and lived eight or ten years in Cambridgeport, Mass., keeper of a livery stable.

Children:
- i JOHN HERBERT, b. Apr. 27, 1880.
- ii RALPH LEROY, b. June 16, 1882.
- iii LILIAN AMELIA, b. Feb. 12, 1888.

IX. 259 William Burkitt Fowler,[9] (*Sidney S.,*[8] *David M.,*[7] *James,*[6] *John*[5] *Lionel,*[4] *James,*[3] *James,*[2] *Lionel*[1]), born below Hampton, N. S., Dec. 24, 1851; m. Sophia Oikle, December 1879; is a farmer and fisherman, two miles below Hampton, Bay of Fundy shore.

Children:
- i HERBERT, b. 1881.
- ii HANLEY, b. 1883.
- iii ERNEST YORKE, b. 1885.
- iv

IX. 260 Frank Lowery, brother to the above, born below Hampton, N. S., September 1855; married Jessie A., daughter of John Eber Chute (136), Nov. 24, 1888, and live on the Bay shore, near Phinney Cove, farmers.

Children:
- i LENA, b. Sept. 1889.
- ii EVA, b. 1891.

IX. 261 Richard Henry,[9] (*Rev. Ariel P.,*[8] *Richard,*[7] *James,*[6] *Daniel,*[5] *James,*[4] *James,*[3] *James,*[2] *Lionel*[1]), born in Woburn, Mass., Mar. 14, 1843; enlisted into Co. C, 35th Mass. Inf., Aug. 7, 1862; promoted to 2nd lieut., of Co. F, 59th Mass., Dec. 4, 1863; 1st lieut., Feb. 14, 1864; and captain June 23. He was taken prisoner at North Anna, Va., May 24, 1864; paroled Dec. 10, and discharged for disability Mar. 1, 1865. Then he went to St. Louis, Mo., and was clerk for Lamb & Quinlan, two or three years, but engaged in lumber business early in 1869. In 1872 he located at Louisianna, Mo., and in 1875, settled in Eau Claire, Wis. He married Nov. 6, 1867, in Georgetown, Mass., Susan Rebecca, daughter of Humphrey and Susan R. (Horner) Nelson.

Children:

    i ARTHUR L., b. Aug. 12, 1869.
    ii MARY N., b. Jan. 28, 1872; d. Nov. 21, 1874.
    iii RICHARD H., b. Feb. 4, 1874.
    iv ROBERT W., b. Dec 24, 1875.
    v REBECCA, b. Aug. 26, 1879.

IX. 262 George Albert,[9] (*Andrew,*[8] *Richard,*[7] *James,*[6] *Daniel,*[5] *James,*[4] *James,*[3] *James,*[2] *Lionel*[1]), born at Orland, Me., Mar. 3, 1843; was in Co. K, 59th Mass., in the late war; wounded May 24, 1864; discharged June 29, 1865; been a salesman in Boston, most of the time since. He married Clara H., daughter of Johnson Wood, Bluehill, Me., Feb. 1, 1872.

Children:

    i ANNE GERTRUDE, b. Nov. 27, 1872, in Cambridge.
    ii ERNEST HOWARD, b. Mar. 25, 1875, in Chelsea.
    iii CLARENCE HASKELL, b. Feb. 27, 1877, Chelsea.
    iv FLORENCE LOUISE, b. June 3, 1881, Chelsea.

IX. 263 Edward Lane, brother to the above, born in Maine, Nov. 27, 1853; having a desire to go into the ministry he entered college at Andover in 1877, and graduated July, 1880; married Julia, adopted daughter of Prof. John P. Cleveland, D. D., July 7, 1880; ordained at Saugus, July 2, 1880; was pastor there two years; Duxbury three years, and at Northborough since; Congregationalist.

Children:

    i HELEN C., b. June 28, 1881.
    ii CHARLES LIONEL, b. Aug. 4, 1882.

iii ALICE E., b. Jan. 22, 1884; d. Aug. 17.
iv MARION H., b. May 4, 1887.
v SARAH GLADYS, b. Oct. 14, 1889.

IX. 264 Charles Hubble,[9] (*James Martin*,[8] *Daniel*,[7] *James*,[6] *Daniel*,[5] *James*,[4] *James*,[3] *James*,[2] *Lionel*[1]), born at Evansville, Ind., Dec. 4, 1843; married Mary B. Henderson, Montezuma, Ind., Sept. 14, 1871; and is a confectioner, at Lawrence, Kan.
Children:

i WILLIAM HENDERSON, b. July 13, 1873.
ii JULIA ABIGAIL, b. Dec. 3, 1876.
iii HENRY FRANK, b. Feb. 21, 1880.
iv RALPH L., b. June 16, 1889.

IX. 265 George Curtis,[9] (*Moses*,[8] *Curtis*,[7] *Josiah*,[6] *Curtis*,[5] *Thomas*,[4] *James*,[3] *James*,[2] *Lionel*[1]), born in Carthage, Me., April 19, 1845; married Martha Ann, daughter of Harvey Freeman, May 10, 1868; she died Oct. 8, 1879, aged thirty-two. He is a merchant at Waldoboro, Me.
Children:

i WALTER S., b. Dec. 1869; d. Feb. 10, 1870.
ii SUSIE L., b. Apr. 17, 1871; m. George E. McGowen, Jan. 23, 1890; son George A. K., b. Nov. 23, 1890.

IX. 266 Charles Moses, brother to the above, born in Carthage, Me., July 3, 1849; married Beulah W., daughter of Abel and Mary P. (Weston) Arnold, son of Gaylon and Sally Arnold, of Duxbury, Mar. 25, 1875; and is a merchant in Rockland, Mass.
Children:

i BERTHA MAY, b. Apr. 20, 1876.
ii FRED ARNOLD, b. July 2, 1880.
iii MARY VIOLET, b. Nov. 15, 1884.
iv ARTHUR MURRAY, b. July 16, 1887.

IX. 267 Edwin Elliott, another brother, born Apr. 8, 1851; married Mary,[6] daughter of Solomon[5] and Martha (Bayless) Foster, son of Capt. Solomon[4] and Polly (Peak) Foster * of Cape Cod, Oct. 8, 1875. Mr. Chute went to Rockland, Mass., 1870, and is in mercantile business there.

* *Joseph*,[3] *John*,[2] *Thomas*,[1] over before 1640.

Children:

 i HARRY FOSTER, b. June 30, 1877.
 ii WALTER EDWIN, b. May 1, 1880.
 iii HOWARD EMERY, b. Apr. 9, 1886.

IX. 268 Curtis,[9] (*John H.*,[8] *Col. Francis*,[7] *Col. Thomas*,[6] *Curtis*[5] *Thomas*,[4] *James*,[3] *James*,[2] *Lionel*[1]), born in Otisfield, Me., Mar. 29, 1845; married Almeda C., daughter of Benjamin Stone, Sept. 6, 1866: moved to Hillhurst, Compton, P. Q. Mrs. Chute died Feb. 17, 1888: he married 2nd, Louisa Brown, 1889.

Children:

 i HANNAH E., b. June 10, 1868.
 ii CARRIE M., b. Feb. 13, 1870.
 iii CHARLES L., b. July 19, 1872.
 iv ALMEDA I., b. Dec. 10, 1875.
 v BERT L., b. Nov. 23, 1877.
 vi CURTIS W., b. June 18, 1882.
 vii EDITH E., b. April 21, 1884.

IX. 269 Albert F.,[9] (*John H.*,[8] *Col. Francis*,[7] *Col. Thomas*,[6] *Curtis*,[5] *Thomas*,[4] *James*,[3] *James*,[2] *Lionel*[1]), born in Otisfield, Me., Jan. 27, 1856; married Eugenia, daughter of Joseph N. Scribner, Sept. 10, 1876; and they live on the farm of his father and grandfather. Mr. Scribner died August 1886, aged fifty-three. One son.

 i ALFRED LEROY, b. Mar. 8, 1877.

IX. 270 Alonzo Franklin,[9] (*James*,[8] *William C.*,[7] *Col. Thomas*,[6] *Curtis*,[5] *Thomas*,[4] *James*,[3] *James*,[2] *Lionel*[1]), born near Naples, Me., Nov. 13, 1843; married Mary, daughter of Nathaniel and Esther (Mann) Staples, Dec. 1866; Raymond, Cumberland Co., Me. Mr. Chute died Oct. 4, 1873; she married 2nd Luther L., son of George W. Longley, of Waterford, Oxford Co., July 3, 1876; and live on the same place. Mr. Longly married 1st, Sophia L. Butler, Jan. 1, 1868, and had Leon M., born Oct. 27, 1869; 2nd, Saida A., born Aug. 23, 1872. Mrs. Longley died Sept. 26, 1874; aged thirty-four.

Children:

 i MILES GRANT, b. Mar. 29, 1868; m. Elvira M. Bickford of New Gloucester, Me., Nov. 24, 1887; son, *Guy Meredith*, b. June 20, 1890; live in Haverhill.
 ii ALBION R., b. Oct. 29, 1869; d. August, 1870.
 iii MARY E. LONGLEY, b. July 7, 1879.

IX. 271 Horace Mann,[9] (*James,*[8] *William C.,*[7] *Col. Thomas,*[6] *Curtis,*[5] *Thomas,*[4] *James,*[3] *James,*[2] *Lionel* [1]), born Oct. 7, 1851; married Inez Florence, daughter of Vernon Miles, Sept. 17, 1873, in Templeton, Mass.; moved to Winchendon, 1881, and is station agent for the Boston and Albany railroad.

Children;

- i BERTHA J., b. Feb. 15, 1875.
- ii SUSIE E., b. Feb. 7, 1878.

IX. 272 Russell E., another brother, born June 28, 1855; married Emma J. Putney, June 5, 1878; she died May 7, 1886, aged twenty-seven; he married 2nd, Ella M., daughter of Rev. A. B. Lovewell, Feb. 27, 1887; is a farmer near Crooked River, below Naples.

Children :

- i IDA MAY, b. October, 1874; d. May, 1885.
- ii GRACE INEZ, b. May 26, 1879.

IX. 273 Quincy Mayberry,[9] (*Fanklin A.,*[8] *William C.,*[7] *Col. Thomas,*[6] *Curtis,*[5] *Thomas,*[4] *James,*[3] *James,*[2] *Lionel* [1]), born near Naples, Nov. 30, 1854; married Melissa D. Lewis, Dec. 20, 1881, and live with his father and mother in Harrison.

Children:

- i BLANCHE, b. 1882.
- ii ROLAND, b. 1884.

IX. 274 Josiah Cobb,[9] (*Edwin,*[8] *Daniel,*[7] *Col. Thomas,*[6] *Curtis,*[5] *Thomas,*[4] *James,*[3] *James,*[2] *Lionel* [1]), born in Otisfield, near Bolster's Mills, Sept. 18, 1850; married Lunetta, daughter of Lewis G. Brackett, Jan. 1, 1879; live in Harrison; farmers.

Children :

- i LYMAN A., b. Jan. 26, 1880.
- ii CHARLES S., b. Mar. 1, 1882.
- iii EDA I., b. July 8, 1884.
- iv MAUD BELLE, b. July 16, 1888.

TENTH GENERATION.

X. 275 Richard Burpee,[10] (*Robert,*[9] *Dea. Abram,*[8] *Dea. Daniel,*[7] *Samuel,*[6] *John,*[5] *Lionel,*[4] *James,*[3] *James,*[2] *Lionel* [1]), born in Clements, Annapolis Co., N. S., Jan. 2, 1845; married Emma Eliza, daughter of Edward Covert, in Lower Granville, Dec. 24, 1865; she died Dec. 24, 1877, aged thirty-three; he married 2nd, Essaphine B. Buffum; a school teacher (born June 11, 1855), Nov. 1, 1878. Mr. Chute, a sailor and a blacksmith, moved to New London, Ct., 1880.

Children:

    i IDA MAY, b. Dec. 6, 1866; m. ——.
    ii BESSIE E., b. Sept. 8, 1869; m. ——.
    iii ETTA, b. Apr. 7, 1873; d. Aug. 12.
    iv HATTIE EUGENIE, b. July 3, 1874; d. Oct. 12.
    v ROBERT E., b. Oct. 8, 1876.
    vi RAYMOND C., b. Oct. 15, 1879.
    vii ELIZABETH H., b. Aug. 5, 1881.
    viii ESSAPHINE M., b. July 23, 1885.
    ix RICHARD B., b. 1887.
    x JAMES BUFFUM, b. 1890.

    The first two were born in Nova Scotia, the third in East Boston, the next three in Providence, R. I.

X. 276 Norman Wilfred,[10] (*Ephraim,*[9] *Dea. Aaron,*[8] *Dea. Daniel,*[7] *Saumel,*[6] *John,*[5] *Lionel,*[4] *James,*[3] *James,*[2] *Lionel* [1]), born in Clements, seven miles from Digby, Jan. 6, 1851; married Cornelia O. Beals (*John,*[8] *Elijah,*[7] *Abel* *), Sept. 7, 1874; Mr. Chute has worked up step by step, from a farmer boy, to a skillful sea captain on the Atlantic Ocean. They live near Bear River in Clements.

Children:

    i DAVID WILFRED, b. June 17, 1876.
    ii ELMER ELSWORTH, b. May 30, 1878; d. June 7.
    iii LIZZIE MAUD, b. July 26, 1880; d. Sept. 27, 1887.
    iv BLANCHE W., b. Oct. 19, 1881; d. Sept. 22, 1887.
    v HORACE DEAN, b. May 7, 1886; d. May 9, 1887.
    vi HERALD DITMAS, b. Mar. 22, 1889; d. June 25.

* Abel,[6] Abel,[5] Andrew,[4] Jeremiah,[3] Jeremiah,[2] John,[1] of Hingham, died 1688; aged 100.

X. 277 Freeman Ezra, brother to the above, born Feb. 2, 1853; married Irene Chute, his father's cousin, by Rev. J. M. Parker, Oct. 4, 1874; and live in "Virginia," in Clements, Annapolis Co.
Children:
> i Cora Belle, b. Aug. 1. 1876.
> ii Edith May, b. May 7, 1880.
> iii Abba Philinda, b. Mar. 24, 1883.
> iv Ethel Maud, b. Apr. 4, 1885.
> v Melinda Beatrice, b. Nov. 1, 1886.
> vi Lilah Lee, b. Aug. 27, 1891.

X. 278 William St. Clair,[10] (*Joseph W.,*[9] *Dea. Aaron,*[8] *Dea. Daniel,*[7] *Samuel,*[6] *John,*[5] *Lionel,*[4] *James,*[3] *James,*[2] *Lionel*[1]), born in Bridgetown, N. S., Sept. 1, 1855; married Emma, daughter of John and Sarah Ward, May 26, 1880, and lived in Lynn, Mass.; he died there Sept. 6, 1885, and the widow lives with her father in Truro, N. S.
Children:
> i Otis St. Clair, b. Apr. 3, 1881.
> ii Maud Frances, b. Aug. 30, 1882.
> iii Harry Walker, b. Oct. 31, 1884.

X. 279 Samuel Gilbert,[10] (*Dea. Everett,*[9] *Daniel,*[8] *Dea. Daniel,*[7] *Samuel,*[6] *John,*[5] *Lionel,*[4] *James,*[3] *James,*[2] *Lionel*[1]), born in Clements, N. S., Feb. 14, 1862; taken to Northfield, Carleton Co., N. B., with his parents about 1868; married Maria V., daughter of John Clark, and live in Upper Woodstock, N. S. She died January 1894.
Children:
> i John Everet, b. Aug. 7, 1886.
> ii Bennett William, b. February, 1888.
> iii Bertha Ellen, b. July 6, 1889.
> iv Archie, b. January, 1891.
> v Son, b. May, 1893.

X. 280 John Nelson,[10] (*Dea. Everitt,*[9] *Daniel,*[8] *Dea. Daniel,*[7] *Samuel,*[6] *John,*[5] *Lionel,*[4] *James,*[3] *James,*[2] *Lionel*[1]), born in Clements, N. S., March 19, 1863; taken to Northfield, N. B., with his parents in 1868; went to Maine 1880; to Malden, Mass., 1881; married there June 17, 1886, Jennie, daughter of William Nangle, of Halifax, N. S.,

I

and they live in Boston; he is a first-class architect, carpenter and builder.

Children:

 i Frank Nelson, b. Jan. 11, 1887; d. Nov. 19, 1889.
 ii Ellen E., b. June 9, 1888; d. Oct. 22, 1889.
 iii Walter Harris, b. Apr. 12, 1891.
 iv Sarah May, b. Sept. 3, 1893.

W. E. C., Jan. 16, 1893.

CLOSING CHAPTERS ON THE CHUTE FAMILY.

I. ON THE ORIGINAL FIRST FAMILY TERMINATING IN THE SECOND OR MIDDLE BRANCH.

Ipswich, Mass., was first settled by English emigrants in 1633. But a tradition seems to say that the Mayflower intended to settle there, but went on to Plymouth, here is the first verse of a poem of six verses by James Appleton Morgan.

> I love to think of old Ipswich town,
>   Old Ipswich town in the East countree;
> Whence on the tide you can float down
>   Thro' long salt grass to the wailing sea.
> Where the Mayflower drifted off the bar,
>   Sea-worn and weary long years ago,
> And dared not enter, but sailed away
>   Till she landed her boats in Plymouth Bay.

Abram Hammatt Esq., (1780-1856), of Ipswich, in his "Hammatt papers," says: It appears from our records "that there was a grammar school set up in Ipswich in ye year 1636," three years after John Winthrop, the younger with his twelve companions commenced a settlement in this place. It was kept by Lionel Chute, who died in 1645.

But the Chute family all seem to have left Ipswich before 1700, and settled in Rowley and Newbury. In the burying yard by the Byfield meeting-house, used to stand a dark stone with the following inscriptions upon it:

Sacred to the memory of Capt. Daniel Chute who died Jan. 6, 1805, in the 83d year of his age, having been a respectable member of the church of Christ sixty-three years.

Mrs. Hannah Chute, relict of Capt. Daniel Chute, died April 28, 1812, in the 90th year of her age. She was distinguished for sound judgement, active, benevolent and sincere piety.

Sacred also to the memory of Dea. James Chute, who died Jan. 31, 1769, in the 83d year of his age.

And of Mary Chute his consort, who died Aug. 12, 1760. Aged 67.

Deacon Chute was the son of Mr. James Chute, who in 1681, commenced a settlement a few rods west of this spot. He was a grandson of Lionel Chute the first of the family in Massachusetts.

The old Chute house — a mile north of the Byfield meeting-house — now owned by James Chute Peabody, which he inherited from his aunt, Sophia Chute, granddaughter of Capt. Daniel Chute, was built by Capt. Daniel Chute, 1780, over the cellar of a garrison house, built by his grandfather a century before, and has always been in the family.

The Chute place, a few rods west of the Byfield meeting-house, went from Capt. Daniel Chute to his son Dea. James; thence to his son Richard, who sold it to Shubael Dummer, who left it to his son David, who sold it to Joseph Strauss, a Jewish priest of Boston, who still owns it, although in New York. The buildings of the latter place are all gone, and three old cellars and two old wells remain as relics of the once famous old house.

II. OF THE OLDEST, OR NEW HAMPSHIRE AND NOVA SCOTIA BRANCH.

Rev. Henry Alline, son of William and Rebecca Alline, was born in Newport, R. I., June 14, 1748; taken to Nova Scotia with his parents in 1756, and lived in Falmouth, Hauts Co. From the time of settlement in Nova Scotia, he was impressed with the importance of being a christian, and these impressions and convictions finally led to his conversion in March, 1775. He immediately professed a call to preach the gospel, and being encouraged, he exercised his gifts and talents with great success; and being in advance of many others in that day, although crude in some things, he was called a New Light, and was ordained to the gospel ministry, as a Congregationalist, in a large barn at Falmouth, in 1779; and traveled extensively (principally on horseback), up and down the Annapolis valley, even to Yarmouth, and other parts of Nova Scotia, in New Brunswick and in Maine; and finally died at the house of Rev. David McClure (1748–1820), Northampton, N. H., Feb. 2, 1784; in his thirty-sixth year. Many of the grandparents of the old folks, now living, were converts of his, and joined the Baptist churches, then organizing in those provinces.

Besides being the instrument in God's hand of leading hundreds, if not thousands, to follow the Lord Jesus Christ, he wrote about four hundred hymns which were published about 1790, a third edition was printed at Dover, N. H., 1797. They were used quite extensively among the New Lights and Free Baptists; but the only hymn among them now in use, we believe is the one commencing

> "Amazing sight the Savior stands,
> And knocks at every door.
> Ten thousand blessings in his hands,
> To satisfy the poor."

Thomas Chute,[6] heard the Rev. Mr. Alline about 1780, from the text "And it shall come to pass in that day that the great trumpet shall be blown and they shall come that are ready to perish in the land of Assyria, and the outcasts in the land of Egypt, and they shall worship the Lord in the holy mount at Jerusalem," Isaiah 28: 13; and it led to his conversion, and he was baptized, if we mistake not, by Rev. Thomas Handley Chipman, in the Annapolis River, near Bridgetown; and probably his older brothers, Samuel and John (perhaps their parents too), were converted and added to the church about the same time. Bear, moose, foxes and other game, besides Indians, were quite plentiful in Nova Scotia in those days.

This same Dea. Thomas Chute on Mar. 6, 1808, at Bear River, went out in the morning and found a bear track, so he and sons, Andrew and Abel — perhaps Calvin and John — with a couple of dogs, went up back of the barn into a swamp, and found a tree partly blown over, so there was a large hollow under the roots. Abel cut a stick and poked down through a hole in the top, and exclaimed "It is soft as a bag of wool." At that the old bear stuck her nose out under the roots looking "savage as a meat ax," when the old gent let go an ounce musket ball into her, at which she sank down with a groan, and a cub crawled up on her back; this was picked up with the hand and taken care of. They got out the dead bear, dressed it, sold the meat at the garrison in Annapolis for six pence a pound; kept the cub till in the summer it got so mischievous they sold it too. For forty to fifty years afterwards the sons would say when the sixth of March came around, "this is the day we got the old bear out of the den."

In 1811 the brothers, Benjamin and Thomas, took a notion to go to Upper Canada (called Canada West, in 1849, and Ontario in 1867), and they went as far as Black Rock, below Buffalo, so they saw the "promised land" across the Niagara River, when Uncle Benjamin was taken sick and they returned.

In 1841, when Andrew Chute sold out at Bear River to go to Canada, some opposed and some ridiculed him. His father-in-law, Eleazer Woodworth, composed a little poem commencing

> Andrew Chute, the old goat,
> Put all his property afloat.

But Deacon Chute always rejoiced that he sold out in Nova Scotia — said there was a providence in it — and went to a country where there was more room and privileges to grow up with the growth of the country in education, wealth and usefulness.

On his seventieth birthday, Sept. 15, 1859, Deacon Chute had a large party at his house, which included, besides the members of his own family, Mrs. Jane Chute, Mrs. Nellie McConnell, Dea. R. Hankinson and wife, Dea. B. J. Timpany and wife, Charles Northrup and some neighbors. This was his last home party. Deacon Chute composed a poem or two in early life, but we believe they are lost. We here insert, however, a favorite poem of his, in heroic verse, to which he composed a tune.

1.

Of all the fools on earth by heaven accursed,
 The drunkard should be reckoned with the worst;
No beast that walks the plain or bird that flies,
 Does act so base a part or so unwise.

2.

The dull, the slow, the poor despised ass,
 In wisdom does the drunkard far surpass;
He drinks no more when nature's satisfied,
 But leaves the stream along the vale to glide.

3.

But drunkards of inferior sense will drink,
 Till they can scarcely walk or talk or think;
What crime will not a drunkard then commit,
 When in this vile intoxicated fit.

4.

Satan can rule him with easy sway,
 And turn him as he pleases in his way;
His health, his wealth, his character and time,
 Are all destroyed by this atrocious crime.

5.

We censure thieves who into houses creep,
   To rob their neighbors while they are asleep;
To purchase poison in the flowing bowl,
   Which brings them all to want and damns the soul.

6.

Stay, sinner, stay before it is too late,
   Reflect with horror on thine awful state;
The blood of Christ will cleanse your sins away,
   O seek his mercy, seek without delay.

About fourteen years after his father's death, his son Freeman, to whom was willed the old homestead, moved away the white house, built by Capt. John McIntyre in 1841, and built a brick house in its place; and as it was finished at the time his wife was forty years old, his brothers, sisters, cousins and neighbors, got up a "surprise party," June 5, 1877, and assembled between forty and fifty to do them honor. As he was on the road to work, being path-master that year, the company sent out a "corporal's guard," captured him and took him in. At that party J. M. Chute read Will M. Carleton's "Out of the Old House into the New," with variations, which were very appropriate.

As the centennial of his father's birthday drew near, Freeman concluded to have a celebration at his place on the occasion; so as the fifteenth of September was Sunday he invited his friends and kindred from far and near, and they assembled on Saturday, Sept. 14, 1889, to the number of sixty-six named Chute, twenty named McConnell and forty-seven others, nearly all related, and they carried out the following program: Assembled at 10 A. M., took dinner under the cherry trees in front of the house; Mr. E. S. Phillips of Aylmer, with his camera took pictures, three or four groups; then they gathered on the east side of the house and had music by a string band of seven violins, a cornet and bass viol; Rev. William Grant being called to the chair, gave a good speech; music, "Old Folks at Home," by the band; speech by Rev. A. T. Sowerby of Aylmer; song, "Look on the Bright Side," by W. E. & J. M. Chute of Michigan; recitation by Sophia Mulholland, a school teacher; anthem, "Holy is the Lord," by the Chute choir; speech by W. E. Chute, sketching the family of John Chute and Judith Foster, who moved from New Hampshire to Nova Scotia in 1759 — of their five sons and three daughters, descendents of five of them were represented as present; "Let every heart rejoice and sing," was then sung, followed by speeches from Deacons E. L. Chute of Aylmer, and J. M. Chute of North Branch, Mich.; song, "The Maid of Dundee," by Loretta Chute, accompanied on a guitar; hymn-anthem, "Jerusalem my glorious home," was sung; speech by Isaiah Chute of Peabody, Mass.; then "Auld Lang Syne," by the band; speeches by Mesdames Sarah A. Harris and Harriet Chute, sisters of " mine host;" musical dialogue, "Teacher and Pupil," by W. E. Chute and his nephew, H. L. McConnell; speeches by C. Chute and F. Chute, Esquires; hymn, "Parting Friends," sung by all; closing speech by Elder Grant, and singing, "God be with you till we meet again," all of which were well done and well enjoyed; and all parted in peace, having spent a fine day, long to be remembered. As most of the names will readily be found by looking at the records we now proceed to name the assembly present:

OF CHUTES.

Freeman and Rhoda Ann, host and hostess; Edgar and Jostella; Warren and Howard Leigh; Ezekiel and Eliza; James Edward and Helen and Mary E., Mary and Harriet; William W. and Caroline; Mahlon and Hannah; Lorinda and Herman; Roy and Edith; James Albert and Matilda; Clarence and Jennie; J. Edward and Anna; Charles P. and Ellen; William B. and Estella; May A. and Charles L., George and Louise and Vernon; Josephine and Hattie; J. M. and Lucy; William E. and D. M.; Walter and Catharine; Charles and Tamer; Ernest and Loretta; Joseph and Augustus; Lichard L. and Elizabeth; Araminta and Clark; Elgin and Mabel; Everett and Abba; William H. and Eliza; Nina and Earle; Walter and Mary Ash; Isaiah and Nathan.

OF McCONNELL.

Reuben and Phebe Jane; Cynthia and Hilly L., Minnie and Ola; Newton and Albert; Milledge and Judson; Augusta and John D., Rachel and Irene; George and Hattie; Ross and Ellen; Chilian and Huldah Ann.

OTHER NAMES.

Sarah A. Harris and Susanna Webb; Rev. A. T. Sowerby and wife and Mabel; Rev. William Grant and wife; George W. Stewart and wife; George and Minard Stewart; Austin Adams and wife; Hiram and Kate Westover; Seretta Foster and Jessie Westover; Ephraim and Emeline Doolittle; John and Hains Saxton; Charles Randall and Mary Adams; George William and Anna van Velzor; Charlie V. V. and Sophia Mulholland; Ezra and Harriet Woodworth; Gertie, George and Wilbert

Woodworth; James and Laleah Marr; Lloyd, Leslie, Norman and Ila Marr; Martha Louise Heron; Wesley and Cortland Wilson; E. S. Phillips and George M. Winn; Daniel Cameron; Elijah, Emma and Mary Hains.

III. OF THE MAINE OR THIRD BRANCH:

Dea. Thomas Chute, who went from Massachusetts to Maine, 1737, was certainly a man of ambition, energy, faith and perseverance, as the records of Boston, Marblehead and Salem, Mass., and those of Portland and Windham, Me., plainly show. A part of his papers and personal effects descended through his grandson Col. Josiah of the Revolution, to his son George W., of Windham; while another part descended through Col. Thomas, and Col. Francis to John W., of Otisfield. At the house of the late John H., is a good size pine board chest with "T. C. 1712," on the inside of the cover, that he had in Boston, the year he married Mary Curtis. At this same John H.'s, is a painting purporting to be the Chute Coat of Arms, but it is pronounced by experts a fraud.

After the Revolution, a good sized porcelain pitcher (probably made in Philadelphia), with blue flowers on the side and the name "Mary Chute," also in blue, was presented to Mary, wife of Josiah Chute, which descended to the daughter Mary Noyes Abbot and from her to Mary Ann Sanborn.

But there is a bad thing in Windham. The church records say that Dea. Tho. Chute died in 1771; Thomas L. Smith (1797-1881), delivered a Centennial address in 1835; enlarged since and called the History of Windham, in which he says that Thomas Chute was born in England, 1690. Then George W. Chute, in view of approaching dissolution, appointed Wm. Goold, Esq., his executor, and ordered two white marble monuments to be erected about fifteen feet high, in the family burying ground, to cost $1,000, with inscriptions of four generations, Thomas, Curtis, Col. Josiah and George W., upon them, in which not only the error of the death of Thos. Chute in 1770 is copied, but his birth—worse than Mr. Smith—is stated as in London, England, 1690. At the same time papers were in the house of George W. Chute explaining and telling better, but only needing and demanding examination and investigation. It is bad enough, when falsehoods are told, but worse to be written, and still worse to be engraved upon stones.

ADDITIONS AND CORRECTIONS.

On page 8, family of Ruth Chute and Wm. Hine, besides the three ch., mentioned were James, Oct. 25, 1724; Joseph, Nov. 13, 1726, and Ruth, Apr. 9, 1732. Of the family of Hannah Chute and Capt. Tim Jackman (James, James), Benj., m. 1st, Dorothy Lunt, Aug. 9, 1744; and Hannah Chute m. David Adams. James Chute jr., m. Mary, da. of Isaiah and Mercy (Thompson) Wood. She was the eldest of fifteen children and b. Oct. 31, 1658.

On page 18, Rebecca, da. of John and Rebecca (Chute) Bodge, m. Wm. Mayberry (Richard, William).

On page 29, for Mattie, da. of James Snow read Hattie, da. of Ingram B. Snow. Phebe Ann, w. of Thomas Brooks, d. in the fall of 1893.

On page 36, Elizabeth Hale Elliott, d. in Dec. 1893. Instead of Jenny Flora, da. of Andrew Baldwin, read Flora Elizabeth.

On page 47, Eliza C., w. of Joseph D. Milbury, d. Christmas 1893. James P. Milbury, on the same page m. Anna Hallowell, w. of George, son of John, son of Sol. Milbury.

On page 58, for Rev. Enoch Townes, read Towner on the next page for Rev. Israel Rise, read Rice. Mrs. S. A. Harris returned from the West to Swampscott, Jan. '94.

On page 69, the name Edgett should be Edgeley.

On page 72, for 1874 read 1884 as the birth of Percy L. Fash.

On page 73, Handley Chute (No. 143), d. Dec. 16, 1893.

On page 74, Rev. O. Chute, d. Feb. 1, 1894.

On page 89, the w. of Joseph Chute, d. May 3, 1894, a. 87.

On page 92, Mrs. Sarah Ann Cummings, d. in Mo., Mar. 5, '93, a. 80.

On page 93, for Asa Wright read Aaron Wright.

On page 94, Mrs. Miriam P. Chute, d. Jan. 20, '94, a. 95.

On the same page, Wm. H. Chute, d. May 16, '94, a. 88.

On the same page, Mrs. Sarah Chute, d. July 10, '94, a. 88.

On page 95, George Wm. Chute, m. July 19, '94, Emma R. Bomberger,[5] (Elias,[4] Benjamin,[3] Benjamin,[2] Charles of New York[1]), and live at Blue Earth City, Minn.

On page 96, Wm. A Medicraft, m. Bessy, da. of Arch. Gillis. Abram M., m. Mary Fredericks.

On page 99, Mrs. G. G. Collins, d. in Boston, May 1, '94, a. 37.

On page 102, the two children of Capt. Spicer, were Christiana and Harry. The other son of Edward and Susan Slocomb was John.

On page 109, at the bottom, the parenthesis should include (Levi and Clarissa Day, David).

On page 110, Carrie Beals, m. Thomas P. Atkins, Jan. 8, '94.

On page 111, Charles Chute, m. Tamer McConnell, Jan. 3, '44.

On page 113, Rev. A. Chute, d. in Ill., Jan. 7, '94. And this is the lineage of his wife: Olive Miner,[7] (Trueman,[6] Reuben,[5] Dea. Jehu,[4] Ephraim,[3] John,[2] Thomas,[1]

b. 1608, over with John Winthrop 1630; m. Grace Palmer, of Rehoboth 1634, had 11 ch., and d. 1690); ancestral lineage—Thomas the emigrant,[10] (Clement,[9] Wm.,[8] Wm.,[7] Thomas,[6] Lodowick,[5] Thomas,[4] Wm.,[3] Henry,[2] Henry[1]), surname Bulman. He was a miner by profession and took one hundred domestics and servants, armed them and escorted King Edward III, through a dangerous pass in Somerset, in 1339; the king acknowledged his service by granting him a coat of arms, and changing his name to Henry Miner.

On page 114, the number to Mahlon Chute, is 233, to Arthur Wm., 235.

On page 116, Harvey H. Chute, m. 1893.

Page 124, tells of three vessels lost, owned by H. H. Chute, Esq., the 3rd, one was in 1870; a 4th was lost in 1873 or 1874, so another verse is added to complete the poem.

6.

And then the brig Phœnix, just in from the sea,
Was capsized while beating into Port Medway;
She fell on the rocks and to pieces was sent,
And so the four vessels to ruin all went.

On page 125, for Charles Warner read Clarence Warner.

On page 128, Robert J. Chute, d. Feb. 19.

On page 140, two ch. more to the family of Rev. A. C. Chute—Austin Aubrey, b. at Austin, Ill., July 28, '92; Marjorie Parker, b. Halifax, N. S., Mar. 13, '94.

On page 141, Mrs. S. M. W. C. Chute, d. at Sharon, Mass., July 21, '94, a. 89.

On page 142, for Sarah Burk read Sarah Buck.

On page 148, Harold W. Davis, b. 1866, read b. 1886.

On page 152, after Robert Chute, Dea. Andrew, in the parenthesis, should be Dea. Abram.

On page 155, 9th line from the top, for lived read lives.

On page 157, of the ch. of R. S. Chute the 1st was b. Aug. 17, '82, the 2nd, Sept. 2, '88.

On page 160, the 3rd ch. of Isaac N. Chute, Lorenzo B., b. Apr. 1, '93.

On page 166, 4th line from top for Bridgeton read Bridgetown.

On page 167, at the middle of page for Wavelock read Havelock.

On page 170, Freeman Chute m. a da. of John and Jane Collins from England.

On page 192, in the list of Chutes, smaller print, Lichard should be Richard.

INDEX

RSONS BEARING THE NAME OF CHUTE.

THE NUMBERS REFER TO THE PAGE.

80, 86, 120.	Alice M., 111, 125.
120.	Alfred, 60, 92, 113, 116.
133, 177.	Alfred E , 114, 172.
55.	Alfred H., 172.
55, 109.	Allen, 55.
)1.	Almeda I., 182.
123.	Almira, 100.
85.	Alonzo, 93.
4, 61, 72, 73, 106.	Alonzo F., 146, 182.
3.	Alphonso B., 147.
100.	Alvin, 136.
35, 68, 70, 72, 135.	Alzina W., 106.
88, 177.	Alden C., 175.
45, 46, 85, 86, 94, 95, 96.	Amanda E., 90.
120, 174.	Amanda M., 101.
44, 83, 84.	Amelia S., 129.
W., 75.	Amoret R., 99.
, 157.	Amoret S., 55.
.	Amos A., 88, 105, 154.
M., 100.	Ann, 8.
30.	Anna B., 158.
21.	Anna E., 157.
., 147.	Anna G., 166.
.. 83, 150.	Anna Jane, 104.
)1.	Anna L., 101, 139.
A., 172.	Anna M. L., 109.
J., 58, 106.	Annie, 161.
	Annie L., 153.
., 75.	Anna M., 125, 126.
.	Annabel C., 152.
145, 182.	Annetta, 127.
104, 165.	Angelina L., 118.
126.	Angie S., 166.
147.	Angus, 36, 73, 139.
35.	Andrew, 35, 58, 74, 83, 95, 141, 150.
52, 74, 102, 140.	Andrew A., 172.
S., 131.	Andrew E., 122.
..	Andrew F., 114, 172.
0.	Andrew M., 65, 126.
15.	Ansley B., 160.

Anzonetta, 106.
Archie, 168, 185.
Archie M., 157.
Armanilla, 53, 59.
Armanilla J., 100.
Arminta, 112.
Ariel P., 74, 140.
Arthur C., 74, 139, 168.
Arthur H., 103.
Arthur N., 100, 164.
Arthur W., 53, 114, 126, 173, 176.
Arnold S., 130.
Asa W., 123, 175.
Augusta, 158.
Austin A., 153.
Austin S., 86, 153.
Avard, 154.
Azor D., 132.
Beatrice, 136.
Benjamin, 20, 31, 32, 45, 55, 56, 70, 90, 96, 160, 167.
Benjamin F., 46, 93.
Benjamin P., 74.
Bertha, 134, 136, 153.
Bertha E., 185.
Bertha J., 183.
Bert L., 182.
Bertrand, 155.
Bernard A., 168.
Bennett, 133.
Bennett W., 185.
Bessie E., 184.
Bessie M., 99.
Betsey, 36, 74.
Betsey Jane, 140.
Binea, 35, 66, 110, 170.
Blanche, 183.
Bœmer, 35, 38, 45.
Brainard A., 134.
Brunelle D., 159.
Burpee E., 168.
Burton, 55, 108.
Burton A., 159.
Calvin, 35, 63, 65.
Caroline, 58, 67, 81.
Caroline H., 36.
Caroline M., 132.
Caroline V., 63, 111, 166.
Catharine, 32, 81.
Catharine B., 62.
Catharine C., 78.

Catharine S., 123.
Catharine T., 101.
Catharine W., 82.
Carrie, 148, 165.
Carrie B., 176.
Carrie E., 131, 167.
Carrie M., 139, 182.
Carey H., 135.
Cassie B., 166.
Celesta A., 158.
Celina E., 154.
Ceretha, 55.
Ceretha Jane, 91.
Ceretha O., 109.
Charles, 52, 58, 102, 110, 111.
Charles A., 56, 82.
Charles P., 67, 130.
Charles B., 75.
C. Harris, 36.
Charles C., 74, 103, 165.
Charles W., 106, 128, 139.
Charles H., 124, 142, 150, 153, 164, 1
Charles E., 129, 150.
Charles L., 130, 154, 165, 182.
Charles R., 141, 142.
Charles M., 144, 181.
Charles F., 162.
Charles D., 162.
Charles & Tamer, 166.
Charles T., 169.
Charles S., 183.
Charlot F., 75.
Charlot A., 37, 107, 137.
Charlot M., 90.
Chester B., 142.
Clarence, 167.
Clarence H., 180.
Clarence W., 163.
Clara A., 100.
Clara G., 164.
Clarissa, 90.
Clark H., 112.
Cleveland, 171.
Cora Bell, 147, 153, 185.
Cora C., 170.
Cora May, 150.
Clyde C., 160.
Crocker, 29, 49.
Curtis, 18, 19, 25, 40, 77, 145, 182.
Curtis W. 182.
Cordelia, 137.

H., 53, 104.
.0.
175.
, 153.
, 22, 23, 28, 37, 38, 39, 43, 45,
2, 91, 148.
161.
48, 97.
90, 155.
136, 178.
38, 39, 40, 45, 92.
40, 101.
58, 136, 164, 179.
35, 72, 73, 89, 139, 143.
97, 161.
99, 138, 163.
100.
fred, 184.

169.

154.
3, 73.

133, 135.
68.
59, 110, 112, 133.
., 161.
., 113.
10, 155.
., 103, 157.
, 138, 179.
., 101.
., 142, 180.
., 96, 159, 160.
, 163.
., 100, 145, 163.
. B., 131.
., 125.
;.
126, 176.
116, 174.
}.
157, 185.
182.

62.
72.
33, 155, 165.
., 115.
0, 58, 102.

Elbridge G., 146.
Elbert, 112, 171.
Elberta, 172.
Elba J., 158.
Elena, 129.
Elgin L., 112.
Elizabeth, 5, 7, 8, 12, 28, 35, 44, 45, 52, 71, 75, 143, 153.
Elizabeth A., 131, 156.
Elisab C., 3, 6, 72.
Elisab H., 184.
Eliza, 62.
Eliza A., 65, 66, 101, 128.
Eliza J., 55, 68, 77, 108.
Eliza M., 70.
Eliza S., 77.
Eliakim, 106.
Elias, 45, 92, 93, 157.
Elias B., 93.
Ella, 130, 148.
Ella A., 147.
Ella B., 159.
Ella E., 158.
Ella G., 154.
Ella O., 176.
Ellen, 163.
Ellen A., 156.
Ellen J., 108.
Ellen M., 141.
Ellen S., 146.
Elmer E., 172.
Emma B., 126.
Emma C., 150, 162.
Emma J., 146, 167, 169.
Emma L., 166.
Emma M., 68, 99.
Emma S., 151.
Emma T., 56.
Emma V. A., 144.
Emeline, 88, 113.
Emery, 169.
Emily J., 90.
Emily L., 147.
Emily N., 81.
Emily R., 98.
Emily V., 107.
Ena F., 154.
Enoch, 70.
Enoch S., 104, 166.
Enola E., 160.
Ensley, 95.

Ephraim L., 87, 93, 158.
Ermina, 96.
Eral C., 172.
Ernest A., 111, 151.
Ernest E., 172.
Ernest G., 167.
Ernest M., 157.
Ernest N., 160.
Essaphene, 153.
Essaphene M., 184.
Essie Inez, 160.
Estella, 130.
Estella S., 176.
Esther, 32.
Esther A., 151, 157.
Ethel E., 172.
Ethel M., 185.
Ethel S., 168.
Etta L., 173.
Euina M., 127.
Eunice, 36.
Eunice A., 94.
Eunice E., 103.
Eunice F. A., 88.
Everitt, 59, 91, 106, 156.
Ezra, 54, 92, 104, 169.
Ezekiel, 32, 35, 55, 60, 73, 92, 108, 115, 130.
Everitt S., 133.
Fanny E., 127.
Fanny M., 51.
Florence E., 133, 157.
Florence L., 151.
Florence M., 162, 166.
Flora, 134.
Flora Lovina, 159.
Flora M., 151.
Flora S., 129.
Frances, 43.
Frances P., 141.
Frances N., 77.
Frank, 115, 158, 174.
Frank S., 123, 144, 175.
Francis, 42, 79, 80, 135, 145.
Frank L., 138, 155, 179.
Frank A., 131, 155, 177.
Foster M., 158.
Franklin A., 81, 146.
Freeman, 60, 110, 116, 170.
Freeman E., 93, 153, 185.
Fred Y., 95.
Frederick, 122, 143, 174.

Freddy S., 135.
Fred Truman, 167.
Freeman G., 173.
George, 36, 58, 67, 109, 130.
George W., 30, 42, 50, 51, 79, 95, 101, 164.
George R., 74.
George H., 75.
George M., 83, 121, 151, 175.
George A., 103, 129, 142, 144, 146, 157.
George E., 104.
George Abel, 106, 169.
George C., 144, 181.
George Otis, 156.
George K., 159.
Georgiana, 96, 166.
Gilbert S., 34, 54, 105.
Gilbert R., 52, 102.
Gilbert F., 54, 55, 108.
Gilbert E., 167.
Gertrude M., 170.
Gray L., 139.
Grace M., 144.
Grace F., 143.
Gracia A., 148.
Grace Inez, 183.
Guifford D., 158.
Hannah, 10, 11, 12, 13, 14, 21, 23, 32, 38, 70, 72.
Hannah A., 70, 166.
Hannah D., 135.
Hannah E., 182.
Hannah M., 94.
Handley, 35, 54, 70, 73, 138.
Handley C., 123, 175.
Haller T., 75.
Harriet, 60, 95, 110.
Harriet A., 114.
Harriet C., 123.
Harriet M., 130.
Harriet S., 89, 111.
Harris O., 96.
Harley E., 163.
Harry, 131.
Harry A., 169.
Harry F., 182.
Harry H., 125.
Harry N., 156.
Harry W., 185.
Harvey F., 135, 178.
Harvey H., 116.

H. Alice, 105.
H. Isabel, 147.
Hattie G., 139.
Hattie L., 136.
Hassel B., 158.
Havelock, 163.
Havilah S., 89, 105.
Helen A., 73.
Helen O., 144.
Henry, 133, 177.
Henry A., 126.
Henry D., 135.
Henry J., 94, 159.
Henry R., 69.
Henry W., 97.
Henrietta M., 56.
Henrietta O., 157.
Herbert E., 151.
Herbert M., 115, 173.
Herbert N., 156.
Herman S., 163, 173.
Hiram, 66, 127, 138.
Hiram E., 93.
Hiram F., 128.
Hiram M., 90, 105, 167.
Horatio N., 57, 111, 170.
Horace M., 146, 183.
Homer H., 104.
Howard, 147.
Howard D., 86.
H. Spurgeon, 106.
Ida E., 154.
Ida J., 148.
Ida M., 136, 167, 170, 184.
Idella R., 147.
Ila Maud, 173.
Inez, 156.
Ira Moody, 127.
Irene, 93, 185.
Irene S., 135.
Isabella, 55, 65, 96.
Isabella C., 101.
Isaac, 65.
Isaac M., 173.
Isaac N., 95, 160.
Isaac R., 69, 132.
Isaiah, 64, 125, 168.
Israel, 58, 67, 70, 107, 110, 132.
Israel James, 132.
Izory M., 101.
Jacob, 34, 35, 69, 70, 133.

James, 1, 2, 5, 6, 7, 8, 9, 10, 11, 12, 15, 21, 22, 26, 31, 35, 36, 37, 43, 50, 53, 72, 76, 81, 82, 104, 145, 166.
James A., 114, 142, 148, 163, 173.
James B., 138.
James C., 151, 173.
James E., 35, 51, 67, 68, 106, 115, 169.
James H., 108, 114.
James K., 127.
James L., 47, 97, 136, 161.
James M., 61, 68, 75, 122, 131, 142.
James P., 69, 96, 128, 131, 161, 176.
James R., 74, 143.
James S., 98, 162.
James T., 76, 143.
James W., 97, 100, 161, 163.
Jane, 142.
Jane C., 75.
Jane G., 52.
Janet G., 77.
Jemima, 11, 89.
Jerusha, 90.
Jerusha M., 167.
Jerome A., 104.
Jervis, 55, 105, 168.
Jessie, 166.
Jessie A., 135, 154.
Jessie E., 91.
Jessie J., 107.
Jessie N., 165.
John, 12, 20, 26, 29, 31, 35, 43, 44, 50, 52, 65, 169.
John B., 64, 94, 115, 159, 174.
John C., 51.
John D., 138, 162.
John E., 29, 53, 103, 185.
John H., 80, 108, 128, 145, 169, 175.
John M., 61, 69, 75, 121, 132, 156.
John N., 46, 94, 156, 159, 185.
John R., 90, 173.
John W., 72, 83, 101, 102, 137, 161.
Joanna, 29.
Jonathan A., 44.
Jordan, 103.
Joseph, 32, 45, 56, 89.
Joseph B., 66, 111, 127.
Joseph C., 79, 144.
Joseph D., 72, 135.
Joseph F., 31, 53, 96, 146, 180.
Joseph H., 53, 103, 165.
Joseph M., 73.

Joseph N., 101.
Joseph W., 61, 87, 104, 123, 158.
Josephine, 132.
Josephine W., 164.
Josie L., 104.
Josiah, 26, 41, 78, 79.
Josiah C., 147, 183.
Joshua M., 72, 136.
Judith, 22, 38.
Judson, 89, 105.
Julia, 115.
Julia A., 91, 181.
Justin R., 123.
Lavinia, 54, 72.
Laleah, 94.
Laughlin I., 98, 162.
Lauretta A., 111.
Laila M., 128.
Lauren O., 130.
Laura M., 86, 160, 167.
Leah F., 31.
Leonvia S., 88.
Levi, 92.
Leander, 94, 158.
Lemuel, 108.
Leoni, 113, 171.
Leroy G., 139.
Lerana J., 152.
Lena E., 156.
Lee, 174.
Libby B., 108.
Lionel, 1, 2, 8, 11, 12, 13, 14.
Lionel J., 113.
Linton, 110.
Lillie, 115.
Lida Mary, 115.
Lizzie F., 126.
Lizzie May, 127.
Lizzie J., 105.
Lizzie L., 144.
Lilian B., 131.
Lila G., 167.
Lilah Lee, 185.
Louisa, 41, 81.
Lovena, 60, 95, 133.
Louise J., 67.
Louise M., 63.
Lois, 69.
Lois E., 157.
Lois H., 66.
Lovenia, 89.

Louisa A., 90.
Louisa L., 99.
Louisa J., 110.
Lottie O., 125.
Lorenzo W., 136.
Louis P., 143.
Lottie G., 157.
Lottie D., 160.
Lucinda, 47, 96, 97, 110.
Lucy A., 151.
Lydia, 11, 30, 73.
Lydia S., 63.
Lyman W., 66, 128.
Lyman H., 74.
Lydia Ann, 96.
Lydia O., 100.
Lycurgus, 103, 165.
Lyman A., 183.
Mary, 1, 6, 8, 9, 10, 11, 15, 18, 19, 23, 30, 31, 37, 40, 46, 50, 58, 80, 94, 96, 169.
Mary A., 67, 71, 83, 90, 102, 130, 133.
Mary C., 146.
Mary E., 85, 87, 89, 90, 97, 99, 105, 132, 133, 138, 161, 162, 164, 168.
Mary F., 50, 166.
Mary H., 107.
Mary J., 53, 62, 93, 104, 131, 143.
Mary K., 69.
Mary L., 123, 143.
Mary S., 101, 111.
Mary V., 181.
Mary E. G., 163.
Madella L., 108.
Mahlon, 114, 172,
Mahlon A., 147.
Mabel Ann, 165.
Mabel L., 167.
Maggie, 160.
Maggie I., 159.
Maggie M., 161.
Margaret, 79, 94, 105, 112.
Marguretta, 154.
Mariam P., 163.
Maribelle, 173.
Margera A. 105.
Marietta, 1 5, 124.
Martha, 8, 32, 70, 134, 137.
Martha A., 55.
Martha E., 109, 141, 151.
Martha L., 93, 135.

H., 143.
., 48.
.., 114, 172.
I, 115.
L., 88.
, 133.
, 185.
D., 172.
e, 36.
n, 91, 157.
B., 185.
J., 87.
90, 95, 167.
W., 146.
38.
55.
, 145.
?., 136, 178.
, 106.
ant, 182.
158.
., 122.
L., 134.
89.
A., 57, 73.
J., 90.
S., 175.
09.
.., 146, 165.
'., 122.
., 127.
'., 142.
V., 138.
14.
78, 143.
38.
., 153.
il, 1.
l.
l., 55, 67, 108, 130.
6.
ane, 158.
'., 81.
h, 91, 156, 168.
13.
, 163.
, 148.
iy, 155.
144.
63.
'., 161.

Norman, 134.
Norman E., 155.
Norman W., 153, 184.
Noble Brown, 156.
Nina Grace, 168.
Obadiah, 89, 155.
Obadiah M., 155.
Obed, 36, 73.
Ociella, 126.
Olive, 47, 110.
Olive A., 163
Oliver, 54, 105, 107, 168.
Oliver C., 95.
Oliver H., 134.
Olivia, 112.
Otis St. C., 185.
Palmer, 170.
Paul, 30, 51.
Paul C., 104.
Peter P., 30, 52.
Percy H. M., 131.
Percy R., 169.
Phebe, 32, 53, 69, 131.
Phebe Ann, 89, 121.
Phebe Jane, 54, 58, 120.
Prior, 28.
Priscilla, 47, 96.
Prudence, 90.
Quincy Mayberry, 147, 183.
Rachel, 28.
Ray Cecil, 163.
Raymond C., 184.
Rebecca, 18, 19, 79.
Rebecca L., 159.
Reuben C., 175.
Reuben P., 135.
Retta D., 162.
Rhoda A., 63.
Rhoda F., 68.
Rhoda V., 157.
Rhupurty, 135.
Richard, 36, 74, 76, 142.
Richard B., 152, 184.
Richard H., 141, 180.
Richard L., 58, 111.
Richard S., 91, 157.
Richardson, 94, 159.
Robert, 72, 85, 135, 138, 152.
Robert M., 143, 166.
Robert O., 153.
Robert S., 115.

Robert E., 184.
Robert F., 163.
Robert J., 66, 125, 128.
Robert R., 164.
Robert W., 128.
Roland, 183.
Roland A. 156.
Rose, 146.
Rose Ella, 158.
Rosilla, 82.
Roxana, 101.
Ruth, 8, 15, 26.
Ruth A., 164.
Ruth S., 78.
Rupert D., 127.
Rupert J., 125.
Russel E., 146, 183.
Rosa M., 169.
Sally, 38.
Samuel, 12, 20, 27, 28, 47, 49, 100.
Samuel, B., 46, 95, 158.
Samuel F., 100.
Samuel G., 156, 185.
Samuel H., 77, 143.
Samuel R., 99.
Samuel S., 143.
Sabra M., 104.
Sadie, 148.
Salina A., 108.
Salina E., 105, 114.
Sarah, 11, 20, 28, 34, 42, 64, 80, 158.
Sarah A., 48, 59, 100, 105, 110, 115.
Sarah A. M., 101.
Sarah B., 141, 142.
Sarah C. R., 76.
Sarah E., 156.
Sarah J., 89.
Sarah L., 87, 120.
Sarah M., 67.
Sarah R., 107.
Satira, 89.
Sileda, 138.
Seraph A., 55.
Seraph O., 97.
Seraphina, 47.
Seretta, 90.
Seth, 32, 54, 71, 134.
Sibyl, 64.
Sibyl Ann, 82.
Sibyl Belle, 167.
Sidney, 36, 60, 89, 114, 137, 155.

Sidney I., 72, 188.
Silas, 35, 69, 105.
Silas P., 94, 158.
Solomon, 71, 134.
Sophia, 35, 38, 68, 73, 86, 88, 138, 161.
Sophronia, 67.
Stanley, 174.
Stephen J., 52.
Susan, 22, 33, 49, 58, 85, 102, 153.
Susanna, 46, 83, 89.
Susan A., 86, 97, 103, 110.
Susan L., 135.
Susan O., 42.
Susan P., 53.
Susie E , 183.
Susie L., 181.
Syrena, 96.
Syrena A., 91.
Syrena N., 78.
Tamer, 68.
Teressa, 95, 133.
Theodore H., 163.
Theodore H. P., 126, 176.
Thomas, 8, 18, 19, 20, 26, 32, 33, 43, 54, 65, 80, 83, 105, 126, 171.
Thomas A., 46, 92, 95, 111.
Thomas F., 106, 168.
Thomas H., 48, 99, 100, 163.
Timothy W. B., 73, 138.
Unie M., 159.
Vernie F., 127.
Vernon, 130.
Virginia E., 151.
Vorus F., 133, 177.
Waity, 94.
Walter, 58, 111.
Walter A., 120.
Walter E., 182.
Walter S., 166.
Wallace G., 104, 111, 166.
Wallace I., 159.
Wallace S., 148.
Warren B., 81, 151.
Warren L., 116.
Warren M., 147.
Watson, 82, 150.
Whitefield, 86, 152.
Willett, 55, 95.
Willett M., 86.
Willie Y., 143.
William, 28, 46, 81, 108, 146, 148, 154.

William A., 67, 76, 104, 128, 130, 134, 147, 161, 176.
William B., 130.
William C., 43, 80, 84.
William E., 60, 116, 120, 136, 153, 164, 179.
William F., 54, 107, 108, 139, 142.
William G., 101, 164.
William H., 46, 65, 66, 94, 106, 107, 127, 128, 168, 169, 181.
William L., 162.
William J., 166.
William M., 105, 127, 155, 167.
William O., 63, 125, 130, 157, 159.
William P., 134, 177, 178.
William R., 103, 153.
William S., 154, 185.
William T., 109.
William W., 82, 112, 128, 148, 170.
William B. F., 138, 179.
Wintfred O., 133.
Xenophon, 112.
Zipporah M., 72, 106,
Zenas E., 91, 156.
Zechariah, 92.
Zededia, 93.
Zephina, 96.

INDEX TO OTHER NAMES.

Abbott, 40, 41, 81, 146, 147.
Abrams, 49.
Adams, 8, 22, 23, 24, 30, 41, 138.
Akeroid, 46.
Akers, 82.
Allen, 76, 81, 108.
Alline, 136, 188.
Allison, 52.
Ally, 51.
Ames, 66.
Andrew, 43, 83.
Andrews, 41, 145.
Anderson, 53, 75, 165.
Ansley 28, 45, 55, 65, 110.
Appleton, 5, 6, 9, 17.
Archer, 68, 131.
Armstrong, 28, 31, 52, 64.
Ash, 106.
Atkins, 148.
Atkinson, 8.
Atwood, 50.
Austin, 88, 161.
Averill, 5.

Babb, 26, 104.
Bacon, 56, 86, 141.
Bailey, 179.
Baker, 1, 9, 42, 75, 102, 165.
Balch, 164.
Balcomb, 22, 85, 133, 158.
Baldwin, 36, 53, 103, 128.
Balsor, 53, 99, 100, 163.
Bancroft, 28.
Barclift, 114.
Banks, 34, 35, 45, 55, 69, 108, 161, 166.
Barnard, 151.
Barnes, 27, 28, 64, 120.
Barrows, 79.
Barteaux, 94, 95, 123.
Bartholomew, 1, 2.
Bathrick, 50.
Baumwart, 92.
Baxter, 71.
Bayless, 181.

Bayley, 15, 37.
Bazley, or Beardsley, 51.
Beals, 87, 110, 184.
Beard, 20.
Belcher, 13.
Benjamin, 74.
Benner, 72.
Bennett, 11, 80.
Benson, 66, 67.
Bent, 105, 155, 161.
Bentley, 115.
Berrick, 82.
Berry, 19, 63, 88, 89, 90, 125, 135, 157, 166.
Betts, 51.
Beveridge, 177.
Bickford, 182.
Billings, 58.
Birsted, 31.
Bishop, 5, 176.
Black, 49.
Blackburn, 65.
Blackmer, 83.
Blake, 78.
Blanchard, 97.
Blunt, 60.
Bodge, 18, 79.
Boeth, 20.
Bogert, 30.
Bohaker, 152.
Bonfeoy, 109.
Booth, 52, 96.
Bower, 172.
Bowers, 46.
Bowman, 169.
Bowlby, 93, 102.
Brabzon, 166.
Bradford, 10, 50, 80.
Bragg, 6.
Brennan, 155, 156.
Bridgham, 6.
Briggs, 41, 70.
Brinton, 70, 71, 72.
Boyce, 63.
Brewer, 100.

Bracket, 183.
Bramhall, 140.
Brocklebank, 8.
Brotha, 32.
Brown, 8, 9, 10, 19, 24, 28, 29, 31, 33, 38, 46, 54, 80, 82, 96, 108, 116, 169, 177, 182.
Brooks, 29, 30, 36, 134.
Brundage, 172.
Bubar, 33.
Buck, 37.
Buffum, 184.
Bulkley, 6.
Burbank, 68.
Burgess, 94, 103, 159.
Burnham, 73, 129.
Burns, 63.
Bunfill, 113, 114.
Burpee, 33.
Burtt, 34.
Busby, 72, 100.
Busey, 42
Butler, 163, 182.
Bridgewater, 113.

Calkins, 93.
Cameron, 73, 177.
Campbell, 30, 110, 115.
Camplin, 110.
Cann, 64, 132.
Capen, 144.
Card, 161.
Carr, 26, 58, 96.
Carson, 47, 98.
Carter, 106.
Carton, 100.
Carver, 40.
Cavalry, 108.
Chandler, 29, 72, 140.
Chaplain, 26, 81.
Chapman, 51.
Chamberlain, 76, 123.
Charlton, 71, 156, 158.
Chase, 68, 93, 105.
Cheney, 5, 8, 10, 13, 14, 15.
Chesley, 21, 31, 68, 107, 136.
Childs, 50, 136.
Chipman, 21, 22, 27, 32, 45, 52, 54, 83, 94, 95, 123.
Choate, 17.
Church, 35, 44, 83.
Churchill, 132.

Clapp, 76.
Clappison, 170.
Clark, 30, 31, 33, 34, 35, 38, 124, 127, 185.
Clarkson, 130.
Clement, 79.
Cleveland, 25, 38, 180.
Cobb, 26, 41, 42, 77, 82.
Cobham, 18, 19.
Coburn, 12.
Colburn, 104.
Coleman, 23, 24, 34, 37.
Coffin, 1, 37.
Coates, 69.
Cogswell, 87, 127, 134, 159.
Cole, 44, 145.
Coldwell, 101.
Collins, 99, 170.
Colt, 92.
Comstock, 141, 166.
Conant, 19, 42.
Connell, 96.
Conner, 62, 173, 174.
Conrad, 49.
Cook, 39, 44, 129, 177, 178.
Cooper, 121.
Constable, 135.
Cornish, 63.
Cornwell, 91.
Cossett, 31, 53.
Cotton, 19.
Covert, 105, 184.
Cowper, 70.
Cox, 73, 139, 159.
Craft, 11.
Craig, 82.
Crandall, 63, 109.
Crane, 76, 100.
Crawford, 33.
Crocker, 29, 156.
Cronk, 30.
Crosby, 131, 167.
Croscup, 57.
Cross, 72, 73.
Cropley, 134.
Crouss, 57, 67, 130, 163.
Crowell, 97, 132.
Cummings, 92, 178.
Cunningham, 90, 162.
Currier, 34, 98.
Currill, 133.

Curtis, 18, 19.
Cushing, 51.
Cutten, 50.

Dakin, 91, 92, 120, 154.
Danford, 24,
Daniels, 86.
Davenport, 13.
Davis, 41, 50, 53, 129, 148.
Davisson, 68, 159.
Dawes, 150.
Dawley, 43.
Day, 109, 143.
De Costa, 40.
Delap, 61, 139.
Delong, 49.
Denison, 5, 6.
Densmore, 34.
Denton, 91.
Devinny, 53.
Dewar, 110, 111.
Dewitt, 36.
Dewolf, 28.
Dexter, 22.
Dickinson, 14.
Dimond, 110.
Dinsmore, 17.
Ditmars, 62.
Divoll, 53.
Dodge, 21, 48, 49, 55, 94, 109, 116.
Doane, 86.
Dolbear, 49, 50.
Dole, 82.
Donavan, 150.
Doolittle, 113.
Doty, 65.
Downs, 107.
Dresser, 146.
Drinkwater, 77.
Driscol, 157.
Dudley, 18.
Dugan, 109.
Dummer, 14, 15, 16.
Duncan, 7.
Dunham, 147.
Dunn, 49.
Durant, 101.
Dyer, 92, 109.
Durland, 65.
Duty, 23.

Eagan, 95.
Eagleson, 106.
Earle, 127.
Early, 90.
Easter, 49.
Eastman, 145.
Eason, 135.
Edes, 150.
Ebinger, 60.
Edgecomb, 51.
Edwards, 6, 9, 39, 101, 139, 148, 171.
Elder, 56, 66, 70, 104.
Eldridge, 86.
Elkins, 36.
Elliott, 36, 70, 100, 129, 164, 177.
Ellis, 29, 30, 78.
Elwell, 51.
English, 99.
Epps, 4, 5, 18.
Estabrooks, 33.
Estey, 33.
Evans, 96.
Everett, 33, 64, 152.

Fairchild, 142.
Farnsworth, 29, 30, 54, 71, 72, 78, 133, 138, 165.
Farris, 162.
Farquharson, 54.
Fash, 54, 72.
Faunce, 40.
Felch, 1, 53.
Fellows, 55, 56.
Felt, 14.
Fisher, 89, 138.
Fitchett, 133.
Fitz Maurice, 22.
Flack, 19.
Flagg, 86.
Fleet, 102.
Fleming, 34.
Fletcher, 33, 147.
Flint, 48, 106.
Fluria, 107.
Forbes, 69, 153.
Forbush, 28.
Ford, 40.
Fonda, 49.
Foss, 162.
Foote, 65.
Fox, 48, 55, 123.

Fowler, 5, 6, 44, 54, 163.
Foster, 5, 20, 22, 28, 30, 31, 35, 38, 45, 46, 62, 63, 66, 68, 70, 71, 72, 77, 89, 99, 103, 104, 109, 122, 123, 133, 134, 161, 166, 177, 181.
Fraser, 101, 125, 168.
Frazier, 17.
Franklin, 162.
Fredericks, 96.
Freeman, 48, 82, 181.
French, 5.
Frisbie, 47.

Gabel, 31.
Gage, 5.
Galup, 33, 34.
Gammon, 18, 19, 77, 83, 151.
Gates, 31, 94.
Gerrish, 6, 23, 24.
Gesner, 71.
Generals, 117.
Gilliat, 55, 73, 166, 168.
Gilliland, 63, 64, 155.
Gillis, 96, 97.
Gilman, 77.
Gilpin, 59.
Gleason, 38.
Glendenning, 110, 111.
Glidden 138.
Glines, 40.
Glover, 48, 107, 112.
Goble, 107.
Godden, 14.
Goldsmith, 43.
Goodnow, 77.
Goodrich, 82.
Goodridge, 8.
Goudey 139.
Gould, 99, 140.
Graffam, 43.
Graham, 66, 124, 156, 167.
Graves, 72, 78.
Gray, 82, 92.
Grant, 117.
Green, 43, 50, 95, 160.
Greenham, 28.
Greeno, 101.
Greenlaw, 136.
Greenleaf, 37.
Greeley, 103.
Griggs, 137.

Grimes, 29.
Groendyke, 143.
Gumb, 171.
Guthree, 36.

Hadley, 50, 164.
Haight, 64.
Haily, 34.
Hale, 10, 14, 16, 17, 24, 25, 36, 153.
Hall, 26, 43, 70, 98, 129, 134, 135, 147.
Hamline, 40.
Hamm, 30.
Hammond, 40, 41.
Hankinson, 60, 130.
Hannah, 34.
Harmon, 40.
Harvey, 29, 30.
Harris, 5, 6, 7, 9, 10, 35, 53, 58, 59, 67, 96, 130, 156, 163.
Harrison, 29.
Hagan, 177.
Haines, 105.
Hamer, 158.
Hamilton, 66, 143 175.
Hancock, 81.
Hanson, 81, 82.
Harding, 123.
Hardwick, 35, 157.
Hassel, 92.
Hasty, 44.
Hauszer 78.
Haven, 78.
Hawkins, 61.
Hawley, 139.
Hayes, 179.
Hazeltine, 9.
Heald, 80.
Heath, 100, 147.
Henderson, 181.
Henshaw, 89.
Heaton, 78.
Hendey, 95.
Heron, 60.
Hersey, 67, 109, 129.
Herrick, 77, 95.
Hepp & Co., 122.
Hicks, 20, 22, 31, 122.
Higginson, 16.
Hills, 38.
Hill, 49, 100, 116.
Hickson, 141.

Hinxman, 31.
Hine, 8.
Howie. 138.
Hobbs, 93.
Hobson, 23.
Hoffman, 135.
Holden, 50, 51, 79.
Holt, 38.
Hooper, 146.
Horner, 180.
Hopkins, 46.
Houghton, 36.
Hovey, 5, 43.
Howard, 80, 136.
Howell, 28.
Hoy, 65.
Hoyt, 48, 82.
Hudson, 135.
Hull, 5.
Hulsemam, 66, 91.
Humbert, 58.
Hunnewell, 18.
Hunt, 140.
Hurd, 73.
Hurst, 165.
Hutchinson, 13, 72, 126.
Hyde. 41.

Ilsley, 94, 159.
Ireland, 113, 114.
Irvine, 34, 127.

Jack, 93.
Jackman, 8, 14, 24.
Jackson, 43, 168.
Jacobs, 88, 143.
Jayne, 137.
Jeffrey, 50.
Jenkins, 75.
Jewett, 5, 12, 13, 14, 15, 23, 34, 37, 52.
Jillson, 147.
Johnson, 85, 102, 131, 124, 137, 146.
Jones, 19, 52, 63, 80, 86, 98, 158.
Jordan, 18, 26, 82, 94, 135, 145, 150.

Karnan, 78.
Karns, 116.
Kemp, 103.
Kenny, 53.
Kean, 126.
Kearney, 167.

K

Keating, 176.
Keene, 146.
Keith, 167.
Kempton, 68, 85, 87.
Kelly, 104.
Kent, 128, 137.
Kerrigan, 132.
Kidder, 44.
Kilburn, 50, 81.
Kilmer, 81.
Kilpatrick, 71.
Kimball, 41, 50, 107.
King, 81, 131, 169.
Kindred, 80.
Kinghorn, 87.
Kingsbury, 5, 41.
Kingsley 66.
Kinney 33.
Kinsman, 115, 121.
Killam, 132.
Kitchen, 33.
Knapp, 62.
Kniffin, 88, 124, 154.
Knight, 79, 80, 144.
Knowles, 65.
Knowlton, 6.

Ladiner, 101.
Ladue, 166.
Lagrange, 92.
Laine, 18.
Lane, 40, 50, 144.
Ladd, 25.
Langley, 31, 32, 131.
Lantz, 90.
Larkin, 50.
Lathrop, 89.
Lawrence, 130, 166.
Leary, 64.
Leavitt. 42.
Lewis. 64, 93, 183.
Leighton, 92.
Leitch, 78.
Leonard, 34.
Leach, 49.
Lee, 53, 117.
Lent, 135.
Letteny, 54.
Libby, 78, 82.
Little, 17, 37.
Littlehail, 26.

Lincoln, 107.
Lingley, 29, 30.
Livermore, 101.
Lloyd, 49.
Lobdell, 64, 65.
Locke, 73.
Lohnas, 103.
Long, 32, 136, 179.
Longley, 24, 34, 101, 182.
Longfellow, 24.
Lonsbury, 175.
Lord, 5, 26, 41, 150.
Lorimer, 157.
Lovewell, 81, 183.
Low, 24, 93.
Lowe, 97, 126.
Lowell, 8, 9.
Loyte, 24.
Lull, 13, 14, 25.
Lunt, 8, 11, 24.
Lynam, 28, 29.
Lynch, 48.

Mabie, 128.
Mackie, 18.
McAlpine, 46, 48, 64.
McAuliffe, 49.
McAdam, 52.
McBride, 143.
McComsky, 104.
McConnell, 60, 61, 62, 106, 111, 115, 116, 30, 73, 174, 175.
McDonald, 46, 60, 83, 134, 167.
McDormand, 59, 113.
McGraw, or McGrath, 33.
McGawley, 46.
McGroom, 50.
McGiffin, 74.
McGregor, 90, 99.
McGee, 116.
McGowen, 181.
McKenzie, 32, 47.
McKim, 106.
McLellan, 26.
McIntyre, 59.
McLeish, 115.
McNinny, 46.
Maning, or Manning, 5, 56, 58, 61, 92.
Maling, 53, 86.
Madden, 69.
Mailman, 96.

Malloch, 136.
Mansfield, 19.
Mann, 97, 143, 145, 182.
Marsh, 6.
Marshall, 28, 32, 34, 35, 46, 64, 65, 6? 102, 105, 108, 123, 131.
Martin, 40, 138.
Marriett, 93, 153.
Markle, 114, 172.
Marr, 130.
Mather, 18.
Masters, 32, 93, 110.
Matthews, 80.
Mason & Hamlin, 122.
May, 85.
Mayberry, 19, 20, 26, 43, 44, 79, 80.
Maybin, 169.
Mayo, 82, 103, 146.
Meekins, 28.
Messenger, 31, 71, 134.
Medcalf, 9.
Merrill, 36, 139.
Merry, 44.
Merritt, 54.
Mead, 79.
Medicraft, 96.
Mercer, 110.
Miller, 29, 30, 71, 100, 128, 129 133.
Mills, 30, 46, 107.
Middleton, 30, 31.
Milledge, 35, 54.
Milbury, 46, 47, 67, 97, 138, 168.
Mitchell, 70, 71.
Milner, 90.
Minard, 90, 155.
Miner, 113, 176.
Miles, 183.
Moody, 25, 65, 101, 142, 161.
Moore, 48, 60, 69, 154.
Morey, 54.
Morgan, 66, 67, 75, 87.
Morehouse, 100, 106.
Monroe, 85.
Morse, 2, 10, 21, 22, 32, 49, 55, 69, 72, 108, 115, 127, 158.
Morton, 42, 43, 75.
Morrison, 31, 113.
Morine, 53.
Mulholland, 111.
Murray, 82.
Mussels, 102.

Nangle, 185.
Nason, 50.
Neily, 21, 168.
Neal, 33.
Nelson, 10, 154, 180.
Newcomb, 21, 69, 70, 73, 138, 157.
Newman, 9.
Nichols, 31, 69, 129, 136, 159, 175.
Nickerson, 52, 69, 132.
Noble, 51.
Northcott, 173.
Norton, 163.
Noyes, 6, 8, 10, 12, 13, 39, 40, 41, 77, 78.
Northern, 23.

Odell, 30, 87, 88.
Ogleby, 28.
Oikle, 179.
Oliver, 102.
Ord, 32.
Osborne, 6.
O'Conner, 30.

Paine, 75.
Palmer, 5, 48, 94, 112, 158, 159.
Parish, 23, 47, 48.
Parker, 21, 48, 49, 67, 69, 93, 94, 105, 111, 128, 185.
Parsons, 17, 24.
Patch, 31.
Patchin, 81.
Patterson, 35.
Parlin, 40.
Parvis, 41.
Paul, 43.
Payson, 70.
Peabody, 38,
Peake, 67, 181.
Parson, 10, 16, 23, 24, 36, 38, 74.
Peasley, 138.
Pearce, 6.
Peery, 120.
Pelham, 53.
Perley, 25, 38.
Perkins, 23, 25.
Pennivet, 18.
Perry, 76, 133, 130.
Peters, 66, 134, 141, 142.
Peterson, 143.
Pettingal, 10, 14.
Pengry, 6.

Pevear, 164.
Philbrick, 11, 20, 138, 147, 148.
Phillips, 15, 90, 91.
Phinney, 70, 108, 134.
Pickard, 16.
Pickup, 22.
Pickering, 37, 38, 92, 107, 114.
Picknell, 157.
Pickles, 128.
Pike, 11, 25, 37, 41, 77, 135, 145.
Pinkham, 64.
Pinkney, 30, 69.
Plumer, 10, 14, 24.
Pierce, 131.
Poole, 6, 106, 144.
Poor, 10, 25, 36, 37, 38.
Porter, 34, 48, 108, 126, 128.
Potter, 61, 65, 85, 86, 88, 90, 91, 93, 95, 105, 108, 110, 128, 152, 154, 156, 161, 167, 175.
Powell, 62, 109.
Pray, 126.
Prickett, 65.
Priestly, 69.
Prince, 40, 132.
Prior, 97.
Proctor, 4, 43, 98.
Prosser, 36.
Purdy, 67, 125.
Purrington, 43.
Putnam, 101.
Putney, 101, 183.
Pyne, 125.

Quereau, 153.
Quick, 48.

Rainforth, 158.
Rand, 97.
Randall, 22, 28, 29, 31, 47, 52, 55, 56, 98.
Randolph, 178.
Raymond, 69, 70, 105.
Rathburn, 78.
Read, 4, 96.
Reagh, 55.
Redding, 59.
Reed, 50, 73, 90.
Reynard, 47.
Reynolds, 78.
Rhodes, 29, 54, 169.
Rice, 26, 31, 52, 59, 66, 67, 87, 88, 124, 154.
Rich, 77, 129.

Richardson, 45, 79, 104.
Richards, 70.
Ridout, 50.
Riley, 161.
Rines, 41.
Ripley, 89.
Ritchie, 108.
Roach, 69, 70.
Robblee, 152.
Roberts, 31, 147.
Robbins, 46, 88, 89, 155.
Robinson, 107, 115, 125, 141, 161, 173.
Rodney, 132.
Rogers, 5, 17, 25, 90.
Rouillard, 65.
Ross, 58, 101.
Rosse, 5.
Rowe, 80.
Royer, 167.
Rudolph, 99.
Rundol, 9.
Ruggles, 63.
Rush, 114.
Russell, 48, 78.

Sabean, 64, 65, 70, 139, 161.
Sabes, 156.
Safford, 14.
Saltonstall, 10.
Sancton, 51, 52.
Savary, 55, 127.
Sanford, 47, 90, 91, 175.
Sanborn, 41.
Saunders, 30, 34, 57.
Saxton, 58, 112.
Sawyer, 41, 79.
Schofield, 47, 96.
Scott, 50, 98.
Scully, 111.
Scammell, 51, 52.
Scribner, 79, 81, 147, 182.
Searle, 15, 25, 38.
Sederquist, 102.
Seeley, 31.
Sewall, 126.
Shaw, 34, 35, 107, 113.
Sharp, 77.
Sherer, 30.
Sherwin, 89.
Shepherd, 129.

Shirley, 14.
Shook, 56.
Short, 5, 59, 60, 70.
Showers, 172.
Simms, 135.
Simpson, 48, 121, 154, 176.
Simonds, 178.
Skinner, 11, 94, 95, 129.
Sleith, 54.
Sloane, 50.
Slocomb, 102.
Smalley, 92.
Smith, 6, 8, 9, 13, 16, 33, 37, 38, 42, 46, 58, 62, 65, 89, 92, 95, 123, 129, 165.
Snell, 47, 80.
Snow, 29, 37, 70, 71.
Snyder, 75, 114, 123.
Somerby, 6.
Southern, 154.
Spearin, 96.
Spears, 137, 138.
Spencer, 87.
Spaulding, 101.
Spofford, 15.
Spooner, 78.
Sponemburg, 173.
Spurr, 32, 33, 34, 55, 91, 105, 110.
Sprowle, 179.
Spicer, 101, 102.
Squair, 60.
Standan, 111.
Staples, 71, 182.
Starratt, 28, 68, 73, 108.
Staniford, 6, 7, 9.
Stacy, 9.
Steadman, 29, 30, 104, 108.
Steele, 114.
Stevens, 16, 51, 64, 75.
Stickney, 8, 10, 11, 12, 13, 14, 15, 24, 37.
Stimpson, 22.
Stinchfield, 18, 42.
Stone, 56, 144, 146, 162, 182.
Stuart, 14, 89, 145, 146.
Stubbs, 41, 78.
Strasser, 93.
Stratton, 154.
Straight, 114, 172.
Strong, 140.
Styrnbrough, 109.
Swett, 19.
Symonds, 1, 2, 4, 5, 6, 39.

n, 19.
y, 31.
:, 21, 46, 47, 48, 49, 79, 98, 99, 106, 143, 157, 162, 174.
leman, 133, 168.
·, 24, 25.
pson, 42.
as, 28, 32, 42, 66, 86.
her, 18, 56.
er, 65, 178.
ton, 15, 22, 36, 37, 38.
e, 111.
n, 23.
ons, 120, 121.
n, 31.
nson, 35.
er, 56, 58, 86.
48, 100.
, 66.
well, 6, 9.
, 18.
108.
oly, 158.
, 56, 69, 87, 89, 130, 134.
36.
dell, 21, 48.
19.
r, 30, 134.
r, 56, 102, 106.
ull, 91.
r, 83, 145.
n, 51.
, 6, 9.
bly, 79.
154.
ll, 62.

wood, 143.
, 79.

23.
mburg, 131.
larcom, 106.
uskirk, 31, 45, 46, 123, 128, 130.
orne, 142.
elzor, 121.
y, 43, 81, 87.
n, 154.
y, 132.
e, 49, 64, 105, 123, 135, 136.
135.
n, 62, 63, 125.

Wade, 7, 96.
Walker, 16, 50, 51, 61.
Waldron, 19, 78, 80.
Wadham, 48.
Waldo, 26.
Wallis, 6, 9.
Waite, 6.
Ward, 5, 30, 185.
Wareham, 53.
Warren, 116, 121, 122.
Warden, 128.
Warner, 125.
Wall 163, 169.
Watkins, 146.
Watson, 31.
Wainwright, 6, 9.
Walton, 101.
Waterman, 97.
Waters, 116, 121, 122.
Wakeling, 67.
Waugh, 55.
Wear, 28, 45, 87, 88, 89, 155.
Webster, 46.
Weddell, 36.
Wentworth, 43.
West, 47, 99.
Wellstead, 29.
Webb, 59, 171.
Welsh, 62.
Webber, 83, 151.
Wells, 139.
Welton, 49.
Weston, 79, 83, 84, 181.
Westover, 62.
Wernau, 109.
White, 2, 13, 46, 47, 54, 73, 88, 100, 139.
Whipple, 6, 9.
Wheeler, 15, 24, 80, 111.
Wheelock, 21, 135.
Whitman, 29, 81, 132.
Whitcomb, 99, 101.
Whittimore, 103.
Wilson, 5, 8, 16, 32, 76, 111, 114, 123.
Willett, 32.
Wicom, 8.
Withington, 37.
Winsor, 44.
Williams, 68, 111, 114, 129.
Williston, 73.
Wilder, 164.
Wight, 145.

Winslow, 140, 144.
Winchester, 78, 88.
Wilkins, 102, 166.
Wilkinson, 113.
Wiswall, 69.
Wisdom & Son, 122.
Witham, 91, 147.
Witt, 108.
Wood, 8, 11, 19, 26, 47, 126, 180.
Woodbridge, 10, 13.
Woodbury, 21, 32, 80, 83.
Woods, 11.
Woolery, 65.
Woodward, 20.
Woodworth, 23, 28, 30, 46, 48, 58, 67, 87, 89, 92, 110, 117.
Wooster, 18.

Worcester, 10, 26, 101, 102.
Wolfe, 12.
Woodman, 5, 31, 48, 66.
Work, 54.
Wright, 35, 36, 80, 93, 102.
Wyer, 80.
Wylie, 173.
Wyman, 93.
Wray, 103.

Yarrigle, 58.
York, 50.
Young, 9, 120, 138, 142, 144.
Younglove, 5, 6.

Zaring, 36.
Zwicker, 125.

LIST OF COLLATERAL TRACINGS.

Andrew, 43.
Banks, 55.
Barteaux, 94.
Beals, 184.
Berry, 63.
Bodge, 18.
Bohaker, 152.
Brown, 8.
Burnham, 129.
Calkins, 93.
Chandler, 140.
Church, 44, Nathan sen., or Rev. Nathan,[5] Benj.,[4] Benj.,[3] Sam.,[2] Richard.[1]
Chesley, 107.
Clapp, 76.
Clark, 124.
Coburn, 12.
Colburn, 104.
Coleman, 37.
Coldwell, 101.
Conant, 42.
Crosby, 131.
Dakin, 120.
Dodge, 21, 55.
Elliott, 36.
Foster, 61, 63, 181.
Fowler, 71.
Gesner, 71.
Green, 160.
Gilliatt, 73.
Hall, 135.
Hankinson, 60.
Harris, 67.
Hill, 116.
Hinman, 62.
Herrick, 95.
Jewett, 15.
Johnson, 108.
Jordan, 18, 26, 82, 150.
Keene, 146.

Keith, 167.
Kniffin, 154.
Lawrence, 166.
Libby, 78, 82.
McConnell, 60.
Marshall, 65.
Milbury, 153.
Morgan, 67.
Newcomb, 69, 73, 157.
Parsons, 140.
Pearson, 16.
Peters, 141.
Perkins, 23.
Philbrick, 147.
Phinney, 70.
Palmer, 112.
Parish, 48.
Parker, 22, 93.
Poor, 38.
Potter, 61.
Rand, 97.
Rice, 52.
Savary, 55, 127.
Saxton, 112.
Smith, 42.
Steadman, 30, 104.
Stickney, 8.
Strong, 140.
Thurston, 8, 37.
Tisdale, 111.
Viditoe, 136.
Vroom, 62.
Warren, 121.
Whitman, 81.
Winchester, 78.
Winslow, 140, 144.
Woodbury, 32.
Woodworth, 23, Chas. sen.,[5] Jona,[4] Step.,[3] Isaac,[2] Walter.[1]
Worcester, 26.

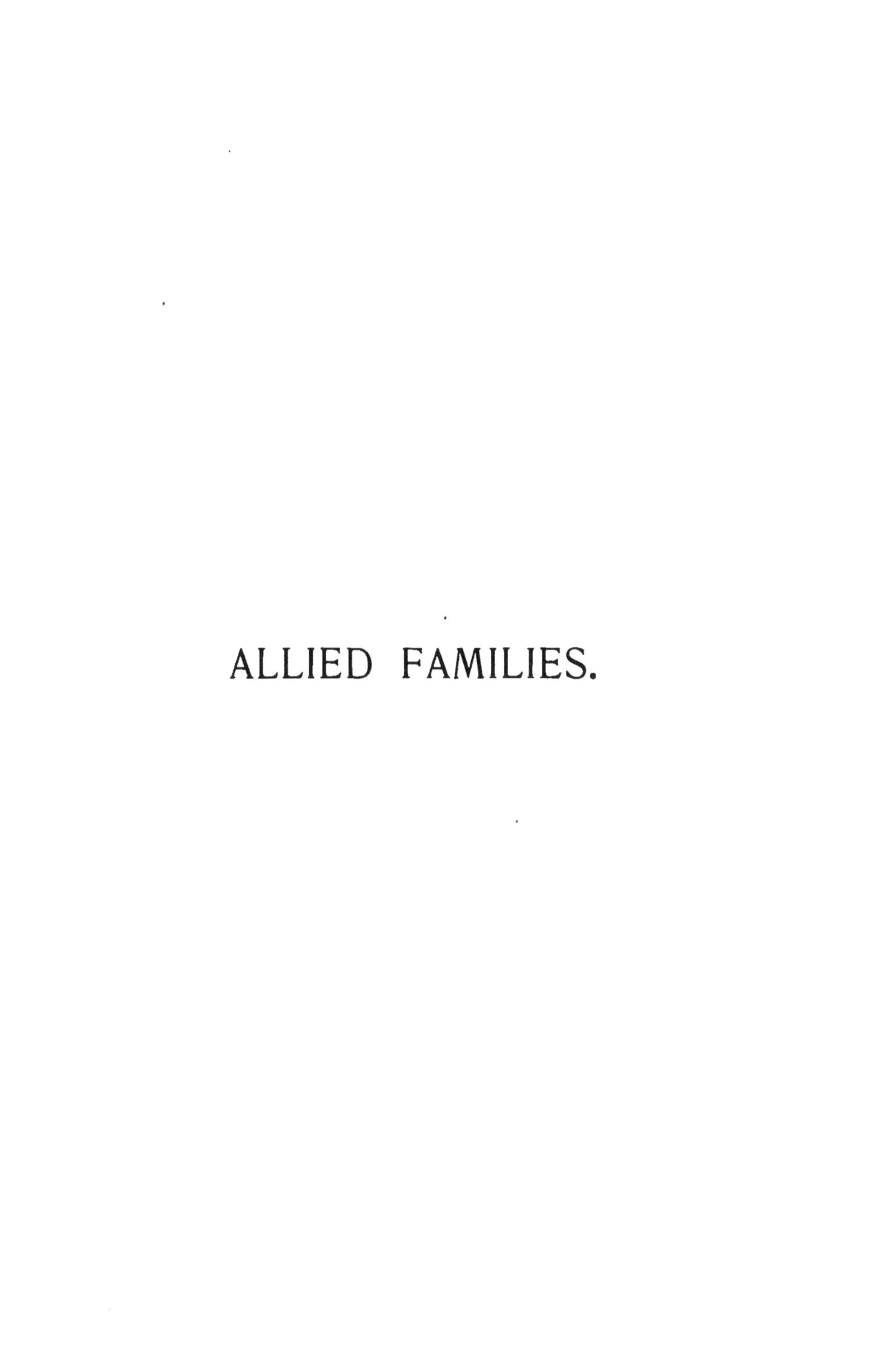

ALLIED FAMILIES.

THE ALLIED FAMILIES.

When the neutral French were driven out of Nova Scotia by their English victors, in 1755, liberal offers were made to loyal subjects of the King of England to occupy the lands. As a consequence, some thousands from Great Britain, Germany, and the New England States, emigrated to that province, the descendants of a large number of whom are connected with the Chute family. During and after the Revolution, thousands of Loyalists, or Refugees, chose to establish themselves in that part of North America, which still remained under the British flag.

Histories of some of these families have been partly written, and published in the United States, and so will not be so fully described here; while the greater part of them are now printed for the first time, and will be in more detail.

ALLIED FAMILIES.

ADAMS.

(From the Welsh of Ap Adam.)

1. i. Robert Adams, from Devon, England (said to be son of Robert (and Elizabeth Shirland), son of Richard, son of John), m. Eleanor ——; settled in Ipswich, Mass., 1635; removed to Salem, 1638; to Newbury, 1640; and settled on land still held by descendants of the name. He was a tailor, and a good citizen. His wife d. June 12, 1677; he m. (2d) Sarah Glover, widow of Henry Short, Feb. 6, 1678, and d. Oct. 12, 1682, aged 81. She d. Oct. 24, 1697.

CHILDREN.

    i JOHN, m. —— Woodman.
    ii JOANNA, b. 1634; m. Launcelot Granger, Jan. 4, 1654; the ancestor of Gideon Grander, a postmaster-general of the United States.
2 iii SERG. ABRAM, b. 1639.
    iv ELIZABETH, m. Edward Phelps of Andover.
    v MARY, m. Jeremiah Goodridge, Nov. 15, 1660.
    vi ISAAC, b. 1648; d. single.
    vii JACOB, b. April 23, 1649; d. young.
    viii HANNAH, b. June 25, 1650; m. William Warham, Feb. 10, 1680.
    ix JACOB, b. Sept. 13, 1651; m. Anna Ellen, April 7, 1677.
    x ARCHELAUS, b. about 1653; m. Sarah ——, March, 1698; m. 2d, Sarah Green (1699-1719), 1717.

2. ii. Sergt. Abram Adams (Robert), b. 1639; m. Mary Pettingall, Nov. 10, 1670, and d. Dec. 12, 1714. She d. Sept. 19, 1705.

CHILDREN.

i MARY, b. Jan. 16, 1672.
ii ROBERT, b. May 12, 1674; m. Rebecca Knight, Aug., 1695, had 8 children.
iii ABRAM, Jr., b. May 6, 1676; m. Ann Longfellow, 1703, had 11 children; a pair of twins were:
    1. Rev. Joseph, b. March 8, 1719; m. Mrs. Mary Greenleaf, 1746.
    2. Rev. Benjamin, b. March 8, 1719; m. Elizabeth Payson, 1748; m. 2d, Rebecca Nichols.
iv ISAAC, b. Feb. 26, 1679; m. Hannah Spofford, 1 08, had 7 children.
v SARAH, b. April 13, 1681; m. John Hutchinson, 1715.
vi JOHN, b. March 7, 1684; m. Elizabeth Noyes (John, Dea. Nicholas) 1707; m. 2d Sarah Pearson, 1713; had 7 children.
vii DR. MATTHEW, b. May 25, 1686; m. Sarah Knight, April 4, 1707; had 7 children.
viii ISRAEL, b. Dec. 25, 1688; m. Rebecca Atkinson, Oct. 15, 1714, and d. Dec. 12, 1714. She m. 2d, Ensign Joseph Hilton, of Exeter, N. H., Oct. 10, 1716.
ix DOROTHY, b. Oct. 25, 1691.
3 x RICHARD, b. Nov. 22, 1693.

3. iii. Richard Adams (Sergt. Abram, Robert), b. 1693; m. Susanna Pike, Dec. 12, 1717, and d. 1770. She d. Oct. 17, 1754.

CHILDREN.

i MARY, b. Oct. 8, 1718; m. Abram, son of Dr. Matthew Adams, March 14, 1738.
ii JOHN, b. Sept. 9, 1720; d. March 20, 1723.
iii HANNAH, b. Nov. 12, 1722; m. Capt. Daniel Chute (James, James, James, Lionel), April 20, 1742. See No. 8.
iv ENOCH, b. Sept. 24, 1724; m. Sarah Jackman[4] (Nicholas, James, James), July 28, 1747; had 2 children: Lieut. Nathaniel m. Mary Pearson and d. 1828, aged 80; Susannah d. young. Mr. Adams d. June 27, 1749.
v RICHARD, Jr., b. Nov. 2, 1726; m. Sarah Noyes, 1755; had 9 children, and d. Nov. 6, 1788.
vi SUSANNA, b. Aug. 5, 1729; d. June 19, 1749.
vii JOHN, b. July 30, 1732; m. Elizabeth Thorla, Dec. 22, 1761; and had 10 children.
viii DANIEL, b. Sept. 4, 1734; m. Edna Noyes, Oct. 26, 1758, and had Hannah, who m. Paul Lunt, 1790. Mr. Adams d. Dec. 1, 1759.
ix MOSES, b. Jan. 17, 1737; m. Ruth Palmer, Feb. 6, 1760.

x EDMUND, b. Oct. 24, 1740; m. Hannah Thurston (John, Daniel, Daniel), Nov. 22, 1764; had 9 children; lived in Londonderry, N. H., and d. Jan. 18, 1825. She d. Sept. 12, 1802. Jacob, the youngest son (1785-1823), founded the Adams Female Academy in Londonderry, N. H.

THE ADAMSES OF BRAINTREE, MASS.

1. i. Henry Adams, said to be a cousin to Robert, of Newbury, m. —— Ambrose, and came over from Devonshire, Eng., 1632, and settled in Braintree, about ten miles south of Boston. In 1639 he had a grant of land at Mt. Wollaston. He d. Oct. 6, 1646.

CHILDREN.

i HENRY, b. 1604; m. Elizabeth Paine, 1643, and was killed in King Philip's War, Feb. 21, 1675-6. She was shot by accident 8 days after. They had 6 children; Henry, had Thomas, whose son Thomas had Hannah (1755-1881), the great American authoress.

ii THOMAS, b. 1612; m. Mary ——; was a lieutenant and d. 1688; 7 children.

iii SAMUEL, b. 1617; m. Rebecca Graves, of Charlestown; d. 1664; m. 2d Esther Sparhawk, of Cambridge, 1668; he was a freeman 1643; was also captain; he lived in Charlestown and Concord, but went to Chelmsford 1654; d. 1689; 14 children.

iv JONATHAN, b. 1619; m. Elizabeth ——; 2d Mary ——; d. about 1691, Medfield.

v PETER, b. 1622; m. Rachel ——; settled in Medfield; d. about 1690; 13 children.

vi JOHN, b. 1624; m. Ann ——, and d. 1706; 8 children. Dr. Daniel Adams, author of Arithmetic, is 7th on this line.

2 vii JOSEPH, b. 1626.

viii EDWARD, b. 1630; m. Lydia ——; d. 1676; lived in Medfield; d. about 1715; 14 children.

ix URSULA.

2. ii. Joseph Adams (Henry), b. 1626; m. Abigail, daughter of Gregory Baxter, 1650, and d. Dec. 6, 1694. She d. 1692, aged 58; freeman 1653; selectman, etc.

CHILDREN.

i HANNAH, b. 1652; m. Samuel Savill.

3 ii JOSEPH, b. 1654.

iii JOHN, b. and d. 1656.

iv ABIGAIL, b. 1658; m. John Bass.

    4 v JOHN, b. 1661.
       vi BETHIA, b. 1661; m. John Webb, 1680.
      vii MARY, b. 1663; sup. d. young.
     viii SAMUEL, b. 1665; sup. d. young.
       ix MARY, b. 1667; m. Samuel Webb; Dea. Samuel Bass; d. 1706.
        x PETER, b. 1669; m. Mary Webb, 1695.
       xi JONATHAN, b. 1671.
      xii MEHITABLE, b. 1678; m. Thomas White, 1697.

3. iii. Joseph Adams (Joseph, Henry), b. 1654; m. Mary Chapin (1662–1687), 1682; 2d Hannah Bass (1667–1705); 3d Elizabeth ——; d. 1740, aged 71. He was selectman of Braintree; d. 1737.

CHILDREN.

        i MARY, b. 1683; m Ephraim Jones, 1714.
       ii ABIGAIL, b. 1684; m. Seth Chapin, of Mendon, and was grandmother of Rev. Dr. Chapin, Columbia Col., Washington.
      iii JOSEPH, b. 1688; H. C. 1710; pastor Newington, N. H., 1715, and was there sixty-six years; d. 1784. John Quincy Adams remembered him at his father's; had 3 sons. A descendant invented the Adams printing press.
    5 iv JOHN, b. 1691.
        v SAMUEL, b. 1693; m. Sarah Paine, 1720.
       vi JOSIAH, b. 1695; m. Bethiah Thompson, 1718; dismissed to the church in Mendon, 1735.
      vii HANNAH, b. 1697; m. Benjamin Owen, 1725.
     viii RUTH, b. 1700; m. Rev. Nathan Webb, 1731.
       ix BETHIA, b. 1702; m. Eben Hunt, as 2d w., Weymouth, 1737.
        x EBENEZER, b. 1704; m. Ann Boylston, of Brookline.
       xi CALEB, b. 1710; d. young.

4. iii. Capt. John Adams (Joseph, Henry), b. 1661; m. Hannah Webb, 1694; 2d Hannah Checkley; he followed the seas; lived in Boston after 1687; merchant there; d. 1711.

CHILDREN.

        i HANNAH, b. 1685; m. Samuel Holbrook, 1710.
       ii JOHN, b. 1687.
      iii SAMUEL, b. 1689; m. 1713, Mary Fifield, of Boston (1694– ——); was a prominent man in Boston and d. 1748; 12 children—only three grew up—son Samuel, b. 1722; m. Elizabeth, daughter of Rev. Samuel Checkley (1725– ——), 1749; 2d, Elizabeth Wells (1736– ——), 1764;

he graduated H. C. 1740; proscribed with John Hancock by Governor Gage; signer of the Declaration of Independence; Lieutenant-Governor of Massachusetts, 1789; Governor 1794-7; d. 1803. Statue in Scolly square, Boston. He assisted Wm. Billings in making singing books. Great statesman.

  iv JOSEPH, b. 1695.
  v MARY, b. 1695; m. Samuel Jones, Boston.
  vi THOMAS, b. 1701.
  vii ABIJAH, b. 1702; m. 1725, Deborah Cutler; d. 1768; clerk of Faneuil Hall Market many years.

5. iv. Dea. John Adams (Joseph, Joseph, Henry), b. 1691; m. 1734, Susannah Boylston (Peter, Dr. Thomas, Thomas, England to America, 1635; died 1653, aged 38), of Brookline; was constable in 1728, selectman 1734, deacon 1747; d. 1761; wife d. 1797, aged 88.

CHILDREN.

  i HON. JOHN, b. 1735; m. Abigail, daughter of Rev. Wm. Smith, and had 5 children, of whom John Quincy (1767-1848) was the 6th President of the United States. He m. Louisa Catharine Johnson (1775-1852), of Maryland, and had 3 sons. Hon. John was educated a lawyer, and became 2d President of the United States (1797-1801). His wife d. 1818, aged 74. He d. July 4, 1826.
  ii PETER B., b. 1738; m. Mary Crosby, 1768.
  iii ELIHU, b. 1741; m. Thankful White, 1765.

BANKS.

Henry F. Waters, of Salem, in his "Gleanings from English Records," 1880, mentions the will of John Bancks of London probably 1630, in which the testator remembers William, Richard, Thomas, George, and Mary, children of his uncle, William Bancks, deceased; also cousin Ralph Fogg.

1. Richard Bankes, who came to America, and settled at Scituate, Mass., about, or before, 1640, may have been connected with the family mentioned above. In 1643 he was a settler in York County, Me., where he was a Provincial Councilor for 1651-2, under Gov. Edward Godfrey; Selectman off and on twenty years; Trial Justice or Commissioner several years; Court Appraiser the best part of thirty years, to 1691; besides other appointments, as

Tax Commissioner, 1652; Overseer of County Prison, 1673, etc. He was made a freeman 1652, and in 1681 appears in a list of inhabitants swearing allegiance to the King. He d., or was carried off by Indians, early in 1692, when 137 of the people of York were either killed or carried captive to Canada. He m. Elizabeth, daughter of John and Elizabeth Alcock, of York, who survived him several years.

CHILDREN.

2 i JOHN.
   ii SAMUEL, b. ere 1659; d. 1692.
   iii JOB, d. 1692.
   iv JOSEPH, b. 1667; m. Elizabeth, daughter of John and Eliza (Cummings) Harmon, of York, 1694; had 8 children, and d. about 1744.

2. ii. John Bankes (Richard), b. about 1657; Selectman, 1693; Grand Juror, 1692-3, and 1701; m. twice; the second wife was Elizabeth, daughter of Peter and Sarah (Saunders) Turbat, of Wells, and d. 1726; she d. 1738.

CHILDREN.

   i ELIZABETH, m. Nehemiah Clausen, of Lebanon, Vt., before 1738.
   ii JOHN, d. probably before 1719.

By second wife:

3 iii MOSES.
   iv HANNAH, m. Benjamin Jacobs, of Salem and Wells, June 13, 1750.
   v AARON, b. about 1695, in York; was a mariner in the service of the Province, 1717, under Sir William Pepperill, and d. at York, 1763. He m. Mary Hains, 1726, and had Aaron, b. 1738; probably more. He m. Mary Perkins, 1764; was in the wars of 1759-63; d. 1823.
   vi MARY.

3. iii. Moses Bankes (John, Richard), b. about 1690; lived upon the family homestead in York through life. He had various offices on land and sea, and was called Lieutenant on the town book. He was in Col. Thomas Westbrook's company, 1722-5, to fight Indians. He m., 1712, Ruth, daughter of Elias and Magdalen (Hilton) Weare, and d. 1750. She d. 1763, aged 66-7.

CHILDREN.

4 i JOSHUA, b. Sept. 13, 1713.
   ii ELIAS, b. Aug. 9, 1715; d. 1725.

ALLIED FAMILIES.

- iii MARY, b. Sept. 12, 1717; m. Francis Betts, Aug. 18, 1735, 1751; lived in York; had two daughters.
- iv JOHN, b. March 12, 1722; m. Hannah Preble.
- v ELIAS, b. Sept. 9, 1725; m. Lydia Dresser, 1748, and lived in Scarboro'. He was Captain of the sloop "Willing Mind," 1747.
- vi JEREMIAH, b. Oct. 7, 1727; d. May 21, 1752, of small-pox.
- vii ZEBEDIAH, b. May 7, 1730; m. Abigail Muchmore, 1753; lived in York; had 13 sons.
- viii MOSES, b. July 24, 1732; m. Phebe, daughter of Jacob and Abigail (Bracy) Curtis, son of Ephraim and Elizabeth (Kilburne) Curtis, of Rowley, 1754, and moved to Arundel (Kennebunkport) about 1760; removed to Scarboro', where he taught school, and was engineer and surveyor. He was in the Revolutionary war, 1775-6, and was 1st Lieutenant in Col. Edmund Phinney's regiment; saw service at Fort George and Ticonderoga, N. Y. After the war he resided at Scarboro'; later in North Yarmouth, and d. in Saco, Me., Oct. 9, 1823, aged 91. His wife died April, 1814; had 9 children. One, Elias, b. 1774, m. Lucretia Prince; had a son, Edward Prince, b. 1811, whose son, Charles Edward, M. D., late of Vineyard Haven, Mass., but now of Portland, Me., has long been hunting Banks and Weare families.
- ix ELIZABETH, b Jan. 11, 1734-5; m. Benjamin Milliken, Aug. 26, 1754.
- x RUTH, b. Jan. 18, 1736-7; m. Elias Weare (Joseph, Elias, Peter), April, 1760. See Weare.
- ix RICHARD, b. about 1738-9; d. Dec. 4, 1762, of a fever contracted in the service during the French and Indian wars.

4. iv. Joshua Bankes (Moses, John, Richard), b. Sept. 13, 1713; m. Mary Muchmore, Sept. 18, 1737, and had a large family, five of whom immigrated to Nova Scotia time of the Revolution.

CHILDREN.

- 5 i JOSHUA, b. Nov. 4, 1750.
- ii JOSEPH, b. May 11, 1752.
- iii ELIZABETH, b. July 24, 1753.
- iv JEREMIAH, b. July 20, 1755.
- 6 v MOSES, b. Oct. 22, 1758.

5. v. Joshua Bankes, Jr., bapt. Nov. 4, 1750; went to Nova Scotia, and probably m. there Dorothy Craft, 1777, and settled on on the "Post Road," a mile below Lawrencetown, Annapolis County, an honest, upright farmer; d. 1846, aged 96. His wife d. 1833, aged 80. His eyesight was good to the last.

ALLIED FAMILIES.

CHILDREN.

7	i	GEORGE, b. March 12, 1778.
8	ii	JOHN.
9	iii	HENRY.
10	iv	JAMES.
11	v	CHRISTOPHER.
12	vi	JACOB.
13	vii	FREDERICK.
	viii	HANNAH, m. Elija Beals (Cooper, Abel), and had Mary Ann, Dolly, and Edward.
	xi	BETSY, m. Bayard Payson (Jonathan, Jonathan, Jonathan, Ephraim, Dea. Edward, over from England to Roxbury, 1636, and d. about 1690).
14	x	WILLIAM.
	xi	MARY, d. young.
	xii	FRANK, d. young.

6. v. Moses Banks (Joshua, Moses, John, Richard), bapt. Oct. 22, 1758; m. —— Saunders, settled in Wilmot, N. S., and is reported to have d. on his birthday, 1857, aged 99.

CHILDREN.

15	i	MOSES, JR.
16	ii	RICHARD.
17	iii	TIMOTHY.
	iv	JANE, b. 1791; m. Dea. Daniel Whitman[6] (Daniel, John, John, Rev, Zachariah, Dea. John, 1637), 1821, and d. 1887. He m. 1st, Ann Dykeman (1792–1817); had 11 children, and d. 1863, aged 72.
	v	JUDITH, d. Jan., 1891, aged 96 or 7.
18	vi	ELIPHALET.
	vii	ANN, m. James Astens, a soldier.

7. vi. George Banks (Joshua, Joshua, Moses, John, Richard), b. near Lawrencetown, Annapolis County, March 12, 1778; m. Betsy, daughter of Francis and Elizabeth (Mason) Nelson, Jan. 10, 1805; lived in Upper Clarence; farmer and cooper; d. March 29, 1860. She d. April 8, 1875, aged 89.

CHILDREN.

i	ELIZA, b. March 9, 1807; d. March 31, 1811.
ii	HANNAH, b. Aug. 25, 1809; m. Burton Chute. (No. 93.)
iii	SALLY, b. Oct. 10, 1811; m. Dea. Silas, son of Frank Jackson, 1831; 4 children.
iv	SAMUEL NELSON, b. April 2, 1814; m. Dolly, da. of Elijah Beals; 4 das.

- v GEORGE CRAFT, b. June 22, 1816; m. Sophia (Marshall) Chute. (No. 18.)
- vi FREDERICK, b. Feb. 9, 1819; m. Naomi Marshall; Seraph Chute. (No. 33.)
- vii ELIZA ANN, b. March 27, 1821; m. William, son of Frank Jackson, May 7, 1848; he d. Sept., 1883, aged 73. She lives in Danvers, Mass.
- viii ISAAC, b. April 25, 1823; d. Oct. 12, 1826.
- ix ELEANOR, b. March 4, 1826; m. Sidney Marshall; Samuel Moore. (See Marshall.)
- x ISAAC, b. March 13, 1828; m. Eliza, daughter of Charles Foster; 5 children.
- xi MARGARET ANN, b. Feb. 4, 1831; m. Howard Mayhew (John P., James); one son; live in Danvers, Mass.

8. vi. John Banks (Joshua, Joshua, Moses, John, Richard), b. 1780; m. Polly, daughter of Joel Farnsworth, and lived on the mountain, above Hampton, and d. 1838. She m. 2d, Dea. Hall, a soldier of Wellington's army, and d. 1888, aged 95. He died 1877, aged 90. He m. 1st, —— Corbitt, and had 2 sons, and a daughter, Elizabeth; m. Parker Viditoe.

CHILDREN.

- i DEACON WILLIAM, b. about 1816; m. Rachel, daughter of William Elliott, and had 7 children.
- ii HANDLEY, b. 1818 (?); m. Armanella Marshall (William, Anthony); 6 children.
- iii MARGARET, b. Sept., 1820; m. Rev. Henry Archelaus.
- iv MARIA, b. Sept., 1822; m. William H. Roach; Arche Burns, Jr.; 5 or 6 children.
- v HENRY, b. 1825; m. Becca, daughter of John Viditoe; 3 sons; Becca Hoffman.
- vi JAMES, b. 1828; m. Elizabeth, daughter of Timothy Banks; 2 daughters.
  Balcomb; 3 children.
- vii ELIZABETH, b. 1831; m. Samuel Judson, son of Reuben
- viii MARY ELIZA, b. 1833; m. Weston, son of Uriah Johnson; 4 children.

9. vi. Henry Banks (Joshua, Joshua, Moses, John, Richard), b. 1782; d. 1880; m. Thankful, daughter of Joel Farnsworth; lived in Upper Clarence, under the North Mountain; she d. about 1870.

CHILDREN.

- i JOEL, J. P., m. Deborah, daughter of Joshua Slocomb, 1831; 4 children.

ALLIED FAMILIES.

    ii MARY, m. Charles Foster, son of Isaac, Jr.; 9 children.
   iii JOSHUA, m. Catharine, daughter of Caleb Slocomb; 4 children; daughter Catharine (?) m. Capt. Charles B. Weaver, who was drowned off the "C. B. Weaver," in Boston harbor. Mr. Banks d. about 1838. She m. 2d, Captain Harvey.
   iv HENRY, JR, m. Catharine, daughter of Jacob Durland; 6 children
    v CALEB, b. 1813; d. Feb. 1, 1831.
   vi LOUISE, b. 1819; m. Wesley Gilliatt* (Michael, Win); 3 children.
  vii FANNY, m. Gideon, son of Samuel Beardsley.
 viii BECCA, m. Parker, son of Joseph Neily; 5 children.
   ix SUSIE, b. 1829; m. George, J. P., son of Joseph Neily; their son, George E., b. 1856, was killed by a railroad train at Pine Grove, Sept., 1874.
    x CALEB, b. 1833; m. Cassie Rafuse, and had 4 children.

10. vi. James Banks (Joshua, Joshua, Moses, John, Richard), b. 1784; m. Sally Rice (see Rice); lived near Marshall's Cove, now Port Lorne, and d. June, 1864. She d. Aug., 1865, aged 75.

CHILDREN.

    i SILAS, d. a young man.
   ii JOSEPH, m. Leah, daughter of Daniel Durland; 2 children; m. 2d, Hettie, daughter of William Phinney.
  iii JAMES, b. 1819; m. Margaret Moody; 11 children; daughter Ellen m. James William Chute.
   iv ELIZA, b. 1821; m. Thomas, son of John Elliott, and had 8 children.
    v JACOB, b. 1823; m. Ruth Ann, daughter of Arche Burns, Jr. (b. 1825), and d. Feb. 6, 1892. Arche Burns, Sr., m. Hannah Brooks.
   vi SIDNEY, b. 1825; m. Sarah, daughter of Deacon Wilbur, son of Abednigo Parker; 13 children.

11. vi. Capt. Christopher Banks (Joshua, Joshua, Moses, John, Richard), b. 1785; m. Phebe, daughter of Daniel Durland, and lived in Wilmot, above Port Lorne. She d. 1836, aged 41; he m. 2d, Jerusha, daughter of Isaac Longley (Israel, William, John, William, William, William), and d. Oct., 1883; she d. Jan., 1889, aged 77.

CHILDREN.

    i ELIZA, b. 1812; m. Reece Worthylake; daughter Sabina, m. John Balsor. Mr. Worthylake m. 2d, Sophia Hoyt.
   ii CHARLES, b. 1814; m. Sarah A., daughter of Dea. Alex. McKenzie; 4 chilnren.

- iii CORNELIA, b. 1816; m. John, son of Alex. McKenzie; 7 children.
- iv WILLIAM, b. May 19, 1818; m. Hannah (b. 1823), daughter of Joseph Rankin, Jan. 12, 1840, and had 10 children; son Robert, b. 1842, m. Nancy, daughter of Arod McNayr, and had 9 children; moved to Beverly, April, 1887. His parents are there, too.
- v ANGELINE, b. 1820; m. Israel Brooks and d. shortly after; he m. 2d, Mary E., daughter of Riley Corbit; have a daughter, Jessie.
- vi GEORGE, b. 1822; m. Rebecca, daughter of Eli Messenger; 5 children.
- vii MARIA, b. 1824; m. Wm. Crocker, at Middleton, N. S.; 2 children.
- viii SALLY, b. 1826; m. Solomon, son of James Charlton; 2 children.
- ix JOHN WARD, b. 1829; m. Rachel, daughter of Alex. McKenzie, 1849; 2 children. She d. 1854, aged 25; m. 2d Emma Frances, daughter of Geo. Warren, and live at Danversport. He was a soldier in the United States Navy.
- x RUSSELL, b. 1831; m. Lovisa Marshall (George, Otis, Isaac); 6 children.
- xi CLARK, b. 1836; d. about 1859.

12. vi. Jacob Banks (Joshua, Joshua, Moses, John, Richard), b. 1787; m. Betsy Witt (1798—1868); lived south of Lawrensetown, south of Annapolis River; d. Aug., 1870.

CHILDREN.

- i JOHN, b. 1820; m. Mary, daughter of Joseph Neily.
- ii LOUISE, m. John C. Wilson, and d. ——; he m. 2d, Ella, daughter of Harvey Saunders, and widow of John Jefferson.
- iii GEORGE, m. Sarah A., daughter of Daniel Durland, Jr.
- iv AMBROSE L., m. Sarah E., daughter of John Whitman; Matilda, a sister, and Armanella, daughter of James Sprowle.
- v BETHIA, m. James A., son of James Sprowle.
- vi MARIA, m. Isaac Whitman, son of John; Alden, son of Timothy Banks.

13. vi. Frederick Banks (Joshua, Joshua, Moses, John, Richard), b. about 1790; m. Hannah (1797—Sept., 1881), daughter of John Graves; lived at Port Lorne, and d. about 1885.

xvi ALLIED FAMILIES.

CHILDREN.

 i PHILO, b. 1820.
 ii GILBERT, b. 1822.
 iii ALEXANDER, b. 1824; d. 1891.
 iv CAPT. ISRAEL, b. 1826; d. Jan., 1857.
 v JOHN, b. 1828; m. Rachel Wilson (Walter, Christopher).
 vi ELIZABETH, b. 1830; m. Aaron, son of Thomas Charlton.
 vii PHINEAS, b. 1832; m. Harriet, daughter of Walter Wilson, 1879.
 viii JANE, m. Wm. Dalton, Jr.
 ix MARGARET ANN, m. Curtis, son of Henry Dalton. (William, Sr., and Henry brothers.)

14. vi. William Banks, youngest of 8 brothers, b. about 1800; m. Margaret Warwick, and lived on the old homestead of his father; d. about 1853. She d. Sept., 1891, over 80.

CHILDREN.

 i MAY ELIZA, b. 1832; m. Desbrisay, son of Eben Balcomb. His mother was a sister of Avard Longley, Esq.
 ii JESSIE, b. 1835; m. Thomas, son of Samuel Chesley.

15. vi. Moses Banks (Moses, Joshua, Moses, John, Richard), b. about 1774-5; m. Olive (b. March 12, 1776), daughter of Dea. Joseph and Eleanor (Blood) Morton, and lived in Aylesford, Kings County, N. S.

CHILDREN.

 i ABRAM, d. at 20.
 ii JOSEPH.
 iii EDMUND, m. Eunice Morton, a cousin; Portland, Me.
 iv JOHN, m. Elizabeth, daughter of Elijah Beals.
 v WILLIAM, m. Harriet, daughter of James Patterson.
 vi MARIAH, m. George Dunkean, a carpenter.
 vii EMILY, m. James Dunkean.
 viii GEORGE, m. Sarah Taylor; Sylvia Marshall (Isaac, William, David, Isaac).

16. vi. Richard Banks (Moses, Joshua, Moses, John, Richard), m. Nancy Patterson, and lived in Aylesford.

CHILDREN.

 i WILLIAM, m. Ruth Collins.
 ii RUTH, m. Charles Palmer.
 iii JANE, m. Peter Martin, from England.
 iv JOHN, m. Mary Martin.

 v ALEXANDER, b. 1812; m. Abbie, daughter of Joseph Collins; 2d, Helen A. Morse (1830—m. 1852); 8 children.
 vi LOUISA, m. Charles Ritchie.
 vii SON, m. Barteaux.

17. vi. Timothy Banks (Moses, Joshua, Moses, John, Richard), m. Margaret, daughter of Joseph Barss, and lived in Aylesford, N. S.

CHILDREN.

 i ELIZA, m. John, son of Paul Crocker.
 ii CAROLINE, m. Parker Baker.
 iii JOHN, m. Ann, daughter of Joseph Spinney.
 iv ALDEN, m. Hannah Cogswell; Seraphina Patterson; Maria (Banks) Whitman.
 v MARY, m. Beniah, son of Joseph Spinney.
 vi DAVID, m. Maria Patterson.
 vii MARGARET, b. 1819; m. John, son of George Burns.
 viii AMORET, m. Wm. Henry Harris, son of Joseph (Captain Henry), at Bear River, N. S.
 ix JOSEPH, m. Dolly, daughter of Bayard Payson.
 x BETSY, m. James, son of John Banks.
 xi DIMOCK, m. Betsy, daughter of Edward Goucher.

18. vi. Eliphalet Banks (Moses, Joshua, Moses, John, Richard), m. Hannah, daughter of Timothy Saunders, and lived in Aylesford.

CHILDREN.

 i SAUNDERS, m. off South.
 ii ABRAM, m. Sarah, daughter of Rev. Israel Rice.
 iii HENRY.
 iv DAVID, m. Maria Payson.
 v OBADIAH, m. Margaret Moody.
 vi EZEKIEL.
 vii THOMAS HANDLEY.
 viii JUDITH, m. James Kinney.
 ix MARTHA, m. —— Robar.

BARNES.

1. Nathaniel Barnes, born about 1720, appears in Granville, N. S., soon after the French were driven out, in 1755.

CHILDREN.

2 i HANNAH, b. 1745; m. Job Young.
3 ii ELIZABETH, b. 1746; m. Joseph Milbury, from Ireland.
 iii SARAH, b. 1748; m. Samuel Chute. (No. 10.)

xviii ALLIED FAMILIES.

4 iv MARY, b. 1750; m. James Ray, from Ireland.
  v NATHANIEL, b. 1752; m., if I mistake not, Jerusha Blackmore (one of 9 children of John and Sarah (Holmes) Blackmore, son of John and Anna (Branch), son of William and Elizabeth (Banks), Blackmore, over from England to Scituate, Mass., 1665, m .1666), over to Nova Scotia before the Revolution, and settled in Cornwallis, Kings Co.
5 vi SPENCER, b. 1755; m. Jane, daughter of Valentine Troop.

2. ii. Hannah Barnes, m. Job Young, and had, in Granville, N. S.:

CHILDREN.

 i WILLIAM, b. 1764; m. Miriam Parker, 1790.
 ii SAMUEL, b. 1765; m. Lydia, daughter of Samuel Morse.
 iii HANNAH, b. 1768; m. James Parker, 1795; no children.
 iv JOSEPH, b. 1769.
 v TIMOTHY, b. 1771; m. Mary ——.
 vi JOB, b. May 26, 1773; m. —— Leonard.
 vii JOHN, b. 1775.
 viii NATHANIEL, b. 1777.
 ix ROBERT, b. 1779; m. Elizabeth McCormack.
 x SARAH, b. 1780; d. young.
 xi ABRAM, b. 1784; m. Hannah Wade.

3. ii. Elizabeth Barnes, m. Joseph Milbury, 1764, and had:

CHILDREN.

6 i THOMAS, b. 1765; m.
7 ii BENJAMIN, b. 1767; m.
8 iii JAMES, b. 1770; m.
 iv MARY, b. 1772; m. Demotte Durland.
 v ELIZABETH, b. 1774.
 vi JOSEPH, b. 1776; drowned.
9 vii HENRY, b. 1778.
 viii SAMUEL, b. 1780.
 ix RICHARD, b. 1782.
 x SARAH, b. 1785.

4. ii. Mary Barnes[2], (from Ireland) m. Joseph Ray, and had in Nova Scotia:

CHILDREN.

 i JANE, m. Joseph Foster. (See Foster.)
 ii JOHN, m. Deborah, daughter of Joel Farnsworth.
 iii MOSES, returned to Ireland.
 iv JAMES, m. Rachel, daughter of John Morris, of Bunker Hill fame.

5. ii. Spencer Barnes, b. 1755; m. Jane Troop (b. 1760), and had:

CHILDREN.

- i KATY, b. May 17, 1779.
- ii JACOB T., b. 1782.
- iii HENRY, b. 1784.
- iv POLLY, b. 1788.
- v JOSEPH T., b. 1790.
- vi NANCY, b. 1800.

6. iii. Thomas Milbury (Joseph, and Elizabeth (Barnes, daughter of Nathaniel.)

CHILDREN.

- i THOMAS, drowned in Annapolis Basin; over 80.
- ii PHEBE, m. Nathaniel Harris (Benj., Samuel, Beverly, Mass., to Yarmouth, N. S., 1763).
- iii JOSEPH, m. Rebecca Weare (Joseph, Elias, Joseph, Elias, Peter).
- iv DAVID, drowned in childhood.

7. iii. Benjamin Milbury (Joseph and Elizabath Barnes), b. 1767; m. Sarah Marshall, b. about 1770, daughter of Solomon, and lived in Wilmot, N. S., near Port George. He d. about 1845; she d. about 1842.

CHILDREN.

- i MERCY, b. Jan., 1798; m. —— Bryan; 2d, Nickerson; 3 children.
- ii WILLARD, b. 1800; m. Eunice, daughter of John Weaver, St. John, N. B.
- iii SAMUEL, b. 1804; m. Mary, daughter of Silas Bent, and d. 1883, at Lawrencetown; 5 children.
- iv SOLOMON, b. 1806; m. Phebe Sprowle, daughter of W. Roach.
- v BENJAMIN, b. 1808; m. Clarissa Viditoe (John, Jesse).
- vi SIMEON,
- vii THOMAS, } b. 1810; d. soon.
- viii J. WESLEY, b. 1812; m. Hannah, daughter of Jonas Ward, and d. June, 1880. Children: (1) C. Willard, 1835; m. Matilda Sears (Joseph, David, Joseph), of Sackville, N. B., Aug. 16, 1856, and lived at Black Rock, N. S., till 1880, when they moved to Reading, Mass; 11 children. (2) J. Wesley, 1837, m. Sarah, daughter of John Rier; 5 children; she d. 1875, aged 36; m. 2d, Rachel Finley; she d. 1888, aged 51; m. 3d, Sarah (Frazer) Porter. (3) James Simeon, 1839, m. Melissa Gower, of Westport, N. S.; 4 children; live in Salem, Mass. (4) Solomon, 1841, d. 1863. (5) Sarah, Nov. 8., 1843; m. James Robert,

son of John Rier; 5 children; Middleton, Mass. (6) Henry, 1846; off to sea, not heard from since 1880. (7) Rachel, 1848; m. Wm. Bryden; 3 children; Reading. (8) David, 1850; m. Alice Reynard; 4 children; he was a sea captain.

- ix LUCINDA, b. 1814; m. Asaph, son of Reis Stronach, Esq.
- x SARAH ANN, b. 1817; m. Edwin Downey.
- xi G. WHITEFIELD, b. 1820; m. Eunice Sprowle, of Westport, N. S.

8. iii. James and Sarah (Fletcher) **Milbury**, had:

CHILDREN.

- i JOSEPH, b. Dec. 14, 1796; m. Priscilla Chute. (See No. 22.)
- ii JAMES, b. July 8, 1798; m. Mary, daughter Henry Milbury; 4 children.
- iii ELIZABETH, b. July 27, 1800; d. young.
- iv HENRY, b. Oct. 18, 1801; m. Mary Young; 7 children; he m. 2d, Phebe Ann, daughter of John and Phebe Palmer.
- v SUSANNA, b. Feb. 22, 1803; m. John Brown; 2 children.
- vi ANNA, b. Jan. 21, 1805; m. Wm. Armstrong; 4 children.
- vii MARY, b. June 21, 1807; m. Wm. Nicholls.
- viii DAVID F., b. Sept. 8, 1810; m. Lucy Marshall (Elisha, Solomon), and had Amanda, David F., Elmira, and John. Mr. D. F. M. drowned April, 1837, and Lucy M. m. 2d, Hugh Williams.
- ix LUCY, b. Nov. 17, 1812; m. Jas. Lyman Chute. (See No. 73.)
- x JOHN, b. Sept. 3, 1814; m. Seraphina Chute. (No. 22.)
- xi ELIZABETH, b. Nov. 2, 1817; m. Harrington Messenger.
- xii FLETCHER, b. July 30, 1819; m. Sarah J. Sprowle; 2 daughters.

9. iii. Henry Milbury, brother to the three preceding, b. 1778; m. Sarah, daughter of John Wade, about 1800. She d. ——; he m. 2d, Sarah Dodge, 1804, and lived at or near Phinney's Cove, Annapolis Co., N. S.

CHILDREN.

- i JOHN, m. Mary Elizabeth, daughter of Israel Longley, Jr., and had a son, John Fletcher, who m. Louise Jane Chute. (See No. 40, Bear R.)
- ii STEPHEN, m. Mary, daughter of Eben Bent, of Sam.
- iii PHEBE, m. Benj. Farnsworth, 2d wife.
- iv SETH, m. Elizabeth ——.
- v MARY, m. James Milbury, Jr.
- vi DAVID, m. Mary Bent, of John, of Sam.

ALLIED FAMILIES.

vii Jas. Priestly, m. Henrietta Clark (William, Richard), and had 3 sons, William, Wesley, and Richard. Mrs. M. d. 1887; he m. 2d, Lucretia (Farnsworth) Chute, 1888.
viii Alfred.
ix Edward, Esq., m. Margaret Holland.

CHENEY.

1. John and Martha Cheney came over from England 1635; settled in Roxbury, and members of the church there, but removed to Newbury, 1636; was made a freeman 1637; d. July 28, 1666, aged about 60. His wife d. July 20, 1663. He is reported as shoemaker. The records at Newbury says, "Aged Sister Cheney was buryed June 3, 1686," and is supposed to be the wife of John Cheney; but if it be so, she must have been 2d wife.

CHILDREN.

    i Mary, b. 1628 (?); m. Nich. Busby, 1652.
    ii Martha, b. 1629 (?); m. Anthony Sadler, 1649.
2 iii John, b. 1631 (?); m.
    iv Daniel, b. 1633 (?); m.
    v Sarah, b. 1635; m. Joseph Plummer, Dec. 23, 1652.
    vi Lydia, b. 1637 (?); m. John Kendrick, Nov. 12, 1657.
4 vii Peter, b. 1639; m.
  viii Hannah, b. Nov. 16, 1642; m. Richard Smith. (See Smith.)
    ix Nathaniel, b. 1645; d. April 24, 1684.
    x Elizabeth, b. 1648; m. Stephen Cross.

2. ii. John Cheney, Jr., m. Mary, daughter of Francis Plummer, May 20, 1660; lived in Newbury, but was drowned near Roxbury, in the Charles R., Dec. 12, 1671. She m. 2d, David Benit, April 29, 1672.

CHILDREN.

  i Mary, b. 1661; m. Isaac Kilborne, a mute, July 24, 1684.
  ii Martha, b. 1663; m. John Leighton, June 4, 1691.
 iii John, b. 1669; d. of smallpox on an expedition to Canada, and thrown overboard at Nantasket, 1691, and his two sisters were appointed to administer upon his estate.

3. ii. Daniel Cheney (John), m. Sarah Bailey, b. 1644, daughter of John, Oct. 8, 1665, and d. Sept. 10, 1694, aged 61.

CHILDREN.

    i SARAH, b. Sept. 11, 1666; m. John Richards, June 16, 1696.
    ii JUDITH, b. Sept. 9, 1668.
5 iii DANIEL, b. Dec. 31, 1670.
    iv HANNAH, b. Sept. 3, 1673; m. Thomas Wiswall (Noah, Thomas), of Cambridge, Dec. 17, 1696. He d. 1709, aged 43; she m. 2d, Dea. David Newman, 1719; 7 children.
6 v JOHN, b. July 10, 1676.
    vi ELINOR, b. March 29, 1679; m. Richard Shatswell, of Ipswich, 1696; she m. 2d, Thomas Safford[3] (John, Thomas[2], of Ipswich 1640), b. 1672, and had Stephen[4], who was the father of Nathan[5], who m. Elizabeth Foster, of Salem, daughter of Capt. Nathaniel, descendant of Reginald. Their son, Nathan Foster[6] (1786-1847), had a son, Nathan Foster[7], Jr., (1815-1891).
    vii JOSEPH, b. 1682; m. Sarah Wiswall (Noah, Thomas, to Mass. 1635), 1702, and died 1749.
    viii JAMES, b. April 6, 1685; m. Lydia Myrick, 1732, and d. 1746; 5 children.

4. ii. Peter Cheney (John), b. in Newbury, Mass., 1639; m. Hannah, daughter of Dea. Nicholas Noyes, May 14, 1663, and d. Jan., 1694, aged 55. She m. 2d, John Atkinson, Sr., June, 1700.

CHILDREN.

    i PETER, b. Nov. 6, 1663.
    ii JOHN, b. May 10, 1666.
    iii NICHOLAS, b. May 23, 1667.
    iv HULDAH, b. 1669 (?); m. Timothy Worster, 1691; Simon Daykin, 1718.
    v MARY, b. Sept. 2, 1671; m. Francis Worster, 1691; Joseph Eaton, 1726.
    vi MARTHA, b. 1673 (?); m. Wm. Worster, 1691; John Pemberton, 1710. (See Worcester.)
    vii NATHANIEL, b. Oct. 2, 1675; d. July 30, 1677.
    viii JEMIMA, b. Nov. 29, 1677; m. —— French; Richard Pettingall, Oct. 10, 1703.
9 ix ELDAD, b. Oct. 24, 1681.
    x HANNAH, b. Sept. 13, 1683; m. Lionel Chute. (No. 4.)
    xi ICHABOD, b. Sept. 22, 1685; m. Ann Chute. (See No. 3.)
    xii LIDIA, b. Nov. 5, 1687; m. Jeremiah Poor (Henry, John), 1709; 2d, Samuel Plummer, or —— Lull, ere 1718, and lived to about 1780.

ALLIED FAMILIES.   xxiii

5. iii. Daniel Cheney, Jr. (Daniel, John), b. Dec. 31, 1670; m. Hannah Dustin, daughter of Thomas and Hannah* (Emerson) Dustin, of Haverhill, son of Thomas, of Dover, N. H., 1698.

CHILDREN.

   i DANIEL, b. July 16, 1699; m. Sarah ——, and had Marcy, 1725, and perhaps more.
  ii JOHN, b. March 10, 1702; m. Johana Pike, 1732; had Daniel, Hannah, Daniel, and Sarah; d. April 27, 1738; she m. 2d, Nathan Chase, Dec 30, 1740.
 iii THOMAS, b. Feb. 25, 1704; m. Harriet Stephens, 1726, and had Daniel, Duston, Thomas, Mary, and Nathaniel
 iv HANNAH, b. Sept. 25, 1706; m. John Coffin, April 28, 1726, and had Dustin, 1727.
  v SARAH, b. Jan. 25, 1708; m. Wm. Calef, Nov. 5, 1728.
 vi NATHANIEL, b. Nov. 25, 1711; m. Kezia Annis, Oct. 25, 1733.
vii MARY, b. Aug. 9, 1714; m. Joseph Homan, Dec. 20, 1734.
viii ABIGAIL, b. Nov. 1, 1719.

6. iii. John Cheney (Daniel, John), b. July 10, 1676; m. Elizabeth ——; d. 1715; m. 2d, Elizabeth Currig, Oct., 1717; m. 3d, Lydia Burrage, 1729.

* Hannah, daughter of Michael and Hannah (Webster) Emerson, was b. Dec. 23, 1657, in Haverhill, Mass; m. Dec. 3, 1677, Thomas Dustin (or Duston), and had 13 children before 1699. On March 15, 1697, nineteen or twenty Indians made a raid upon the town, burned half a dozen houses, murdered and captured about thirty-nine persons, including Mrs. Hannah Dustin, her nurse, Mary Corliss, widow of Wm. Neff, and an English boy, Sam Lennardson. Her baby, Martha, only 6 days old, had its brains dashed out against a tree, in its mother's sight! Mr. Dustin, seeing the savages coming, ran with his gun, got between them and the children—eight of his own and several others along with them—and got them to a place of safety. The captured ones were marched seventy-five or eighty miles north, through the woods, to an island in the Merrimack river, at Pennacook, above Concord, N. H. The Indian family were twelve—two stout men, three women, and seven children—and while there in camp, fearing and dreading worse usage, Mrs. Dustin planned their escape. So on the night of the 29th, while they were asleep, Mrs. Dustin and her nurse, with tomahawks, brained ten of them; one, seeing the fate of the others, up and run, and one was spared. She then took the ten scalps and her captor's gun, as trophies, and they paddled down the Merrimack in a canoe, arriving at home the 31st, finding their house burned, but the husband and children all safe. She was awarded £50 by the General Assembly at Boston, and some presents from Colonel Nicholson, governor of Maryland. Mr. Dustin was living in 1729, and it is said that she survived him several years. The children were: Hannah, 1678; Elizabeth, 1680; Mary, 1681; Thomas, 1683; Nathaniel, 1685; John, 1686; Sarah, 1688; Abigail, 1690; Jonathan, 1692; Timothy, 1694; Mehitable, 1694; Martha, 1697; Lydia, 1698.

A monument has been erected in Haverhill to the memory of Hannah Dustin, with appropriate inscriptions upon it.

CHILDREN.

- i JOHN, b. Jan. 10, 1704; m.
- ii SARAH, b. Oct. 7, 1706; m. Isaac Shepherd, 1727.
- iii DANIEL, b. Dec. 28, 1710; d. 1743.
- iv TIMOTHY, b. April 18, 1713.
- v MOSES, b. Oct. 20, 1715; m. Hannah Woodward, 1755.

SECOND FAMILY.

- vi WILLIAM, b. July 8, 1719; m. Lydia Flagg, 1745.
- vii ELIZABETH, b. Nov. 2, 1721; m. Stephen Hastings, 1750.
- viii ELEANOR, b. Feb. 6, 1724.
- ix SAMUEL, b. Jan. 31, 1726; d. 1761.
- x ABIGAIL, b. Aug. 20, 1727.
- xi LYDIA, b. Dec., 1731.

7. iii. Peter Cheney, Jr. (Peter, John), b. Nov. 6, 1663; m. Mary, daughter of Nathaniel Holmes, 1691; lived at Worcester, 1704.

CHILDREN.

- i NICHOLAS, b. March 14, 1693; m. Hannah Tenny, 1717, and had Abigail, 1718; Samuel, 1720; Gersham, 1722; Eldad, 1724; Benjamin, 1725; David, 1729; Hannah, 1733; Hannah, 2d, 1736.
- ii MARY, b. 1695; d. soon.
- iii BENJAMIN, b. Jan. 6, 1698; m. Elizabeth Long, 1724; lived at Hartford.

8. iii. John Cheney (Peter, John), b. May 10, 1666; m. Mary Chute (James, James, Lionel), March 7, 1693.

CHILDREN.

- 10 i EDMUND, b. June 29, 1696.
- ii MARTHA, b. July 3, 1700; m. Tristram Coffin, Nov. 17, 1715, Newbury.
- iii MARY, b. Nov. 14, 1701; m. Francis Brocklebank, July 25, 1719.
- 11 iv JOHN, b. May 23, 1705.

9. iii. Eldad Cheney (Peter, John), b. Oct. 24, 1681; m. Mary Walker, of Bradford, Dec. 31, 1707; she d. about 1730; m. 2d, Joanna Woodbury, March 28, 1734; m. 3d, Martha Palmer, widow of Joseph Worcester (Samuel, Rev. William), 1747.

CHILDREN.

- i ICHABOD, b. March, 1709; m. Rebecca Smith, 1739.
- ii HANNAH, b. May 25, 1712; m. Daniel Spofford, 1735.
- iii MARY, b. 1735.
- iv JOANNA, b. 1738.

ALLIED FAMILIES.

10. iv. Edmund Cheney (John, Peter, John), b. June 29, 1696; m. Mary Plummer, Nov. 18, 1714.

CHILDREN.

12 i Moses, b. Nov. 26, 1715.
    ii Nathaniel, b. July 22, 1717; m. Lidia Bartlett, Aug. 19, 1741, and had Elizabeth, 1744; Richard, 1746.
    iii Edmund, b. May 15, 1719; m. Susanna Middleton (1713-1753), Oct. 9, 1740; had Mary, 1743; Dorothy, 1744.
    iv Peter, b. April 3, 1721; m. Ann Poor, 1748.
    v Mary, b. March 3, 1723; m.
    vi John, b. July 13, 1731; m. Sarah Colby, Haverhill, 1760.
    vii Sarah, b. Jan. 19, 1735.

11. iv. John Cheney (John, Peter, John), b. May 23, 1705; m. Elizabeth Dakin, 1725; m. 2d, Mary, daughter of Noah Clapp, Dec. 25, 1730; she d. 1744; he m. 3d, Kezia Kendall, 1745.

CHILDREN.

13 i Tristram, b. 1726.
    ii John, b. 1727.
    iii Elizabeth, b. 1729.
    iv Elias, b. 1734; d. young.
    v Esther, b. 1748.
    vi Jesse, b. 1754.
    vii Abigail, b. 1759.
    viii Elias, b. 1765.

12. v. Moses Cheney (Edmund, John, Peter, John), b. Nov. 26, 1715; m. Sarah Whitten, Oct. 23, 1740.

CHILDREN.

14 i Elias, b. Feb. 20, 1742.
    ii Moses, b. 1745.

13. v. Tristram (John, John, Peter, John), b. 1726; m. Margaret Joyner, 1745.

CHILDREN.

  i Elizabth.   iv Sarah.
  ii John.   v Mary, m. —— Johnson.
  iii William.   15 vi Elias, b. 1760.

14. vi. Elias Cheney (Moses, Edmund, John, Peter, John), b. Feb. 20, 1742; m. Jane Plummer, of Rowley, Sept. 7, 1762, and had:

CHILDREN.

16 i Elias, b. 1768.   ii Samuel.

15. vi. Elias Cheney (Tristram, John, John, Peter, John), b. 1760; m. Deborah Winchester, and had 12 children, of whom Dea. Franklin was the youngest.

16. vii. Elias Cheney (Elias, Moses, Edmund, John, Peter, John), b. 1768; m. Sarah Burbank (b. 1766), about 1790, and had:

CHILD.

18 i Moses, b. 1793.

17. vii. Dea. Franklin Cheney (Elias, Tristram, John, John, Peter, John), b. Dec. 25, 1812; m. Sarah Abrams, of Lowell, 1846, and had:

CHILDREN.

  i Rev. Wm. Franklin, b. Oct. 6, 1847; m. Lucy Elizabeth Chickering, who d. young.
 ii Geo. Abrams, m.

18. viii. Dea. Moses (Elias, Elias, Moses, Edmund, John, Peter, John), b. 1793; m. Abigail Morrison, b. 1796 (Jonathan, Bradbury, John, David; to America ere 1700; settled near Haverhill, and from there spread into New Hampshire and other states), 1816.

CHILDREN.

   i Rev. Oren B., b. 1817; D. C., 1839; professor in Bates Col., Lewiston, Me.; m. Catharine A. Rundlett, 1840, who d. 18.6; m. 2d, Nancy St. Clair, daughter of Rev. Thomas Perkins; 3 children.
  ii Esther M., b. 1818; m. John M. Merrill; 6 children.
 iii Sarah B., b. 1821; m. Rev. S. G. Abbott; 2 children.
 iv Moses, b. 1822; m. Martha Smith; son Charles in Boston.
  v Abigail M., b. 1823; m. Geo. Washburn.
 vi Charles G., b. 1826; D. C., 1848; m. Sarah E. Smith; 4 children.
 vii Person C., b. 1828; m. S. Anna Moore, 1850; m. 2d, Sarah (White) Keith, 1859; he was governor of New Hampshire.
viii Ruth E., b. 1830; m. Jos. W. Lord; 8 children.
 ix Elias H., b. 1832; m. Susan M. Youngman; 4 children.
  x Maria A., b. 1834; m. James P. F. Smith; 2 daughters.
 xi Harriet O., b. 1838; m. Dr. C. F. Bonney; 1 son.

William Cheney, of Roxbury, supposed brother of John, of Newbury, b. 1604; m. Margret ———; came over from England in 1635, and d. 1667. She m. 2d, Mr. Burge.

CHILDREN.

i THOMAS, b. in England; m. Jan. 11, 1655, Jane Atkinson, and lived in Cambridge; 10 children.
ii WILLIAM, b. in England; m. Deborah Wiswall, daughter of Elder John Wiswall; lived in Medfield and Dorchester; 9 children.
iii ELLEN, b. in England; m. 1643, Humphrey Johnson.
iv MARGARET, b. probably in Roxbury; m. April, 1651, Dea. Thomas Hastings, of Watertown, and had 7 sons and 1 daughter. He d. 1685, aged 80. She survived him.
v JOHN, b. and d. 1639. (Ancestors of the Hastings family.)
vi JOHN, b. 1640.
vii MEHITABLE, b. 1643.
viii JOSEPH, b. 1647; m. Hannah Thurston, of Medfield, and had 14 children. The descendants of this family are quite numerous, and are sometimes mixed with the descendants of John, of Newbury.

CHIPMAN.

Thomas Chipman, b. near Dorchester, Dorset Co., Eng., about 1567; m. after 1590, and d. about 1623. His wife d. 1637.

CHILDREN.

i HANNOR (Hannah?)
ii TUMSON (Thomasine?)
iii JOHN.

1. John Chipman, b. near Dorchester, Eng., about 1614; came to America in the ship "Friendship" of Barnstable, Eng., and arrived at Boston, July 14, 1631; lived in Plymouth till 1646; Yarmouth till 1649; then in Barnstable 30 years; and near 30 years in Sandwich. He bought property in Barnstable of Edward Fitz Randolph, 1649, that is yet held by the family and name, to the 7th and 8th generations. He was Selectman, Justice of the Peace, Deputy to the Court, etc., 1652 to 1669, and seems to have been a Deacon of the church in Barnstable, which he joined in 1652, and a Ruling Elder from 1670. He m. Hope, daughter of John Howland, of Plymouth, 1646. She must have d. about 1680. He m. 2d, Ruth, daughter of Wm. Sargent and wife of Jonathan Winslow, son of Josiah, and nephew of Gov. Edward (1595-1655), and Rev. Richard Bourne, who d. 1682, and d. April 7, 1708. She d. 1713, aged 71.

CHILDREN.

 i ELIZABETH, b. June 24, 1647; m. Hosea Joyce (his 2d wife), of Yarmouth.
 ii HOPE, b. Aug. 13, 1652; m. John Huckins, Aug. 10, 1670, and d. in 1678.
 iii LYDIA, b. Dec. 25, 1654; m. John Sargent of Malden as his 3d wife.
 iv JOHN, b. March 2, 1657; d. in June.
 v HANNAH, b. Jan. 19, 1659; m. Thomas Huckins, May 1, 1680, and d. Nov. 4, 1696.
2 vi SAMUEL, b. April 15, 1661.
 vii RUTH, b. Dec. 31, 1663; m. Eleazer, son of Deacon William Crocker, 1682; had 10 children, and d. 1698. He m. 2d, Mary Phinney, 1716.
 viii BETHIAH, b. July 1, 1666; m. Shubael Dimock (?).
 ix MERCY, b. Feb. 6, 1668; m. Nathan Skiff, of Chilmark, 1699.
3 x JOHN, b. March 3, 1669-70.
 xi DESIRE, b. Feb. 26, 1673; m. Col. Melatiah Bourne, 1692.

2. ii. Dea. Samuel (Dea. John), b. 1661; m. Sarah, 12th child of Dea. Henry Cobb, Barnstable (from Kent, Eng., d. 1697), Dec. 27, 1686; was a cordwainer, and d. 1723. She d. 1743, aged 80.

CHILDREN.

 i THOMAS, b. Nov. 17, 1687; was a Justice of the Peace of Stonington, Groton, and Salisbury, Conn.
4 ii SAMUEL, b. Aug. 6, 1689.
5 iii JOHN, b. Feb. 16, 1691.
 iv JOSEPH, bap. March, 1692.
 v MARY, bap. June 5, 1693.
 vi JACOB, b. Aug. 30, 1695.
 vii SETH, b. Feb. 24, 1697.
 viii HANNAH, b. Sept. 24, 1699; m. Barnabas Lothrop, Jr., 2d wife, Dec. 25, 1715.
 ix SARAH, b. Nov. 1, 1701; d. young.
 x BARNABAS, b. March 24, 1703; m. Elizabeth Hamblin, 1727; had 5 children.

3. ii. Hon. John (Dea. John), b. 1669-70, m. Mary, daughter of Capt. Stephen Skiff, Justice of the Peace, of Sandwich (1671-1711); m. 2d, Elizabeth, daughter of Capt. Thomas Handley and Miss Young, of Boston, who was widow of ——Russell, and —— Pope. She d. 1725. He m. 3d, Hannah Hookie or Hoxie, of Rhode Island, and d. Jan. 4, 1756. She d. Feb. 21, 1747. Hon. John was b. at Barnstable, but lived at Sandwich, 1691 to 1712, and 1714 to 1720; at Chilmark, 1712 to 1713; after that at Newport, R. I. In

Mass. he was Justice of the Peace, Military officer, Member of the General Court, 1719; Justice of the Court of Common Pleas, 1722; Agent of the English "Society for the Propagation of the Gospel," 1723. In R. I. he held several important offices of trust, etc.

CHILDREN.

    i JOHN, b. 1692; d. young.
    ii JAMES, b. Dec. 18, 1694.
    iii JOHN, b. Sept. 18, 1697.
    iv MARY, b. Dec. 11, 1699: m. Shubael Smith, Sept. 6, 1724.
    v BETHIA, b. Dec. 11, 1699, m. Samuel Smith, Oct. 6, 1717.
    vi PEREZ, b. Sept. 28, 1702; d. in Del., 1781.
    vii DEBORAH, b. Dec. 6, 1704.
    viii STEPHEN, b. June 9, 1708.
    ix LYDIA, b. June 9, 1708; m. Zephaniah Swift of Conn.; and Pres. Moore of Williams College.
    x EBENEZER, b. Nov. 18, 1709.
6   xi HANDLEY, b. Aug. 31, 1717.
    xii REBECCA, b. Nov. 10, 1719.

4. iii. Dea. Samuel Chipman (Dea. Sam., Dea. John), b. 1689; m. Abiah, daughter of John Hinkley, Jr., Dec. 8, 1715. She d. July 15, 1736, aged 40. He m. 2d, Mrs. Mary Green, of Boston, and d. 1753. She was living in 1763.

CHILDREN.

    i SETH, b. Aug. 10, 1717; d. soon.
    ii HANNAH, b. July 1, 1719.
    iii SAMUEL, b. 1721; m. Ruth Baker, 1746; lived in Conn., had 12 children; d. 1780.
    iv DEA. TIMOTHY, b. 1723; m. Elizabeth Bassett, 1751; had 8 children; d. 1770.
    v EBENEZER, b. 1726.
    vi JOHN, b. 1728.
    vii MARY, b. 1731; m. Samuel Jenkins, 1750, to Gorham.
    viii NATHANIEL, b. 1733.
    ix THOMAS, b. 1736 (?).
    x JOSEPH, b. 1740; d. soon.

5. iii. Rev. John (Dea. Sam., Dea. John), b. 1691, H. C. 1711; m. Rebecca, daughter of Robert Hale (1701-1751), 1718; m. 2d, Hannah, daughter of James Warren, son of Peter. Her brother, Joseph, was father of the orator and patriot of Bunker Hill (Gen. Joseph Warren, M. D., 1741-1675), and also of John, whose son John C., was a professional M. D., and author of the "Warren Genealogy." She d. 1769, aged 62; he d. March 28, 1775.

CHILDREN.

i   ELIZABETH, b. 1719; m. Rev. John Warren (1704, H. C. 1725, ordained pastor of the church in Wenham, 1732, d. 1749); m. 2d, Rev. Joseph Swain (1721, H. C. 1744, d. 1792), pastor in Wenham.

ii   SARAH, b. and d. 1721.

7   iii   JOHN, ESQ., b. 1722; of Salem, 1743.

iv   SARAH, b. 1724; m. John Leech, Jr., of Salem, 1743.

v   SAMUEL, b. 1726; m. Anstice (1725–89), daughter of Capt. Richard Manning, and had 9 children. Samuel was a sea Captain.

vi   REBECCA, b. 1728; m. Rev. Nehemiah Porter (1719, H. C. 1745; pastor in Ipswich, 1750; dismissed June, 1766; founder and installed pastor of a Congregational Church at Yarmouth, N. S., 1767; pastor of a church at Ashfield, Mass., 1774; d. 1820). Eunice, a daughter of Nehemiah Porter, Jr., m. Hon. Joseph Shaw, of Yarmouth, a step-son of Capt. and Dea. Zachariah Chipman.

vii   ROBERT, b. 1730; d. 1736.

viii   HENRY, b. 1732; m. Mary, daughter of Samuel Carr, and widow of Zachariah Newell, 1755; he was a tinner at Newburyport, and d. before 1800. She d. 1817.

ix   BYLEY, b. 1734; d. in Boston, 1752.

x   ROBERT H., b. 1736; d. at sea.

xi   JOSEPH, b. 1738; m. Elizabeth Obear, 1807; 2 children; m. 2d, Elizabeth Fowler, 1809, who d. 1852.

xii   MARY, b. 1740; m. Timothy Leech, of Beverly, and d. 1775.

xiii   HANNAH, b. 1742; m. Miles Ward, Salem, 1772, and d. 1829.

xiv   ABIGAIL, b. 1744; m. Capt. William Groves, 1776, and d. 1816.

xv   BENJAMIN, b. 1751; m. Anna, daughter of Jonathan Porter, 1779; had 2 children, and d. 1783. She m. 2d, Dea. John Dike, 1798, of Beverly and Salem.

6. iii. Handley Chipman (Hon. John, Dea. John), b. in Sandwich. Mass., Aug. 31, 1717; m. Jean, daughter of John and Margaret Allen, April 24, 1740, and had 11 children in Newport, R. I. Mr. Chipman was a cabinetmaker, Justice of Peace, and a pious Congregationalist. He left Newport, R. I., May 7, 1761, sailed to Nova Scotia, and settled in Cornwallis, Kings County, where his wife d. April 5, 1775, aged 53. Col. John Allen, her father, of Martha's Vineyard, d. 1765, aged 87; his wife, daughter of Rev. William Homes, d. about 1768, aged nearly 80. Mr. Chipman m. 2d, Nancy, daughter of Stephen and Elizabeth (Clark) Post, Dec. 14, 1775; had 5 more children. Mr. Chipman was Jus-

ALLIED FAMILIES.

tice of Peace, and Judge of Probate in Nova Scotia; left some comments on the New Testament; d. May 27, 1799. His wife d. 1802, aged 51. Mr. Post d. 1762.

CHILDREN.

- i ELIZABETH, b. in Newport, R. I., Feb. 19, 1741; m. William Dexter, of Cranston, R. I., and d. Feb. 9, 1764.
- ii JOHN, b. July 21, 1742; d. soon.
- iii MARGARET, b. July 17, 1743; m. Richard Bacon, Providence, R. I., and d. May 4, 1761.
- 8 iv JOHN, b. Dec. 18, 1744.
- v CATHARINE, b. Nov. 11, 1746; m. John Beckwith, Jr., 1764; 7 children, and d. 1812; he d. 1816.
- vi HANDLEY, b. Oct. 9, 1748; d. in Nov.
- vii REBECCA, b. Nov. 8, 1750; m. Samuel Beckwith (Samuel, James, Matthew, Matthew), Aug. 6, 1767; 11 children.
- viii ANTHONY, b. 1754; was a soldier in the American army under Colonel Tucker; after deserting the British naval service at Halifax, into which he had been impressed, he went to Gloucester, Mass., 1780; m. Anna Lurvey, 1783, and d. since April, 1790. She m. 2d, Samuel Wonson, 1792, and lived in Rockport; had Anthony, 1786, and James, Aug. 12, 1788.
- 9 ix THOMAS HANDLEY, b. Jan. 17, 1756.
- 10 x WILLIAM ALLEN, b. Nov. 8, 1757.
- xi Nancy, b. Oct. 6, 1772; m. Capt. Abner Morse, May 27, 1793, and d. Dec. 30, 1851.
- 11 xii HOLMES, b. Jan. 17, 1778.
- 12 xiii ZACHARIAH, b. March 20, 1779.
- 13 xiv MAJOR, b. Dec. 4, 1780.
- 14 xv STEPHEN, b. June 29, 1784.

7. iv. John Chipman, Esq. (Rev. John, Dea. Samuel, Dea. John), b. at Beverly, Mass., 1722, H. C., 1738; m. Elizabeth, daughter of Rev. John Brown, and sister of Rev. Cotton Brown, and lived in Marblehead; d. 1768. She d. June 17, 1765, aged 42.

CHILDREN.

- i JOHN, b. 1745; d. in infancy.
- ii NATHANIEL, b. 1747; d. in childhood.
- iii ABIGAIL, b. 1749; m. Capt. Peter Bubier, and d. 1815.
- iv JOHN, b. 1750; d. young.
- v REBECCA, b. 1752; m. Capt. William Blackler, 1773, and d. 1823, in Marblehead.
- vi WARD, b. 1754, H. C., 1770; teacher in Roxbury, 1771; sided with the Royalists; wrote for them in the Revolution, and so left Boston in 1776, with the British, when they evacuated; was a good and useful officer in the Government of New Brunswick, filling var-

ious offices, up to Lieutenant-Governor; m. about 1785, Elizabeth, daughter of Hon. William Hazen (1739–1814), of St. John, N. B., and thus inherited a large estate in that city. They had one son, Hon. Ward Chipman, LL. D., b. in St. John, July 21, 1787; H. C., 1805; d. Nov. 26, 1851. He was a learned and useful member in the Courts of New Brunswick; m. Elizabeth, daughter of W. Wright, Esq., Collector of Customs, St. John. The Prince of Wales "guested" there in Aug., 1860. Mrs. Chipman d. July 4, 1876, aged 84.

vii ELIZABETH, b. 1756; m. Hon. William Gray, Jr. (b. in Lynn, 1750; d. 1825), 1782, at one time the largest ship-owner in the United States; lived in Salem and Boston. His fleet of commercial vessels at one time numbered 44, some of them the largest ships running. He was one term Lieutenant-Governor of Massachusetts.

viii NATHANIEL, b. 1758; d. in infancy.

ix SAMUEL,
x MARY, } b. 1759; d. in infancy.

xi JOANNA, b. 1761; m. Capt. William Ward, of Salem and Medford (1761–1827), 1790; he m. 1st, Martha Proctor, 1785; she d. 1788.

xii JOHN, b. 1763; d. young, after studying in Harvard Col.

8. iv. John Chipman (Handley, John, John), b. in Newport, R. I., Dec. 18, 1744; taken to Cornwallis, N. S., with his parents, 1761; m. Eunice Dixon, and had:

CHILDREN.

i JOHN HANCOCK, b. May 9, 1770; m. Elizabeth, daughter of Samuel and Sarah Osborn, Dec. 3, 1789.

ii HANDLEY, b. Aug. 26, 1771.

iii CHARLES, b. July 9, 1772; m. Eunice Cogswell (Mason, Hezekiah, Samuel, Samuel, John, John), Cornwallis.

iv GEORGE, b. April 23, 1774; m. Mrs. —— Frazer.

v ELIZABETH, b. June 18, 1775; d. soon.

vi ELIZABETH, b. May 30, 1776; m. S. Herman Burbridge, Cornwallis.

vii EUNICE, b. Aug. 9, 1777; d. soon.

viii EUNICE, b. June 30, 1778; m. David, son of John and Elizabeth Whidden, Oct. 6, 1794.

ix ALLEN, b. March 26, 1780; m. ——, daughter of Capt. Gardner, Liverpool, N. S.

x DANIEL, b. April 21, 1782; m. Sarah Bishop; 7 children.

xi LOVENIA, b. Nov. 21, 1783.

xii JANE, b. March 19, 1785; m. Timothy, son of Timothy and Elizabeth Barnaby, Sept. 8, 1802.

xiii WILLIAM, b. Dec 9, 1786.

xiv JARED I., b. May 22, 1788.

xv OLIVIA, b. March 8, 1790.

9. iv. Thomas Handley (Handley, John, John), b. in Newport, R. I., Jan. 17, 1756; m. Mary, only daughter of John Huston, Esq., of Cornwallis, Sept., 1776; she d. 1784; he m. 2d, Jane Harding of Boston, Oct., 1786; she d. 1813; he m. 3d, Mrs. Mary Briggs, Portland, Me., Sept., 1820; she d. 1826; he d. Oct. 11, 1831, and is buried near the Baptist Church, Nictaux. Mr. Chipman was a convert of the renowned Henry Alline, and was baptised by Rev. Mr. Piersons, from England, 1778, and was ordained into the Baptist ministry at Annapolis, 1779, and for more than 50 years was a faithful preacher of the Gospel of Jesus Christ.

CHILDREN.

i JANE, b. Oct. 20, 1777; m. Nov, 1798, John M. Morse. (See Morse.)
ii MARGARET, b. Sept. 8, 1779; m. George Troop, of Annapolis; 10 children.
iii JOHN H., b. June 12, 1781; m. March, 1801, Hopestead Barnaby; 4 children.
iv ANN, b. May 6, 1784; m. Daniel Lovett, a Baptist Licentiate preacher.
v THOMAS.
vi HELEN, m. Wm. D. Randall, J. P., Sept. 1814; 11 children.
vii MARY, m. Geo. Fitch of Wilmot, June, 1815; 9 children.
viii DEA. SAMUEL L., b. 1803; m. Nancy Randolph of Annapolis, Oct. 25, 1827, and d. April 29, 1875.
ix JOSEPH WHEELOCK, m. Theresa, daughter of Robert Charlton, Jan. 25, 1824, and had George W. and Robert H.
x ELIZA, m. John Quick, Feb., 1822; 6 children.

10. iv. Wm. Allen, J. P. (Handley, John, John), b. in Newport, R. I., Nov. 8, 1757; m. Ann, daughter of Samuel and Sarah Osborn, by Rev. B. Phelps, Nov. 20, 1777; he d. Dec. 23, 1845; she d. Nov. 3, 1847, having been married seventy years. Mr. Chipman was an honorable and very useful member of society, an M. P. P., etc.

CHILDREN.

i REBECCA, b. June 28, 1779; m. John Barnaby, April 28, 1795.
ii REV. WILLIAM, b. Nov. 29, 1781; m. Mary McGowen, daughter of Matthew and Jean Dickey, Feb. 24, 1808; m. 2d, Eliza A., daughter of his uncle, Thomas Holmes Chipman, who d. Oct. 23, 1853, aged 46. He d. July 14, 1865. They had twenty-one children. Rev. Mr. Chipman was at first a captain of militia, but for about sixty years was an able, pious, and useful minister in the Baptist church.

 iii HANDLEY, b. July 25, 1784; m. Polly Burbridge, Oct. 4, 1809; she d. about 1813; m. 2d, Anne Hoyt (Jesse, James, Joseph, Dea. Zerubbabel, Walter, Simon, of Charlestown, Mass., 1623), June 19, 1814.

 iv SARAH, b. Aug. 10, 1788; m. Thomas, son of Phineas Lovitt, Sept. 3, 1805.

 v SAMUEL, the Centennarian, b. Oct. 18, 1790; m. Elizabeth, daughter of Col. Henry and Sarah (Pineo) Gesner, son of John, May 11, 1815; she d. 1826; he m. 2d, Jessie W., daughter of Thomas Hardie, 1842; he d. Nov. 10, 1891, having been blind about five years. Mr. Chipman was elected to the "House of Assembly" for Kings county, 1830, succeeding his father, and again in 1840. In 1844 he was defeated by Mayhew Beckwith, but re-elected again in 1851. He was financial secretary 1855, and member of the Executive Council, from which he retired in 1857. In 1859 he was again elected for the north riding of Kings. In 1863 he was appointed a member of the Legislative Council, where he sat till 1870, when he was appointed Registrar of Deeds for Kings county, which he held till 1887, and was succeeded by a Mr. Brown. He built the bark *Cornwallis* in 1848. He was baptised and joined the Baptist church when he was 97. Children: (1) Ann, b. Dec. 14, 1816; m. Dr. John Primrose. (2) Sarah Rebecca, b. Sept. 9, 1820; m. Samuel J. Sharp. (3) William A., b. June 30, 1818; m. Margaret Dodge. (4) Adelaide Elizabeth, b. Aug. 30, 1822; m. John E. Wilder; 3 children; m. 2d, Marshall S. Shedd, and live in Malden. Second family of Mr. Chipman: Fanny, Russell, Samuel, Isaac, Joseph, and Mary.

 vi ANNA, b. Dec. 16, 1795; m. Thomas Lovitt, Jan. 5, 1815.

2. iv. Thomas Holmes Chipman (Handley, John, John), b. in Cornwallis, N. S., Jan. 17, 1777; m. Elizabeth, daughter of Israel Andrews, Nov. 10, 1798, and d. May 28, 1862.

CHILDREN.

 i HANDLEY,
 ii ISRAEL, } b. and d. 1799.

 iii WM. HANDLEY, b. Feb. 10, 1801; m. Lurane, daughter of Dr. Jonathan Woodbury.

 iv JAMES ANDREWS, b. Dec. 26, 1802; d. 1823 of consumption.

 v WENTWORTH ALLEN, b. Nov. 10, 1804; m. Mary Jane Troop, June 23, 1831.

 vi ELIZA A., b. July 3, 1807; m. Rev. Wm. Chipman.

 vii NOBLE, b. Feb., 1810; d. soon.

 viii JOHN ANDREW, b. May 18, 1812; m. Elizabeth, daughter of Alpheus Harris, Feb. 25, 1836.

ALLIED FAMILIES. XXXV

  ix ZACHARIAH, b. April 18, 1814; m.
   x SARAH M., b. April 22, 1816; d. in May.
  xi HARRIET N., b. Aug. 19, 1818.

12. iv. Capt. Dea. Zachariah (Handley, John, John), b. in Cornwallis, March 20, 1779; m. Abigail, dau. of James and Mary (Dodge) Brown, of Wenham, Mass., and widow of Dea. Joseph Shaw, of Annapolis, Nov. 29, 1800, and lived in Yarmouth 60 years, a good and useful citizen, and a pious member of the Baptist Church. She d. Sept. 22, 1853, aged 78. He d. July 1, 1860.

CHILDREN.

    i BETHIAH, b. Dec. 10, 1801; m. Sept. 11, 1828, Dea. John C. Wilson, of Wilmot, and lived in Clements; they had (1) Eliza, b. 1829; m. Joseph Warren Chute. See No. 110. (2) Naomi, b. 1831; m. John G., son of Isaac and Martha (Chute) Woodbury. See No. 12. (3) Zachariah, b. 1833, d. 1847. (4) Abigail Ann, b. 1836; m. Justin Rideout. (5) Rachel, b. 1838; m. Handley Bishop. (6) Lemma, b. Sept. 2, 1840, m. (7) Harriet, b. 1842; m. John Benson. Dea. John Wilson, Esq., m. 1st, Elizabeth Morse, and had six children:
15 ii THOMAS DANE, b. July 27, 1803.
16 iii DEA., REV. HOLMES, b. Dec. 10, 1804.
    iv ABIGAIL, b. May 3, 1806; m. Jan. 27, 1825, Capt. Jacob Flint.
    v ZACHARIAH, b. May 17, 1813, d. in Oct.
    vi NANCY JANE, b. April 25, 1816; m. Capt. Obed McKenney.

13. iv. Hon. Major Chipman (Handley, John, John), b. in Cornwallis, Dec. 4. 1780; m. Elizabeth, daughter of Wm. Bishop, Nov. 25, 1802, and lived near Lawrencetown, Annapolis county, N. S., a good old Christian gentleman; was a member of the House of Assembly; d. March 28, 1871; she d. Oct. 14, 1855, aged 74.

CHILDREN.

    i DEA. SAMUEL B., b. Aug. 2, 1803; m. Levicia Marshall (John, Wm.), 1825; 5 children; d. Aug. 22, 1855; she d. 1877.
    ii NANCY, b. March 2, 1805, d. young.
    iii EDWARD, b. Nov. 2, 1807, d. young.
    iv LEVINIA, b. Feb. 2, 1811; m. Wm. Morse (Aaron, Samuel, Obad, Daniel, Daniel, Daniel, Samuel), and had four children.

14. iv. Stephen Chipman, Esq. (Handley, John, John), b. June 29, 1784; m. March 24, 1805, Nancy Tupper, daughter of ——, and d. May 5, 1849.

CHILDREN.

i Miner, b. Dec. 9, 1805; d. Nov. 2, 1826.
ii Maria, b. Jan. 15, 1807; d. Aug. 11, 1824.
iii Alfred, b. Aug. 9, 1809; d. March 29, 1831. Mr. Chipman m. 2d, Jane Tupper, of St. John, N. B., October, 1847, and had
iv Nancy Maria, b. July 2, 1848; m. a Presbyterian minister.

15. v. Thomas Dane (Dea. Zachariah, Handley, Hon. John, Dea. John), b. in Yarmouth, N. S., July 27, 1803; m. Nov. 25, 1824, Mary Alice, daughter of Rev. Harris Hardin (1761–1854), son of Israel and Sarah Harris (Lebbeus, James, James, of Connecticut); she d. the winter of 1837–8; he m. 2d, Dec. 13, 1838, Emily, daughter of Rufus Hibbard, and d. July 26, 1882.

CHILDREN.

i Maria, b. Sept. 12, 1825; m. Peter Parker, of Cornwallis.
ii Miner, b. May 30, 1827; d. 1848.
iii Ludowick, b. April 30, 1829; m. Hannah Churchill and two more.
iv Mary Alice, b. Jan. 26, 1831; m. Roland Porter, of Yarmouth.
v Thos. Dane, b. Dec. 29, 1832; m. Cecilia Cann, of Yarmouth, and d. 1868.
vi Laleah, b. April 5, 1834; d. 1853.
vii Sarah E., b. April 10, 1837; d. 1857.
viii Harriet, b. Dec. 18, 1839; m. Geo. Washington Saunders.
ix Susan H., b. March 12, 1841; m. Capt. Wm. E. Trefrey.
x Abbie, b. May 16, 1844; m. Asa Porter, and d. Nov., 1884.

16. v. Rev. Holmes (Dea. Zach., Handley, John, John), b. Dec. 10, 1804; m. Jan., 1827, Eliza, daughter of Capt. Alexander Bayne, and lived some in Clements and some in Massachusetts; d. about 1870.

CHILDREN.

i Xerxes Zachariah, b. Nov. 27, 1827; m.
ii Xenophon Alexander, b. Sept. 12, 1829; m.
iii Vortigern George, b. Jan. 13, 1833; m.
iv Origen Holmes, b. July 7, 1835.
v Elizabeth Rowena, b. March 27, 1839.
vi Stephen, b. May 7, 1841; d.
vii William Wentworth, b. Aug. 15, 1843.
viii James Locke Judson, b. 1846.

COGSWELL.

Robert and Alicia Cogswell, of Wiltshire, England, flourished there the middle of the sixteenth century; he d. 1581; she d. 1603. They had 8 children. Edward, the youngest, m. Alice ——; both d. 1616. Of their 14 children, John, the eighth, b. 1592, d. 1669, m. Elizabeth, daughter of Rev. William and Philis Thompson, 1615; she d. 1676. He settled at Chebacco, 1635, now Essex, three or four miles southwest of Ipswich. The "Cogswell House," built by William Cogswell, 1782, still stands there.

CHILDREN.

  i A DAUGHTER, b., m., and remained in London, Eng.
  ii MARY, m. Godfrey Armitage, 1649; lived in Boston.
  iii WILLIAM, b. March, 1619; m. Susanna Hawkes, 1650; lived in Chebacco; d. 1700. She d. 1696, aged 63.
2 iv JOHN, b. July, 1622.
  v HANNAH, m. Dea. Cornelius Waldo, 1652, said to be a descendant of the Rev. Peter Waldo, of Waldensian fame; d. 1701. From them has descended Ralph Waldo Emerson.
  vi ABIGAIL, m. Thomas Clark.
  vii EDWARD, b. 1629; of him little is known.
  viii SARAH, b. 1637; m. Simon Tuttle, 1663; d. 1782; he d. 1692.
  ix ELIZABETH, m. Nathaniel Masterson, 1657.

2. ii. John Cogswell, Jr., b. July, 1622, d. 1653; m. —— ——, 1647, who d. 1652.

CHILDREN.

  i ELIZABETH, b. 1648; m. Abram Wellman; d. 1736.
  ii JOHN, b. 1650; m. Margaret Gifford; d. 1724.
3 iii SAMUEL, b. 1651.

3. iii. Samuel Cogswell (John, John), b. 1651; m. Susanna, daughter of Richard and Susanna (Newhall) Haven, 1668, and d. 1700.

CHILDREN.

	i	HANNAH.		vi	JOSEPH.
	ii	SUSANNA.		vii	NATHANIEL.
	iii	WASTALL.		viii	JOHN.
4	iv	SAMUEL, b. 1677.		ix	JOSHUA.
	v	ROBERT.			

4. iv. Samuel (Samuel, John, John), b. 1677; m. Ann, daughter of Capt. John Mason, and widow of John Denison, Jr., in Lebanon, Vt.; lived some in Saybrook, Ct. Mr. Cogswell m. 2d, Abigail ——; lived in Canterbury, Ct.; d. 1752. She d. 1753.

CHILDREN.

i	Samuel.	5	v	Hezekiah, b. 1709.
ii	Anna.		vi	Robert
iii	Hezekiah.		vii	Jedediah.
iv	Samuel.		viii	James.

5. v. Hezekiah (Samuel, Samuel, John, John), b. Lebanon, Ct., 1709; m. Susannah Bailey, 1730; had 11 children; moved to Cornwallis, N. S., 1761; was an elder in the Presbyterian Church there; d. in 1806. She died about 1800, aged 90.

CHILDREN.

	i	Daniel.	vii	Naomi.
	ii	Ezra.	viii	Ann.
	iii	Aaron.	ix	Diadama.
6	iv	Oliver, b. 1740.	x	Martha.
	v	Sarah.	xi	Mason.
	vi	Christiana.		

6. vi. Oliver (Hezekiah, Samuel, Samuel, John, John), b. about 1740; m. Abigail, daughter of Joshua Ells, 1773, and lived in Cornwallis, N. S.; d. 1783. She d. about 1840.

CHILDREN.

7	i	Samuel.	iii	Mary.
	ii	Elizabeth.	iv	John

7. vii. Samuel Cogswell (Oliver, Hezekiah, Samuel, Samuel, John, John), b. in Cornwallis, N. S., Dec. 9, 1774, m. Eunice, daughter of John and Hannah Loveless, April 11, 1805, and lived in Horton, N. S.

CHILDREN.

8 i Oliver Hezekiah, b. Feb. 21, 1806.
  ii John F., b. May 4, 1807.
9 iii Joshua B., b. Dec. 4, 1808.
  iv Mary A., b. Sept. 1, 1810; m. Richard R. Crowe, Jan. 19, 1830; 9 children.
  v Hannah M., b. Nov. 1, 1812; m. Alden Banks.
  vi William E., b. March 21, 1815; d. Oct. 31, 1830.
10 vii Enoch L., b. May 9, 1817.
11 viii Aaron, b. May 26, 1820.
  ix Samuel, b. May 29, 1826; d. in Aug.

ALLIED FAMILIES. xxxix

8. viii. Dea. Oliver H. (Samuel, Oliver, Hezekiah, Samuel, Samuel, John, John), b. Feb. 21, 1806; m. Rebecca, daughter of Ezra E. and Penelope M. Crowe, March 11, 1828; lived in Morristown, King's county, N. S. He d. Nov., 1888. She d. 1884, a. 75.

CHILDREN.

i Lavina, b. Dec. 18, 1829; m. Seth Chute. No. 134.
ii Mary Ann, b. Dec. 18, 1831; m. Rev. Adoniram J. Cogswell, 1857.
iii Abner W., b. Dec. 28, 1833; m. Louisa A. Turner, 1856.
iv Rachel A., b. July 20, 1836; d. Feb. 13, 1861.
v Rebecca P., b. July 20, 1836; m. Edwin Skinner.
vi Julia E., b. June 8, 1838; m. Rev. James Palmer, 1856.
vii Charles M., b. Oct. 16, 1840; m. Jane, daughter of Elijah Palmer, 1865.
viii Fanny M., b. April 2, 1843; m. Richardson Chute, 1862. See No. 189.
ix Hannah M., b. Nov. 5, 1845; m. Benjamin, son of John West.

9. viii. Rev. Joshua Borden, brother to the preceding, b. Dec. 4, 1808; m. Ann Potter, daughter of Rev. Israel, Sen., Sept. 18, 1832; lived in Nova Scotia till 1853, when he returned to Bridgewater, Me. He entered the Baptist Ministry in 1829, and for more than 40 years witnessed for Christ. He also practiced medicine 40 years, retiring at 65. He d. March, 1886. She d. Aug. 12, 1890, aged 82.

CHILDREN.

i Burton, b. Nov. 11, 1833; m. Sophronia Heminway, Nov. 6, 1871.
ii Adoniram J., b. March 2, 1835; m. Mary A. Cogswell, 1857.
iii Wallace W., b. July 22, 1836; m. Margaret M. Marshal, April 22, 1859.
iv Zenas E., b. Aug. 2, 1841; d. July 15, 1858.
v Jerusha Ann, b. Aug. 2, 1841; m. Charles Kidder, Esq., Jan. 16, 1866.
vi Mary Emma, b. March 29, 1843, m. Sumner D. Seavey, Oct. 18, 1871, Charlestown, Mass.
vii Frances F., b. July 9, 1845; m. William H. Mills, Dec. 2, 1862.
viii Joshua Byron, b. Sept. 15, 1850; m. Lena ——, and lives in Chicago.

10. viii. Enoch Leander, another brother, b. May 9, 1817; m. Mary Ann, daughter of William and Elizabeth (Parker) Graves,

1839, and lived in Aylesford, King's county. He was a farmer and singing teacher, and d. Oct. 24, 1871. She d. March 13, 1879, aged 60.

CHILDREN.

i   HANDLEY PARKER, b. Dec. 15, 1840; m. Lavinia, daughter of Edward Gates, 1866. He was a sea captain.
ii   ELIZABETH, b. 1842; m. E. M. Chute, Nov., 1871, and d. Feb. 27, 1889. See No. 193.
iii   EMMA, b. Oct. 22, 1845; m. Henry Palmer, 1864. He d. Oct. 31, 1876, aged 87. She m. William Brown.
iv   BERIAH B., b. 1848; m. Maria Dawes, 1880. He, a sea-captain, was lost at sea, Aug, 1887.
v   MIRIAM L., b. Dec. 6, 1851; m. Joseph F. Chute, Dec 18, 1876. See No. 194.
vi   WM. BRUCE, b. July 1, 1853; m. Lilla Bell, daughter of Charles McAuley, May 20, 1884. He, a sailor, to Charlestown, 1864, but now in Malden.
vii   HAVELOCK, b. 1855; d. June 14, 1861.
viii   HARVEY, b. 1858; d. Nov. 5, 1884.

11. viii. Rev. Aaron Cogswell, the youngest brother, b. May 26, 1820; m. Lydia Ann, daughter of Samuel and Jane (Lowry) Beckwith, Oct. 29, 1842. She d. March 8, 1875, aged 55. He m. 2d, Griselda, daughter of Dea. James and Susan A. Messenger (b. 1839, at Bridgetown), July 19, 1875. Mr. Cogswell began to preach at 18, was ordained when 23, preached 2 years in Hantsport; 5 in Hampton; 13 in Clements; 10 at Beaver River; 7 at St. Mary's Bay; and over 7 at Lake George; and now for some time at Clementsport.

CHILDREN.

i   EMMA JANE, b. Aug. 3, 1843; m. Wm. W. Berry, May 6, 1862.
ii   SAMUEL BECKWITH, b. Jan. 8, 1845; d. May 28, 1853.
iii   SAMANTHA S., b. Dec. 5, 1850; m. George C. Tedford, Dec. 24, 1870.
iv   ALICE MATILDA, b. July 31, 1852; m. Busby W. Ray, Nov. 13, 1871.
v   SAMUEL B., b. Dec. 4, 1854; m. Annie M. Cleveland, Feb. 6, 1876.
vi   PAMELIA ANN, b. Dec. 2, 1856; d. Nov. 21, 1864.
vii   MARY HASELTINE, b. Aug. 9, 1859; m. —— Ray, and d. 1887.
viii   EVA V. WENTWORTH, b. Sept. 6, 1860; m.
ix   CLEMENTS BAKER, b. Dec. 13, 1865; d. July 21, 1866.

CROUSS.

John H. Crouse, b. Aug. 28, 1782; left Hamburg, Germany, in the morning. This was in 1806. He came to America and settled at Bear River, N. S., near the head of the tide; m. Sarah E., a sister to Dr. Frederick Beeler, from Savannah, Ga., 1807, and there lived, an honest, industrious farmer. He d. about 1863. She d. 1865, aged 80.

CHILDREN.

i JOHN, b. April 7, 1808; m. Hannah Rice (Jonas, Levi, Joseph, Beriah, Thomas, Thomas, Dea. Edmund), and d. at sea about 1842. Five daughters. She m. 2d, Jacob Dodge (Stephen, Tristram, Tristram, Tristram), who d. 1866, aged 80. She d.

ii SUSAN, b. Sept. 2, 1809; m. Rev. Israel Rice, Jan. 1, 1829; had 14 children; d. May 22, 1891. He d. Feb. 18, 1866.

iii CHRISTIANA, b. Jan. 1, 1811; m. Capt. David M. Quigley, son of Wickworth Q., and had 11 children. He d. 1877, aged 74. She d. 1884.

iv WILLIAM, b. Sept. 22, 1812; m. Harriet Harris (James, Capt. Henry), and d. 1864. She m. 2d, Capt. William Anthony. He d. 1888.

v MARY, b. July 17, 1814; m. Elijah Harris (Wm. H., Capt. Henry); 3 children, and both d.

vi ELIZA A., b. Oct. 7, 1816; m. Nelson Chute; 2d, Ezekiel Croscup (Ludowick, Ludowick from Germany); had 4 sons.

vii LEAH, b. Feb. 24, 1818; m. Capt. John Rice (Wm., Capt. John, Matthias, Gershom, Thomas, Dea. Edmund); 3 children, and d. He m. 2d, Jane Sweney.

viii HENRY, b. Jan. 13, 1821; m. Lovena Dodge (Jacob, Stephen, etc.). 4 children.

ix DOROTHY, b. May 15, 1823; d. 1893.

x MARGARET E., b. Jan. 13, 1825; m. Chesly Thomas. 4 children.

xi JACOB D., b. July 16, 1827; m. Sophia Kinney. 1 daughter.

FARNSWORTH.

1. Matthias Farnsworth, b. 1612, in Lancaster, Eng.; came over to Lynn, Mass., about 1647; was a weaver by trade; moved to Groton about 1660; d. Jan. 21, 1689. His wife, Mary, d. 1716-17. (One Joseph Farnsworth of Shirley, 1639, by some has been quoted as the father of Matthias, but the best authority says he was a brother.)

CHILDREN.

i   ELIZABETH, b. about 1647; m. James Robinson, Jan. 16, 1667, and d. Dec. 22, 1729. He d. Dec., 1720, aged 88. They had a daughter, Elizabeth, 1668, who m. William Lakin, Jr., 1685; 5 children.
ii MATTHIAS, b. 1650; m. Sarah Holden; 5 children.
iii JOHN, b. 1652; m. Hannah Aldis, Dec. 8, 1686, of Dedham, aunt of John and Sarah Aldis. (Sarah Aldis was daughter of Philip Eliot, brother of the Apostle John (1603-1690), and had 4 daughters and 5 sons.) He was a man of property and influence, both in church and State; Ensign in the militia; Deacon, 1709 to 1715; represented Groton in the General Court, 1709-10, 1712-13; Selectman several years, and frequently Moderator in the town meetings.
2 iv BENJAMIN, b. about 1654.
v   JOSEPH, b. Nov. 17, 1657; d. Oct. 31, 1674.
vi MARY, b. Oct. 11, 1660; m. Samuel Thatcher of Watertown, April 11, 1676, and d. Aug. 17, 1725. He d. Oct. 21, 1726, aged 78.
vii SARAH, b. 1663-4; m. Simon Stone of Watertown, and d. Sept. 16, 1731. He d. Dec. 19, 1741, aged 85.
viii SAMUEL, b. Oct. 8, 1669; m. Mary Whitcomb, w. of Simon Willard of Lancaster, 1706, and lived at Turkey Hill, Lunenburg; d. 1730.
ix ABIGAIL, b. Jan. 17, 1671; m. John Hutchins, b. June 3, 1668.
x   JONATHAN, b. June 1, 1675; m. Ruth Shattuck (b. June 24, 1668); 15 children; d. June 16, 1748, in Howard.
xi JOSEPH, 1677-87.

2. ii. Benjamin Farnsworth (Matthias), b. about 1654; m. Mary (b. Feb. 3, 1674), daughter of Jonas (John) and Mary (Loker) Prescott, 1695, and d. Aug. 15, 1733, Groton, Mass.

CHILDREN.

i   MARY, b. June 5, 1696; m. Lieut. Wm. Tarbell (b. June 10, 1689), 1718, and d. Feb. 29, 1784.
ii MARTHA, b. Jan. 6, 1698; d. July 11.
3 iii BENJAMIN, b. Jan. 16, 1699.
iv ISAAC, b. July 14, 1701; m. Sarah Page, April, 1723, and d. Dec. 17, 1744, Lunenburg, Mass.
v   EZRA, b. Jan. 17, 1703; m. Elizabeth Lakin (b. Aug. 23, 1707), April 25, 1726. 3 children. She d. He m. 2d, Abigail Pierce, Sept. 23, 1733, in Concord, and had 4 more. He d. June 10, 1788. She d. Jan. 8, 1800, a 80.

ALLIED FAMILIES.

4 vi Amos, b. Nov. 27, 1704.
  vii Lydia, b. Sept. 26, 1706; m. Samuel Tarbell, April 19, 1725, and d. Nov. 11, 1778. He d. May 23, 1776, aged 79.
  viii Aaron, b. Aug. 29, 1709; m. Hannah Barron, March 29, 1739; m. 2d, Sarah ———; m. 3d, Mrs. Elizabeth Parker, and she d. Dec. 12, 1760.
  ix Martha, b. May, 1711; m. Capt. John Stephens of Townsend, Oct. 11, 1728. He d. April 17, 1759.
5 x Jonas, b. Oct. 14, 1713.
  xi Deborah, b. 1715; m. Samuel Bowers, Jr., March 19, 1735. He d. Dec. 16, 1768, aged 57.

3. iii. Benjamin Farnsworth, Jr., b. Jan. 16, 1699, m. Patience ———. She d. July 10, 1733. He m. 2d, Rebecca Pratt of Malden, March 19, 1736, and d. Sept. 18, 1757. She d. Oct. 1. 1756.

CHILDREN.

  i Oliver, b. Nov. 9, 1727; m. Sarah Tarbell (b. April 14, 1726), Dec. 15, 1749, and d. 1802, at Shelburne.
  ii Susannah, b. Nov. 29, 1729.
  iii Benjamin, b. Oct. 24, 1736; d. Aug. 31, 1757.
6 iv Solomon, b. Oct. 13, 1738.
  v Ebenezer, b. Nov. 22, 1739; m. Sarah Nicholls. She d. April 13, 1782. He m. 2d, ——— ———.

4. iii. Amos Farnsworth (Benj., Matthias), b. Nov. 27, 1704; m. Lydia Longley (John Longley[4], the redeemed captive, William[3], William[2], William[1], m. Joanna, sister to Dep. Gov. Thomas Goffe, in England; came over to Lynn about 1636; made a freeman, 1638; moved to Groton, 1660; and d. Nov. 29, 1680. William[2] m. Deliverance ———; had 8 children. The parents and 5 children were slain by Indians, July 27, 1694, and 3 others taken into captivity. The daughter Betty d. of starvation, Lydia went into a nunnery at Montreal, while John was ransomed and reluctantly returned in 1699. A monument at Groton has this on it: "Here dwelt Wm. & Deliverance Longley, with their 8 children. On the 27th of July, 1694, the Indians killed the father & mother, & five of the children, & carried into captivity the other three."), and lived at Groton, Mass. About 1764, he went to Nova Scotia, but having some difficulty with real estate business in Massachusetts, he returned again before the Revolution, and was drowned crossing the Nashua River, Dec. 5, 1775.

xliv ALLIED FAMILIES.

CHILDREN.

i SARAH, b. Oct. 10, 1736; d. Sept. 19, 1756.
ii RACHEL, b. Jan. 29, 1738; m. Capt. Jabez Holden (descendant of Richard—over to Watertown, 1684), June 16, 1761, and d. 1829. He d. Aug. 11, 1783.
iii LYDIA, b. Nov. 24, 1739; m. Wm. Shedd, Sept. 26, 1765, and d. June 30, 1774. He m. 2d, Elizabeth ——, and d. March 18, 1806, a 71.
iv SUSANNA, b. Aug. 25, 1741; m. John Sawtell, Jr., Aug. 25, 1761, of Groton, and d. 1815.
v LUCY, b. Nov., 1743; m. Solomon Farnsworth. See Farnsworth, No. 6.
vi AMOS, b. June 24, 1746; d. July 9, 1749.
vii LT. JONAS, b. Aug. 18, 1748; m. Jane, daughter of James and Mary (Kelly) Delap, 1774, Granville, N. S., and d. July 16, 1805. She d. May, 1826, aged 74.
viii MARY, b. 1751; m. Joseph Potter, Jr. See Potter.
ix AMOS, JR., b. April 28, 1754; m. Elizabeth Rockwood, May 7, 1782, and d. Oct. 29, 1847. She d. Dec. 11, 1847, nearly 91. This Amos was at the battle of Bunker Hill, June 17, 1775, where he, with Samuel Lawrence and —— Bancroft, was posted in the night at the extreme east line of battle to watch the war-ships lying off there, and report to Col. Wm. Prescott. They remained there until driven away by the guns of the vessels. He was shot through the right arm and side, while on the retreat from the hill. Afterwards he was in the army that retreated from Ticonderoga to Saratoga before Burgoyne, and was present at Burgoyne's surrender. Being a Lieutenant, he served afterwards in New Jersey; was Major in the Artillery, and got a pension of $113 per month from the Government.
x BENJAMIN, b. Oct. 24, 1757; drowned with his father.

5. iii. Jonas (Benjamin, Matthias), b. Oct. 14, 1713; m. Thankful Ward* (Obadiah, Richard, William, to Sudbury, 1639), 1739, and d. Dec., 1803. She d. May 1, 1799, aged 87, Worcester, Mass.

CHILDREN.

i AZUBAH, b. June 3, 1740; m. Benj. Tarbell, June 20, 1761, and d. March 4, 1838.
ii MARTHA, b. May 21, 1742; m. Edwin Phelps; m. 2d, —— Jocelyn, both of Leominster.

---

* The Ward family trace their origin back to the Conquest, 1066. From 1379, they claim a succession of heads of families as follows: Ralph, Richard, John, John, Richard, William, Thomas, Thomas, John, Richard, Thomas, who had sons John and William.

ALLIED FAMILIES.

iii JONAS, JR., b. April 2, 1744; m. Sarah Delap, Granville, N. S., June 13, 1775. She d. Nov. 30, 1785. He m. 2d, Mrs. Peggy Lewis, and d. April 5, 1808. He was one of the first settlers of Machias, Me., and had Thomas, Catherine, Sarah, and Deborah.

iv DEBORAH, b. Sept. 15, 1746; m. Joseph Wheelock (Obadiah, Obadiah, Benj., Rev. Ralph), 1769.

v DANIEL, b. Aug. 14, 1748; deserted from the American side, and went over to Nova Scotia; was proscribed, 1778, with the death penalty.

7 vi ISAAC, b. Aug. 9, 1750.

vii THANKFUL, b. Aug. 3, 1752; m. —— Beaman, April 10, 1770, and lived in Leominster.

viii PETER, b. Aug. 18, 1754; m. Margaret Marshall, Bath, Me.; to Norridgewock, 1780; d. 1803.

8 ix JOEL, b. May 28, 1759.

6. iv. Solomon (Benj., Benj., Matthias), b. in Groton, Mass., Oct. 13, 1738; m. Lucy Farnsworth, a cousin, Dec. 6, 1770, in Nova Scotia, and lived near Chute's Cove, now Hampton. His wife d. June, 1800, aged 57. He m. 2d, Mary Chute (John, John, Lionel, James, James, Lionel), May 23, 1801, and d. Nov. 19, 1812. She m. 2d, John Ellis. See No. 111.

CHILDREN.

i SARAH, b. June 4, 1773; m. Michael Miller, had 5 sons, and d. He m. 2d, Susan, daughter of Patrick Grimes, and had 3 sons and a daughter. Children: (1) Solomon, b. 1794, m. Sally Tuck, and had (a) Julia Ann, m. John M. Wade; (b) Jane, m. —— Fowler, St. John, N. B.; (c) Betsy; (d) Olivia, m. Henry Bent; (e) John, went to sea; (f) Wm. Elder, m. Jane Eaton; (g) Aaron; (h) Solomon, m. up St. John River, N. B.; (i) Parker. Mrs. Sarah Miller d. 1844. Mr. Miller d. 1854, aged 60. (2) Harris, b. 1796, m. Sarah Gaskell; 2d, Sarah (Potter) Spurr, and had (a) Sophia, b. 1819, m. Dea. Eaton Chute, Dea. Solomon Chute; (b) Michael, b. 1823, m. Elizabeth, daughter of Handley Chute (No. 44), and d. 1849; (c) Wm. Doane, m. Elizabeth Saunders; (d) Mary, m. Alex, son of George Witt, and Joseph Potter. (3) William, b. 1798; a shoemaker; d. about 1868, aged 70. (4) James, m. Eleanor Chandler. See No. 11. (5) Edward, d. before 1830. By 2d, wife: (6) Michael, m. Lucy Ann Merry, and had 7 children in Granville. (7) Rees. (8) Handley. (9) Salome.

ii FRANCES, b. Oct. 11, 1774; m. Rev. James Manning (1763–1818), 1796. She m. 2d and 3d, Henry Troop and Aaron Morse, and d. March 7, 1872. Children, besides losing 2 or 3 in childhood: (1) James Edward, b. 1804, m. Catherine Boyd of Falmouth, and d. about 1840. Children: (a) James Edw., m. Isabel Fitch, daughter of Archie Hicks; (b) John B., m. Adaline Pierson, Mrs. Annie Flagg; (c) Ann, m. Ansley Brown (John, Wm., from Eng), who d. She m. 2d, Israel Foster, who had m. 1st, Minnetta (Foster) Morse; (d) Ellen; (e) Catherine; (f) Victoria, m. Isaac Freeman; (g) Dena, m. Charles Chase. (2) Benjamin W. C., b. about 1808, m. Waity Newcomb, b. 1819 (Dea. Wm. N., Eddy, John, Eddy, John, Simon, Andrew, Andrew, over to Boston about 1635), 1840, and lived at Bridgetown, N. S. Children: (a) Rev. James Wm., b. 1841, Baptist minister in Halifax; m. Sarah A. Bigelow, b. 1850 (Wm. J., Daniel, Amasa, Isaac, Isaac, Samuel, John, over to Watertown from England about 1630; m. Mary, daughter of John Warren, over from England about the same time; a descendant of Cerdic, the Saxon general, over to England in 495, d. 534. Queen Victoria is traced back to the same origin), Sept. 12, 1872; (b) Capt. Leigh Richmond, b. 1843, m. Mary Keating; (c) Johnston E., b. 1845, m. Lois, daughter of Gilbert Sanderson; (d) Celina R., b. 1847, d. 1851; (e) Frances A., b. 1850, m. George Sanderson; m. 2d, T. T. Keefler; (f) Adelia A., b. 1852, m. Daniel Benjamin, M. P. P.; (g) Leander C., b. 1854, m. Florence Lovett, Chester, N. S.; (h) Laura C., b. 1858, d. soon; (i) Arthur T., b. 1859, m. Mary Rebecca (McIntosh) Inness, lives in Everett, Mass.; (j) Capt. Edmund E., b. 1862, on the bark Zebina Gondey; m. Isabel J. Mosher, Bridgetown, March 2, 1893. (3) Lucy Ann, m. William Henry, son of Henry Troop, and had (a) Mary Troop, m. Rev. J. J., son of Isaac Skinner; (b) Charlotte L., m. Avard Longley, M. P. P., etc. (Asaph, Israel, William, John, William, William, William); 6 children. (4) Frances, m. Israel Longley (brother to Avard); he d. 1871; she m. 2d, Levi Woodworth. Children: (a) James Wilberforce, b. 1849 (Attorney-general of Nova Scotia), m. Annie, daughter of Newton Brown; 4 children.

iii Lucy, b. June 15, 1777; m. James Eaton (David, James, Jonathan, Thomas, John), June, 1799, and had (1) Nancy, b. 1801; m. 1821, Henry Holt; 8 children; d. 1879; he d. (2) Harriet, b. 1803; m. 1829, Aaron Hardy; 2 children, Ruth and Prudence. (3) Edward, b. 1804; m. 1840, Sarah Jane, daughter of John and Deborah (Eaton) Manning, lived at Bridgetown, a merchant; d. 1892. (4) Fanny, b. 1806; m. James Huntley, Canning, N. S.; 5 children. (5) James, b. 1808; d. at 3 or 4. (6) Rebecca b. 1811; m. Capt. Guy Moreten Newcomb (Joseph, Joseph, John, John, Simon, Andrew, Andrew), April 24,

1833; had 9 children. He sailed for St. John, N. B., Jan., 1872; vessel and all lost; he aged 62. (7) Caroline, b. 1814; m. Benjamin Sanford (John, Benjamin, Esbon, Samuel, John, over to Boston, 1631), about 1835; 3 sons, 2 daughters. Mr. Eaton, b. 1767, m. 1st, Nancy, daughter of John Manning* of Falmouth, Hants county, N. S., 1793, and had (1) Ruth, b. 1794; m. 1814, William, son of Asael Bentley of Billtown; 6 children and d. 1847; he d. 1864, a. 74. (2) May Ann, b. 1796; m. 1817, Benjamin Steadman (Enoch, John, John); 8 children; d. 1869; he d. 1865, a. 79. Mrs. Eaton d. Dec., 1798; he d. May, 1813. His 2d wife, Lucy, m. 2d, John Sanford (Benjamin, Esbon, Samuel, John), as his 2d wife, 1814, and had 4 more children.

iv MARY, b. 1779; m. John Brown (William, from England before the Revolution, b. 1757), in 1800. He d. about 1840. She d. 1855. They had (1) Lucy, m. —— Strong. (2) Fanny, m. Isaac Marshall (Otis, Isaac). (3) Sarah, m. Thomas, son of George Brown, a cousin. (4) Charles, d. young. (5) Abba, m. James, son of Samuel Cornwell; 4 children. (6) Louise, m. William Tupper, Jr. (7) J. Manning, m. Mary Ann Foster (Oliver, Isaac, Benjamin, Jacob, Isaac, Reginald of Ipswich, Mass., 1638). (8) Ansley, m. Ann Manning (James, Edward, Rev. James, John); had Ada, Lucy, and Wayland. John Brown had a brother, George, b. 1759; m. Anna Clark, and d. 1857. Anna d. 1858, aged 96. (Another brother, William, Jr., d. 1852, aged about 90.) Children: (1) Thomas, m. Sarah, daughter of John Brown, cousin. (2) Mary, m. James Hall (John, William, from England before the Revolution). (3) Joseph, m. Helen Gates (Joseph, Jonas, Capt. Oldham, Amos, Simon, Stephen, over to Hingham, 1638). (4) George, m. Harriet Longley, daughter of Asaph; 2 children. (5) William, m. Mary, daughter of Jacob Cornwell, and wife of William Allen and James Johnson; had 5 children. She d. 1850, aged 41; he m. 2d, Mary Helen, daughter of William Shaw; had 5 more, and d. April 22, 1887, aged 82, and the widow lives in Lynn. (6) Seth, m. Jane, daughter of Sylvanus Snow; 6 children. (7) Eliza, m. Daniel, son of Thomas Harris; 12 children. (8) Loretta. (9) Susan, d. young. (10) Sophia, m. Syl-

---

*Of the family of John Manning of Falmouth, besides Rev. James, was ohn (1764–1858); Nancy, that m. James Eaton; and Rev. Edward (1766–852, a stout, tall, powerful man, both in the pulpit and elsewhere. H was instrumental, under God, of winning many souls to Christ, in the Baptist :hurch in Cornwallis, and other places in Nova Scotia. He m. Rebecca, aughter of Charles Skinner, and had (1) Nancy, m. Hezekiah J. Cogswell, and nd d. soon after; he m. 2d, Ann, daughter of John Bentley. (2) Eunice, . young. (3) Mary, m. Peter Carruthers, 1834. Mrs. Manning d. April 5, 857, aged 86.

    vanus Snow, Jr.; 7 children. (11) Ann, m. Joseph, son of Jonas Rice. (12) Simon, m. Rachel Dill; 7 children.
  v SOLOMON, b. 1781; d. 1782.
9 vi BENJAMIN, b. Feb. 1, 1802.
10 vii PETER, b July 19, 1803.
11 viii JOHN CHUTE, b. Oct. 11, 1805.
  ix MARY, b. 1807; m. William Hall (John, William, b. in Somersetshire, England, 1748, over to America before the Revolution), and lived in Wilmot, N. S. Children: (1) Solomon F., b. 1825; m. Mary J. Fisher. (2) Edward M., b. 1827; d. about 1849–50. (3) John W., b. 1829; m., to Australia. (4) Mary Eliza, b. 1831; m. Capt. Samuel Hains, of Freeport, N. S. He was run down off New Orleans, and lost, with 2 children, 1856–7. (5) Capt. Jacob R., b. 1833; m. Sarah A., daughter of John and Sally (Gates) Reagh, 1855; 3 children, besides losing several; live at the Spa Springs, Wilmot, N. S. (6) Hannah Ann, b. 1835; m. Elkanah Bowlby. (7) William H., b. 1837. (8) Joshua C., b. 1839; d. young. (9) George B., b. 1843; d. young. Mr. Hall d. 1842, aged 42. She d. 1851, aged 44.
12 x SOLOMON, b. Oct. 9, 1809.

7. iv. Isaac Farnsworth (Jonas, Benjamin, Matthias), b. in Massachusetts, Aug. 9, 1750; went to Nova Scotia in youth, m. Hannah Hill, April 21, 1773, and lived in Granville. She d. He m. 2d, Martha Barth, and lived in Jonesboro', Me.; d. 1832. She d. March, 1830.

CHILDREN.

13 i DANIEL, b. about 1774.
  ii ICHABOD, b. about 1776.
  iii ROYAL, b. about 1878.
  iv ASA, b. about 1780; m. Betsy Weston; had (1) Sybil, m. Nathan Libby; (2) Kezia, m. Hiram Libby.
  v AMAZIAH, b. about 1782.
  vi ISAAC, b. about 1784.
  vii MARTHA, b. about 1786; m. Reuben Libby.
  viii HANNAH, b. about 1788; m. Joseph Libby.
  ix MARY, b. about 1790.

8. iv. Joel Farnsworth (Jonas, Benjamin, Matthias), b. in Massachusetts, May 28, 1759; m. Abigail Fales (sister to Benjamin, Daniel, and 2 or 3 sisters who m. Gateses), and lived in Wilmot, N. S., now Clarence. She d. 1826, aged 65. He m. 2d, Sarah (Dewolf) Perkins, and d. 1843, aged 84. She d. 1865, aged 92.

ALLIED FAMILIES. xlix

CHILDREN.

i DEBORAH, m. John, son of James and Mary (Barnes) Ray.
ii THANKFUL, m. Henry Banks. See Banks.
iii SALLY, m. Silas Gates. See Gates.
iv RELIEF, m. John Hurst, a school-teacher; m. 2d, Elias Gates. See Gates.
v RACHEL, m. Fred, son of Dea. Joseph Morton.
vi BETSY, b. 1791; m. Joshua U. Slocomb (Capt. John, John, Simon), and d. 1852; he d. Sept. 10, 1850, aged 66; 11 children.
vii POLLY, m. John Banks.
viii LUCY, d. young.
ix FANNY, d. young.
x MARTHA, m. James Adams.
xi AZUBA, m. Joseph Ogilvie; daughter Naomi m. John Henry Hall (Dea. Henry, John, William).

9. v. Benjamin Farnsworth (Solomon, Benjamin, Benjamin, Matthias), b. at Phinney's Cove, below Hampton, Annapolis county, N. S., Feb. 1, 1802; m. Anna Matilda, daughter of John and Rebecca (Raymond) Ellis, 1822, and lived on the "Bay Shore," near his native home. She d. May 15, 1861, aged 55. He m. 2d, Phebe, daughter of Henry Milbury, 1862, and d. Feb. 4, 1880. She, at Phinney Mountain.

CHILDREN.

i SERAPHINA, b. Dec. 10, 1823; m. James Lowry, Sept. 27, 1852. He d. Oct. 25, 1886, aged 62. She is in Danvers, Mass.
ii MARY, b. April 19, 1825; m. Daniel Gunnison, 1850; 6 children, and d. Christmas, 1890. He d. 1861.
iii EZRA, b. Oct. 26, 1827; m. Mary Jordan, 1854; 4 children, and d. about 1875. She is at Petite Passage, N. S.
iv LUCRETIA, b. Oct. 24, 1829; m. Sidney S. Chute. No. 142.
v MATILDA ANN, b. 1831; d. 1834.
vi JACOB E. R., b. June 4, 1834; m. Louise, daughter of Isaac and Elizabeth (Patterson) Foster, 1861; had a daughter, Anna M., m. George W. Davis, Lynn, Mass. Mr. Foster moved there, 1867. She d. April 6, 1894.
vii ELLEN ANN, b. 1838; m. Merrill Tufts, 1859; 2d, James Mowatt, 1875; daughter Saville, b. 1880.
viii ABIJAH, b. 1840; m. Anna Whalin, 1870; and d. Nov. 24, 1874. She m. 2d, James Knowlin in California.

10. v. Peter Farnsworth (Solomon, Benjamin, Benjamin, Matthias), b. July 19, 1803; m. Mary, daughter of Michael and Abigail (Simpson) Holden, April 29, 1827, and lived near Hampton; d. 1886. She d. Jan., 1890, aged 84.

4

ALLIED FAMILIES.

CHILDREN.

i MICHAEL HOLDEN, b. April 25, 1828; d. in May.
ii SOLOMON, b. May 27, 1830; d. in 1837.
iii MICHAEL HOLDEN, b. April 23, 1834; m. Terrissa Chute. See No. 132.
iv STEPHEN THOMAS, b. Sept. 18, 1836; m. Mary Fraser; had 2 daughters, Rose and Bessie. She d. Jan. 26, 1876, aged 42. He m. 2d, Mrs. Maggie Waters, and was killed at sea, 1889; a sea captain.
v JAMES WELLINGTON, b. Feb. 5, 1844; m. Sarah A., daughter of Joseph Corbit; two sons, Handley C., and Joseph P. Capt. J. W. Farnsworth went to Lynn, May, 1892, and d. in July, 1893.
vi LALEAH, b. Nov. 2, 1852; m. Avard, son of Francis Brinton, 1872. He d. Nov. 4, 1873, aged 23. She m. 2d, Elias Messenger.

11. v. John Chute Farnsworth, another brother, b. Oct. 11, 1805; m. Mary Cecelia, daughter of Job Park, Feb. 15, 1826. She d. 1839, aged 32. He m. 2d, Nancy, daughter of James and Phebe Chute, Jan. 14, 1841. She d. Jan. 31, 1856, aged 55. He m. 3d, Elizabeth Charlotte Chute. See No. 45.

CHILDREN.

i MARY AMELIA, b. May 5, 1827; m. William Rhodes; had 5 children. He d. Aug., 1885, aged 62. She m. 2d, Franklin Rice (as his 3d wife), 1887, and lives at the head of the tide, Bear River.
ii JOB, b. June 6, 1829; m. Lucy, daughter of William and Lucy (Foster) Woodworth, 1850, and d. 1891. She d. 1886, aged 60. Children: (1) William Morrill, b. 1851,—home on the old farm, Trout Cove, N. S. (2) John Abel, b. 1853; m. Annis Haight, Digby Neck. (3) Thomas Henry, b. 1855, m. Emma Jane Winslow; 2d, Lalia Daily, Digby. (4) George A., b. June, 1857; m. Mary Ellen Gilliland (Jacob, William, William, Joseph), and lives in Lynn. (5) Mary Cecelia, b. 1859; m. Charles D., son of Capt. William Hull, and is in Lynn. (6) Darius Lord, b. 1861; m. Emeranda Smith.
iii HENRIETTA, b. July 23, 1831; m. William H. Denton, Trout Cove, son of Edward.
iv CHARLOTTE, b. Oct. 4, 1834; m. Daniel D. Morton, and had (1) Anna, m. Simon Soulis. (2) Lloyd, m. Amelia Morehouse, and d. 1864. He m. 2d, Adelaide, daughter of Daniel Jordan. 4 more children.
v FOSTER, b. April 23, 1836; m. Elizabeth, daughter of Timothy Brooks, Jr., and had 12 children.
vi JOHN EDWARD, b. 1838; m. Phebe R., daughter of Timo-

thy Brooks. Children: (1) Reed, m. Hannah Munroe. (2) Edith, m. Albert Tolen. (3) Timothy Hugh, m. Emma Jane, daughter of Alonzo Foster, and lives in Lynn.

12. v. Dea. Solomon Farnsworth, the youngest, b. Oct. 9, 1809; m. Anna B., daughter of James Cummings, Digby county, Nov. 19, 1833; had 4 children. She d. 1843. He m. 2d, Phebe, daughter of Abram Bogert; lived at Stony Beach, below Annapolis Ferry. He d. 1888.

CHILDREN.

i JAMES, b. 1834; m. Eliza, daughter of Daniel Kennedy; m. 2d, Elsie Condon, widow of A. Judson, son of Rev. John J. Woodworth.
ii REED, m. Prudence, daughter of Henry Hardy.
iii SOLOMON, m. in Pa.; d. 1888.
iv NAOMI, m. Jacob, son of Joseph Hardy; m. 2d, Stephen Blaney, and d.
v WALLACE S., b. 1844; d. in 1847.
vi MARY EMMA, d. in childhood.
vii GEORGE BURTON, m. Lavina, daughter of David Mills.
viii JOHN, m. May, daughter of Alfred Winchester.
ix MARGARET JANE, m. Duncan Cummings.
x LAVINIA, m. Alfred, son of David Mills.
xi E. STANLY, m. Nellie, daughter of Alfred Winchester.
xii MARY EMMA, m. Lebaron Mills, Nov. 9, 1892.
xiii RUPERT.

13. v. Daniel Farnsworth (Isaac, Jonas, Benjamin, Matthias), b. in Aylesford, N. S., 1775; m. Jerusha Earl of Horton, Dec. 8, 1803; lived in Aylesford. She d. Feb. 3, 1861, aged 77. He d. Nov. 24, 1866, aged 92.

CHILDREN.

i SARAH, b. May 21, 1804; m. Thomas Jaques, Aug. 27, 1828.
ii NELSON, b. Dec. 25, 1806; m. Harriet Orpin, Dec. 28, 1828.
iii THOMAS, b. March 16, 1808; m. Lydia Dugan, Dec. 17, 1838.
iv ISAAC, b. May 6, 1811; d. young.
v WILLIAM, b. March 23, 1814; m. Louise, daughter of Charles Van Buskirk.
vi LOIS, b. Oct. 13, 1816; d. young.
vii ROBERT JAMES, b. March 5, 1820; m. Rachel, daughter of Ezekiel Marshall, wid. of Benjamin, son of John Wilson; had 2 or 3 children; live in Dorchester, Boston, Mass.
viii JOHN L., b. Aug., 1824; m.; d. 1855, Dayton, Ohio.
ix SAMUEL B., b. Jan. 23, 1828; m. —— ——, Peabody, Mass.; 4 children; went to York, Me., about 1862.

FOSTER.

1. i. Reginald Foster, b. about 1595; is reported to have come from Exeter, Devon, England, with his wife Judith, 5 sons, and 2 daughters, and settled in Ipswich, Essex county, Mass., 1638. He lived near the "East Bridge," which stood where the stone bridge is now. His wife Judith d. Oct. 1664. He m. 2d, Sarah, widow of John Martin, Sept., 1665, and d. 1681. She m. 3d, William White of Haverhill, 1682, and d. 1683.

CHILDREN.

 i MARY, b. 1618; m. Lieut. Francis Peabody; had 14 children, and d. at Topsfield, Aug. 9, 1705. He d. Feb. 19, 1697-8, aged 83.

 ii SARAH, b. 1620; m. William Story; had 6 children, and d. Jan., 1702-3. He d. 1702, a. 79; was the ancestor of Dr. Story of Boston, and of the late Judge Story.

 iii ABRAM, b. 1622; m. Lydia, daughter of Caleb and Martha Burbank, of Rowley, and had, in Ipswich, Ephraim, Abram, James, Isaac, Benjamin, Ebenezer, Mehitable, Caleb, and Ruth.

2. iv ISAAC, b. 1630.

 v WILLIAM, b. 1633; m. Mary, b. Feb. 8, 1639, daughter of William and Joanna Jackson; moved to and lived in Rowley, and was a man of wealth and influence there and in Boxford, Haverhill (where his son David moved to in 1705), and elsewhere, besides a Christian gentleman; d. 1713. Children: Mary, Judith, Hannah, Jonathan, William, Timothy, David, Samuel, and Joseph.

 vi JACOB, b. 1635; deacon of the first church in Ipswich; m. Martha Kinsman; had 7 children. She d. Oct. 15, 1666; m. 2d, Abigail, daughter of Robert and Mary (Waite) Lord, Feb. 26, 1667, and d. "July ye 9th 1710, in ye 75 yr of His Age." She d. June 4, 1729. Children: Judith, John, Jacob, Sarah, Mary, Abram, Jacob, Amos, Abigail, Nathaniel, Samuel, Joseph, James, and Mary.

 vii REGINALD, b. 1636; m. Elizabeth, daughter of John Dane, and lived in Chebacco parish, Ipswich. Children: Elizabeth, Isaac, Judith, Mary, John, Rebecca, Naomi, Ruth, Eleanor, Hannah, and Nathaniel.

2. ii. Isaac Foster (Reginald), b. 1630; m. Mary Jackson, May 5, 1658; d. Nov. 27, 1667; m. 2d, Nov. 25, 1668, Hannah Downing, who d. Nov. 27, 1677; m. 3d, Martha Hale, March 16, 1679, who survived him. He lived in Ipswich, near Topsfield, at the east end of "Symond's Farm," the town line dividing the farm.

CHILDREN.

   i JONATHAN, b. Jan. 9, 1658–9; d. young.
  ii MEHITABLE, b. Sept. 19, 1660; d. Feb., 1661.
3 iii JACOB, b. Feb. 9, 1662–3.
  iv BENJAMIN, b. June, 1665; d. 1700.
   v ELIZABETH, b. April 20, 1667.
  vi MARY, b. June 26, 1669; m. Richard Grant, Feb. 27, 1688.
 vii DANIEL, b. Nov. 14, 1670; d. about 1753.
viii MARTHA, b. Aug. 1, 1672; m. Thompson Wood, Dec. 8, 1691.
  ix RUTH, b. Feb. 20, 1673–4; m. —— Grove.
   x PRUDENCE, b. May 23, 1675; m. Jos. Borman, Feb. 17, 1696.
  xi HANNAH, b. Oct. 24, 1676.
 xii ELEAZER, b. April, 1684; d. Nov. 15, 1771.
xiii SARAH, b. March 19, 1687.

3. iii. Jacob Foster (Isaac, Reginald), b. in Ipswich, near Topsfield, Feb. 9, 1662–3; moved to Topsfield, 1686; m. Sarah, daughter of Isaiah Wood, Sept. 12, 1688; d. Sept. 27, 1697; m. 2d, Mary Edwards, May 20, 1700. Mr. and Mrs. Foster were dismissed from the church in Topsfield, Jan. 29, 1718, and admitted to the church in Lebanon, Ct., July 6, 1718.

CHILDREN.

4 i BENJAMIN, bapt. Oct. 6, 1689.
  ii MARY, b. May 13, 1691.
 iii ISAAC, b. March 13, 1701; d. Dec. 23, 1703.
  iv JOHN, b. Sept. 11, 1702; m. Hannah Thorpe, Aug. 26, 1724, and returned to Lebanon,* Ct., where he owned the covenant, 1729. She did the same, 1727.
   v EZEKIEL, bapt. Dec. 31, 1704; d. Oct. 20, 1727, Lebanon, Ct.
  vi MARTHA, bapt. —— 24, 1709.
 vii DAVID, bapt. April 29, 1711; m. Althea ——, Lebanon, Ct.; had 4 children.
viii JONATHAN, b. June 3, 1714; to Lebanon, Ct.

4. iv. Benjamin Foster (Jacob, Isaac, Reginald), b. in Topsfield, Mass., Oct., 1689; m. Sarah, daughter of Ezekiel Woodward,

---

*The home of Jonathan Trumbull, Jr. (Jonathan, Joseph, Dea. John, John Trumble, d. 1657, Cumberland county, England; to Roxbury, Mass., 1639, freeman, 1640, thence to Rowley), b. 1740; Harvard University, 1759: paymaster to the Northern department of the army, 1775 to '78; in 1780 was 1st aid to General Washington, and Secretary; Member of Congress 1789 to '95; Speaker, 1791 to '95; United States Senator, 1795 and '96; Lieut.-Governor of Connecticut, 1796 to '98; and Governor, 1798 to 1809. When in need of ammunition, Washington said "Let us consult Brother Jonathan." And from that mere joke it became a byword, and has since been applied to the whole Yankee nation. John Trumbull (1750–1831), the poet, was a brother.

Jr., and Abigail, in Ipswich, March 15, 1725, and seems to have moved from Essex county, Mass., into Rockingham county, N. H., about 1740, when four of them married, as stated in the Hampstead town records; and in 1760, the old folks, with 2 sons and 2 daughters, moved to Granville, Annapolis county, N. S. Mr. Foster d. the day after landing, and the old lady — an honest, industrious, pious woman — after living 45 years a widow, d. in 1805, aged 104. She used to spin flax on the "little wheel," and when she got tired and faint would make a little hasty-pudding in the skillet, over some coals on the hearth of the old fireplace, saying she " only wanted a few bites to content natur."

CHILDREN.

  i   JUDITH, b. 1726; m. John Chute. See No. 7.
5 ii ISAAC, b. 1728.
6 iii EZEKIEL, b. 1730.
  iv ELIZABETH, b. 1733; m. Francis B. Lecain, 1761, and lived in Annapolis, where he d. 1806, aged 84. Children: (1) Francis, b. 1762; m. Margaret, daughter of Andrew Ritchie. (2) Benjamin, b. 1764; m. Mary, daughter of Nath. Winchester. (3) Nicholas, b. 1765; m. Catherine ———. (4) William, b. 1767; m. Sarah Henshaw, and d. 1830. Francis, Jr., d. 1843.
  v   SARAH, b. 1737; m. Abel Wheelock. See Wheelock.
  vi JEREMIAH, b. 1740; m. Jemima Kent, Jan. 5, 1768. He went to Nova Scotia some years after the older ones went; came back again, and is reported to have settled in Winthrop, Me.

5. v. Isaac Foster (Benjamin, Jacob, Isaac, Reginald), b. in Massachusetts, 1728; m. Mehitable Worthing,* by Rev. Henry True, in Hampstead, N. H., Oct. 31, 1754; moved to Granville, N. S., 1760, and there lived, a hearty old couple, more than half a century. He d. Jan. 29, 1819. She (danced in 1822) d. in 1826, aged 93.

CHILDREN.

7 i BENJAMIN, b. May 24, 1755.   ii JACOB, b. 1657; d. 1759.

---

*Samuel Worthen, or Worthing, m. Mehitable Heath, 1732, and lived in Hampstead, N. H., which was organized into a town in 1749. Mr. Worthen d. Sept., 1756, aged 45. Children: (1) Mehitable, b. Oct. 12, 1733; m. Isaac Foster, 1754. (2) Samuel, b. April 26, 1739; m Deborah Johnson, 1764. (3) Oliver, b. March 11, 1743. (4) Amos, b. Jan. 1, 1746. (5) Mary, b. Sept. 16, 1751. Perhaps more.

Moses Worthen m. Abigail ———, 1744; and had (1) Martha, b. March 12, 1745. (2) Mary, b. March 16, 1747. (3) Samuel, b. Jan. 15, 1749. Abigail, wife of Moses Worthen, received into church fellowship July 4, 1760. "Payed out to Moses Worthen sixteen pounds, old tenor, for his wiffs ceeping of scool." Sandown, 1763.

iii SARAH, b. Oct. 15, 1760; m. John Adams, 1779; had a son James, b. Aug. 4, 1780; m. Eleanor, daughter of John Chute, Jr. See No. 11.
8 iv ISAAC, b. Aug. 24, 1763.
v MEHITABLE, b. March 23, 1766; m. Thomas, son of Isaac and Anna (Thomas) Phinney, Oct. 29, 1786; and lived in Granville. He d. Dec. 16, 1845, aged 80. She d. April 1, 1858. Children: (1) Isaac, b. 1787; m. Sarah Borden, 1819; 7 children. She d. March 5, 1847, aged 57. He d. April 14, 1867. (2) William, b. 1789; m. Rebecca (Goucher) Starratt. (3) Ann, b. 1791; d. 1794. (4) Cynthia, b. 1793; m. Thomas Horsfield, 1825; 3 children; d. June 12, 1863; he d. March 8, 1836. (5) Betsy, b. 1795; d. 1796. (6) Ann, b. 1797; m. William, son of Andrew Walker, 1816; 6 children, and d. Dec. 17, 1878. (7) Walter W., b. 1799; d. 1826. (8) Caroline, b. 1801; m. David Dill, and d. Dec. 13, 1863; he d. 1849, aged 59. (9) Elizabeth, b. 1803; m. Daniel Felch, Jr., March 12, 1833; 6 children; he d. 1868, aged 67. (10) Phineas, b. 1805; m. Jerusha Foster (Isaac, Jr.); 4 children, and d. July 14, 1873.
vi ELIZABETH, b. Dec. 17, 1768; m. Jordon, son of Abednego Ricketson, Dec. 24, 1789, and lived in Granville. She d. July 31, 1795; he m. 2d, Hannah Parker, 1796, and d. 1832, aged 67. Children: (1) Henry, b. 1790; m. Charlotte Thomas, 1814. (2) Phebe, b. 1792; m. Theodore Hill. (3) Sarah, b. 1794; d. young. (4) Abednego, b. 1797; d. about 1814. (5) Betsy, b. 1799; m. Frederick, son of Matthew Roach, from Ireland, 1817; 7 children. (6) Mary. (7) Shadrach, m. Sally E. Thorn, and d. She m. 2d, Henry Blakeslee. (8) Charlotte, m. William R., son of Benjamin Wheelock, Feb. 14, 1827. (9) Miriam. (10) James Parker, m. Eliza, daughter of Michael Bohaker. (11) Ann. (12) Susan, m. Jacob Low.
9 vii SAMUEL, b. Oct. 1, 1770.
10 viii OLIVER, b. May 1, 1773.
11 ix ASA, b. Nov. 24, 1776.
x JAMES, b. Jan. 24, 1780; m. a widow in Massachusetts.*

6. v. Ezekiel Foster (Benjamin, Jacob, Isaac, Reginald), b. in Massachusetts about 1730; m., by David Little, Esq., July 17,

---

*Family of Isaac and Anna (Thomas) Phinney, from Cape Cod to Granville, about 1760. He d May 13, 1785, She d. April 18, 1781. Children:
i Mehitable, b. Jan. 8, 1764; m. Major Ruloffson.
ii Thomas, b. July 1, 1765; m. Mehitable Foster, 1786; 10 children.
iii Lott, b. April 6, 1767; m. Betsy, daughter of Daniel Durland, May 4, 1786; 10 children.
iv Levi, b. Feb. 27, 1769; off to the States.
v Abigail, b. Jan. 17, 1771; m. Capt. Walter Willett.
vi Elijah, b. April 6, 1773; m. Hepzibah Chesly, 1800.
vii Desiah, b. April 22, 1776; m. David, son of Moses Shaw.

1755, Mary Roberts,* Hampstead, N. H.; went to Granville, N. S., with parents, brother Isaac, and two sisters, 1760. She d. July 31, 1765, aged 29. He m. 2d, Ruth Farnsworth, b. 1740 (William, Ebenezer, Matthias, Matthias), Sept. 30, 1770. Dates of death not learned.

CHILDREN.

  i SARAH, b. 1756; d. 1760, Hampstead, N. H.
  ii MARTHA, b. Aug. 13, 1757; m. Benjamin Chute. See No. 12.
12 iii JOHN, b. March 29, 1760.
13 iv EZEKIEL, b. March 30, 1763.
14 v JOSEPH, b. Oct. 18, 1771.
15 vi EZRA F., b. Aug. 1, 1773.

7. vi. Benjamin Foster (Isaac, Benjamin, Jacob, Isaac, Reginald), b. in Hampstead, N. H., May 24, 1755; m. Elizabeth, daughter of Col. Philip Richardson, Jan. 23, 1776, and lived in Granville, N. S. She d. Nov. 28, 1828, aged 70. He m. 2d, Mary Pamelia, daughter of Edward Robinson and Mary Chandler (sister to Richard from England), and widow of Job Park, Nov. 3, 1831, and d. Nov. 13, 1842. She d. 1854, aged 67.

CHILDREN.

  i MEHITABLE, b. May 6, 1778; m. Abram Chute. See No. 21.
  ii ELIZABETH, b. Sept. 1, 1780; m. James Taylor. See Taylor.
16 iii BENJAMIN, b. Aug. 2, 1782.
17 iv SAMUEL, b. Sept. 9, 1784.
  v SUSANNA, b. Aug. 31, 1786; m. Francis Tupper (Charles, Capt. Eliakin, Eliakin, Thomas, Capt. Thomas, Sandwich, England, to Sandwich, America, 1635; d. 1676, aged 98), 1801; had 6 children. He d. Nov. 17, 1842, aged 61. She d. Dec. 15, 1882.
  vi MARY, b. Dec. 29, 1788; m. Samuel Tupper, brother to Francis. He d. April 23, 1817; she m. 2d, Augustus Tupper, another brother, March 25, 1818, and d. Oct. 20, 1849. He d. April 11, 1850.
18 vii ISAAC, b. April 9, 1791.
19 viii ABNER, b. May 9, 1793.
  ix LUCY, b. May 24, 1795; m. William Woodworth. See Woodworth.
20 x SOLOMON, b. Aug. 3, 1797.
  xi PHILIP, b. July 3, 1799; m. Susan, daughter of William Frail, and had a son, William, m. Rebecca A. Fuller.

---

*Daniel Roberds, or Roberts, m. Martha Heath, 1724, and lived in Hampstead, N. H. She d. Aug., 1757, aged 50. They had (1) Daniel, b. 1724; m. Meribah Davis, 1747, and had 3 or 4 children. (2) Dorothy, 1725. (3) Priscilla, 1733. (4) Mary, 1736, m. Ezekiel Foster, 1755. (5) Hannah, 1740. (6) Sarah, 1745, m. Philip Emerson, 1761. (7) Samuel, 1748. Perhaps more.

ALLIED FAMILIES. lvii

  Mrs. Foster d. April 10, 1871, aged 78. He d. Oct. 10, 1890.
xii HELEN F., b. Aug. 3, 1801; d. Dec. 10, 1833.
xiii CATHERINE, b. Nov. 28, 1804; m. Enoch, son of Gardiner Dodge, March 21, 1822; had 4 children, and d. Sept. 18, 1875. He d. May 9, 1868, aged 70, Bridgetown, N. S.

Job Park (whose widow Benjamin Foster m. for his 2d wife) was b. in New York (of parents from England), 1777; went to Nova Scotia in his youth; m. Mary Pamelia Robinson, 1806, and d. in Granville, 1822.

CHILDREN.

i JOB, b. Sept., 1807; m. Pelina Morrison, and had a son, Charles Morrison, b. 1830; became a sea captain. The father drowned April, 1830; and the widow m. Morrison Burns, 1833, St. John, N. B.
ii MARY SISSILIA, b. Nov. 20, 1809; m. John C. Farnsworth.
iii NELSON, b. April 8, 1812; m. Eliza, daughter of Henry Ricketson; 11 children. He d. in Salem, Mass., May 7, 1892.
iv EDMUND, b. May 22, 1814; m. Caroline, daughter of Esq. Payson; 7 children.
v FITZ WM., b. Christmas, 1816; m. Pamelia Woodworth, 1855; d. in Salem, Dec. 9, 1893.
vi JOHN EDW., b. March, 1819; m. Azuba Foster, 1846; 7 children.

8. vi. Isaac Foster (Isaac, Benjamin, Jacob, Isaac, Reginald), b. in Granville, N. S., Aug. 24, 1763; m. Betsy, daughter of William Gilliatt, 1790; moved to Wilmot, 1802, where she d. He d. in Clarence, June 3, 1852.

CHILDREN.

i CHARLES, b. about 1795; m. Mary Banks (Henry, Joshua, Joshua, Moses, John, Richard), 1820; m. 2d, Mary Ann Green, daughter of a Quaker preacher. Children: (1) Elnora, m. David Edgeley. (2) Eliza, m. Isaac, son of George Banks. (3) Maria, m. Joshua, son of John Ray. (4) Abba, m. David Morrison. (5) Mary, m. Henry, brother to Silas Jackson. (6) Louise, m. Isaac Moore. (7) Becca, m. William Neily. (8) Emma, m. Arthur, son of Benjamin Rumsey. (9) Norman, m. Agnes, daughter of George Burbridge.
ii MARY, b. 1797; m. Charles, son of John Dunn, from England, and d. 1840. He d. 1873, aged 78. Children: (1) Susan, m. Ambrose, son of Ichabod Corbit. (2) Elizabeth, m. Stephen T., son of Samuel Foster. (3) Isaac Foster, b. Oct. 9, 1824; m. Eliza J., daughter of David

ALLIED FAMILIES.

  Spinney; 3 children; to Lynn, Mass., 1869; to Cliftondale, Oct., 1887. (4) Charles H., m. Eunice, daughter of Solomon Bowlby.
- iii BETSY M., b. 1799; m. Daniel Vaughan.
- iv HANNAH, b. 1801; m. Edward, son of Samuel Foster.
- v ANN, b. Aug. 20, 1803; d. in Clarence, Sept. 15, 1889.
- vi ARCHIE G., b. 1805; killed in 1811.
- vii JERUSHA, b. April 7, 1807; m. Phineas, son of Thomas Phinney, March 15, 1832.
- viii WILLIAM, b. Dec. 27, 1813; m. Hannah Huntington (Ebenezer, Ezra, Caleb, Caleb, Lieut. Samuel, John, William, Simon, over from Norwich, England, 1633; d. on the way, and buried in the sea), and had (1) Elizabeth, m. William Rumsey. (2) B. Watson, m. Melintha Douglass. (3) Emma Lovina, m. Major, son of Daniel Messenger; m. 2d, John W. Jenness, and lives in Lynn. (4) Lewis Johnson, m.; Cincinnati, Ohio. (5) William Bartlett, m. Alice Zaar. (6) Delacy E., m. Sophia, daughter of John A. and Mary J. (Chute) Vroom. (7) Annie Laurie, m. Burton Bowlby, Lawrence, Mass.

9. vi. Samuel Foster, another brother, b. in Granville, Oct. 1, 1770; m. Betsy Wilson.

CHILDREN.

- i EDWARD W., m. Hannah, daughter of Isaac Foster, Jr., 1826.
- ii MARGARET, m. Ariel Corbit.
- iii CLARK.
- iv MARY, m. Edward Bruce.
- v ZIPPORAH, m. Edward Gilliatt.
- vi MATILDA, m. John Millner.
- vii ELIZA, m. Richard Armstrong.
- viii JOHN, drowned.
- ix CORBIT, m.

10. vi. Oliver Foster, another brother, b. in Granville, May 1, 1773; m. Cynthia, daughter of Israel Fellows, Nov. 13, 1796; lived in Granville. She d. Nov. 8, 1813; he m. 2d, Betsy, daughter of Daniel Saunders, Jan. 1, 1817, and d. June 5, 1827.

CHILDREN.

- i DAVID, b. June 19, 1797; m. Mary Clark, 1827; 7 children. She d. Feb. 23, 1840, aged 37; he m. 2d, Azuba Wheelock (Joseph, Obadiah, etc.), and d. Dec. 27, 1862. See Wheelock.
- ii CYNTHIA, b. March 24, 1799; m. Job Randall. See Randall.
- iii ARCHIBALD MARSDEN, b. April 14, 1801; m. Eliza Bent.
- iv ANN, b. July 1, 1803; m. William (b. 1794), son of Fred Fitch.

ALLIED FAMILIES. lix

- v MARIA, b. Aug. 28, 1807; d. April 25, 1822.
- vi JERUSHA, b. May 19, 1809; m. Henry, son of William Ruffee, July 18, 1829; had 3 children.
- vii ROBERT H., b. March 5, 1812; m. Elizabeth Hall (John, John, William), and d. 1849.
- viii SUSAN, b. Nov. 8, 1813; m. Israel, son of Joseph Bent.
- ix OLIVER, b. 1817; m. Betsy Woodbury.
- x ISRAEL, b. 1819; m. Minetta, daughter of Asa Foster, widow of Obadiah Morse, Jr. She d. Jan. 2, 1890, aged 77; he m. 2d, Ann Manning, widow of Ansley Brown, and d. Oct., 1892, aged 73.
- xi MARY ANN, b. 1821; m. William Morse; 2d, J. M. Brown; 4 children; Lawrencetown, N. S.
- xii DANIEL J., b. 1824.
- xiii CHARLES WILLIAM, b. 1826.

11. vi. Asa Foster, the youngest brother, b. in Granville, Nov. 24, 1776; m. Roby, or Rhoda, daughter of Thomas and Sarah (Chute) Hicks, by Rev. T. H. Chipman, July 26, 1798, and lived a mile below Bridgetown; farmer and miller; d. Sept. 20, 1854. She d. July 1, 1863, aged 81½ years.

CHILDREN.

- i HARRIET, b. April 26, 1799; m. Nathan, son of Amos and Susan (Chute) Randall, Jan. 21, 1819; and d. Aug. 21, 1889. He d. 1864, aged 73.
- ii IRENE, b. March 17, 1802; m. Charles, son of Maurice Peters, Jan. 11, 1826; 6 children; d. Oct. 9, 1865. He d.
- iii AVISA, b. Oct. 12, 1804; m. Capt. James Peters, brother to Charles, 1821, and d. 1880. He d. 1885.
- iv WILLIAM WORTHING, b. Aug. 15, 1806; m. Harriet Calvert, 1837. She d. 1840; he m. 2d, Hannah Wheelock[7] (Asaph, Capt. Obadiah, Obadiah, Obadiah, Benjamin, Rev. Ralph), March, 1843, and d. July 20, 1873. She d. Dec. 24, 1890, in her 86th year.
- v SUSAN ANN, b. Sept. 16, 1808; m. Jacob, son of Benjamin Foster, Jr., of Cornwallis, 1833, and d. He d. March, 1892, aged 82.
- vi LOUISE JANE, b. May 4, 1811; m. Binea Chute. See No. 40.
- vii MINETTA, b. Feb. 7, 1813; m. Obadiah Morse, Jr., Sept. 11, 1834. See No. 7.
- viii OLIVER G., b. Dec. 11, 1816; m. Eliphal A. Chute (see No. 37), and d. in Bayham, Ont., April 8, 1894.
- ix S. MATILDA, b. Dec. 16, 1818; m. J. E. Chute. See No. 41.
- x LEAH, b. Jan. 27, 1820; m. J. M. Chute. See No. 109.
- xi ELIZA, b. March 5, 1823; m. Charles, son of Theodore Hill, Jan. 30, 1850, and had 6 children; live in Lynn, Mass.

ALLIED FAMILIES.

12. vi. John Foster (Ezekiel, Benjamin, Jacob, Isaac, Reginald), b. in Hampstead, N. H., March 29, 1760; taken to Granville, N. S., that year; m. Elizabeth, daughter of Abednego Ricketson, Dec. 26, 1781; lived in Aylesford, and in that town, Wilmot, and Nictaux preached the gospel of Christ in the Methodist church. He d. Sept. 29, 1827. His widow d. April 7, 1852, aged 89.

CHILDREN.

i PHEBE, b. May 28, 1783; d. June 6.

ii JOHN, b. April 11, 1784; m. Sarah Brown, July 14, 1813, and d. Feb. 21, 1857. Children: (1) Willis, b. 1814; m. Charlotte Baker, 9 children; 2d, Margaret Ryer, 6 children. (2) Ezra, b. 1816; m. Elizabeth Spinney. (3) Marsden, b. 1818; m. Mary, daughter of Fred Foster; 2d, Eleanor Middlemas, widow of Martin Gates. (4) Elizabeth, b. 1820; m. Edward, son of George Orpin. (5) Mary A., b. 1822; m. John Earl. (6) John W., b. 1824; m. Mary Ann, daughter of Matthew Clark; 6 children. (7) Phebe, b. 1827; m. William Selfridge, Jr.

iii RUTH, b. Aug. 12, 1787; m. Walter Wilkins, May 21, 1807; had 11 children, and d. Nov. 24, 1865.

iv PHEBE, b. Jan. 28, 1790; m. James Roach, 1823; 4 children.

v FREDERICK, b. May 13, 1792; m. Rachel Benedict, daughter of Jabez, 1814; 5 children, and was killed by ice falling on him on the Bay Shore, April 16, 1825. Children: (1) Elizabeth, b. 1815; m. John Warwick. (2) William, b. 1817; m. Mary Jane Roach (Dea. Zebina, Matthew, Patrick). (3) Charles, b. 1819; m. Mary Jane Woodbury. (4) Mary, b. 1821; m. Marsden Foster. (5) James, b. 1823; m. Charlotte, daughter of Wm. Patterson.

vi WILLIS, b. Nov. 15, 1794; m. Susanna, daughter of William Pierce, 1826; m. 2d, Nancy, daughter of Ezra F. Foster, Jan. 20, 1835, and d. Jan. 29, 1875. Susanna d. July 12, 1834; aged 42. Children: (1) George, b. 1827; m. Adelaide, daughter of Ezra Foster. (2) John, b. 1830; m. Susan, daughter of Zebulon Neiley. (3) Susanna, b. 1834; d. Oct. 9. Mrs. Foster d. July 15, 1834; he m. 2d, Nancy, daughter of E. F. Foster, Jan. 20, 1835, and had (4) William Rufus L., b. Nov. 15, 1835.

vii ELIZABETH, b. Dec. 23, 1796; m. James, son of William Pierce, Oct. 10, 1817; 3 children, and d. Dec. 30, 1825; he m. 2d, Nancy Patterson. 1828; 6 children.

viii HENRY, b. May 29, 1799; m. Jane Truesdell, March 15, 1827, and d. Nov. 5, 1870.

ix EZEKIEL, b. July 26, 1801; m. Eliza, daughter of John and Margera (Barss) Dugan, Sept. 5, 1822, and lived in Aylesford, a farmer. She d. April 21, 1878, aged 72. He d. April 21, 1889. Children: (1) Mary Ann, b. 1824;

ALLIED FAMILIES.

    m. Ingersoll Patterson. (2) Albert Desbrisay, b. 1828; m. Martha Larkin, Elizabeth Parsons, Margaret Reed, and Agnes Neily. (3) Susan, b. 1831; m. Willett Chute. See No. 95. (4) Elizabeth, b. 1838; m. (5) Lucy, b. 1842; m. Charles Proctor. (6) Lydia, b. 1849; m. Charles Doyle; to Mass., 1872, and live in Lynnfield.

x MARY ANN, b. Jan. 10, 1804; m. Zebulon Neily, Jan. 1, 1829; 4 children, and d. Jan. 9, 1871.

xi BAYARD, b. July 8, 1808; m. Mary Ann, daughter of Ezra F. Foster, and d. Aug. 12, 1885. She d. Oct. 5, 1879, aged 75.

13. vi. Ezekiel Foster, Jr., brother to the preceding, b. in Granville, March 30, 1773; m. Elizabeth, daughter of Joseph Dring, May, 1803, and d. Aug. 26, 1829. She m. 2d, Benjamin Rhodes, and d. Jan. 17, 1854, aged 69.

CHILDREN.

i THOMAS, b. 1804; m. Mary Wheelock[6] (Benjamin, Abel, Joseph, Gershom, Rev. Ralph), Feb. 12, 1827; had Elizabeth, Sarah Ann, Louisa, and Ezekiel B.); Southbridge, Mass. She d. Aug. 16, 1859.

ii EZRA, b. 1807; m. Hannah Bohaker (Michael, Andreas, from Germany before the Revolution), Nov. 8, 1831; 6 children. He d. April, 1880.

iii ELIZABETH ANN, b. 1809; m. Abel Wheelock, brother to Mary, who m. Thomas Foster, and had a son, Joseph Israel, b. Jan. 1, 1828, m. Elizabeth, daughter of Thomas Foster. She d., and he m. 2d, Ruth Bent.

iv MARY F., b. 1811; m. William Banks, and d. Jan. 1, 1877.

v TAMER, b. 1814; m. Benjamin Randall; 4 children.

vi ATHALINDA, b. 1816; d. May 9, 1846.

vii ADOLPHUS W., b. 1818; m. Caroline, daughter of Jonathan Woodbury; 4 children.

viii ISRAEL, b. 1821; d. 1822.

ix MARTHA, b. 1824; m. Rev. Isaac, son of Lewis McAnn, of Vermont.

14. vi. Joseph Foster, another brother, b. in Granville, Oct. 18, 1771; m. Jane, daughter of James and Mary (Barnes) Ray, Nov. 25, 1795; and lived at Nictaux, Annapolis county, N. S.

CHILDREN.

i RUTH, b. 1796; killed by the falling of a tree, March, 1814. Joseph Woodbury (Foster, Dr. Jonathan from Portsmouth, N. H.) wrote a poem on her death as follows:

Young people all, pray lend an ear,
And don't forbear to shed a tear;
While to your minds a scene I bring,
That happened early in the Spring
The last of March, the sky serene,
In eighteen hundred and fourteen,
This tragedy was brought to view,
And worse than many ever knew.

One afternoon two damsels fair[*]
Did walk abroad to take the air,
When turning back for home that day,
Death took one of them for his prey.
A tree was suffered from above
To fall upon this harmless dove;
She fell beneath that awful rod,
And had no time to call on God.

The ground was covered o'er with blood,
That from her mouth ran in a flood;
And tears did melt the snow around,
While mourning made the woods resound.
Her paren's wept, but all in vain,
Their sighs can't bring her back again;
Her friends and kindred, all as one,
Their much belovèd now bemoan.

The youth[†] on whom her tho'ts were bent,
And in deep mourning did lament
The loss of his intended bride,
Who now is severed from his side.
But she has gone and left him here
To mourn for her, year after year;
The deep impressions, he will find,
Will never be worn out of mind.

Her young companions now are left,
Of a good friend they are bereft;
This should to all a warning be—
Make ready for eternity.
How short our lives! how brief, alas!
Peter[‡] compares them to the grass,
The grass doth wither and decay,
The flower thereof doth fade away.

This was the text upon that day,
The damsel mingled with her clay;
When gloomy looks with griefs attend
The faces of her many friends.
Now to conclude — It was her lot —
So let this scene be ne'er forgot,
The awful tree! that shocking blow!
The fatal spot will ne'er outgrow.

 ii Ezekiel, b. 1799; m. Mary A. Waters, June 21, 1821; 5 children.
 iii Jane, b. 1801; m. Abel Wheelock (John, Abel, Joseph, Gershom, Rev. Ralph); 8 children. See Wheelock.

[*] Sally Banks was the other.   [†] Robert, son of John Eaton.   [‡] 1. Peter, 1 : 24.

- iv HANNAH, b. 1802; m. Newcomb Bent.
- v JOSEPH, b. 1805; m. Zilpah, daughter of Michael Martin, the singing teacher.
- vi JOHN M., b. 1807; m. Lucilla, daughter of Fairfield, son of Dr. Jonathan Woodbury. She d. 1870, aged 64.
- vii SOPHIA ANN, b. 1807; m. Edward, son of Michael Martin, He m. two other wives, and d. Feb., 1892, aged 92.
- viii EZRA, b. Sept., 1814; m. Mary Ann Burkitt, and Mercy Ann Van Buskirk.

15. vi. Ezra Farnsworth Foster, the youngest brother to the preceding, b. in Granville, Aug. 1, 1773; m. Susanna, daughter of John and Eunice (Fellows) Troop, Jan. 24, 1798, and lived in Aylesford.

CHILDREN.

- i NANCY, b. Jan. 25, 1799; m. Willis, son of John Foster, Jan. 20, 1833.
- ii GILBERT, b. Sept. 16, 1800; d. about 1865.
- iii RUFUS, b. June 3, 1802; m. Christiana Tough, Aug. 4, 1838; 2 sons.
- iv MARY ANN, b. April 22, 1804; m. Bayard Foster.
- v WILLIAM YOUNG, b. May 22, 1806; m. Minetta, daughter of Seth Leonard, 1835, Bridgetown.
- vi GEORGE, b. Aug. 18, 1808; d. about 1870.
- vii LUCY, b. Aug. 2, 1810; m. William Tough.
- viii EUNICE, b. Oct. 25, 1812; m. Fred. Vroom (George, John, Hendrick, Hendrick, Cornelius Peter, of New York about 1650), June 15, 1836; 5 children.
- ix ISRAEL, b. May 8, 1815; d. Dec. 18, 1817.
- x F. ELIZA, b. July 6, 1817; m. William Vroom, brother to Frederick; 3 children.
- xi SUSAN, b. July 1, 1822.

16. vii. Benjamin Foster (Benjamin, Isaac, Benjamin, Jacob, Isaac, Reginald), b. in Granville, Aug. 2, 1782; m. Mary, daughter of Samuel Randall, 1804, and lived in Cornwallis, Kings county, a good old farmer; d. Aug. 5, 1882, aged 100 years, 3 days. She d. March, 1871, aged 85.

CHILDREN.

- i ABRAM, b. Aug. 23, 1805; m. Rachel Morton, 1825; 6 children and d. July, 1886, New Gloucester, Me.; he d. 1880.
- ii ISAAC, b. Oct. 27, 1806; m. Rebecca, daughter of Dea. Stephen Taylor, and had (1) Mary Olivia, m. John L. Sandford. (2) Robert, d. (3) Rev. Joseph Morton, b. 1833; m. Elizabeth Johnson, Jane Baker. (4) Rev. Paoli, b. 1835; m. Addie, daughter of Dr. Crocker. (5)

ALLIED FAMILIES.

Stephen Taylor, b. 1836, to Cal. (6) Carr, b. 1838; d. young. (7) Jacob, b. April 16, 1840; m. Henrietta, daughter of Donald and Lettie (Parker) McPherson, Jan. 1, 1866, Brookfield, N. S.; 7 children. Mr. Foster, a blacksmith, went from Aylesford, N. S. to Methuen, Mass., Oct., 1889; to Watertown, 1890. (8) Esther, b. 1842; m. Anthony Stephens. (9) Benjamin, b. 1843; d. 1844. (10) Benjamin P., b. 1845; m. —— ——, to Fall River, Kan. (11) Sikes, d. young. (12) Lillia, b. 1848; m. George, son of Christopher Randall. See Randall.

iii JACOB, b. April 27, 1810; m. Susan Ann, daughter of Asa Foster, Dec. 23, 1835, and d. June 10, 1892.

iv WILLIAM W., b. Aug. 2, 1812; m. Sarah Marshall (David, Isaac), and had a daughter, Anna.

v ROBERT, b. Dec. 13, 1813; m. Martha Morton; had 2 children. She d. June 25, 1855, aged 34; he m. 2d, Elizabeth, daughter of Elijah Taylor, and had a daughter, Martha.

vi EDWARD CLARK, b. May 27, 1817; m. Harriet Tupper (John, Miner, Elias, Eliakim, Thomas, Capt. Thomas, of Sandwich, England, to Sandwich, Mass., 1635; d. 1676), Oct., 1847, and is postmaster and merchant at Berwick, N. S. Children: (1) John Rupert, b. 1849; m. Isabel McDonald, 1879. (2) Miner Tupper, b. 1850; m. Sarah Randolph. (3) Mary Eliza, b. 1852; m. Lorenzo F. Darling, lives at Riverside, Cal. (4) Thomas Harris, b. 1856; d. 1857. (5) George Edward, b. 1861; m. Lora F. Underhill, in Boston. (6) Douglass Benjamin, b. 1864; m. Addie Cole, a descendant of John Hopkins (over in the *Mayflower*, 1620) and lives in Somerville, Mass.

17. vii. **Samuel Foster**, brother to the preceding, b. in Granville, N. S., Sept. 9, 1784; m. Lydia Chute (John, John, Lionel, James, James, Lionel), March 17, 1805, and lived at Hampton, Annapolis county; a farmer. She d. Dec. 20, 1833, aged 49, nearly; he m. 2d, Catherine, daughter of Thomas Crips, Dec. 4, 1835, and d. July 29, 1879. She d. April 10, 1881, aged 70.

CHILDREN.

i THOMAS, b. 1807; d. 1818.

ii SAMUEL, b. April 22, 1809; m. Mary Marshall, 1830.

iii J. VAN BUREN, b. Feb. 17, 1811; m. Elizabeth Marshall, 1835.

iv LUCY, b. Sept. 30, 1813; m. John Sampson, 1835; m. 2d, James Taylor, Jr., 1845.

v DEA. HARRIS, b. June 28, 1815; m. Martha Chute, see No. 44; m. 2d, Lavinia, (Cogswell) Chute, see No. 134; m. 3d, Mary A. (Brown) Chute, see No. 251. Harris Foster, Esq., is a merchant and a Baptist deacon at Hampton.

ALLIED FAMILIES.

- vi   RUBY ANN, b. April 12, 1817; d. 1893; m. William Henry Maccaboy, April 23, 1840; 6 children; lives on the North Mountain, near Annapolis.
- vii   ABIGAIL, b. Feb. 1, 1819; m. Abram Brooks Smith, 1838.
- viii   DEA. STEPHEN TAYLOR, b. Oct. 20, 1821; m. Elizabeth, daughter of Charles Dunn, son of John from England, and d. July 11, 1857.
- ix   ABNER, b. March 3, 1823; m. Louise, daughter of Josiah and Sarah (Randall) Dodge, 1846.
- x   SUSAN, b. May 9, 1826.
- xi   JACOB, b. Feb. 29, 1828; m. Ann McCabe; m. 2d, Theresa Eagleson.
- xii   LYDIA, b. April 6, 1836; m. James, son of Sylvanus Snow.
- xiii   THOMAS H., b. July 20, 1837; m. Elizabeth Ann, daughter of Benjamin and Eliza M. (Chute) Foster, May 12, 1861 (see 44); had 9 children. One, Dudley, b. 1877, only 27 inches high.
- xiv   JOSEPH J., b. Feb. 28, 1839; drowned June 30, 1860.
- xv   MELISSA, b. Dec. 6, 1841; m. Ingram, son of Sylvanus Snow.
- xvi   HENRIETTA, b. Aug. 16, 1842; m. John, son of Parker Viditoe.
- xvii   DAVID M., b. June 24, 1844; m. Henrietta Dunn; 2d, Adelia Foster, sister to Elizabeth Ann.
- xviii   ALONZO, b. March 10, 1846; m. Fidelia Glass, April 16, 1871; had 8 children.
- xix   ELLEN, b. Feb. 16, 1848; m. Gilbert Viditoe (Parker, Jesse).
- xx   ADONIRAM JUDSON, b. Dec. 7, 1851; m. Susan, daughter of George Walter Wilson.

18. vii. Isaac Foster (Benjamin, Isaac, Benjamin, Jacob, Isaac, Reginald), b. in Granville, April 9, 1791; m. Elizabeth, daughter of John Patterson, Oct. 6, 1814; and lived on the Bay Shore, near Hampton; d. Nov. 19, 1867. She d. April 8, 1868, aged 76.

CHILDREN.

- i   JAMES P., b. July 7, 1815; m. Mary T., daughter of Phineas Graves, 1853.
- ii   BENJAMIN, b. June 21, 1816; m. Eliza M. Chute. See No. 44.
- iii   ELIZABETH, b. Nov. 22, 1817; m. Benjamin Rumsey.
- iv   AUGUSTUS, b. Nov. 23, 1819; d. about 1850.
- v   AMBROSE, b. April 16, 1821; m. Martha Knowles of Liverpool, N. S.; m. 2d, Ellen Holland, Lawrence, Mass.
- vi   WILLIAM, b. April 26, 1824; m. Hannah Bogert, and d. 1890.
- vii   PHILIP R., b. May 16, 1826; m. Martha Hogan; 6 children.
- viii   JOHN, b. June 1, 1828; m. Diadama, daughter of Josiah

Spurr, and had Zebuda and Dawson. He m. 2d, Harriet, daughter of William and Sarah (Chute) Marshall. See No. 13.

ix MARY J., b. June 1, 1830; m. Fred Benedict, 1851; m. 2d, Thomas Roland.

x LOUISE, b. May 22, 1834; d. in Lynn, April 6, 1894; m. Jacob E. R. Farnsworth, 1861. See Farnsworth.

xi MARIA, b. Dec. 23, 1837; m. Peter White; 2d, Napoleon Wood. Live in Lynn.

19. vii. Abner Foster, another brother, b. May 9, 1793; m. Sarah, daughter of Benjamin Wheelock, Oct. 29, 1818, and lived in Granville. She d. Feb. 3, 1838, aged 44; he m. 2d, Katie Elliott, and d. Aug. 12, 1875. She d. June 20, 1880, aged 85.

CHILDREN.

i AMBROSE, b. 1820; d. 1821.

ii MARY ELIZABETH, b. Nov. 3, 1821; m. Elijah Phinney[7], (James, Zaccheus, Benjamin, John, John, John, about 1630.)

iii ABEL, b. Aug. 28, 1823; m. Evaline Young.

iv HELEN, b. Nov. 28, 1828; m. John Newcomb, son of John, Jr.

v CATHARINE, b. Aug. 11, 1830; d. Jan., 1894; lived on the old Chute place, 2 miles below Bridgetown.

20. vii. Solomon F. Foster, the youngest brother, b Aug. 3, 1797; m. Susan Phinney (Zaccheus, Benjamin, John, John, John), Aug. 1, 1821, and lived in Granville; d. Jan. 29, 1862. She d. Sept. 6, 1884, aged 82.

CHILDREN.

i ANN, b. May 24, 1823; m. David, son of John Hall, Jr.

ii MARTHA, b. Nov. 28, 1825; m. James Cropley.

iii ZACHARIAH, b. 1829; m. Hannah Saunders.

iv ZERUAH, b. 1833; d. 1852.

GATES.

1. i. Stephen Gates, of Hingham, came over from England in the ship, *Diligent*, with wife and two children, 1638, and went to Lancaster; was made a freeman, 1653; to Cambridge, 1656; Constable, 1657; d. 1662. His wife Ann m. 2d, Richard Woodward of Watertown, April 18, 1663, and d. in Stow, 1683. (Richard Woodward, aged 45, and wife Rose, aged 50, Ipswich, England; to Watertown, Mass., 1634; 2 sons, George and John. Rose d. 1662, aged 80; he m. 2d, Ann Hill, widow of Stephen Gates, and d. Feb. 16, 1665, aged 76.)

CHILDREN.

    i   ELIZABETH, b. in England; m. John Lazell, 1649.
    ii MARY, b. in England; m. John Maynard (over before 1638), April 5, 1658; 11 children; he d. 1711.
    iii STEPHEN, b. about 1640; m. Sarah, probably daughter of George Woodward, and lived in Cambridge, Boston, Marlboro', and Stow; had 8 children.
    iv THOMAS, b. about 1642; m. Elizabeth, daughter of Edmund Freeman, 1670, and lived in Sudbury, Marlboro', and Stow; d. 1707; had 8 children.
2 v   SIMON, b. about 1645.

2. ii. Simon Gates (Stephen), b. Lancaster, Worcester county, Mass., 1645; m. Margaret ——, and lived in Cambridge, Lancaster, 1686, and Muddy River; d. 1707.

CHILDREN.

    i   ABIGAIL, b. 1671; m. Nathaniel Sparhawk.
    ii   SIMON, b. 1673; d. 1675.
    iii SIMON, b. 1675; m. Sarah Woods, 1710, lived in Marlboro', and d. 1735.
    iv   GEORGE, b. 1678; d. 1679.
3 v   AMOS, b. 1680.
    vi   JONATHAN, b. 1683; m. Persis——, lived in Cambridge and Worcester.
    vii SAMUEL, b. Aug. 11, 1685.
    viii MARGARET, b. Aug. 13, 1689; m. James How.

3. iii. Amos Gates (Simon, Stephen), b. about 1680, in Cambridge; m. 1703, Hannah (b. 1681), daughter of Samuel Oldham (by his wife, Hannah Dana, whom he m. 1670), and settled in Brookline; thence to Cambridge, and bought 100 acres of Edward Wilson, in 1729, for £650—the Charles Trowbridge Farm—where he settled; was a Selectman; d. 1754.

CHILDREN.

    i   HANNAH, b. 1706; m. John Edmunds, Newton.
    ii   MARGARET, b. 1708; m. Thomas Spring, 1729, Newton.
    iii ABIGAIL, b. 1710; m. Jonathan Peerson, Andover.
    iv   MARY, b. 1712; m. Nehemiah Wright, 1733, Framingham.
    v   CAPT. AMOS, b. 1714; m. Mary, daughter of John Trowbridge, 1744; 12 children; d. 1800. She d. 1798.

ALLIED FAMILIES.

    iii RUTH, m. John, son of David and Amy (Payson) Randall; 12 children; all d. young.
    iv MARY, m. Alex. Clark; 4 or 5 children; lived on Stronach Mountain.
    v ELLA, m. Samuel Miller; he m. 2d, Lydia Winner.
16 vi OLDHAM.
    vii RACHEL, d. about 1822.
    viii DANIEL, m. Harriet, daughter of Stephen Jefferson, and had Rachel, Theresa, Charlotte, Daniel, and Harriet.
    ix ELIZA, d. a young woman.
    x EDWARD, m. Sarah, daughter of John Hayes, and had Frances, Sarah, Elizabeth, Lavenia, and John.

7. v. John Gates, another brother, b. 1756; m. Judith Baker, and lived at Nictaux, Annapolis county, N. S., a farmer; d. 1841. She d. 1837, aged 76.

CHILDREN.

17 i LIEUT. JAMES, b. 1783.
18 ii ELIAS, b. 1785.
19 iii JACOB, b. March 7, 1788.
    iv AZUBA, b. 1789; m. Ward Wheelock (Elias, Obadiah, Obadiah, Benjamin, Rev. Ralph), 1804, and had 9 children.
    v ANN, m. Jonathan, son of Austin Smith; 11 children.
    vi SUSANNA, m. William Pierce, Jr., 7 children.
20 vii SILAS.

8. v. Oldham Gates, Jr., b. 1765; m. Rachel, daughter of George Stronach, and lived on the "Gates Mountain," in Wilmot; had 2 children; then she d. He m. 2d, Eleanor Slocomb (Capt. John, John, Simon of Wrentham, Norfolk county, Mass., 1700), Jan. 13, 1814, and d. 1850, aged 85. She d. Aug. 22, 1849, aged 59.

CHILDREN.

    i GEORGE, b. 1807; m. Louisa (1840–91), daughter of Isaac Landers, Sen., and d. June, 1871. Children: (1) Ratchford, b. 1835; d. 1856. (2) Frances, b. 1837; d. 1857. (3) Amos, b. 1841; m. Jane, daughter of Willis Foster; to Danvers, 1891. (4) William, b. 1843; d. 1845. (5) John Scott, m. Ida Graham; to Danvers, 1891.
    ii RACHEL, m. Samuel, son of Richard Bowlby; 4 children.
    iii LAVINIA, b. Jan. 3, 1815; m. John, son of Richard and Betsy (Hawksworth) Bowlby, and had Sarah, Eleanor, and Sidney.
    iv MARIA, b. Sept. 5, 1816; m. John H. Potter (John, Rev. Israel, Joseph, Joseph, Ephraim, Robert, Robert, Nicholas of Lynn, 1633), of Clements; 6 children. See Potter.

ALLIED FAMILIES.   lxxi

- v WILLIAM, b. 1818; m. Sarah E., daughter of Ambrose Gates; m. 2d, Susan, daughter of Wm. Hawkins.
- vi AMOS, b. 1820; thrown from a horse and killed July 23, 1848.
- vii SARAH E., b. 1822; m. William Van Buskirk (Jerry, John, Lawrence); 2 sons.
- viii CALEB, b. 1824; m. Anna, daughter of Andreas Bohaker, Jr., and lived in Wilmot. One son, Andreas, m. Bessie Ruggles. Caleb Gates was the proprietor of "Life of Man Bitters" (said to have been invented by his mother); he d., and his wife m. 2d, Hugh Chambers.
- ix SUSAN, b. 1827; m. George, son of Isaac Roach.
- x JOHN SLOCOMB, b. 1830; m.

9. v. Samuel Gates, another brother, b. 1772; m. Sarah, daughter of William Marshall, July 16, 1797; lived in Wilmot; d. July 24, 1830. She d. Aug. 5, 1853, aged 77.

CHILDREN.

- i ELIZABETH, b. July 16, 1799; m. Dea. Williard Graves, 1818; 13 children; d. 1878. He d. 1858.
- ii AMBROSE, b. Dec. 20, 1802; m. Rachel, daughter of John Cropley, 1830; 11 children; d. 1858. She d. April, 1853, aged 44.
- iii AMORET, b. Jan. 26, 1804; m. Edward, son of Joseph Brown; 2 children; d. 1840; he m. 2d, Irene, daughter of Joseph Neily, 1842, and d. March, 1885.
- iv SAMUEL, b. Aug. 8, 1807; m. and went off to the West.
- v WILLIAM, b. Sept. 26, 1810; m. Mary, daughter of John Clark, had 5 or 6 children; moved to Michigan, 1842.
- vi WILLETT, b. Aug. 25, 1814; m. Mary, daughter of Joseph Neily, 1844; 7 children; d. July 30, 1860.
- vii SARAH ANN, b. Dec. 18, 1819; m. Daniel, son of Enoch Wood; 7 children; he d. June, 1884.

10. vi. John Gates (Jonas, Capt. Oldham, Amos, Simon, Stephen), b. in Wilmot, N. S., about 1785; m. Elizabeth Fales, lived near Malvern Square, and d. about 1835. She d. about 1850.

CHILDREN.

- i RUTH, m. Levi, son of Lot Phinney. She d. He m. 2d, Betsy Marshall (William, Isaac).
- ii ANN, m. Thomas, son of Richard Bowlby.
- iii CAROLINE, m. Joseph, son of Stephen Goucher.
- iv JOSEPH DIMOCK, m. Eliza, daughter of James and Rachel (Harris) Ray.
- v BURTON, d. young.
- vi ENOCH, b. 1825; m. Mary Eliza Marshall (William, Wil-

liam, Isaac), and had (1) Rev. George O., Baptist minister, St. John, N. B. (2) Bella L., at Colorado Springs, Col. (3) James A. (4) Rev. E. Lewis, b. March 23, 1863, Baptist minister, Fiskdale, Mass. (5) J. Macauley, also in Colorado.

vii EVALINE, m. George Phinney, and had George and Lewis.
viii MARY, m. Oliver, son of Job Randall.
ix ELIJAH, m. Eliza, daughter of John Eagan.
x HEPZIBAH, m. John, son of Sam Spinney.

11. vi. Thomas Gates, another brother, m. Ann Van Buskirk (Garrett, Lawrence), June 18, 1804, and lived in Aylesford; d. in May, 1838, aged 50. She went to Yarmouth, Ont., about 1840; m. 2d, David Sibley (his 2d wife), 1845, and lived in Bayham, near Port Buswell; d. in 1849, aged 63. Mr. Sibley d. 1850, aged 76.

CHILDREN.

i HANDLEY CHIPMAN, b. June 15, 1805; m. Mary Marshall (Obadiah, Solomon).
ii MEHITABLE, b. Oct. 2, 1806; m. Oliver Brown, Margaretville; 2d, Joseph Borden.
iii PHEBE, b. June 10, 1808; m. William Cook.
iv BATHSHEBA, b. March 15, 1800; m. Elijah Downey and d.; he m. 2d, Hepsy (Gates) Stronach.
v THOMAS A., b. March 6, 1812; m. Eliza Downey.
vi ELIZABETH, b. March 25, 1814; m. John Baker, Jr.
vii HENRY, b. Dec. 7, 1815; m.
viii ALBERTIS, b. Feb. 3, 1818; m. in Maine.
ix GEORGE NEILY, b. Feb. 23, 1820; m. in Maine.
x REV. LAWRENCE B., b. 1823; m. twice; d. 1890.
xi SUSAN, b. 1827; m. Geo. Baynton, 1847, in Ontario, and d.

12. vi. Joseph Gates, another brother, m. Hulda Brown, 1812; lived in Wilmot. She d. about 1841, aged 50; he d. about 1860, aged 70.

CHILDREN.

i ABRAM, } d. young men.
ii ISAAC,
iii JACOB, m. Mary Wood; 2 children.
iv HELEN, m. Joseph Brown, Jr.
v SARAH, m. John Roy, Boston.
vi HENRY, m. Ruth, daughter of Sam Spinney.
vii THOMAS, m. Harriet Gates, daughter of Daniel; lives at Malvern Square.
viii JOSEPH A., m.; lived at Weymouth, N. S.
ix LORAINE, m. Hezekiah Hall (James, John, William from England); 4 children. She d., and he m. 2d, Carrie, daughter of John Dale. He d., and she m. 2d, J. D. Chute. See No. 138.

ALLIED FAMILIES.

13. vi. Henry Gates, the youngest, m. Mary Van Horne Tupper, and lived below Annapolis; had 5 children; then she d. He m. 2d, Mercy, daughter of William Barteaux. He was a blacksmith and made axes. He was also M. P. P. 3 years, and d. about 1847.

CHILDREN.

i HARRIET, m. William Fairn, Jr.; had 3 children. He was drowned in 1868 or 1869, aged 50.
ii AVARD, m. Maria Lecain.
iii JERUSHA T., m. Jacob Slocomb (John P., John, John, Simon), 1843.
iv MARY ELIZABETH, d. single.
v HENRY ALBERT.
vi EDWIN, b. March 31, 1836; m. Horatia, daughter of George E. G. Ryerson; was mail contractor at Annapolis; has a livery, etc.
vii THOMAS LEANDER, b. 1837.
viii MARIA, b. 1839; m. Augustus Fullerton, school-teacher, collector of customs at Annapolis, etc.; had 6 children. She d. Feb. 8, 1876; he m. 2d, Maggie M. Munroe, from Scotland.

14. vi. John Gates, Esq. (James, Capt. Oldham, Amos, Simon, Stephen), b. at Malvern Square, Wilmot, N. S., about 1788; m. Catharine Smith (Frank, Austin), 1810, and lived in Aylesford; d. about 1864. She d. about 1871 or 1872.

CHILDREN.

i GILBERT, b. 1811; m. Mary, daughter of Jonas Ward, and d. 1868.
ii MARY ANN, b. 1813; m. Rev. James H. Tupper[7] (Thomas, brother to Rev. Dr. Charles, Charles, Eliakim, Eliakim, Thomas, Thomas), Dec. 11, 1828; had 9 children. He was called to preach in 1841; ordained to the Baptist ministry, 1844, in Jacksontown, N. B.; but preached in a dozen places in that province; d. July 27, 1892, aged 84.
iii THERESA, b. 1815; m. Jonas Ward, Jr.
iv MATILDA, m. Christopher Randall. See Randall.
v HARRIET, m. Elias Graves, Jr.
vi THOMAS IRA, m. Mary Ann Traverse.
vii JOHNSON, d. aged 25 or 26.
viii ELIZA, m. James Trites.
ix AUSTIN, m. Mary A. Banks. See Banks.
x CHARLES, m. Beals.
xi SIMEON, killed by a tree.

15. vi. Benjamin Gates, a brother to the above, m. Elizabeth, daughter of Stephen and Mary (Gage) Goucher, and lived at Malvern Square. He went to sea in the schooner *Margaret*, Feb., 1841; was shipwrecked and all lost but the captain, Nelson Dodge, who got ashore on the coast of New Brunswick. She m. 2d, Robert Neily, 1851; and d. April, 1865, aged 71; he d. Jan., 1862, aged 77. See No. 7.

CHILDREN.

i JAMES, b. 1816; m. Margaret Dodge (William); m. 2d, Jane Martin.
ii WILLIAM, b. 1818; m. Louisa Goucher (Edward, Stephen); had Maria and Walter. He d. 1880.
iii STEPHEN, b. 1821; m. Sarah Ann Dodge, a school-teacher, daughter of Cyrus and Sarah. He was a sea captain, and left St. John, N. B., on a foreign voyage, brigantine *Reciprocity*, Jan., 1856, and were all lost near Borneo. The widow d. 1889, aged 70; left 2 sons, Alonzo and William Leander, who went to Rock Island, Ill.
iv HENRY, b. 1825; m. Mary, daughter of William Dodge; 4 daughters.
v EMERSON, b. 1828; m. Nancy, daughter of Thomas Nichols; Mary Roland; and Rebekah S., daughter of Alex. Morse.
vi ALFRED, b. 1830; m. Catharine Ward of Australia, and went to Rock Island.
vii CAROLINE, b. 1834; m. George, son of William Kirkpatrick; had 5 children. She d. 1871; he m. 2d, Rebecca McPhee; 3 more children.

16. vi. Oldham Gates, another brother, m. Lavinia McNeil (John and Lavinia Slocomb — John, Simon — McNeil), and lived in Wilmot. She d. Aug. 27, 1849, aged 48; he m. 2d, Betsy, daughter of John McGregor.

CHILDREN.

i LAVINIA A., b. May 30, 1819; m. George W. Busteed, 1843; had Willard J., b. 1846; d. 1847.
ii ELIZA E., b. 1820; m. James Griffin, and d. 1847.
iii CHARLOTTE E., b. 1822; m. John Synder.
iv PROF. CHARLES, b. 1824; music teacher.
v ELKANAH H., b. 1826; m. Margaret Petrie, Mary A. Lawrence, Mary E. Phinney.
vi CAROLINE M., b. 1829; m. Benjamin F. Ward.
vii WILLARD A., b. 1832; m. Mary A., daughter of James Henry North; moved to South Boston, 1850; son, Charles W., b. 1855.
viii ARABELLA O., b. March 16, 1836; m. Dr. A. E. McDonald, Boston.
ix DEA. WELLESLY J., m. Mary O. Locke.
x WILMOT NASH, m. Lizzie Honeywell.
xi GEORGE OUTHOT, m. Mary A. Armstrong.
xii ANNA, b. since 1850; m. —— Bill.

ALLIED FAMILIES. lxxv

17. vi. James Gates (John, Capt. Oldham, Amos, Simon, Stephen), b. 1783; m. Mary, daughter of John Ward of Peekskill, N. Y., and lived near Port George on Gates Mountain; d. April, 1849. She d. 1840, aged 50.

CHILDREN.

i MARY, m. David son of Isaac Landers; had a daughter, Hetty, m. William Gates, son of Silas; m. 2d, Joel Slocomb, J. P. (Joshua U., John, John, Simon).
ii FRANCES, m. Isaac Landers, Jr.; son, James Gates Landers, b. 1831; m. Fanny L. Heffler; have one son; live in South Boston.
iii WALTER, m. Mary, daughter of John Pierce; have 2 children.
iv HARRIS, b. about 1813; d. 1892.
v MARTIN, b. 1815; m. Eleanor, daughter of Peter and Eleanor (Sprague) Middlemas, 1844, and had 6 children. Mary Lavinia, the eldest, b. 1846; went to Boston, 1865; m. Charles W. Miller, and has 2 sons in East Boston. (Charles Wallace, son of William Miller, b. 1839; m. 1st Sarah E. Cromley, and had 4 children. Live in East Boston.) Mr. Gates d. 1870; and the widow m. 2d, Marsden Foster, and d. 1888.
vi SUSAN, b. 1817; m. John Emslie; adopted a daughter, Mary, and d. 1891.
vii BETSY, b. 1819; d. 1862.
viii SARAH, b. 1821; d. 1886.
ix JAMES, b. Oct. 2, 1823; m. Elizabeth, daughter of John Pierce, son of William, Dec. 22, 1853; 4 children; live in Charlestown.
x JUDSON, b. 1825; d. about 1882.
xi LOUISE, m. John, son of William Saunders.
xii JOHN, d. young.

18. vi. Capt. Elias (John, Capt. Oldham, Amos, Simon, Stephen) b. 1785; m. Hannah, daughter of John Ward, and lived on the mountain above Port George. They had 8 children. Then she d., and he m. 2d, Relief, daughter of Joel Farnsworth, and widow of John Hurst.

CHILDREN.

i WARD, b. 1813; d. about 1878.
ii AZUBA, b. 1814; m. Joshua Morgan; lived in East Boston; 5 children.
iii HENRY, b. 1816; m. Sarah Nickson, widow of Capt. Potter of Brier Island, and was drowned at Gates' Breakwater, Port George, soon after, about 1844.
iv ROBERT, b. 1818; m. Fanny Saunders; lived at Patterson's Mills, New Albany.

ALLIED FAMILIES.

- v MAJOR, b. 1820; lost at sea.
- vi THOMAS, b. 1822; lost at sea.
- vii CHARLOTTE, b. 1824; m. John Grimes, Esq. (Hugh, Patrick), Aug. 11, 1842; 5 children; daughter Irene, b. 1844, m. George M. Phinney, 1863, had 5 children, and d. Sept. 18, 1876.
- viii MARY, b. April 6, 1826; m. Samuel J. Peters' (Dea. Peter Edmund, Samuel, John, John, William, William, Andrew of 1657); 9 children. Mr. Peters, b. in Baddock, Cape Breton, 1832; m. Mary Gates in Boston, 1854; went to Providence, R. I., 1880; to Roxbury, Boston, 1883.

19. vi. Jacob Gates (John, Capt. Oldham, Amos, Simon, Stephen), b. March 7, 1788; m. Mary, daughter of Ezekiel and Mary (Gates) Brown, by Rev. T. H. Chipman, July 11, 1811, and lived a mile above Port George, a farmer. Mrs. Gates d. 1820; he m. 2d, Margaret, daughter of William Pierce, April, 1821, and d. Jan. 28, 1854. She d. Dec. 12, 1870, aged 76.

CHILDREN.

- i FRANCIS, b. May 28, 1812; m. Jane, daughter of Harris Ward; 4 children.
- ii SILAS, b. Oct. 10, 1824; m. Susan, daughter of Charles Williams; 6 children.
- iii CHARLES, b. Oct. 16, 1815; m. Mary, daughter of Isaac Landers, Jr.; 2 daughters, and d. 1891.
- iv MARY, b. Aug. 25, 1817; m. Johnson, son of John Turner; 6 or 7 children.
- v OLDHAM, b. March 8, 1819; d. soon.
- vi JOHN, b. May 22, 1822; m. Naomi Slocomb (Joshua Upham, John, John, Simon of 1700); 5 children.
- vii Edwin, b. July 1, 1825; m. Mary, daughter of Lawrence Harris; 5 children.
- viii JANE, b. Feb. 1, 1827; m. Walter Wheelock; 2d wife.
- ix MARGARET, b. March 22, 1832; m. Dea. Samuel Wheelock. See Wheelock.

20. vi. Silas Gates (John, Capt. Oldham, Amos, Simon, Stephen), b. about 1795; m. Sarah, daughter of Joel Farnsworth, and lived in Nictaux, on his father's old place.

CHILDREN.

- i ELEANOR, m. William Baker; James Douglass.
- ii LUCY, m. James, son of Edw. Morton.
- iii WILLIAM, m. Hettie, daughter of David Landers; he d., and she m. 2d, Joel, son of Joshua U. Slocomb.
- iv BUSBY, m Abbie, daughter of William Wade.
- v MARY, m. Walter Wheelock; 1st wife.

ALLIED FAMILIES. lxxvii

   vi SERAPH, d. about 20.
  vii MARGARET, m. Edward Saunders.
 viii SARAH JANE, d. about 20.
  ix ALBERT, m. Syretha, daughter of Hardy Parker, and lives on the old Gates farm.

When the question is asked, "Was Gen. Gates of the Revolution any relation of this family?" answer "No." Gen. Horatio Gates, who fought and won the battle of Saratoga in 1777, was b. in England, 1728; d. in New York city, April 10, 1806.

An English musician, Bernard Gates, Jr. (1685–1773), was singer and teacher of the children in the Chapel Royal; d. and was buried in Westminster.

HAINS. [Haines]

1. i. Matthew Hains, b. about 1700; jumped overboard from an English man-o'-war off Long Island, and swam ashore. He was a rope-maker in New York. His children were:

2   i MATTHEW, b. about 1728.
3 ii BARTHOLOMEW, b. about 1730.
4 iii ALEXANDER, b. about 1733.

2. ii. Matthew Hains, Jr., m. —— ——, and had:

    i ELIZABETH, b. 1751; m. Benjamin McConnell, 1770, N. Y.
   ii SOLOMON.
  iii JOSHUA.
   iv SAMUEL.
    v PHEBE, m. Elijah Weeks, Annapolis, N. S., and had (1) Tamer, a school mistress. (2) Martha, m. Capt. Pardon Saunders.
   vi ANNA, m. Elisha Budd.
  vii CHARITY, m. Charles Budd, N. Y.

3. ii. Bartholomew Hains, b. about 1730; m. Mary ——, and had:

5   i BARTHOLOMEW, b. 1750.
   ii CHARLES, b. about 1751. ⎫
  iii THOMAS, b. about 1753. ⎬ Slain in the war of the Revolution.
   iv SAMUEL, b. about 1755. ⎭
    v TITUS (?), b. about 1757.
   vi ELIZABETH (?), b. about 1760.

4. ii. Alexander Hains, b. about 1733; m. Clarine Purday, and lived near Weymouth, Digby county, N. S.; farmer.

ALLIED FAMILIES.

CHILDREN.

 i ANNA, b. 1765; d. Sept. 20, 1850; Bayham, Ont.
6 ii CALEB, b. 1766; m. Sarah McConnell, 1800.
 iii MARGARET, b. Nov. 4, 1768; m. Rev. John Saxton, 1786.
 iv HANNAH, b. 1770; m. John Backhus, and d. Sept. 10, 1850, in Bayham, Ont. Mr. Backhus, from England, m. 1st, Margaret Longbotham, and had William, Mary, Esther, Elizabeth, Thomas, John, Abram, and Mina. He m. 2d, Jane More, lived in the States awhile, then moved and settled in Malahide, Elgin county, Ont., and had Henry, Jane, and Nancy; m. 3d, Hannah Hains, and d. in Ont., 1826, aged 85. William Backhus came from England in 1796, and d. 1863, aged 85. Margaret Longbotham, daughter of William, m. Levi Johnson (1801-1867); 2d, Abram Countryman (1798-1876); 3d, —— Gilbert; 4th —— ——.
 v ELIZABETH, b. 1772; m. James Russell, lived in Bayham, near Port Burnwell, and d. Dec. 9, 1862. He d. 1834, aged 79.

5. iii. Bartholomew Hains (Bartholomew, Matthew), b. in Westchester county, N. Y., Sept. 16, 1750; m. Gloranah Sniffin, or Kniffin (b. Sept. 19, 1754), Feb. 18, 1776; migrated to Long Island, Digby county, N. S., and d. there. (He was a Loyalist in the Revolution, and with about 100 others signed a petition to be true and loyal to George III, at Rye,* N. Y., 1774. *C. W. Baird's History of Rye, 1871.*)

CHILDREN.

 i MARTHA, b. 1777; d. young.
7 ii JAMES, b. 1778.
8 iii NICHOLAS, b. 1780.
9 iv BARTHOLOMEW, b. 1782.
 v ROBERT, b. 1784; d. young.
 vi MARY E., b. 1786; m. John A. Timpany, son of Major Robert,† 1807, and lived on Digby Neck, farmer and fish-

---

* Gottfir, or Gottfrie Hans, or Hanes, from Holland to Westchester county, N. Y., before 1710, lived at Rye, a rope-maker. His wife, Anne, was of the town of Mamaroneck. In the cemetery near Milton, N. Y., are the following described monuments. "In memory of Godfrey Hains, who departed this life July 22, 1768, aged 93 years." "In memory of Anne, wife of Godfrey Hains, who departed this life Feb. 19, 1758, aged 68. *Baird's History of Rye.* Godfrey Hains, Jr., went to Nova Scotia.

† Major Robert Timpany, b. in Ireland, 1742, was educated at the University of Glasgow, Scotland; came over to Philadelphia about 1760, and taught school at Hackensack, N. J., till the Revolution, when he became Major in the 3d battalion of New Jersey Volunteers; was at the battle of Long Island, 1776; led the party that took the Parker House in New Jersey; fought at Guilford, Cowpens, Eutaw, and Charleston, and was wounded in the

ALLIED FAMILIES.   lxxix

erman. She d. 1847; he m. 2d, Pelina Covert, and d. 1860, aged 79. Children: (1) Robert Kingsly, b. 1808; m. Clarissa Burns; 8 children, and d. 1887. She d. 1878, aged 65. (2) Bartholomew John, b. 1810; m. Sally McConnell, and lived in Bayham, Ont. (3) James Henry, b. 1812; m. Isabelle McKay, and d. 1881. She d. 1891, aged 82. (4) Sophia Jane, b. 1814; m. George, son of Jonathan Hurd; 5 children; d. 1852. He d. 1859, aged 48. (5) Sarah Ann, b. 1816; m. James E. Delap, and d. 1864; he m. 2d, Emeline, daughter of James Mullin, and d. Jan. 21, 1890, aged 80. (6) Mary Emeline, b. 1818; m. David, son of James Cowan, from Scotland to New Brunswick, 1822, when he was 4 years old; 5 children, and d. 1871. (7) Margaret, b. 1821; m. Benjamin Wade, and d. 1892. (8) Clark Augustus, b. 1824; d. 1891.

10 vii THOMAS, b. 1789.
11 viii CHARLES, b. 1791.
12 ix JOHN, b. 1794.
   x SOPHIA, b. 1798; m. John Spring; Samuel Young, Jr.

6. iii. Caleb Hains (Alexander, Matthew), b. 1766; m. Sarah McConnell about 1800, and lived at Weymouth, N. S.; went to Bayham, Ont., summer of 1828, and d. there Sept. 13, aged 62. She d. 1868, aged 92.

CHILDREN.

i CLARINE, b. Aug. 24, 1801; m. James Thomas Hawkinson, see Hawkinson.
ii ALEXANDER, b. Feb. 10, 1803; m. Fanny, daughter of Henry Willis, and had Elizabeth, Dea. Caleb, William Elijah, Clarine, Alexander, and Benjamin. Mr. Hains d. in Bayham, Ont., March 27, 1893.
iii BENJAMIN, b. 1805; m. Susan, daughter of Adonijah, and Nancy (Williams) Edison; had a daughter, Hannah, m. Samuel Newel Cameron. Mr. Hains d. April 21, 1851. She d. Feb. 13, 1883, aged 71.

groin and foot. In 1776 he m. Sarah Clark, and at the peace of 1783, went to Nova Scotia in the transport, *Atalanta*, and settled at the head of St. Mary's Bay, Digby county, 1787, but spent the latter years of his life at Yarmouth; d. 1844, aged 102, having his faculties to the last, even reading without glasses.

CHILDREN.

i SARAH, m. Col. Robinson, a British officer; m. 2d, Dr. Charles Abell.
ii JANE, m. James Hains.
iii KINGSLY, m Margery, daughter of Robert Huston; 3 children.
iv MARY ANN, m. William Roach; 5 or 6 children; one of them a minister.
v CHARLOTTE, m. Gabriel B. Van Norden (Gabriel, John); 7 children; Yarmouth, N. S.
vi JOHN ADDISON, m. Mary Eliza Hains, 1807.

ALLIED FAMILIES.

- iv JOHN, b. April, 1807; d. in Malahide, Feb. 18, 1856.
- v ELIZABETH, m. Rev. George, son of William Backhus.
- vi SUSAN, m. John, son of Moses Edison.*
- vii MARGARET, m. Elijah, son of Rev. John Saxton.
- viii CHARITY, m. Hains, son of Moses Edison.
- ix HANNAH, m. Alexander (Sandy) Saxton.
- x TAMER, m. Thomas, son of Peter Weaver. He d. 1877, aged 66.

7. iv. James Hains, b. about 1781; m. Jane, daughter of Major Robert Timpany, Long Island, N. S. He d. 1858. She d. 1867.

CHILDREN.

- i SARAH ANN, b. 1809; m. James Inglis Marshall (Solomon, Anthony), and had Martha J., Solomon, Alden, Charlotte, Edward, Harvey, Sophia, and George. Mr. and Mrs. Marshall d. 1884, he 79, she 74.
- ii ROBERT, b. Sept. 22, 1810; m. Rachel Saxton (David, George, William); 10 children; Marblehead.
- iii SOPHIA, b. 1812; m. Stephen Marshall.
- iv J. EDWARD, b. 1814; m. Emily Wiser.
- v CHARLOTTE, b. 1816; m. George Saxton, son of David.
- vi WILLIAM H., b. 1818; m. Eleanor Saxton, daughter of David
- vii J. KINGSLEY, b. 1820; m. Hannah Baxter.
- viii CHARLES A., b. 1824; m. Lalea, daughter of Edmund Jones.

8. iv. Nicholas Hains, b. about 1779; m. Mary, daughter of Thomas and Sarah (Chute) Hicks (see No. 7), and lived on Long Island, N. S.

CHILDREN.

- i BARTHOLOMEW R., b. 1806; m. Edith Ann McGray; 6 children; m. 2d, Sarah Lent, and d. May 27, 1893.
- ii JOSEPH, m. Catherine Israel, daughter of Belshazzar.
- iii LOUISA, m. Arche McNeil; m. 2d, James C., son of Shippy Spurr.
- iv MARY ANN, m. William, son of Dea. Andrew Coggins.
- v CHARLES.

---

* Of the family of John Edison of New Jersey, there were Samuel, Moses, Adonijah, Thomas, Margaret (m. William Saxton), Catherine, (m. Peter Weaver), and Mary (m. Dennis Dowling), who all lived in Bayham, Ont., since the American War. Capt. Samuel lived at Vienna, Ont.; d. 1865, aged 103. He had 2 wives and had 2 families. One son, Samuel, Jr., b. Digby, N. S., 1803, also had 2 wives, and lived in Ohio. By his 1st wife, Thomas Alva, the great electrician, was born in 1847, whose wonderful lights we are all enjoying.

ALLIED FAMILIES.

9. iv. Bartholomew Hains (Bartholomew, Bartholomew, Matthew), b. 1777; m. Mary Kniffin, widow of —— Daniels, and lived on Long Island, Digby county, N. S.

CHILDREN.

i   NICHOLAS, m. Margaret Delancy, and had (1) Wesley, m. Eliza Tibert. (2) Elizabeth, m. Edwin Springs Hains. (3) Effie, m. Lyman Hains.
ii JAMES G., m. Lydia Stevens, and had (1) Capt. Amasa C., m. Annabel, daughter of Rev. —— Oram, and he d. in South America, 1893. (2) Capt. Israel, m. Randelia Dixon. (3) Lyman, m. Effie, daughter of Nicholas Hains. (4) Syretha, m. Waitstill Perry. (5) Edwin, m. Armanella Whiteneck. (6) Agnes, m. Norman, son of Abram Lent.
iii LINDA G., m. George Lee.
iv PHEBE, m. —— Pines.

10. iv. Thomas Hains, b. about 1784; m. Mercy Moore on Long Island, and had:

i   JOHN MILTON, m. Fanny, daughter of Charles Hains.
ii   SAMUEL, m. Eliza Hall (William, John, William).
iii THOMAS. } Lost at sea.
iv   HOLLAND. }
v   HETTIE, m. Samuel Outhouse, son of Peter.
vi   JANE, m. Israel Blackford, son of Anthony.
vii CELIA, m. Simonson Outhouse, son of Simon.
viii LINDA, m. Wesley Outhouse, son of William.
ix   MARGARET, m. James McKay, son of Capt. William.

11. iv. Charles Hains, b. about 1786; m. Margaret Robinson, Long Island, N. S., and had:

i   FANNY, m. John M. Hains.
ii MARGARET JANE, d. in Boston about 1875.
iii TAMER BUDD, m. Thomas Wrighter, Gloucester, Mass.
iv JOHN. } Lost at sea.
v   NELSON. }
    Four more daughters d. young.

12. iv. John Hains, b. about 1788; m. Abigail, daughter of Samuel Young, Long Island, N. S.

CHILDREN.

i AUGUSTUS, m. Sophia Wyman; m. 2d, Matilda Stenderson.
ii CAPT. SAMUEL YOUNG, m. Maria Antoinette Israel; was run down off New Orleans, and lost with two children, 1856 or 1857.

   iii LYDIA, b. 1840; m. James T. Raymond (John, Peter, Peter); had a daughter, Florence A., who d. Oct., 1886, aged 17. The mother d. May 9, 1886; he m. 2d, Alice Chute. See No. 86.

   iv ELIZA ANN, m. Zachariah C. Doty, and d. He m. 2d, Emma Jane Burns; to Somerville, 1873; since then in Everett, Mass.

   v ANNIE S., m. Capt. John Daniels; m. 2d, Capt. J. W. Murphy; daughter Katy m. George F. Potter in Lynn.

   vi EDWARD S., m. Elizabeth, daughter of Nicholas Hains.

HALE.

1. i. Thomas Hale, b. near Coadicote, Hertfordshire, Eng., 1606; m. about 1680, Thomasine ——; came to America 1636, and settled in Newbury, Essex county, Mass. He was a leather dresser and glover, and seems to have removed to Haverhill, 1645 or '46; returned again in 1651; to Salem 1658; to Newbury again, 1661; d. 1682. His widow d. 1683.

CHILDREN.

   i THOMAS, b. in Eng., Nov. 18, 1633; m. Mary, daughter of Richard and Alice (Bosworth) Hutchinson of Salem (first of the name over from Eng. to Am., 1634), May 26, 1657, and had Thomas, Mary, Abigail, Hannah, Lydia, Elizabeth, Joseph, and Samuel. Mr. Hale d. Oct. 22, 1688; his widow went to Boxford with son Joseph, 1692; m. 2d, Wm. Watson (Joseph's father-in-law), and d. Dec. 8, 1715; he d. 1710.

2 ii JOHN, b. in Eng., April 19, 1635.

   iii SAMUEL, b. in Newbury, Feb. 2, 1639; m. Sarah, daughter of Wm. and Barbara Ilsley, of Newbury, July 21, 1673, and had 2 daughters. Sarah and Mary. He was a constable, tax collector, J. P., judge, and useful generally in church and state, and lived most of his life in Woodbridge, N. J. She d. Jan. 16, 1681, aged 26; he d. Nov. 5, 1709.

   iv APPHIA, b. 1642; m. Benjamin Rolfe, Nov. 3, 1659; had 12 children; he was a weaver, 1637 to '40. She d. Dec. 24, 1708. He d. Aug., 1710, aged 70.

2. ii. John Hale, b. in Eng., 1635, known as "Sergeant John;" m. Rebecca, daughter of Richard Lowle, or Lowell, of Newbury. She d. June, 1662, aged 20; he m. 2d, Sarah, daughter of Henry and Judith (Greenleaf) Somerly, Dec. 8, 1663; she d. June 19, 1672, aged 27; he m. 3d, Sarah, daughter of Hon. Samuel Symonds of Ipswich, 1673; she d. Jan. 19, 1699, aged 63; he d. June 2, 1707.

CHILDREN.

    i   JOHN, b. Sept. 2, 1661; m. Sarah Jacques, 1683.
    ii   SAMUEL, b. Oct. 15, 1664; d. May 15, 1672.
    iii HENRY, b. Oct. 20, 1666; m. Sarah Kelly, Sept. 11, 1695; 10 children; d. 1724; she d. 1741, aged 72.
    iv THOMAS, b. Nov. 4, 1668; d. probably before 1710.
    v   JUDITH, b. July 5, 1670; m. Thomas Moody (Caleb, Wm.), Nov. 24, 1692; 6 children.
3 vi JOSEPH, b. Nov. 24, 1674.
    vii BENJAMIN, b. Aug. 11, 1676; d. Aug. 31, 1677.
    viii MOSES, b. July 10, 1678; m. Elizabeth, daughter of Richard and Elizabeth (Appleton) Dummer of Newbury, 1702; she d. Jan. 15, 1703-4, aged 22; he m. 2d, Mary, daughter of Dea. Wm. and Mehitable (Sewall) Moody, and had 10 children. Mr. Hale became a minister in the Congregational church in Byfield parish, Newbury, and labored there 41 years. Rev. Moses Hale d. Jan. 16, 1743-4. His widow d. July 17, 1757, aged 72.

3. iii. Joseph Hale (John, Thomas), b. in Newbury, known as Capt. Joseph Hale, cordwainer; m. Mary, daughter of Caleb and Judith (Bradbury) Moody, Dec. 25, 1699; d. Jan. 24, 1755; she d. 1758, aged 75.

CHILDREN.

    i   JUDITH, b. Sept. 22, 1700; m. —— Moody.
    ii   MARY, b. Nov. 22, 1703; m. Edmund Greenleaf.
    iii ELIZABETH, b. April 9, 1705; m. Geo. Thurlow.
    iv SARAH, b. Oct., 1707; m. Joshua Noyes.
    v   ABIGAIL, b. March 5, 1709; m. Richard Coffin.
4 vi JOSEPH, b. Sept. 8, 1712.
    vii MOSES, b. Jan. 18, 1715; m. Mehitable Dummer, daughter of Nathaniel and Sarah (Moody), of Newbury, Nov. 8, 1744; had 8 children. Two daughters, Sarah and Mehitable, married respectively Rev. Nat. Noyes and Rev. Levi Frisbie. This Moses Hale graduated H. C., 1734; was minister at W. Newbury; d. Jan. 18, 1779. She d. Jan. 18, 1796, aged 76.
    viii ANNIE, b. Aug. 4, 1717; m. Richard Kent, 1736.

4. iv. Joseph Hale (Joseph, John, Thomas), b. in Newbury, Sept. 8, 1712; m. Mary Noyes, May, 1736, and had 13 children — 10 d. in infancy, of "throat distemper." Mr. Hale was styled Capt. Joseph, as was his father, and was a "cordwainer" in Byfield parish, Newbury. He d. March 9, 1776; she d. Sept. 19, 1794, aged 85.

lxxxiv ALLIED FAMILIES.

CHILDREN.

5 i Joseph, b. Jan. 8, 1742.
  ii Daniel, b. June 3, 1745.
  iii Stephen, b. Jan. 10, 1747–8.

5. v. Joseph Hale (Joseph, Joseph, John, Thomas), b. in Newbury, 1742; m. Mary, daughter of Samuel and Mary (Boynton) Northend (Ezekiel, Ezekiel), of Rowley, Nov. 19, 1765. He was known as Dea. Joseph, of Byfield parish, Newbury, and d. Dec. 25, 1818. She d. Oct. 8, 1830, aged 90.

CHILDREN.

  i Mary, b. Nov. 24, 1766; m. Rev. Elijah Parish, D. D. (b. Lebanon, Ct., Nov. 7, 1762, graduate Dart. Col., 1785; was an able learned divine and author; d. in Byfield, Oct. 15, 1825), Nov. 7, 1796. She d. May 30, 1831, aged 65.
6 ii Daniel, b. April 3, 1768.
7 iii Joseph, b. Dec. 14, 1781.

6. vi. Daniel Hale (Joseph, Joseph, Joseph, John, Thomas), b. in Newbury, Mass., April 3, 1768; m. Betsy Chute (James, Daniel, James, James, James, Lionel), Dec. 8, 1796; was a deacon, farmer, and J. P., in Newbury, on the old homestead—that has been in the family over two hundred years. Mrs. Hale d. in the fall of 1806, aged 30. He m. 2d, in 1811, Ruth Searle, daughter of Joseph and Mary Coleman, and widow of George Thurlow, who d. 1809, aged 50, and d. May 16, 1846. She d. May 15, 1866, aged 82.

CHILDREN.

  i Eliza, b. 1797; m. John Howes, M. D., of Madison, Ind.
  ii George, b. 1800; drowned 1810.
  iii Henry O., b. 1802; d. Sept., 1806.
  iv Samuel, b. and d. 1806.
  v Mary Ann, b. Aug. 23, 1812; m. Aaron K. Hathaway, Aug. 29, 1836, who had a classical school and Academy at Medford, Mass. Had 3 children; he d. 1861, aged 50; she d. 1881.
  vi Annette Woodward, b. Dec. 7, 1816; m. A. L. Weymouth, M. D., April, 1875; he d. in Boston, April, 1879, aged 68.
  vii Sarah Searle, b. July 18, 1820; m. Geo. A. Todd, Nov., 1863. He d. Sept., 1882, aged 71.

7. vi. Joseph Hale (Joseph, Joseph, Joseph, John, Thomas), b. Dec. 14, 1781; m. Eunice Chute, sister to the wife of Daniel

ALLIED FAMILIES. lxxxv

Hale, 1806; was a merchant in Salem, school-teacher, trader on the sea, etc. In one trip at sea he was taken by pirates, and by cute manœuvring was let off without robbery or bloodshed. He d. June 18, 1820; she d. June 20, 1868.

CHILDREN.

8   i   JOSEPH, b. Jan. 6, 1807.
9   ii   HENRY, b. Feb. 18, 1808.
    iii   MARY, b. May 14, 1809; m. Samuel Warren Stickney. Col. Stickney was president and treasurer of three or four institutions, deacon, etc. He d. in Lowell, March 24, 1875, aged 70; she d. 1877.

8. vii. Joseph Hale (Joseph, Joseph, Joseph, Joseph, John, Thomas), b. in Byfield (Newbury), Jan. 6, 1807; m. Mary Downing (b. May 31, 1816), 1836; had a hardware store in Salem many years, but went to California in 1849; returned in 1856; went to Brooklyn, N. Y., in 1862, and to Passaic, N. J., 1885, where he still resides.

CHILDREN.

   i   JOSEPH, b. Feb. 1, 1839; went as a private into the late war, was at Bull Run, wounded at Spotsylvania, promoted to captain, and is in the United States 3d Inf. at Fort Snelling, Minn. He m. Patti W. Palmer, of Detroit, and has 2 or 3 children.
  ii   EDWARD MANN, b. March 31, 1841; was also in the army; taken to the War Department in Washington after the war; was in a bank; now in Passaic, N. J., and sometimes in New York City.
  iii   RUTH DOWNING, b. Aug. 4, 1843.
  iv   GEORGE HENRY, b. Aug., 1845; m. Hattie Stoddard, 1884, New York City.
  v   SAMUEL, b. 1845; d. soon.
  vi   RICHARD D., b. Jan. 18, 1848; m. Helen Hurst; 2 children. Tea merchant at Ridgewood, N. J.
  vii   MARY ALICE, b. Feb. 5, 1857.

9. vii. Henry Hale, brother to the preceding, b. Feb. 18, 1808; m. Sarah Winn Appleton, Oct. 2, 1833, and was a hardware merchant in Salem, where he d. July 8, 1890; his wife d. there Dec. 1, 1875, aged 68 nearly.

CHILDREN.

  i   SARAH ELLEN, b. July 2, 1834; d. Jan. 24, 1870.
  ii   HENRY APPLETON, b. 1836; d. March, 1838.
  iii   MARY STICKNEY, b. March 18, 1839.

iv   HENRY APPLETON, b. July 15, 1840; m. Sarah E., daughter of John Kinsman. Mrs. Hale d. Aug. 28, 1885, aged 45; he m. 2d, Alice P., daughter of Nathaniel M. and Dolly A. (Potter) Jackman. Mr. Hale was in the 8th Mass. in the late war, 1st lieutenant in the 19th, then captain, then brigade inspector, then assistant adjutant general, 23d A. C., and latterly lieutenant-colonel of volunteers. He was in 25 battles, wounded twice—once in the mouth; has now his father's hardware store, Essex street, Salem. Children: Henry A., b. June 23, 1888; John K., b. March 2, 1879; d. July 16, 1889.

v   JOSEPH STONE, b. March 8, 1842; m. Mary E., daughter of Jacob Kinsman, and lives in California. Member of the 50th Reg. M. V.

Thomas Hale, the emigrant, was son of William, son of Richard, son of Thomas, of Coadicote, Herts, Eng., about 1610.

i. Robert Hale, deacon and founder of the church in Charlestown, 1632, is said to have been a brother to Thomas of Newbury; and the two as cousins to Sir Matthew Hale of Gloucester, Eng., 1609-1676, Lord Chief Justice of England.

ii. Rev. John Hale (Robert), b. June 3, 1636; H. C, 1657, first pastor of the church in Beverly, ordained Sept. 20, 1667, and filled the office near 40 years. In 1692, his wife was accused of witchcraft, and he wrote "Modest inquiry into the nature of Witchcraft," which was published 1702. He d. May 15, 1700.

iii. Samuel, 3d son (Rev. John, Robert), b. Aug. 13, 1687; m. Apphia Moody, May 29, 1714, and settled in Newbury.

iv. Richard (Samuel, Rev. John, Robert), moved to Coventry, Conn.; was deacon there.

v. Rev. David (Richard, Samuel, Rev. John, Robert), Yale, 1785, settled as pastor of Congregational church, Lisbon, Conn., 1790. On account of failing health he gave up preaching and taught a select family school, 1803-4, and d. Feb., 1822. He was J. P., and Judge of the County Court. His wife Lydia d. 1850.

v. Nathan, an older brother of Rev. David, b. 1754; Yale, 1773; taught school, New London and East Haddam; was a Capt. of Light Infantry under Col. Knowlton; was arrested as a spy by the British, and hanged at or near New York, Sept. 22, 1776. At his death he said: "I regret that I have but one life to lose for my country." He had a twin brother, Rev. Enoch, Y. C., 1773, too; ordained pastor at Westhampton, Mass., Sept. 29, 1779; d. Jan. 14,

1887, leaving 3 sons (1) Hon. Nathan, LL. D., editor of the *Boston Daily Advertizer*; d. at Brooklyn, N. Y., Feb. 8, 1863, aged 78. (2) Enoch, M. D. (3) Richard.

vi. David, of New York, only son of Rev. David, b. 1791; m. Lucy Sargent Turner, a descendant of the Vintons of Braintree.

HANKINSON.

1. Robert Hankinson, born in the Cove of Cork, Ireland, about 1730; came to New York and New Jersey; his children were Reuben, Thomas, Daniel, Kenneth, and Sarah. Richard, Ambrose, and Daniel were brothers, of another family, and cousins to the five above named. Some lived in Richmond, Va., and others lived in New Jersey, while some went to Nova Scotia.

2. ii. Reuben Hankinson (Robert), b. Feb. 28, 1758; was a sergeant and an ensign in the New Jersey Volunteers in the Revolution; was taken prisoner on Staten Island, 1777, and sent to Trenton, N. J. At the peace of 1783 he went to Weymouth, Digby county, N. S. He m. Gertrude, daughter of Francis Peter and Sarah Leroy, 1785. (She had brothers — Henry, Daniel, Peter, and Levi—of whom three settled and lived in Michigan, Peter lived in New York.) Mr. Hankinson d. in the winter of 1833-4. Benjamin McConnell, Jr., John T., and Kenneth Hankinson, and their mother went to Malahide, Ont., in 1834, where the widow d. July, 1856, aged 89.

CHILDREN.

- i FRANCIS, b. Nov. 22, 1786; m. Martha Olds, and lived at Rochester, Mich.; had 7 children.
- 3 ii ROBERT, b. Jan. 29, 1788.
- 4 iii REUBEN, b. Dec. 27, 1789.
- iv SARAH, b. May 23, 1791; m. Wm. B. McConnell (see McConnell).
- v DANIEL, b. Dec. 30, 1792; m. Sarah Anderson, and lived in Minnesota; 10 children. A son Richard is a man of wealth and honor at Hankinson, Richland county, N. D.
- vi GERTRUDE, b. Dec. 23, 1794; m. M. H. McConnell (see McConnell).
- vii JAMES THOMAS, b. June 7, 1796; m. Clarine Hains (see Haines), and had Wm. H., Charity, Sarah, Caleb Hains, Hannah, Thomas, Margaret, and John. He d. Nov. 26, 1875; she d. July 2, 1862, aged 61.
- viii CATHERINE, b. Oct. 14, 1798; d. young.

- ix RICHARD, b. Aug. 28, 1801; m. Elizabeth, daughter of Joseph McConnell, 1823, and had Maria, Edwin, Ann, Charles B., and Daniel. Prof. Charles B. was an eminent and eloquent teacher in the Woodstock Institute, Ont., and d. June 3, 1867, aged 36.
- x JOHN TAYLOR, b. Aug. 11, 1802; d. in Malahide, 1845 or '46.
- xi ANN, b. July 7, 1804; m. Peter, son of Geo. Saxton, and had Reuben, John, David, and Anna. He froze to death in 1832, and she m. —— Powell, and —— Vrooman.
- xii JANE, b. Aug. 5, 1806; d. in Nova Scotia, 1830.
- 5 xiii KENNETH, b. Sept. 19, 1808.
- xiv ELLEN, b. Aug. 2, 1811; d. in Nova Scotia, 1833.

3. iii. Robert Hankinson (Reuben, Robert), b. in Weymouth, N. S., Jan. 28, 1788; m. Elizabeth McConnell, Jan. 16, 1809; lived a farmer at Weymouth; d. 1862; she d. March 17, 1851, aged 61.

CHILDREN.

- i ROBERT, b. April 19, 1811; d. July 1, 1836.
- ii WILLIAM, b. Oct. 2, 1812; m. Mary Ann Timpany (Robert K., John A., Major Robert, b. in Ireland, 1742; d. Yarmouth, N. S., 1844), Oct., 1851; had 2 daughters. She d. Dec. 10, 1879, aged 49.
- iii SUSANNA, b. 1814; d. May 11, 1819.
- iv JOHN, b. Nov. 10, 1815; lives on old farm at Weymouth.
- v REUBEN, b. Aug. 10, 1817; m. Ellen, daughter of Geo. Taylor, Jan., 1847; had 15 children; all d. in infancy.
- vi SAMUEL, b. March 29, 1819; lives in Elgin county, Ont.
- vii SUSAN, b. Nov. 5, 1820; d. 1889.
- viii CAROLINE, b. April 20, 1823; lives on the old farm.
- ix GEORGE, b. Nov. 20, 1824; m. Sarah Timpany, sister to Mary Ann. One daughter, Bessy
- x JOSEPH, b. Jan. 16, 1826; m. Nancy M. Roy, 1864; d. 1889.
- xi JANE, b. Jan. 29, 1828; m. Wm. H. Allen, Lynn, Mass.; d. 1879; he d. 1884.
- xii ELIZABETH, b. Dec. 8, 1830; m. Dr. B. R. Green, Wilton, N. H.
- xiii BENJAMIN, b. Feb. 2, 1832; d. July 8, 1836.
- xiv GILBERT, b. Oct. 14, 1836; m. Mary, daughter of Enoch Grant, 1877.

4. iii. Reuben Hankinson, Jr., b. Dec. 27, 1789; m. Christiana Shook (Dea. David, Martin), 1814; was a deacon in the Baptist Church, and a farmer. She d. Oct., 1830, aged 36; he m. 2d, Charity, daughter of David and Isabella Grant, and widow of D. W. Newcomb (Joseph, John, John, Simon, Andrew, Andrew), who d.

1831, aged 46, and d. Sept. 6, 1865. She* d. April 22, 1879, aged 75.

CHILDREN.

i HARTSHORN, b. July, 1815; went to the West Indies and Virginia; d. of yellow fever about 1837.
ii ELLEN, b. 1818; m. Jacob Wyman, Jr., and had 6 children.
iii ELIJAH, b. June, 1820; m. Rachel, daughter of Peter Cosmond; 7 children,
iv DAVID SHOOK, b. Dec., 1822; m. Mary H. Clements; some children.
v GERTRUDE, b. Aug. 10, 1825; m. Isaac Kinney; 6 children.
vi DANIEL, b. Feb. 10, 1828; m. Mary, daughter of Dea. Henry Charlton Sabean.
vii MARTIN, b. Sept. 22, 1830; m. Abba Saxton (David, George, Wm.), 1859; had a daughter Jane. Mrs. H. d. July 30, 1864, aged 27. He m. 2d, Melinda, daughter of Joseph Kinney, and widow of John Lecain (2 children), Nov. 26, 1866; have a daughter Helen. Mr. Hankinson is a painter in East Boston.
viii SABINA JANE, b. Feb. 3, 1836; m. Joseph Randall (see Randall).
ix SAPPHIRA AUGUSTA, b. Feb. 3, 1836; m. A. D. Gruber; 3 children; live in Everett, Mass.
x THOMAS EDWARD, b. 1839; m. Sarah Lent.
xi WILLIAM CHIPMAN, b. 1841; m. Catharine John.

5. iii. Kenneth Hankinson (Reuben, Robert), b. Sept. 19, 1808; m. Christina McConnell, 1831, and lived in Malahide, Ont., a farmer, and an active, pious deacon in the Baptist Church; d. May 19, 1874. She d. Nov. 28, 1890, aged 82.

CHILDREN.

Besides Caroline, Sarah Jane, Harriet, Elizabeth, and Avarintha, who died young, were:

i SUSAN C., b. Feb. 20, 1834; m. Wm., son of Craig Haggan, 1855; had 3 sons and 4 daughters. He d. a Christian man and a farmer in Malahide, Feb. 13, 1890, aged 60.
ii JAMES, b. May 9, 1836; m. Abbie McConnell (Dea. Moses, Joseph, Benjamin); 4 children. He was a good, pious

---

* Her Newcomb children were (1) Guy, b. 1820; (2) Sabina Ruth, b 1821; m. Andrew Layton, Falmouth, N. S.; (3) Joseph, b. 1823; m. Mary and Sarah Jane Bennett, sisters; (4) Grant, b. 1828; d. 1835; (5) Charlton, b. 1830, a Baptist deacon; m Rachel, daughter of Enoch Grant; (6) Daniel Webster, b. 1831; m. Zilphia P. Kinney, 1856; he was a skillful sea captain, circumnavigated the globe in 1863, and d. at home 1872; she m. 2d, Joseph R. Raymond. (See No. 43).

Newcomb children: (1) Robert, b. 1857; (2) Edina Agnes, b. 1862; (3) Louisa Kinney, b. 1864, Weymouth, N. S.

deacon in the Baptist Church, and a farmer; d. March 22, 1889.
iii ELLEN V., b. March 16, 1838; m. Charles P. Chute. See No. 123.
iv ROWLAND TAYLOR, b. May 8, 1853; m. Mattie, daughter of Charles and Mary (Clark) Gilbert, of New York State; had 2 daughters and 2 sons, and has lived on his father's old farm in Malahide, Ont.

HARRIS.

1. Arthur Harris, of Plymouth, Devon, England, was at Duxbury, Plymouth county, Mass., in 1640; was one of the original purchasers and proprietors of Bridgewater, and among the first settlers of West Bridgewater, 1651-2; m. Martha ——, perhaps Martha Lake, and d. in Boston, June, 1674.

CHILDREN.

2 i ISAAC, b. about 1644.
 ii SAMUEL, b. about 1646; lived in East Bridgewater.
 iii MARTHA, m. Thomas Snell from England, nephew of Dea. Samuel Edson, West Bridgewater, 1665; 9 children.
 iv MARY, m. John Winchcomb of Boston.

2. ii. Isaac Harris (Arthur), b. probably at Duxbury, resided in Bridgewater; m. Mercy (b. 1650), daughter of Robert Latham (m. Susanna, daughter of John Winslow, brother to Gov. Edward), and granddaughter of the famous Mary Chilton, who is said to be the first female who set foot on Plymouth shore. She d., and he m. 2d, Mary, daughter of Robert, and sister to Peter Dunbar, of Hingham. He d. in 1707.

CHILDREN.

i ARTHUR, probably d. at sea subsequent to 1703.
ii ISAAC, b. about 1667; m. Jane (1689-1717), daughter of Caleb Cook of Plymouth. She d. He m. 2d, Elizabeth, daughter of Joseph Shaw, and widow of Noah Washburn, 1719. Children: (1) Arthur, b. 1707; m. Mehitable, daughter of Samuel Rickard of Plympton, 1730; 3 children; m. 2d, Bethia, daughter of Dea. Thomas Hayward, 1741; a daughter, Mehitable, b. 1747. (2) Abner, b. 1710; m. Mary, daughter of Micah Pratt of Taunton, 1735; a daughter, Betty, b. 1737. He enlisted in the French war, 1755, under Gen. Winslow, at the seizing of the neutral French. (3) Ann, b. 1712; m. Capt. John, son of Colonel John Holman, 1734; 6 children; he d.

1755; she d. 1757. (4) Elizabeth, b. 1714; d. young.
(5) Jane, b. 1716; m. James Johnson, Middletown, Conn.
(6) Isaac, b. 1720; d. young.

3 iii SAMUEL, b. about 1669.
  iv DESIRE, b. about 1670; m. John Kingman, Jr.; 4 children.
  v JANE, b. about 1671; m. James Dunbar; had Robert; and he d. 1690; she m. 2d, Pelatiah Smith; 9 children.
  vi SUSANNAH, m. Jeremiah Newland, 1696.
  vii MARY, m. Daniel Packard, 1713; 7 children.
  viii MERCY, b. 1680; m. Josiah Sears, and d. 1712; 3 children.
  ix BENJAMIN, by 2d wife, was at Hingham, 1722; Bridgewater, 1724.
  x MARTHA.

3. iii. Samuel Harris (Isaac, Arthur), b. about 1669; m. Abigail Harden, 1710.

CHILDREN.

  i SUSANNA, m. Joseph Wilbur, 1741.
  ii ABIGAIL, m. Thomas Drew, 1739.
  iii MARY, b. 1725.
  iv SETH, b. 1726, Bridgewater; m. at Middleboro', 1751, Abiah, daughter of Samuel Alden, and moved to Abington; 7 children. She d. July 11, 1776, aged 47; he m. 2d, Mary, daughter of David Howard, and widow of Eliphalet Phillips, and d. July 10, 1797. She d. 1816, aged 74.
4 v SAMUEL, b. 1728.

4. iv. Samuel Harris (Samuel, Isaac, Arthur), b. in Bridgewater, Mass., 1728; moved to Plympton, thence to Boston; was a trader and shipper on the ocean; m. about 1757, Sarah Cook, probably daughter of Robert, a descendant of Francis Cook, who came to Plymouth with the Pilgrims in 1620. He removed to Mt. Pleasant, Annapolis county, N. S., 1763; thence to Granville Ferry. He purchased a large tract of land of Col. Hoar, southwest of Allen's Creek, where he spent the balance of his life, a good and useful citizen, and d. 1801. She d. 1809, aged 85.

CHILDREN.

5 i JOHN, b. 1758; Boston, Mass.
  ii LYDIA, b. 1759, Boston; m. Robert Laidley, 1792, Annapolis, N. S.; had 8 children.
  iii SYLVIA, b. 1760, Boston; m. in Annapolis, N. S., John Wright, from Halifax, and d. Jan. 3, 1822. They had (1) John, m. —— Katherns; 6 children. (2) Betsy, b. 1780; m. James Chute. See No. 14. (3) Sarah,

m. Joseph Balcomb. (4) Ann, m. —— Hoffman. (5) Sophia, m. William Sweet. (6) Stanley. (7) Harriet, m. Peter Cress.

iv SARAH, b. 1761; m. Samuel Hill, Machias, Me., and had Samuel and Josiah. He d. She m. 2d, in Machias, Joseph Hitchins, and had Obadiah and Julia. She d. there.

6 v SAMUEL, b. at Mt. Pleasant, N. S., April 21, 1763.

7 vi BENJAMIN, b. at Granville Ferry, N. S., 1764.

8 vii CHRISTOPHER P., b. at Granville Ferry, N. S., Aug. 8, 1767.

viii JOSIAH, b. in Annapolis, Aug., 1770; killed by pirates in the West Indies, 1791.

5. v. John Harris, (Samuel, Samuel, Isaac, Arthur), b. in Boston, 1758; to Nova Scotia, with parents and three sisters, 1763; purchased lands at Saw-mill Creek, now Mochelle, above Annapolis, where he lived, a government surveyor, J. P., M. P. P., etc. His large estate was still owned by his son, Philip Richardson, and grandsons, Alex., John, and Arthur, a few years ago. He, with Col. James Millidge and others, run the boundary line between Maine and New Brunswick. He m. Abigail, daughter of Michael Spurr, at Annapolis, by Rev. Jacob Baily, Oct. 30, 1785. She d. Nov. 21, 1802, aged 34; he m. 2d, at Digby, Anna, daughter of William Lettenay (who came over with the refugees), Aug. 3, 1806, and d. Sept. 30, 1822. She d.

CHILDREN.

i SARAH, b. Aug. 20, 1786; m. Robert Jefferson, Jr., grandson of Judge Evans, and nephew of Thomas Jefferson, 3d president of the United States (1743–1826), 1810; lived in Clements, a farmer; d. April, 1876, aged 92. She d. about 1865. Children: (1) Abigail, b. Aug. 23, 1811; m. James Fitz-Gibbons, a school-teacher. They went to New York, where he d. She m. 2d, Charles D. Strong, who moved to St. Paul, Minn., about 1850, and became a wealthy merchant. He d. Feb., 1890, aged 89. He had 5 children by a first wife. (2) George Henry E., b. July 3, 1813; m. Sarah, daughter of Elijah Purday; m. 2d, Mary Welch, widow of Capt. Asa Peters (Capt. Charles, Maurice). (3) James Edmund H., b. Feb. 5, 1816; m. Mary, daughter, of Dea. Aaron Potter, June, 1840. (4) Robert John, b. March 5, 1817; m. Jane, daughter of Dea. John Wilson, Esq., 1842. (5) Charles Clensy, b. Aug. 19, 1819; m. Frances Betts, daughter of Elijah Purday, July 3, 1844; 8 children. She d. Oct. 11, 1861, aged 37; he m. 2d, Elizabeth Adelaide Ruggles, widow of

Israel, son of John Lent, Nov. 6, 1861; 4 children. They moved to Revere, Mass., 1887. (6) Caroline A., b. Dec. 8, 1821; m. George Edmund Johnson (Edmund W., William, William, Nathaniel, Dea. Samuel, Dea. William, Robert of New Haven, 1637), and d. about 1850; he m. 2d, Louise Harris (Joseph, Capt. Henry), Dec. 1, 1863; m. 3d, Mary, daughter of Joseph Taylor, widow of Thomas Hunter and Charles Partlock. Mr. Johnson is a mechanic in Roxbury, Boston, Mass. (7) Elizabeth E., b. March 8, 1824; m. Anthony, son of Dea. Aaron Potter, and d. 1872; he m. 2d, Sarah A. Wright; 3d, Lucinda (Chute) Potter. (8) William Jesse, b. April 29, 1826; m. Emeline, daughter of Charles D. Strong. (9) Helen S., b. May 11, 1828; m. John Wilson, Jr. He d., and she m. 2d, Wallace, son of David Lent, June, 1862; 3 children, and d. 1877; he m. 2d, Belle Dunbar. (10) Sarah Louise, b. April 12, 1830; m. Chas. Campbell.

9 ii JOHN SPURR, b. Dec. 23, 1787.
  iii JOSIAH, b. Dec. 24, 1789; d. Sept. 22, 1808.
  iv HENRIETTA, b. Dec. 27, 1791; m. Edmund W. Johnson (William, William, Nathaniel, Dea. Samuel, Dea. William, Robert), of Digby, about 1813, and had William Moore, Caroline, George Edmund, and Henrietta. He d. 1823, aged 35. She d. July 26, 1873.
  v GEORGE, b. May 20, 1794; m twice, but no children.
  vi AZABELAH M., b. Feb. 13, 1796; m. Anna Vaughn, Providence, R. I., and d. in Boston.
  vii ANNA, b. Feb. 25, 1798; m. Asaph Whitman (Daniel, Dea. John, John, Rev. Zachariah, Dea. John), Feb. 22, 1821, and had Caroline and Abigail A. Mr. Whitman d. 1828. She m. 2d, John Whitman, a brother, and had Emily and Thomas Ainsley. She d. 1846.
  viii HORATIO NELSON, b. April 20, 1800; m. Anna Maria, daughter of John Robinson, Jan. 23, 1829; and had John R., James R., Susan Ann and Caroline Amelia (twins), Louisa, William, George, Nelson, Berthia, and Mary Esther. He d. Feb. 27, 1876. She d. Oct. 10, 1882, aged 80.
  ix CAROLINE NELSON, twin with the above, m. Spinney Whitman, 1819; had Jacob, and d. at Cape Canseau, N. S., Sept. 20, 1825. He d. Dec. 15, 1873.
  x EVANS, b. Sept. 5, 1807; d. Sept. 23, 1808.
  xi SIDNEY SMITH, b. Dec. 8, 1808; m. Sarah Allen about 1834, and had Allen Smith, Eliza Ann, Mary Emma, and John William.
  xii ARTHUR WILLIAMS, b. Jan. 7, 1810; m. Caroline, daughter of Phineas Oakes, J. P., at New Albany, N. S., Oct. 22, 1833, and had Rachel Ann, Lydia Eliza, Amanda Fitz-Allen, George Augustus, Amelia Jane, and Cynthia Louise.

ALLIED FAMILIES.

- xiii ALEXANDER, b. March 24, 1813; m. Helen Augusta Barteaux (George, William, Philip), Jan. 1, 1840, and had Elizabeth, Anna Maria, Alexander, Sarah Williams, John, Helen Augusta, George B., Ernest Osburn, and Arthur. Mr. Harris d. March 24, 1878. She d. 1888.
- xiv HANNAH ELIZA, b. Feb. 16, 1815; m. Phineas Lovett Oakes, Dec. 15, 1834, and had Harris L., Sidney A., Rachel A., Deborah Louisa, Willard J., Wellesley Johnson, Sarah Elizabeth, John Henry, Georgiana, and Edith S. Mr. Oakes d. 1872, aged 72.
- xv MICHAEL, twin brother, b. and d. Feb. 16, 1815.
- xvi PHILIP RICHARDSON, b. Jan. 16, 1818; is J. P., Commissioner of the Supreme and County Court for Annapolis, P. M. at Saw-mill Creek, and chief door-keeper, House of Commons, at Ottawa, Canada; m. Charlotte A., daughter of Jasper Williams, from Wales, Oct. 14, 1841, and had Alfred B., Sidney Smith, Anna Eliza, James, Charles Evans, Margaret Williams, Henry, Seraph, and Mary. Mrs. Harris d. Feb. 13, 1884, aged 68.

6. v. Samuel Harris (Samuel, Samuel, Isaac, Arthur), b. at Mt. Pleasant, Annapolis county, N. S., April 21, 1763; m. Elizabeth Evans, daughter of Robert Jefferson, Sen., Jan. 4, 1798, and lived near Annapolis; d. Nov. 8, 1834. She d. July 29, 1845, aged 66.

CHILDREN.

- i ELIZABETH J., b. Dec. 12, 1798; d. April 25, 1855.
- ii HENRY J., b. Sept. 11, 1800; d. July 27, 1839.
- iii STEPHEN, b. Oct. 22, 1802; d. Sept. 22, 1803.
- iv SARAH J., b. Aug. 6, 1804; d. June 22, 1846.
- v MARY A., b. July 14, 1806; d. Nov. 25, 1889.
- vi JOSIAH, b. Sept. 19, 1808; d. July 27, 1822.
- vii HENRIETTA, b. March 26, 1811.
- viii ROBERT JEFFERSON, b. May 18, 1813; m. Rebecca, daughter of Col. Isaac Ditmars, and grand-neice of Gov. Peter D. Vroom of New Jersey, Dec. 13, 1843, and had Dr. John Henry; Ernest Augustus; Isaac D., b. 1848; William V.; Charles S.; Alice R.; Vorus E., an Episcopal clergyman, B. A., M. A., and dean at Amherst, N. S.; Fenwick Williams, b. Aug. 10, 1858, m. Susanna E. D. Rolston, and is a grocer at Melrose, Mass. (for several years he has been hunting up the Harris family); Robert Edward, Queen's Council; Lemmia E.; Emma Blanche; and Florence Mabel. Mr. Harris d. Nov. 19, 1888.
- ix SAMUEL, b. April 16, 1815; d. May 29, 1877.
- x JOHN, b. Feb. 3, 1818; m. Sarah, daughter of Richard W. Jones of Weymouth, N. S., Aug. 9, 1860, and had Minnie Eliza. She d. Oct. 16, 1889.
- xi WILLIAM, b. April 21, 1820; Queen's Surveyor, Clerk of

the County Court, J. P. of the county of Elgin, Ont., and P. M. at Iona; m. Phebe Ann, daughter of James Weatherspoon of New Caledonia, N. S., and had Richard Cowan, William Albert, Minnie, and William James. Mrs. Harris d. July 21, 1863, and he followed 6 days after. A fine monument is erected to their memory by the citizens of Iona and vicinity.

7. v. Benjamin Harris (Samuel, Samuel, Isaac, Arthur), b. at Granville Ferry, N. S., 1764; m. Rachel Balcomb, adopted daughter of Thomas Harris, Esq., of Annapolis, 1790. Their deaths we have not learned.

CHILDREN.

i THOMAS, b. about 1792; m. Leafy, daughter of John Roop, and had John Van Buren, Susan, and Benjamin. Mr. Harris and 13 others were lost on the *Caroline*, Dec. 18, 1831. Mrs. H. d. June, 1848, aged 52.

ii SYLVIA, b. July 16, 1794; m. Dea. James Manning Potter, Esq., son of Rev. Israel, Sr., Nov. 3, 1825. See Potter.

iii FREDERIC, b. about 1797; d. about 1828.

iv CHRISTOPHER, b. about 1800; d. about 1830.

v JAMES STANLEY, b. Oct. 25, 1803; m. Louisa Ann, daughter of Benj. Wilson of Dorchester, N. B., Nov. 8, 1836, and had Julia, Eliza, Augusta J., Louisa E., Clara Lottie, James S., Anna Gertrude, Caliste C. H., Alice Maud, and Laura Pauline. Mr. Harris was a pioneer foundryman and car builder of the maritime provinces, at St. John, N. B. He manufactured bar iron, cut nails, car wheels, saw-mills, pig iron, farming implements; was a J. P., etc., etc.; d. June, 1888. She d. March 26, 1887, aged 75.

8. v. Christopher Prince Harris (Sam., Sam., Isaac, Arthur), the youngest of Samuel and Sarah Cook, b. at Granville Ferry, Aug. 8, 1767; m. Elizabeth, daughter of Abram Spurr, July 25, 1791, and lived in Hillsborough, on the Digby side of Bear River, a sturdy old farmer, known far and near as "Uncle Kit Harris;" d. Jan. 31, 1853. She d. Aug., 1862, aged 89.

CHILDREN.

i ROBERT LAIDLEY, b. June 9, 1792; m. Lucy Hall, daughter of Captain Henry Harris, April 25, 1816, and had Henry Christopher, b. Oct. 5, 1818, m. Mary Ditmars; Elizabeth Hall, Wm. Robert, James Edwin, Martha Ann, George Robert, and Emma Jane. Mr. Harris d. from falling from a tree in Roxbury, Mass., Sept. 30, 1854. She d. in Jersey City, N. J., July 6, 1887, aged 91.

ii MARY AMELIA, b. June 25, 1794; m. Andrew, son of John Heniger, Feb. 19, 1824, and had Eliza Ann, Mary Jane, Maria V., James H., Harriet S., and Christopher. She d. Nov. 14, 1869; he d.

iii JANE ELIZABETH, b. Dec. 23, 1796; m Capt. Joel, son of Thomas McDormand, Jan. 24, 1819, and had James H., Diadama, Charlotte Ann, Elizabeth, Freeman, Thomas, Penn Williams, Edwin, Sarah Jane, and Leonard. Mrs. McD. d. Aug. 1, 1882; Capt. Joel d. Feb. 2, 1883, aged 90.

iv ANN, b. Sept. 20, 1799; m. Thomas P. Williams, Jr., Nov. 25, 1825, and had Mary Elizabeth, Susan Ann, Thomas Penn, Henry Heniger, Thomas Penn, 2d, Margaret Ann, and Henrietta. Mrs. Williams D. at Moncton, Westmoreland county, N. B., Feb. 27, 1883. He d. Oct. 2, 1844, aged 42.

v ELIZA, b. Feb. 9, 1802; d. Oct. 19, 1808.

vi MICHAEL SPURR, J. P., b. Sept. 22, 1804, Moncton, N. B.; was mayor, shipper, etc.; m. in Annapolis, N. S., Sarah Ann, daughter of John Troop, Esq., May 11, 1826, and had Sarah Jane, Geo. Michael, Mary Eliza, John L., Christopher P., Joseph A., Isabella H., Joseph A., and Isabella H., 2d. He d. Jan. 26, 1866. She d. Nov. 13, 1864, aged 58.

vii GEORGE DAVIS, b. May 20, 1808; m. Sophia H. M., daughter of Fred Rupert, of St. John, N. B., July 27, 1832, and had Robert Boyle, Wm. Edgar, Helen Augusta, Gilbert Spurr, and Margaret Leah. He d. Aug. 27, 1866. She d. Oct. 8, 1854, aged 37.

viii EDMUND REECE, b. Jan. 23, 1811; m. Susan, daughter of Rev. Henry Saunders, Dec. 23, 1840, had Henry Christopher, Cynthia A., Joseph E., Elizabeth, Charles R., George D., Maggie S., and Michael Spurr. He d. 1888.

ix ELIZA MARIA, b. Sept. 7, 1814; m. Wm. Short, from Plymouth, Eng., Jan. 15, 1839, and had Wm. Henry, Benjamin James, Wm. Henry, 2d, Frederic, Mary Elizabeth, Alice Davy, Henry, and Charles Spurgeon. She d. Feb. 25, 1859. He m. 2d, Maria Clark (Wm., Richard), and d. 1870.

x BENJAMIN JAMES, b. March 2, 1817; m. Susan Amanda, daughter of Joseph Potter, Sept. 11, 1854, and had Albert Bent, Wm. Sears, Maggie Spurr, Orilla G., Christopher P., Leonora E. P., Theodosia D., Eliza M., Florence N., Alberta M., Susan B., Carrie T., and Lottie D.

9. vi. John Spurr Harris (John, M. P. P., Sam., Sam., Isaac, Arthur), b. near Annapolis, Dec. 23, 1787, was a king and queen's surveyor, lived in Clements, near the head of Bear River, a farmer; m. Christiana, daughter of John Conrad Heteric, Jan. 28, 1814; d. Feb., 1839. She d. 1873, aged 81.

CHILDREN.

i ANDREW HETERIC, b. Dec. 3, 1814; m. Sarah A. Chute. See No. 36.
ii JOSIAH, b. Dec. 20, 1816; d. April, 1883.
iii JOHN HENRY, b. Aug. 4, 1818; is a surveyor and civil engineer at Bear River, in Clements; m. Lemmia, daughter of Charles Van Buskirk, Jan. 14, 1847, and had Mary Ann, Emma Josephine (m. Wm. Albert Chute), Flida Jane, Henrietta A., John Ingles, Charles Henry, Orville Augustus, and Marietta. Mrs. Harris d. March 28, 1877, aged 58; he m. 2d, Catharine, daughter of Thomas Miles, widow of Joseph Copeland, Oct. 31, 1877.
iv JAMES EDWARD, b. Aug. 14, 1820; he run a sawmill near the head of Bear River many years; lives now near Smith's Cove, Digby county; m. Clarissa Ruggles, a school-teacher (see Ruggles), July 3, 1858, and had Harriet Ellen, Wm. Edward, and George Heterick.
v ELEANOR CAROLINE, b. July 19, 1822; m. Stephen Bampford, son of Henry Heniger; had 6 children; d. Oct., 1857; he m. 2d, Drusilla, daughter of Charles Van Buskirk, and had 3 more children. Mr. Heniger m. 1st, Ann Purdy, St. John, N. B., and had a daughter, Mary Ann.
vi SUSANNA S., b. March 14, 1825; d. June 22, 1833.
vii GEORGE CANNING, b. Aug. 18, 1827; m. Mary Ann, daughter of James W. Spurr (Michael, Abram, Michael), and widow of Caleb Goodwin, Nov. 17, 1860, and had John Spurr, Henry Bertrand, Mary Anna, Frank Harvey, Arthur Wellesley, and Canning. She d. Sept. 2, 1874, aged 43; he m. 2d, Mary Ann, daughter of John Combs of Norfolk, Va., Feb., 1876, and had Teressa Blanche, Herman Sylvanus, and Susanna. They live at Bear River.

HETERICK.

John Conrad Heterick, came from Innispruck, chief town of Tyrol, Austria, and on the ship coming across the Atlantic fell in with Eleanor Lindsay, widow of —— Schenck, and married her. They lived at Bear River, in Clements. She d. about 1830, aged 70; he d. Jan. 25, 1839, aged about 88.

CHILDREN.

i MARY ELIZABETH HENRIETTA SCHENCK, b. July 31, about 1777; m. Elijah Purday (Gabriel, Samuel, Francis, Francis, d. at Fairfield, Ct., 1658), a farmer and tanner, and lived in Hillsborough, on the Digby side of Bear River. He d. Dec. 5, 1837, aged 70; she d. Oct. 15,

1849, aged about 72. Children: (1) Eleanor Ann, b. 1803; m. Richard Ruggles, Jr. See Ruggles. (2) Lewis, b. 1805; m. Sarah Robinson. (3) Bethiah, b. 1807; m. Rev. John C. Austin, 1840. (4) Mary E., b. 1808; m. Abner Morse. See Morse. (5) Sarah, b. 1810; m. Geo. Henry E. Jefferson. (6) Stearns, b. 1813; m. Betsy, daughter of Wm. Dukeshire. (7) Susan G., b. 1816; m. Capt. James T. Hinnman (Thomas, Charles, from Eng.); 4 children; d. Aug. 24, 1854. He m. 2d, Bethiah Woodman. (8) William, b. 1820; was a sailor; d. of yellow fever, and buried at home. (9) Fanny B., b. 1822; m. Charles C. Jefferson, and d. 1861; he m. 2d, Elizabeth A. (Ruggles) Lent. (10) Robert, b. 1825; m. Susan Croscup, daughter of Daniel Croscup.

ii HANNAH HETERIC, b. 1789; m. Wm. H. Harris, Esq.; d. 1829. See the next family.
iii CHRISTIANA, b. 1792; m. John S. Harris.
iv ANDREW, b. 1795; d. 1816.

Henry Harris, b. in England, Feb. 4, 1757; went to New York before the Revolution, and (Lorenzo Sabine (1800-1877), says in his "American Loyalists") was taken prisoner on Staten Island, and sent to Trenton, N. J. Residence unknown, but we find Capt. Henry Harris at Bear River, N. S., right after the Revolution, spoken of as a good citizen, farmer, etc. He m. Elizabeth Hall (b. March 31, 1761; d. Dec. 18, 1820) Oct., 1780; he m. 2d, Mary, daughter of Joseph Potter, and widow of Capt. John Rice, and d. May 12, 1831. She d. Dec. 3, 1858, aged nearly 93.

CHILDREN.

i MARY, b. July 30, 1781; m. Edward, son of George and Ann Morgan (from England), 1802, and had Thomas, Henry H., Maria, Jane, Edward, Samuel, Ascenath, and Charles. He d. Jan. 2, 1867, aged 80. She d. July 8, 1858.
ii JOSEPH, b. Oct. 18, 1784; m. Betsy, daughter of Richard Clark, 1810, and had Richard, William Henry, Mary, Henrietta, Ethalinda, Elizabeth, Louise, and Abigail. He d. March 22, 1871. She d.
iii JAMES, ESQ., b. July 29, 1786; m. Maria, daughter of Richard Clark; 7 children. She d.; he m. 2d, Sarah, daughter of Benjamin and Leah (Fowler) Green, and d. 1866; had Edward, Nancy, Louise, Setliffe, Harriet, Matilda, Susan, Isaac, Albert, Leah, Robert L., and Emma.
iv CAPT. WILLIAM HENRY, ESQ., b. May 30, 1788; m. Hannah Heterick; 6 children; m. 2d, Ann Pyne (Alpheus,

Daniel); she d. Dec. 6, 1868, aged 66; he d. Aug., 1870. Children: Samuel Andrew, Elijah Purday, Thomas Henry, Eliza Ann, Thomas H., Milledge, Hannah, and Wallace.

v SAMUEL, b. May 5, 1792; m. Debby Ann McAllister of Halifax, 1816; went into Kent county, Ont., about 1830, and d. at Kingsville, Essex county, Aug. 22, 1876. She d. at Chatham, Aug. 10, 1882, aged 87. Children: (1) Eliza Frances, b. Jan. 5, 1817, Southwold, Ont.; m. William D. Maynard, Sept. 5, 1841; 5 children; Ruth, b. 1846, m. Rev. H. J. Iler(Rev. Jacob, Jacob, Jacob), 1864; 6 children. She d. Feb. 9, 1885, in Michigan; he m. 2d, Mary A. Rowley, (b. 1845), 1890, and lives near Clayton, Mich. (2) Samuel Henry, b. Sept. 18, 1818; m. Sabina C. Girty, 1844, and lives in Essex county, Ont.

vi ELIZABETH, b. March 29, 1792; m. John, son of James Carty.

vii JOHN VAN KIRK, b. May 17, 1794; went to Southwold, Ont., a young man; m. Jane, daughter of Bryan Holmes, from England; and had Mary, Henry, Margaret, Alice, Jane, Sarah, and John. He d. Dec., 1870. She d. 1882, aged 87.

viii LUCY HALL, b. Aug. 31, 1796; m. Robert L. Harris. See that branch.

ix AMELIA, b. Sept. 16, 1798; d. single.

x ANN, b. Jan. 14, 1801; m. Abram Spurr (Abram, Michael), and d. June 10, 1872.

HICKS.

Robert and Thomas Hicks, b. in England about 1575; sons of James, about 1550; son of Baptist, about 1526; son of Thomas; son of John, about 1470, descendant of Ellis Hicks, knighted by Edward, the Black Prince, at the battle of Poictiers, 1356.

1. i. **Robert Hicks,** came over to Plymouth, Mass., in the ship *Fortune*, 1621; had lands there in 1623; went to Duxbury about 1630; to Scituate after, and d. March 24, 1647. He was a leather-dresser at Bermondsy, Southwark, London, and m. Elizabeth ———, who d. early; he m. 2d, Margaret ———, who came over in the *Anne*, 1623, bringing the children, who were probably her own. Mr. Hicks made his will, May 28, 1645; his inventory amounted to £39, 18 s., his wife Margaret executrix. Her will was July 8, 1665.

CHILDREN.

2 i SAMUEL.
  ii EPHRAIM, m. Elizabeth Howland, Sept. 13, 1649, and d. Dec. 12. She m. 2d, John Dickarson, 1651.
  iii LYDIA, m. Edward Banges, over in the *Anne*, 1623, to Eastham, 1644, and d. winter of 1677–8, aged 86; 10 children.
  iv PHEBE, m. George Watson.

Thomas, brother to Robert, probably from London, England; came in the ship *Anne*, 1623; Scituate, 1640, and d. 1652. He m. Margaret ——, and had:

  i ZACHARIAH, b. 1628; m. Elizabeth, daughter of John Sills, Cambridge, Mass., 1652, and d. 1702; She d. 1730, aged 94. Children: (1) Elizabeth, b. 1654; m. John Needham, and d. 1691. (2) Zachariah, b. 1657; m. 1685, Ruth, daughter of John Greene (1673–1708); m. 2d, Seeth, widow of William Andrew, and d. 1752; had, by 2d wife, Ruth, Zachariah, Elizabeth, Margaret, John, Ruth, Thomas, and Zachariah; the last one, H. C., 1724, was an eminent schoolmaster in Boston; d. 1761, aged 53. (3) John, b. and d. 1660. (4) Joseph, b. 1662. (5) Thomas, b. 1664; d. 1676. (6) Hannah, b. 1666. (7) John, d. young.
  ii DANIEL, m. Elizabeth, daughter of John Hanmore, 1659.
  iii SAMUEL, of Dorchester, m. Hannah Evans, 1665, and had Peter, who m. Sarah, widow of Joseph Mather, moved to and founded Dorchester, S. C.

2. ii. Samuel Hicks (Robert), lived in Plymouth, and was able to bear arms 1643; m. Lydia, daughter of John Doane, 1645, and moved to Eastham; was representative, 1647–8–9, and later went to Barnstable, and to Yarmouth before 1670, where he engaged in promoting the settlement of Dartmouth, Bristol county.

CHILDREN.

3 i THOMAS, b. 1650.
  ii DORCAS, b. 1652.
  iii MARGARET, b. 1654; probably more.

3. iii. Thomas Hicks (Samuel, Robert), of Dartmouth, Mass., went to Portsmouth, R. I.; m. Mary, daughter of John and Dorothy Albro. He was a carpenter, 1673, and d. 1698. She d. 1710.

CHILDREN.

  i SARAH, m. 1693, John Anthony, Jr. (1671–99), and d. June 16, 1694.

ALLIED FAMILIES. ci

4 ii THOMAS.
   iii SAMUEL, m. 1702, Susan, daughter of Abram and Alice
       (Woodell) Anthony (1674-1736), and had Samuel,— his
       father's executor — Sarah, Alice, Leah, Susanna, Abigail,
       and Mary; at Tiverton, R. I.
   iv EPHRAIM.
   v   SUSANNA.
   vi ABIGAIL.
   vii ELIZABETH, m. 1719, John Cascy, and had Mary and Elizabeth.

4. iv. Thomas Hicks (Thomas, Samuel, Robert), b. about 1677; m. 1704, Ann, daughter of Weston and Mary (Easton) Clarke; m. 2d, Elizabeth ———, and d. Nov. 20, 1759.

CHILDREN.

   i   THOMAS, b. 1705; to whom was willed wearing apparel and
       part of homestead.
   ii WESTON, b. 1707; executor, to have all housing and lands
       in Portsmouth, lands in Tiverton, and rest of personal;
       his daughter Ann, £50, her brother Thomas, cane and £50.
   iii BENJAMIN, b. 1709; part of homestead by deed.
   iv MARY, b. 1711; m. ——— Hathaway, and received negro
       Betty, and £200; sons, Joseph and Benjamin, £50
       apiece.
   v   MARGARET, b. 1713; m. ——— Aikin, to have £100, and
       daughter Anne, £50.
5 vi JOHN, b. 1715; to have housing and land by deed; his son
       Thomas, silver spoon and £50.
   vii ANN, b. 1720; m. ——— Parker, and rec'd £200; son Jeremiah, a little desk; daughters, Comfort and Ann, £50
       each.
   viii ELIZABETH, b. 1723; m. ——— Smith, and received negro
       boy and girl, £100, and all household goods the father
       had at death of first wife; Mary Hathaway and Ann
       Parker to have rest of household goods, got or purchased since death of first wife Ann. To Ann, daughter of Thomas, £50; her brother Clarke, £100, and their
       brother Thomas, bible and £50. "Whereas my wife,
       Elizabeth, hath eloped from me, and carried away considerable quantity of my goods, I give her nothing but
       what she can get by law." The father's will. Inventory,
       £2263, 12 s., 3 d.

5. v. John Hicks (Thomas, Thomas, Samuel, Robert), b. Portsmouth, R. I., April 23, 1715; m. Elizabeth Russell, 1740, and moved to Falmouth, Hants county, N. S., 1759, but seems to have lived in Annapolis county some time, as he is reported a member of

ALLIED FAMILIES.

the House of Assembly for Granville, 1768.   He d. March 6, 1790, aged 75.

CHILDREN.

i   HANNAH, b. 1748; d. young.
ii EPHRAIM, b. 1744.
iii RUSSELL, b. 1745.
iv SETH, b. 1746.
6 v   BENJAMIN, b. 1750.
vi PATIENCE, b. 1752.
7 vii JOHN, b. 1755.
8 viii THOMAS, b. 1758.
ix WESTON, b. 1760; m. Catee, daughter of Valentine and Katy Troop, and widow of Rev. Joseph Fellows*, and had (1) Weston, d. young. (2) Ann, m. Rev. Alex. Fowler, and had Priscilla, m. Robert Troop; and Weston, m. Ann Hall; 4 children.
x   HANNAH, b. 1763; m. John Hall(?).
xi RUTH, b. 1765; d. single, 1856.

6. vi. Benjamin Hicks (John, Thomas, Thomas, Samuel, Robert), b. Portsmouth, R. I., Nov. 4, 1750; to Falmouth, N. S., with parents, brothers, and sisters, 1759; m. Elizabeth Morrison (b. Nov. 6, 1752), Aug. 5, 1772, and lived in Annapolis county. He d. Aug. 2, 1826.

CHILDREN.

i   JOSEPH, b. April 18, 1773.
ii ARCHIBALD, b. June 16, 1774; m. Dec. 15, 1808, Helen Benson (Christopher, Col. Christopher). He d. March 31, 1846. She d. April 30, 1851, aged 65. They had (1) Elizabeth, b. Oct. 5, 1804; m. William Smith, Nictaux. (2) Russell, b. Feb. 14, 1806; d. April, 1888. (3) Rebecca A., b. Dec. 8, 1807; m. Capt. Joshua Croscup. (4) Margaret S., b. March 9, 1810; d. Oct. 3, 1875. (5) Eleanor, b. March 17, 1812. (6) Theresa Church, b. July 8, 1814; m. Robert Bent. (7) William, b. July 5, 1816; m. Eliza Ann Messenger; 3 children. (8) Lucy, b. Oct. 6, 1819; m. John, son of Asaph Rice. (9) Finley, b. Dec. 29, 1821; d. Nov. 29, 1822. (10) John, b. Sept. 27, 1823. (11) Caroline S., b. Aug. 10, 1825; m. Abner, son of Obadiah and Hannah (Chute) Morse. (12) Arabel, b. April 22, 1829; m. James E. Manning. (13) Charles E., b. Jan. 5, 1832; m. Margaret Ann, daughter of Carr L. Drake, M. D.; 3 children; live in Chelsea, Mass.
iii RUSSELL, b. March 4, 1776.
iv FINLEY, b. Nov. 10, 1777; reported wealthy in the South.
v   BENJAMIN, b. July 18, 1779.
vi NANCY, b. May 20, 1781; m. Parker Oakes; daughter Caroline d. Feb. 8, 1845.
vii SETH, b. April 1, 1783; d. March 1, 1800.

*Rev. Joseph Fellows' children were Joseph, Israel, George, and Benjamin.

ALLIED FAMILIES.

viii RUTH, b. Dec. 24, 1784; d. March 11, 1812.
ix HANNAH, b. April 10, 1786.
x PRUDENCE, b. Feb. 19, 1789; d. Sept. 5, 1790.
xi JOHN, b. Sept. 6, 1790.

7. vi. **John Hicks, Jr.**, b. Nov. 14, 1755; m. Oct. 28, 1777, Sarah Church, and lived near Bridgetown, N. S.; d. May 18, 1815. She d. Jan. 9, 1819, aged 62.

CHILDREN.

i HANNAH, b. Oct. 19, 1778; m. Daniel Morse. See Morse.
ii ELIZABETH, b. July 9, 1780; m.
iii CONSTANT, b. Dec. 11, 1782; m. —— Johnson, and d. about 1820. She m. 2d, Jeremiah Sabean, and had Willoughby and Philinda. Children: (1) Edward, m. Appalonia Graves (David, Phineas), and had James Edward, and Burpee. (2) Rebecca, m. James Harvey, Avondale, N. S., and had Constant and Weston. (3) Thomas Ansley, b. 1812; m. Mahala Ann, daughter of Edward Harrington, St. John, N. B., and d. May 10, 1881. She d. Feb. 15, 1890, aged 74; had Rebecca H., b. 1839; Elizabeth Ann, b. 1841; James E., b. 1843; Jesse B., b. 1845; William Thomas, b. 1848; Henry, b. 1850; Lucinda Ruth, b. 1852; Weston M., b. 1854; Catharine A., b. 1856; Harvey H., b. 1858; Constant, b. 1862. (4) William, d. 1884. (5) Henry, 1805–1849; m. Elizabeth, daughter of Silas C. and Ann (Graves) Charlton, and had John Weston, Capt. James Harvey (1843), William Edward, Charles S., As nath Rebecca, and Henry Burpee. Their mother m. 2d, Gavin Harvey, and went to Malahide, Elgin county, Ont. (6) James, d. at about 30. (7) Hiram, d. young.
iv MARTHA, b. Dec. 31, 1784; m. David Jess, and d. 1843.
v REBECCA, b. Feb. 7, 1787.
vi JOHN, b. March 16, 1789; m. July 20, 1820, Phebe Church. She d. July 21, 1821, aged 23; m. 2d, Theresa, daughter of Obadiah and Hannah (Chute) Morse, March 6, 1834, and d. 1863. She d. 1868, aged 65; had (1) Phebe Ann, b. May 24, 1836. (2) Maria Helena, b. Oct. 29, 1838; d. about 1870. (3) John Herbert, b. March 24, 1844; school-teacher, Bridgetown; m. Sarah Collins, daughter of Rev. Thomas Harris Davies, April 29, 1875, and have 3 sons.
vii SARAH, b. Sept. 3, 1791.
viii MARY, b. Jan. 23, 1794; m. John Lockhart.
ix LUCINDA, b. March 31, 1796; m. John Church.
x MARGARET, b. Aug. 20, 1798; m. Abner, son of Obadiah and Hannah (Chute) Morse; 3 children.

8. vi. Thomas Hicks, brother to the two preceding (see page 20), b. 1758; m. Sarah Chute, and had

    i   PATIENCE, b. April 1, 1778; m. James Chesley, and had (1) Dea. Hicks. See No. 42. (2) Nancy, m. Capt. John Rice. (3) Russell, m. —— Barnaby. (4) Hanson, m. Eliza C. Woodworth. (5) Robert, m. Harriet Marshall (Andrew, William). (6) Mary m. —— Archibald. (7) Edward, m. Mary Ann Morse and Jerusha Tupper.

    ii SARAH, b. Feb. 11, 1780; m. John Rice.

    iii MARY, b. Feb. 23, 1783; m. Nicholas Hains. See Hains.

    iv ROBY, b. Jan. 26, 1785; m. Asa Foster. See Foster.

    v   JOBE, b. Feb. 3, 1786; m. Bridget Burrows, and had Thomas, Mary, Georgiana, Charles, George.

    vi SUSAN, b. April 5, 1788; m. John Rice.

    vii CHARLES, b. April 7, 1790; m. Mary Kirk, Halifax, N. S. but lived near Bridgetown, and d. at Westport, Digby county, 1873. She d. 1863. They had (1) Thomas, d. at about 30, Westport. (2) Amelia, b. 1815; d. Melrose, Mass., 1888. (3) Margaret, m. Capt. Jeremiah Gilliatt (Dea. Thomas, William), and he was lost at sea. (4) Joseph, m. Amanda Tilton of St. John, N. B.; 2 children, and d. at Westport; she m. 2d, John Tolman, Dorchester, Mass. (5) Charles, m. Almira Utley of Yarmouth; 5 or 6 children; Westport. (6) Walter D., b. 1828; m. Sarah Ellen Skerry, 1856, of Salem, Mass.; had 4 children who all d. in childhood. He moved to Melrose, 1862, furniture dealer. (7) Susan, at Westport. (8) Harriet, m. Charles Coggins, and d. at Westport; 3 children.

    viii AMELIA, b. June 9, 1793; m. David Welch; 4 children.

    ix GILBERT, b. Feb. 1, 1795; drowned 1834.

    x   HARRIET, b. Feb. 7, 1797; m. John, son of George and Elspeth Murdock (Scotland to London, Eng., thence to Nova Scotia about 1810), Feb. 20, 1824, and lived at Bridgetown, a merchant. They had (1) George, b. Nov. 28, 1824; m. Alvenia, daughter of John Tupper; 7 children. (2) Margaret, b. March 21, 1826; m. Edward Wheelock Payson (Guy C., Jonathan, Jonathan, Jonathan, Ephraim, Dea. Edward); 8 children; live in Boston. (3) John, b. Dec. 19, 1827; m. Cornelia Bent; 4 children; m. 2d, Barbara St. Clair; 1 child. (4) Susan, b. June 9, 1829; m. John Power, and had John M. and James. (5) Henry Albert, b. March 8, 1831; d. about 1861. (6) Harriet, b. Oct. 20, 1832; m. Aaron Buckminster. (7) Mary Ann, b. July 29, 1834; d. 1838. (8) Elspeth, b. Nov. 28, 1836; over to Chelsea, 1865, dressmaker. (9) Janet, b. Feb. 23, 1839; m. George Wooley in England; 3 children. (10) Bessie, b. Feb. 9, 1844; m. Warren Sheldon; 2 children; Medford, Mass.

ALLIED FAMILIES.

xi Joseph, b. June 10, 1799; m. Lovena Langley.
xii Horatio Nelson, b. July 29, 1801; m. Elizabeth Mongard, and d. 1872. She d. 1892, aged 87.

MULLIN.

Peter Mullin, of Poughkeepsie, N. Y., about 1750, m. Eleanor, daughter of John Van Kleek, and had

i Rachael, b. 1778; m. George Saxton. See Saxton.
ii James, b. 1780; m. and settled near Albany, N. Y.
iii John, b. June 18, 1782; m. Mary, daughter of John Grant, 1804, and d. 1849. She d. 1861, aged 77. Children: (1) David, b. 1805; m. Betsy Sabean (Benjamin, Jeremiah, Jeremiah, Benjamin, William of Rehoboth, Mass., 1643, from Wales, or South England; d. about 1687). (2) James, b. 1807; m. Catharine Sabean, a sister; 10 children. (3) Henry, b. 1809; m. Elmira Hobbs. (4) Rachel, m. Benjamin Sabean, Jr. (5) George, m. Betsy Prime. (6) John, m. Christina Warner. (7) Mary Jane, m. George Gilliland, Jr.; 1 child. (8) Emily, m. Michael Prime. (9) Enoch, m. Henrietta Sabean, daughter of Robert, brother to Benjamin. (10) Peter, m. Lydia, daughter of John McNeil.

Peter Mullin, Sen., moved from New York to Nova Scotia about 1782, and settled on St. Mary's Bay, Digby county, and d. there about 1783. The widow m. 2d, Deacon David Shook, son of Martin, from Pennsylvania, 1784, and they went to Malahide, Ont., in 1834, where he d. Nov. 1, aged 78. She d. 1838, aged 88.

CHILDREN.

i Mary, b. Dec. 26, 1784; m. Joseph McConnell, 1800.
ii Catharine, b. May 14, 1787; m. Benjamin McConnell, Jr., 1805.
iii Eleanor, b. Dec. 21, 1789; m. Elijah McConnell, 1807.
iv Jane, b. Jan. 16, 1792; m. Thomas Chute, Jr. See No. 35.
v Christina, b. Jan. 9, 1794; m. Reuben Hankinson, Jr., 1814.

1. Benjamin McConnell and his twin brother Joseph were b. in Ireland, 1742, came to Long Island, N. Y., about 1765. Joseph d. young. Benjamin m. Elizabeth, daughter of Matthew Hains, Jr., 1770, and went to Weymouth, N. S., at the time of the Revolution, where he d. Dec. 28, 1808, and was buried in the Church of England Cemetery. His widow d. in 1828, aged 77.

CHILDREN.

    i JOHN, b. March 19, 1771; m. Sarah Hailey, and d. Dec. 22, 1850.
    ii SUSAN, b. Jan. 16, 1773; m. Capt. John Cosmond, Nov. 6, 1794, and d. 1870. He d. about 1830.
    iii MOSES, b. May 30, 1774; d. in the West Indies about 1800.
    iv SARAH, b. April 5, 1776; m. Caleb Hains. See Hains.
2 v JOSEPH, b. April 7, 1777.
3 vi BENJAMIN, b. May 18, 1779.
4 vii ELIJAH, b. May 23, 1781.
    viii SAMUEL, b. May 3, 1785; d. in 1829 or 1830.
    ix CHARITY, b. April 1, 1787; m. Joseph Sprague, and d. about 1822. He d. about 1866.
    x ELIZABETH, b. April 4, 1790; m. R. Hankinson. See Hankinson.
5 xi MATTHEW HAINS, b. June 8, 1792.
    xii WILLIAM BROWN, b. Feb. 13, 1795; m. Sarah Hankinson, and was drowned in the Sissiboo River, March, 1819. She m. 2d, Dea. Henry Charlton Sabean, Esq., (Benjamin, Jeremiah, Jeremiah, Benjamin, William, over from South of England about 1640; was of Rehoboth, Mass., 1643. Had 2 wives and 20 children; d. 1687. Jeremiah[4] went to Nova Scotia) and had (1) George Prime, b. 1823; m. Becca, daughter of David Sabean. (2) John Taylor, b. March 5, 1825; m. Cynthia, daughter of Samuel Warne. (3) Haines, b. Oct. 21, 1827; m. Satira, daughter of Michael Weaver. (4) Henry C., b. July 1, 1829; m. Margaret Ann, daughter of Rev. Charles Randall. (5) Helen Jane, b. 1831; d. young. (6) Mary, b. 1833; m. Daniel, son of Dea. R. Hankinson. Mr. Sabean m. 1st, Jane Prime, and had 1 daughter, d. young. Children by William B. McConnell: (1) Benjamin, b. 1817; d. about 1847. (2) Eliza, b. 1819; m. Simon D. Sabean (Benjamin) and had 9 children.

2. ii. Joseph McConnell (Benjamin), b. on Long Island, N. Y., April 7, 1777; m. Mary Shook, 1800, and moved from Weymouth, N. S., to Malahide, Ont., 1829; good old farmers and Baptists. He d. March 5, 1851; she d. June 2, 1856.

CHILDREN.

    i ELIZABETH, b. 1801; m. Richard Hankinson, 1823. He d. July, 1836, aged 36. She d. in Ontario, Nov. 29, 1877. They had Maria, Edwin, Ann, Charles B., and Daniel.

ALLIED FAMILIES.   cvii

ii ELEANOR, b. Feb. 26, 1803; m. Nelson, son of James* McDormand, 1824, and went to Bayham, Ont., in 1827. Had Mary, Joseph, Margaret, William (a Baptist minister in Kansas), and Sarah Ann. Mr. McDormand was drowned in Otter Creek, near Port Burwell, March 22, 1837, aged 38. She m. 2d, Peter Shoemaker, Esq. (as his 2d wife), 1842, and d. Sept. 14, 1883. He d. 1877, aged 90.

iii MOSES, b. 1805; m. Tamer Northrup (Jacob, Joshua), 1830, and had 5 children in Malahide, Ont. He was a pious, exemplary deacon in the Baptist Church, and d. Nov. 8, 1857. She d. May 3, 1888, aged 73. They had Jehiel, Mary, Abigail, George, and Aletta.

iv JANE, b. Aug. 31, 1808; m. George Cameron (John†, Angus from Scotland), 1826; went to Bayham, Ont., 1827. Lived at Port Burwell several years, he a ship carpenter, but for more than 50 years on a farm 2 miles west of Port Burwell. He "experienced religion" and joined the Baptist Church at the age of 77, and d. Jan. 29, 1889, aged 95. She d. Nov., 1889. They had Lucy, James, Thomas, Samuel Newell, William Hebron (was a Baptist minister), Richard (a school-teacher and preacher), Ellen Jane, George, John, and Lucy.

v MARTIN SHOOK, b. 1811; m. Margaret, daughter of Peter Godfrey, and had 5 children. Before he was 10 years of age he was the subject of religious impressions, which finally developed into a hope unto eternal life, when he made the noble confession and was "buried with Christ" in baptism by Rev. Joseph Merrill (1784–1842), in 1836, in Bayham, Ont. He soon commenced to prepare for the ministry, and was ordained to preach the gospel of Christ in Sept., 1837. He was pastor in St. Thomas, Ont., 2 years; Boston, Ont., 9 years; then in Malahide, among his old friends and kindred, 25 years or more, retiring about 1876. Besides these pastorates he traveled and preached considerably abroad. He bought the Barteaux farm in Malahide, 1848, and lived there over 30

---

* The family of James McDormand and Ann, his wife, daughter of Jude and Ann Rice of Brier Island, Digby county, N. S., were Sarah, James, Mary, Rachel, Elizabeth, Jane, Charlotte, Frances, Nelson, Dea. Sidney (1801–1879). The parents, with the last four, and Rachel, went to Port Burwell, Ont., about 1830, and in that vicinity and elsewhere are their descendants. Robert McDormand, an older brother of James, m. Mary Morrill, and moved to Canada West about 1811. Their children were Nancy, Mary, Rev. Cormack, Dea. Robert, Dea. Thomas, Wilson, Jane, Dea. James, and Rev. William (1801–1879). We believe most of the family went to Canada, settled and d. in Norfolk, Elgin, and Kent Counties, leaving many descendants.

† The family of John Cameron, of Cape Breton, N. S., were John, Joseph, Charles, Lucy, George, James, Nancy, Mary, Alex, and Eliza. John, the father, d. in New Brunswick, 1835, aged 93.

ALLIED FAMILIES.

years. He was a very pious, zealous, successful minister in the Baptist Church, and doubtless was the instrument under God of leading some hundreds of precious souls to the Lord Jesus Christ. We well remember the great revival in the Jubilee Church of Malahide in 1853, when 68 followed their Divine Master down the "banks of Jordan." He d. in Hamilton, Ont., Aug. 2, 1889, at the house of a son-in-law.

- vi DEA. JAMES, b. 1814; m. Jerusha, daughter of William Parks, from Queens county, N. S., 1847, and had 4 children; one, Delia, m. Rev. T. S. Johnson. Dea. McConnell still lives on his father's old farm in Malahide, Ont.; but she d. Oct. 1, 1890, aged 67½ years.
- vii HARDING, b. 1816; m. Viletta, daughter of Richard Edward, Sen., and had 5 children. She d. and he m. twice after; 1 child by the last one.
- viii WILLIAM, b. 1818; m. Philena Palmer (see Palmer), March 10, 1842, in Bayham, Ont. Had 4 children.
- ix MARIA, b. 1820; m. James, son of William Parks, Oct. 20, 1850; had 3 children. Lived in Malahide, where he d. Jan. 20, 1882, a. 74.
- x CATHARINE, b. 1823; m. Walter Chute. See No. 98.
- xi TAMER, b. 1825; m. Charles Chute. See No. 99.
- xii JOSEPH, b. 1828; m. Matilda Palmer, Sept. 16, 1854, and had 7 children.

3. ii. Benjamin McConnell, Jr., b. Long Island, N. Y., May 18, 1779; m. in Weymouth, N. S., Catharine, daughter of Dea. David Shook, 1805, and emigrated to Malahide, Ont., 1834. They were a happy, Christian couple. He d. June 30, 1859; she d. Aug. 21, 1856, aged 72.

CHILDREN.

- i SUSAN, b. 1806; d. in Ontario, Oct. 31, 1834.
- ii CHRISTINA, b. 1808; m. Dea. R. Hankinson, Jan. 11, 1831.
- iii DEA. JOHN, b. 1810; m. Almira, daughter of Henry Willis, 1839, and had William Burton, Heman A., in Bayham, Ont., and Catharine. Heman A. m. Sarah Bennett, 1867, and have 2 children. He is a Baptist minister in Indiana and Michigan. They had a silver wedding April 20, 1892, at Leslie, Mich. Mrs. Almira McConnell d. May 21, 1858, aged 41. He m. 2d, Eliza, daughter of Joseph Bennett, and widow of L. D. F. Nash, Dec., 1858, and d. Nov. 20, 1879.
- iv BENJAMIN, b. 1813; m. Elizabeth, daughter of John and Catharine (Saxton) Marr, 1841, and had Mahlon, Adolphus, and Chileon. Mrs. McConnell d. March 10, 1856, aged 40. He m. 2d, Huldah Ann Van Velzor

ALLIED FAMILIES.

(John, Jacob), Oct. 25, 1864, and d. in Bayham, on the town line of Malahide, June, 1887.

v SARAH ANN, b. 1816; m. March 4, 1838, Dea. Bartholomew J. Timpany (John Addison, Maj. Robert), and lived on the fourth concession of Bayham, town line of Malahide; good, industrious farmers and pious Baptists. Their children were Mary Jane, Americus Vespucius Charles, Sarah Jane, Euretta C., John, and May Eliza. The second one, Rev. Americus V. Timpany, b. Dec. 21, 1840; m. Jane, daughter of Rev. John Bates, and went as a missionary among the Felugus in Hindostan, where he was instrumental in doing much good. He returned in 1875 and recruited both in health and funds for two years, and then returned; d. of cholera in Cocanada, Feb. 19, 1885. Three children. She returned soon after and m. 2d, Dea. William Booker (son of Rev. Alfred, who perished in the dreadful Desjardin bridge disaster near Hamilton, Ont., March 12, 1857). He d. about 1890 or 1891.

vi CHARLES, b. 1820; m. Hester, daughter of Finley Burns, about 1865, and have Leslie D. and Emery.

vii ELISHA, b. 1825; m. Cynthia Chute, No. 36.

viii AMELIA JANE, b. 1828; m. Dea. John, son of Craig Haggan, 1855, and had 5 children.

4. ii. Elijah McConnell, b. on Long Island, N. Y., May 23, 1781; m. Eleanor Shook, 1808, and moved to Malahide, Ont., 1829. Settled on a place near the present Lakeview, and d. Jan 21, 1836. She d. Nov. 9, 1869, aged 80.

CHILDREN.

6 i DAVID, b. 1809.

ii CHARITY, b. 1811; m. Levi, son of William Raymond; had 1 daughter and 5 sons. He d. 1869, aged 60; she d. 1873.

iii RACHEL, b. Jan. 29, 1813; m. Robert, son of John Eakins, and had 7 children. Mr. Eakins went to Western Canada (from Digby county, N. S.) before the American War, and was a lieutenant there in the British service. After the war he took up and settled a farm in Houghton, Norfolk county, 3 or 4 miles below Port Burwell. He was baptized by Rev. William McDormand in 1840, and since 1865 a deacon in the Baptist Church. They celebrated their golden wedding in 1880. He d. at his home, Cherry Grove, April 22, 1882, aged 89; she d. March 9, 1888, after being a pious church member 45 years.

iv MARY, b. March 19, 1815; m. George Northrup (Jacob, Joshua), 1836; had 2 sons and 1 daughter. The eldest, Charles, was a preacher of the gospel in Illinois some years. Mr. Northrup was a well-to-do farmer in Malahide more than 40 years; deacon in the Baptist Church

        since 1862. He moved to Aylmer since 1880, where she d. April 17, 1887.
- v EDWARD, b. Feb. 16, 1817; m. Eliza Jane, daughter of Henry Willis; had 4 children. She d. 1867, aged 41. He m. 2d, Sarah, daughter of Andrew McLeash and widow of Robert Scott, and had 2 daughters. He lived on his father's old homestead in Malahide; d. of apoplexy May 25, 1891.
- vi HARRIET, b. 1820; m. Alex Saxton, Esq. (Rev. John, William), and had Henrietta (d. young) and Mary Eliza, m. Dr. John Kingston, Aylmer, Ont. See Saxton.
- 7 vii REUBEN, b. 1822; m.
- viii ELIZA, b. Oct. 8, 1825; m. Dea. E. L. Chute. See No. 104.
- ix ELIJAH, b. 1828; m. Ann Schoffe, and had 5 children.

5. ii. Matthew Hains McConnell (Benjamin), b. at Weymouth, Digby county, N. S., June 8, 1792; m. Gertrude Hankinson (Reuben, Robert), 1814, and moved to Malahide, Ont., 1846, then to Watervleit, Berrian county, Mich., 1855, but some of the family remained in Ontario. He d. in Michigan, Feb., 1856; she d. March 17, 1775, aged 81.

CHILDREN.

- i FRANCIS, b. June 3, 1815; m. Eliza Cyphers, and had 7 children. Mobile, Ala.
- ii CATHARINE, b. Dec. 19, 1818; m. Thomas Pollard; 5 children.
- iii RICHARD, b. Sept. 2, 1820; m. Charity, daughter of James Thomas Hankinson (Reuben, Robert); 2 children. He d. June, 1856; she d. Sept. 11, 1891.
- iv SOPHIA M., b. Nov. 2, 1823; m. William H. Hankinson, brother to Charity; 9 children.
- v MARY, b. Aug. 10, 1825; m. Thomas Smith; 6 children.
- vi JANE, b. July 15, 1827; m. Henry, son of William Puntine; 3 children.; he d. She m. 2d, Isaac Wills; 3 children more.
- vii JOANNA, b. May 1, 1829; m. George, son of William Puntine; 6 children.
- viii WILLIAM, b. Feb. 10, 1831; m. Elizabeth Fowler; 7 children.
- ix GERTRUDE, b. May 1, 1833; m. Thomas Major; 9 children.
- x MOSES, b. March 4, 1836; m. Mary ——; 2 children.
- xi JOHN, b. March 22, 1839; m. Sophronia Beals; 2 children.

6. iii. David McConnell (Elijah, Benjamin), b. Weymouth, N. S., 1809; m Rachel, daughter of John and Catharine (Saxton) Marr, Feb., 1833, in Malahide, Ont., and lived near the Lake Erie shore; a farmer. She d. May 8, 1849, aged 35. He m. 2d, Ellen Chute (see No. 35), Dec. 23, 1849, and d. Oct. 17, 1881.

CHILDREN.

i   JOHN D., b. April 16, 1834; m. Lovena Chute. See No. 36.
ii   SUSAN, b. July 3, 1836; m. William H. Hamilton, 1858; 7 children. The eldest, Grace P., m. George M., son of Aaron Chute. See 107.
iii   GEORGE MILTON, b. Aug. 13, 1838; m. Phebe L., daughter Ira Doolittle, Oct. 21, 1861; had a daughter and 2 sons. The daughter Hettie m. John Saxton (Elijah, John, William), April 29, 1891.
iv   EMELINE, b. 1842; d. 1849.
v   HETTIE, b. Feb. 17, 1845; m. Henry Dakin (George, Daniel, Abram), May 21, 1867; 3 or 4 children.
vi   EMMA ELIZA, b. Jan. 7, 1851; m. Elijah Hains (Alex, Caleb, Alex, Matthew), Feb. 25, 1877.
vii   ADONIRAM JUDSON, b. Aug. 5, 1853.
viii   AUGUSTA ALBINA, b. Dec. 21, 1856.

1. iii. Reuben McConnell, brother to David, b. at Weymouth, N. S., 1822; m. Phebe Jane Chute, sister to Ellen, Feb. 17, 1850, and have lived over 40 years in Malahide, Ont., across the road from the Jubilee meeting house, as farmers.

CHILDREN.

i   LEONIDAS BURWELL, b. Feb. 3, 1851; m. Rachel, daughter of Capt. James and Mary (McDormand) White, Oct. 11, 1876, and is a merchant in St. Thomas, Ont.
ii   THERESA ALBINA, b. July 28, 1852; d. Oct. 5, 1853.
iii   ADONIRAM J., b. Jan. 15, 1857; d. March 5, 1863.
iv   ROGER WILLIAMS, b. Aug. 23, 1858; m. Hattie A. McConnell (Elisha, Benjamin, Benjamin), Dec. 19, 1883, and are living in Assa, west of Manitoba.
v   AMERICUS V., b. June 14, 1862; d. April 5, 1881.
vi   THOMAS MILLEDGE, b. May 31, 1869; m. Etta Lorenda, daughter of Mahlon Chute, Sept. 23, 1891, and lives with his parents on the old farm.

McKENZIE.

1. i. Alexander McKenzie, b. in Scotland, 1733, came over to Halifax, N. S., about 1747; from there went to Granville; m. Mary, daughter of Walter Wilkins (b. in Halifax, 1750) in 1765, and they settled at Stony Beach, 2 miles below Granville Ferry; a good Christian man and a farmer. Rev. Henry Alline made his home there considerably during his ministry. He d. July 14, 1820; she d. in the fall of 1843, aged 93.

ALLIED FAMILIES.

CHILDREN.

i SARAH, b. June 24, 1766; m. June 15, 1786, Joseph Thomas, b. in Pennsylvania, 1752; d. in Granville, Nov. 28, 1811. She m. 2d, Dea. Thomas Chute, 1829. See No. 13. Children: (1) Betsy, b. Dec. 6, 1788; m. George, son of John Hall, and had 7 children. (2) Mary, b. Dec. 5, 1791; m. Frederick Rickitson, son of Abednego, Feb. 15, 1810, and had Walter, Armanella, Joseph, Havilah, Mary Ann, Huldah, John, and Elizabeth. (3) Charlotte, b. June 23, 1793; m. Henry Rickitson (Jordan, Abednego), Sept. 1, 1814, and lived in Clarence till 1820, at St. Croix Cove till 1828, then in Granville, where he d. 1865, aged 75; she d. July, 1882, past 89. Children: (a) Eliza Ann, b. June 8, 1816; m. Nelson Pack (see Benjamin Foster). (b) Jordan Alfred, b. 1818; m. Irene, daughter of Guy Payson; 3 children. (c) Hannah R., b. Nov. 16, 1819; m. Alex, son of James Healy, son of Alex, July 22, 1847; 6 children; he d. Feb. 7, 1889, aged 67, in Lynn. (d) Joseph, b. 1821; m. Maggie Yule, and went to Australia. (e) Mary, b. 1823; m. Benjamin Todd, Lynn, Mass. (f) Sarah, b. 1825; m. Charles Anderson. (g) Henry, b. 1827; m. Catharine Staniford; went to Australia. (h) Frederick, b. 1830; m. Lizzie Yule; also went to Australia. (i) Susanna, b. 1832; m. Charles Healey. (j) Zeruah, b. 1838; d. about 1863. (4) Walter, b. Oct. 28, 1795; m. Eleanor, daughter of Abram Lent; 5 children; m. 2d and 3d, Betsey and Eleanor, daughters of Rev. Thos. Delong. (5) Sarah, b. May 1, 1797; m. James, son of Alexander Healy, Feb. 12, 1820; 7 children. (6) Eleanor, b. June 7, 1799; d. young. (7) Joseph, b. Feb. 20, 1802; d. 1821. (8) Susan Ann, b. Feb. 27, 1804; m. James, son of Henry Messenger; 6 children. (9) Alexander, b. May 20, 1809; m. Sarah Rebecca, daughter of Joseph Allen, Aug. 17, 1841; lived in St. Catharine, Ont., several years, blacksmith; she d. Oct. 28, 1860; he m. twice after, and d. Feb. 23, 1875. Children: (a) Annie, d., aged 25. (b) William, d., aged 19. (c) Hattie M., b. 1843, came to Lynn, 1872; m. Joseph Skinner, policeman, May, 1886, and live in Peabody.

ii MARY, b. 1768; d. soon.

iii WALTER, b. May 4, 1770; a sea captain; d. on his own vessel in Annapolis River, Dec. 24, 1799.

2 iv WILLIAM, b. May 4, 1770.

v ABBA, b 1773; d. 1776.

vi ELIZABETH, b. 1776; m. George, son of Gideon Witt (from Lynn, Mass., to Granville, N. S.), Oct. 3, 1799, and had 13 children. She d. May 19, 1827. He m. 2d, Eleanor, daughter of Abram Lent, and had 3 children more.

vii JOHN, b. about 1779. A preacher after Henry Alline.

ALLIED FAMILIES.

viii NANCY, b. 1781; m. Paul Chesley; 6 children.
3 ix ALEXANDER, b. 1784.
  x SUSAN, b. Sept. 26, 1786; m. James C. Steadman. See Steadman.
  xi POLLY, b. 1790; m. Henry, son of Abednego Rickitson; no children.

2. ii. William McKenzie (Alex), b. in Granville, May 4, 1770; m. Hannah, dau. of Ebenezer Corning, 1795; lived at Stony Beach, and d. March, 1859. She d. Oct., 1842, aged 72.

CHILDREN.

i ALEXANDER, b. May 4, 1796; m. Mary, daughter of Dr. Andrew Sideler. She d. 1889, aged 85. Children: (1) William Henry, b. 1824; m. Mary, daughter of Gilbert Post; 1 daughter; m. 2d, Catharine, daughter of Joseph Dunbar; 3 children; merchant in Lynn. (2) Anne, b. 1826; m. Stephen McColl; 9 children. (3) Elizabeth, b. 1828; m. Thomas Pearson; 2 children. (4) Hannah, b. 1830; m. Cyrus Varney; 3 children. (5) Mary, b. 1832; m. William Halliday; 1 son. (6) Emeline, b. 1834; m. Robert Halliday. (7) Wilhelmina, b. 1839; m. Olney Roberts; 1 daughter; d. 1880. (8) Sophronia, b. 1841; m. James Van Blaricom; 1 son. (9) Alexander, b. 1845; m. Mary Smith (Col. Aaron G., John). (10) John Sideler, b. 1848; m. Dora Kennedy; 7 children. She d. 1888.

ii BETHIAH, b. Sept. 15, 1797; m. Dea. John, son of Manasseh Litch, and lived at Littlefield, N. S., and d. Feb., 1835. He married 2d and 3d, Polly and Amelia, daughters of Dea. Daniel Hains, and d. Children: (1) Hannah, m. Francis Halliday. (2) Manasseh, m. Elizabeth, daughter of Jacob Turpel. (3) Susan, d. soon. (4) Susan, m. Capt. Thomas Mussels. (5) Eben Corning, m. Henrietta Furbush. (6) Edwin R., m. Mary O. Peters. (7) James, m. Isabel Clark. (8) Bethiah, b. Dec. 10, 1834; m. John W. Johnson, son John W.; m. 2d, Rev. George W., son of John Sederquist; 5 children.; live in Lynn.

iii ABIGAIL, b. Sept. 1, 1799; m. James Martin, who d. suspiciously only 7 months after. A daughter Ann, b. Dec. 1, 1822; m. Capt. John Perry, of Beaver River.

iv MARY, b. Aug. 3, 1802; m. Gilbert Cross; 7 children.
v HANNAH, b. June 7, 1804; m. James Litch; 8 children.
vi ELSIE, b. April 5, 1807; m. William Turpel; 7 children.
vii ELENOR, b. June 27, 1809; m. Thomas Sprowle, Jr.; 9 children.
viii ELIZA M., b. Jan. 18, 1812; m. John B., son of Jonathan McKinnea; 7 children. He d. 1862, aged 49; she m. 2d, James Killam.

ix Sarah A., b. May 1, 1813; m. Rev. John J. Woodworth.
x Margaret Jane, b. Sept. 5, 1815; m. Thomas, son of John Perry; 3 children. A son Thomas William at New Haven, Ct.

3. ii. Alexander McKenzie, Jr., b. 1784; m. Polly, daughter of Willoughby Sollows, of Yarmouth. She d. about 1831. He m. 2d, Edith, daughter of Joseph Saunders (Henry, Joseph), and widow of William Harris, and d. about 1834.

CHILDREN.

i Walter, m. Mary, daughter of Ancel Crosby.
ii William, m. Rachel, daughter of John Landers.
iii Eleanor, m. Nathan, son of Jabez Landers.
iv Ruth, m. William, son of Isaac Balcomb.
v Mary Caroline.

MARSHALL.

1. i. Sometime before the Revolution, probably about 1770, four brothers Marshall went to Granville, N. S., and located, three of them in Wilmot, the other, Anthony, at Marshalltown, Digby county. Their parentage we have not satisfactorily ascertained. Solomon is reported to have come from Pennsylvania to Massachusetts and thence to Nova Scotia, while Anthony is reported to have come over from Long Island. William is said to have got his wife, Lydia, in Roxbury, Mass., so it is difficult to arrive at precise data to trace them. That they were brothers was always said by their children in Nova Scotia.

CHILDREN.

2 i William, b. about 1740.
3 ii Solomon, b. about 1743.
4 iii Anthony, b. about 1745.
5 iv Isaac, b. June 10, 1748.
v Elizabeth, b. 1751 (?); d. young.

2. ii. William Marshall, m. Lydia, daughter of George Willett, Roxbury, Mass., April 22, 1761, and lived in Wilmot, Annapolis county, N. S. He is reported to have d. in New Brunswick about 1815. She d. Sept. 1, 1828, aged 91.

CHILDREN.

i Sybil, b. Feb. 3, 1762; m. Dea. Thomas Chute. No. 13.
ii William, b. Oct. 21, 1763; d. Sept. 6, 1764.

ALLIED FAMILIES.

  iii WILLIAM, b. Aug. 5, 1765; d. Sept. 30, 1776.
  iv CATHARINE, b. Sept. 10, 1767; d. Jan. 5, 1779.
6 v ANDREW, b. Feb. 28, 1770.
7 vi JOHN, b. April 20, 1772.
8 vii ABEL R., b. May 13, 1774.
  viii ELIZABETH, b. March 28, 1776; m. William Marshall, son of Isaac.
  ix CALVIN, b. April 16, 1778; m. Helen Phinney (Zaccheus, Benjamin, John, John, John, of Barnstable county, Mass., about 1630), and lived at Petticodiac, N. B.; had John and 3 or 4 more children.
  x SARAH, b. Aug. 27, 1780; m. Samuel Gates. See Gates.

3. ii. Solomon Marshall, m. —— Simpson in Pennsylvania, and had a daughter Sarah, b. about 1770; m. Benjamin Milbury, See Barnes. Mrs. Marshall d. He m. 2d, Hannah Kendall (Elisha, Thomas, Thomas, Francis, of Woburn, Mass., 1640; d. 1708, aged 88), and went to Wilmot, N. S.

CHILDREN.

9 ii ELISHA, b. 1773 (?).
10 iii OBADIAH, b. 1775 (?).
  iv SOLOMON, b. 1777; m. Rachel Chute. See No. 10.
11 v SAMUEL, b. 1779.
  vi SETH, b. 1782 (?).
  vii SOPHIA, b. 1785 (?); m. Levi Cole.
12 viii LEVI, b. 1788 (?).

4. ii. Anthony Marshall, m. Rachel Morse, 1764; and lived at Marshalltown, Digby county, N. S. She d. 1825, aged 70; he m. 2d, Mrs. Margera Ingles, widow of Thomas Bacon, 1826; and d. 1829. She d. 1830, aged 80.

CHILDREN.

  i ABIGAIL, b. 1765; m. John Henry Snyder*, and had (1) Stephen, m. Manassah Spinney. (2) Mary, m. Henry Merry. (3) Abba, m. John McColly. (4) Henry, m., and drowned in the Bay of Fundy. (5) Rachel, m. Daniel, son of Peter Hamm; 8 children. (6) Solomon. (7) Joseph. (8) Becca, b. 1807; m. Thomas Morgan (Edward, George); 5 or 6 children.
13 ii JOSEPH, b. 1766.

---

* Mary Elizabeth Cunningham m. Mr. Schofield, who was drowned, leaving a daughter, Sarah Clarissa, who m. Robert Saxton. The Widow Schofield then m. Nathan Rogers, and a daughter, Susanna, m. Benjamin Chute. Mr. Rogers d., and the widow m. John Henry Snyder, as his second wife.

ALLIED FAMILIES.

  iii RICHARD, b. Jan. 30, 1768; m. Hannah Bacon. She d. 1847, aged 70; he m. 2d, Martha (Ingles) Marshall, and d. 1855. She d. 1862, aged 81.
14 iv ISAAC, b. March 12, 1770.
  v RACHEL, b 1771; m. Richard Collins; several children.
  vi POLLY, b. 1773; m. John, son of William Cropley, Nov. 1, 1792; 2 children.
15 vii WILLIAM, b. 1776.
16 viii SOLOMON, b. 1779.

5. ii. Isaac Marshall, b. June 10, 1748; m. Mary Robbins, 1772; lived in Clarence. She d. Jan. 7, 1817, aged 65; he m. 2d, Ruth Parish, widow of Dea. Joseph Morton, 1820, and d. Dec. 6, 1824. She d. May 23, 1846, aged 80.

CHILDREN.

17 i OTIS, b. Feb. 21, 1773.
  ii LUCY, b. Jan. 6, 1775; m. George Gardner, and had a daughter, Catharine, m. Henry Charlton; 6 children. Mr. Gardner d. 1850, aged 93. Henry Charlton d. 1842, aged 52. She d. 1883, aged 89.
18 iii WILLIAM, b. Aug. 14, 1777.
  iv MARY, b. Sept. 10, 1779; m. William Chute. See 22.
  v CYNTHIA, b. Nov. 27, 1781; m. Elisha Marshall. See Marshall.
  vi PRISCILLA, b. Nov. 29, 1783; m. Henry, son of John Dunn, 6 children. She d. Dec. 3, 1877. He d. July 13, 1884, aged 92.
19 vii DAVID, b. Sept. 17, 1786.
  viii CATHARINE, b. July 2, 1791; d. young.

6. iii Andrew Marshall (William), b. Feb. 23, 1770; m. Susanna, daughter of Major Samuel Chesley, Jan. 29, 1792, by Dr. Charles Ingles, and lived in Clarence, Annapolis county, a sturdy farmer. He d. Sept. 28, 1865. She d. Dec. 2, 1858, aged 89.

CHILDREN.

  i NANCY, b. Aug. 27, 1793; m. Jeremiah, son of Jacob Calnek, Oct. 23, 1821, and d. March 25, 1858. He d.; had 7 children. The eldest, William A., b. 1822, d. June, 1892, was an excellent surveyor, school-teacher, editor, historian, and genealogist.
  ii ANDREW, JR., b. Oct. 31, 1795; m. Abigail Morse (Capt. Abner, Abner, Obadiah, Daniel, Daniel, Daniel, Samuel), Oct. 21, 1819, and had Henry, Benjamin, Harriet, Maria, Eliza, William Burton, Charlotte, and Rose. Mr. Marshall d. March 7, 1868. She d. March 9, 1844, aged 53.

ALLIED FAMILIES.

iii CALEB, b. Nov. 30, 1797; m. Eliza, daughter of William Bent, Nov. 11, 1823, and had (1) Maria Augusta, b. 1824; m. Rev. Jeremiah Bancroft. (2) Selina Elizabeth, b. 1827; m. Dea. Edw. Marshall. See No. 13. (3) Susan Amelia, b. 1830; d. 1850. (4) Abigail Jane, b. 1835; m. Isaiah Dimock. (5) William Lovett, b. 1839; m. Susan Leonard (Benjamin, Seth). Mr. Marshall d. Jan. 8, 1862. She d. Aug. 31, 1882, aged 82.
iv SUSAN, b. Aug. 24, 1800; m. Joseph Starrett, July 11, 1847; d. He d. 1871.
v ELIZA, b. Aug. 16, 1802; m. Daniel, son of Richard Nicholls, Nov. 4, 1829, and d. April, 1876. He was a merchant and postmaster at Clarence; d. 1885, aged 80.
vi BENJAMIN, b. July 10, 1804; m Eliza Beattie, 1830.
vii HELEN, b. Feb. 11, 1807; d. May 24, 1849.
viii SIDNEY, b. April 16, 1809; d. Nov. 8, 1811.
ix SIDNEY, b. May 31, 1814; m. Tamer Chute. No. 42.

7. iii. John Marshall (William), b. April 20, 1772; m. Nancy, daughter of Abednego and Phebe (Tucker) Rickitson, Oct. 17, 1797, by Rev. T. H. Chipman, and lived a mile below Bridgetown, south side of the Annapolis river, a farmer; d. July 15, 1858. She d. March 17, 1853, aged 76.

CHILDREN.

i MARIA, b. Oct. 14, 1798; m. John, son of Alvin Corbit, Feb. 8, 1820, by Parson Perkins; had several children, and d. He d. about 1870.
ii SUSANNA, b. March 9, 1800; d. 187–.
iii WILLETT, b. Feb. 9, 1802; m. Margaret, daughter of Joseph Johnson, 1826; and d. about 1870.
iv LEVICIA, b. Nov. 8, 1803; m. Samuel B., son of Hon. Major Chipman. See Chipman.
v WILLIAM, b. April 22. 1805; m. Maria, daughter of William Bent, May 10, 1831, and d. She d. about 1870.
vi CALVIN, b. April 2, 1807; d. Jan. 17, 1815.
vii SOPHIA, b. Aug. 14, 1810; m. William, son of Joseph Johnson, Dec. 19, 1838; several children.
viii ELIZA, b July 31, 1812; m. Thomas A., son of Antonio Gavazza, Jan. 4, 1848, and d. Oct. 2, 1891. He d. 1877.
ix MARY ANN, b. Feb. 10, 1816; m. William Freeman Marshall (Solomon, Anthony), June 22, 1847; had 2 daughters, and d. July 7, 1891. He m. 2d, —— Shamper.
x JOHN JAMES, b. June 7, 1818; m. Maria Randolph, Dec. 16, 1852, and lived on the old place; d. in N. Y., 1894.

8. iii. Abel R. Marshall (William), b. May 13, 1774; m. Esther, daughter of Daniel Felch, Esq. (came over to Annapolis, N.

S., in the sloop, *Charming Molly*, in May, 1760), Jan. 4, 1798, and lived in Clarence.

CHILDREN.

i WILLIAM, b. Sept. 27, 1798; m. Mary Fritz, July 4, 1822; 8 children.
ii SAMUEL, b. Nov. 25, 1800; m. Rachel, daughter of John Elliott.
iii DEA. THOMAS A., b. Nov. 7, 1802; m. Margaret Elliott, a sister; 11 children; Lawrencetown.
iv LYDIA, b. Feb. 12, 1805; m. William, son of James Charlton.
v RUFUS, b. Sept. 15, 1810; m. Mary Jane Webster.

9. iii. Elisha Marshall (Solomon), b. about 1773; m. Cynthia, daughter of Isaac Marshall, and lived in Wilmot.

CHILDREN.

i ELIZA, m. Oldham, son of Benjamin Fales; 7 children. See Gates.
ii CAROLINE, m. —— Sullivan.
iii LUCY, m. David F. Milbury (James, Joseph). See Barnes.
iv REV. LEVI H., b. 1811; m. —— Collins; was an active, useful minister in the Baptist church in New Brunswick; d. April 15, 1866; 7 children.
v SETH, m. Susan, daughter of John Fritz.
vi EMILY, m. William Locke.
vii JACOB, m. Mary, daughter of Thomas Ward; 5 children.
viii MERCY, m. James Locke; 3 children.

10. iii. Obadiah Marshall, brother to the above, b. about 1775; m. Margaret, daughter of John Eaton; lived in Wilmot.

CHILDREN.

i AMELIA, m. James, son of Andrew Brown.
ii MARY, m. Handley C. Gates. See Gates.
iii LUCY, m. Phineas Hudson.
iv MARGARET, m. Rufus, son of John Robbins.
v SARAH ANN, m. Daniel Whitman.
vi EUNICE, m.
vii JOHN, m. Sarah, daughter of Levi Marshall.
viii WILLIAM, m. Margaret, daughter of James Flanigan.
ix ROBERT, m. Margaret Moore.
x ELIAS, m. Nancy Freeman.

11. iii. Samuel Marshall, another brother, b. 1779; m. Nancy, daughter of Joseph Rustine; 2d, Anna Tufts; 3d, Mary

ALLIED FAMILIES. cxix

(Marshall) Chute (see No. 22); 4th, Cynthia, daughter of James Harris, and widow of Hughy Gray,* and d. 1859.

CHILDREN.

i Sophia, m. Edwin Arminson.
ii William, m. Hannah, daughter of Thomas Ward.
iii Elizabeth, b. 1808; m. Stephen, son of Andrew Brown; 4 children. He d. 1844, aged 42; she m. 2d, Nelson Baker, and lives in East Boston.
iv Louise, m. Stephen Tufts.
v Rebecca, m. James Mitchell, 1837.
vi Joseph, m. Rebecca Walker.
vii Samuel, m. Fanny Welton.
viii Mary Ann, m. John Hawksworth.
ix Catharine, m. James Devinny.
x Salome, m. Israel Bent, Jr.
xi Abigail, m. Robinson, son of John Palmer.

12. iii. Levi Marshall, youngest brother, b. about 1788; m. Catharine, daughter of Rev. John White, and lived in Wilmot. She d. about 1830; he m. 2d, Mary White, a sister; d. about 1840. He d. 1865.

CHILDREN.

i Lamitty Ann, d. single.
ii James Manning, m. Mary Whitman, 6 children; m. 2d, —— Bruce; and live in Georgia.
iii Maria, m. Jabez Morton.
iv Henry, m. Phebe Morton, daughter of Jabez by a 1st wife.
v Sarah, m. John, son of Obadiah Marshall, and live at Centre Harbor, N. H.
vi Edward Manning, b. 1821; m. Margaret Moffat; 2 children.
vii Catharine, b. 1823; m. James P., son of William Pierce; 13 children. They came from New Brunswick to Boston, Mass., 1869; daughter Martha m. James Milledge Chute. See 127.
viii Adoniram Judson, m. Barbara Rafuse (Frederick and Betty (Morton) Rafuse); he d. on Gates Mountain, March 23, 1893, aged 88.

13. iii. Joseph Marshall (Anthony), b. near Digby N. S., 1766; m. Temperance Eldridge* (Barnabas, over to Yarmouth, N. S., from Cape Cod, Barnabas, Gideon, Robert, to Yarmouth, Mass., from Norwich, Eng., 1643), 1789. He went to New London,

---

* See Cynthia, daughter of Richard Ruggles.

Conn., 1793 or 4, and was not heard from afterwards. His widow, about 1800, m. Benjamin Ellis.

CHILDREN.

i BARNABAS, b. Aug., 1790; m. Mary S., daughter of Thomas Bacon, and lived at or near Marshalltown, a shoemaker; d. Nov., 1863. She d. May 3, 1884, aged 94. Children: (1) Thomas, b. Oct., 1811; m. Mahala, daughter of James Smith; 11 children, and d. 1889. (2) Martha, b. 1813; m. Robert Foster (Irish); 6 children. (3) Abba, b. 1815; m. Eliab Bell, Jr.; 6 children. (4) Mary, b. 1818; m. Marr Porter; 7 children. She d. Aug., 1864. (5) Stephen B., b. 1820; m. Matilda, daughter of Stephen Bacon; 10 children. (6) Margera, b. 1823; m. Washington, son of Jabeth Dunbar; 6 children; Mt. Serrat. (7) James E., b. 1825; m. Lydia, daughter of James Smith; 8 children. (8) Sarah A., b. 1828; m. Benjamin Marshall (Joseph, William, Anthony); 7 children. (9) Joseph B., b. 1831; m. Esther, daughter of James and Esther (Savary) Smith, 1858; had 5 children; lived at Dover, N. H., and d. Sept. 18, 1892. (10) Robert W., b. Aug. 12, 1834; m. Mary C., daughter of William Zeigler, Dec. 16, 1860; 8 children; live in Marblehead, a shoemaker.

ii ABBA, b. 1792; m. Isaac Dakin, 1808; had a child that d. with its mother soon. He m. 2d.

14. iii. Isaac Marshall (Anthony), b. March 12, 1770; m. Rachel, daughter of James and Elizabeth (Potter) Goudey, and lived at or near Marshalltown. She d. 1797; he m. 2d, Abigail, daughter of Josiah Winchester, and d. 1835. She d. spring of 1855.

CHILDREN.

i RACHEL, b. March 8, 1797; m. Dea. Thomas Bacon, son of Thomas; 8 children. Dea. Bacon m. 1st Abigail Eldridge, sister to Capt. Stephen Eldridge, and had a son, Samuel Trask, b. 1814, a school-teacher, J. P., and Baptist deacon; m. Susan, daughter of Thomas Harris (lost on the *Caroline*, 1831), and had 6 children. She d. Feb., 1893, aged 76. Dea. Thomas Bacon killed by a tree March 8, 1844, aged 58.

ii ELIZA ANN, b. 1799; m. Towner Odell, and had a daughter, Abba Elizabeth, m. George Troop, son of Frank and Mary (Barnes-Gilliland) Armstrong. Mr. Odell d. She m. 2d, William Gilliland (eldest son of Joseph, from Ireland), and had 6 children. Mr. Gilliland m. 1st, Marsena Ann, daughter of Gideon Van Emburgh, and had 3 children.

iii ANTHONY, b. 1802; lost at sea about 1830.

iv GEORGE, b. 1806; m. in Trinidad, West Indies.
v MARIA, b. April 29, 1809; m. John Potter (his 2d wife), 1853, and lives at Swampscott.
vi JOSEPH, b. 1811; m. Mary Pickel, St. John, N. B.; 5 children.
vii JAMES, b. 1813; m. Amelia Ann Poole.
viii HANNAH, b. 1815; m. Benjamin Hardy, 1st wife.
ix ALFRED, b. 1817.
x HOWARD, b. 1819; m. Lavinia Poole; 6 or 7 children.
xi CECILIA, b. 1822; m. Benjamin Hardy, 2d wife.

15. iii. William Marshall, brother to the preceding, b. 1776; m. Becca White (b. Dec. 12, 1779), and lived at "South Range," Digby county; d. Jan. 4, 1828. She m. 2d, Richard Mott (b. Oswego, N. Y., June 9, 1767; d. July 10, 1844), and d. about 1867, aged 90. Mr. Mott m. 1st, Susanna White (b. Sept. 9, 1769; d. March 20, 1836), sister to Aunt Becca, and had several children.

CHILDREN.

i HANNAH, b. Jan. 12, 1800; m. William Zeigler; 14 children. He d. Feb., 1883, in his 95th year.
ii JOSEPH, b. 1804; m. Eunice Hains[4], Daniel[3], John[2], Walter[1], from Wales; 3 children.
iii WILLIAM H., b. 1806; m. Hannah Wilson, 5 children; m. 2d, Caroline Lambertson, 4 children.
iv ROSANNA, b. 1808; m. Samuel Hains, brother to Eunice; 6 children; live in Maine.
v CHRISTIANA, b. 1810; m. Eli, son of Ezekiel Messenger, and had (1) William Edward, b. April 16, 1830; m. Harriet Eliza Bacon (Dea. Thomas, Thomas), and had 6 or 7 children. He is a grocer in Beverly, Mass. (2) Mary Rebecca, m. George, son of Christopher Banks. (3) James Eli, m. Armanella Leach. (4) Armanella, m. Alfred Parker. (5) John. (6) Idelbert, m. Jenny Carter. (7) Joshua, m. Emma ——. Mr. Eli Messenger d. May, 1851, aged 45. She m. 2d, Michael Gilliatt (his 2d wife), and had Fanny Melinda, m. Israel, son of Daniel Hall, Port Williams, N. S., and had a son, Capt. William Hall. Mr. Gilliatt d. 1865, aged 75. She d. 1885.
vi JAMES MOODY, m. an English lady, had 2 children, and lived in New York city.
vii MARY ANN, d. about 1860, aged 40.
viii MARTHA, m. Daniel Hains, Jr.; 6 children, and lived in Granville.
ix JOHN, m. Maria, daughter of James Fleet; 3 children.
x RICHARD MOTT, m. Emma, daughter of William Fleet; 3 children.
xi ARMANELLA, m. Handley, son of John Banks; 5 children. Port Williams.
xii SHAW, m. Minetta Haskell; 2 children.

ALLIED FAMILIES.

16. iii. Solomon Marshall (Anthony), b. 1779; m. May 13, 1802, Martha, daughter of James Inglis, from Glasgow, Scotland, and lived at Marshalltown, a farmer, merchant, tanner, and sawyer, near the head of St. Mary's Bay. With Capt. James Bryant, and son Benjamin, Charles Thomas, Elijah Carty, a Mr. Westcoat, and Thomas Harris, he started for St. John, N. B. (Harris and Marshall were passengers), on the packet schooner *Caroline*, and were all lost, Dec. 18, 1831. The vessel belonged to James Crowley, merchant, Digby. Mrs. Marshall m. 2d, Richard Marshall.

CHILDREN.

i JAMES INGLIS, b. 1804; m. Sarah A. Hains (James, Bartholomew, Bartholomew, Matthew), and had Martha J., Solomon, Alden, Charlotte, Edward, Harvey, Sophia, and George. The parents both d. in 1884. She was 75.
ii RICHARD, m. Elizabeth Crowley; 2 children.
iii EDWARD, m. Clarissa, daughter of James Everet; 6 children.
iv ELIZA, m. Edward, son of James Everet; 6 children.
v STEPHEN, m. Sophia Hains; 2 children.
vi SOLOMON, m. Anna Wade; Sophia Corbit.
vii LOUISE E., m. John Ervine, 2 sons; Alfred Troop.
viii WILLIAM FREEMAN, m. Mary Ann Marshall; 2 daughters.
ix GILBERT, d. aged 3 years.
x ALPHEUS, m. Tamer, daughter of Alexander Hardwick, Esq.; 4 children.
xi HANNAH M., b. 1827; m. Edward Hardwick; Daniel Nichols. Son Melbourn H. Hardwick, in Boston with his mother.
xii THOMAS WHITEFIELD, m. Dorinda Inglis.

17. iii. Otis Marshall (Isaac), b. in Clarence, Feb. 21, 1773; m. Silence, daughter of Daniel Felch, Esq., July 12, 1796; and lived at Marshall's Cove, now Port Lorne. He d. 1868. She d. Oct. 1, 1856, aged 79.

CHILDREN.

i DANIEL, b. 1797, m. Amoret McKean, 1834, and had Leonora, Ansley, Mary A., Oliver, Isabel, James E., and Amoret.
ii LUCY, b 1799.
iii POLLY, b. 1802; m. William, son of Jesse Viditoe; 9 chn.
iv ISAAC, b. Oct. 14, 1804; m. Frances Brown (John, William), and d. 1870.
v REBECCA, b. Oct. 14, 1804; m. Allen Clark; 6 children.
vi JOHN, b. 1806; m. Rachel Katherns; 5 children.
vii OLIVER, m. Mary, dau. of Jesse Viditoe; 10 children.

ALLIED FAMILIES. cxxiii

- viii DIADAMA, m. Elkanah McLeod; 6 children.
- ix GEORGE, m. Caroline, daughter of Jesse Viditoe.
- x LOVISA, m. Chesley Sturk.
- xi ALLEN, m. Rachel, daughter of John Henry Snyder. She m. 2d, Thomas W. Marshall; 3d, James Morton.
- xii CALVIN, m. Lucy, daughter of Peter Strong; 11 children.
- xiii ELIZA, m. Alex. Jackson; 5 children.

18. iii. William Marshall, brother to the above, b. Aug. 14, 1777; m. by Rev. T. H. Chipman, Oct. 16, 1801, Elizabeth, daughter of William and Lydia (Willett) Marshall, and lived in Clarence; farmer. She d. June 26, 1811, aged 35; he m. 2d, by Rev. James Manning, Dec. 16, 1811, Sarah, daughter of Dea. Thomas Chute. See No. 13.

CHILDREN.

- i ASAPH, b. Aug. 27, 1802; m. Eliza Morse[8] (Jonathan, Samuel, Obadiah, Daniel, Daniel, Daniel, Samuel), April 18, 1830. He was a pious, active deacon in the Baptist church, Justice of the Peace, and farmer; d. Nov. 14, 1880; she d. Jan. 31, 1871, aged 66. Children: (1) Howard Douglass, b. Feb. 19, 1831; was an excellent school-teacher; d. in Boston, Dec. 15, 1856. (2) Melbourne E., b. Dec. 26, 1837; m. Lydia C., daughter of Leonard Weston, Nov. 2, 1868; 4 children; live on the old farm, Paradise. (3) Susan Elizabeth, b. April 24, 1840; m. Dennis Weston, May 31, 1865; 5 children; live in California.
- ii WILLIAM, JR., b. July 17, 1804; m. Grace Smith (Frank, Austin), Feb., 1827, and lived in Clarence. He d. in or near Bangor, Me., about 1845; she m. 2d, Dea. James Messenger (son of Henry), April 20, 1858, and d. 1878, aged 78. He d. at Bridgetown, 1880, aged 91. Children: (1) Mary Eliza, b. 1828; m. Enoch Gates (see Gates). (2) Charles Stewart, b. Dec. 14, 1830; m. Rachel Knapp, widow of Lambert Van Alstyne (4 children by Van Alstyne); m. 2d, Anna M., daughter of Andrew Dunn; he has lived in Ontario and in Boston. (3) Angeline F., b. 1833; m. Rev. John Goucher.
- iii CALVIN, b. and d. 1808.
- iv ELIZABETH, b. Jan. 12, 1811; m. Levi Phinney (Lot, Isaac, from Cape Cod), 1867; d. April 13, 1877; he m. 1st, Ruth Gates.

19. iii. David Marshall, youngest brother to the preceding, b. Sept. 17, 1786; m. Elizabeth, daughter of Col. B. R. Beardsley, Aug. 23, 1806, and lived near Port Lorne; farmer; d. about 1872; she d. about 1863.

CHILDREN.

   i   Enoch, m. Jane Handspiker.
  ii   Robinson, m. Susan, daughter of Ezekiel Messenger.
 iii   Ebenezer, d. young.
 iv   Mary, m. Samuel Foster, Jr.
  v   Betsy, m. Van Buren Foster.
 vi   Wellington, m. Hannah Balsor.
vii   David, Jr., d. young.
viii   Lovina, m. Joseph, son of Thomas Durland.
 ix   Sarah Ann, m. Warren, son of Benjamin Foster.
  x   Olive, m. Henry Dalton, Jr.
 xi   Isaac William, m. Fannie, daughter of David Eason; 9 children.

MAYBERRY.

1. i. William Mayberry, the first of the name of whom we have any account in this country, came with his family from the North of Ireland, and settled at Marblehead, Mass., about 1730. He was a blacksmith by trade, and had acquired considerable property in Marblehead when he joined the grantees of New Marblehead—now Windham, Me.,—and became one of the first actual settlers of that plantation in 1740. He was the first of his trade in the new township, and one of the most honored of the citizens during his life. His wife was Bathsheba ——, and he d. March 15, 1764.

CHILDREN.

2   i   John, b. 1716.
3 ii   Thomas.
   iii   Seafair, m. Stephen Manchester, Dec. 21, 1749.
4 iv   Richard.
    v   Nancy, b. 1740; m. Gershom Winship, June 29, 1759.

2. ii. John Mayberry* (William), b. in Ireland, about 1716, m. Elizabeth Dennis at Salem, Jan. 17, 1740; settled in Windham, Me., about 1745; d. March 12, 1805.

---

* This is according to the best information from records, traditions, and the memoirs of aged members of the families 30 years ago. *Rev. G. M. Bodge.*

CHILDREN.

i WILLIAM, m. Jane Miller, April 7, 1763, Cape Elizabeth.
ii ELIZABETH, m. James Webb, Oct. 19, 1762; m. 2d, Stephen Hutchinson, July 10, 1776.
iii CHARITY, b. Aug. 30, 1755; m. Enoch Graffam, 1784.
iv BATHSHEBA ⎫ twins. ⎰ m. James O. Mayberry, Dec. 1, 1785.
v REBECCA. ⎭

3. ii. Thomas Mayberry (William), b. probably in Ireland, went to Windham, Me., with his father, 1740; m. Bethia Spear, Jan. 17, 1744; she d. June 14, 1767. He m. 2d, Anne Swett, Dec. 3, 1767; she d. April 6, 1770. He m. 3d, Margaret Weeks, Sept. 9, 1770, and d.

CHILDREN.

i WILLIAM, b. Feb. 1, 1745; d. April 26.
5 ii WILLIAM, b. April 12, 1746.
iii JOHN, b. March 28, 1748; d. Aug. 27.
iv SARAH, b. July 12, 1749; m. Joshua Lowell, Oct. 28, 1768.
v THOMAS, b. July 17, 1751; m. Mary Wooster, April 28, 1774.
vi BATHSHEBA, b. July 14, 1753; m. Abram Osgood, Dec. 29, 1774.
vii MARY, b. Sept. 21, 1762; m. Col. Thomas Chute. See No. 18.
viii RICHARD, b. Aug., 1764; m. Miriam Thompson, Feb. 19, 1789.
ix JAMES, b. 1765; m. Bathsheba Mayberry, Dec. 1, 1785.
x JOHN, b. June 13, 1767.
xi HANNAH, b. Feb., 1770.
xii MARGARET, b. Dec., 1771.

4. ii. Richard Mayberry (William), m. Martha Bolton of Falmouth, Feb. 23, 1756, and d.

CHILDREN.

i MARY, b. Nov. 10, 1756; m. Edward Anderson, Aug., 1774.
6 ii WILLIAM, b. Dec. 12, 1758.
iii THOMAS, b. May 21, 1761; m. ——.
iv BATHSHEBA, b. Nov. 13, 1763; m. Abijah Purinton, Feb. 9, 1793.
v ANNA, b. Feb. 9, 1766; d. Feb. 18.
vi RICHARD, b. April, 1767; m. Mary Jordan (b. 1772), Jan. 20, 1793. She d. 1799.

cxxvi ALLIED FAMILIES.

 vii ANNA, b. Nov. 30, 1769; m. Ezekiel Jordan⁶ (1770–1852, Dominicus, Nathaniel, Dominicus, Dominicus, Rev. Robert, over to Cape Elizabeth, 1640) March 31, 1793; Ezekiel m. 2d, Mehitable Maxwell.
 viii DANIEL, b. March 4, 1778.
 ix EDWARD, b. Sept. 9, 1775.
 x MARTHA, b. Sept., 1778; m. John Lakey, 1803.

5. iii. William Mayberry (Thomas, William), b. April 12, 1746; m. Rose Walden, or Waldron, Feb. 4, 1768, and lived in Windham, Me.

CHILDREN.

 i BETHIA, b. Aug. 10, 1768; m. Ebenezer Proctor, Nov. 20, 1790.
 ii ANNA, b. April 15, 1770; m. Amos Rodgers, Aug. 14, 1790.
 iii DAVID SPEAR, b. May 1, 1772; m. Mary Cash, Oct. 12, 1794, Marblehead.
 iv ROBERT, b. March 25, 1774; m. Elizabeth Crockett, Dec. 19, 1801.
 v THOMAS, b. July, 1776; m. Katharine Goodwin, June 22, 1797.
 vi MOSES, b. 1778; m. Sarah Mitchell, June 6, 1799.
 vii ZEPHANIA, m. ———.
 viii ABRAM, m. Ann White, 1809; Fannie Harmon.
 ix ISAAC, m. Mary Mayberry, March 8, 1807.
 x ROSA, b. May, 1789; m. William C. Chute. See No. 54.
 xi MARY, m. David Waterhouse, June 26, 1814.
 xii BATHSHEBA, b. Sept., 1794; m. Daniel Chute. See No. 55.
 xiii SALLY, b. Nov., 1782; had right leg sawed off in a mill, 1791; taught school, and d. March 18, 1857, aged 75.

6. iii. William Mayberry (Richard, William), b. Dec. 12, 1758; m. Rebecca Bodge⁴ (John, Rebecca (Chute), Benjamin, Henry), and lived near a spruce swamp in Windham; hence he was called "Spruce Bill" to distinguish him from the other Williams. He d. June 8, 1850; she d. Oct., 1854, aged 97.

CHILDREN.

 i MARTHA, b. March 27, 1784; m. Col. Francis Chute. See No. 53.
 ii FRANCIS, b. 1786; m. Susan Stewart, 1810.
 iii BENJAMIN, b. 1788; m. Lois Buzzell.
 iv MARY, b. 1790; m. Richard Cook, Feb. 23, 1811.
 v BETSY, b. Oct. 13, 1792; m. Daniel Walker, and d. July, 1886. Mr. Walker, a soldier in the American War, d.

ALLIED FAMILIES. cxxvii

        1858, aged 62; son George, b. 1828, m. Mary G., daughter of John Sawyer, Jr.; was drowned in Coffee Pond, Nov., 1884.
- vi OLIVER, b. 1794; m. Betsey Haskell, 1823.
- vii REBECCA, b. 1797; d. Feb. 8, 1855.
- viii LUCY, b. 1799; d.
- ix NANCY, b. 1802; m. Charles Turner, and had only a daughter, Mary Augusta; m. George William, son of William Bicknell, Otisfield, Me. Mr. Turner d. 1862, aged 70.

A Richard Mayberry, probably brother of William, m. Elizabeth Meek, in Salem, Mass., Feb. 7, 1740, and had:

- i SARAH, baptized Nov. 7, 1740; m. John Whitefoot, Jr., Aug. 24, 1760.
- ii JANE, baptized Sept. 12, 1742; m. Thomas Delgado, June 9, 1768.
- iii ELIZABETH, baptized Aug. 5, 1748; m. Ebenezer Whitefoot, June 14, 1763.
- iv RICHARD, baptized Sept. 21, 1746; m. Elizabeth Reeves, Sept. 3, 1765.

MORSE.

In 1596 Rev. Thomas Morse, of Foxearth, Essex county, England, made his will, and mentions sons John, Samuel, Daniel, Joseph, Jeremye, James, Nathaniel, and Philip, and daughter Sarah. Samuel and Joseph undoubtedly came to America and settled, one in Ipswich, the other in Dedham.

1. Samuel Morse, b. in England, 1585; m. Elizabeth ———; came over to America in the ship *Increase*, 1685, and settled at Dedham, about 10 miles southwest of Boston; d. at Medfield, April 5, 1654. She d. June 20, 1655, aged 68.

CHILDREN.

- i JOHN, b. 1611; m. Annis Chickering, and d. in Boston, 1657; she d. 1693.
- 2 ii DANIEL, b. 1813.
- iii JOSEPH, b. 1615; m. Hannah Phillips of Watertown, 1638, and d. 1654. She m. 2d, Thomas Boyden, 1658, and d. 1676.

ALLIED FAMILIES.

    iv ABIGAIL, m. Daniel Fisher, Speaker of the House of Deputies.
    v SAMUEL, m. Mary Bullen.
    vi JEREMIAH.

2. ii. Daniel Morse (Samuel), b. 1613, in England; m. Lydia ——, and lived in Dedham, Medfield, and Sherborn; d. June 5, 1688; she d. 1690, aged 70.

CHILDREN.

    i OBADIAH, b. June 8, 1639; m. Martha Johnson, and only 1 son, Obadiah, who d. in infancy. Mr. Morse was a deacon, Town Clerk of Sherborn, schoolmaster in 1699, etc.; d. March 4, 1704; she d. 1714.
3 ii DANIEL, b. 1640.
    iii JONATHAN, b. 1643; m. Mary Barbour, 1666; 7 children. He was a lieutenant, and d. Aug. 30, 1727; she d. 1700.
    iv LYDIA, b. 1645; m. Ephraim Wight, 1667, Medfield.
    v BETHIAH, b. 1648; m. John Perry, of Sherborn, May 23, 1665, and d. June 8, 1717.
    vi MARY, b. 1650; m. Alexander West, Medfield and Sherborn, and d. 1736.
    vii BATHSHEBA, b. 1653; m. Benjamin Fisk, Medfield, 1674, and d. 1737.
    viii NATHANIEL, b. 1656; m. Mary ——; 10 children. Dea. Nathaniel d. 1728.
    ix SAMUEL, b. 1661; m. Deborah ——; 10 children, and d. Oct. 5, 1719.

3. iii. Daniel Morse, Jr., b. 1640; m. Elizabeth Barbour, 1669, Sherborn, Mass., and d. Sept. 29, 1702. She d. 1714.

CHILDREN.

    i ELIZABETH, b. 1670; Medfield.
4 ii DANIEL, b. July 10, 1672.
    iii ESTHER, b. May 21, 1674; Sherborn.
    iv ELIZABETH, b. Oct. 29, 1677; m. Richard Sanger, 1697; Sherborn.
    v JOHN, b. Aug. 27, 1679; d. Feb. 17, 1718.
    vi NOAH, b. April 20, 1681; m. Mary Johnson, July 12, 1705; 2d, Abigail Gleason, 1714; 4 children by each.
    vii MARGARET, b. Sept. 30, 1683; m. Ezra Clark, 1707; Medfield.
    viii HANNAH, b. Dec. 15, 1685; m. Arthur Clark, 1719; Sherborn; 4 children.
    ix MARY, b. Jan. 23, 1687; drowned in "Mary's Pond."
    x SARAH J., b. June 8, 1689; m. John Robinson, 1703; Weston.
    xi DAVID, b. Dec. 10, 1692; d. in infancy.

ALLIED FAMILIES.   cxxix

4. iv. Daniel Morse (Daniel, Daniel, Samuel), b. in Sherborn, July 10, 1672; m. Susanna Holbrook, 1696, and inherited his father's place, Sherborn, and d. 1717.

CHILDREN.

    i SUSANNA, } twins. { b. Aug. 14, 1696.
   ii BATHIA, } { b. Aug. 14, 1696; d. May 2, 1740.
  iii DANIEL, b. Nov. 22, 1699; m. Esther ——, 1724, in Walpole. She d. July 8, 1725; he m. 2d, Mary Bullard, Aug. 26, 1726, and d. Sept. 16, 1734.
5 iv OBADIAH, b. Aug. 15, 1704.
   v PATIENCE, b. Nov. 19, 1707.
  vi ANN, b. May 2, 1710.

5. v. Obadiah Morse (Daniel, Daniel, Daniel, Samuel), b. in Sherborn, Aug. 15, 1704; m. Mercy Walker, 1728, and d. in 1753.

CHILDREN.

    i DANIEL, b. 1729; m. Hannah Eames, Framingham, Mass., 1755; lived in Nova Scotia, 1760, and Natick, Mass.; had 12 children; 7 d. in 1777 in 43 days of "heart distemper."
6 ii ABNER, b. 1731.
  iii OBADIAH, b. March 20, 1733; m. Grace Fairbanks (1734-1772), July 10, 1755. He m. 2d, Abigail Death of Framingham, 1776. He d. by a fall from a scaffold, Jan. 7, 1800.
  iv MERCY, b. 1735; m. Ezra Whitney, Feb. 14, 1754, and lived at Douglass, Worcester county.
   v BENAIAH, b. 1737; m. Betsy Eames; 7 children; lived at Douglass; was killed by a cart, 1771.
7 vi SAMUEL, b. 1739.
  vii SARAH, b. 1741; m. Ezra Cook; lived at Warwick.
 viii JOHN, b. 1743; m. Eunice ——; Douglass and Sherborn; 4 children. He was a soldier in the Revolution; called "40 foot," and d. about 1825.
  ix HANNAH, b. 1745; m. Ezra Taylor, Southboro'.
   x MARY, b. 1747; m. Asahel Newton, and lived at Warwick.

6. vi. Abner Morse (Obadiah, Daniel, Daniel, Daniel, Samuel), b. in Sherborn, Mass., 1731; m. Anna Church, 1754, and moved to Annapolis county, N. S., on the sloop *Charming Molly*, 1760, and settled in Granville, as farmers, and most of them members of the Baptist church. He d. Dec. 28, 1803; she d. 1811, aged 75.

CHILDREN.

8 i ABNER, b. Dec. 6, 1756.
  ii ANNA, b. Nov. 30, 1758; m. Jacob Troop, 1774; 9 children.

CXXX ALLIED FAMILIES.

  iii ELIZABETH, b. March 2. 1761; m. James Chute, No. 14.
  iv OBADIAH, b. Feb. 13, 1763; m. Hannah Chute. See No. 7.
  v JONATHAN, b. July 6, 1765; m. Margaret Beckwith; m. 2d, Lucy Grant; 2 daughters.
9 vi DEA. SILAS, b. Aug. 26, 1767.
  vii MERCY, b. Feb. 3, 1770; m. George, son of Valentine and Katy Troop, Jan. 17, 1787; 13 children. She d. Nov. 17, 1819; he m. 2d, Margaret Chipman, Oct. 24, 1822.
10 viii DANIEL, b. Feb. 5, 1772.
11 ix JOHN MARTIN, b. July 21, 1774.
12 x DAVID, b. Jan. 16, 1777.
  xi ABIGAIL, b. April 18, 1779; d. Aug. 18.
  xii HANNAH, b. Oct. 14, 1780; m. Henry Alline Parker.

7. vi. Samuel Morse, brother to Abner, b. in Sherborn, Mass., 1739; m. Lydia Church about 1765; settled in Annapolis county, N. S.; d. Jan. 13, 1798.

CHILDREN.

13 i SAMUEL, b. about 1768.
14 ii AARON, b. Dec. 5, 1770.
15 iii JONATHAN C., b. about 1773.

8. vii. Capt. Abner Morse (Abner, Obadiah, Daniel, Daniel, Daniel, Samuel), b. Sherborn, Mass., Dec. 6, 1756; went to Nova Scotia with his parents in the *Charming Molly*, 1760, to Annapolis; m. Elizabeth Saunders, daughter of Timothy, Sen., 1774, and settled near Bridgetown. She d. early in 1793; he m. 2d, Nancy, daughter of Handley Chipman, Esq., May 27, 1793, and d. Dec., 1840; she d. Dec. 31, 1851, aged 78.

CHILDREN.

  i ANNA, m. Henry Balcomb.
16 ii CHURCH, b. 1777; m.
  iii DIADAMA, m. Nathaniel Parker, Jr.
  iv HANNAH, m. Moses Rice; 10 children.
  v RACHEL, b. 1788; m. William McGregor.
  vi HANDLEY C., b. May 7, 1795; m. Jerusha, daughter of Asa Tupper, and d. 1862. They had Asa, James, John L., Margaret A. (m. Edmund Chesley), Phebe, Jerusha (m. Edmund Gilliatt), Harris H., and Alfred C.
  vii ELIZABETH, b. March 2, 1797; m. Dea. John Wilson, Esq., 1813, and d. 1827.
  viii REBECCA, b. April 9, 1799; m. William, son of Dea. Thomas Bishop.
  ix ABIGAIL, b. April 23, 1801; m. Andrew Marshall, Jr.
  x LUCY, b. April 15, 1803; m. John Van Norden.

xi CAROLINE, b. March 7, 1805; m. Abel Banks.
xii EMELINE, b. July 4, 1807; m. Edward Bauckman; 4 children.
xiii HARRIET, b. June 22, 1809; m. Ambrose Poole. A son, Adoniram Judson, m. twice; is in Indianapolis, Ind.
xiv ABNER, b. Nov. 15, 1811; m. Sarah Ann, daughter of David Morse; 6 children.
xv EUNICE, b. March 24, 1814; m. Stephen Harris (George, John), Bear River; 3 children. He d. 1849, aged 38; she m. 2d, Dea. James Purdy; 3d, John Bennett, and now lives in Roxbury, Boston, Mass.

9. vii. Dea. Silas Morse (Abner, Obadiah, Daniel, Daniel, Daniel, Samuel), b. in Granville, N. S., Aug. 26, 1767; m. July 25, 1791, Helen, daughter of Capt. Grant; 5 children, 3 d. in infancy. She d. Aug. 6, 1801, aged 31. He m. 2d, Elizabeth Osborn, widow of John H. Chipman; 7 children; she d. He m. 3d, Sarah Bishop, widow of Daniel Chipman, and d. April 30, 1849; she d. Aug. 10, 1826, aged 53.

CHILDREN.

i ROBERT GRANT, b. 1794; d. about 1820 in the East Indies.
ii WILLIAM HALIBURTON, b. 1796; d. 1872; m. 1824, Catharine, daughter of Jacob Troop, and had (1) Amelia, m. James Phinny. (2) Charlot, m. James, son of Dea. Benjamin Fellows. (3) Robert, d. young. (4) Maria, m. John Jones. (5) Sarah, m. Charles Jones. (6) Charles. (7) James.
iii SILAS L., b. 1804; lawyer, Bridgetown; d. 1871.
iv JOHN OSBORN, b. 1806; m. Rhoda Parker; 3 children; m. 2d, Harriet Stephens; 2 more children.
v HELEN G., b. 1808; d. 1876.
vi SARAH, b. 1812; d. 1865.
vii CHARLES, b. 1815; m. Margaret Henderson; 5 children.
viii ELIZABETH, b. 1816; m. James Smith, Windsor; 4 children.
ix THOMAS A., b. Jan. 23, 1820; m. Marguretta Maria, daughter of George B. Oxley; 6 children, one a Baptist minister. Mr. T. A. Morse, a ship-builder, moved to Charlestown, Mass., 1879.

10. vii. Daniel Morse, another brother, b. in Annapolis county, N. S., Feb. 5, 1772; m. Jane, daughter of Isaac Woodbury, and setttled near Bridgetown; a farmer.

CHILDREN.

i SAMPSON, drowned at 4 years.
ii SUSAN, m. Dea. Abel Parker (William, Major Nathaniel, William).

  iii SERAPH, m. Amos Patterson. He d. 1871.
17 iv DANIEL, m. Susanna Parker (William, etc.), 1829.
  v ISABEL, m. Dea. Sidney Welton (Cephas, Ezekiel, Thomas, John, John and Mary (Upson), England, to America, 1667; to Waterbury, Conn., 1679); son, Daniel Morse Welton, D.D., b. 1831; Prof. of Hebrew, Bap. Col., Toronto, Ont.
  vi JANE, m. Rev. David Chase.
  vii LEVERETT, m. Hannah Chase. She d. 1867.

11. vii. John M. Morse, brother to the above, b. in Nova Scotia, July 21, 1774; m. Jane, daughter of Rev. T. H. Chipman, Nov., 1798; was a farmer and a good, pious deacon in the Baptist church; d. 1823. She d. 1845.

CHILDREN.

 i WILLIAM HUSTON, b. 1799; m. Miriam Parker (Samuel, Abijah, Obadiah, Nathaniel, Dea. Thomas), (b. 1801), 1828, and had 5 children.
 ii MARY A., b. 1801; m. Capt. Jonathan Crane, Topsham, Me.
 iii LOUISA, b. 1805; m. Elijah Parker, son of Samuel.
 iv MARGARET, b. 1809; m. John Balcomb, son of Henry.
 v EVALINE, b. 1811; m. Edward Parker, son of William.
 vi GAINES, b. 1813; d. young.
 vii M. ROSENBLAD, b. Aug. 23, 1815; m. Charlotte Johnson (b. March 29, 1825), Rockport, Mass.; 2 daughters, 1 son; d. March, 1894. The son, Richard Burpee, lives in Marblehead.
 viii JOHN CHIPMAN, b. 1819; m. Isabel, daughter of Abner Woodworth; m. 2d, Fanny Dakin. Rev. John C. Morse has labored faithfully at Sandy Cove, Digby county, more than 50 years, a Baptist minister; 6 children.
 ix ELIZA Q., m. Isaac Hamilton.

12. vii. David Morse, another brother, b. Jan. 16, 1777; m. Hannah, daughter of John Hicks, Jr., and lived near Bridgetown.

CHILDREN.

 i CONSTANT, m. Sarah Songster.
 ii EDWARD, m. —— ——, widow of —— Ditmars.
 iii JOHN A., m. Sarah Smith; a son is Dr. John A.
 iv WILLIAM, still living.
 v LUCINDA, m. James, son of Stephen Bent.
 vi MARY, m. Ansley, son of John Brown.
 vii SARAH ANN, m. Abner Morse, 2d, Jr.

ALLIED FAMILIES.

13. vii. Samuel Morse (Samuel, Obadiah, Daniel, Daniel, Daniel, Samuel), b. about 1768; m. Amoret Wheelock (Elias, Obadiah, Obadiah, Benjamin, Rev. Ralph), 1796, and lived near Bridgetown; d. about 1850. She d. May 12, 1825.

CHILDREN.

i Elias, b. 1798; m. Lucy Boener; 2 children.
ii Samuel, b. 1800; m. Eliza, daughter of Stephen Boener; 5 children.
iii Major, b. March 16, 1802; m. Margaret Kennedy; 4 children; d. March 11, 1894.
iv Abigail, b. 1805; d. of measles, 1823.
v Martin, b. 1808; m. Susan Leonard; 5 children.
vi Sophia, b. 1810; m. Stillman Bent; 4 children.

14. vii. Aaron Morse, brother to the above, b. Dec. 5, 1770; m. Eleanor McGregor, 1796. She d. May 9, 1827, aged 51. He m. 2d (as her 3d husband), Frances Farnsworth, widow of Rev. James Manning, and also of Henry Troop, and d. Aug. 1, 1838. She d. March 7, 1872, aged 98.

CHILDREN.

i Aaron, b. 1796; m. Seraph, daughter of Michael Martin, the singing teacher (1770–1853); 12 children.
ii Lydia A., b. Dec. 2, 1797; m. Ezekiel Chute. See No. 33.
iii William, m. Lovena, daughter of Major Chipman; 4 children.
iv Edward M., m. Mary A., daughter of William Bishop; 6 daughters; 1 son, Capt. Edward M., Jr., b. about 1830; m. Caroline Wentworth, a school-teacher from Dover, N. H., who d. at West Paradise, N. S., Oct. 30, 1889, aged 57. Capt. E. M. Morse is a man of good repute in that place.
v Joseph, d. over 40.
vi Eleanor, m. James, son of John Starratt; 6 children.
vii Henry Alline, m. Mary Elizabeth, daughter of Peter, son of John Starratt; 2 daughters; daughter Henrietta m. William Fowler Chute, a carpenter in Lynn. Mrs. M. E Morse d. in Lynn, March, 1893, aged 69.

15. vii. Jonathan C. Morse, another brother, b. about 1773; m. Susanna Longley (William, Israel, William, John, the Redeemed Captive, William, William, William of Lynn, Mass., 1636), and lived at or near Paradise, N. S.

CHILDREN.

    i   EDWARD, m. Sarah A. Elliott, daughter of John.
   ii   ISRAEL, m. Susan Sturmey.
  iii   ELIZA, b. May 23, 1805; m. Asaph Marshall (William, Isaac, William (?), or John (?)), April 18, 1830; 3 children.
   iv   HARRIET, m. David Morse, Jr.
    v   LUCY, m. Lawrence Phinney.
   vi   CAROLINE, m. Gideon, son of John I. Palmer.
  vii   MENETTA, m. Warren Longley (William, Israel).
 viii   MARY CECELIA, m. Jacob Miller, Jr.

16. viii. Church Morse (Capt. Abner, Abner, Obadiah, Daniel, Daniel, Daniel, Samuel), b. 1777; m. Elizabeth Parker (Major Nathaniel, William), 1800, and lived near Bridgetown. He was drowned May 1, 1817. She m. 2d, Samuel Felch (1776–1852), and d. May, 1866, aged 85. 7 Morse children; 1 Felch.

CHILDREN.

    i   HELLEN, b. April 6, 1801; m. Abner Parker, May 24, 1825; 10 children.
   ii   BENAIAH, b. Dec. 22, 1802; m. Elizabeth, daughter of John Robinson, March 31, 1825; Wilmot, N. S.; had 8 children; m. 2d, Elizabeth Cutten, 1864.
  iii   JONATHAN, b. July 15, 1805; m. Elizabeth, daughter of Samuel Spinney; 10 children.
   iv   ELIZABETH, b. Jan. 17, 1807; m. James Saunders; 2d, William Copeland, 1829; 2 children.
    v   NATHAN PARKER, b. Dec. 12, 1809; m. Mary A. Roach (d. 1860); m. 2d, Mary Elizabeth Elliott, 1861, and d. 1880, in Clarence; 4 children.
   vi   CHARLOTTE, b. and d. 1812.
18 vii   ABNER, b. July 1, 1813.
 viii   EUNICE SALOME FELCH, b. 1824; m. Joseph L. McKenne, 1843; Kingston, N. S.; 9 children.

17. viii. Daniel Morse, Jr. (Daniel, Abner, Obadiah, Daniel, Daniel, Daniel, Samuel), b. near Bridgetown, N. S., 1805; m. Susan Parker (William, Major Nathaniel, William), 1829, and d. Sept. 30, 1881. She d. 1884, aged 76.

CHILDREN.

    i   SARAH J. B., b. Dec. 11, 1829; d. April 17, 1859.
   ii   ISAAC WATTS, b. Oct. 14, 1831; m. Rebecca, daughter of Capt. John Shafner, 1858; 7 children; to Watertown, Mass., 1885.

ALLIED FAMILIES. CXXXV

iii LYDIA SALOME, b. Aug. 17, 1833; m. William W. Balcomb, 1860.
iv LUCY ISABEL, b. Oct. 30, 1835; d. March 6, 1844.
v WILLIAM ALLINE, b. Oct. 14, 1837; m. —— ——, 1861.
vi ROBERT DANIEL, b. Sept. 6, 1841; d. June 28, 1842.
vii JAMES SHANNON, b. May 14, 1843.
viii MARY ANN H. JUDSON, b. Jan. 15, 1847.

18. ix. Abner Morse (Church, Capt. Abner, Obadiah, Daniel, Daniel, Daniel, Samuel), b. July 1, 1813; m. Mary Elizabeth, daughter of Elijah Purday, Nov. 9, 1834, and lived at Bear River, a blacksmith. She d. 1882, aged 74. He d. April 25, 1894.

CHILDREN.

i ALLISTER, b. 1836; m. Mary Ann, daughter of Daniel and Elizabeth (Phinney) Felch, 1859; 3 children. He d. 1871; she to Boston, 1881.
ii ELIZABETH HELEN, b. 1838; m. William T., son of Obadiah Morse, Jr. He d. 1862; she m. 2d, Henry J. Rice (b. 1829), and have 5 children.
iii MARY ADALINE, b. 1842; d. 1845.
iv WILLIAM CHURCH, b. 1844; m. Sarah Rogers, 1865; and d. 1870.
v FANNY ANN, b. 1846; m. Ezra, son of Nelson Miller, 1866, and d. 1873; 4 children.
vi LAVINIA C., b. 1848; m. Abram Chute Potter, 1874; one daughter, Kizbro F., b. 1874. Mr. Potter d. Sept. 2, 1877. She m. 2d, Israel Balcomb, 1885.
vii ABNER PURDY, b. 1850; d. 1871.

19. Rev. Arsarelah Morse was in Granville, N. S., between 1770 and 1800; said to be a Presbyterian minister. His history is a little uncertain, but from the best information within reach, it appears that his descent is this: Arsarelah, Theodore, Joshua, Joshua, Joshua, William of Newbury, Mass., b. 1608, in Marlboro,' Wilts, Eng.; m. Elizabeth ——, about 1635; and d. at Newbury, Nov. 29, 1683.

This Rev. A. Morse was b. in Massachusetts, Jan. 16, 1745, H. C., 1767; m. Hephzibah Hall, July 4, 1771, a descendant of Gov. Thomas Dudley and Gov. John Winthrop. She d.; he m. 2d, Mrs. Susan Phinney, Granville, N. S.

Joshua[2] was Chaplain to Sir William Phipps, 1689.
Joshua[3], b. 1692, Joshua 2d b. 1694.
Joshua[4] m. Elizabeth Doten, Plymouth, Mass.
Theodore[5], b. Aug. 20, 1714; was a Captain; m. Thankful Crocker (1717–1762), and d. Dec. 19, 1794.

CHILDREN OF REV. A. MORSE.

i ABIGAIL, b. July 2, 1772.
ii THANKFUL, b. 1774.
iii DIADAMA, m. Michael Spurr, Jr.

20. **Anthony Morse**, brother to William, b. May 9, 1606, in Marlboro,' Eng.; came over to Newbury, Mass., 1635; d. Oct. 12, 1686. Anthony[2] d. 1678. Peter[3] moved to Roxbury, d. 1721. John[4] m. Sarah Peak (1701–1801). Jedediah[5], 1726–1819. Jedediah[6], D.D., 1761–1826, author of American Geography, 1784, etc.; m. Elizabeth Ann Breeze, 1789, in Charlestown; had 11 children; only three grew up to manhood:

i SAMUEL FINLEY BREEZE, 1791–1872, was the great professor, and inventor of the telegraph. He m. Lucretia Pickering (1800–1825); m. 2d, Sarah E. Griswold. They visited St. John's, N. F., in 1855, when at a banquet there the following toast was given:

> "The steed called Lightning," says the fates,
> Was tamed in the United States;
> 'T was Franklin's hand that caught the horse,
> 'T was harnessed by Professor Morse."

ii SIDNEY E., 1794–1871; author of *Morse's Geography*, etc.
iii RICHARD C., 1795–1868; d. in Bavaria; established *New York Observer*, etc.

NOYES.

1. i. **Rev. William Noyes**, rector of Cholderington, or Salisbury, Wilts, Eng.; d. about 1616, aged 30, and was succeeded by his son Nathan, who d. 1651. His widow, Ann (sister of Rev. Robert Parker, called a very learned Puritan, who was driven to Holland for not complying with Queen Elizabeth's forms), d. March 7, 1657, aged 82. They left, besides Nathan, sons James and Nicholas.

2. ii. **Rev. James Noyes** (Rev. William), b. 1608; was educated at Oxford; m. Sarah, daughter of Joseph Brown of Southampton; came over in the brig *Elizabeth*, to Ipswich, 1634; preached a year in Medford; was invited to Watertown in May, 1635; removed to Newbury, and was colleague there with Rev. Thomas Parker, his cousin. He d. Oct. 22, 1656.

CHILDREN.

i JOSEPH, b. Oct. 15, 1637; d. at Bermuda.
ii REV. JAMES, b. March 11, 1639: H. C., 1659; m. Dorothy, daughter of Thomas Stanton, Sept. 11, 1674; was pastor over the First Congregational Church, Stonington, Conn.; had 7 children; d. 1719. She d. 1743, aged 91.
iii SARAH, b. Aug. 12, 1641; d. young.
iv MOSES, b. Dec. 6, 1643; H. C., 1659; m. Ruth, daughter of John Picket.
v JOHN, b. June 3, 1645; d. young.
vi THOMAS, b. Aug. 10, 1648; m. Martha Pierce, 1669; Elizabeth Greenleaf, 1677.
vii JOHN, b. June 4, 1649; went to Bermuda.
viii REBECCA, b. April 1, 1651; m. John Knight, Jan. 1, 1671.
ix DEA. WILLIAM, b. Sept. 22, 1653; m. Mrs. Sarah Cogswell, Nov. 6, 1681.
x SARAH, b. March 21, 1656; m. Rev. John Hale, son of Dea. Robert of Beverly, 1684.

3. ii. Dea. Nicholas Noyes (Rev. William), b. 1614; came over with his brother, Rev. James, 1634; to Newbury, May, 1635; made a freeman, 1637; Representative to the General Court at Boston, etc.; m. Mary, daughter of John Cutting, 1640, and d. Nov. 21, 1701, aged 87.

CHILDREN.

i MARY, b. Oct. 15, 1641; m. John French.
ii HANNAH, b. Oct., 1643; m. Peter, son of John Cheney, May 14, 1663; he d. 1694, aged 55; she m. 2d, John Atkinson, June, 1700. Three of this family m. three children of James Chute. See Cheney.
iii JOHN, b. Jan. 20, 1645; m. Mary, daughter of John Poor (Wiltshire, to Newbury, Mass., 1635; d. 1684, aged 69); 9 children; d. 1700. She m. 2d, Eliphalet Coffin.
iv REV. NICHOLAS, b. Dec. 22, 1647; H. C., 1667; to Salem, 1682; had a hand in the "Salem Witchcraft," 1692; d. Dec. 13, 1717.
v CUTTING, b. Sept. 23, 1649; m. Elizabeth Knight, Feb. 25, 1673; had 6 children; m. 2d, Elizabeth Tappan, 1702.
vi SARAH, b. Sept. 13, 1651; d. soon.
vii SARAH, 2d, b. Aug. 22, 1653; m. Matthew Pettingall, Sept. 13, 1674.
viii TIMOTHY, b. June 23, 1655; m. Mary Knight, Jan. 13, 1680; had 11 children, and d. 1718.
ix CAPT. JAMES, b. May 16, 1657; m. Hannah Knight, March 31, 1684; 12 children.
x ABIGAIL, b. April 11, 1659; m. Simeon French.

xi RACHEL, b. March 20, 1661; m. James Jackson, 1682.
xii THOMAS, b. June 20, 1663; m. Sarah ——; 2 daughters.
xiii REBECCA, b. May 18, 1665; d. 1683.

John Knight, b. 1622, came over to America; m. Bathsheba, daughter of Richard Ingersoll of Salem, 1647; and d. 1678. She d. Oct. 25, 1705.

CHILDREN.

i JOHN, b. Aug. 16, 1648; m. Rebecca Noyes, 1672.
ii JOSEPH, b. June 21, 1652; m. Deborah Coffin, 1677.
iii ELIZABETH, b. Oct. 18, 1655; m. Cutting Noyes, 1674.
iv MARY, b. Sept. 8, 1657; m. Timothy Noyes, 1681.
v SARAH, b. April 13, 1660.
vi HANNAH, b. March 22, 1662; d. soon.
vii HANNAH, b. Aug. 30, 1664; m. James Noyes, March 31, 1684.
viii CAPT. RICHARD, b. July 26, 1666; m. Elizabeth Jacques.
ix BENJAMIN, b. Aug. 21, 1668; m. Abigail Jacques.
x ISAAC, b. Aug. 31, 1672; d. 1690.

After much correspondence and research for a tracing of the Noyes family of Maine back to the parent stock of Newbury, Mass., we arrive at this conclusion: Mary Noyes (David and Elizabeth Newman, Daniel and Judith Knight, John and Mary Poor, Dea. Nicholas and Mary Cutting, Rev. William and Ann Parker), b. in Portland, 1763; m. Col. Josiah Chute of Windham, Me., 1781, a soldier of the Revolution.

PALMER.

1. i. William Palmer, b. 1605; from England, 1648; and was a citizen of Mamaroneck, Westchester county, N. Y., 1650 and d. about 1670. His children were:

   i JOSEPH.   ii BENJAMIN.
2 iii SAMUEL, of Mangopson Neck. iv OBADIAH.
   v THOMAS.

2. ii. Samuel Palmer (William), of Mangopson Neck, had:

   i OBADIAH, b. 1649; m. Anne ——, and d. 1748.
   ii NEHEMIAH, m. —— ——, and had a son, and daughter May; d. 1760.
3 iii SYLVANUS.   iv SOLOMON.
   v JOSEPH.   vi THOMAS.
   vii BENJAMIN.

ALLIED FAMILIES. cxxxix

3. iii. Sylvanus Palmer (Samuel, William), m. Mary ——— and d. 1741.

CHILDREN.

    i Robert, m. Mary ———.   ii Sylvanus.
4 iii John.   iv Marmaduke.
   v Edward.   vi Anne.
 vii Susanna.   viii Charity.
  ix Mary.

4. iv. John Palmer (Sylvanus, Samuel, William), m. Rebecca ———, and had:

    i Joseph.   ii Martus.
  iii Benjamin.   iv Esther.
   v Philip.   5 vi Lewis.
 vii Thomas.   viii Martha.

5. v. Lewis Palmer (John, Sylvanus, Samuel, William) was a Loyalist in the Revolution, and lost £600 by adhering to the Crown; went to Shelburne, N. S., after 1780; m. Rachel Fowler before 1750, and the children were all born in Westchester county, New York.

CHILDREN.

    i Capt. Edmund, was taken and shot by the Whigs, as a spy, leaving a son.
6 ii Alpheus.   7 iii Benjamin.
8 iv Theodore.
   v Mary, m. Peter Bonett, Annapolis.
  vi Milcah, m. David Denison; lived in Horton; 6 or 7 children.
 vii Euphemia, m. Peter de San Croix; 4 children.

6. vi. Alpheus Palmer (Lewis, John, Sylvanus, Samuel, William), b. at Mamaroneck, Westchester county, N. Y.; m. about 1775 Bathsheba, daughter of John Turner (1728–1817), and lived in Aylesford, Kings county, N. S. He went with sons John and Gideon to Canada West, 1831.

CHILDREN.

    i Betsy, m. Charles Card.
  ii John, d. away off in the West.
  iii James, killed by a falling tree.
  iv Lewis, drowned in youth.
   v Bathsheba, m. ——— ———; lived and d. in Ohio.

ALLIED FAMILIES.

9 vi ALPHEUS, b. 1799; m. Margaret Palmer.
   vii GIDEON, b. July, 1804; m. Margaret, daughter of William Creelman, and moved to Euphemia, Lambton county, Oct., 1831, and d. there about 1870; a farmer and pious deacon in the Baptist church; had 8 sons; 1 daughter.
   viii MARY, m. Wentworth Robinson, and lived at Miramichi, N. B. A great fire there 1826.
   ix RACHEL, m. John Inglis Palmer.

7. vi. Benjamin Palmer (brother to the above), b. 1751; m. Philena, daughter of Enoch and Betsy (Fowler) Hunt, and settled in Aylesford, N. S., as farmers. He d. 1847; she d. 1850, aged 88.

CHILDREN.

   i ENOCH, d. young.
   ii RACHEL, m. William Henry, son of Robert and Margaret Robinson, Dec. 11, 1806; 8 children.
10 iii ELIJAH, b. 1784.
   iv BETSY, m. John Taylor, from Ireland.
11 v ENOCH LEWIS, b. 1788.
12 vi BENJAMIN, b. 1790.
   vii PHILENA, b. 1799; m. John William Creamer, 1818; 2 children; Henry Pitcher; son John William.
   viii MARGARET, m. Alpheus Palmer, Jr.
13 ix JOHN INGLIS, b. 1802.
   x MARY P., b. 1806; m. John Dunn, 1832; 5 children.

8. vi. Theodore, the youngest brother, m. —— Denison, and lived in Wilmot, Annapolis county, N. S.

CHILDREN.

   i EDMUND, b. about 1788; m. Rachel Smith, and d. 1875. Children: Amanda, Caroline, Eliza, James, and Mrs. Avery.
   ii MARY, b. about 1789; d. about 1880.
   iii RACHEL, b. about 1790; m. —— Witter; 2 sons.
   iv JOHN, b. about 1792; m. Phebe Elliott, and d. 1862; she d. 1877, aged 80. Children: (1) Arthur, m. Lucy Morse; 6 children. (2) Robinson, m. Susanna Pierce. (3) Phebe Ann, m. Henry Milbury. (4) Joseph, m. Caroline, daughter of Sam Chesley; 6 children. (5) Edward, m. Phebe, daughter of Sam Chesley; 2 children. (6) Margaret, m. Edward Drew; 5 children. (7) Eunice, d. about 11. (8) Zephaniah, b. 1826; m. Maria Ann Starratt (Sam, John, John, from Ireland); 9 children, and d. Sept. 20, 1886; the widow went to Beverly that year. (9) Edmund, m. May Ann Johnson; 4 children. (10) Sarah, m. William Nichols, Jr.; 6 children.

ALLIED FAMILIES.

9. vii. Alpheus Palmer, Jr., m. Margaret Palmer, and d. 1860, aged 61. She d. 1870, aged 72.

CHILDREN.

   i Edwin W., b. 1833; m. Angelina Ward; 9 children.
   ii Elizabeth L., b. 1835; m. William B. Palmer (Benjamin, Enoch L., Benjamin); 1 daughter.
   iii Melinda A., b. 1838; m. William Dazelle; 6 children.
   iv Benjamin W., b. 1841; m. Evalina, daughter of Richard Woodworth; 1 daughter.

10. vii. Elijah Palmer (Benjamin, Lewis, John, Sylvester, Samuel, William), b. in Nova Scotia, 1784; m. Elizabeth, daughter of Robert and Margaret Robinson, 1811, and lived in Aylesford.

CHILDREN.

   i Mary Jane, b. 1812; m. Robert Jackson; Handley Parker.
   ii Benjamin Lawrence, b. 1817; m. Charlotte, daughter of Frank Tupper, and had Leander, Hanley, Edgar, Amelia, Armina, Euphemia, Arabel, Helen, and James Reed.
   iii Eliza, b. 1819; m. Frank Jackson, 3 sons; —— Nelson, 2 children.
   iv Ann, b. 1822.
   v Louisa, b. 1824; m. Charles, son of Robert Nichols; 5 children.
   vi Ann, b. 1826; m. Eliakim Collins; 4 children.
14 vii Thomas R., b. 1829, } twins.
   viii Sarah N., b. 1829, } m. Ambrose, son of Robert Nicholas; 6 children.

11 vii. Enoch Lewis Palmer (Benjamin, Lewis, John, etc.), was b. in Aylesford, Kings county, N. S., April 24, 1788; m. Margaret, daughter of Robert Robinson, by Parson John Wiswall, March 11, 1811, and lived on a farm in Morristown, where he d. Dec. 10, 1869; she d. March 9, 1882, aged 88.

CHILDREN.

   i Maria, b. July 11, 1812; m. Lawrence, son of William Creamer from Connecticut, 1837, and had 6 children.
15 ii Elijah, b. Sept. 28, 1813.
16 iii Benjamin, b. Sept. 3, 1815.
   iv Elizabeth L., b. May 1, 1817; m. Robert, son of Joseph Collins, 1836; 9 children; she d. 1874. He m. 2d, Adaline Fisher, 1877, and d. April, 1886, aged 71; son Harvey G. Collins, blacksmith, Somerville, Mass.
   v Margaret P., b. March 5, 1819; m. Joseph Kelly, Dec. 25, 1845.

ALLIED FAMILIES.

    vi MARY CAROLINE, b. Feb. 22, 1821; m. Dea. Edmund Chute. See No. 101.
   vii PHILENA HUNT, b. Jan. 20, 1823; m. William McConnell (Joseph, Benjamin), March 10, 1842; 4 children.
  viii DEA. JOHN H., b. May 6, 1825; m. Margaret, daughter of Robert Robinson, Jan., 1851; 5 children; and d. Nov. 12, 1891.
    ix WILLIAM H., b. Feb. 27, 1827; d. April 28, 1840.
     x MATILDA, b. Nov. 5, 1829; m. Joseph McConnell, Jr.
    xi ENOCH L., b. April 17, 1832; m. Rebecca Parish, 1853; 3 children.
   xii SUSANNA, b. Jan. 6, 1835; m. James Henry Barteaux (Robert, Charles, William, Philip), Nov. 15, 1854; 5 children.
  xiii REV. JAMES, b, April 6, 1837; m. Julia E., daughter of Dea. Oliver H. Cogswell, 1856; one daughter, Laleah, b. 1858; m. her cousin, Theodore McConnell of Ontario. Rev. Mr. Palmer was a zealous minister in the Baptist church, but d. young, Aug. 4, 1865; she d. Dec. 13, 1876, aged 38.
  xiv HENRY, b. Aug. 29, 1839; m. Emma, daughter of Enoch L. Cogswell, 1864, and d. Oct. 31, 1876.

12. vii. Benjamin Palmer, another brother, b. 1790; m. Isabel Dunn (John Dunn from Ireland), and had

     i SARAH.
    ii ELIZABETH; d. young.
   iii SAMUEL, m. daughter of Henry Ogilvie.
   iv JAMES, m. Charlotte Rosencranz.
    v CHARLES, m. Ruth Banks (Richard, Moses, etc.).
   vi AMANDA, m. Lawrence Creamer, as 2d wife.

13. vii. John Inglis Palmer, the youngest brother, b. in Aylesford, 1802; m. Rachel, daughter of Alpheus Palmer, and lived in Aylesford; d. 1886; she d. some time before him.

CHILDREN.

     i JOHN INGLIS, m. in Ontario.
    ii GIDEON, m. Caroline, daughter of John C. Morse.
   iii MERINDA R., m. Benjamin Wood; 6 children.
   iv JOSEPH, m. daughter of Parker Welton, son of Cephas.
    v JANE, m. Edward P. Lloyd; 4 children.
   vi ZACHARIAH, m. Abigail Taylor (William, James, Eldad, Edward); 5 children.
   vii WILLIAM, Boston.
  viii SELINA, m.

ALLIED FAMILIES.

14. viii. Thomas R. Palmer (Elijah, Benjamin, Lewis, John, Sylvester, Samuel, William), b. in Aylesford, 1829; m. Mary Ann, daughter of George Nicholls.

CHILDREN.

i MARY E., m. Edmund C., son of Benjamin and Mary J. Palmer.
ii ANNETTA, m. Foster, son of Joel Parish; 2d, Jr.
iii GEORGE, m. Maggie McEmerson.
iv AMBROSE, m. Sarah, daughter of Leander Chute; she a school-teacher.
v CHARLES.
vi ELIZABETH, d. at 19.
vii LATHAM, d. at 15.
viii EMMA, m. Fred Webb.
ix ISAIAH, m. Victoria Sanford (George W., James, John N.).
x HANDLEY, m. Martha E. Sanford (William H., John N.).
xi THOMAS.
xii CHARLOT, m. Lysander Thomas.
xiii ROBERT.

15. viii. Elijah Palmer (Enoch L., Benjamin, Lewis, John, Sylvester, Samuel, William), b. in Morristown, N. S., Sept. 28, 1818; m. Margaret, daughter of James Hamilton, Nov., 1841, and settled at Welsford, in Cornwallis, N. S.; farmer.

CHILDREN.

i JANE, b. 1842; m. Charles Maynard, son of Dea. O. H. Cogswell, 1866; 6 children.
ii CAROLINE, b. 1844; m. James Read; 4 children.
iii JAMES, b. 1847; d. about 1877.
iv REUBEN, b. 1850.
v RICHMOND, b. 1853; m. Amanda, daughter of George Borden.
vi MAGGIE, m. George West.

16. viii. Benjamin Palmer (Enoch, Lewis), b. Sept. 3, 1815; m. Mary J., daughter of Eleazer and Mary Woodworth, by Rev. William Chipman, Dec. 22, 1838, and lived on the South Mountain, Cornwallis, N. S.; a farmer and Baptist exhorter; d. Sept. 10, 1889.

CHILDREN.

i JOHN ALBERT, b. Sept. 4, 1840; m. Anna McGranihan, 1863; 5 children; she d. He m. 2d, ——.
ii WILLIAM BURPEE, b. Dec. 8, 1841; m. Elizabeth L. Palmer (Alpheus, Alpheus, Lewis, John, etc.), Dec. 23, 1863, and

had one daughter, Melinda A., b. 1869; m. John W. Moore, Lynn, Mass. Mr. Palmer is a mechanic in Lynn, and Mrs. Palmer is a writer for the papers.

iii   EDMUND CHUTE, b. Aug. 16, 1843; m. Mary Eliza, daughter of Thomas R Palmer, Jan. 8, 1868; 8 children; Waterville, N. S.

iv   MARY AMY, b. April 24, 1845; d. 1846.

v   EZEKIEL K., b. Oct. 18, 1846; m. Eliza, daughter of James Bent, June 25, 1879; 3 children.

vi   JOEL P., b. July 2, 1848; m. Anna, daughter of William H. Barnaby, 1880, and d. at Chipman Brook, 1884. She m. 2d, Willard Rudolph, 1885, and d. 1888.

vii   JAMES R., b. June 8, 1850; m. Martha Reed, Florida, 1880.

viii   ROBERT W., b. Jan. 27, 1852; killed in the Modoc War, 1872.

ix   MARGARET E., b. Dec. 27, 1853; m. William Ridout Marshall (Isaac, William, David, Isaac), 1876; 3 or 4 children; Cambridge, Mass.

x   MARY OLIVIA, b. Dec. 27, 1855; m. Walter R. Simmons, June 17, 1886, Boston, Mass.; have a daughter Pauline, besides 2 daughters he had by a 1st wife.

PARKER.

1. i. About the year 1700, or before, lived in Shrewsbury, Mass., a family of Parkers; of whom William is mentioned as marrying, Oct. 23, 1739, Mary D. Maynard (Sergt. Simon, Simon, John, one of the 47 who shared in the division of Sudbury meadows, 1638; selectman, and a petitioner for the grant of Marlboro', 1656; moved there, where his children were b., and d. 1711. His wife was Mary, daughter of Stephen Gates). She was b. 1719, and admitted to the church in Shrewsbury 1742.

CHILDREN.

i   WILLIAM, b. March 18, 1740; m. Tabitha Sawyer, Dec. 11, 1761, and had: (1) Parnal, a daughter, b. July 4, 1763. (2) Eunice, b. Dec. 8, 1764; d. Aug. 11, 1770. (3) Joseph Sawyer, b. Feb. 21, 1770; d. April 14, 1771.

ii   JOAB, b. April 20, 1741.

2 iii   NATHANIEL, b. March, 1743.

2. ii. Major Nathaniel Parker (William) was a soldier in the British army, 1759–1763, at the taking of Quebec, etc.; went to Granville, N. S., after the war; m. Anna Hardy about 1766, and they

ALLIED FAMILIES.   cxlv

had 6 children; she d. about 1778. He m. 2d, Salome Whitman, 1779 (Dea. John, Dea. John, Rev. Zachariah, Dea. John of Weymouth, Mass.), widow of Major Ezekiel Cleveland (Lemuel, Isaac, Edward, Moses of Woburn, Mass., 1640), and lived at Nictaux, Annapolis county; an honest, pious farmer; d. 1830; she d. June 5, 1831, aged 76.

CHILDREN.

- 3 i WILLIAM, b. about 1770.
- 4 ii NATHANIEL, b. 1772.
- 5 iii HENRY ALLINE, b. 1774.
- iv MOLLY, b. 1775; m. Daniel Benjamin, Horton, N. S.
- v MIRIAM, b. 1776; m. Elias Graves, and had William, Willard, Elias, and 2 daughters, who m. George West and William West.
- vi LUCY, b. 1778; m. Dea. Cephas Welton, and had Allen, killed by a falling tree; Sidney, m. Isabel Morse; Erie, m. Mary Spinney; William, m. Louisa Willett; Parker, m. Mary Neily; Walter, m. Helen Dodge; Lucy Ann, m. Jacob Neily.
- vii HENRY, b. 1780; m. Eleanor Starratt; 4 children; 2d, Sophia (Tupper) Prentiss (1793–1849); 4 children, and d. 1835, Nictaux, N. S.
- viii ELIZABETH, b. 1781; m. Church Morse, 1800; 9 children; m. 2d, Sam Felch (1776–1852); she d. May, 1866.
- ix PARNEY, b. 1783; m. Abel Wheelock, 1801. See Wheelock.
- x IRENE, b. 1785; m. Hugh, son of Patrick Grimes, and d. 1823; 10 children.
- xi MITTIE, b. 1788; m. John Wheelock. See Wheelock.
- xii LOVE FRI, b. 1790; m. Capt. Beriah Bent, lost at sea about 1820; m. 2d, Simeon Freeman (1762–1847), 1828, and d. 1836; 6 children.
- xiii CHARLOTTE, b. 1792; m. Dea. Zoheth Freeman (1794–1848 — Peleg, Simeon, Elisha, Dea. Samuel, Dea. Samuel, Samuel of 1630), 1819; he m. 1st, Rebecca Kempton (1797–1818). Mrs. Charlotte Freeman d. 1863. A son, Rev. David Freeman, b. 1820, m. Annie E., daughter of Dea. Abel Parker (1832–1884), 1857; 5 children; he graduated Acadia College, N. S., 1850; is a Baptist minister.
- xiv LETITIA, b. 1794; m. Donald McPherson (1793–1874), 1818; had 9 children, and d. 1880.
- xv REV. MAYNARD, b. 1795; m. Catharine Spurr (1805–1851), 1821; m. 2d, Margaret (Miller) Norwell, and d. 1860; 13 children.
- xvi MARIA, b. 1800; m. Dea. Luther Leadbetter (1790–1866); lived in Brookfield, Queens county, and d. 1874; 5 children.

3. iii. William Parker (Maj. Nathaniel, William), b. about 1770; m. Lydia Benjamin, 1790; lived in Aylesford, farmer, and d. 1846; she d. 1847.

CHILDREN.

i SILAS, b. Dec., 1790; m. Nancy Balcomb, and d. 1860. She m. 2d, Dea. Joseph Wade (son of Sylvanus, son of John, went to Nova Scotia time of the Revolution), and the good old deacon d. in Granville, 1887, aged 101.
ii MARY, b. Jan., 1792; m. Job Randall; had a son Oliver, then he d. She m. 2d, Dea. Joseph Wade.
iii DEA. ABEL, b. Nov. 8, 1793; m. Susan, daughter of Daniel Morse, Jan. 25, 1821; lived at Berwick, in Cornwallis; 9 children, one of whom is Rev. David O. Parker, Baptist. He d. 1868; she d. 1876.
iv SALOME, b. Sept. 2, 1796; m. Jonas, son of Henry Balcomb, Feb. 25, 1823, Wilmot.
v MIRIAM, b. Sept. 1, 1799; m. William Chase; B. F. Chute. See No. 67. She d. Jan., 1894.
vi REV. OBADIAH, b. Nov. 24, 1803; m. Hannah Maria Morse; see No. 7; m. 2d, Mary, daughter of Reuben Balcomb, Jan. 24, 1837; 2 daughters more. He d. July 1, 1890; she d. 1888, aged 89.
vii SUSANNA, b. Nov. 24, 1805; m. Daniel Morse, Jr., Nictaux.
viii EDWARD, b. March 1, 1808; m. Evalina, daughter of John M. Morse, W. Cornwallis.
ix NATHANIEL, b. Oct. 14, 1810; merchant in Wilmot; d. July 18, 1880.
x REV. JAMES, b. Aug. 25, 1813; m. Phebe Durland, daughter of Zebulon, son of Daniel, July 12, 1842; d. Jan. 26, 1876; she d. Feb 15, 1878.

4. iii. Nathaniel Parker, Jr., b. 1772; m. Diadama Morse, daughter of Captain Abner, 1799; lived in Aylesford. He m. 2d, 1855, Sarah Ann, daughter of Stephen Parker, and widow of George Harris (1788-1854); lived at Bear River, and d. 1860; she d. 1876, aged 84.

CHILDREN.

i ABNER, m. Helen, daughter of Church Morse; he d. 1873.
ii EDWARD, m. Betsy, daughter of Henry Balcomb; he d. 1876.
iii ALFRED, m. Jane McGee.
iv LUCY, m. Samuel Balcomb.
v WILLIAM, m. Eliza, daughter of Foster Woodbury, Jr., and d. She m. 2d, John, son of Jesse Viditoe.
vi HARRIET, m. John, son of Shippy Spurr.

ALLIED FAMILIES. cxlvii

 vii NATHANIEL, m. Abba Morse.
 viii MARY, d. at about 18.
 ix BENJAMIN HARDY, m. Abigail, daughter of Alex Morse.
 x JOHN, m. Minetta, daughter of Alex Morse.
 xi ELIZABETH A., m. Jacob Wood.

5. iii. Henry Alline Parker (Maj. Nathaniel, William), b. 1774; m. Hannah Morse (Abner, Obadiah, Daniel, Daniel, Daniel, Samuel); lived in Aylesford; he d. 1871.

CHILDREN.

 i DIADAMA, m. Enoch, son of Joel Parish.
 ii STEPHEN, m. Irene Grimes (Hugh, Patrick).
 iii BETSY, m. Ezekiel, son of Thomas Banks.
 iv RACHEL, m. John Hodges, from Ireland.
 v HANDLEY, b. 1813; m. Mary J., daughter of Elijah Palmer and widow of R. T. Jackson.
 vi DANIEL, d. young.
 vii REV. WILLARD G., b. 1816; m. Lois Ruggles (James, Joseph, Joseph—brother to Gen. Timothy—Rev. Timothy, Capt. Samuel, Capt. Samuel, Thomas, 1638); he d. Dec., 1878.
 viii CHURCH MORSE, b. April, 1819; m. Lydia, daughter of James Porter.
 ix SOPHIA, m. Henry Ewing.
 x ANDREW, m. Ruth Miner.
 xi REV. WARREN, m. Sarah Ewing.

POTTER.

Nicholas and Robert Potter—supposed to be brothers, and sons of Robert Potter, b. in England, 1577;— came over to Lynn, Mass., in or before 1634. Robert was made a freeman of Massachusetts, Sept. 3, 1634, and spoken of as a farmer; but he moved to Roxbury, and on account of church troubles, he being a Quaker, he moved again to Portsmouth, R. I., and was joined by others afterwards, and founded Warwick. Mr. Potter m. Isabel ——, and had 3 daughters and a son, John, from whom have sprung some noble ministers, bishops, generals, and other noted persons. He d. in 1655.

1. i. Nicholas Potter, is said to be one of 50 persons or families who settled Saugus and Lynn, soon after 1630. He was a mason and was interested in iron works in Lynn, but moved to Salem in 1660. He had 60 acres of land in Lynn, which were given to his first family. He m. Emma Knight (?), and had 2 children. She d.

He m. 2d, Alice, widow of Thomas Weeks, with 2 children —Bethiah, b. 1642, and Hannah, b. 1645, — and she d. soon after. He m. 3d, Mary, daughter of John G. and Sarah Gedney (who came to Salem, 1637), and d. Oct. 18, 1677. She m. 2d, Joseph Boice, Jr., of Salem.

CHILDREN.

2   i   ROBERT, b. before 1630.
    ii   ELIZABETH, b. before 1630; m. Thomas Newhall (first white child b. in Lynn, 1630), Dec. 29, 1652, and d. Feb. 22, 1687. He d. April 1, 1687; 6 sons, 3 daughters.
    iii   MARY, b. Jan. 4, 1659–60; d. in October.
    iv   HANNAH, b. March 25, 1661; d. Oct. 28, 1662, in Salem.
    v   SARAH, b. Oct. 4, 1662; d. Sept. 29, 1688.
    vi   MARY, b. Nov. 10, 1663; m. Samuel Elson; 3 children.
    vii   SAMUEL, b. Jan. 9, 1664–5; d. Jan. 10, 1666.
    viii   HANNAH, b. March 27, 1666; m. William Roach; 4 children.
    ix   LYDIA, b. Feb. 26, 1667; d. Sept. 17, 1668.
    x   BETHIAH, b. May 23, 1668; m. Thomas, son of John and Sarah Witt, Feb. 26, 1685; had Mary and Thomas, and d. 1691.
    xi   SAMUEL, b. April 22, 1669; m. Rebecca Trask, and d. 1693.
    xii   LYDIA, b. July 16, 1670; d. April, 1671.
    xiii   BENJAMIN, b. Nov. 6, 1671; d. single.
    xiv   JOSEPH, b. June 9, 1673; d. young.

2. ii. Robert Potter (Nicholas), b. in England before 1630; m. Ruth, 6th child of Robert and Phebe Driver of Lynn, Jan. 25, 1660. He was a carpenter, and took the oath of allegiance with his son Robert, and brother-in-law, Robert Driver, Jr., 1677. In 1675, these two Roberts, brothers-in-law, went into the regular army in King Philip's war. For more than 20 years Mr. Potter was a man of confidence and integrity in Lynn, being selectman, surveyor, fence-viewer, etc. Ten or more different lots were given him in the town, till he must have had 25 or 30 acres. His wife d. March 18, 1704, aged 67. He d. March 21, 1709.

CHILDREN.

3   i   ROBERT, b. March 18, 1661.
    ii   NATHANIEL, b. April 14, 1663; d. in Boston after 1726.
    iii   JOHN, b. Sept. 13, 1665; m. Elizabeth Norwood, 1692; moved to Leicester about 1720; 6 children.
    iv   ELIZABETH, b. Feb. 9, 1668; d. young.
    v   ELIZABETH, b. Aug. 3, 1670; m. Joseph Floid.
    vi   RUTH, b. Feb. 27, 1673; m. John Ivory, 1698.

ALLIED FAMILIES. cxlix

- vii JOSEPH, b. Dec. 25, 1676.
- viii BENJAMIN, b. April 11, 1680; m. Ruth Russell, 1705; one child, Anna, d. at 4 years, 4 months. Capt. Benjamin Potter d. April 25, 1745.
- ix SAMUEL, b. May 8, 1682; m. Elizabeth Hart, April 1, 1709.

3. iii. Robert Potter, Jr., b. March 18, 1661; m. Martha Halle, 1682, in Lynn, Mass.; d. 1704. She d. "July ye 7th, 1709," aged 49.

CHILDREN.

- 4 i EPHRAIM, b. April 5, 1683.
- ii MARTHA, b. June 21, 1685; d. May 17, 1710.
- iii SARAH, b. April 12, 1687.
- iv RUTH, b. 1688; d. soon.
- v RUTH, b. March 16, 1690; m. Nathaniel Collins, 1714.
- vi ELIZABETH, b. March 13, 1692.
- vii ROBERT, b. Oct. 11, 1694; m. Mary Bird or Breed, 1721; d. 1733; 3 children.
- viii REBECCA, b. Oct. 24, 1696; m. Jonathan Collins, 1719.
- ix MARY, b. March 26, 1699; d. 1700.
- x NATHANIEL, b. July 16, 1701.
- xi ELIZABETH, b. May 4, 1704.

4. iv. Ephraim Potter (Robert, Robert, Nicholas), b. April 5, 1683; m. Sarah Witt, 1708, and d. 1731.

CHILDREN.

- i MARY, b. Sept. 11, 1709; Marlboro', Mass.
- ii MARTHA, b. Sept. 1, 1711.
- 5 iii JOSEPH, b. Feb. 3, 1713.
- iv PERSIS, b. Aug. 29, 1715.
- v EPHRAIM, b. March 5, 1718; m. Esther —— (1732–1810), and d. 1792.
- vi SARAH, b. Jan. 26, 1721; m. Joseph Stone, Marlboro'.
- vii THEOPHILUS, b. Jan. 26, 1725; m. Lois Walker, 1748, and d. 1814.
- viii ELIZABETH, b. Jan. 25, 1728; m. Thomas Walkup of Sudbury.

5. v. Joseph Potter (Ephraim, Robert, Robert, Nicholas), b. in Marlboro', Middlesex county, Mass., Feb. 8, 1713; m. —— ——, 1735; d. April 1, 1791. She d. April 4, 1788, aged 70.

CHILDREN.

- i MARY, b. July 3, 1736.
- ii BETTY, b. June 22, 1738.
- 6 iii JOSEPH, b. Aug. 23, 1741.

iv ROBERT, b. Nov. 7, 1745.
7 v BENJAMIN, b. May 9, 1749.
vi EBEN, b. Aug. 11, 1751.
vii SARAH, b. Nov. 21, 1753.
viii JOHN, b. March 31, 1757.
ix REUBEN, b. Dec. 9, 1759.

It is rather mysterious what became of this family. Joseph and Benjamin went to Nova Scotia, and with Joseph must have gone over a family Bible, printed in London, 1712, in which are recorded the deaths of Joseph and his wife. But her name is not mentioned.

6. vi. Joseph Potter (Joseph, Ephraim, Robert, Robert, Nicholas), b. in Marlboro', Mass., Aug. 23, 1741; m. Zebudah Hayden,* 1761, and for a few years lived in Sudbury, where the first family was born. Mr. Potter enlisted in a regiment of troops raised by Gov. William Shirley, and commanded by Col. Jonathan Bailey, and was at the battle of Fort Ticonderoga, Lake Champlain, July 8, 1758, where Gen. Lord Howe was killed. Mrs. Potter d. Jan. 24, 1767, in her 34th year. About 1770 he moved to Nova Scotia, and settled in Clements, Annapolis county, where he m. 2d, Mary Farnsworth (see Farnsworth) from Groton, Mass., 1772. She d. June 30, 1790, aged 39. After the Revolution Mr. Potter went to New York to get help to build iron works, or a foundry, which was worked for some time at Moose River, now Clementsport, and was lost at sea on a trip to New York about 1800.

CHILDREN.

i AARON, b. July 11, 1762; m.
8 ii ISRAEL, b. July, 1763.
iii MARY, b. Feb. 7, 1766; m. Capt. John Rice (see Rice), April 21, 1785. He d. May 2, 1811, aged 73; she m. 2d, Capt. Henry Harris, 1821 or 2, and d. Dec. 3, 1858. He d. May 12, 1831, aged 74.
9 iv JOSEPH, b. June 14, 1773.
v SAMUEL, b. Dec. 9, 1774.
vi SARAH, b. Aug. 4, 1776; m. John Dyer about 1800, and went to Marietta, Ohio.

---

*John Hayden, England to America, 1634, and settled in Braintree; moved to Saybrook, Conn., 1664; m Susanna ——, and had 9 children.
John, b. 1635; m. Hannah Ames, and d. 1718; 8 children.
Josiah, b. June 19, 1669; moved to Sudbury, Mass.; m. Elizabeth Goodnow, March 6, 1691, and had Josiah, John, Elisha, and Ebenezer.
Ebenezer, m. Thankful Parmenter, May 11, 1727; and had:
  i ZEBUDAH, b. June 26, 1734; m. Joseph Potter, Marlboro'.
  ii HANNAH, b. April 7, 1737; m. Elias Hayden.
  iii LOIS, b. June, 1740.

ALLIED FAMILIES.   cli

10 vii BENJAMIN, b. Dec. 11, 1777.
   viii LYDIA, b. Oct. 29, 1779; m. William Gilliatt, Jr., 1801, and d. 1818; 6 children.
11 ix FRANKLIN, b. April 28, 1781.
   x MARTHA, b. April 9, 1783; m. Thomas Rice. See Rice.
   xi SUKEY, b. Feb. 18, 1785; m. John Gilliatt; 7 children.
   xii ESTHER, b. March 16, 1787; m. John Armstrong, 1809; m. 2d, Dea. Stephen Taylor. See Taylor.

7. vi. Benjamin Potter, brother to the preceding, b. in Marlboro', Mass., May 9, 1749; m. Sarah Angier, 1773, and must have raised his family in Massachusetts. The death of Mrs. Potter I do not find in Nova Scotia, but he d. in Clements, Jan. 16, 1823.

CHILDREN.

   i HANNAH, b. 1774; m. John Burns; 4 children. He d.; she m. 2d, John Early, and had 2 sons.
   ii SARAH, b. 1776.
   iii MARY E., b. 1778; m. David Spinney and had (1) Jane, m. Joseph, son of Benjamin Brown. (2) Sarah, m. James McLachlan. (3) Henry. (4) Betsy, m. John Rier (Isaac, Dennis), and had Charlotte, 1834; John, 1837; Sarah, 1840; James R., 1842; and Elizabeth, 1845.
   iv JOSEPH, b. April 5, 1781; m. Sukey, daughter of Samuel Cutting, 1811, and settled in Framingham; d. Aug. 31, 1858. She d. Oct. 7, 1856. They had (1) Louisa, b. Nov. 7, 1813; m. Joseph Town of Saxonville, and d. 1867. (2) Angier, b. Dec. 1, 1815; m. Jane M., daughter of Walter H. Stone, and d. Dec. 23, 1885. She d. March 14, 1886, aged 66. (3) Orlando H., b. Jan. 28, 1818. (4) Anna, b. May 13, 1819; m. George Clapp of Scituate.
   v LOUISE, b. July 22, 1784; m. Jonathan Millner, and had (1) Ann, b. April 9, 1800; m. Daniel Millner. (2) John, b. Sept. 8, 1810.
   vi ASA, b. 1786; into the British army, in Newfoundland.
12 vii BENJAMIN, b. Aug. 10, 1789.

8. vii. Israel Potter (Joseph, Joseph, Ephraim, Robert, Robert, Nicholas), b. in Sudbury, Middlesex county, Mass., July, 1763; in 1780 he joined a company of six-months' men in Shrewsbury, Worcester county, to reinforce the Continental Army, and marched from Springfield with Lieut. Taylor of the 2d Mass. Regt., July 6. After the war he went to Nova Scotia, and settled on his father's estate, called Potter's Point, in Clements, where he carried on farming and fishing. He was captain of militia in the war of 1812, and served through the last of the reign of George III, into the reign of

George IV. He m. Mary, daughter of Capt. John Rice (see Rice), Jan. 7, 1786, and they lived together over 61 years. I do not know what year he was converted and joined the Baptist church, but he wrote a letter to Dr. T. Baldwin (1758-1826), of Boston, in 1810, telling of a "powerful reformation" in Clements, when about 200 were converted to the Lord; and the glorious work spread away "up the river" to Bridgetown and elsewhere. He was called to preach about this time, and was ordained to the gospel ministry in 1822, and continued a faithful minister of Jesus Christ to the end. He d. Aug. 17, 1847. She d. March 7, 1849, aged 81.

CHILDREN.

13 i AARON, b. Sept. 3, 1786.
   ii ZEBUDAH, b. March 22, 1788; m. Josiah Spurr, 1807, and had William, John, Mary Ann, Eleanor, and Eliza; and d. Jan. 11, 1816.
14 iii ISRAEL, JR., b. Jan. 7, 1790.
15 iv JOHN, b. Jan. 17, 1792.
16 v JOSEPH, b. Jan. 31, 1794.
   vi MARY, b. May 16, 1796; m. James Balcomb, and d. Oct. 2, 1880; 9 children.
   vii SARAH, b. Dec. 17, 1798; m. Josiah Spurr, his 2d wife, and had Letitia, Diadama, Israel, Charles, and Sarah.
   viii FANNY, b. Jan. 11, 1800; d.
17 ix JAMES MANNING, b. April 7, 1802.
18 x JACOB, b. Feb. 10, 1804.
   xi SUSANNA, b. Feb. 10, 1806; m. Henry Watkeys, and had Henry, Mary, Susan, William Edward, and Harriet, and d. Nov., 1866. He d. before her.
   xii ANN, b. Nov. 15, 1808; m. Rev. J. B. Cogswell. See Cogswell.
19 xiii JOSIAH SPURR, b. Feb. 22, 1810.
   xiv ZERUAH, b. Dec. 24, 1812; m. Thomas, son of Jonathan Hurd, and had Abijah and Albert. She d. March 9, 1840; he m. 2d, Jane, daughter of Edward Morgan.
20 xv ISAIAH S., b. Oct. 9, 1814.

9. vii. Joseph Potter (Joseph, Joseph, Ephraim, Robert, Robert, Nicholas), b. at Potter's Point, near Goat Island, Clements, N. S., June 14, 1773; m. Lois Hayden, 1796. She d. Nov. 3, 1833, aged nearly 53. He m. 2d, Olive, daughter of John Balcomb, and d. Aug. 26, 1848.

CHILDREN.

   i WARREN, b. July 15, 1797; m. Martha Lewis of Long Island, N. S., Dec. 20, 1827; d. 1859. She d. 1889, aged 80.

ii Sophia, b. March 25, 1799; m. Abel Chute. See No. 37.
iii Eliza, b. Aug. 7, 1801; m. John Chute. See No. 39.
iv Louisa, b. March 3, 1804; m. Dea. James Purday, Feb. 6, 1825; a daughter Louisa, m. Francis Rice (Joseph, Silas, Capt. John); 9 children. Mrs. Purday d.; he m. 2d, Eliza, daughter of John and Sukey (Potter) Gilliatt, and had Edmund, Jacob, Israel, Josiah, Albert, Rebecca, and Mary Eliza. Mrs. Purday 2d d.; he m. 3d, Eunice Morse, widow of Stephen Harris (George, John), and after his death she m. 3d, John Bennett, and lives in Boston, aged 79.
v Joseph Lyman, b. May 30, 1807; m. Lydia Witt (George, Gideon, from Lynn, Mass.), Oct. 9, 1834, and had George, Allen, Joseph, Mary Elizabeth, Lois Ann, Eunice Matilda, Martha Jane, and Joseph Edgar. Mr. Potter d. 1859, aged 52. She m. 2d, Elliott Ritchie (1816–1880); m. 3d, Nathan R. Chute (1815–1891), and since then she has lived near Boston, Mass.
vi William Franklin, b. Oct. 16, 1809; m. Mary Ann, daughter of William Gilliatt; she d.; he m. 2d, Mrs. Phebe (German) Kennedy.
vii Mary, b. Jan. 23, 1811; m. Ashael Howard; m. 2d, Solomon, son of George Bowlby.
viii Sally, b. March 6, 1814; m. Israel, son of William Gilliatt, 1836.
ix Silas, b. Nov. 5, 1816; m. Catharine, daughter of Dea. Thomas Gilliatt, and d. May, 1891.

10. vii. Dea. Benjamin Potter, J. P., brother to the above, b. Dec. 11, 1777; m. Jane Spurr (Abram, Michael), and lived at Smith's Cove, Digby county, good, pious people, and farmers. He d. June, 1861. She d. 1864, aged 86.

CHILDREN.

i Eliza, b. 1799; m. Caleb Soulice (John, Daniel, John, John, of the French Pyrenees in France, 1670); and had Benjamin Potter, 1830; Cynthia, 1831; Henry Harris, 1833; Eliza Deborah, 1835; John L., 1837; James Albert, 1839; Amanda J., Mary Emily, and Annetta. Mrs. Soulis d. 1848; he m. 2d, Olive, daughter of John Potter (she was drowned, 1868); he m. 3d, Mrs. Roop.
ii Thomas, b. April 1, 1800; m. Sarah A., daughter of Jeremiah Smith, Jr., and had Henrietta Jane, Charles Thomas (m. Susan Ann Chute), Eliza Abigail (m. B. P. Soulice), Oratia Adelia, Sarah Ann, Emma Amelia, Cynthia, Jeremiah Smith, and Louise Maria.
iii John L., b. 1802; m. Caroline Hunt (Elijah, Benjamin); 10 children. He d. March 24, 1867, aged 65; she in Boston.

- iv WILLIAM F., b. about 1804; m. Abigail O., daughter of Capt. Simpson; 4 children.
- v HENRY, b. about 1807; m. Polly Rice (Silas, Capt. John); 5 children.
- vi CYNTHIA, b. about 1810; m. William Jones, Jr., and d. 1843; son, Benjamin Potter Jones, b. Sept. 6, 1842; m. Sept. 29, 1872, Abbie F., daughter of William Butterfield of Vermont (b. May 17, 1851); to Boston, 1864, cabinetmaker; have Walter Alford, b. Jan. 26, 1874, and Clinton Havelock, b. Nov. 20, 1888; lost 3 or 4.
- vii JANE, b. about 1812; m. John, son of Jeremiah Ditmars; 3 children.
- viii JAMES M., b. about 1815; m. Elizabeth Sharp; went to Fonthill, Ont., 1851; then to St. Catherine's, as principal of a high school, 25 years; but since 1880 to California; 6 or 7 children.
- ix EDWARD W., b. about 1818; m. Abigail Soulice[e] (Daniel, John, Daniel, John, John); 3 children.
- x EMELINE, b. about 1822; m. George S. Soulice (Daniel, John, etc.); 3 children. She d. 1860; he m. 2d, Minerva Sypher.

11. vii. Dea. Franklin Potter, another brother, b. April 28, 1781; m. Cynthia Boice, in Clements, 1805, and soon after moved to Brier Island, Digby county, where, after having 4 children, she d. He m. 2d, Abigail O'Brien; after having 6 children she d. He m. 3d, Mrs. (Robbins) Durkee, of Yarmouth; she d. Sept., 1859; he d. 1862.

CHILDREN.

- i DEA. GEORGE BOICE, Justice of the Peace, b. 1807; m. Sarah Payson (Elisha, Jonathan, Jonathan, Ephraim, Dea. Edward, over to Roxbury 1636; m. Ann Parke, d. Sept. 10, 1641; m. 2d, Mary, daughter of Philip Eliot, brother to the Apostle John Eliot, and d. about 1695), and was a good and useful citizen in civic and religious society at Westport; d. April, 1893; she d. 1868, aged 64. Children: (1) Abigail, m. Thomas Titus (Enoch, James, Isaac, Timothy, Jacob, John, Edmund, Robert, b. in England 1600; to America 1635; d. about 1670); 8 children, of whom Rev. George B. is pastor of the Baptist church, Everett, Mass. (2) Orinda, m. John Peters; 12 children. (3) Cynthia, m. Maurice Peters, a brother; 12 children. (4) Sarah Caroline, m. Jesse Peters, another brother; 7 children. (5) Eliza Jane, m. William Welch; 2 sons. (6) Ann, m. George Coggins; 6 children. (7) Helen, d. young.
- ii MARY ANN, m. Capt. Holland E. Payson (Elisha, Jonathan, etc.); 4 children.

ALLIED FAMILIES.

- iii MEHITABLE, m. Ethel Davis (3d of 4 wives).
- iv WILLIAM, m. Ann Welch; 2 children.
- v JOSEPH J., d. on a passage from Jamaica to Wilmington, N. C.
- vi EDWARD J., m. Ellen Budreau.
- vii CHARLES J., m. Cynthia White.
- viii CAPT. FRANKLIN, m. Rachel Payson (Elisha, Esq., Jonathan, etc.), and d. 1853.
- ix CYNTHIA, m. John D. Southern, Jr.; light-keeper; 8 children; she d. 1875, aged 58.
- x THOMAS RANKIN, d. in Guadeloupe, W. I.
- xi PHEBE SUSAN, m. Dea. Joseph Southern, son of John; 4 children; he d. Oct., 1883, aged 62.

12. vii. Dea. Benjamin Potter (Benjamin, Joseph, Ephraim, Robert, Robert, Nicholas), cousin to the four preceding, b. in Clements, Aug. 10, 1789; m. Ruth Wear (see Weare), Jan. 21, 1811; d. there Nov. 27, 1850; she d. Jan. 18, 1886, aged 97.

CHILDREN.

- i PHEBE, b. Aug., 1811; m. John, son of Philip Lightizer, and d. May 24, 1884; he d.
- ii ANN, b. June 24, 1813; m. Elijah, son of James Berry, and had Asa and Eliza; d. April 22, 1884; he d. March, 1883.
- iii SARAH E., b. May 14, 1815; m. J. Edward Woodworth. See Woodworth.
- iv ASA, b. April 30, 1817; m. Elizabeth, daughter of Abram Bowlby, Jan. 1, 1847; 3 children, and d. Jan. 27, 1889, in Bayham, Ont.
- v EMELINE, b. Sept. 7, 1819; m. Joseph Wear Robbins; 8 children; he d. 1889, aged 77.
- vi DEA. EZRA, b. Oct. 26, 1821; m. Zebudah Potter (Dea. Aaron, Rev. Israel, etc.), Oct. 28, 1852; she d. Jan. 4, 1872, aged 52. He m. 2d, Luvisa Wright, widow of Thomas H. Millner, Feb. 24, 1872; she d. July 21, 1882, aged 66. He m. 3d, Elizabeth, daughter of Joseph Lightizer, July 1, 1883; live near Clementsvale, on his father's old farm.
- vii JOHN, b. Oct. 18, 1823; m. Elche, daughter of Thomas Millner; 9 children.
- viii MARIA, b. March 24, 1825; m. John Henry, son of Benjamin Lecain; 3 children; d. 1881; he d. 1878.
- ix REBECCA, b. June 13, 1827; m. Aaron Potter, Jr.; 6 children, and d. 1891.
- x BENJAMIN, b. June 10, 1830; m. Mary, daughter of Joseph Lightizer; 2 children. He lost a leg by fever sore, and d. 1882.
- xi RUTH, b. Nov., 1835; m. John Henry, son of Daniel Millner; have a daughter Ruth.

clvi ALLIED FAMILIES.

13. viii. Dea. Aaron Potter (Rev. Israel, Joseph, Joseph, Ephraim, Robert, Robert, Nicholas), b. in Clements, Sept. 3, 1786; m. Susanna, daughter of Anthony Purday, and lived near Clementsvale; farmer; d. Sept. 21, 1860; she d. March 22, 1874, aged 87.

CHILDREN.

i Dea. James Edward, Esq., b. 1810; m. Mary M., daughter of Isaac Ditmars, and had Isaac, 1837; Abram D., 1838; Alexis, 1841; Lemma L., 1843; Rachel E., 1845; Sarah I., 1848; James Edward, 1851; Mary M., 1852; Hubert V., 1854; Caroline E., 1857; George, 1862. She d. 1863. He m. 2d, Naomi Chute (see No. 59); had a son, George F., b. 1865. Dea. Potter d. Aug. 1, 1890, and she lives in Lynn.
ii Fanny G., b. 1812; m. James Snell.
iii Mary Ann, b. 1815; m. James E. Jefferson (see Harris); 6 children.
iv Anthony, b. 1816; m. Elizabeth E. Jefferson; m. 2d, Sarah A. Wright; m. 3d, Lucinda (Chute) Potter, 1889; he d. July 31, 1890; she d. Dec. 24, 1892. Children: Sophia, Julia, Elizabeth, Helen, Charles, William, Georgiana, Robert, Anna, Bertha, David, and Florence.
v Israel, b. 1818; m. Caroline Lecain; Susan Roup.
vi Zebudah, b. 1821; m. Dea. Ezra, son of Dea. Benjamin Potter.
vii Jacob, b. 1823; b. and d. in March.
viii Susannah, b. 1824; d. 1855.
ix Reuben D., b. 1826; m. Sarah Dyer, daughter of John Gilliatt, Jan. 24, 1850; 7 children.
x Aaron, b. 1828; m. Rebecca, daughter of Dea. Benjamin Potter; 6 children, and d. Feb. 2, 1892.
xi Elizabeth, b. 1831; m. John H. Millner, Oct. 29, 1857.
xii Moses, b. 1833; d. young.

14. viii. Rev. Israel Potter, Jr., brother to the above, b. Jan. 7, 1790; m. Catharine, daughter of John Ditmars, and lived at Clementsvale; farmer and Baptist minister. He was ordained to the ministry in 1835, and d. June 26, 1860; she d. about 1870.

CHILDREN.

i Dea. John Douglass, b. 1815; m. Lucinda Chute (see No. 59), Jan. 4, 1840.
ii Dea. Dowe Ditmars, b. 1817; m. Mary Ann, daughter of Josiah Spurr; 2 children; she d. April, 1885. He m. 2d, Elizabeth Everett, widow of Robert Chute (see No. 171), Dec. 10, 1885. Live near Clementsvale.

ALLIED FAMILIES. clvii

iii DAVID H., m. Elizabeth Bacon; 5 children.
iv JEREMIAH V., m. Sophia Chute, Feb. 10, 1848. See No. 59.
v REBECCA, b. 1825; m. Richard H. Sanford, March 25, 1847. See Sanford.
vi JOSEPH, m. Sarah D., daughter of James Rice, a schoolteacher. See Rice.
vii ISRAEL, d. young.
viii MARY CATHARINE, m. Edward Jones; one son, Fred.
ix ABIGAIL S., d. young.
x DEA. JOSHUA C., m. Clarissa Chute. See No. 63.
xi ZENAS AARON, b. April 20, 1840; d. Feb. 20, 1865.

15. viii. John Potter, another brother, b. Jan. 19, 1792; m. Mary, daughter of John Balcomb, 1814; she d. 1851, aged 56. He m. 2d, Maria Marshall (see Marshall), 1853, and d. March 15, 1878. He was blind 18 years.

CHILDREN.

i HELEN, b. 1815; m. James H. Carty, son of John and Elizabeth (Harris) Carty, M. D., 1837, and d. in Chelsea, Mass., Jan. 3, 1891. They lived in Salem and Chelsea since 1846.
ii JOHN H., b. June, 1818; m. Maria Gates, daughter of Oldham, Jr.; 6 children; she d. He m. 2d, Letitia, daughter of Josiah Spurr, and widow of James V. Hogan.
iii OLIVE, b. Dec. 8, 1820; m. Caleb Soulice (see Dea. Benjamin Potter, No. 10), as his 2d wife, 1863; she was drowned at the wreck of the schooner *Deering*, off Cape Ann, Oct., 1868, with Capt. Charles Soulice, James Soulice, Walker Vroom, Horatio Vroom, Mrs. Margaret Craig and child, a colored man, and 4 more; Rufus Goodwin and another Charles Soulice only escaped. Mr. Soulice m. 2d, Sarah, widow of —— Perry; and —— Roop and the old gent. (b. 1803) still live at Smith's Cove.
iv WILLIAM, b. Aug., 1822; m. Ann, daughter of Edward Barteaux.
v JAMES D., b. Feb., 1826; m. Elizabeth, daughter of Jacob Potter.
vi MARY ANN, b. Dec. 14, 1828; m. Christopher, son of Dea. Thomas Gilliatt.
vii ROBERT, b. Nov., 1830; m. Jane Witherspoon.
viii SARAH, b. 1832; d. 1846.
ix CAPT. SAMUEL, b. 1835; m. Alice Woodbury (John G., Isaac, Jr.).

16. viii. Joseph Potter, another brother, b. Jan. 31, 1794; m. Margaret, daughter of John Balcomb, and lived in Upper Clement; d. Oct. 19, 1829. She m. 2d, John Rice (see Rice), and d. about 1853.

CHILDREN.

   i JERANE, b. about 1819; m. William Jones, and had Edward and Frank.
   ii CATHARINE, b. about 1821; m. Stephen Harris (George, John); 2 children, and d. He m. 2d, Eunice Morse, and had Sarah Ann, Chipman, and Emma; he d. about 1853, aged 40. She m. 2d, Dea. James Purday; he d. 1859. She m. 3d, John Bennett.
   iii AMBROSE, b. about 1823; m. Emeline (Everett) Ring; 8 children.
   iv AMANDA, b. Feb. 26, 1826; m. Benjamin Harris (see Harris); 13 children.
   v JACOB, b. 1827; m. Anna Trefetheren.
   vi CAPT. JOSEPH, b. 1829; m. Martha Gavazza, widow of Michael Brown; 2 children; m. 2d, aArtmesa Brown; 1 child; m. 3d, Lizzie Ackley.
   vii JOHN, m. Armanella Ruggles; 5 children. See Ruggles. She d.; he m. 2d, Maggie Ray.
   viii MAGGIE A., m. Charles Inglis; 6 children.

17. viii. Dea. James Manning Potter, Esq., another brother, b. April 7, 1802; m. Sylvia Harris (see Harris), 1828, and lived near Goat Island in Clements; she d. Oct. 15, 1849, aged 55. He m. 2d, Caroline, daughter of Benjamin Wilson, St. John, N. B.; he d. at Bear River, Dec. 27, 1888; she d. Aug. 31, 1890, aged 71.

CHILDREN.

   i PETERSON, b. 1825; d. 1829.
   ii JOHN POLHEMUS, b. Dec. 3, 1828; m. Ellen, daughter of John Balcomb, and had Louise, Emma, and John W., a sailor. Mrs. Potter d. He m. 2d, Emma, daughter of George R. Whittemore,* and had Fred M. and Albert; live in Lawrence, Mass.
   iii JAMES HARRIS, b. 1832; m.; live in St. John, N. B.
   iv FREDERICK, b. Feb. 26, 1835; m. Margaret, daughter of Willoughby Bath.
   v MARY LOUISE, b. April 7, 1837; m. William Henry Chute. See No. 119.

18. viii. Jacob Potter, another brother, b. Feb. 10, 1804; m. Catharine Warn; she d. He m. 2d, Maria, widow of Captain Cook.

---

* Isaac, Isaac, Ebenezer, of Tewksbury, Mass.

ALLIED FAMILIES.

CHILDREN.

- i HARRIET, b. 1832; m. Albert Butler.
- ii ALFRED, m. Ellen Currier.
- iii ELIZABETH, m. James D. Potter, cousin.
- iv JOSEPH, m. Mary Allen; out West.
- v MARY CATHARINE, m. Capt. Henry, son of Dr. William Webster.
- vi PETERSON, m.; out West.

19. viii. Josiah Spurr, another brother, b. Feb. 22, 1810; m. Louisa, daughter of Edward Barteaux (William, Philip); lived in Clements. She d. May 16, 1852, aged 32; he m. 2d, Naomi G——, widow of Eliakim Bent. She d. July 19, 1877, aged 54. He d. in Boston, Nov. 25, 1890.

CHILDREN.

- i ELIZA JANE, b. Feb. 2, 1842; d. 1855.
- ii GEORGE M., b. Dec. 11, 1843; m. Anna Maria Cunningham, and had 6 children. He keeps a hotel in Boston.
- iii MERCY M., b. 1847; d. 1851.
- iv ANNA LOUISA, b. Oct. 6, 1849.
- v EMMA, b. Jan., 1852; d. in May.
- vi EMMA Z., b. March 28, 1854; m. Arthur Ball.

BIRTHDAY POEM ON THE OLD HOMESTEAD, FEB. 22, 1884.

The farmhouse wore a modest mien,
The small size windows, quaint and red,
And through a tangled web of green,
I think I see the old woodshed!
The orchard bloom in white and pink
Was handsome to the children's eye,
Sweet music of the bob-'o-link
Gave pleasure in a sunlit sky.

The lofty height of hard wood trees,*
That used to grow upon the hill,
Was kept to burn — we did not freeze —
For the fireplace we used to fill!
The nightingale — her ringing song —
Upon those trees in summer time,
We heard it all the evening long,
She'd almost charm us with her rhyme.

Of clover red and new-mown hay,
A fragrance on the air swept by;
The old brick yard and miry clay
Would sometimes cause us boys to sigh!
The sunset spread its rose-red glare,
The stars upon the upland play,
Through dreary paths of purple air
North Mountain ranges stretch away.

* Ash, beech, birch, maple, and oak.

Beside the bars, close to the wood,
Within the mellow twilight gloam,
How oft a barefoot boy I stood,
To wait until the cows came home.
The battle of my life I've fought,
'Part from the scenes of boyhood's time,
Yet even in this time I sought
To clasp a stronger hand than mine.

J. S. P., in Boston.

20. viii. **Capt. Isaiah Shaw Potter**, the youngest of the family of Rev. Israel Potter, Sen., b. Oct. 9, 1814; m. Sarah A. Lecain, and lived at Clementsport, and followed the sea; d. Jan., 1885.

CHILD.

i EMMA, b. Jan. 1, 1852; m. William F. Mowatt, March 26, 1888; have 2 children; live in Chelsea, Mass.

RANDALL.

1. i. **John Randall**, of Westerly, R. I., d. there about 1684–5. His wife, Elizabeth ——.

CHILDREN.

i JOHN, b. 1666; m. Abigail ——, of Stonington, Conn., 1695; she d. 1705; he m. 2d, Mary, daughter of John and Rebecca (Palmer, b. 1675) Baldwin, 1706, and d. 1711. (Rebecca Palmer, mother of Mary Baldwin, was daughter of Walter and Rebecca (Short) Palmer; m. 1st, Elisha Cheesebrough, 1666; he d. 1671; she m. 2d, John Baldwin.) Children: (1) Elizabeth, b. 1696, m. James Brown, and d. 1786; he d. 1750; 9 children. (2) Jonathan, b. 1698. (3) Mary, b. 1700; m. Stephen Wilcox; 5 children. (4) John, b. 1701; m. Elizabeth Cottrell, 1727; 4 children; she d. about 1740; he m. 2d, Mary, daughter of Joshua and Fear (Sturgis) Holmes, and widow of Elias Palmer, 1741; 6 children more, and d. 1761. (5) Dorothy, b. 1703; m. (6) Abigail, b. 1705; m. John Brown, 1729. (7) Sarah, b. 1707; d. 1712, Stonington, Conn. (8) Nathan, b. 1709; m. Mary Cottrell, 1730; 2 children; she d. 1735; he m. 2d, Eleanor, a sister, 1736; had 6 in Stonington, and 2 in Voluntown. They seem to have d. before the Revolution. (9) Ichabod, b. 1711; was a corporal in Capt. Giles Russell's company, in the Havanna Expedition, under Admiral Pocock, and Lord Albermarle. He m. —— ——, settled in Horton, N. S., and had Ichabod, Charles, Benjamin Green,

ALLIED FAMILIES.   clxi

      Humility, and John. (10) Sarah, b. and d. 1714. (11) Joseph, b. and d. 1715. (12) Benjamin, twin, b. 1715; m. Ruth Brown, 1733, and d. 1811. She d. at Colchester, Conn., 1791; 11 children. (13) Rebecca, b. 1717. (14) Joseph, b. 1720.
2 ii STEPHEN, b. 1668.
   iii MATTHEW, b. 1671; m. Eleanor ——, 1698, and d. at Hopkinton, R. I. She d. 1763. Children: (1) Eleanor, b. 1694. (2) Mercy, b. 1696. (3) Mary, b. 1700; m. Caleb Pendleton, 1716; 4 children; Westerly, R. I. (4) Benjamin, b. 1698 or 1702; m. Mary Badcock, 1735, and d. at Hopkinton, R. I., 1744; 8 children. (5) Elizabeth, b. 1704; m. Edward, son of Thomas and Sarah (Rogers) Wells, 1725.
   iv PETER, b. 1673-4; m. Elizabeth Polly; 3 children at Stonington, Conn.; m. 2d, Phebe Benjamin, 1719, and lived at Preston, Conn. Children: (1) Prudence, b. 1709. (2) Peter, 1711-1712. (3) Peter, b. 1713; m. Keturah Ellis, 1732; 13 children at Preston. (4) Elizabeth, b. 1720. (5) Greedfield, b. 1722; m. Ann Bellows, 1745; 3 children. (6) Samuel, b. 1726.

2. ii. Stephen Randall (John), b. 1668; m. —— ——, and lived at Stonington, Conn.

CHILDREN.

    i ABIGAIL, b. 1698.   ii SAMUEL, b. 1701.
  iii STEPHEN, b. 1704.   iv JONATHAN, b. 1707.
   v ELIZABETH, b. 1709; d. 1711. vi PHEBE, b. 1712.
 vii WILLIAM, b. 1715.   3 viii DAVID, b. 1719.

3. iii. David Randall (Stephen, John), b. Stonington, Conn., May 4, 1719; m. Kezia Davidson, Nov. 6, 1739, at Preston, Conn.; 3 children b. at Stonington, 7 or more at Preston. They moved to Kings county, N. S., in 1766, and there lived and died, good old farmers.

CHILDREN.

   i NATHAN, b. May 27, 1741; must have d. young.
  ii KEZIA, b. March 4, 1743; m. —— Murchant in New York.
 iii LUCY, b. Feb. 4, 1744.
 iv SARAH, b. Jan. 2, 1746; m. John Newcomb (Eddy, John, Simon, Andrew, Andrew), 1769. Children: son Eddy, b. 1769; m. Waity Sanford, 1790-91; m. 2d, Mary, daughter of Cyrus West, 1792; 7 children. She d. 1811, aged 38; he m. 3d, Alice, daughter of Simeon and Sarah Porter, 1812; 2 children, and d. 1850. Sarah, the 6th,

ALLIED FAMILIES.

   m. William Bowles Masters (b. 1801), 1824; 3 children, and d. 1832, aged 27. John Newcomb d. She m. 2d, John Smith, and went to New York.
4 v DAVID, b. Jan. 17, 1748.
  vi JONATHAN, b. April 2, 1751; m. a daughter of Dr. Willoughby.
5 vii SAMUEL, b. Sept. 10, 1753.
6 viii AMOS, b. Dec. 30, 1755; m. Susan Chute. See No. 7.
  ix HEZEKIAH, b. Jan. 29, 1758; m.
  x ELISHA, b. 1760; m. Mary ——; had James and ——.
  xi JOHN, b. 1762; d. young.
7 xii NATHAN, b. May 7, 1764.

4. iv. Dea. David Randall (David, Stephen, John), b. in Preston, Conn., Jan. 17, 1748; m. Amy Payson, Nov. 23, 1775, in Nova Scotia, and settled in Aylesford. He d. 1831. She d. 1830, aged 78.

CHILDREN.

  i JOHN, b. Sept. 10, 1777; m. Ruth Gates (James, Capt. Oldham, etc.), 1804, and had James, William Silas, Mary, Emily, Eliza, and Helen. He m. 2d, Nancy Downey; 3d, Polly (Baker) Goucher.
  ii LUCY, b. July 28, 1780; d. at one month.
  iii JONATHAN, b. Aug. 15, 1781; m. —— ——, and lived in Maine.
8 iv WILLIAM D., b. Oct. 16, 1783.
  v GEORGE, b. Aug. 28, 1785; drowned in a spring about 1816.
  vi LUCY, b. Nov. 19, 1787; m. Peter P. Chute. See No. 27.
  vii AMY, b. Sept. 15, 1789; m. Rev. Ebenezer Stronach, of Wilmot; he d. Nov. 25, 1858.
  viii EUNICE, b. Aug. 8, 1791; d. young.
  ix DAVID, b. March 28, 1793.
  x OLIVE, b. April 27, 1797; d. Nov. 13, 1798.

5. iv. Samuel Randall (David, Stephen, John), b. Sept. 10 1753; m. Sarah Ann, daughter of Col. Benjamin Prince, 1783, and lived in Aylesford; he d. 1847; she d. 1834.

CHILDREN.

  i ELIZABETH, b. July 12, 1784; m. Samuel Chute, Jr. See No. 23.
  ii MARY, b. 1786; m. Benjamin Foster, Jr. See Foster.
  iii JOB, b. 1788; m. Cynthia Foster, cousin to Benjamin. See Foster. One son, Oliver. Job m. 2d, Mary, daughter of William Parker, Esq.
9 iv PAOLI, b. July 11, 1791.

ALLIED FAMILIES. clxiii

- v SARAH, b. 1794; m. Cyrus Dodge, Nictaux; 5 children. She m. 2d, Henry McGee.
- vi NAOMI, b. 1796; m. Rev. Clark Alline (Joseph, William, from R. I.); a daughter; m. William Rice of Brigdetown.
- vii ROBERT, b. Oct. 28, 1798; m. Hannah, daughter of Samuel Hall, and widow of Robert Delap, 1832; had (1) Samuel, b. Nov. 2, 1833; m. Anna S., daughter of Robert Carter, 1867; moved to Mass. Nov., 1863; live in Everett. (2) Job, b. May 13, 1835; m. Lovena Goucher (Manly, Stephen), Aylesford, N. S.
- viii RUTH, b. 1800; m. William Steves, a sailor, Petticodiac; she m. 2d, Israel Steves, a cousin, and sailor, too.
- ix MARIA, b. 1803; d. 1816.
- 10 x CHRISTOPHER, b. 1805.

6. iv. Amos Randall (David, Stephen, John); m. Susan Chute (No. 7), 1788.

CHILDREN.

- 11 v JAMES, b. July 3, 1798.
- 12 x BENJAMIN, b. May 23, 1810.

7. iv. Nathan Randall (David, Stephen, John), b. May 7, 1764; m. Susan Gates (Jonas, Capt. Oldham), 1795, Aylesford, N. S., and d. Sept. 25, 1840; she d. July 18, 1816, aged 38½ years.

CHILDREN.

- i HETTIE, b. 1796; d. March 4, 1824.
- ii SARAH, b. April 13, 1799; m. Rev. Henry Saunders (Timothy), Nov. 13, 1817, and d. Aug. 15, 1880, aged 90; she d. Aug. 20, 1880. Children: (1) Susan, b. 1818; m. Edmund Reis Harris (Christopher P., Samuel, Samuel, Isaac, Arthur); 8 children; Mr. Harris d. 1888, aged 77. (2) Nathan R., b. 1820; m. Abigail Ann Whitman (Asaph, Daniel, Dea. John, John, Rev. Zachariah, Dea. John), 1844; had 4 children; she d. 1855, aged 30. He m. 2d, Harriet McGregor, and d. 1882. (3) Rev. Joseph Henry, b. Sept. 13, 1824; m. Sept. 15, 1852, Caroline, daughter of William H. Harris, and had William H. H., 1854; Sarah A. E., 1857; Carrie A., 1859; Frank Burton, 1867; Mr. Saunders is editor of the *Messenger and Visitor*, St. John, N. B. (4) Elizabeth, b. Nov. 22, 1822; d. at Hebron, N. S., 1850. (5) Sarah Jane, b. April 20, 1827; d. in Aylesford. (6) Thomas H. C., b. May 23, 1829; m. Jane Neily; 5 children. (7) Margaret Ann, b. 1831; m. William Snell, Bear River. (8) Martha, b. Jan. 2, 1835; d. May 17, 1836. (9) Cynthia, b. Aug. 2, 1837; d. Sept. 18, 1841. (10) Charles William, b. Sept.

30, 1840; m. Mary Elizabeth Sloan of Lynn, Feb. 21, 1869; 2 children in Boston.
iii THOMAS, b. 1801; m. Hannah Dennett, and d. 1850; had Edwin, Alfred, and Sarah.
iv OLIVE, b. 1803; d. 1817.
v SUSAN, b. Dec. 30, 1804; m. Manly, son of Stephen Goucher, 1825, and lived in Aylesford; he d. March, 1866, aged 62. Children: (1) Ambrose D., b. 1826; m. Helen Amanda, daughter of Edmund Palmer; and Mary, daughter of Samuel Tilly. (2) George N., b. 1828; m. Augusta, daughter of Thomas Nichols; and Lavenia, daughter of Richard Nichols. (3) Sidney W., b. 1831; m. Fanny, daughter of David Goucher; 4 children. (4) Margaret A., b. 1833; d. 1834. (5) Sarah J., b. 1835; m. Samuel Patterson; 2 children. (6) James E., b. 1837; m. Abbie D., daughter of Jonas Parker; 6 children, Minneapolis, Minn. (7) Charles W., 1839–1840. (8) Mary L., b. 1841; m. Job, son of Robert Randall, Melvern Square. (9) Sophia W., b. 1845; d. 1848. (10) Charles A., b. 1848; m. Edna F., daughter of James Burkitt of Maine, Oct. 22, 1872, and lives at Quincy, Mass.
13 vi REV. CHARLES, b. Jan. 4, 1807.
vii MARGARET, b. May 29, 1809; m. Robert Neily; no children, and d. May 26, 1831. He m. twice after.
14 viii WILLIAM HENRY, b. June 16, 1811.
15 ix JAMES DWIGHT, b. April 19, 1813.
x REV. SAMUEL MARTIN, b. Sept. 15, 1815; m. Mary Nichols; and Sarah Roop.

8. v. William D. Randall, J. P., (Dea. David, David, Stephen, John), b. Oct. 16, 1783; m. Helen, daughter of Rev. T. H. Chipman, Sept., 1814; lived in Wilmot; d. 1870; she d. 1875, aged 84.

CHILDREN.

i SELINA JANE, m. Handley Shafner.
ii AMANDA M., m.
iii HARRIET NEWELL, m. Alfred, son of John Dodge.
iv MARY ELIZA, m. Jonathan Woodbury, Jr., M. D.
v WILLIAM, M. D., m. Sarah, daughter of Capt. Allen of Yarmouth.
vi THOMAS HARDING, m. Cassie A. Beckwith (Mayhew, Handley, John, John, James, Matthew, Matthew).
vii MARY CHIPMAN, m. George Fitch.
viii ELIZABETH, m. Capt. Quick, of Bridgetown.
ix WHEELOCK, m. daughter of Robert Carlton.

9. v. Paoli Randall (Samuel, David, Stephen, John), b. July 11, 1791; m. Rebecca, daughter of Green and Lydia (Rand) Randall, Jan. 30, 1816; she d. Aug., 1843, aged 46. He m. 2d, Theresa (Randall) Chute (No. 34), Jan. 5, 1845. Mr. Randall was a prosperous merchant in Portland, Me., where he d. April 12, 1864; she d. Feb. 17, 1872, aged 64 years 3 months.

CHILDREN.

i MARY E. A., b. Dec. 23, 1816; m. Capt. James W. Taylor, and had James Henry and William George. Capt. Taylor was lost off the ship *Alamance*, 1848, aged 33. She m. 2d, Daniel Dimock Chute. See No. 47.
ii LYDIA A., b. March 28, 1818; m. William Simonton; lived in Portland; had 3 children, and d. Aug. 28, 1891; he d. 1890.
iii DR. BENJAMIN PRINCE FRANKLIN, b. June 15, 1819; d. in Boston, Aug. 29, 1855.
iv C. WILLIAM, b. Aug. 5, 1821; d. 1859.
v THOMAS S., b. May 23, 1824; d. Dec. 3, 1827.
vi MARY E., b. April 17, 1826; m. John Clark; 4 or 5 children, and both are dead.
vii SIMON F., b. Feb. 16, 1828; m. Harriett Cobb; 3 children.
viii JOHN P., b. Aug. 12, 1847; d. Aug. 23.
ix MARIA R. A., b. Feb. 3, 1850; d. March 30, 1856.

10. v. Christopher Randall, brother to the above, b. Feb. 15, 1805; m. Matilda Gates (John, James, Capt. Oldham), June 30, 1830; lived in Aylesford; she d. May 11, 1882, in her 70th year. He m. 2d, Susannah Johnson, July 10, 1882, and d.

CHILDREN.

i SARAH, b. Sept. 26, 1831; m. Alfred Trites.
ii MARY J., b. Oct. 23, 1833; m. Jeremiah Lutz; Christopher Harmon.
iii HARRIET A., b. Jan. 11, 1836; m. Allen Steves; Martin Black.
iv RUTH, b. Oct. 1, 1837; m. George Wilson.
v ISABEL, b. June 25, 1839; d. young.
vi SAMUEL, b. April 7, 1841; m. Eunice Horseman, in N. B.
vii MARGARET, b. Dec. 5, 1842; d. 1844.
viii ELISHA, b. Sept. 7, 1844; m. Judith Smith, in N. B.; d. July 16, 1873.
ix ISABEL, b. June 24, 1846; m. Beriah Bent.
x KIMBALL, b. April 16, 1848; m. Martha Trites, Coverdale, Albert county, N. B.; she d. He m. 2d, Ettie Trites.
xi DR. EDWARD C., b. April 16, 1851; m. Maggie McClatchy, Hillsboro', N. B.
xii GEORGE E., b. April 23, 1851; m. Esther Foster (Isaac, Benjamin, Jr.), daughter of Isaac Foster and Rebecca daughter of Stephen Taylor.

xiii CHRISTIANA, b. Sept. 29, 1853; m. John Carroll, Moncton, N. B.

11. v. James Randall (Amos, David, Stephen, John), b. July 3, 1798; m. Mary Pickup (George, Samuel), Feb. 3, 1831, and lived in Clements, above Moose River; had 3 sons, 3 daughters; 2 of the sons and the 3 daughters d. in infancy and youth; while George, b. 1834, m. Mary E. Roblee, and has Bessie, Ada, Marilla, Mary Olivia (school-teacher), and Irwin; live a little below Goat Island, in Clements.

12. v. Benjamin Randall, brother to the above, b. May 23, 1810; m. Tamer, daughter of Ezekiel Foster, Jr., Feb. 1, 1838; lived in Granville; d. Dec., 1885; she d. July 17, 1884, aged 70.

CHILDREN.

i MORDANT H., b. June 10, 1841; m. Mary P. Anderson, 1861; she d. He m. 2d, Adelia M. Conway, 1870, and d. Oct. 19, 1882.
ii JOHN LEANDER, b. July 1, 1843; m. Mary P. Richardson, Aug., 1869, and d. April 28, 1879, Bath, Me.; 2 daughters.
iii ETHALINDA ELIZABETH, b. July 23, 1846; m. William A. McKenzie, Sept. 5, 1867; he d. about 1874, aged 30; she lives in Boston.
iv CHARLOTTE ANZONETTE, b. Dec. 28, 1853; d. April 23, 1857.

13. v. Rev. Charles Randall (Nathan, David, Stephen, John), b. Jan. 4, 1807; m. Cynthia, daughter of Jonas Ward, 1834, and lived at Weymouth, Digby county; an active, energetic minister in the Baptist church. He was ordained to the ministry 1833, so was engaged in the Master's service 45 years; he d. March 24, 1878; she d. Jan. 2, 1890, aged 87.

CHILDREN.

i CHARLES WILLIAM, b. June 6, 1835; } d. April 25, 1857.
ii JOSEPH HENRY, b. June 6, 1835; } m. Sabina Jane Hankinson (Dea. Reuben, Reuben, Robert), and d. Jan. 8, 1875; 3 children. He was a school-teacher and a sea captain.
iii MARGARET ANN, b. Sept. 25, 1836; m. Dea. Henry Charlton Sabean, Esq. (Henry C., Benjamin, Jeremiah, Jeremiah, Benjamin, William), Oct. 22, 1857; farmer and postmaster, New Tusket, Digby county, N. S. See Hankinson.
iv MARY ELIZABETH, b. April 30, 1838; m. Capt. George Grant, who was lost in the brig *Confederate.*

ALLIED FAMILIES. clxvii

14. v. William Henry Randall, brother to the above, b. June 16, 1811; m. Susan A. Tupper (John, Miner, Elias, Eliakim, Thomas, Thomas); (John Tupper m. Elizabeth Longley (Israel to Nova Scotia, from Mass., 1760—William, John, the redeemed captive, William, William, William, to Lynn, 1636). Mr. Randall was a blacksmith; moved to Marblehead, Mass., about 1850, where the wife d., Oct. 9, 1876, aged 62; he returned to Digby Joggins, N. S., 1877; m. 2d, Agnes Jane (Woodman) Seeley (see No. 11), 1880.

CHILDREN.

i CAPT. JOHN F., b. March 4, 1834; m. Sarah Bassett, 1860, and d. at sea March 16, 1863. A son, John Fletcher, Jr., b. Nov., 1862; m. Emma W. Bowden, Oct. 18, 1888.
ii EMMA J., b. Dec. 2, 1835; m. Samuel Roundy, 1855; d. 1856; m. 2d, Jepthah Rice, 1863, and was drowned Nov., 1864. Mr. Rice m. 2d, —— Balcomb.
iii ELIZABETH ANN, b. Oct., 1838; m. George Haynes (Amos, Luke, John), 1859. A daughter, Carrie Grata, b. Aug., 1874, m. Armeanus Thorner, Nov. 24, 1892; all of Marblehead.
iv CHARLES ALBERT, b. Nov. 11, 1840; m. Sarah Trefry; 2 children.
v MARIA L., b. May 26, 1844; m. John Gallaher, and d. Oct. 14, 1892; 2 children.
vi HARRIET A., b. March 29, 1849; m. Russell Peddrick.

15. v. James Dwight, brother to the two preceding, b. April 19, 1813; m. Maria Henrietta Patterson (April 26, 1817-May 10, 1886), widow of Elijah Nichols, Nov. 10, 1842, Aylesford, N. S., and d. March 2, 1889.

CHILDREN.

i CYTHIA JANE, b. Dec. 7, 1843; m. Bradford Dodge, April 10, 1870, and d. in Boston, March 11, 1871.
ii SUSANNA MATILDA, b. Sept. 18, 1845; m. Melbourne Welton, Aug. 30, 1865; 9 children.
iii ASA HAMILTON, b. July 31, 1847; m. Elizabeth Cook; 4 children; 2 d.; then he, with Charles and Harry, went to New York City.
iv RUNA MARIA, b. Aug. 25, 1849; m. Peter Copeland, Boston, and d. April 6, 1875; 2 children.
v SABRA KNOWLES, b. June 8, 1852; m. John Anderson, Boston.
vi FRANCES ZERUIAH, b. Oct. 19, 1856; d. Feb. 12, 1876.
vii CLARABEL, b. Oct. 5, 1859; dressmaker, Boston.

RICE.

1. i. Edmund Rice was living at Berkhampstead, Hertfordshire, Eng., 1627; came to America about 1638, and settled in Sudbury, Mass. He brought with him from England his wife Thomazine, and 7 children. He was a selectman in 1644, and several years after; deacon of the church 1648, and after. His wife d. June 13, 1654; he m. 2d, "Mercia" Hurd, widow of Thomas Brigham of Cambridge, March 1, 1655, and d. at Marlboro', May 3, 1663, aged 69. She m. 3d, William Hunt, an early settler in Concord (where he had children, 1640, and wife Elizabeth, who d. there Dec. 27, 1661), who d. at Marlboro', Oct., 1667, and the old lady d. Dec. 28, 1693.

CHILDREN.

i	HENRY, b. 1616.	ii	EDWARD, b. 1618.
iii	EDMUND.	iv	THOMAS.
v	MARY.	vi	LYDIA, b. 1627.
vii	MATTHEW, b. 1629.		
viii	DANIEL, b. 1632. } twins.		
ix	SAMUEL, b. 1632.		
x	JOSEPH, b. 1637.	xi	BENJAMIN, b. 1640.
xii	RUTH, b. 1659.	xiii	ANNE, b. 1661.

2. ii. Thomas Rice (Dea. Edmund), b. in England, 1622; came over with his parents about 1638; m. Mary ——, and lived at Sudbury, but removed to Marlboro' about 1664, where he d. Nov. 16, 1681, aged 70. His children were Grace, Thomas, Mary, Peter, Nathaniel, Sarah, Ephraim, Gershom, James, Frances, Jonas, Grace, and Elisha.

3. iii. Gershom Rice (Thomas, Edmund), b. at Marlboro', Mass., May 9, 1667; m. Elizabeth, daughter of Henry and Elizabeth (Balcom) Haynes (who were m. at Charlestown, Aug. 12, 1646). She was b. Aug. 16, 1672, and they removed to Groton, Conn., about 1697, where their children, except the first, were born. They returned to Marlboro' in 1713, where he and his brother Jonas commenced the 3d and permanent settlement of Worcester, two previous settlements being broken up by Indians. In 1715 he was there, and had 80 acres of land granted him in 1718. Mr. Rice d. Dec. 19, 1768, aged 101 years, 7 months, 10 days. Mrs. Rice d. 1752, aged 80. Their children were Gershom, Elizabeth, Abishai, Sarah, Matthias, and Ruth. His father d. aged 70; his mother 84; had 14 children, of whom Peter lived to 97; Thomas, 91; Mary, 80;

Nathaniel, 70; Ephraim, 71; James, 72; Sarah, 80; Fanny, 96; Jonas, 84; Grace, 94; and Elisha, 60.— *Worcester paper, Dec. 19, 1768.*

4. iv. Matthias Rice (Gershom, Thomas, Edmund), b. Jan. 26, 1707; m. Mary ——, and lived several years at Worcester. He moved to Sudbury about 1747, and was enrolled on the alarm list, Sudbury company, 1756. Children: John, Bathsheba, Ithamar, Bathsheba, Josiah, Solomon, Matthias, Luke, and Artemas.

5. v. Capt. John Rice (Matthias, Gershom, Thomas, Dea. Edmund), b. in Worcester, Mass., Dec. 26, 1738; went over to Annapolis, N. S., 1759; m. Sarah, daughter of Zephaniah and Eunice Smith, May 6, 1761. She d. April 29, 1784, aged 41; he m. 2d, Mary, daughter of Joseph and Zebudah (Hayden) Potter, April 21, 1785, and d. May 2, 1811; she m. 2d, Capt. Henry Harris (his 2d wife), 1821–2. He d. May 12, 1831, aged 74; she d. Dec. 3, 1858, aged nearly 93.

CHILDREN.

6   i   SILAS, b. 1762.
    ii   JOHN, b. 1764; d. 1784.
    iii   SARAH, b. 1766; d. 1784.
    iv   MARY, b. 1769; m. Rev. Israel Potter, and d. 1849. See Potter.
    v   JOSEPH, b, 1771; d. 1784.
7   vi   WILLIAM, b. 1774.
8   vii   THOMAS, b. 1779.
    viii   JOSEPH, b. 1787; d. 1795.
9   ix   JAMES, b. 1790.

6. vi. Silas Rice (Capt. John, Matthias, Gershom, Thomas, Dea. Edmund), b. at Annapolis, N. S., 1762; m. Sarah Kniffin (George, George, George, George, of Stratford, Conn., 1666). Her mother was Sarah, daughter of Col. Jacob Baker, of Philadelphia before the Revolution. Silas Rice was a sturdy old farmer of Hillsburg, Digby county, N. S., and used to tell of the Dark Day of May 19, 1780. He d. in 1853, aged 91; she d. 1856, aged 90.

CHILDREN.

    i   JOHN, b. 1786; m. Polly, daughter of Aaron Hardy; 2d, Margaret Balcomb, widow of Joseph Potter; 3d, Elizabeth Chute, widow of John Balsor Rice; by 1st wife had (1) Alfred, b. July 11, 1819; m. Martha, daughter of Thomas and Martha (Potter) Rice. (2) James. (3) Eliza, m. Samuel A. Harris (William H., Esq., Capt.

Henry). (4) Caroline. (5) Emily. For 2d family, see Potter. For 3d family, see No. 28.
ii SALLY, m. James, son of Joshua Banks, and had James, Joshua, and Sidney; the latter m. Sarah, daughter of Dea. Wilbur Parker.
iii GEORGE, a sea-captain, m. Harriet Clark, daughter of Richard, and had Sally Ann, Robert, Capt. Isaiah, Edward, and Minetta.
iv BETSY, b. 1794; m. William, son of Thomas Berry; 7 children.
v JOSEPH, b. 1798; m. Sophia, daughter of Francis Miller, and had Mary Ann, Rachel, Francis, Thomas, Whitefield, Sophia, Leonard, William Henry, Edward, and Norman. Mrs. Rice d. 1853; he m. 2d, Anna Brown, and d. 1871. She d. 1892, aged 90.
vi POLLY, m Henry, son of Dea. Benjamin and Jane (Spurr) Potter; 5 children.
vii HENRY ALLINE. b. 1803; m. Zebudah, daughter of Thomas and Martha (Potter) Rice, and had Lois, David, Henry, Aaron, Thomas, Wesley, Melissa, Melvina, Mary Elizabeth, and Alexander. Mrs. Rice d. 1877, aged 70; he m. 2d, Leonora, daughter of Dea. Aaron Chute, July 12, 1881, and d. 1892. She d. July 5, 1890, aged 48.
viii DOLLY, b. 1806; m. Oldham, son of James Armstrong; had 2 children, William and Maxie, and d. Jan., 1892. He d. about 1870.
ix CHARLOTTE, m. Dea. Wilbur, son of Abednego Parker; 12 children.
x AARON, b. Dec. 22, 1813; m. Ann Aymar, daughter of William, and had James, William, Charles, and Herbert.

7. vi. William Rice, brother to the preceding, b. 1774; m. Ann, daughter of Aaron Hardy, and lived in Clements, on the east side of Bear River, a farmer; d. about 1884; she d. 1843.

CHILDREN.

i NANCY, b. about 1800; d. about 1820.
ii STEPHEN, m. Martha, daughter of George and Sarah (Robinson) Kniffin.
iii WILLIAM, m. Jane, daughter of Benjamin Cushing. Children: (1) Benjamin, b. about 1822. (2) Ambrose, b. 1824. (3) Leafy. (4) Stephen. (5) Charles, besides 3 or 4 that d. in infancy. Mr. Rice d. about 1868. She d. about 1863.
iv MARY, m. Ambrose, son of James Taylor, Jr.
v JAMES, m. Eliza McMullin; to Eastport, Me.
vi CAPT. JOHN, m. Leah, daughter of John Crouse; m. 2d, Jane Sweeney; 3 children.

ALLIED FAMILIES. clxxi

8. vi. Thomas Rice, another brother, b. May 23, 1779; m. Martha Potter (Joseph, Joseph, Ephraim, Robert, Robert, Nicholas), 1800, and lived near the head of Bear River. He was the first settler there, built the first bridge across the river, built vessels, made brick, burnt lime, and had a mill on the West Branch brook at the head of the tide, in front of his son Israel's house. One vessel he built was called *Temperance*, and went to sea under Capt. Leonard Troop and mate Asa Goodwin, and was never heard from, 1834–5. He d. Dec. 18, 1861. She d. Oct. 12, 1847, aged 74½ years..

CHILDREN.

i DAVID, b. 1801; m. Mary, daughter of George and Sarah (Robinson) Kniffin, and lived on the Digby side of Bear River, and became wealthy by ship building. About 1855 he moved to Bear River, and was there a merchant. Mrs. Rice d. 1877; he m. 2d, Elizabeth Harris (Joseph, Capt. Henry), widow of William Turnbull (whose first wife was Gloriana Wright), Nov. 27, 1878; and d. Jan. 12, 1881. (William Turnbull, son of Robert from Scotland, d. June 1, 1871, aged 68.) Children: (1) Elizabeth, b. 1823; m. Dea. H. H. Chute, M. P.P. (2) Ethelon, b. 1825; m. Dea. Richard Clark (William, Richard), who d. 1892. (3) Thomas, m. Cordelia Potter (William, Esq., Dea. Benjamin). (4) Edward E., m. Annie Riordan. (5) William R., m. Elizabeth Dunn (Dea. Israel, Edward, John). (6) Charles, m. Irene, daughter of Israel Dunn, and Anna, daughter of Richard Dunn. These sons are all doing good business at Bear River.

ii REV. ISRAEL, b. 1803; m. Lois Whitman (Daniel, Dea. John, John, Rev. Zachariah, Dea. John), and had Sarah, b. 1824 (m. 1848, Abram Banks; 7 children); and Lois, d. young. Mrs. Rice d. 1828, aged 24; he m. 2d, Susan, daughter of John Crouse, Jan. 1, 1829, and lived at the head of the tide, Bear River, an active, energetic, business man. About 1882–3, he and William Turnbull built the Mic-Mac mill (so named from a tribe of Indians that lived near by), on the West Branch brook. This mill was for the manufacture of lumber, staves, and shingles, but somehow it proved a failure, and now there is scarcely a sign on the banks that a mill or a dam ever was there. For nearly 20 years Mr. Rice was an active deacon in the Baptist church; then when the Millerite doctrine was proclaimed in 1843, he went with them, and was an ordained minister among the Second Adventists for over 20 years. He was also a worker in the temperance cause, and d. Feb. 18, 1866; his wife d. near Boston, Mass., May 22, 1891, aged 82. Their children were (1)

Zebudah, b. 1829. (2) Asaph, b. 1830; had 5 wives. (3) William Franklin, b. 1832. (4) Joseph C., b. 1834. (5) Obadiah, b. 1836; d. young. (6) Adoniram Judson, b. 1837. (7) Eliza A., b. 1839. (8) Wallace, b. 1842; d. young. (9) Susan, b. 1844; d. soon. (10) Margaret E., b. 1845. (11) Mary Sophia, b. 1847; d. young. (12) Israel Lemuel, b. 1849. (13) Wallace M., b. 1851. (14) Ida L., b. 1853.

iii MARY, b. 1805; m. John, son of Abram Lent; 9 children. He d. 1842, aged 43; she m. 2d, Isaac Cornwell, Digby Neck, N. S.

iv ZEBUDAH, b. 1807; m. Henry Alline Rice, a cousin, 1829; 10 children.

v DIADAMA, b. 1809; m. John Copeland, Jr.; 9 children.

vi FRANKLIN, b. 1811; m. Susan, daughter of Silas Hardy, and had Moses, Harriet, Ruth, Eunice, and Susan. Mrs. Rice d. about 1839; he m. 2d, Eliza Hardy, a sister, and had William Henry, James, Adelbert, and Ella. Mrs. Rice 2d, d. 1886; he m. 3d, Mary Amelia (Farnsworth) Rhodes, 1887 (see Farnsworth). They live at the head of the tide, Bear River.

vii JANE, b. 1814; m. Harris Morgan (Edward, George, from England); 6 children.

viii ESTHER ANN, b. Nov. 25, 1816; m. William Reed, a son of Samuel, of London, Eng.; 6 children. She d. Dec. 3, 1862; he m. 2d, Mary Ann Minard, widow of Capt. Joseph Anthony, and is a merchant.

ix MARTHA, b. April 19, 1819; m. Alfred Rice (John, Silas, etc.), and had (1) Joshua F., b. 1844; m. Agnes A. Armstrong. (2) Botsford, b. 1847; m. Cynthia Harris. (3) Israel Burpee, b. 1849; m. Margaret E., daughter of Capt. William Anthony; live in Cambridge, Mass. (4) Horatia L., 1851–1860. (5) James E., b. 1853; m. Lovenia, daughter of Capt. John Littlewood. (6) Alice E., 1855–60. (7) Georgietta, 1857–58. (8) Charles S., b 1866; m. Ella, daughter of Capt. Littlewood.

x CATHARINE, b. March 18, 1822; m. Thomas, son of Rev. John McLearn. Children: (1) Eva G., b. May 2, 1857; m. James E., son of James Clarke, Feb., 1884, and have Edward E., b. Dec. 25, 1884; Harvey M., b. April 3, 1886; and Fannie P., b. Jan. 26, 1890. (2) Sarah D., b. Jan. 2, 1861; m. Edward K. Marshall (James, Solomon, Anthony), Feb., 1880; James Edward, b. 1883. Mr. McLearn d. 1836, aged 36; she m. 2d, Dea. Edward, son of Dea. Edwin Christopher; he d. 1870, aged 47; she m. 3d, Joel H. Prescott (Samson, David, David, Ebenezer, Jonas, Jonas, John, b. at Wygan, Lincolnshire, Eng., 1604; m. Mary Platts, 1629; over to Watertown, 1640), Sept. 24, 1887, as his 2d wife, and lives in Cambridge, Mass. [William H. Prescott, LL.D., the historian, b. 1796; H.C., 1814;

ALLIED FAMILIES. clxxiii

   d. 1858, William, Col. William (of Bunker Hill fame, 1726-1795), Hon. Benjamin, Jonas, Jonas, John.]
xi SILAS, m. Elizabeth Hews; a daughter Mary m. James Manning Rice (Robert, George, Silas).
xii CYNTHIA, m. Alexander Ross, Esq., deacon and schoolteacher. She d. about 1868; he m. 2d, Lydia (Harris) Chute.

9. vi. James Rice, youngest of the four brothers, b. near Annapolis, 1790; m. Feb. 11, 1813, Dorothy Tupper (Miner, Elias, Eliakim, Thomas, Capt. Thomas, b. in England, 1578; came over to Sandwich, Mass., 1635; d. 1676; wife Anne d. 1676, aged 90). She d. April 16, 1816; he m. 2d, Ann Evans, June 18, 1818, and d. Feb. 14, 1886, aged 96. She d. 188–.

CHILDREN.

i JOHN L., b. 1813; m. Eliza Lecain, and d. 1882.
ii MARY D., b. 1815; m. Stephen Young, and d. 1857.
iii ELIZABETH S., b. 1819; m. Arthur Ruggles, son of Richard, Jr.; 6 children.
iv CHARLOTTE A., b. 1821.
v SARAH D., b. 1823; m. Joseph Potter (Rev. Israel, Rev. Israel, etc.).
vi ESTHER R., b. 1825; d. 1826.
vii WILLIAM E., b. 1826; d. 1833.
viii HENRY J., b. 1829; m. Elizabeth, daughter of Abner Morse.
ix REBECCA W., b. 1830; m. Harvey Heniger.
x ARTHUR S., b. 1832; d. 1833.
xi CATHARINE, b. 1835; d. 1837.
xii HARRIET A., b. 1837.

10. iv. Beriah Rice (Thomas, Thomas, Dea. Edmund), cousin to Matthias, b. Aug. 20, 1702; m. Mary Goodnow (Samuel, Samuel, Thomas (1608-1664), came over in the ship *Confidence*, of London April, 1638, and settled in Sudbury); lived in Westboro', Mass.; moved to Annapolis, N. S., about 1748, where they d., he in 1764, and their family scattered, some into Digby county, and some into Kings county.

CHILDREN.

i JUDE, b. 1781; m. Sarah ——, Briar Island, N. S.
ii ASAPH, b. 1783; m. Mary, daughter of Rev. Ebenezer Morse; 8 children.
iii TIMOTHY, b. 1785; m.
iv STEPHEN, b. 1737; m. Dorothy Woods, 1763, and had 7 children.

ALLIED FAMILIES.

 v MARY, b. 1739; m. Paul Hazeltine.
 vi SARAH, b. 1741; m. Elias Wheelock (Obadiah, Obadiah, Benjamin, Rev. Ralph).
 vii LUCY, b. 1743; m.
 viii RACHEL, b. 1745; m. Obadiah Wheelock, 2d, Jr. See Wheelock.
 ix BERIAH, b. 1747; m. —— McSweeny; to Cape Breton.
 x BENJAMIN, b. 1749; m.
 xi JOSEPH, b. 1752; m. —— Fairn.

11. 5. **Abishai Rice** (Abishai, Gershom, Thomas, Dea. Edmund), b. 1740, cousin to Capt. John; m. Rebecca ——, and lived in Sandisfield, Berkshire county, Mass., 30 miles west of Springfield. They had Erastus, Chester, Submit, Watson, Frances, Huldah, and Rebecca. He d. in 1795. The wife must be the one who m. Jeremiah Jordan (James, Jeremiah, Jeremiah, Rev. Robert, over from England to Cape Elizabeth, near Portland, Me., 1640), No. 5211 in the "Jordan Memorial," the successor to Ruth Chute, see No. 9; and Watson Rice must have been the one on the Yankee *Enterprise*, that captured the British *Boxer*, off Portland, Sept. 5 1813.

RUGGLES.

Ruggles, de Ruggle, de Ruggele, and de Ruggeley is a name traced back to early in the 13th century. Robert de Ruggele lived in England time of Henry III., 1220. Then in the 26th of Edward I., 1298, William de Ruggele was honored for faithful service to the king, in his army in Flanders. Then in the 10th, 13th, and 14th of Edward III. mention is made of Simon De Ruggeley, sheriff of the counties of Salop, Stafford, etc.

1. Thomas Ruggles of Sudbury, Suffolk, Eng., 1547, besides a sister Isabella and brother William, had children Nicholas, John, Ann, and Elizabeth.

2. Nicholas had Roger, George, Thomas, Edward, Margery, William, and Robert.

3. Thomas m. Margaret Whatlocke, and had 8 children between 1564 and 1591.

1. **Thomas** (Thomas, Nicholas, Thomas) of Nazing, Essex, Eng., b. 1584; m. Mary Curtis (sister to William, the first one of

ALLIED FAMILIES. clxxv

that ame that came over), Nov. 1, 1620; came over to Roxbury, Mass., 1637; made a freeman 1639; d. Nov. 16, 1644. His widow m. Mr. Roote, and d. 1674, aged 88. John, a brother to Thomas, b. 1591, came over to Roxbury 1635; while John of Boston, another one, came over in the fleet with Gov. John Winthrop, 1630. Besides these were Jeffrey, George, and Samuel, who came over. Children of Thomas:

    i   Son, d. in England.
    ii SARAH.
    iii JOHN, b. 1625; m. Abigail, daughter of Griffin Crafts, 1651, and d. 1658. She m. 2d, Edward Adams.
2 iv SAMUEL, b. 1629.

2. ii. Capt. Samuel Ruggles (Thomas), b. 1629; m. Hannah, daughter of George Fowle, of Charlestown, 1655; she d. Oct. 24, 1669. He m. 2d, Ann, daughter of Henry and Ann (Goldstone) Bright (1644–1711), May 26, 1670, Watertown, Mass. He was a prominent man in Roxbury; served as selectman and representative, 1689–1692; had the rank of captain, and was actively engaged in deposing Gov. Sir Edmund Andros (1637 in England, Gov. of New England 1686 to 1690—tyranical and very unpopular—then Gov. of Virginia and Maryland, 1692 to 1698; d. in England 1713), and d. Aug. 15, 1692.

CHILDREN.

   i   HANNAH, b. Jan. 21, 1656; d. soon.
   ii MARY, b. Jan. 10, 1657; d. young.
3 iii SAMUEL, b. June 1, 1658.
   iv JOSEPH, b. Feb. 12, 1660.
   v   HANNAH, b. Dec. 22, 1661; d. Nov. 6, 1669.
   vi SARAH, b. Nov., 1663; d. 1664.
   vii MARY, b. Dec. 8, 1666; m. Ebenezer Pierpont; 2d, Isaac Morris.
   viii SARAH, b. Aug. 30, 1669; d. Nov. 16.
   ix REV. THOMAS, b. March 10, 1671; m. Sarah Fisk; 2d, Mary Hubbard.
   x   ANN, b. Sept. 30, 1672; m. William Heath.
   xi NATHANIEL, b. Sept. 22, 1674; d. young.
   xii ELIZABETH, b. May 1, 1677; m. James Bayley (James, John, John).
   xiii HENRY, b. July 7, 1681; d. 1702.
   xiv HULDAH, b. July 4, 1684; m. Samuel Hill.

3. iii. Capt. Samuel Ruggles (Samuel, Thomas), b. June 1, 1658; lived in Roxbury; succeeded his father as captain, selectman, representative to the general court, etc. He was one of the first proprietors of the territory now Warwick; the deed was dated Dec., 1686. He m. July 8, 1680, Martha Woodbridge (daughter of Rev. John, son of Rev. John, of Wilts, Eng., who came over in 1634 with his uncle, Rev. Thomas Parker, first minister of Newbury. Mr. Woodbridge was b. in 1613, ordained at Andover 1644, and d. 1695. His wife Mercy, youngest daughter of Gov. Thomas Dudley (1576-1652), of Mass., who came over in 1630. Of her two older sisters, Ann (1612-1672) m. Gov. Simon Bradstreet (1603-1697), and was celebrated as a poetess. Patience (1619-1689), m. Maj. Daniel Denison (1612-1682); and their only brother, Joseph (1647-1720), became Governor of Massachusetts, and father of Paul (1675-1751), chief justice of the state, and F. R. S.), who d. in Billerica, 1738; he d. Feb., 1715-1716.

CHILDREN.

- i REV. SAMUEL, b. Dec. 3, 1681; m. Dec. 19, 1710, Elizabeth Whiting; m. 2d, 1728, Elizabeth Williams (Samuel, Samuel, Samuel, Robert), and d. March 1, 1749.
- ii LUCY, b. Sept. 8, 1683; m. Joseph Stevens.
- 4 iii REV. TIMOTHY, b. Nov. 3, 1685.
- iv HANNAH, b. April 16, 1688; m. William Noyes.
- v PATIENCE, b. Nov. 9, 1689; m. James Robinson.
- vi MARTHA, b. 1691; m. Job Lane.
- vii SARAH, b. 1694; m. John Holbrook.
- viii JOSEPH, b. 1696; m. Joanna White.
- ix MARY, b. 1698.
- x REV. BENJAMIN, b. July 4, 1700; m., and d. May 12, 1782.

4. iv. **Rev. Timothy Ruggles** (Samuel, Samuel, Thomas), b. Nov. 3, 1685; H. C. 1707; settled in Rochester, Plymouth county, 1710, and had a large estate in Hardwick; pastor of the church there; m. Sept. 27, 1710, Mary, daughter of Benjamin and Susanna (Cogswell) White (1688-1750); m. 2d, Anne Woodworth; d. Oct., 1768.

CHILDREN.

- 5 i TIMOTHY, b. Oct. 11, 1711.
- ii CAPT. BENJAMIN, b. May 19, 1713; m. Alice Merrick; 9 children; m. 2d, 1778, Mary Smith; 3 children, and d. Oct. 11, 1790.
- iii SAMUEL, b. July 5, 1715; m. Alice Sherman.
- iv JOSEPH, b. June 23, 1717; m. Hannah Cushman; 6 children, and d. Jan. 28, 1791; son Joseph, b. at Hardwick, April 8, 1748; was a Loyalist; went to Aylesford, N. S., 1768;

ALLIED FAMILIES. clxxvii

      m. Lois Nichols, and had Joseph, William, Thomas R., James, and John. Lois, a daughter of James, m. Rev. Willard G. Parker.
v MARY, b. Jan. 1, 1719; m. John Hammond, Jr.
vi SUSANNA, b. Jan. 6, 1722; m. Paul Mendell (1723-1809), and d. Dec. 16, 1813. He was selectman 11 years, assessor 16, town clerk, representative to the Provincial Congress, 1774-1775, etc.
vii HON. EDWARD, b. Aug. 30, 1723; m. Lucy Spooner (Dea. Samuel, d. 1797, aged 103; Samuel, d. 1739, aged 84; William, son of John and Ann of Leyden, Holland, 1616; came over 1637, and d. 1684), and d. May 21, 1778; she d. 1821, aged 92; 8 children.
viii NATHANIEL, b. April 12, 1725; m. Deliverance Barrow, and d. Dec. 25, 1776; 8 children.
ix THOMAS, b. 1727; d. young.
x HANNAH, b. 1728; d. young.
xi THOMAS, b. 1730; m. Mary Loring, and d. 1776.
xii JOHN, b. Sept. 2, 1731.

5. v. Brigadier-General Timothy Ruggles (Rev. Timothy, Capt. Samuel, Capt. Samuel, Thomas), b. at Rochester, Plymouth county, Mass., Oct. 11, 1711; H. C., 1732; m. a Miss Humphrey, 1735; was an able lawyer, 1736. His wife d. 1750, and soon after he m. 2d, Bathsheba, only daughter of Meletiah Bourne, and widow of William Newcomb (Peter, Andrew, Andrew), who d. April 8, 1736, aged 34, leaving seven children. Mr. Ruggles moved to Sandwich about this time, opened a tavern and attended bar and stable, and continued the practice of law and the courts. About 1753-4, he moved to Hardwick, Worcester county, and entered the British Army, and led a body of troops to join Sir William Johnson in 1755, as Colonel, and was in the expedition to Crown Point and the battle of Lake George. He remained in the army till 1760, the last three years brigadier-general, under Lord Amherst. He represented Hardwick several years in the Legislature, and was speaker in the House, 1762-3. In 1765 he was made President of the Congress of nine colonies at New York, at which Otis and Partridge were delegates from Massachusetts. In 1774 he was made a "Mandamus Councillor," at Salem, Mass. He was a good scholar, shrewd, brave, and witty. He was a Loyalist or Tory and had to leave his extensive estates in Hardwick, which were confiscated. He accompanied the British army to Halifax, N. S., in 1783. In 1784, he received a grant of land in Wilmot, Annapolis county, N. S., and commenced a settlement near the top of the North Mountain, called clxxviii   ALLIED FAMILIES.

Ruggles Mountain; but being bought by Lot Phinney about 1800, it has since been called Phinney Mountain, and there he d. Aug. 4, 1795, aged 84.

CHILDREN.

    i   MARTHA, b. Aug. 10, 1736; m. John Thafts (Tufts?).
6 ii TIMOTHY, b. Jan. 7, 1738.
   iii MARY, b. Feb. 10, 1740; m. Dr. John Green.
7 iv JOHN, b. Sept. 30, 1742.
8 v RICHARD, b. March 4, 1744.
   vi BATHSHEBA, b. Feb. 13, 1746; m. Joshua Spooner, and d. 1778.
   vii ELIZABETH, b. May 15, 1748; m. Gardner Chandler.

6. vi. Timothy Ruggles (Gen. Timothy, Rev. Timothy, Samuel, Samuel, Thomas), b. in Rochester, Mass., Jan. 7, 1738; m. Sarah Dwight (Col. Simeon, Capt. Henry, Capt. Timothy, John, who came over in 1634 from Dedham, Eng., to Dedham, Mass.; wife Hannah d. 1656; he m. 2d, Elizabeth, widow of William Ripley and Thomas Thaxter, 1657, and both d. 1660), b. May 1, 1746, and d. 1842. He d. 1831. They lived at Belle Isle, Annapolis county.

CHILDREN.

   i SARAH, b. Feb. 2, 1768; m. Judah Hinkley.
   ii ANNA, b. June 8, 1769.
   iii SOPHIA, b. Jan. 19, 1771; d. young.
   iv BETSY, b. Nov. 15, 1772; d. young.
   v TIMOTHY, b. Dec. 1, 1773; d. young.
   vi TIMOTHY, b. March 7, 1776; m. Jane, daughter of Edward Thorne, and d. 1831. He was M.P.P. of Annapolis county, and had (1) Jane R., b. 1811; m. Abel Sands. (2) Harriet, b. 1813; m. Thomas Bartlett; William J. Starr. (3) Armanella, b. 1816. (4) Timothy Dwight, b. 1818; m. Havilah Jane Thorne; 9 children; she d. 1892; he is a lawyer in Bridgetown, N. S. (5) Edward Thorne, b. 1820; d. single. (6) Stephen Thorne, b. 1823; m. —— Wade.
   vii SOPHIA, b. Oct. 20, 1777; m. Christian Tobias; John T. Smith.
   viii SIMEON D., b. Jan. 23, 1780; m. Margaret Robinson, and d. 1812; had (1) William R., b. 1808; m. Seraph Cutter; 4 children. (2) Dr. Henry D., b. 1810; m. Sarah Campbell; 14 children. (3) Mary Adelia, b. 1811; m. James Runciman. (4) Elizabeth Johnston, b. 1812; d. single.
   ix HARRIET, b. Feb. 23, 1782; m. Stephen De Wolf.

ALLIED FAMILIES. clxxix

 x CLARISSA, b. April 3, 1784; m. Dr. George W. Shepherd.
 xi ISRAEL WILLIAMS, ESQ., b. Aug. 27, 1786; m. Elizabeth Millidge, 8 children; m. 2d, Maria Owen, 3 children, and d. 1880 (?).

7. vi. John Ruggles, brother to the above, b. in Rochester, Mass., Sept. 30, 1742; m. Hannah, only daughter of Dr. Thomas Sackett of Long Island, N. Y., and being proscribed and banished, settled in Wilmot, N. S., in 1778, where he d.; she d. 1839, aged 76.

CHILDREN.

 i BATHSHEBA, b. 1777; d. about 1865.
 ii TIMOTHY AMHERST, b. 1781; was captain of the N. S. "Fencibles," and d. 1838.
 iii ELIZA BAYARD, b. 1797; m. Austin Woodbury, Wilmot.
 iv FRANCES MARY, b. 1802; m. Jonathan, son of Fairfield Woodbury.

8. vi. Richard Ruggles, another brother, the youngest son of the Brigadier-General, b. in Rochester, Mass., March 4, 1744; m. in 1771 Welthea, daughter of Capt. Ebenezer and Welthea (Gilbert) Hathaway, and had their family partly in Massachusetts and partly in Annapolis, N. S. He d. Oct. 21, 1832; she d. Dec. 4, 1824.

CHILDREN.

 i BATHSHUA, b. Sept. 21, 1772; m. John Hutchinson; one child.
 ii CYNTHIA, b. April 15, 1774; m. John Durland; James Harris; daughter Cynthia m. John Gray.
 iii THOMAS HUTCHINSON, b. Nov. 19, 1775; m. Sarah (Helms) Fowler; 8 children.
9 iv RICHARD, b. Sept. 25, 1780, } twins. { m. Charles Tucker; 9 children.
 v WELTHEA, b. Sept. 25, 1780, }
 vi SOPHIA, b. Jan. 31, 1785; m. John Ryerson; 11 children.
 vii TRYPHENA, b. May 24, 1786; d. May 20, 1844.
 viii GILBERT, b. June 14, 1788; m. Mary Morehouse, and d. May 22, 1841; 6 children.

9. vii. Richard Ruggles (Richard, Gen. Timothy, Rev. Timothy, Samuel, Samuel, Thomas), b. Sept. 25, 1780; m. Eleanor Ann, daughter of Elijah Purday, Oct. 18, 1820, Bear River, N. S., and lived in Clements. He was a school-teacher and farmer; d. Nov. 19, 1853; she m. 2d, Henry F. Vroom, Esq. (as his 2d wife), 1879, and d. Feb., 1884, aged 80; he d. 1892, aged 84.

CHILDREN.

i Josiah Jones, b. Nov. 4, 1821; m. Mary, daughter of Dea. Thomas Gilliatt; Adelia Whitman.
ii Clarissa, b. Sept. 24, 1823; m. James Edward Harris, July 3, 1858; 3 children.
iii Arthur, b. 1825; m. Elizabeth S., daughter of Joseph Rice; 6 children.
iv William Spurr, b. 1828; m. Rebecca Berry (Thomas), and d. 1891; 3 children.
v Elizabeth Adelaide, b. Sept. 22, 1830; m. Israel Lent (John, Abram); 2d, Charles C. Jefferson (as his 2d wife); live at Beechmont, Mass.
vi George Albert, b. Jan. 26, 1833; m. Lydia Sophia Chute. See No. 37.
vii Armanella, b. June 2, 1835; m. John Rice, Jr., and d. April, 1872; he m. 2d, Maggie Ray.
viii Charles, b. July 28, 1837; m. Bessy, daughter of Thomas Lee, Lynn, Mass., May 19, 1867; 4 children.
ix Rev. Gilbert, b. Aug. 19, 1839; m. Eunice, daughter of Franklin Rice; 3 children.
x Cecilia, b. 1841; m. William Gwyer, Weymouth, N. S.
xi Timothy, b. April 24, 1844, } twins. { m. Maggie ——.
xii Richard, b. April 24, 1844, }   { m. Abba (Hayward) White; 3 children, Wakefield, Mass.

SANFORD.

1. i. John Sanford, son of Samuel and Eleanor, of Alford, Lincolnshire, Eng., came in the ship *Lyon,* arriving in Boston, Nov. 3, 1631, and is numbered 115 on the list of church members; a freeman of the colony, April 3, 1632, and the same year commander at the fort. He was one of the 58 church members disarmed in 1637 (being a supporter of Rev. John Wheelwright (1594-1679) and Mrs. Anne (Marbury), wife of William Hutchinson (1591-1644)), on account of an Antinomian Schism. Mr. Sanford went to Rhode Island in 1638, and was one of the 19 signers of the civil compact dated March 7, 1638, for the settlement of Aquidneck, now the island of Rhode Island. He was Constable, Secretary, Treasurer, and General Recorder, 1647-49, and was President of the Colony in 1653, and d. between June 22 and Nov. 16, 1653. He m. 1st, Elizabeth Webb and had 2 children; m. 2d, Bridget, daughter of William and Anne Hutchinson; she m. 2d, William Phillips, who d. 1683; she d. 1698.

ALLIED FAMILIES. clxxxi

CHILDREN.

- i JOHN, b. June 4, 1633, in Boston; m. Elizabeth, daughter of Henry Spachurst, Aug. 8, 1654. She d. Dec. 6, 1661; he m. 2d, April 17, 1663, Mary, daughter of Samuel Gorton and widow of John Green, Jr.; 3 children by each.
- 2 ii SAMUEL, b. July 14, 1635.
- iii ELIPHAL, b. Dec. 9, 1637; m. Bartholomew Stratton, and d. 1724; 4 children.
- iv PELEG, b. May 10, 1739, Portsmouth, R. I.; m. Mary, daughter of Gov. William Brenton; m. 2d, Mary, daughter of William and Ann Coddington, and d. 1701. He was Governor of Connecticut 1680 to 1683.
- v ENCOME, b. Feb. 23, 1640, Rhode Island; d. young.
- vi RESTCOME, b. Jan. 29, 1642, Dutch Island; d. 1667.
- vii WILLIAM, b. March 4, 1644; Rhode Island.
- viii ESBON, b. Jan. 25, 1646, Rhode Island; m.
- ix FRANCES, b. Jan. 9, 1648; m. Elisha Hutchinson, grandfather of Gov. Thomas Hutchinson.
- x ELISHA, b. Dec. 28, 1650; Rhode Island.
- xi ANNE, b. March 12, 1652, Rhode Island; d. Aug. 26, 1654.

2. ii. Samuel Sanford (John), b. in Boston, July 14, 1635; m. Oct. 1, 1662, Sarah, daughter of William and Mary Woodell. She d. Dec. 15, 1680; he m. 2d, April 23, 1686, Susannah, daughter of William and Elizabeth Spachurst of the Bermudas, and d. March 18, 1712–13; she d. Nov. 13, 1723.

CHILDREN.

- i ELIZABETH, b. Oct. 2, 1663; m. Samuel Allen, and d. April 14, 1743.
- ii JOHN, b. June 10, 1668; m. Sept. 6, 1689, Frances, daughter of Jeremiah and Ann Clark, and d. 1728; she d. 1702.
- iii BRIDGET, b. June 27, 1671.
- iv MARY, b. April 27, 1674; m. Josiah Arnold, and d. July 15, 1711.
- v WILLIAM, b. May 21, 1676; m. 1699, Hope, daughter of George and Sarah Sisson; 8 children.
- vi SAMUEL, b. July 14, 1678; d. Oct., 1704.
- vii RESTCOME, b. Feb. 26, 1687; m. Honoria Stringer, 1710; 2 children, and d. at sea Feb. 6, 1713.
- viii PELEG, b. Aug. 16, 1688; m. Sarah, daughter of Capt. Josiah Arnold, 1718, and d. at St. Kitts, 1730; she d. Dec., 1726–7.
- ix ELISHA, b. Feb. 24, 1690; m. 1715, Rebecca, daughter of William and Martha Wood, and widow of Charles Ware; she d. May 16, 1745.
- x ENCOME, b. Nov. 19, 1691; d. at sea, June 13, 1717.

ALLIED FAMILIES.

3 xi   Esbon, b. Oct. 30, 1693.
   xii   Frances, b. Oct. 24, 1695.
   xiii   Joseph, b. Aug. 13, 1698; m. 1721, Lydia, daughter of John Odlin, and d. Oct. 1, 1765; she d. 1781, aged 80.
   xiv   Benjamin, b. June 4, 1700; drowned at Eutacea, Nov. 21, 1730.
   xv   Joshua, b. April 18, 1702; d. at Martinico, Nov. 13, 1721.
   xvi   Elizabeth, b. Dec. 7, 1706.

3. iii. Capt. Esbon Sanford (Samuel, John), b. Oct. 30, 1693; m. Sept. 27, 1716, Mary Woodward. He was a freeman at Newport, R. I., 1718; captain, 1735; deputy from Newport, 1736–43; appointed to the General Assembly, 1739–40, and d. Aug. 22, 1743; she d. 1745.

CHILDREN.

   i   Mary, b. 1719.
   ii   Eneas, b. 1721.
   iii   Woodward, b. 1723.
   iv   Hannah, b. 1725; m. June 28, 1759, Joseph Phillips.
   v   Esbon, b. 1728; m.
4 vi   Benjamin, b. 1732.
   vii   Lydia, b. 1735.
   viii   Joshua, b. 1737.
   ix   Joseph, b. Feb. 18, 1740; m. Mary Clark, June 13, 1764.

4. iv. Benjamin Sanford (Esbon, Samuel, John), b. Newport, R. I., 1732; m. Amelia ——, 1754; went from Newport, R. I., to Falmouth, N. S., in the sloop *Sally*, Jonathan Lovatt, master, May, 1760, passage paid £8, 15s. Joshua Sanford went over the same time — paid £3, 15s. Afterwards Joshua, Joseph, and Encome followed. Woodward Sanford went 1772, Esbon and Peleg in 1781. Benjamin Sanford bought property of Benjamin Borden, Dec. 13, 1763. Mrs. Sanford d. about 1800; he m. 2d, Lydia Strong (Stephen, Stephen, Jedediah, Jedediah, Elder John), widow of Jonathan Rand (Caleb, John, Thomas, Robert), Oct. 4, 1804.

CHILDREN.

   i   Susanna, b. Dec. 4, 1754; m. Nathan, son of Elnathan and Elizabeth Palmeter, Feb. 27, 1772.
   ii   Mary, b. Feb. 1, 1756; m. Jonathan, son of Stephen and Hannah Loomer, Feb. 8, 1776.
5 iii   Daniel, b. Jan. 26, 1758.
   iv   Abigail, b. Nov. 17, 1759; m. Benjamin Newcomb (Joseph, John, John, Simon, Andrew, Andrew), June 6, 1776, and d. 1840; he d. Aug. 6, 1821, aged 58. Several

ALLIED FAMILIES. clxxxiii

of the children m. and settled in or near Falmouth, N. S.: (1) James, b. 1777; m. Rachel Cunnabell, widow of Stephen Sheffield (Preserved, Samuel, John, London to Boston about 1673); d. 1845; 4 children. (2) Catharine, b. 1778; m. Jonathan Colwell, and d. 1819; he d. 1820; 7 sons. (3) Sarah, b. 1780; m. John Bigelow and d. in N. B. 1850; 8 children. (4) Susanna, b. 1782; m. Gideon Davisson, 1816; 5 children. (5) David, b. 1784; m. Elizabeth Fisher, 1807, and d. 1854; she d. 1865, aged 76; had (a) William Edward, b. 1807. (b) John Sampson, b. 1809; m. Sarah Ann Bronson, 1846 (lost on the steamer *Lady Elgin*, off Racine, Wis., in Lake Michigan, Sept. 8, 1860), and was killed by the accidental discharge of his gun in New York city, 1861; was a soldier in the Milwaukee Light Guards, and left 5 children. (c) Matthew F. (d) David B. (e) Mary E., b. 1816; m. 1842, John, son of Wilmot Osborn (1812, to Boston, 1869); to Worcester after; 8 children. (f) Matthew F. (g) Simon B. (h) Samuel H. (i) Rebecca F. (j) Alfred W. (k) Willey Ann. (l) Gideon E. (6) Barnaby, (1786-1821), m. 1810, Rebecca Pinneo; 2 children. (7) Elizabeth (1787-1841), m. 1813, Elijah, son of David and Rebecca Pineo; 6 children. (8) Benjamin (1789-1858). (9) Eddy (1791-1855), m. Sarah Ilsley, widow of Benjamin Sanford; 3 children. (10) Alice (1793-1822), m. John Marsh. (11) John (1795-1852), m. Rebecca, daughter of David and Rebecca West. (12) Mary (1797-), m. Harris Crocker; 8 children; 2d, Samuel Rand. (13) Eleanor (1798-1816). (14) Hezekiah (1800-1832), tanner and shoemaker, Frederickton, N. B.; willed $4000 to his nephew David Barnaby Newcomb. (15) Simon (1803-1844), m. 1827, Lydia (1808-), daughter of Jedediah and Sarah Ells; she m. 2d, Andrew Weathers; 7 children.

v EDWARD, b. March 16, 1761; m. —— Beckwith, and had, if we mistake not, a son James, m. Sarah Jane Best, and lived near Harborville. Children: (1) William, m. Sarah Bennett; she m. 2d, Ebenezer, son of Stephen Strong. (2) George W., m. Phebe Graves. (3) Julia A., m. William John McNeily. (4) Ruth, m. John McKay. (5) James, d. about 24. (6) Stephen B., b. 1832; m. Melissa, daughter of Henry Ray; 4 children, and d. Nov., 1869. She went over to Boston, 1870, m. Nathaniel Ross, June, 1891, and lives in Brighton, Mass. Edward Sanford had a daughter Abigail, b. 1787; m. Benjamin Newcomb (Joseph, John, John, Simon), 1807, and had Edward, David, Phebe, and Daniel. Mr. Newcomb d. before 1820, and she m. 2d, Charles Cox.

6 vi BENJAMIN, b. April 2, 1763.

ALLIED FAMILIES.

- vii AMELIA, b. Aug. 30, 1764; m. Samuel, son of Joshua and Mary Ells, 1784.
- 7 viii SAMUEL, b. April 24, 1766.
- ix SARAH, b. Nov. 6, 1767; m. Amasa Keller, Nov. 13, 1795.
- x ELIZABETH, b. Jan. 25, 1771; m. Samuel Loomer.
- xi WAITY, b. Aug. 20, 1772; m. Eddy Newcomb, an only son (John, Eddy, John, Simon, Andrew, Andrew), 1790, and d. 1791; he m. 2d, Mary, daughter of Cyrus West, 1792; 7 children; she d. 1811, aged 38; he m. 3d, Alice, daughter of Simeon and Sarah Porter, 1812; 2 children, and d. 1854, aged 85; she d. 1850. Sarah, the 6th, m. William Bowles Masters (b. 1801), 1824; 3 children; d. 1832, aged 27.
- xii DEBORAH, b. May 8, 1774; m. Ira Woodworth. See Woodworth.
- 8 xiii JOHN, b. April 1, 1776.

5. v. Daniel Sanford (Benjamin, Esbon, Samuel, John), b. Newport, R. I., Jan. 26, 1758; m. Ruby Strong, Feb. 16, 1780 (Stephen, Stephen, Stephen, Jedediah, Jedediah, Elder John, over in 1630, lived with his wife 58 years; 16 children; d. 1699, aged 94; she — Abigail Ford — d. 1688, aged 80), and lived in Upper Pero, Kings county, N. S. He d. about 1833; she d. 1848, aged 80.

CHILDREN.

- i DAVID, b. Jan. 1, 1781; d. young.
- 9 ii JOSHUA, b. Jan. 10, 1783.
- iii JOSEPH, b. Oct. 26, 1784; m. Welthea Palmeter, Nov. 15, 1806; daughter Welthea Jane m. William Lyons, and had 15 children.
- iv ELIZABETH, b. Nov. 26, 1786; d. 1800.
- v BENJAMIN, b. Dec. 1, 1788; m. Sarah Ilsley, Sept. 3, 1812, and d. after having 2 sons; she m. 2d, Eddy Newcomb (1791-1855), and had 3 more children.
- vi WAITY, b. May 4, 1791; m. Thomas, son of Daniel Johnson, Feb. 7, 1811, and had James B., Eben S., Sarah A., Rebecca A., Waity Melissa, William Henry, Daniel W., John Alfred, Mary Jane, and Lucy Ann. Two or three live in Boston.
- vii STEPHEN, b. May 5, 1793; d. young.
- viii DEBORAH, b. May 2, 1795; d. young.
- ix LYDIA, b. Sept. 2, 1796; m. Asa Huntley, Scotch Bay; 4 children.
- 10 x DANIEL, b. Jan. 20, 1799.
- xi RUBY, b. Jan. 22, 1801; m. Daniel, son of Daniel Johnson; 10 children.
- xii EBER, b. Sept. 3, 1803; bled to death about 1824.

ALLIED FAMILIES. clxxxv

6. v. **Benjamin Sanford,** brother to the above, b. Horton, N. S., April 2, 1763; m. Freedom Strong, daughter of Dea. Abel (she was a niece of Ruby, his sister-in-law), March 25, 1790, by Dr. Graham, and lived in Cornwallis. He lived to nearly 100. She d. about 1860, aged 98.

CHILDREN.

11 i JAMES, b. Jan. 2, 1791.
   ii BETSY, b. Oct. 2, 1792; m. Nathan Loomer, and had Wellington, Eben, Henry, and Freedom.
12 iii JOHN, b. Sept. 25, 1794.
   iv MARY, b. Dec. 6, 1796; m. John McDonald; lived at Pero, and had (1) Benjamin, b. 1817; m. Mary Witham, Moultonboro', N. H. (2) William, in Cambridge, Mass. (3) Lois, m. James Ryan; 5 children; 2d, Angus McDonald, 1 child. (4) John, m. Catharine McDonald; 9 children; near Boston. (5) James, killed in the late war. (6) Duncan, m. —— ——; 8 children in Connecticut. (7) Eleanor, a twin, m. John Dow; 8 children. (8) Thomas Henry, to Australia. (9) Richard, to Australia. (10) Mary, m. Samuel Rodoch. (11) Rebecca, in Boston. (12) Nathan, off West.
   v SALLY, b. Sept. 12, 1798; m. Henry, son of Thomas Borden.
   vi DANIEL, b. Aug. 4, 1800; m. Eliza, daughter of Joseph Dimock of Newport, N. S., and d. in California. They had (1) Harriet, m. Learly Dodge of Aylesford; 2 children; to Stockton, Cal. (2) Rebecca, m. Charles Nichols. (3) Jane, m. Rev. D. A. Dearborn, Baptist minister, Worcester, Mass. (4) Selina, m. Albert Horne. (5) Lucilla, m. Edward Nichols. (6) William Judson, m. Mary Rand; 6 children; to Boston, where she d. suddenly, 1889; he to Minnesota, and m. again.
   vii AMELIA, b. Aug. 2, 1802; m. Dea. Daniel Sanford, a cousin.
   viii LOIS, b. July 2, 1805; m. Thomas, brother to Dr. Borden, Sen.
   ix DRUSILLA, b. June 20, 1807; m. William McPhee, and had Lewis, James, Margaret Ann, Freedom R., Mary, and Elizabeth.
   x CINDERELLA, a twin, m. Donald McDonald, Somerset, N. S.; had Mary Ann, Freedom, John, Benjamin, Melinda, Daniel, and Wallace.
   xi REBECCA ANN, b. July 2, 1814; m. Charles Sanford, a cousin.

7. v. **Samuel Sanford,** another brother, b. Horton, N. S., April 24, 1766; m. Ruth Newcomb (John, John, Simon, Andrew,

Andrew), Feb. 14, 1787, and lived in Cornwallis; d. about 1822; she d. 1830.

CHILDREN.

13   i   JOHN NEWCOMB, b. Dec. 25, 1788.
     ii   DAVID, b. Feb. 10, 1790; m. Betsy Bowen, widow of John Waggoner (with 3 children, Jacob, John, and Sarah), about 1819, and had Henry, Nelson, Eadie, Harriet, and Emeline.
14   iii   JONATHAN, b. Nov. 10, 1792.
     iv   MARY, b. Sept. 11, 1795; m. Samuel Beckwith, Esq. (Samuel, James, Matthew, Matthew, b. in England, 1610; over to Hartford, Conn., 1639; d. at Lyme, Conn., Oct. 28, 1680), farmer and singing teacher, and d. 1876. He d. 2 or 3 years before; 3 children.
     v   JACOB, b. Aug. 25, 1796; m. Eunice Dexter, and had Enoch and Edward.
     vi   ELIZABETH, b. June 3, 1798; d. about 1866.
     vii   AMELIA, b. March 18, 1800; m. Enoch Cleveland, and d.; he m. 2d, Mrs. Charlotte Downey.
     viii   SARAH, b. about 1804; m. Henry Borden, March 21, 1821, as his 2d wife.

8. v. John Sanford, the youngest brother, b. at or near Horton, N. S., April 1, 1776; m. Waity (b. March 11, 1781), daughter of Charles and Hannah (Huntley) Palmeter, 1800, and lived in Pero, Kings county, N. S. She d. in May, 1813; he m. 2d, Lucy Farnsworth, widow of James Eaton, Nov. 24, 1814.

CHILDREN.

     i   JAMES GORDON, d. July 17, 1802; m. Hannah Weaver.
     ii   BENJAMIN, b. Oct. 12, 1803; m. Caroline, daughter of James and Lucy (Manning) Eaton, and had (1) Judah, m. —— Tupper. (2) Walter Manning, m. Rebecca Martin. (3) Lucy Ann, m. Colin Dewolf, and d. 1892. (4) John M., m. Sarah Ann Tupper, widow of Eben Sanford. (5) George. (6) Julia, m. George Whalin.
     iii   WILLIAM PALMETER, b. April 20, 1805; m.
     iv   MARIA ANN, b. Feb. 17, 1807; m. George, son of Dea. Daniel Sanford.
     v   EUNICE ELIZA, b. June 28, 1809; m. John Witt.
     vi   CHARLES, b. March 18, 1811; m. Rebecca Ann, daughter of Benjamin Sanford, Jr.
     vii   NATHAN, b. Feb. 13, 1813; m. Rachel Jane Newcomb (James, Benjamin, John, John, Simon, etc.).
     viii   JAMES, b. Aug. 22, 1816; m. Angelina Sophronia Newcomb (Joseph, Joseph, John, John, Simon, etc.), 1840,

ALLIED FAMILIES.

and had Rufus, Adaline, Noble, Ruth Ann, Watson, Burpee, and Lucy.

- ix WAITY, b. June 19, 1817; m. Ebenezer Bigelow (Eben, Amasa, Isaac, Isaac, Samuel, John), 1848; vessel builder at Canning, N. S.; 10 children; both d. 1889.
- x MANNING, b. July 25, 1819; m. Harriet Corbit.
- xi HENRY, b. Aug. 2, 1821.

9. vi. Joshua Sanford (Daniel, Benjamin, Esbon, Samuel, John), b. in Cornwallis, Kings county, N. S., Jan. 10, 1783; m. Betsy Weaver, 1806, and lived at Woodville; d. about 1844; she d. June, 1849, aged 60.

CHILDREN.

- i WELTHEA, b. 1808; m. Benjamin, son of Amos Porter; 7 children.
- ii ERASTUS P., b. 1810; m. Mary Porter, a sister; 9 children.
- iii JEREMIAH, m. Eliza, daughter of James Porter; 6 children.
- iv DANIEL, m. Waity, daughter of Amos Porter; 6 children.
- v LYDIA, m. Charles, son of Amos Porter; 5 children.
- vi RUBY, b. 1821; m. William H. Loveless (Handley, William); 4 children, and d. Sept. 5, 1887.
- vii MARY, m. Rufus, son of Samuel Wood; 6 children.
- viii JAMES, m. Eunice, daughter of Nathan Schofield; 10 children; m. 2d, Hannah Dunn; 3 children.
- ix JANE, m. Andrew, son of William Mahar; 7 children.
- xii MARILLA, m. Thomas, son of William Mahar; 3 children.

10. vi. Dea. Daniel Sanford, brother to the above, b. June 20, 1799; m. Amelia, daughter of Benjamin Sanford, a cousin, and lived in Pereau, where they d.; he, 1874; she, before.

CHILDREN.

- i RUBY, m. Charles Golden.
- ii BENJAMIN, was in the Mexican war, 1846.
- iii GEORGE, m. Maria Ann, daughter of John Sanford; to California.
- iv EBER, m. Sarah Ann Tupper; 2 children, Eber and Emily.
- v WELLINGTON, m. Mary Conners.
- vi FREEDOM, m. Samuel Damon; Gilbert Crocker.
- vii SHEFFIELD, m. Amelia Lyons.
- viii WILWORTH, m. Mary Bryant.
- ix UDAVILLA, m. James Stewart; Asaph, son of Rev. Israel Rice.

11. vi. James Sanford (Benjamin, Benjamin, Esbon, Samuel, John), b. in Cornwallis, Jan. 2, 1791; m. Sarah Woolaver (Caleb,

John), and lived between Rawdon and Douglass. He d. 1884; she d. 1886, aged 88.

CHILDREN.

i NATHAN, b. Aug. 24, 1815; m. Melissa White; 3 children. He moved to Humboldt county, Cal., 1854, and d. there.
ii MARY, b. May 12, 1818; m. Henry Murdock; 5 children.
iii MELINDA, b. Sept. 14, 1819; m. Alexander Lavers; Robert Fenton; 3 children each.
iv JAMES MUNRO, b. Nov. 21, 1821; in Prescott or Williams, Arizona.
v MARIA, b. Jan. 8, 1823; m. William McDougall, Jr., Oct. 24, 1843; he d. Aug., 1869; she m. 2d, Rev. John McDonald, 1873; he d. Feb. 10, 1881, aged 66. Children: (1) William James, b. Feb. 21, 1845; to Boston, 1864; supposedly in the late war. (2) Ursula, b. May 22, 1846; d. young. (3) Rev. John, b. June 6, 1847; m. Margaret Ryan; 7 children. (4) Sarah Amelia, b. Nov. 17, 1849; m. Thomas Loney; 7 children; to Grass Valley, Nevada, Cal. (5) Rev. Donald, b. Sept. 28, 1851; m. Lizzie McDonald; 9 children. (6) Mary Melinda, b. Sept. 1, 1853; m. Peter McDonald; 4 children; 2d, Jacob Mason; 3 children. (7) Nancy Jane, b. Nov. 10, 1855. (8) Rachel Assenath, b. June 26, 1857; m. Albert Burgess; 4 children. (9) Nathan, b. July 7, 1859; drowned 1861. (10) Esson Monroe, b. Oct. 17, 1861; m. Myrtle Wallace; 2 children (11) Lois Ann, b. Sept. 21, 1864; is a school-teacher. (12) Austin Everett, b. June 18, 1867; in Haverhill, Mass.
vi LEVI, b. May 31, 1826; m. Mary Hight; 6 children; Grass Valley, Cal.
vii CATHARINE A., b. Sept. 22, 1829; m. Samuel Alderman; 8 children.
viii BENJAMIN, b. April 25, 1832; m. Euphemia Wallace; 7 children.
ix LOIS, b. July 7, 1833; m. Thomas Loney; 1 child; d. in California.
x AMELIA J., b. May 31, 1835; d. young.
xi RACHEL DIENA, b. Nov. 8, 1836; m. Josiah Wallace; 5 children; he d. 1871.

12. vi. **John Sanford**, brother to the preceding, b. Sept. 25, 1794; m. Roxana, daughter of James Langley and lived at Billtown; d. March, 1847; she d. 1863, aged 59.

CHILDREN.

i ESTHER, b. Nov. 21, 1824; m. Fred H. Flynn, Feb. 9, 1854; he d. Feb. 18, 1870, aged 40; she m. 2d, Daniel Carr,

1871; he d. 1878; she went to Boston, 1841, and lives in Dorchester. Children: (1) William Edward, b. Nov. 13, 1854; m. Lizzie Simpson, June 6, 1877; in South Boston. (2) Florianna, b. June 8, 1858; m. George W. French; 2d, F. N. Kimball. (3) Hattie Lorena, b. April 15, 1861; m. John W. Prescott (George W., John, Jeremiah, Nathaniel, John, James, over 1665; d. 1728), Sept. 28, 1881, and live in Dorchester.

ii SAMUEL STEPHENS, b. 1826; m. Susan, daughter of Joseph McLellan, 1852, Cornwallis, N. S. They had (1) Esther, b. Dec. 20, 1853; m. William Rockwell. (2) Nathan Henry, b. Sept. 20, 1856; m Clara, daughter of Samuel McPherson. (3) Samuel W., b. 1858; m. Lizzie, daughof Frank Robblee. (4) Martha, b. 1860; m. Alfred Allen. (5) Stephen Noble, b. March 4, 1862; m. Jane (Spears) Glynn. (6) Edward, b. 1864. (7) Emily, b. 1870.

iii MARK, b. 1828; m. Hannah Rodick; 9 children.
iv CHARLES, b. 1830; m. Maggie Walton; 5 children.
v EBOR, b. 1832; off in 1848; unknown.
vi ELIZABETH, b. 1836; m. Charles M. Abbot; 4 or 5 children.
vii BENJAMIN H., b. July 15, 1838; m. Jerusha Ann, daughter of Daniel, son of Joseph Sanford; 2d, Maria, daughter of Thomas Langley, 1873; Hattie, b. July 16, 1874. Mr. Sanford to Boston, 1859.
viii EUNICE MALINDA, b. Feb. 28, 1841; m. Charles M., son of Charles Flynn, brother to F. H. Flynn; 3 children.
ix JOHN LEANDER, b. March 1, 1843; m. Eliza McLearn; to Humboldt county, Cal.; 5 children.

13. vi. John Newcomb Sanford (Samuel, Benjamin, Esbon, Samuel, John), b. in Cornwallis, N. S., Xmas, 1788; m. Sophia, daughter of David Condon, by Rev. Edward Manning, March 13, 1813, and lived at Horton; she d. March 24, 1820, aged 30; he m. 2d, Charlotte Woodworth (see Woodworth), March 7, 1821, by Rev. Edward Manning, and d. May 15, 1831; she d. in Clements, Sept. 19, 1861, in her 68th year.

CHILDREN.

15 i WILLIAM HENRY, b. Dec. 22, 1813.
16 ii JAMES, b. May 28, 1816.
iii SOPHIA, b. Jan. 1, 1818; m. Solomon, son of Abner Woodworth, Oct. 11, 1836, and lived at Somerset, West Cornwallis, but moved to Lawrence, Mass., about 1870, and d. June 14, 1884, aged 76; she d. July 31, 1884. They had (1) Abner, b. Dec. 15, 1837; m. Susan, daughter of

William Selfridge, Jan. 12, 1858; 9 children. (2) Perry, b. 1842. (3) William Henry, 1844-1853. (4) Hathron, b. Aug. 26, 1846; m. Sarah, daughter of James and Ann Jane (Shaw) McMaster, Aug. 12, 1871; live in Everett, Mass.; 4 children. (5) Rachel, b. Aug. 2, 1850; m. Thomas Henry, son of William Pickles, Aug. 20, 1881, photographer in East Cambridge, Mass.; 5 children. (6) Alice, b. Sept. 21, 1853; m. Ingram, son of Wells Phinney, Nov. 28, 1872; he d. March 3, 1877, aged 27, Lynnfield, Mass.; 2 children; she m. 2d, George R. Whittemore, (Isaac, Isaac, Ebenezer), b. 1824, Aug. 15, 1884; 2 children. (7) Henry, b. Jan. 30, 1856; d. Dec. 13, 1858. (8) John S., b. Sept. 15, 1858; m. Mattie Jackson, June 21, 1879; she d. Feb. 23, 1891, aged 33, leaving (a) Gladdis, b. May 10, 1880. (b) Gertrude, b. Aug. 10, 1881. He m. 2d, Levinia, daughter of Robert Matthews from England, and live at and work in one of the factories in Waltham, Mass. (9) Fred W., b. Dec. 8, 1861; m. Alice, daughter of John Hudson, Oct. 19, 1881; 2d, Laurie, daughter of John Gettie, Nov. 4, 1890, Lawrence, Mass.; Charles Henry, b. June 3, 1886.

    iv MARY ANN, b. Feb. 22, 1822; m. Joseph Chute. See No. 62.
17 v RICHARD H., b. April 24, 1824.
18 vi JOHN BURTON, b. Aug. 26, 1826.
19 vii EZEKIEL PRIOR, b. April 27, 1828.
20 viii EDWARD MANNING, b. May 16, 1830.

14. vi. Jonathan Sanford, brother to the preceding, b. in Cornwallis, N. S., Nov. 10, 1790; m. Melinda Woodworth (Dan, Soloman, Silas, Ichabod, Benjamin, Walter, Walter), March 19, 1819, and lived at Somerset, Kings county, N. S., a farmer; d. Oct. 17, 1884; she d. April 30, 1865, aged 69.

CHILDREN.

  i JOHN BURTON, b. Feb. 25, 1820; d. Oct. 2, 1829.
  ii EBER PORTER, b. Dec. 12, 1821; m. May 10, 1823.
  iii WILLIAM STANHOPE, b. May 9, 1824; m. Linda Taylor from Wisconsin, about 1850; she d. July 8, 1858, aged 45; he m. 2d, Emma Jane Lucas, and had 4 children; 3 d. in infancy, while the 4th is a smart young man named Loren. The parents are mutes.
  iv EUNICE AMELIA, b. Oct. 12, 1826; m. Clark Neily; 4 children, and d. Sept. 1, 1872. He d. March 26, 1873, aged 50.
  v CHARLES EDWARD, b. June 7, 1829; m. Alice, daughter of

ALLIED FAMILIES.

William H. and Elizabeth Ann (Woodworth) Skinner; 6 children.

- vi CAROLINE AMANDA, b. May 19, 1831; m. Nathan Vaughn.
- vii JONATHAN DOUGLASS, b. Oct. 30, 1834; m. Sarah J. Chase.
- viii GEORGE WOODWORTH, b. Jan. 25, 1838; m. Emma J. Ellis; 6 children; she d. Aug. 20, 1885, aged 47. He is a blacksmith in the Boston Rubber works, Malden, Mass.

15. vii. William Henry Sanford (John N., Samuel, Benjamin, Esbon, Samuel, John), b. in Horton, Kings county, N. S., Dec. 22, 1813; m. Rachel, daughter of Enoch and Eunice (Davison) Condon, March 6, 1844; she d. Oct., 1860, aged 39; he m. 2d, Sarah A. Pineo (Augustine, William, Peter, James), Feb., 1861, and d. June, 1890; she d. March, 1890, aged 75.

CHILDREN.

- i PRUDENCE, b. Aug. 2, 1846; m. Nathan, son of T. Best, 1862.
- ii JOSEPH, b. Aug. 28, 1848; m. Ceretha Margeson; live in Merrill, Iowa.
- iii PRYOR, b. April 19, 1850; m. Annie Jarvis; Ruth Charlton.
- iv MARY JANE, b. Aug. 19, 1852; m. James Alonzo Durland (b. Sept. 15, 1849, son of Charles S., Thomas, Daniel); 4 children; Arlington, Mass.
- v JOHN WILLIAM, b. Oct. 15, 1856; m. Annie, daughter of William Molloy, 1887; live in Brighton, Mass.
- vi STEWART NOBLE, b. Oct. 27, 1859; m. Alice Thompson, Somerville.
- vii NOBLE H., b. March, 1862; d. Sept., 1866.
- viii WILLARD N., b. Dec., 1863; m. Maggie, daughter of Ezekiel Parish, 1889.
- ix MARTHA E., b. Sept. 15, 1866; m. Handley, son of Thomas Palmer, 1889.

16. vii. James Sanford, brother to the above, b. May 28, 1816; m. Harriet, daughter of Robert Lyons, Dec. 20, 1837, and lived near Waterville, Cornwallis, N. S.; she d. March, 1869, aged 47; he m. 2d, Emily, daughter of David Sanford, and widow of John McDougall, and d. March, 1874.

CHILDREN.

- i WESLEY, m. Sarah Nicholls; Waterville.
- ii PRUDENCE, m. Obed Taylor; 2d, —— ——.
- iii JAMES, m. Anna Eaton; Merrill, Cass county, Iowa.

   iv FLORENCE, m. George, son of William Forsythe.
   v LALEAH, d. at 20.
   vi CORNELIA, b. 1847; m. Joseph, son of David and Sally (Wear) Minard; 7 children; Dorchester, Boston.
   vii MARY JANE, m. Jason, son of John Nicholls; 3 children; Merrill, Iowa.
   viii FREEMAN, d. at 30.   ix WELCOME, d. at 20.
   x SOPHRONIA, d. young.   xi ARTHUR, off West.
   xii ERNEST MEAD, by 2d wife; off West.
   xiii HASTINGS.   xiv CHARLES.
   xv GEORGE.   xvi WELCOME.

17. vii. Richard Harding Sanford (John N.—and Charlotte Woodworth —, Samuel, Benjamin, Esbon, Samuel, John), b. in Cornwallis, April 24, 1824; m. Rebecca Potter (see Potter), March 25, 1847, and lived in Clements, Annapolis county, N. S.; she d. April 6, 1866, aged 40; he m. 2d, Jerusha Chute (see No. 63), and d. March 5, 1883. The widow is merchant and postmistress at Clementsvale.

CHILDREN.

   i DEA. EDWARD PRYOR, b. March 2, 1848; m. Maggie C. Wade (William, John, John), a school-teacher; live in Allston, Mass.
   ii EMMA ORATIA, b. Feb. 17, 1849; m. Joseph F. Berry (Peter, Thomas), 1872.
   iii JOHN MILTON, b. Feb. 2, 1851; m. Serena A. Chute; Amanda E. Chute (see No. 63); and lived on Brookline street, Cornwallis, N. S.; to New Hampshire, 1879; to Allston, Mass., 1891; to Linden, 1892.
   iv THOMAS ANSLEY, b. Dec. 5, 1852; m. Althea, daughter of William Long, Oct., 1876; 3 sons; live in Allston, Mass.
   v PRUDENCE JANE, b. Feb. 13, 1855; m. Handley C. Chute. See No. 243.
   vi ABBA CHRISTINA, b. Sept. 20, 1856; m. Samuel, son of David Pine, Sept., 1876.
   vii ELIZABETH EUGENIA, b. Jan. 25, 1859; m. John, son of Charles Dondale, Oct., 1880.
   viii IDA LILIAN, b. May 23, 1861; m. Capt. Herbert A. Henshaw, Sept. 2, 1890, and d. at sea of ship fever, April 24, 1891, near the West Indies.
   ix ZENAS ARMSTAN, b. April 19, 1863; m. Laura, daughter of David Frazer, 1887.
   x ADAH REBECCA, b. May 23, 1865; m. John, son of Gilbert Hicks, 1888.

18. vii. John Burton Sanford, the next brother, b. Aug. 26, 1826; went over to Marblehead, Mass., about 1850; m. Ann M., daughter of William Clark, a whitesmith from Devon, Eng., July 2, 1856; she d. at or near Middleton, Aug. 7, 1882, aged 48 years.

CHILDREN.

  i JUDSON C., b. Oct. 9, 1857; m. Lizzie A., daughter of D. Thomas Martin, Sept. 21, 1880, and is a bookkeeper in Boston, but lives in Marblehead.
  ii CARRIE A., b. Oct. 27, 1859; d. 1869.
  iii WILLIAM EDWARD, b. March 10, 1864; m. Carrie Hutchinson, and she d. April 7, 1891, aged 26.
  iv DANIEL C. B., b. Dec. 6, 1866; m. Jennie Hutchinson (George R., Jacob, John, John, Joseph, Joseph, Joseph, Richard, 1602–1682). Ancestral line on the other side: Thomas of Arnold, England, Thomas, Thomas, Lawrence, Thomas, Anthony, William, James, Bernard of Cowlam, York county, Eng., 1280; live in Danvers, Mass.
  v LIZZIE R., b. Jan. 10, 1870; m. Otis Williams, 1889.

From the Hutchinson family of New England have descended some high, honorable, and pious personages. Perhaps the most noted are the celebrated "Hutchinson Family" of New Hampshire, popular 40 years ago as a band of concert singers. Jesse, the father (Elisha, Joseph, Joseph, Joseph, Joseph, Richard), b. at Middleton, Mass., 1778; m. Mary Leavitt, 1800; moved to Milford, N. H., 1824; had a family of 16 children; 13 of them grew up, and united as the band of singers. The father d. 1851; the mother in 1868, aged 83. Jesse (1813–1853), the chief composer, and Andrew B. (1808–1860), were pious members of the Baptist church. John Wallace, the only one left, is living in Lynn. Jesse wrote "The Old Granite State," "Good old days of Yore," "Slave's Appeal," and "Congressional Song." We well remember some of these in days of yore, espescially "The Old Granite State," one stanza of which is here appended:

> David, Noah, Andrew, Zeppy,
> Caleb, Joshua, Jesse, and Benny,
> Judson, Rhoda, John, and Asa,
> And Abby are our names;
>   We're the sons of Mary,
>   Of the tribe of Jesse,
>   And we now address you
> With our native mountain song.

19. vii. Ezekiel Pryer Sanford, another brother, b. April 27, 1828; m. Louisa, daughter of Jonathan Millner, July 12, 1853, and lived in Clements, east of Bear River. She d. 1856, aged 24; he m. 2d, Harriet Amanda Brown (William and Mary, George and

Mary, the last Mary daughter of Jacob Cornwell and widow of William Allen and James Johnson of Digby county), March 31, 1858, and d. July 7, 1890.

CHILDREN.

i JAMES S. S., b. 1854; d. 1865.
ii CHARLES W., b. June 15, 1859; m. Laura, daughter of John Henshaw, Nov., 1888.
iii EDITH ANN, b. Feb. 6, 1862; m. William Crowell, Dec. 14, 1881, and d. Jan. 17, 1886; he d. 1885, aged 25, leaving a son Ralph, b. 1883.
iv CLARENCE R., b. Aug. 22, 1871; m. Euphemia (Yarrigle) Hiltz, March 25, 1891.

20. vii. **Edward Manning Sanford,** the youngest and last one, b. May 16, 1830; m. Ann O., daughter of Thomas Millner, March 29, 1854, and lives near Clementsvale.

CHILDREN.

i JANE SOPHRONIA, b. 1855; m. Priestly, son of William Long, Feb. 14, 1876, and d. Jan., 1882; he m. 2d, Ellen Wallace, Oct. 9, 1882; m. 3d, Mary L., daughter of Saunders Millbury.
ii NOBLE, m. Emma, daughter of Robert Miller, 1891.
iii MANNING, m. Lovisa, daughter of Edward Berry, 1885.
iv THADDEUS, m.
v ZILLAH O., m. Michael A. Donovan, April 20, 1892.
vi LOUISA.

The last two were school-teachers.

SAXTON.

Long before the Revolution lived at White Plains, Westchester county, N. Y., a family named Saxton or Sexton. George Sexton, cordwainer, of Rye, sold property in White Plains to Jeremiah Fowler, 1735. Lorenzo Sabine (1800–1877), in his "American Loyalists," 1864, says George Saxton of White Plains, N. Y., lived within half a mile of Washington's headquarters; at the peace of 1783, went to Digby, N. S. His son George d. there 1860, very aged. Whether the father's name was George is questionable. The grandsons in Ontario said his name was William, and William's wife was Jane Jones. They had two sons, John and George, and a daughter Jane.

1. i. **Rev. John Saxton,** was b. near Montauk Point, Long Island, N. Y, July 4, 1758; went to Digby, N. S., a young man; m. Margaret, daughter of Alexander and Caroline (Purdy) Hains, 1786, and had 6 or 7 children. In 1811 he moved to Upper Canada, then so-called, and settled in the London District, since called Malahide, Elgin county, Ont. The old folks belonged to the Baptist church. He d. June 11, 1847; she d. June 4, 1855, aged 87.

CHILDREN.

i JANE, b. May 6, 1787; m. Moses, son of John Edison, and had Mary, John, Hains, William, Isaac, Jane, Russell, and George. They moved from Bayham, Ont., to Grand Rapids, Mich., in 1842, where some of them still live.

ii WILLIAM, b. April 25, 1789; m. Margaret, daughter of John Edison, and had Clara, Sandy, John, Sweyn, Clarinda, Hannah, Sally, Jane, Mary, and Eliza Ann. In 1843 he moved 50 miles northwest, and settled in Carradoc, Middlesex county, near Strathroy, where he d. about 1874. She d. about 1880, aged 91.

iii JOHN HAINS, b. July 6, 1796; m. Ann, daughter of Samuel and Mary (McDormand) Teed, and like William, settled in Bayham. They had Jane, Elijah, Isaac, and Alexander. They moved to Port Rowan, Norfolk county, about 1850, and kept a hotel there.

iv ALEXANDER, b. May 16, 1800; m. Elizabeth Saunders; lived in Bayham, and had Leafy, John, Margaret, Hannah, George, Francis, Mahlan, and Charles. Mrs. Saxton d. in spring of 1842; he m. 2d, Jan. 29, 1846, Harriet, daughter of Elijah and Eleanor (Shook) McConnell, and had 2 daughters; he d. 1872.

v ISAAC HATFIELD, b. Oct. 18, 1802; m. Elizabeth, daughter of Adonijah and Nancy (Williams) Edison, and lived in Bayham, near Vienna. They had Clarine, Lot, James, and John. Mrs. Saxton d. July 3, 1857, aged 55; he m. 2d, Mrs. Lucretia Olmstead, and d. 1881; she d. March 25, 1881, aged 73.

vi ELIJAH, b. May 4, 1807; m. Margaret, daughter of Caleb and Sarah (McConnell) Hains, and lived in Malahide; inherited his father's farm. They had William, Abigail, Mary Ann, John, and Susan. He d. Nov. 2, 1884; she d. Oct., 1890, aged 76.

2. ii. **George Saxton** (William), b. near Montauk Point, N. Y., 1766; m. Rachel, daughter of Peter and Eleanor (Van Kleek) Mullin, near Digby, N. S., April 10, 1791, and lived at Weymouth, N. S. Mrs. Saxton d. Dec. 30, 1807; he m. 2d, Mehitable (Trask) Hubbard, about 1812; she d. about 1846. When he was about 90

he had an excellent visit among friends and kindred in Western Canada, and d. Dec. 25, 1860. They had:

- i CATHARINE, b. Nov. 1, 1792; m. John, son of James Marr, Oct. 20, 1810, and lived at Grovesend in Malahide. He d. May 28, 1835, aged 50; she d. Sept. 19, 1849. They had Rachel, Betsy, John, James, Asaph, and William.
- ii ABIGAIL, b. Nov., 1795; m. Jacob, son of Joshua Northrup, and lived in Malahide, Ont., farmers. He d. Aug. 25, 1867, aged 73; she d. May 4, 1888. They had Tamer, George, Moses, Rachel, Ellen, John, and Robert.
- iii DAVID S., b. 1796; m. Jane Trevoy, and lived at Weymouth, Digby county, N. S. He d. 1868; she d. They had Elizabeth Jane, George, Ellen, Rachel, Emeline, W. Mehitable, Zilphia, and Abigail.
- iv ELEANOR, b. Aug. 26, 1799; m. Anthony, son of Thomas Seeley, April 3, 1818, and lived in Malahide, near the shore of Lake Erie, till about 1850, when he sold out there, and bought the David Sibley farm in Bayham; she d. Aug. 26, 1878, exactly 79; he d. Dec. 25, 1884, aged 80. They had George, Katy, Rebecca, Isaac, Margaret, Moses, and Orlo.
- v ROBERT, b. 1801; m. Sarah Clarissa Schofield, and lived in Houghton, Norfolk county, Ont., east of Vienna. They had Eliphal, John, William, and David. Mrs. Saxton d. 1844, aged 40; he m. 2d, Mary Elizabeth van Buskirk, 1845, and d. Oct. 2, 1880. They had two daughters and a son.
- vi PETER, b. 1803; m. Ann Hankinson, and had Reuben, John, David, and Anna.
- vii MARGARET, b. 1805; m. Enoch, son of David Grant; 7 children.
- viii GEORGE, b. 1807; m. Rebecca Grafton; 10 children.

SMITH.

1. i. Richard Smith, of Shropham, Norfolk, Eng., came over to Ipswich, Mass., 1638 or 1639. He is reported to have returned to England about 1650. He deeded land to his son Richard in Ipswich, 1658, witnessed by Nicholas and Ann Smith, supposed to be a brother of his.

CHILDREN.

- i ELIZABETH, b. about 1625; m. Sept., 1647, Edward Gilman, Jr., who settled in Exeter, N. H. He was lost at sea, 1653.
- 2 ii RICHARD, b. about 1629.

ALLIED FAMILIES.　　　　　cxcvii

   iii MARY, b. about 1631; m. Philip Call, who d. June 14, 1662, leaving Philip (d. 1691) and Mary. She m. 2d, John Burr; m. 3d, Henry Bennett, and d. Jan. 12, 1707-8. Mr. Bennett m. 1st, Lydia, daughter of John Perkins, about 1651; 5 children; she d. 1672. He was living in 1708, aged 79.

   iv MARTHA, b. about 1633; m. John Rogers.

2. ii. Richard Smith, Jr., b. in England about 1629; m. Hannah, daughter of John and Martha Cheney, Nov. 16, 1660 (she was b. Nov. 16, 1642, and d. May 9, 1722), and d. 1714.

CHILDREN.

   i A CHILD, b. July, 1670; probably d. young.
3 ii DANIEL, b. 1673.
   iii MARTHA, b. 1674; m. Jacob, son of Thomas and Elizabeth (Perkins) Boardman (1671-1756), and d. 1740.
   iv NATHANIEL, b. 1676; m. Elizabeth, daughter of James and Mary (King) Fuller (b. 1678), 1702, and had Elizabeth, Richard, Hannah, Nathaniel, John, Dorothy, Lucy, and Daniel.
4 v JOHN, b. 1677.
   vi HANNAH, b. 1678-9; m. —— Chadwell of Lynn; had Eunice, Margaret, and Mary.
   vii DOROTHY, b. 1680; m. Robert Rogers of Rowly, 1702.
   viii ELIZABETH, b. about 1682; d. in 1747.
   ix JOSEPH, b. July 16, 1685; m. Joanna, daughter of Isaac and Joanna Fellows, April 9, 1710, and d. in Sudbury, May 3, 1754. Children: Joanna, Anna, Joseph, Jemima, Isaac, Martha, Ephraim, Margaret, and David.
   x RICHARD, b. about 1688; d. June 22, 1700.

3. iii. Daniel Smith (Richard, Richard), b. 1673; m. Elizabeth, daughter of Robert and Elizabeth (Reiner) Paine (1677-1717), of Ipswich; m. 2d, Deborah Wilcomb of Ipswich, 1721, and d. June 8, 1755.

CHILDREN.

   i ELIZABETH, b. 1703; d. before 1755.
   ii RICHARD, b. and d. 1704.
   iii DANIEL, b. 1705; m. Mary, daughter of Moses and Susanna (Goodhue) Kimball, and moved to Exeter, N. H., about 1748; living in 1755. Children: Daniel, Jeremiah, Ebenezer, Susannah, and Paine.
   iv JEREMIAH, b. Dec. 6, 1707; d. Dec. 13, 1731.
   v JABEZ, b. Dec. 20, 1709; m. Elizabeth ——, and was living at Hampton, 1738.
   vi MOSES, b. July 9, 1711; d. April 18, 1715.

vii AARON, b. Aug. 25, 1713; d. April 18, 1715.
viii EZEKIEL, bapt. Nov. 2, 1714; d. April 12, 1715.
ix AARON, b. about 1715; m. Martha, daughter of Joseph Allen, Esq.; ordained at Marlboro', 1740, and d. at East Sudbury (Wayland) 1781; daughter Martha m. Rev. Mr. Bridge of Sudbury.
x DOROTHY, b. May 5, 1717; m. Joseph Sargent, Jr., 1738, of Gloucester, who d. 1791.
5 xi MOSES, b. May 19, 1724; d. 1783.
xii DEBORAH, bapt. Sept. 19, 1725; d. after 1755.
xiii MARY, b. Oct. 9, 1727; m. —— Dane, who d. 1756, and she survived him.
xiv JEREMIAH, bapt. July 27, 1735; d. young.

4. iii. John Smith (Richard, Richard), b. 1777; m. Mercy, daughter of Nathaniel and Mercy Adams of Ipswich, Feb. 4, 1702, and d. May 20, 1713. He was a weaver, and at his death willed to his wife his loom; she m. 2d, Arthur Abbot, Jr., of Ipswich (1694-1767), Sept. 1, 1716, and d. Sept. 11, 1735.

CHILDREN.

i MERCY, b. April 11, 1702; m. Nathaniel Treadwell, Jr., 1725; 5 children.
6 ii CAPT. JOHN, b. Jan. 28, 1707; d. July 11, 1768.
iii NATHANIEL, b. Feb. 27, 1710; a tailor; d. 1739.
iv CHENEY, b. March 2, 1712; was of Hampton, 1735.

5. iv. Moses Smith (Daniel, Richard, Richard), b. 1724; m. Elizabeth, daughter of Dr. Samuel Wallis of Ipswich (1721-1753) m. 2d, Ruth Little (1729-1777); m. 3d, Mrs. Mary Hodgkins, and d. on the Kennebec River, Me., 1783.

CHILDREN.

i A CHILD, b. 1747; d. soon.
ii MOSES, JR., b. 1748; m. Ruth, daughter of Purchase Jewett (1751-1844), 1770, and d. 1829. Children: Moses, 1770, Jeremiah, 1772, Purchase, 1774, Isaac, 1777, Isaac, 1779, Daniel, 1782, Daniel, 1783, Ruth, 1786; Elizabeth, 1789, Patience, 1792, Katharine, 1795, and Sarah, 1797.
iii ELIZABETH, b. 1751; m. John Cole, son of Purchase Jewett, 1769.
iv RUTH, b. 1756; m. John Stanwood, 1774.
v MARY, b. 1757; m. —— Harris: 3 sons.
vi DANIEL, b. 1761; m. —— ——; daughter Elizabeth, and d. about 1783.

ALLIED FAMILIES.

7 vii AARON, b. Sept. 16, 1763.
   viii JABEZ, b. 1764; m. Sarah Hervey; Mrs. Ruth Taylor, and d. about 1813.
   ix ABIGAIL, b. 1767.

6. iv. Capt. John Smith (John, Richard, Richard), b. in Ipswich, Mass., Jan. 28, 1707; m. Hannah Treadwell (Nathaniel, Nathaniel, Thomas), 1728; m. 2d, Mrs. Susan How, 1762, and d. July 11, 1768.

CHILDREN.

   i JOHN, b. 1729; d. 1730.
   ii HANNAH, b. 1731; m. Isaac Burnham.
   iii MERCY, b. 1733; m. William Dodge, the sheriff; daughter Mary m. Capt. Eben Caldwell.
   iv SARAH, b. 1735; m. Seth Dodge, 1758, Lunenburg.
   v CHARLES, b. 1737; m. Martha Rogers, 1759; 6 children.
   vi CHENEY, b. 1739; m. Lydia Potter.
   vii ABIGAIL, b. 1741; m. Thomas Dodge, 1762, Lunenburg.
   viii EUNICE, b. 1744; m. Joseph Wells, 1766.
   ix AARON, b. 1747; m. Dorothy ——.
   x JOSIAH, b. 1749; m. Margaret Staniford.
   xi SAMUEL, b. 1751; m. —— ——; daughter Abigail m. Capt. William Caldwell.

7. v. Aaron Smith (Moses, Daniel, Richard, Richard), b. Sept. 16, 1763; m. Eunice, daughter of Ebenezer and Sarah Lord (1771-1825), Oct. 3, 1794, and d. Nov. 9, 1849. Mr. Lord d. 1836, aged 96.

CHILDREN.

   i MARGARET, b. Aug. 25, 1795; m. Robert, son of Aaron and Hannah Kimball (1790-1857), and d. July 20, 1873, in Salem; 11 children.
8 ii AARON, b. Sept. 20, 1798.
   iii LUCY, b. April 18, 1807; m. John, son of Jeremiah and Elizabeth Pingree, Nov. 24, 1825, and d. May 30, 1856; 9 children.

8. vi. Aaron Smith (Aaron, Moses, Daniel, Richard, Richard), b. Sept. 20, 1798; moved to Danvers, 1820; to Salem, 1821; m. Mehitable, daughter of Jeremiah and Elizabeth (Kimball) Pingry (1795-1876), and d. May 3, 1879.

CHILDREN.

   i MEHITABLE, b. Sept. 30, 1823; m. George B, son of Luther and Clarissa (Frye) Stedman, Sept. 17, 1846; daughter Clarissa M., b. Jan. 30, 1849; m. John Buckley since 1870; 3 children.

ii Eunice Lord, b. Aug. 19, 1825; d. Dec. 11, 1877.
iii Elizabeth P., b. Jan. 22, 1828; m. Henry W., son of Daniel and Mary (Stacy) Thurston, April 30, 1868.
iv Aaron Augustus, b. Sept. 10, 1830; bookseller and stationer some years in Salem, now inspector and assistant clerk in the Water Department; m. Maria Foster (Isaac P., Moses, Jonathan, Caleb, Abraham, Reginald), Sept. 22, 1858, and had Stephen, Augustus, Eddie, and Arthur Foster. She d. Jan. 5, 1890, aged 57.
v Lucy Ann, b. June 28, 1835; d. Aug. 11, 1876.

SPURR.

1. i. Michael Spurr was one of 45 passengers that embarked from Boston, May 17, 1760, for Annapolis, N. S., on the sloop *Charming Molly*. He had with him Ann Bird, his wife, and they settled in the township of Annapolis, near Round Hill.

CHILDREN.

2 i Abram, b. 1756.
ii Ann, m. William, son of Philip Barteaux.
iii Abigail, m. John Harris, M.P.P. See Harris.
iv Shippy, m. Letitia Vorss.
v Michael, m. Diadama, daughter of Rev. Arsarelah Morse.
vi Thomas, m. Mary, daughter of Robert Hood.
vii Eleanor, m. Abram Lent.
viii Elizabeth, m. Jacob Fritz, Nov. 15, 1787; she d. 1788. He m. 2d, Ann Bent, Feb. 5, 1789.

2. ii. Abram Spurr (Michael), b. in Mass., 1756; m. Mary Lecain*, and lived near Round Hill, Annapolis county, N. S. He d. Jan., 1831; she d. 1846, aged about 80.

CHILDREN.

i Mary, m. George Davis, 1791.
ii Michael, b. 1775; m. Elizabeth, daughter of John Roach, Aug. 9, 1798, and d. Jan. 23, 1878, in his 103d year.

---

* Francis Lecain m. Elicia, daughter of Col. Thomas Hyde and lived at Annapolis.

CHILDREN.

i John, m. Sarah Providence.
ii Elicia, m. John Ritchie—Judge Thomas Ritchie was their son.
iii Ann, m.
iv Elizabeth, m. Thomas Harris.
v Thomas, m. Martha Wilkie.
vi Mary, b. 1766; m. Abram, son of Michael Spurr, and d. about 1846.

iii ELIZABETH, b. 1773; m. Christopher P. Harris. See Harris.
iv JANE, m. Dea. Benjamin Potter. See Potter.
v THOMAS, d. young.
vi ANN, m. Henry, son of Michael Heniger; 6 children.
vii ABIGAIL, b. 1785; d. April 20, 1871; m. Thatcher Sears (Nathaniel, Joshua, Samuel, Paul, Richard). He m. 1st, Rebecca Smith, and d. at St. John, 1819, aged 67; 9 children.
viii REV. GILBERT, b. July 9, 1787; m. Esther Chute. See No. 13.
ix DIADAMA, m. Elijah, son of Benjamin Hunt, 1808, and lived near Smith's Cove, Digby county, N. S.; 6 children b. in N. S. and 4 b. in St. John, N. B. He d. 1847, aged 63. Children: (1) Mary Ann, b. 1809; m. Michael Heniger, Jr. (2) William, b. 1812; m. Frances Horbury, of England, Dec. 14, 1837; 6 children b. in St. John, and 2 in Boston. (3) Rev. Abram S., b. April, 1814; m. Catharine Johnston (Dr. Lewis, William Moreton, Dr. Lewis, the last Royal Governor in Georgia), of Halifax, and d. Oct. 23, 1877; 6 children: (a) Eliza Theresa, b. 1850; m. Judge A. W. Savary (Sabine, Nathan, Uriah, Thomas, Samuel, Thomas, over to Plymouth, Mass., 1634). (b) Dr. Lewis Gibson, m. Flora Vaughan. (c) James Johnston, barrister at Halifax, m. Minnie Anderson. (d) Aubrey Spurr, a merchant. (e) Ella Maud, m. Rev. A. C. Chute; see No. 147. (f) Rev. Ralph M., Jamaica Plain, Mass.; Baptist minister. (4) Maria, b. 1816; m. James Clark. (5) Benjamin, b. 1818; m. Sarah E. Peters, Boston; 7 children. (6) Caroline, b. 1820; m. John L., son of Dea. Benjamin Potter, Esq. (7) Charles M., b. 1823; m. Harriet Worden. (8) Abigail, b. 1827; m. Rev. John D. Caswell, St. John, N. B. (9) Henry Gilbert, b. 1830; m. Jane Babbitt, St. John, N. B., 1861. (10) Julia, b. 1832; m. Benjamin Price, Boston.
x MARIA, m. Samuel McColly.
xi ELICIA, m. John Soulis (John, Daniel, John, John, France to America about 1700).
xii ABRAM, m. Ann, daughter of Capt. Henry Harris, 1820.

STEADMAN.

1. i. John Steadman, b. about 1720, was of S. Kingstown, R. I.; m. Parthenia Gracey, 1746, in Shrewsbury, Monmouth county, N. J.; had 4 children when Mrs. Steadman d., and he m. 2d, Frances Congdon of N. Kingstown, R. I., and went to Cornwallis, N. S., 1760.

CHILDREN.

    i MARTHA, b. about 1747; m. Jan. 12, 1769, Worden Beckwith (John, James, Matthew, Matthew) of Norwich, Ct., who went to Cornwallis, N. S., from S. Kingstown, R. I., in 1760. Children: John Steadman, 1770; Parthenia, 1771; Thomas Worden, 1772; Rebecca, 1776, and Enoch, 1779.

    ii PARTHENIA, m. and lived off South.

    iii MARY, m. and lived off South.

    iv BENJAMIN, m. Sarah Cogswell (Aaron, Hezekiah, Samuel, Samuel, John, John), 1787.

2 v ENOCH, b. 1761.

    vi HANNAH, b. Feb. 5, 1763; d. April 10, 1786.

3 vii JOHN, b. April 19, 1765.

    viii ELIZABETH, b. Dec. 20, 1767; m. Maj. Abram Gesner, son of John; a soldier in the Revolution; from N. Y., of German descent, to Nova Scotia, 1783, and had (1) Hannah, b. 1787; (2) Jacob; (3) Henry; (4) Elizabeth; (5) Famicha; (6) Caroline; (7) Isaac; (8) Maria; (9) Abram; (10) Horatia; (11) Delancy M.; (12) George P. The Major d. April 29, 1824, aged 67. Col. Henry Gesner, twin brother to Abram, also a Loyalist, m. Sarah, daughter of David and Rebecca Pineo (Peter, James), 1786, and had (1) Rebecca; (2) John H.; (3) Elizabeth; (4) David H.; (5) Famicha; (6) Abram; (7) Gibbs H.; (8) Sarah C.; (9) Henry; (10) Ann Maria; (11) Lucy; (12) Charlotte Ann.

    ix THOMAS, b. Jan. 30, 1771.

    x SARAH, b. Sept. 30, 1774.

4 xi WILLIAM, b. March 25, 1777.

5 xii JAMES CONGDON, b. June 2, 1781.

2. ii. Enoch Steadman (John), b. about 1760; m. Ellison Cogswell (sister to Sarah, who m. his brother Benjamin), and lived in Cornwallis.

CHILDREN.

    i SUSANNAH, b. March 1, 1785; m. March 22, 1814, Elisha Eaton (Elihu, David, James, Jonathan, Thomas, John); a son David Owen, b. and d. May 5, 1857; he d. Oct. 3 1846, aged 66.

6 ii BENJAMIN, b. Aug. 2, 1786.

    iii HANNAH, b. June 10, 1789; m. Isaac, son of Joseph and Phebe Jackson, Jan. 22, 1808, and d. in Illinois, Feb. 3, 1856; 7 children; he d. about 1875.

    iv SARAH, b. April 5, 1791; m. Peter Pineo (John, Peter, James), and d. Jan. 17, 1870; he d. about 1859; 11 children.

    v FRANCES, b. May 9, 1794; m. Benjamin B. Sheffield (Amos, Amos, John, Amos, Isaiah, Amos), and d. March 1, 1856.

ALLIED FAMILIES.

  vi NANCY, b. Feb. 23, 1798; m. George Cox (Capt. Henry and Susanna (Eaton) Cox), Aug. 21, 1821, and d. Dec. 24, 1824; 2 children.
  vii DANIEL B., b. Nov. 7, 1802; m. Harriet Gilmore, of Horton, and d. in Illinois, 1845; 6 children.
  viii MARY, b. Nov. 21, 1807; m. Aaron A. Sheffield, brother to Benjamin B., and d. 1892; he d.

3. ii. John Steadman, brother to the above, b. April 19, 1765; m. Hannah Harris, and lived in Cornwallis.

CHILDREN.

  i HANNAH, b. July 11, 1793; m. John Van Buskirk, 1814.
  ii BETSY, b. Jan. 23, 1795; m. John McLachlin; 1821(?); m. 2d, Timothy Haggarty, Nov. 7, 1821.
7 iii CHARLES CHIPMAN, b. April 5, 1797.
  iv THOMAS, b. March 9, 1799; m. Trites Horsman, Petticodiac, N. S.
  v JAMES, b. March 4, 1802; m. Betsy Hicks.
  vi WILLIAM, b. Aug. 2, 1804; m. —— Beckwith.
8 vii BENJAMIN, b. Feb. 12, 1807.
  viii MARY ANN, b. May 21, 1809.
  ix SUSAN, b. July 16, 1811; m. Arthur Armstrong; 2 daughters; m. 2d, Edward Charlton, son of John.
  x GEORGE, b. Feb. 14, 1815; m. —— Perkins; m. 2d, Thomas' widow, Moncton, N. B.

4. ii. William Steadman (John and Parthenia), b. in Cornwallis, N. S., March 25, 1777; m. Hannah T. Coutch, Nov. 18, 1803, and d. in Moncton, N. B., Nov. 18, 1854.

CHILDREN.

  i JOHN, b. Moncton, N. B., Sept. 28, 1804; m. Catharine Harper; was engaged in lumber, ship-building, and mercantile business; d. Jan. 13, 1882; she d. 1860; had George, Mary, and Catharine.
  ii MARY, b. Sept. 30, 1806; m. Stephen H. Shaw, and d. Jan. 14, 1849; several children.
  iii WILLIAM, JR., b. April 1, 1809; m. Charlotte McCormack; 8 children. He was farmer, miller, and lumberman; d. Jan., 1870.
  iv ELIZABETH, b. March 28, 1811; m. James Goldrup, and had 9 children.
  v ENOCH, b. June 10, 1813; was drowned in Pitticodiac River, April 29, 1831.
  vi MARGARET, b. Dec. 15, 1815; m. Charles Black, and d. March 16, 1847; 4 children.

vii JAMES, b. March 27, 1818; studied law and became an attorney, 1844; moved to Frederickton, N. B., 1866; was elected to the Provincial Legislature from Westmoreland, 1854; member of the executive council, 1860, with the office of postmaster general till 1865; was appointed a judge of the county court, 1887. He is an earnest advocate of temperance and prohibition. He m. Julia Beckwith of Frederickton; m. 2d, Emma Jane, daughter of William and Leafy (Tucker) Turnbull of Bear River, N. S., and widow of —— Ring.

viii NANCY, b. June 7, 1820; m. James Beck, and d. May, 1847, her husband and 2 children having preceded her a short time.

ix JANE, b. May 14, 1823; d. Jan., 1828.

x CAROLINE, b. June 10, 1825; m. Joseph Ricketson of Round Hill, N. S. (Fred, Abednego). He d. 1860, leaving a son James; she m. 2d, David Crandall.

xi FRANCES, b. March 15, 1828; m. Joseph Crandall, a merchant and postmaster; 6 children.

5. ii. James C. Steadman, another brother, b. June 2, 1781; m. Susanna, daughter of Alex. McKenzie, 1805; lived in Granville, Annapolis county, and d. near Bridgetown, Sept. 28, 1868; she d. Dec. 9, 1870, aged 84.

CHILDREN.

i FRANCES, b. March 20, 1807; m. Ezra Chute. See No. 85.

ii MARY, b. Feb. 2, 1809; m. Calvin Gidney, and d. about 1885; a daughter Caroline m. Alex. McKay, supervisor of schools for Halifax county, living at Dartmouth.

iii WALTER, b. Feb. 20, 1811; m. Margery Rose, daughter of Capt. John Frazer of Liverpool, N. S., and d. at Bridgetown, March 1, 1889; she d. Sept. 11, 1886.

iv ENOCH, b. May 26, 1813; m. Sophia Mack (Stephen, Samuel, Samuel), b. Nov. 20, 1822; d. Nov. 21, 1886; 7 children.

v ELIZABETH, b. Nov., 1815; m. Joseph, son of Elias Bent; 3 children, and d. July 4, 1887.

vi HAVILAH, b. 1818; m. Nathan R. Chute. See No. 94.

vii HORATIA, b. 1820; m. Ambrose, son of Obadiah Parker; had Obadiah, Susan, James, and Walter, and d. about 1885.

viii CAROLINE, b. 1822; m. Allen T. Mack (Stephen, Samuel, Samuel), near Bridgetown; 3 children.

ix SUSAN, b. 1825; m. William McGochin, Granville Ferry. Three more children must have d. in infancy.

6. iii. Benjamin (Enoch, John), b. Aug. 2, 1786; m. March 13, 1817, Mary Ann Eaton (James, David, James, Jonathan, Thomas,

John), b. May 3, 1796; she d. Sept. 7, 1879; he d. and was buried at Billtown, 1865.

CHILDREN.

i EUNICE, b. Jan. 16, 1818; still living in Cornwallis.
ii ENOCH, b. June 3, 1820; m. Abbie C. Woodbury, United States Hotel, Boston; she d. Two children; one, Fred, is conductor on the Old Colony R. R.
iii NANCY, b. April 1, 1822; d. of measles, 1840.
iv DANIEL, b. April 3, 1826; d. in South Boston.
v RUTH, b. July 30, 1828; m. William Harrington (George, Stephen, Stephen, John, Benjamin), July 18, 1850, and had Charles, Ann, and Fanny.
vi EDWARD M., b. Aug. 30, 1832; m. Sarah Jane Robinson (July 10, 1842–April, 1866), Feb. 4, 1863; daughter Fannie b. Dec. 13, 1863; d. Feb. 16, 1883. He m. 2d, Melissa Elizabeth, daughter of Stephen North, March 6, 1867. They had Frank Elmer, Stephen North, Frederick Webster, Harriet Eleanor, Wilbert Dimock, Harry Cogswell, and William Norman.
vii HARRIET, b. Aug. 21, 1834; m. Robert Harrington, brother to William, and had Ruth, Alice, George William and Mary Blanche, twins, and Enoch Steadman.
viii FANNIE, b. Aug. 26, 1838; m. Frederick Webster (Dr. William, Dr. Isaac, Moses, Noah, George, Thomas, Gov. John), as his 2d wife; had 4 children, and d. March 17, 1882.

7. iii. Charles Chipman Steadman (John, John), b. April 5, 1797; m. Frances, daughter of Major Abram Van Buskirk, and lived in Aylesford.

CHILDREN.

9 i JAMES G., b. March 1, 1824.
ii CHARLES, b. 1826; m. Selina Ritchie, Annapolis; 5 or 6 children.
iii WILLIAM, b. 1829; m. Catharine Etherington; 3 children; m. 2d, Amanda ——.
iv HORATIA D., b. 1833; m. James E. Miller (James, Michael), Nov. 12, 1853; 5 children; Lois Amanda, m. William E. Woodworth; is in Salem.
v JULIA ANN, b. 1837; m. Israel D., son of Timothy Brooks, Jr.; 6 children; he d. 1869 (?). She m. 2d, William Loyte, as his second wife, and live in Swampscott. She came to Lynn, Mass., 1870; her father and mother in 1872. The old lady d. in Nova Scotia, Oct., 1873, aged 65; he d. in Lynn, 1876, aged 79.

8. iii. Benjamin Steadman, brother to the above, b. Feb. 12, 1807; m. Eliza Harris (b. Jan. 2, 1808); d. Aug. 3, 1870. He m. 2d, a sister, Abba (Harris) Ring, 1874, and d. June 7, 1880.

CHILDREN.

i JOHN, b. March 12, 1830; drowned March 12, 1851.
ii MARIA, b. Sept. 21, 1831; d. Nov. 17.
iii INGERSOLL, b. Oct. 22, 1833; m. Eliza Scribner, April 7, 1860; 11 children; Canada Creek, N. S.
iv WILLIAM A., b. Feb. 3, 1836; m. Mary Grace.
v ALONZO, b. June 22, 1838; m. Maggie Grace, daughter of Patrick.
vi MELISSA, b. Sept. 4, 1840; d. 1858.
vii AMELIA, b. May 14, 1842; d. 1858.
viii ASA H., b. Sept. 24, 1844; m. Nancy Grace, daughter of Patrick.
ix EDWARD, b. Jan. 10, 1847.
x ENOCH R., b. Aug. 4, 1850; drowned Jan. 23, 1871.
xi EUNICE A., b. July 11, 1852; m. Donald McDonald, his second wife, 1876.

9. iv. **James Gordon Steadman** (Charles Chipman, John, John), b. March 1, 1824; m. Mary, daughter of John Beach, Brookfield, N. S., June 17, 1847, and lived in Aylesford, but moved to Boston about 1867; he d. Jan., 1887. The widow is in South Boston.

CHILDREN.

i FRANCES JANE, b. April 30, 1848; m. William Wear (d. 1873); m. 2d, James B. Duffy, 1874.
ii ADA HAVILAH, b. April 30, 1849; m. James M., son of Henry Spinney, March 8, 1882.
iii JOSHUA, b. Nov. 26, 1850; d. Jan. 20, 1852.
iv GEORGIANA, b. March 29, 1852; m. Ezra Palmer, South Boston.
v CHARLES CHIPMAN, b. July 11, 1853; m. Nellie Powers.
vi AUGUSTA MARY, b. Oct. 31, 1854; m. William Henry Wear, Boston.
vii JAMES PARKER, M. D., b. July 13, 1856; m. Marion Estelle Webster; live in Milford, Mass.
viii WILLIAM ALLINE, b. May 17, 1858; m. Minnie R. Locke, Lynn.
ix GEORGE ALBERT, b. Sept. 7, 1859; m. Mary Gray, Boston.
x ROBERT LAWSON, b. Sept. 17, 1863; m Christina Rich, Boston.
xi HARVEY EUGENE, b. May 7, 1866.
xii CORA BELLE, b. April 25, 1868; m. Robert McArthur.

TAYLOR.

1. i. **Edward Taylor**, b. in Coventry, Eng., 1642; to Boston, 1668; H. C., 1671; became a settled minister at Westfield, 1679.

ALLIED FAMILIES. ccvii

Unable to buy books, he borrowed, and copied them with his pen, and left at his death thousands of pages in quarto, bound in parchment by himself. He m. Elizabeth, daughter of Rev. James Fitch, of Norwich, Nov. 5, 1674; she d. July 7, 1689, aged 38; he m. 2d, Ruth, daughter of Samuel Willys, of Hartford, June 2, 1692, and granddaughter of Gov. George Willys, of 1642, and d. 1729.

CHILDREN.

i SAMUEL, b. Aug. 27, 1675; m. Margaret, daughter of John Moseley, Jan. 5, 1704, Westfield.
ii ELIZABETH, b. Dec. 27, 1676; d. Dec. 25, 1677.
iii JAMES, b. Oct. 12, 1678.
iv ABIGAIL, b. Aug. 6, 1681; d. Aug. 22, 1682.
v BATHSHEBA, b. Jan. 17, 1683; m. John Pynchon of Springfield, Feb. 18, 1701.
vi ELIZABETH, b. Feb. 5, 1685; d. July 26, 1705.
vii MARY, b. July 3, 1686; d. May 15, 1687.
viii HEZEKIAH, b. Feb. 18, 1687; d. March 3, 1688.
ix RUTH, b. April 16, 1693; m. Rev. Benjamin Cotton, West Hartford.
x NAOMI, b. March 30, 1695; m. Rev. Ebenezer Devotion (John, Edward), of Roxbury; of Suffield, Conn., 1720.
xi ANN, b. July 7, 1696; m. Rev. Benjamin Lord of Norwich, 1720.
xii MEHITABLE, b. Aug. 14, 1699; m. Rev. William Gager of Lebanon.
xiii KEZIAH, b. April 4, 1702; m. Rev. Isaac Stiles (1697-1760) (John (1665-1753), John (1633-1683), John (1595, over 1635, to Windsor, Conn.; m. Rachel ——, and d. 1662), New Haven, Conn., June 1, 1725; one son, Ezra, b. Nov. 29, 1727; the mother d. Dec. 4; he m. 2d, Esther Hooker, 1728; she d. 1779, aged 77. Rev. Isaac was a member of Yale College; his 2d family were 10 in number — 3 of them, Esther, Leverett, and Hamlin, are said to have gone to New Brunswick. Rev. Ezra Stiles, LL.D., president of Yale College, m. Elizabeth, daughter of Col. John Hubbard, 1767; had 8 children; she d. May 29, 1775, aged 44; he m. 2d, Mary, widow of William Checkley, Providence, R. I., Oct. 12, 1782, and d. May 12, 1795, a great scholar and author.
2 xiv ELDAD, b. April 10, 1708.

2. ii. Dea. Eldad Taylor (Rev. Edward), b. Westfield, Mass., April 10, 1708; m. Rhoda, daughter of Jeremiah Dewey, Nov. 1, 1732. She d. June 22, 1740, aged 27; he m. 2d, Thankful, daughter of Maj. John Day of Springfield, 1742, and lived in Weston, Mass., a prominent man in civic and religious society. He d. while attending General Court in Boston, May 21, 1777; she d. Aug. 12, 1803, aged 82.

CHILDREN.

    i ELDAD, b. Sept. 5, 1733; m. Esther Day, Aug. 5, 1754.
   ii RHODA, b. July 10, 1735; d. young.
  iii MEHITABLE, b. Aug. 4, 1736; m. Aaron Ashley, June 12, 1764, Westfield.
  iv RACHEL, b. June 11, 1740; d. young.
   v EDWARD, b. Jan. 5, 1744; m. Sarah Ingersoll, March 2, 1769.
  vi SAMUEL, b. Nov. 26, 1745; m. Tirzah Holcomb, 1786.
 vii THANKFUL, b. Jan. 21, 1748; m. Bohan King, Jan. 3, 1771.
3 viii JAMES, b. Aug. 18, 1750.
  ix JEDIDIAH, b. Oct. 27, 1752; m. Abigail, daughter of Stephen Fowler, Jan. 16, 1783.
   x JOHN, b. April 30, 1755; d. July 21, 1756.
  xi ANNA, b. July 30, 1757; m. Zadoc Bush, 1775, and d. 1845, Westfield.
  xii ELIZABETH, b. Aug. 12, 1760; m. Andrew Perkins, 1789, Norwich, Conn.
4 xiii JOHN, b. Dec. 23, 1762.

3. iii. James Taylor (Dea. Eldad, Rev. Edward), b. Westfield, Mass.; m. Mary Ann, daughter of David Mosely, Nov. 21, 1771. He is reported to have gone to Rhode Island, and thence to Nova Scotia, in time of the Revolution; settled in Granville; m. Becca Smith.

CHILDREN.

   i AMY, b. about 1779; m. Andrew Brown, from Massachusetts and Scotland, and lived in Wilmot, N. S.; d. 1854. Children: (1) James R., m. Amelia, daughter of Obadiah Marshall; 8 children. (2) Andrew, m. Sally, daughter of John Banks; 2 children. (She was with Ruth Foster when killed by the tree, see Foster.) (3) Mary, (4) Amy, (5) Becca, d. 3 old maids. (6) Betsy, m. Samuel McConnell, Protestant from Ireland. (7) Stephen (1802–1844), m. Elizabeth, daughter of Samuel Marshall (b. 1808), and had (a) Mary, 1836, m. Charles Moore (Edward, Thomas) 1855, had 5 children; live in East Boston, and her mother with them. (b) Louise J., b. 1837; m. James Ross. (c) Stephen Edward, b. 1839; m. Mary Tuttie. (d) Abigail, b. 1841; m. Beriah Baker. (8) Thomas.
5 ii JAMES, b. 1780.
6 iii STEPHEN, b. 1785.

ALLIED FAMILIES.

    iv BECCA, b. 1787; m. Joshua Beals (Abel, Abel, Andrew, Jeremiah, Jeremiah, John, from Norfolk, Eng., to Hingham, Mass., 1638; d. 1688, aged 100), and lived on "Beals' Mountain," south of Nictaux; he d. 1865, aged 81. They had (1) Abba, m. Fred Taylor, son of James, Jr. (2) Sarah, m. John Whitman. (3) Amy, m. Dennis Bent, and d. 1850. (4) Isaac, b. April, 1815; m. Mary Harris (Joseph, Capt. Henry.) (5) Stephen, b. 1817; m. Mary Ann, daughter of Edwin Payson, and d. 1891. (6) Rachel, b. Oct. 22, 1819; m. William Henry Harris, brother to Mary. She d. Dec. 26, 1858; he m. 2d, Amoret, daughter of Timothy Banks. (7) Becca, m. William Phinney, Jr.; he d. 1888. (8) Eleanor, m. Edwin Payson, Jr.; he d. 1891.

    v BETSY, b. 1789; m. Caleb Read, and had Robert, Joshua, and William.

7 vi BENNET INGRAM, b. May 13, 1792.
8 vii WILLIAM, b. 1794.

4. iii Rev. John Taylor, brother to the preceding, b. in Westfield, Mass., Dec. 23, 1762; graduated at Yale, 1784; settled minister in Deerfield, as successor to Rev. Mr. Ashley, Feb. 14, 1787; m. Elizabeth, daughter of Col. Nathaniel Terry, of Enfield, Conn., June 14, 1788. On account of ill-health he was dismissed from the church Aug. 11, 1806. He published "Appendix to the Redeemed Captive," 1793, and "A Journey of a Missionary Tour in Western New York." In this trip he visited many settlements on the Mohawk and Black Rivers. He traveled about 1000 miles on horseback, during 3 months' absence, preached 5 or 6 times a week, organized churches, ordained deacons, visited schools, the sick, and the dying. With all these he took time to examine historic places, and make drawings, notably the ruins of ancient forts found in the town of Ellisburg, near Lake Ontario. In 1807 he engaged in farming in Enfield, Conn., and was prominent in civil affairs; several times representative. About 1817 he moved to Mendon, N. Y., and in 1833 to Bruce, Mich., preaching occasionally meanwhile. He was an active, ardent anti-slavery man, too, and d. Dec. 20, 1840, in Bruce, McComb county, Mich.

CHILDREN.

    i ELIZABETH T., b. April 16, 1789; m. Rev. James Taylor of Sunderland, 1810.
    ii JABEZ TERRY, b. Sept. 21, 1790; m. Esther Allen of Enfield, Conn., 1814, and had a son, Gilbert Allen.
    iii JOHN, b. June 30, 1792; m. Phebe Leach, Lima, N. Y., 1814.

iv HARRIET, b. May 18, 1794; m. Roderick Terry of Hart, 1814.
v HENRY WYLLYS, b. Feb. 2, 1796; m. Martha C., daughter of Thomas Masters of New York City, 1832. He graduated at Yale in 1816, and was an able lawyer, judge, and deacon. In 1818 he settled at Canandaigua, N. Y. He was elected to the Assembly in the Legislature of New York in 1837, '38, '39, and '40. In 1840 he moved to Marshall, Mich., as land agent, but returned again, 1848, and resumed law. He retired in 1861. He wintered in Charleston, S. C., 1868, '69, '70, and '71. In 1882 his "Golden Wedding" was celebrated at his home in Canandaigua. In 1871 he published "The Times of Daniel," in which he predicted perilous times near the close of the present century. Mrs. Taylor d. Feb. 27, 1884, and he followed, Dec. 17, 1888.
vi MARY D., b. March 27, 1798; m. Josiah Wright, Syracuse, N. Y., 1827.
vii NAT. TERRY, b. May 16, 1800; m. Laura Winchell of Lima, 1823.
viii ALICE, b. 1802; d. soon.
ix x xi. Three children d. in infancy.

5. iv. James Taylor (James, Eldad, Edward), b. in Granville, N. S., 1780; m. Elizabeth Foster (Benjamin, Isaac, Benjamin, Jacob, Isaac, Reginald), March 10, 1801, and lived in Annapolis county; d. Sept., 1857. Mrs. Taylor d. at the house of her son John in Cornwallis, N. S., March 9, 1888. In 1876, at the age of 96, she was thrown from a carriage and injured. The following poem was written by her when she had passed her 100th birthday.

> God has lengthened out my span
> Beyond the common age of man.
> He has saved me by his power,
> And has kept me to this hour.
>
> One hundred years gone o'er my head,
> The seven last I've kept my bed.
> A hundred years has passed away
> As quickly as a winter day.
>
> Long days and nighs I lie in pain,
> But I've no reason to complain,
> For it is done to let you see
> How good my God has been to me.
>
> The Lord was pleased to place me where
> I have received the best of care,
> And night and day they watch my bed;
> May God reward them when I'm dead!
>
> Now that my days are almost gone,
> I soon shall join that heavenly throng,
> And walk that narrow, happy road,
> That brings me nearer to my God.

ALLIED FAMILIES.

When the Lord is pleased to call me,
I'll be ready for to go,
Believing he will not forsake me,
When I leave this world of wo.

When my days on earth are done,
I shall go down like the sun,
To rise in Heaven above the sky,
A place where love can never die.

When I reach that blessed shore,
There will I my God adore.
God grant that I his face shall see,
And praise him thro' eternity.

CHILDREN.

i AMBROSE, b. Jan. 11, 1802; m. Mary Rice. See Rice.
ii ELIJAH, b. Sept. 28, 1803; m. Abba Ash; 14 children (4 pairs of twins). She d. 1844, aged 44; he m. 2d, Matilda Bishop; 9 children, and d. 1884.
iii MEHITABLE, b. Nov. 2, 1805; m. John Bayne; Digby county.
iv JOHN, b. Oct. 4, 1807; m. Mary Chute. See No. 21.
v JAMES, b. Feb. 15, 1809; m. Lucy (Foster) Samson. See Foster.
vi WILLIAM H., b. July 3, 1811; m. Matilda, daughter of Artemas Odell.
vii ABNER, b. Oct. 22, 1813; m. Eliza Chatner.
viii STEPHEN, b. Sept. 9, 1815; m. Betsy Burden, 1844; 8 children.
ix FRED. WILLIAM, b. Feb. 3, 1819; m. Abba, daughter of Joshua Beals, and d. 1891; 6 children.
x BENJAMIN F., b. Oct. 22, 1822; m. Elsie Armstrong; 2 children.
xi HENRY H., b. Nov. 10, 1823; drowned about 1840.
xii ABBA T., b. Jan. 19, 1829; d. 1830.

6. iv. Dea. Stephen (James, Eldad, Edward), b. near Digby, N. S., Feb. 28, 1785; moved to Wilmot, Annapolis county, 1806, and lived near Middleton, farmer and deacon in the Baptist church; m. Tamson, daughter of Dea. Joseph Morton (b. Feb. 2, 1788), April 25, 1807; she d. April 30, 1816; he m. 2d, Sarah, daughter of Daniel Wood (b. Jan. 24, 1786), Sept. 28, 1816; she d. Feb. 14, 1827; he m. 3d, Olive Wood, a sister (b. April 17, 1796), June 14, 1827; she d. May 1, 1831; he m. 4th Lovina Morse (see Morse) (b. Aug. 14, 1801), Sept. 1, 1831; she d. Oct. 19, 1838; he m. 5th, Esther (Potter) Armstrong (b. March 16, 1791), Feb. 5, 1841; she d. March 26, 1851; he m. 6th, Fanny A. Gabel (b. Sept. 11, 1807),

June 11, 1851; finally, the deacon d. also, Sept. 23, 1859, and the widow m. 2d, Silas Bishop.*

CHILDREN.

i RUTH, b. May 10, 1808; m. Jonathan Hodges, his 2d wife; 8 children.
ii REBECCA, b. Dec. 6, 1809; m. Isaac, son of Benjamin Foster, Jr.; 12 children.
iii JOSEPH M., b. Aug. 11, 1811; m. Eunice Bishop; 4 children.
iv OBADIAH M., b. Sept. 4, 1832; m. Love M., daughter of Nathan Parker, Jan. 14, 1858, and have 4 daughters. He is J. P., and has other town offices.
v LAVINIA H., b. March 8, 1835; d. April 25, 1837.
vi FANNY, b. 1852; m. Engene Fitch, 1869.

7. iv. Bennett Ingraham Taylor, brother to the above, b. near Digby, May 13, 1792; m. Eleanor B., daughter of Dea. Joseph Morton, Jan. 30, 1812, and lived in Wilmot, N. S. He d. June 2, 1859; she d.

CHILDREN.

i SOLOMON BENNETT, b. Sept. 8, 1813. See No. 23.
ii HARRIET ALETHIA, b. July 28, 1816; m. Daniel Gould; 10 children. She d. June, 1878; he d. 1889, about 78.
iii SAMUEL ALWOOD, b. Nov. 6, 1818; m. Maria S. Lysate; 5 children, and d. about 1869.
iv PHINEAS BLOOD, b. Oct. 24, 1820; m. Sarah A. Joyce; 6 children.
v JAMES SMITH, b. May 13, 1822; m. Eliza B. Read, and d. Feb., 1884, in Chicago.
vi EDWARD MANNING, b. Feb. 2, 1824; m. Harriet Morehouse; had 3 daughters, and d. Feb. 12, 1890, Cambridge, Mass.
vii MELUZINE, b. Jan. 16, 1826.; m. Harris L., son of Capt. Harris H. Crocker, May 1, 1860; 5 sons.
viii ISRAEL MORTON, b. May 23, 1828; m. Eleanor Hamlin; m. 2d, Lucinda Baker.
ix MARY ELIZABETH REBECCA, b. Aug. 3, 1830; m. William J. Long (Joseph, William from Ireland), May 1, 1860; he d. Sept. 16, 1869, aged 40, Burlington, Vt.; 5 children.

8. iv. William Taylor (James, Eldad, Edward), b. 1794; m. Lydia, daughter of Ezekiel and Mary (Gates) Brown, and lived in Wilmot; she d.; he m. 2d, Anna Turner, and d.

* Silas Bishop m. 1st, Tamson, daughter of William Taylor, and m. 2d, her aunt.

CHILDREN.

i SARAH, m. George, son of Moses Banks, Jr.
ii TAMSON, m. Silas Bishop.
iii JAMES, m. —— Young.
iv BETSY, m. William H., son of Jonathan Hodges.
v WILLIAM BURTON, m. Anna Reinard.

By 2d wife.

vi ENOCH, m. —— ——; was in the late war.
vii JAMES.
viii STEPHEN.
ix ABBA, b. 1850; m. Zachariah Palmer (John, Benjamin, Lewis, John, Sylvanus, Samuel, William), 1867; 4 children.

THURSTON.

Daniel Thurston, b. in England about 1601, came over to America 1637, and was granted a house lot, Nov. 24, 1638, in Newbury. He m. Ann Lightfoot, Aug. 24, 1648, and d. without issue 1666.

1. i. Daniel Thurston, his nephew, heir, and successor, b. about 1638; m. Ann, daughter of Joseph Pell, of Lynn, Oct. 20, 1655; lived in Newbury. He was a trooper in Capt. Appleton's company; d. Feb. 19, 1693; 8 children besides

2 iii DANIEL, b. Dec. 18, 1661.
  vi JOSEPH, b. Sept. 14, 1667; m. Mehitable Kimball, 1695; m. 2d, Elizabeth, daughter of John Woodbury.
  xi ABIGAIL, b. March 27, 1678; m. Joseph, son of Aquilla and Esther Chase of Newbury, ancestor of Salmon P. Chase, 1699; moved to Littleton, Mass., 1726; 9 children.

2. ii. Daniel Thurston, Jr., b. in Newbury, Dec. 18, 1661; m. Mary, daughter of Lieut. John Dresser of Rowley, and d. Feb. 18, 1738; she d. very suddenly Dec. 7, 1735, aged 69; 9 children besides

  iii MARY, b. Jan. 7, 1694; m. James Chute. See No. 5.
3 xi RICHARD, b. Oct. 16, 1710.

3. iii. Dea. Richard Thurston (Daniel, Daniel), b. Oct. 16, 1710; m. Mehitable Jewett (Jonathan, Joseph, Joseph), May 5, 1731, and was a farmer in Rowley, now Georgetown, and a deacon in the 2d church 50 years. In Oct., 1735, the "throat distemper" broke out in Rowley, and in a short time there were 190 deaths— one-eighth of the whole population. In a memorandum book he says: "My venerable grandfather d. March 14, 1724, in his 85th year. My honored mother [his wife's mother], Mary Jewett, d. Jan. 22, 1742, in her 63d. My honored father, Jonathan Jewett, d. July 25, 1745, in his 67th." He d. July 12, 1782; she d. May 18, 1789, aged 79.

Dea. Thurston was a pious, exemplary man, and in his family devotions was wont to pray "That the Lord would be a God to him and his descendants to the latest generation, as long as the sun and moon endure." Rev. David Thurston, D. D., a grandson, said concerning these prayers, "They have been greatly blessed as regards their spiritual interests; quite a number are or have been deacons and deacon's wives, ministers and minister's wives, etc." Dea. Thurston was a Captain of the 2d foot company of Rowley, June, 1757. In March, 1770, he, with Capt. John Pearson, was on a committee for the consideration of measures to prevent British importations. His estate was valued £3268 3s 9d.

CHILDREN.

 i STEPHEN, b. March 4, 1733; shipwrecked and drowned on Cape Ann bar, May 19, 1762.
 ii MARY, b. Oct. 26, 1734; m. Dea. Jeremiah Searle, 1756, and d. Aug. 20, 1804; 6 children, Georgetown.
 iii EUNICE, b. Oct. 4, 1736; m. John Harris (John, Dea. Timothy, John), and d. Sept. 21, 1775; he d. Sept. 20, 1808, aged 78; 6 children; one, Phebe, b. Dec. 23, 1769, m. Dea. Joshua Jewett, of the Congregational church, Rowley, and d. Oct. 12, 1854; he d. Jan. 3, 1861, aged 93. (I remember him well in Sept., 1857, and sung with him in the old Village Harmony of 1798. W. E. C.)
 iv HANNAH, b. May 16, 1738; d. Nov. 9, 1739.
 v JONATHAN, b. Sept. 26, 1739; d. Jan. 22, 1740.
 vi PHEBE, b. Dec. 14, 1741; m. Rev. David Jewett.
 vii HANNAH, b. Jan. 4, 1744; m. John Adams of Andover, 1773, and d. Jan. 22, 1875.
4 viii DANIEL, b. Dec. 14, 1745; m. Judith Chute. See No. 8.
 ix SARAH, b. April 14, 1748; m. Capt. John Pearson (Capt. John, Joseph, Capt. John, Dea. John), June 13, 1775; 7 children; d. April 28, 1818; he d. Sept. 15, 1807, aged 61.
 x DAVID, b. March 19, 1751; m. Mary Bacon (Rev. Jacob and Mary (Wood) Bacon, Thomas and Hannah (Fales) Bacon); 2 sons; she d. Oct. 21, 1790, aged 40; he m.

ALLIED FAMILIES. CCXV

2d, Chloe Redington (Abram, Asa, Asa), 1791; 6 daughters, 5 sons. Mr. Thurston was a farmer in New Rowley, now Georgetown, till 1795, when he bought property in Sedgwick, Me., and moved there 1796, and d. Aug. 26, 1821. She d. at Bucksport, with her daughter, Mrs. Mary Blodgett, Oct. 12, 1862, in her 96th year.

xi MEHITABLE, b. Sept. 25, 1753; m. Dea. James Chute. See No. 15.

4. iv. Daniel Thurston (Richard, Daniel, Daniel), b. in Georgetown, Dec. 14, 1745; m. Judith Chute (Daniel, James, James, James, Lionel); she d. Dec. 13, 1788, aged 46; he m. 2d, Mrs. Margaret Kinsman of Ipswich, Nov. 5, 1789, and d. there April 30, 1817; she d. Feb. 27, 1822, aged 75.

CHILDREN.

i SUSANNA, b. Nov. 1, 1768; m. Dea. William Coleman (Benjamin, Thomas), May 17, 1792; 9 children, and d. Oct. 8, 1808; he m. 2d, Zerviah, daughter of Zebulon and Abigail Richardson of Woburn, and widow of William Temple of Reading, Mass., Oct. 15, 1809 (Mr. Temple d. April 27, 1802 leaving a son William, b. Sept. 15, 1801. Daniel Chute of Reading was his guardian, and after Dea. Coleman went to live at Boscowen, N. H., he went to live with him, and in 1880 was in Montvale, Mass.); she d. July 25, 1815, aged 35; he m. 3d, Hannah Brown, 1816, and d. at Boscowen, May 23, 1820, aged 52; she d. Aug., 1843, leaving 3 sons. Dea. Coleman was a wheelwright in Byfield.

ii DEA. STEPHEN, b. in Rowley, Jan. 2, 1770; m. Philomela, daughter of Elijah and Eunice (Foster) Parish of Windham, Conn., June 26, 1794. (Mrs. Parish was daughter of Nathan Foster, and granddaughter of Dea. Josiah Standish, son of Capt. Josiah Standish, son of Capt. Myles Standish, b. in Lancashire, Eng., 1584, came over in the *Mayflower*, 1620; his wife Rose d. in January, 1621; he m. 2d, Barbara ———, who came over in the *Ann*, 1621; he settled in Duxbury, and d. there Oct. 3, 1656; had a son Alexander by 1st wife, and 4 sons, 1 daughter by 2d wife). Hannah Standish, daughter of Dea. Josiah, was wife of Nathan Foster, and grandmother of Hon. Lafayette S. Foster of Norwich, Conn., Vice-President, *ex-officio*, of the United States, after the death of President Lincoln. [Lafayette Sabine Foster (Capt. Daniel, Nathan, Abram, Abram, Reginald), b. 1806; d. 1880.] Elijah Parish had brothers Samuel and Lemuel of Canterbury, Conn., and a sister, besides the wife of Dea. S. Thurston; he had sons, Rev. Dr. Elijah of Byfield, and

Rev. Ariel of Manchester-by-the-Sea. Mrs. Eunice Parish d. Dec. 13, 1799 (day before the death of Washington), aged 66; he d. 1817, aged about 83. Mrs. Thurston d. at Bedford, N. H., July 24, 1818; he m. 2d, Sarah Burge, April 14, 1821; she d. Sept., 1825; he m. 3d, Hannah Worcester (Capt. Noah, Rev. Francis, Francis, Samuel, Rev. William), 1826, and d. of cholera, at Bedford, Sept. 13, 1833; she m. 2d, Jonathan Ireland of Dunbarton, N. H., and d. in Elmira, N. Y., Dec. 28, 1871. Mr. Thurston was a farmer in Rowley, then in Andover, 1799, after that in Bedford, Mass., till 1809; deacon and elder in the Presbyterian church. He organized the first Sunday School there, a temperance society, and was a strictly conscientious, pious man. Children: (1) Philomela, b. in Rowley, April 11, 1795; embarked as a missionary for Bombay, East Indies, Oct. 2, 1817; m. Rev. Samuel Newell, son of Ebenezer and Mary (Richardson) Newell of Durham, Me., March 26. 1818. He d. of cholera at Bombay, May 30, 1821, aged 37; she m. 2d, March, 1822, James Garrett, from Trenton, Oneida county, N. Y. He was a printer at the Bombay mission, where he d. 1831. In 1832 she returned, and d. at Poughkeepsie, N. Y., Sept. 16, 1849. She had a daughter Harriet by Mr. Newell, and a daughter and son by Mr. Garrett. James Garrett, Jr., b. 1830, was a soldier in the late war, taken a prisoner at Cold Harbor, from Richmond to Andersonville, and Florence, S. C., where he died. (2) Delia, b. in Rowley, 1796; d. Bedford, N. H., Sept. 24, 1823. (3) Clarissa, b. in Andover, 1801; was an eminent school-teacher more than 40 years, and authoress of several religious books. On Sunday morning, Jan. 6, 1884, she was crushed by a moving train at the R. R. crossing in Elmira, on the way to church, and d. aged 83. (4) Lucinda, b. in Bedford, Mass., July 21, 1805; d. March 23, 1806. (5) Mary Coleman, b. in Bedford, Sept. 23, 1806; d. in Eatonton, Georgia, July 23, 1825. (6) Ariel Standish, b. in Goffstown, N. H., June 11, 1810; m. Julia Clark, daughter of Dr. Erastus L. Hart of Goshen, Conn., 1836; 3 children. She d. April 17, 1844, aged 31; he m. 2d, Cornelia Sophia, daughter of Andrew C. Hull, of Nelson, Madison county, N. Y., 1846; 5 children. She d. at Brooklyn, N. Y., June 27, 1865, aged 45; he m. 3d, Georgiana (Converse) Gibson, April 15, 1867, she being 40 years old. (7) Mary Delia, b. at Bedford, 1827; d. at Elmira, N. Y., 1866.

iii JUDITH, b. Dec. 31, 1771; m. Samuel Pearson, 1793; 9 children; she d. Oct. 18, 1824.
iv DANIEL, b. Dec. 18, 1772; d. April 19, 1792.
v HANNAH, b. May, 1774; d. in childhood.

VAN BUSKIRK.

1. i. Laurens Andressen, to which he added Van Boskirck, came from Holstein, in Denmark, 1655, and settled in New Amsterdam, afterwards called New York. By trade he was a turner, but became a draper. About 1660, he settled in Bergen, N. J., took the oath to the king, Nov. 20, 1665. He was a man of more than ordinary skill and ability for the times, as a pleader for justice for himself and neighbors before the Council and Court. He was a member of the Bergen Court, 1677 to 1680, president of the same, 1681, president of the County Court, 1682. He was also a member of the Governor's Council several years from 1672. With others, he purchased a large tract of land known as New Hackensack in 1676, and lived there in 1688. He m. Jannetje Jans, widow of Christian Barentsen, Sept. 12, 1658, and obtained 4 sons of her 1st husband, 1400 florins, and other property. Both d. 1694.

CHILDREN.

  i ANDRIES, bapt. March 3, 1660; was a member of the 6th Provincial Assembly of New Jersey; d. 1724.
2 ii LAURENS.
  iii PIETER, b. Jan. 1, 1666; m. Trintje Harmanse, and d. July 21, 1738; she d. Nov. 7, 1736; 8 children. Jannetje, the 4th, m. Cornelius Corson Vroom of Staten Island.
  iv THOMAS, m. Margrietje Hendrickje, and d. 1745; 10 children.

2. ii. Laurens Van Buskirk (Laurens A.), b. about 1663; m. Hendricke Van Derlinde, and represented Bergen in the 5th Provincial Assembly in 1709; lived at Saddle Rock about 1690, and d. 1724.

CHILDREN.

  i FITJE, m. Arie Banta, 1712.
  ii JOOST, bapt. 1695; m. Trintje Martese; had Laurens and Martin.
  iii ANDREW, m. Jacomintje Davidse Demarest, 1717.
  iv JOHN, bapt. Feb. 26, 1699; m. Geesje Jurrianse Westervelt, 1720; m. 2d, Maritje Van Derlinde, 1749; had Antje and Laurens.
  v JACOBUS.
  vi JANNETJE.
  vii BENJAMINE.
3 viii LAURENS.

3. iii. Laurens Van Buskirk, Jr., m. Eva ———, and d. 1774.

CHILDREN.

i Thomas.	4 ii John.
iii Aeltje.	iv Antje.
v Jannetje.	vi Mary.
vii Margaret.	5 viii Abram.

4. iv. John Van Buskirk (Laurens, Laurens, Laurens A.), m. Theodosia ———, had a family, and d. 1783.

CHILDREN.

6   i   Lawrence, b. about 1729.
     ii   Abram, b. about 1740; was Colonel of the 4th battalion of N. J. Volunteers, and 2d to Brigadier-General Arnold at Saratoga; settled at Shelburne, N. S., 1784; was its first mayor, and received half pay. His son Jacob, in the Revolution and American war, had a daughter Sarah, m. Mr. Bingay, and a son Thomas, b. 1814.

5. iv. Abram Van Buskirk, brother to the above, m. ——— ———, and d. 1794.

CHILDREN.

   i   Thomas.
  ii   Cornelius, b. June 10, 1743; m. Jane, daughter of David Demarest, of Schraalenburg, N. J., and d. April 28, 1829; she d. 1844, aged 95. Before 1800 he left Bergen, and settled in Bayonne, Hudson county. They had Cornelius, Peter, and Abram.
 iii   Helena, m. Cornelius J. Bogert.
 iv   Margaret, m. Henry Fredericks, and d. before 1788; had Margaret, Rachel, and Henry.
  v   Jannetje, m. Lawrence Van Buskirk, cousin.
 vi   Elizabeth, m. Peter Van Buskirk.
 vii   Rachel, m. Thomas Cooper.
viii   Catharine, m. Thomas Boggs.

6. v. Lawrence Van Buskirk (John, Laurens, Laurens, Laurens A.), b. in Hackensack, Bergen county, N. J., 1729; was a farmer and owner of slaves before the Revolution; he was captain in the King's Orange Rangers, so, being a Loyalist, he fled to St. John, N. B., in 1783, and soon after removed to near Kentville, Kings county, N. S., thence to Aylesford, and bought a farm of Daniel Bowen, and d. 1803. He m. Jannetje Van Buskirk, a cousin, who d. 1791.

CHILDREN.

    i   CAPT. ABRAM, b. about 1750; was of the King's Orange Rangers of New Jersey, 1782; m. Ann Corson, and went to Nova Scotia at the peace, but returned soon after, and was a merchant at Athens on the Hudson; d. in New York about 1820, leaving two sons and two or three daughters (one must have been Frances, who m. Charles C. Steadman). She m. 2d and 3d, Jacob Benson and Lewis Ryas, and d. 1825.

    ii   LIEUT. THOMAS, b. 1752; m. —— Van Buskirk; went to Nova Scotia, but returned.

7 iii   JOHN, b. 1754.

8 iv   GARRETT, b. 1756.

    v   DAUGHTER, b. 1761; m. —— Ryerson, in Aylesford, N. S., and d. in 1849.

    vi   THEODOSIA, m. James Harris; 6 children; N. S.

9 vii   HENRY, b. 1767.

7. vi. John Van Buskirk (Lawrence, John, Laurens, Laurens, Laurens A.), b. about 1754, m. —— ——, and had:

    i   LAWRENCE, m. Polly Brymer. Children: James, Mary, Louise, Matilda, Arabel, Johnson, Charlot, Clarissa, Colin Campbell.

10 ii   CHARLES, b. 1784 (?).

    iii   HENRY.

11 iv   JEREMIAH, b. 1788.

8. vi. Garrett Van Buskirk, brother to the above, b. 1756; m. Betsy Potts, time of the Revolution, and thence to Aylesford, N. S.; d. 1843.

CHILDREN.

    i   LAWRENCE, b. 1780; m. —— Van Horne; 2d, —— Van Buskirk.

    ii   JOHN, b. 1782; m. Betsy West; 2d, —— ——; had a daughter Ann, b. 1806; probably more.

    iii   DOROTHY, b. 1784; m. Ezekiel Brown. See Gates.

    iv   ANN, b. 1786; m. Thomas Gates. See Gates.

12 v   SAMUEL, b. 1788.

    vi   CATHARINE, b. 1790; m. Edwin, son of John Morgan; 8 children, and d. in Chicago, 1875; he d. in Yarmouth, Ont., 1859, aged 73.

    vii   JEMIMA, b. 1792; m. Martin Ryerson.

    viii   ABRAM, b. Sept. 5, 1794; d. in youth.

    ix   HENRY, b. June 13, 1797; m. Ruth, daughter of John Morgan, March, 1819; went to Yarmouth, Ont., 1824; to London, 1826; to St. Thomas, 1845; 8 children; 4 only grew up; one is Dr. William Van Buskirk, St. Thomas, Ont. Unctle Henry d. 1881; his wife d. 1872, aged 73.

ALLIED FAMILIES.

  x Nelson, b. June 13, 1799; m. Betsy Chute. See No. 21.
13 xi Charles, b. April 2, 1804.

9. vi. Henry Van Buskirk, J. P. (Lawrence, John, Laurens, Laurens, Laurens A.), b. about 1767; m. Isabella Donking, Feb. 20, 1797, and lived in Aylesford. She d. June 6, 1829; he m. 2d, Nancy Potter, Nov. 30, 1829, and d. March 16, 1841, aged 74.

CHILDREN.

 i William Henry, b. May 1, 1798; m. Elizabeth Watson, and d. 1823.
 ii Dr. Lawrence E., b. Nov. 6, 1799; m. Mary E. Handley, and d. 1867, Halifax.
iii Elizabeth, b. Jan. 14, 1802; d. 1824.
 iv Dr. Robert, b. March 13, 1804; m. Ann, daughter of James R. Dewolf.
  v Dr. George Pitt, b. April 15, 1806; m. Margaret Reed, St. John, Montreal, and d. 1866.
 vi Charlotte, b. June 14, 1808; m. Thomas Spurr, Bridgetown, and d. 1857.
vii Abram, b. Jan. 4, 1811; m Eliza Harris, and d. 1865.
viii Dr. Inglis, b. April 9, 1813; m. Eliza, daughter of James Barss, and had (1) James B., b. 1837; m. Mary Harding. (2) Henry D., b. 1839; m. Julia, daughter of John Fitz-Randolph of Digby; 5 sons, 1 daughter. He came to Boston, 1866; he m. 1st, Mary Jayne, 1 son. (3) Edward L., b. 1840; d. 1861.
 ix James Donking, b. May 4, 1816; m. Catharine, sister to Rev. H. L. Owen.

10. vii. Charles Van Buskirk (John, Lawrence, John, Laurens, Laurens, Laurens A.), b. about 1784; m. Harriet Vroom (George, John, Hendrick, Hendrick, Cornelius Peter), and lived in Clements till about 1845, when he crossed Bear River, and settled at Bloomfield, Digby county.

CHILDREN.

14 i John, b. Aug. 4, 1801.
 ii H. Vroom, m. Catharine Davenport; 3 children.
iii Ann, m. Silas Balcomb; 8 children.
 iv William, m. Rachel Tallman; 4 children.
  v Charles, m. Caroline Christopher, and had Charles, Frances Ann, Edward, Henry, Abba, and Augusta.
 vi Sarah Jane, m. George Vroom, Jr.; 9 children.
vii Samuel, killed by a tree at about 30.
viii Lemma, b. April 2, 1819; m. John Henry Harris. See Harris.

ALLIED FAMILIES.

ix JEREMIAH, m. Elizabeth Merry; 5 children; son Charles m. Abbie Mary Chute. See No. 110.
x FRANK, m. Mary R. Farer; 4 children.
xi DRUSILLA, b. 1829; m. Stephen B. Heniger as 2d wife; 3 children.

11. vii. Jeremiah Van Buskirk, brother to the preceding, b. 1788; m. Mehitable Welton*, and lived in Aylesford, farmers. Both d. 1876, aged 88.

CHILDREN.

i GEORGE, b. 1813; m. Maria Phinney, and had Charles and Frank.
ii JAMES, m. Kate Owen, in New Brunswick.
iii MERCY ANN, m. Ezra Foster, son of Joseph; 4 children.
iv ERIE, b. 1813; m. Henrietta, daughter of Wells Congdon; 6 children, and d. 1862.
v BERIAH, m. Harriet Wheelock; 4 children.
vi WILLIAM, m. Sarah E. Gates, and had Amos and George.
vii JOHN, b. 1822; d. 1889.
viii WALLACE, m. Elizabeth, daughter of John McGregor; 4 children.
ix CATHARINE, m. John Porter, in New Brunswick.
x MARY, d. single.
xi ADELAIDE, m. Henry, son of John McGregor; 4 children.
xii OLIVIA, m. Bill Jacques (John, Alexander), and had Henry and William.

12. vii. Samuel Van Buskirk (Garrett, Lawrence, John, Laurens, Laurens, Laurens A.), b. in Aylesford, N. S., 1788; m. Mary, daughter of Paul Crocker, Jr., Dec. 26, 1814, and were farmers and pious Christians. He d. about 1845; she d. about 1850.

CHILDREN.

i JAMES, b. March 19, 1816; m. Tamer Clark; 8 children; m. 2d, Lydia, daughter of Moses Langley; m. 3d, Sarah, daughter of Thomas Langley, and widow of Samuel McPherson, and d. Nov. 19, 1882, leaving a son and daughter. Her daughter, Clara A. McPherson, b. June 25, 1862, m. Nathan Henry, son of Samuel Sanford, 1881, and live in S. B. Sons Charles and Samuel Van Buskirk live in Somerville.
ii JOHN, b. Aug. 4, 1818.
iii MARY ELIZABETH, b. Oct. 29, 1822; m. Robert Saxton, 1845, as 2d wife, and lived in Houghton, Ont. Children: Emeline, Eleanor, and Robert. See Saxton.
iv THOMAS, b. about 1826; m. Martha McGaffey, in Ontario; was in the late war, and is reported of in Minneapolis.

* Mehitable, Erie, Ezekiel, Thomas, John, John, from England, 1667; d. Waterbury, Conn., 1679.

13. vii. Charles Van Buskirk, the youngest brother, b. in Aylesford, April 2, 1804; m. Rebecca, daughter of Wells and Abba (Phinney) Condon, and lived in Morristown, Aylesford, N. S. He d.; she d.

CHILDREN.

- i Louise, b. 1828; m. William Farnsworth. See Farnsworth.
- ii Garrett, b. 1830; m. Elizabeth, daughter of Enoch Parish.
- iii Henry, b. March 10, 1832; m. Rebecca, daughter of Enoch Parish.
- iv Elijah, b. Jan. 26, 1834; d. about 1854.
- v Lawrence, b. June 14, 1838; m. Rebecca Porter.
- vi Elizabeth, m. Enoch Hutchinson.
- vii Obed P., m. Julia, daughter of William Banks.
- viii Dorothy, m. Spurr Brennan.

14. viii. John Van Buskirk (Charles, John, Lawrence, John, Laurens, Laurens, Laurens A.), b. in Clements, N. S., Aug. 4, 1801; m. Delphina, daughter of Eliab Bell, and lived at Bloomfield, Digby county, N. S.; she d. May 5, 1875, aged 61.

CHILDREN.

- i Sarah Jane, m. Israel Woodman.
- ii William Vroom, m. Melissa, daughter of Stephen Wilson.
- iii Mary E., d. at about 33.
- iv Welthea A., m. James, son of Nelson Harris.
- v Harriet D., b. 1844; m. Charles, son of William H. Marshall.
- vi Cynthia M., b. 1846; m. Isaac G. Hutchinson.
- vii Elizabeth B., m. Maria, daughter of Edward Vroom.
- viii Caroline S., m. L. Richmond Harris (John D., George, John), to Newton, Mass., 1881.
- ix Lemma H., d. at 3.

WEARE.

1. i. Peter Weare, b. in England, 1618; came over to America about 1638, and was settled at York, Me., about 1650. He is said to have been a prominent man at York, recorder of deeds, 1667, etc., and may have been a brother or cousin to Robert of Dedham, and the same also of Nathaniel of Hampton, N. H. And it is possible that they came of a family that has lived in Devonshire and Somersetshire, England, since the 14th century. Peter

m. Ruth, daughter of John and Ruth Gooch; she d. about 1664; he m. 2d, Mary, daughter of Dep. Gov. John Davis of York, Me., 1666, and was killed or captured by Indians, Jan. 25, 1692, when over 100 of the settlers perished. The wid. d. Jan. 28, 1718–19, aged 85.

CHILDREN.

- i ELIZABETH, m. Thomas, son of Henry and Frances Donnell; he d. 1699.
- ii MARY, m. —— Drury; 2d, —— Brown.
- iii HANNAH, m. Michael Shaller of Boston; was living a widow, 1716.
- iv PHEBE, m. Isaac Marion about 1681, and d. about 1724.
- v PETER, m. Elizabeth ——; 2d, Abigail ——; 3d, Elizabeth Fetherly; 4th, Abigail ——.
- vi NATHANIEL, d. probably before 1667.
- vii RUTH, m. —— Cunningham of Boston, and d. about 1745.
- viii DANIEL, b. about 1667; m. Hannah Boaden; 3 children; d. 1697; 2d, Lydia Hiller, 1698; 1 child; 3d, Mary ——, 1706; 4 children.
- ix JOSEPH, b. about 1668; was a mariner; m. Hannah Purington; 4 children, and d. 1700.
- x MARY, b. about 1670; m. Charles Roberts, 1690.
- 2 xi ELIAS, b. about 1672.
- xii SARAH, b. about 1675; m. Peter Nowell, 1698, and d. about 1725.
- xiii HOPEWELL, b. 1678; m. Lydia, daughter of Job and Sarah (Austin) Young, and d. 1721; had Joseph and John.

2. ii. Elias Weare (Peter), b. 1672 (?); m. Magdalen, daughter of Manwaring and Mary (Moulton) Hilton, and widow of Nathaniel Adams, Jan. 6, 1696. (Magdalen Hilton was b. about 1672, m. about 1692, Nat. Adams, and had a son Nat. She was captured by Indians, Jan., 1693, and was returned by an exchange of prisoners, Oct., 1695. Adams d. in her absence.) Mr. Weare, while in company with friends, "returning from Boston to Wells, between York and Cape Neddock, were all slain by the Indians," Aug. 10, 1707. The wid. m. 3d, John Webber, 1710, had a daughter Hannah, Sept. 18, 1711, and d. Feb. 4, 1725–6.

CHILDREN.

- i RUTH, b. Jan. 6, 1697; m. Moses Banks. See Banks.
- ii ELIAS, b. Jan. 10, 1699; m. Elizabeth Sayward.
- iii JEREMIAH, b. Feb. 13, 1701.
- iv JOHN, b. Jan. 16, 1703.
- 3 v JOSEPH, b. March 17, 1705.

ALLIED FAMILIES.

    vi MARY, b. March 27, 1707; m. Alexander McIntyre.
    vii ELIZABETH, b. about 1710; m. David Bennett.

3. iii. Joseph Weare (Elias, Peter), b. March 17, 1705; m. Mary, daughter of Samuel Webber, Jr. (b. 1710), and lived in York, Me.; d. about 1791. Mr. Webber, Jr., was the 3d, in a family of 11 children. His father was killed by Indians, 1712.

CHILDREN.

    i JEREMIAH, b. March 17, 1728-9.
4 ii ELIAS, b. March 6, 1730-1.
    iii JOHN, b. Nov. 29, 1732.
    iv JOSEPH, b. Oct. 21, 1734; m. Elizabeth Stone.
    v MARY, b. Nov. 22, 1736.
    vi BATHSHEBA, b. Oct. 31, 1738; m. Stephen Paul.
    vii MERCY, b. Dec. 6, 1740; m. Jeremiah Wardwell.
    viii SARAH, b. June 6, 1743; m. Thomas Bragdon.
    ix DANIEL, b. Jan. 24, 1746-7; m. Abigail Littlefield.
    x PHEBE, b. Dec. 5, 1748; m. Capt. Joseph Perkins, 1770, and d. Aug. 20, 1815.

4. iv. Elias Wear (Joseph, Elias, Peter), b. in York, Me., March 6, 1730-1; m. Ruth Banks (Joshua, Moses, John, Richard), 1760; moved to Granville, N. S., 1761, and sometime after that, probably 1790, they crossed the Annapolis river into Clements, and lived near Moose river. He d. 1804; she d. 1805, aged about 70.

CHILDREN.

    i ELIAS, b. June 30, 1762; d. abroad, unknown.
5 ii JOSEPH, b. April 9, 1764.
6 iii JAMES, b. Nov. 12, 1766.
    iv ELIZABETH, b. April 13, 1769; m. about 1787, —— Newcomb, and had a daughter Olive. He d. about 1790; she m. 2d, John Hale (John, Joseph, Thomas, Thomas of Newbury, Mass., 1636), Nov. 9, 1791, and lived in or near Annapolis, N. S. Mr. Hale of Boxford, Mass., b. 1745, m. 1st, in Ipswich, Mass., 1765, Sarah Lord; as no children are reported it is probable that she d. about 1774, and then he went to N. S. He d. about 1803-4; she m. 3d, Edward Brine, and had a son James. Hale children: (1) Gilbert, b. about 1796; m. Sarah Griffin, and lived at Billtown, N. S.; had (a) Charles Nelson, b. 1820; d. Aug. 3, 1893; m. Rebecca, daughter of Wm. and Nancy (Jackson) Peddrick, live in Somerville (went there 1850), Mass.; 7 children. (b) James Israel, b. 1821; m. Sarah Lavenia Miner (James E., Thomas G., Thomas, Sylvanus, Thomas, Manassah of Stonington, Conn., son of Thomas,

the emigrant ancestor, 1630), Dec. 16, 1843; 5 children, and d. June 5, 1871; she m. 2d, Jonathan Woodbury Smith (m. 1st, Marcy G., daughter of Zalmon Briggs; 2 children), and live in Weymouth, Mass. (c) Elizabeth, m. T. Ripley; Sam Shepherd. (d) Rachel, m. Henry Ballou. (e) William, m. Clarissa Davis, Scotch Bay, N. S. (f) Elias, m. Margaret Sullivan. (g) Ruth. (2) James, b. about 1799; m. Rebecca Ward, and lived up the St. John river, N. B. (3) Joseph William, b. Sept. 12, 1802; m. Sarah Quereau (Joshua, Joshua), Feb. 25, 1826; lived in Granville; to Bear River about 1842; to Newburyport, Mass., 1848, and d. May 22, 1873; she d. Oct. 17, 1882, aged 76. Children: (a) Ruth Elizabeth, b. July 2, 1828; m. Ephraim L. Chute. See No. 174. (b) Samuel Dudney, b. April 26, 1830; to Newburyport, Oct., 1849; m. Mary F. Fowler, April 7, 1853 (a son d. in infancy). She d. Aug. 14, 1854, aged 24; he m. 2d, Sarah Ann, daughter of James William Dunning, Sept. 21, 1855; 7 children; live in Groveland, Mass. (c) Mary Ann, b. Aug. 2, 1832; m. John James Thurlow, Oct., 1850; 4 children. (d) Albert D., b. April 17, 1834; m. Emma Nowell, Newburyport. (e) Phebe Arabel, b. 1836–37. (f) David Turner, b. Aug. 16, 1837; m. ——— ———; lived in Boston. (g) Helena Celesta, b. March 28, 1840; m. James Fegan; 6 children. (h) Sarah Lucy, b. Oct. 7, 1842; m. John P. Rundlett; 2 children. (i) Rachel Wilhelmina, b. Sept. 17, 1844; m. John Reed; 2 children; m. 2d, Fred Morton. (j) Joseph William, b. June 4, 1845; m. Elizabeth Currier. (k) Emma F., b. Dec. 22, 1848; d. young.
- v DANIEL, b. Nov. 21, 1770; in the "States"; unknown.
- vi MARY, b. Nov. 28, 1772; m. Ezra, son of John and Grace (Kelly) Dunn, Jan. 7, 1790, and lived south of Annapolis; he d. about 1850; she d. about 1860. Children: (1) Betsy, m. John Mulligan. (2) Grace, m. Joseph Thorne. (3) Sarah. (4) Ruth. (5) John. (6) Robert, m. Sarah Berry (James).
- 7 vii JOHN, b. Feb. 24, 1775; m. Catharine Chute. See No. 13.
- viii SARAH, b. April 16, 1777; m. Dea. Daniel Chute. See No. 20.

5. v. Joseph Wear (Elias, Joseph, Elias, Peter), b. in Granville, N. S., April 9, 1764; m. Elizabeth Chute (see No. 10), by Rev. Jacob Baily, Nov. 20, 1787, and lived in Clements, an exemplary Christian couple, as farmers; d. Nov. 4, 1844; she d. April 30, 1842, aged 74.

CHILDREN.

- i RUTH, b. Jan. 1, 1789; m. Dea. Benjamin Potter. See Potter.

8 ii SAMUEL, b. March 6, 1791.
iii FRANCES, b. May 8, 1793; m. William Robbins (Abial, James, Jeduthen, Jeduthen, John, Nicholas, and Ann, of Duxbury, 1638), Jan. 18, 1810; 6 children, and d. May 6, 1864; he d. Dec. 26, 1862, aged 70.
iv SARAH, b. Oct. 8, 1795; d. 1797.
v PHEBE, b. Jan. 16, 1798; m. Jacob, son of Joseph Rawding, July 20, 1817, and d. Sept., 1881; he d. May 11, 1880, aged 84; lived in Kempt, Queens county, N. S. Children: (1) Eliza Ann, b. 1818; d. 1887. (2) Joseph, b. 1819; m. Sarah More. (3) John, b. 1820; m. Leonora, daughter of Daniel Dukeshire. (4) Rebecca, b. 1822; m. George Ringer, Jr. (5) Austin, b. 1824; m. Esther Dukeshire, sister to Leonora; 2d, Janette Apt; 3d, Mary Marshall Cress. (6) Ruth, m. John, son of Rev. Thomas Delong. (7) Sarah, m. Israel Wear; 2d, William Toole. (8) Alva, m. Susan Dukeshire, another sister. (9) Andrew, m. Letitia, daughter of Ezra Dunn. (10) Phebe Jane, m. James Verge.
9 vi JOB, b. Jan. 22, 1800.
10 vii JAMES, b. Dec. 5, 1803.
viii SOPHIA A., b. June 15, 1805; d. 1807.
ix ELIZABETH, b. July 2, 1807; m. Andrew, son of James Christopher, from England, June 20, 1826; he d. April 30, 1847, aged 43; she m. 2d, Henry, son of George Apt, April 5, 1849; he d. Jan. 6, 1870, aged 70.; she m. 3d, Joseph Chute, July 2, 1877. (see No. 62). Children: (1) Sophronia, b. April 18, 1827; m. James McGregor, 2d Jr., Oct., 1846; 13 children; moved to Lynn, Mass., 1877. (2) Phebe, b. 1831; m. Manasseh McGrath; 2 children; m. 2d, Thomas McGrath, a brother; 4 daughters and a son named William Hicks. (3) John, b. 1833; m. Lizzie Hammond; son Ellsworth in Marblehead. (4) Elizabeth, b. 1835; m. Henry Maughn; 5 children. (5) Emeline, b. 1837; m. Eber Ring; 3 children. (6) Emma A., b. 1839; m. Stephen, son of Ambrose Taylor (see Taylor); 8 children. (7) Ruth S., b. 1842; m. Smith Apt; 5 children. (8) Henry Apt, b. 1852; m. Ida, daughter of William Ford; 7 children.
x SARAH, b. Oct. 2, 1810; m. David, son of Levi Minard, Sept. 25, 1828, and lived in Kempt, Queens county, but about 1860 moved to Brooklyn street, Cornwallis, Kings county. He d. Dec. 10, 1880, in his 81st year; she d. in Boston, Feb. 25, 1887. Children: (1) Elijah, b. July 10, 1829; m. Ellen, daughter of Fred Freeman; she d. 1853, aged 22; he m. 2d, Janet, daughter of Jesse Harding and widow of Capt. Foster Page (with 4 children), 1874; moved to Boston, 1874. (2) Allen, b. Dec. 19, 1830; m. Mercy, daughter of Francis Kempton. (3) David, b. Dec. 19, 1833; m. Louisa Chute. See No. 63.

(4) Elizabeth W., b. Dec. 6, 1836; m. Whilden C., son of Edward Burke, 1857; had 9 children. They went to St. John, N. B., 1877,— were there time of the big fire — and to Boston, 1878, carpenter and builder; he d. Oct., 1883, aged 55. (5) Joseph, b. Nov. 25, 1841; m. Cornelia Sanford. See Sanford. (6) Rebecca, b. Sept. 6, 1843; m. D. R. Chute. See No. 180. (7) Sarah Jane, b. Dec. 3, 1845; m. Joseph B. Cook.

xi REBECCA, b. June 25, 1812; m. Joseph Milbury (Thomas, Joseph), July 3, 1830, and d. Oct, 1866; he d. Feb., 1877, aged 70. They had 3 or 4 children.

6. v. James Wear (Elias, Joseph, Elias, Peter), b. Nov. 12, 1766; m. Rachel Graves about 1790, and lived at Port Medway.

CHILDREN.

i CHARLES, has son Leonard, has a son William, who lives in Annapolis, N. S.
ii PHINEAS, m.
iii POLLY, m.
iv JOSEPH, m.
v CHIPMAN, m. Catharine Crows.
vi DAVID, m. Mrs. Myrick.
vii EZRA, m. Elizabeth Wentzel; 8 children.
viii SUSAN, m.
ix SETH.
x REBECCA.

7. v. John Wear, another brother, b. Feb. 24, 1775; m. Catharine Chute (see No. 13), 1794, and lived near Paradise, Annapolis county; had one child only:

11 i ELIAS, b. Aug. 15, 1795.

Mr. Wear, being a blacksmith, went to St. John's, N. F , about 1805, and is reported to have d. about 1814. So his widow m. 2d, Philip Barteaux (William, Philip), by Rev. Roger Victs of Digby, Dec. 12, 1808, and lived on the Sissiboo Road several years; after the American war to Marshalltown; in 1828 they moved to near Paris, on the Grand river, Ont.; then in 1834 they moved to Shelby county, O.; in 1837 moved again to Ont., and bought a farm east of London, where the asylum now is, but moved again to Malahide, and bought a farm reaching the shore of Lake Erie, 1838. In 1847 they had a splendid visit with old friends and kindred in Nova Scotia. He sold out there to Rev. M. S. McConnell, 1849, and lived in Bayham, on the farm of Dea. Andrew Chute, till the spring of 1854, when they moved to Houghton, Norfolk county, below Port

Burwell, where she d. Nov. 8, aged 75. He removed again to Malahide and lived with Charles Chute, Esq. (whom they brought up from childhood), and d. there March 12, 1867, aged 87.

8. vi. Samuel Wear (Joseph, Elias, Joseph, Elias, Peter), b. in Clements, N. S., March 6, 1791; m. Dorothy Pick, by Rev. Theodore Seth Harding, March 30, 1812; she d. July 23, 1830, aged 36; he m. 2d, Elizabeth Woodworth, by Rev. T. S. Harding, Sept. 16, 1833, and moved to Kempt, Queens county, and there lived, a farmer and a pious Christian in the Baptist church. He d. Dec. 6, 1873.

CHILDREN.

i Sarah Elizabeth, b. Jan. 20, 1813; m. John Trainham, 1838.

ii Joseph Robert, b. Oct. 30, 1815; d. Aug., 1837.

iii Caroline, b. Sept. 22, 1817; m. Benjamin, son of William Skinner, May, 1842; he d. near Buffalo, N. Y., 1867.

iv Asa, b. Oct. 4, 1819; d. Dec., 1833.

v Mary J., b. Feb. 2, 1821; d. Aug., 1832.

vi Frances, b. Aug. 17, 1823; m. William White, Jr.

vii Sophia A., b. June 6, 1826; d. 1832.

viii Rebecca, b. May 27, 1828; d. since 1860.

ix Margaret A., b. July 9, 1830; d. Aug. 6.

x Asa Freeman, b. Sept. 16, 1834; m. Lucy, daughter of Ezra Wear, June, 1857, and had (1) Samuel. (2) Miner. (3) John. (4) Emma Jane. (5) Ethelon Eunice. (6) Frances, b. July 12, 1869; m. Andrew H., son of Mark Sanford, and live in Brookline. (7) William. (8) Charles. (9) Mary. (10) Arthur B.; besides 4 d. in infancy. He d. Aug. 30, 1880; she m. 2d, Robert Pettitt, May 10, 1882, and live at Tupperville, near Round Hill, N. S.

xi John Prior, b. Aug. 7, 1836; m. Matilda L. Chute. See No. 60.

xii Joseph Aaron, b. Feb. 24, 1839; m. Mary, daughter of James Finton, April 9, 1872; 8 children; he d. Jan. 12, 1891.

xiii George Albert, b. June 3, 1841; m. Martha Jane, daughter of J. W. Robbins, Sept. 22, 1864; 10 children; live at Digby.

xiv Pelina Adaline, b. Feb. 10, 1844; m. Aaron Butler, Oct. 22, 1872; 2 daughters.

xv Sarah Amanda, b. Sept. 18, 1848; m. James Forrest, June 12, 1867; 6 children; m. 2d, William, son of Nathaniel Mott, Aug. 20, 1884. Mr. Mott m. 1st, Lucy Jane Andrews, and had a son Charles, b. Aug. 28, 1878; she d. March 23, 1884, aged 38; live at Laquille, near Annapolis.

ALLIED FAMILIES.

9. vi. Job Wear, brother to Samuel, b. Jan. 22, 1800; m. Elizabeth Potter, Nov. 4, 1824, and lived in Clements, pious farmers; d. Jan. 22, 1846; she d. Oct. 10, 1874, aged 75.

CHILDREN.

 i JAMES, b. 1825; m.
 ii JOSEPH ELIAS, b. 1827; m. Charlotte A. Chute. See No. 60.
 iii ISRAEL, b. 1830; m. Sarah Rawding; 2 children, and d.; she m. 2d, William Toole.
 iv SALLY ANN, d. young, about 1853–4.
 v LEMMA, m. Beecher Milbury (Joseph, Thomas, Joseph); 4 children, Beecher, Saunders, Fanny Jane, and Charles.
 vi FANNY, m. John Combs, and d.; he m. twice since.
 vii BENNY, m. Nancy, daughter of Manasseh McGrath.

10. vi. James Wear, the youngest brother, b. Dec. 5, 1803; m. Sarah Robinson, Dec., 1825, and lived in Clements, but moved to Frederickton, N. B., about 1835, since which time little is known of them.

CHILDREN.

 i PHEBE JANE, b. 1827. ii DIMOCK.
 iii HANNAH. iv MARIA.
 v JAMES. vi ALFRED.
 vii SARAH JANE.

11. vi. Elias Wear (John, Elias, Joseph, Elias, Peter), b. near Paradise, N. S., Aug. 15, 1795; lived near Bridgetown a dozen years or more, then went over to the south shore of Nova Scotia, and lived at Liverpool, Port Medway, and Port Maton; belonged to the Baptist church; very ambitious and energetic, but rather unfortunate. He m. Lucinda, daughter of Martin and Bethiah (Smith) Peach, by Rev. John Payzant, Liverpool, June 30, 1825. They moved over to Bear River in 1848; then to Elgin county, Ont., 1853, and lived in Malahide and Bayham, and d. in Houghton, Norfolk county, May 15, 1883; she d. May 23, 1883, aged 76.

CHILDREN.

 i JOHN HENRY, b. Oct. 20, 1832; calker by trade, went back to Nova Scotia, 1856; m. Sarah E. Gardner, 1857, and since 1880 went into Maine.
 ii ELIAS, b. Nov. 9, 1834; m. Angeline Durkee, June 26, 1859, in Malahide, Ont.; had a son and daughter. She d. Aug., 1864, aged 22; he m. 2d, Sarah C. Meadows, Feb. 12, 1865, and had a son and 4 daughters; she d. March 14, 1883; he d. March 25, 1885.

 iii DELINA, b. Nov. 13, 1836; m. Hiram McComb, in Michigan, 1856, and lived there 35 years, having 7 children. He d. Sept. 16, 1885; she moved with 2 or 3 of the children to Oklahoma, 1891.
 iv JANE, b. Nov. 7, 1838; m. Alfred Patient, Dec. 17, 1864; 9 children in Houghton, Ont.; live at Mabee.
 v ELNORAH, b. Jan. 2, 1842; m. Hiram, son of James Sharp, Jan. 9, 1863, in Houghton.
 vi AZUBA, b. Oct. 14, 1846; m. John Billington, 1866, and d. 1878; he m. 2d, Mrs. Dorcas Ryer, 1878, and live at Colpoy's Bay, south side of Lake Huron.
 vii NAOMI, b. June 18, 1849; m. William van Scythe, Sept. 23, 1869, and d. Nov. 2, 1881, at Staynor, Norfolk county; he m. 2d, Lucinda A., daughter of Elias and Angeline Wear, May 31, 1882.

WHEELOCK.

1. i. Rev. Ralph Wheelock, "the founder of Medfield," was b. in Shropshire, Eng., 1600; bred at Clare Hall, Cambridge University; A. B., 1626; A. M., 1631; came over, 1637, probably with wife Rebecca and daughter Rebecca; first to Watertown, then to Dedham, 1638; made a freeman, 1639; clerk of the writs (town-clerk), 1642; solemnized marriages in Medfield and Mendon, 1645; selectman, 1651 to 1655; school-teacher, J. P., and filled other offices from that time onward. He built a house in Medfield, 1651–2, and d. 1683. His wife d. 1680.

CHILDREN.

 i REBECCA, b. about 1632; m. John Crafts, June 7, 1654.
 ii PEREGRINA, b. about 1634; m. Jonn Warfield, 1669, and d. 1671.
2 iii GERSHOM, b. 1636.
 iv MARY, b. 1638; m. Joseph Miles, 1661.
3 v BENJAMIN, b. 1640.
 vi SAMUEL, b. 1642; m. Sarah Kendrick, 1678; 7 children, and d. 1628; she m. 2d, Josiah Rockwood, 1703. Their children were (1) Sarah (1679–1716); m. 1700, Henry Guernsey. (2) Samuel (1680–1698). (3) Rebecca (1681-82). (4) Drodat, b. and d. 1684. (5) Mercy, b. 1685; d. young. (6) Mehitable, b. 1689; m. 1709, Benoni Partridge. (7) Thomas, b. and d. 1699.
 vii RECORD, b. 1644; m. Increase Ward, 1672.
 viii EXPERIENCE, b. 1648; m. Joseph Warren, 1668.
4 ix ELEAZER, b. 1654.

ALLIED FAMILIES.

2. ii. Gershom Wheelock (Rev. Ralph), b. in England, 1636; m. Hannah, daughter of John Stodder of Hingham, 1658, and lived in Medfield; d. 1684.

CHILDREN.

    i   HANNAH, b. and d. 1659.
    ii SAMUEL, b. and d. 1660.
   iii HANNAH, b. and d. 1661.
   iv SAMUEL, b. 1664; lived in Marlboro' and Shrewsbury.
    v   JOHN, b. 1670; d. 1684.
5 vi JOSEPH, b. 1672.
  vii TIMOTHY, b. 1673; d. 1761.

3. ii. Benjamin Wheelock (Rev. Ralph), b. in Medfield, 1640; m. Elizabeth, daughter of Samuel Bullen, 1668; moved to Mendon, 1685.

CHILDREN.

    i   ELIZABETH, b. 1671.
    ii MARY, b. 1674.
   iii ALICE, b. 1676.
   iv BENJAMIN, b. 1678.
6   v OBADIAH, b. 1685.

4. ii. Capt. Eleazer Wheelock (Rev. Ralph), b. 1654; m. Elizabeth Fuller of Rehoboth, 1678; she d. 1689; he m. 2d, Mary Chenery, who d. 1732. Capt. Eleazer Wheelock was a hunter of wolves (killed 4 in 1676); selectman 1720, and prominent in town affairs; d. 1731.

CHILDREN.

    i   ELIZABETH, b. 1679.
    ii DEA. RALPH, 1682–1748; m. —— ——, and had a son Eleazer, b. April 22, 1711; graduated at Yale, 1733; m. Sarah, daughter of Rev. John Davenport, and widow of Capt. William Maltby of New Haven, April 29, 1735; 6 children, 3 d. in infancy. She d. 1746, aged 43; he m. 2d, Mrs. Mary Brinsmead, Nov. 21, 1747, of Milford, Conn., and had 5 children at Lebanon, Conn. Rev. Eleazer Wheelock, D.D., was the first president of Dartmouth College, Hanover, N. H., 1766, which grew originally out of an Indian school of 1754. Dr. Wheelock d. Saturday, April 24, 1779. Children: (1) Theodora, b. 1736; m. 1751, Alex. Phelps; m. 2d, 1777, Capt. John Young; d. 1786, aged 70. (2) Ruth, b. 1740; m. Rev. William Patton, Hartford, Conn., who d. 1775, aged 87. She survived 56 years, and d. 1831. (3) Rodolphus, b.

1742; graduated Yale, 1765, and d. 1817. (4) Mary, b. 1748; m. Prof. Bezaleel Woodward, 1772, and d. 1807. (5) Abigail, b. 1751; m Prof. Sylvester Ripley, and d. at Fryeburg, Me., 1818. (6) John, LL.D., b. 1754; succeeded his father as president of the college, and d. 1817. (7) Eleazer, b. 1756. (8) James, b. 1759.

iii MARY, b. 1686; m. David Clark, 1708, and d. 1714.
iv ELEAZER, b. 1690; d. 1705.
v REBECCA, b. 1692; m. John Fisher; Jeremiah Adams, 1715, Medway.
vi EPHRAIM, b. 1697; deacon, 1738, prominent in town affairs, etc.; m. 1721, Miriam Bullen (Elisha, Samuel, to Watertown 1636, freeman 1641, owned a house 1646, which was burnt by Indians 1675, selectman, 1682; m. Mary Morse, and both d. 1691); she d. 1727, aged 25; he m. 2d, 1729, Priscilla Plimpton (Joseph, Joseph, John); she d. 1740, aged 36; he m. 3d, Experience Bullard (John, Joseph, John); she d. 1755, aged 45; he m. 4th, Mary Partridge (Nathaniel, William), widow of Samuel Ellis (Eleazer, John); she d. 1762, aged 62; he m. 5th, 1766, Elizabeth Colburn of Dedham, and d. 1785; she d. 1775. Children: (1) Ebenezer (1724–1812), called "Master Wheelock," as he was a great school-teacher, 1756 to 1775; he m. 1790, Sarah Plimpton (Sylvester, Jonathan, Joseph, John), who d. 1844, aged 94. (2) Ralph, b. 1726; settled in Sturbridge. (3) Abigail, b. 1730; m. Lemuel Kollack, 1752. (4) Joseph, b. 1732; m. 1770, Sarah Clark; taught school, 1763; selectman, 1767 to '70; to Sherborn, and d. 1787; 6 children; widow m. 2d, Samuel Sanger, 1789. (5) Ephraim, b. 1733; was 4 years in the French and Indian war; captain at Louisburg, 1758; colonel in the Revolution; m. 1767, Mary Clapp of Walpole (d. 1808), and d. 1826; 6 children. (6) Moses, b. and d. 1736. (7) Moses, 1737–1801; settled in Westboro'. (8) Ichabod, b. and d. 1740. (9) Priscilla, 1743–1834; m. 1762, Silas Mason (Thomas, Ebenezer, Thomas).
vii ABIGAIL, b. 1699; m. 1723, Peter Cooledge.

5 iii. Joseph Wheelock (Gershom, Rev. Ralph), b. 1672; settled in Lancaster, Worcester county; m. Abigail ——, 1725; member of the first church, 1748; d. July 19, 1752; she d. Feb. 9, 1751.

CHILDREN.

i OLIVE, b. Jan. 7, 1726; m. Jonathan Broadstreet of Lunenburg, July 2, 1741.
ii OLIVER, b. Dec. 7, 1727; m. Lucretia Smith, 1782.

		iii	JOSEPH, b. Feb. 14, 1729; m. Alice Page, Lunenburg, 1751; 10 children; m. 2d, Olive ——. He was a soldier in the Revolution, and d. March 10, 1778.

    iii JOSEPH, b. Feb. 14, 1729; m. Alice Page, Lunenburg, 1751; 10 children; m. 2d, Olive ——. He was a soldier in the Revolution, and d. March 10, 1778.
    iv PHINEAS, b. Nov. 9, 1731.
    v JOHN, b. Sept. 9, 1733; fifer, drummer, and sergeant in the Revolution, and d. Feb. 7, 1778.
    vi ABNOR, b. Nov. 16, 1735; m. Mary Brown, April 12, 1758; 5 children, Lunenburg.
    vii PRUDENCE, b. Nov. 28, 1737; m. John Warner, 1757.
7 viii ABEL, b. June 29, 1739; went to Nova Scotia.
    ix ELIJAH, b. May 26, 1741, Leominster; m. Anna Wilds of Shirley, July, 1775, and d. from a fall from a cart, 1775.
    x ELISHA, b. March 26, 1743.

6. iii. Obadiah Wheelock (Benjamin, Rev. Ralph), b. 1685; m. Elizabeth Darling, 1708, and was a man of note in Rehoboth and Milford.

CHILDREN.

    i ELIZABETH, b. July 11, 1709; m. Ephraim Daniels, 1733.
8 ii OBADIAH, b. Sept. 21, 1712.
    iii SAMUEL, b. Sept. 6, 1714; m. Hannah Ammidown, 1738.
    iv HANNAH, b. Aug. 18, 1716; m. Joshua Underwood, 1737.
    v EBENEZER, b. Aug. 13, 1718; m. Mary Slocum, 1738.
    vi REBECCA, b. Aug. 30, 1720; m. Benjamin Fisk, 1747.
    vii MARGARET, b. Feb. 18, 1723; m. James Albee, 1789.
    viii JOSIAH, b. March 30, 1725; m. Ephraim Clark, 1748.

7. iv. Abel Wheelock (Joseph, Gershom, Rev. Ralph), b. in Lancaster, Mass., June 29, 1739; went to Annapolis county, N. S., 1760; m. Sarah Foster (Benjamin, Jacob, Isaac, Reginald), April 26, 1764, and lived in Granville, as farmers.

CHILDREN.

9 i BENJAMIN, b. Jan. 26, 1765.
    ii JOSEPH, b. July 7, 1767; d. young.
10 iii JOHN, b. April, 1769.
    iv SARAH, b. Feb. 24, 1771; m. Thomas Wheeler Banks. Children: (1) William, b. March 17, 1791; m. Harriet, daughter of Asaph Wheelock. (2) Sarah (with Ruth Foster when she was killed by the tree), m. Andrew Brown, Jr. (3) Abel, m. Susan Freeman of Brookfield. (4) John, m. Nancy, daughter of Jacob Benjamin. (5) Betsy, m. Clark Felch. (6) Ezekiel, m. Elizabeth, daughter of Allen Parker, and Elizabeth, daughter of Jonas Ward. (7) Rufus, m. Annie Hemming. (8) Sophia, m. Benjamin, son of Samuel Wheelock. (9) Dea. Thomas, m. Salome, sister to Nancy Benjamin. (10) Clarinda, m.

Robert Barteaux (Charles, William, Philip). (11) Zachariah, m. Mary, daughter of Samuel Dodge.

11 v SAMUEL, b. Jan. 6, 1773.
vi ELIZABETH, b. 1775; m. Major Ezekiel Cleveland, Jr. See Whitman.
12 vii ABEL, b. April 23, 1777.
viii ABIGAIL, b. 1779; m. Samuel Felch (Daniel, Ebenezer, John, Henry, Henry), and had (1) Daniel, d. an old bachelor. (2) Sarah, m. Charlton Beals (Elijah, Abel). (3) Hannah, m. Elijah Roop. (4) John, m. Lieut. ——, son of Rev. Thomas Delong.
ix OLIVER, b. 1782; d. young.

8. iv. Obadiah Wheelock (Obadiah, Benjamin, Rev. Ralph), b. Sept. 21, 1712; m. Martha, daughter of Joseph and Sarah (Lovett) Sumner, Oct. 26, 1738; lived in Mendon, Mass.

CHILDREN.

i ZIPPORAH, b. May 12, 1734.
ii MARTHA, b. March 17, 1736.
13 iii OBADIAH, b. July 7, 1738.
14 iv JOSEPH, b. July 17, 1740.
15 v ELIAS, b. April 17, 1743.
vi ABIGAIL, b. April 24, 1746; m. —— Moulton.
vii JESSE, b. Oct. 2, 1748; m. Abigail Lovett, and d. Saco, Me., 1816; 6 children.
viii AMARIAH, b. Sept. 18, 1752.

9. v. Benjamin Wheelock (Abel, Joseph, Gershom, Rev. Ralph), b. in Granville, N. S., Jan. 26, 1765; m. Elizabeth, daughter of John and Elizabeth (Roundtree) Jacques, 1790, and lived in Granville.

CHILDREN.

i ELIZABETH, b. March 28, 1791; m. George Wade and had (1) Gilbert, b. 1811. (2) Phebe, b. 1813. (3) Churchill, b. 1815. (4) Benjamin, b. 1817. (5) Sylvanus, b. 1819. (6) Abel, b. 1821. (7) George, b. 1823. (8) Mary Elizabeth, b. 1827. (9) Lucretia, b. 1833.
ii SARAH, b. 1794; m. Abner Foster. See Foster.
iii ABEL, b. Aug. 27, 1797; m. Elizabeth Ann, daughter of Ezekiel Foster, Jr., and had Joseph Israel, b. Jan. 1, 1828; m. Elizabeth Ann Foster (cousin), daughter of Thomas Foster; she d.; he m. 2d, Ruth Bent. Mr. Wheelock d.; she d. Aug. 16, 1859.
iv MARY, b. Aug. 7, 1799; m. Thomas, son of Ezekiel Foster, Jr. See Foster.
16 v WILLIAM K., b. Sept. 14, 1804.

ALLIED FAMILIES.

10. v. John Wheelock (Abel, Joseph, Gershom, Rev. Ralph), b. April, 1769; m. Mary Gilliatt, daughter of William and Rebecca (Appleby) Gilliatt, from England, and lived at Torbrook, N. S.; four children; she d.; he m. 2d, Mittie, daughter of Maj. Nat. Parker, and d. Aug., 1845; she d. 1863, aged 75.

CHILDREN.

17 i SERGT.-MAJ. ABEL, b. 1793.
    ii ANN, b. 1704; m. John Hoffman, and had (1) Abel, m. Charlotte, daughter of William Allen. (2) Mary Ann, m. William Copeland. (3) John, m. Ann Shipp, widow of D. Robinson. (4) Rebecca, m. Henry, son of Handley Banks. (5) Sarah, m. Joseph Wheelock (Samuel, Abel); 2d, Dea. Leason Baker. (6) Joseph, m. Sophia, daughter of Parker Viditoe. (7) Silas, m. Elizabeth, daughter of Benjamin Rumsey; 2d, Amanda Banks, widow of Archibald Kendall.
    iii REBECCA, b. Sept. 10, 1796; m. Guy Carleton Payson (Jonathan, Jonathan, Jonathan, Ephraim, Dea. Edward, over to Roxbury, 1636, d. about 1690), and d. Nov. 10, 1843; he d. April 15, 1830, aged 40. Children: (1) Cynthia, b. 1818; m. Elias Grimes, Esq. (Hugh, Patrick), and live near Lawrence, Mass. (2) Edward W., b. 1820; m. Margaret, daughter of John Murdock, in Boston. (3) Guy C., b. 1822; m. Mary P. Ames; Fanny Nichols. (4) Jane, b. 1826; m. Asaph, son of Dea. Daniel Whitman. (5) Holland, b. 1829; m. Mary F. Goodwin.
    iv MARY, b. 1799; m. Peter, son of Obadiah and Hannah (Chute) Morse, and had (1) Waity, m. Elliott, son of Abednego Sprowle. (2) Obadiah, m. Mary Eliza, daughter of Stephen Henry Jefferson. (3) Valentine. (4) Demaris, m. Silas Viditoe (William, Jesse). (5) Mary Eliza, m. James, son of Richard Armstrong. (6) John, m. Margaret, daughter of Abednego Sprowle. (7) Sarah Jane, d. about 40. (8) Salome, m. —— Armstrong. (9) Almira, m. Abednego, son of John Allen. (10) Edward, m. Charlot, daughter of Henry Marshall. (11) Isaiah, d. young.

11. v. Samuel Wheelock (Abel, Joseph, Gershom, Rev. Ralph), b. in Granville, N. S., Jan. 6, 1773; m. Mary, daughter of Walter Wilkins; lived at Torbrook, and d. July, 1850; she d. 1832, aged 49.

CHILDREN.

    i JOSEPH, b. 1807; m. Sarah, daughter of John Hoffman, and d. 1873; she m. 2d, Dea. Leason Baker.
    ii BENJAMIN, b. 1809; m. Sophia, daughter of Thomas W.

Banks, and d. at Torbrook, 1891. They had (1) Mary E., b. 1836; d. 1837. (2) Albert, b. 1838. (3) Clarinda, b. 1840; d. 1889. (4) Malinda, b. 1842; m. Abner B., son of Abner Parker, and d. 1888. (5) Rufus W., b. Nov. 9, 1844; m. Emma J., daughter of Eben Woodbury, 1873; 4 children; to Lawrence, 1870. (6) James, b. 1846; d. 1860. (7) Josephine, b. 1848.

iii SARAH, b. 1811; scalded to death, 1815.

iv WALTER, b. April 1, 1813; m. Mary, daughter of Silas Gates; 2d, Jane, daughter of Jacob Gates (two cousins), and had (1) John Whitefield, b. Aug. 14, 1849. (2) Ingram Bill, b. Nov. 4, 1851; m. Hattie, daughter of Alex. Bowey, 1875; Portland, Me. (3) Maggie I., b. March 15, 1853; d. March, 1877. (4) Clara E., b. April 7, 1860; m. Samuel Hooper, 1880. (5) Charles A., b. April 15, 1867; d. in July. Mr. Wheelock moved from Nictaux Falls, N. S., to Boston, 1869; to Lawrence, 1871.

v JAMES, b. 1815; m. Henrietta (Freeman) Smith; had Josephine, b. about 1845; m. William, son of George Miller, Middleton, N. S. Mrs. W. d.; he m. 2d, Lydia Palfrey, widow of John Crisp, and d. Oct. 29, 1882.

vi WILLIAM, b. 1817; m. Love, daughter of Samuel Roberts, and had (1) Lovena, m. W. H. Hamilton, and d. Sept., 1892. (2) Ann, m. John, son of Nathaniel Parker. (3) George Whitefield, m. Annabel Brown (John, Andrew), and d. Oct., 1892. (4) Sarah. (5) Samuel, m. Mary, daughter of Benjamin Prince. (6) Handley, m. Adelia Pierce, widow of Reuben Roberts, son of Acel. (7) William, 1856–1873. (8) Bronte, m. Arthur, son of James Spinney. (9) Charles O., d. aged 17. (10) Winnie A., m. Albert H. Winslow (William Henry, Henry B., Aaron, Zebulon, Elisha, Samuel, Ephraim, Samuel Winsley, over to Salisbury, Mass., 1638, d. 1663), and live in Lynn.

vii WESLEY, b. 1819; m. Mary Jane Masters (Rev. Ezekiel, Abram, Ezekiel), and d. in Boston, Feb. 11, 1892. Children: (1) Guilford D., m. Jessie, daughter of John Pierce. (2) Syretha, m. Nelson Pierce (Henry, Willis, from Ireland), and live in West Roxbury. (3) James Wesley; d. young. (4) Mary Frances, m. Jesse A., son of Edward Van Horne, and live in South Boston.

viii REV. GEORGE WHITEFIELD, b. 1822; d. in the Bahamas, a Methodist, 1846.

ix ANTHONY, b. 1824; m. Josephine ——, Deep Creek, Va.; 3 children.

x SAMUEL, b. 1826; d. soon.

xi DEA. SAMUEL, b. Dec. 24, 1828; m. Maggie, daughter of Jacob Gates, June 24, 1858; went to Boston, 1872; to East Boston and Winthrop, 1885. They had (1) Arthur Brinton, b. 1861; m. Ada Hall. (2) George W., b. 1862;

m. (3) Joseph H., b. 1865; m. Euphemia Kezia Lee, Brooklyn, N. Y. (4) Ida May, b. 1873.
xii Rev. John, b. 1831; d. in Nova Scotia, a Baptist, about 1855.

12. v. Abel Wheelock (Abel, Joseph, Gershom, Rev. Ralph), b. April 23, 1777; m. Parney, daughter of Maj. Nat. Parker, Nov. 20, 1801, and lived at Nictaux; d. Aug. 30, 1856; she d. Feb. 24, 1875, aged 92.

CHILDREN.

i Dea. Samuel, b. Feb. 20, 1803; m. Eliza Ann Barteaux (Charles, William, Philip), 1829, and d. Feb. 27, 1872; she d. 1885, aged 82.
ii Lucinda, b. Sept. 22, 1804; d. Jan. 28, 1827.
iii Olive, b. Dec. 24, 1806; m. Robert Barteaux, 1827, brother to Eliza Ann; had 7 children, and d. May 31, 1857; he d. 1875, aged 71.
iv Parney, b. Jan. 20, 1808; m. James Barteaux, twin to Robert, 1829; had 11 children, and d. June 1, 1875; he d. 1875 also.
v John, b. July 28, 1811; m. Emily J. Dodge (Charles, Stephen, Tristram, Tristram, Tristram), 1838; she d. 1882, aged 67; he m. 2d, Adelaide C. Cosgrove, 1883.
vi Dea. Abel Maynard, b. Dec. 28, 1813; m. Eliza, daughter of Walter Wilkins, 1840; she d. 1882, aged 69; he m. 2d, Elizabeth Cutten, widow of Beniah Morse, April 24, 1883. Maynard, son of William and Mary (Wilkins) Brown, was adopted by Dea. A. M. Wheelock, at Berwick, N. S.; educated at Arcadia College, and is a Baptist minister in Nova Scotia.
vii Letitia, b. July 15, 1816; m. James Spinney, 1834, Torbrook; 13 children.
viii Mittie, b. July 15, 1816; m. James P. Wiswall (1801-1878), 1839; 10 children.
18 ix Ezekiel Cleveland, b. Oct. 3, 1818.

13. v. Capt. Obadiah Wheelock (Obadiah, Obadiah, Benjamin, Rev. Ralph), b. in Mendon, Worcester county, Mass., July 7, 1738; taken to Nova Scotia, on the schooner *Charming Molly*, from Boston to Annapolis, May, 1760, and settled near Bridgetown; m. Rachel Rice (Beriah, Thomas, Thomas, Dea. Edmund), and d. 1807.

CHILDREN.

i Asaph, m. 1797, Mary Church, and had (1) Thomas, b. Jan. 6, 1799; m. Caroline, daughter of Ward Wheelock, (2) Hoyt, off unknown. (3) Harriet, m. William, son of

Thomas W. Banks. (4) Morton, m. Elizabeth O'Brien. (5) Hannah, b. 1804; m. William W., son of Asa Foster, and d. 1890. (6) Obadiah, d. in California. (7) Constant, m. (8) Mary, m. William Miller. (9) Sally, m. Samuel, son of Robert Neily.

ii LUCY, m. Elkanah Morton, M.P.P.
iii CALVIN, m. Mary Pennell; he was a singing master.
iv MARY, m. Walter Willett.
v SAMUEL, m. Ann Eliza ——.
vi IRENE, m. Jesse Hoyt (Jesse, James, Joseph, Dea. Zerubabel, Walter, Simon of Charlestown, Mass., 1628).
vii AMERICUS.

14. v. Joseph Wheelock, brother to the above, b. in Mendon, Mass., July 17, 1740; m. Deborah, daughter of Jonas and Thankful (Ward) Farnsworth, Nov. 5, 1769; m. 2d, Sibyl Tarbell (1769-1856), of Groton, Mass., June 16, 1795, and d. Aug. 9, 1820 in Nova Scotia.

CHILDREN.

i WELCOME, b. June 23, 1796; was high sheriff of Annapolis county, N. S.; m. Mary Eliza Andrews, and d. June 8, 1856. Children: John Andrews, Isabel, Edward C., Kate, James, and Thomas.
ii JOSEPH, ESQ., b. 1798; was a merchant, ship-builder, and owner in Bridgetown, N. S.; he m. Mercy Whitman (Abram, John, John, Rev. Zach., Dea. John), 1824; she d. July 9, 1869, aged 62; he m. 2d, Hannah Whitman, sister to Mercy, widow of George Norris of Halifax (who d. 1865, leaving 3 children); she d. 1877, aged 73; he d. April 27, 1880. Children: (1) John, b. 1825; m. Mary F. Adams, 1867; firm of J. W. Wheelock & Co., oil-merchants, New York City; 4 children. (2) James A., b. 1827; m. Harriet W. Savage, 1857; Middletown, Conn.; maker of firearms; d. at Cromwell, Conn., Nov. 10, 1875. (3) Abram W., b. 1829; farmer, St. Paul, Minn. (4) Joseph A., b. 1831; editor the *Pioneer Press*, St. Paul, Minn.; m. 1861, Katharine French; 4 children. (5) Charlotte L., b. 1832; m. William A. Miller, St. Paul; 4 children. (6) Jesse T. W., b. 1834; d. 1835. (7) Hannah M., b. 1836; m. 1860, Edward W. Chipman, St. Paul; 6 children. (8) Jesse E. W., b. 1838; d. 1879, St. Paul, Minn. (9) Mary E., b. 1840; d. 1865; St. Paul, Minn. (10) Anna A., b. 1842; m. 1877, Edwin Ruggles, lawyer, Bridgetown; 2 children. (11) William A. B., b. 1844; m. 1866, Minnie A. G. Ward; merchant, St. Paul, Minn.; 5 children.
iii AMARIAH, b. 1800; d. off to sea, about 1821.

ALLIED FAMILIES. ccxxxix

   iv AZUBAH, b. 1803; m. 1848, David, son of Oliver Foster (his second wife); had a son James A.
   v TARBELL, b. 1805; m. Mary Fisher, daughter of John Easson.
   vi SIBYL, b. 1808; d. young.
   vii REV. JESSE, b. 1811; d. 1841; Methodist.

15. v. Elias, Esq., the other brother, b. April 17, 1743; m. Sarah Rice, daughter of Beriah, and lived at Nictaux, Annapolis county, N. S.; farmer; d. July 9, 1821.

CHILDREN.

   i ABIGAIL, b. 1766; m. Michael Martin, the celebrated singing master (1770-1853); she d. 1859. Children: (1) Edward, b. 1800; m. Ann, daughter of Joseph Foster; 3 children, Mary Ann, Michael, and Edward; m. 2d, Sophia Starratt, wid. of Zeb. Durland; 3d, Cecelia Beals, wid. of —— Rathburn. (2) Fanny, m. George Merry; 4 children. (3) Ambrose, d. at about 30. (4) Amoret, m. James, son of Silas Bent; 9 children. (5) Zilphia, m. Joseph Foster, Jr.; 4 children. (6) Harriet, m. John Viets. (7) Sarah, m. Botsford Viets, two cousins.
   ii SOPHIA, m. Lieut.-Col. James Eager.
   iii WARD, m. 1804, Azuba Gates, and had Caroline, Armanella, Artemas, Beriah, Dean, Maurice, Elias, Susan, and Louise.
   iv ELIAS, m. Mary Hook (?), and d. in England.
   v SUMNER, m. Mary, daughter of Walter (?) Willett.
   vi SARAH, m. Elkhanah Morton, M. P. P.
   vii CHARLES, b. June 17, 1791; m. Hannah B. Balsor (Foster, Christopher, from Germany), Nov. 1831, and had (1) Sybilla, b. 1833. (2) Rupert Canning, b. 1835. (3) Sophia, b. 1837. (4) Elias, b. 1839. (5) Priscilla, b. 1842. (6) Jessie M., b. 1850. Mr. Charles Wheelock, a merchant and teacher, d. 1880. She came to Mass., 1881; to Middleton, 1885.
   viii AMORET, m. Samuel Morse. See Morse.
   ix BETSEY, d. single, over 80.

In an obituary notice in the *Royal Gazette*, 1821, it is stated that the brothers of Joseph and Elias Wheelock were all present at the capture of Quebec, 1759.

16. vi. William Ker Wheelock (Benjamin, Abel, Joseph, Gershom, Rev. Ralph), b. in Granville, Sept. 14, 1804; m. Charlotte Ricketson (Jordan, Abednego), Feb. 14, 1827, and d. May 16, 1870; she d. Sept. 12, 1890, aged 82.

CHILDREN.

i JAMES EDWARD, b. Aug. 17, 1828; was a school-teacher; m. Oct. 17, 1861, Maria, daughter of Isaac Phinney.
ii MIRIAM ELIZABETH, b. Jan. 28, 1831; m. Nov. 8, 1855, Perry Phinney, brother to Maria.
iii SUSAN AMELIA, b. Oct. 8, 1832; m. September 6, 1870, Elisha Coates, and d. Oct. 8, 1876.
iv MARY ANN, b. Nov. 11, 1835; m. Oct. 29, 1861, William R. Ray.
v ROBERT PARKER, b. Sept. 6, 1838; m. Jan. 1, 1867, Mary E. Ray.
vi HARRIET SOPHIA, b. May 28, 1840; m. April 10, 1860, Ezekiel B. W. Foster.
vii ABEL BENJAMIN, b. Feb. 9, 1843; m. Dec. 3, 1863, Mary E. Healy.
viii WILLIAM EVERITT, b. May 24, 1845; m. Oct. 8, 1870, Clara Cisson.
ix CHARLOT EUPHEMIA, b. Aug. 2, 1847; m. June 4, 1867, Hiram Purdy.
x HANNAH MARIA, b. April 8, 1849; d. young by accident.
xi ALICE MINETTA, b. Aug. 19, 1851; d. about 1871.
xii ISRAEL LONGLEY, b. Sept. 22, 1853; m. April 8, 1877, Bertha Atwood.

17. vi. Sergt.-Maj. Abel Wheelock (John, Abel, Joseph, Gershom, Rev. Ralph), b. at Torbrook, N. S., 1793; m. Jane Foster (Joseph, Ezekiel, Benjamin, Jacob, Isaac, Reginald), 1822, and lived there as farmers; d. Feb., 1870; she d. March 4, 1877, aged 75.

CHILDREN.

i ELIAKIM, b. 1824; m. Lavenia Beals (Charlton, Andrew, Abel, Abel, Andrew, Jeremiah, Jeremiah, John, Norfolk, Eng., to Hingham, Mass., 1638; d. 1688, aged 100); 4 children.
ii MIRIAM, b. 1826; m. Simpson Woodbury (Foster, Jonathan); 13 children.
iii EZRA, b. 1828; d. of small-pox, March, 1848.
iv FLETCHER, b. 1830; m. Harriet Hemming; had Arthur and Leander.
v JOHN, b. 1832; m. Charlot, daughter of Joseph Hoffman; 8 children.
vi HANNAH, b. 1834; m. Samuel, son of Edward Sprowle; 2 sons.
vii MAJ. CLEVELAND, b. 1837; m. Mary L. North (Stephen, William, Isaac); 12 children; live in Lawrence, Mass.
viii MARY JANE, b. 1840; m. Charles, son of Isaac Marshall; 5 children.

ALLIED FAMILIES.

18. vi. Dea. Ezekiel Cleveland Wheelock (Abel, Abel, Joseph, Gershom, Rev. Ralph), b. at Nictaux, N. S., Oct. 3, 1818; m. Amy Elizabeth Dodge (Charles, Stephen, Tristram, Tristram, Tristram, of Block Island, R. I., 1659), May 10, 1842; besides being a pious, exemplary man in the Baptist church, he was a good mechanic and wheelwright. They moved from Torbrook, N. S., to Boston, Mass., 1860, and he met a sudden death on Kingston street by having a chisel thrust through him, working at a turning lathe, Sept. 3, 1866; she d. in Boston, Sept. 5, 1883, aged nearly 60.

CHILDREN.

i Rev. Isaac Robinson, b. Jan. 24, 1843; graduated Brown University 1869, Newton 1872, pastor Pleasant street Baptist church, Worcester, 1875, then to Fitchburg 10 years, then to Meriden, Conn., till 1892, when he moved to Boston. He m. Rosalie H., daughter of Geoge Washington and Cynthia Ann (Hayes*) Hutchins, of Tallahassee, Fla., in Providence, R. I., June 13, 1872, and had (1) Elmore Hayes, b. July 29, 1873; d. May 24, 1874. (2) Merton Hayes, b. Feb. 15, 1876. (3) Howard Bradford, b. Feb. 6, 1878. (4) Rosalie Hutchins, b. June 24, 1884.
ii Emma Jane, b. Sept. 21, 1844; m. Sept. 26, 1869, John W. Larry of Maine; live at Whitewood, N. W. T.
iii Genevieve, b. Feb. 11, 1847; m. June 1, 1880, John Maxwell Brown, printer, Boston.
iv Estelle, b. July 21, 1850; d. Jan. 24, 1852.
v Edna Graham, b. Feb. 12, 1853; m. Sept. 23, 1873, Charles Liffler, insurance agent, Boston.
vi Howard Stanley, b. Sept. 26, 1855; insurance agent in Boston; m. June 2, 1880, Fanny Allen, daughter of Chester Houghton; son, Howard Maxwell, b. Feb. 8, 1882.
vii Lauretta Hayden, b. March 20, 1858; m. Jan. 21, 1878, George William Blish, Prof. of Elocution in Boston.
viii Nessy, b. May 16, 1861; d. May 27.

WHITMAN.

1. i. Deacon John Whitman (probably grandson of John, a martyr, burnt at Ostend, 1572, aged 49), of Holt, Coventry, or Hertfordshire, England; came over in 1637 or 8, and settled in Weymouth, 12 miles south of Boston, and d. Nov. 13, 1692, aged about 90. His wife Ruth d. Aug. 17, 1662. Their children were

* Cousin to President R. B. Hayes.

Sarah, Thomas, John, Mary, Elizabeth, Judith, Hannah, Zachariah, and Abiah. All married and had families.

2. ii. **Rev. Zachariah**, (Deacon John), b. 1644 (H. U. 1668), m. Sarah, daughter of Dr. John Alcock (H. U. 1646) of Roxbury, 1670, and d. Nov. 5, 1726; she d. "April ye 3rd 1715," aged 65. Their children were Zachariah, John, Joanna, Rev. Samuel, Sarah, Elizabeth, John, Mary, and Eunice.

3. iii. **Deacon John**, b. 1688; m. Mary Graves, Charlestown; she d. 1716, aged 18; he m. 2d, Dorcas, daughter of Capt. Jacob Green and widow of Thomas Chitty; she d. 1718, aged 34; he m. 3d, Margaret, daughter of Rev. Thomas Clark and widow of John Damon; she d. 1758, aged 66. He was a J. P., deacon in the church, and a wealthy useful man in the town; d. 1772. Their children were Jacob, John, Lucy, Thomas, Zachariah, Jean, and Charles.

4. iv. **Deacon John**, b. 1717, in Stow, Mass.; m. Mary, daughter of Rev. Mr. Foster, of Stafford, Conn., 1747, and went over to Annapolis, N. S., in the sloop *Charming Molly*, June, 1760, with 45 others, and settled on a tract of land on Saw Mill Creek, south of Annapolis, that extended to the Wilmot line. He d. Sept. 12, 1763; she m. 2d, Samuel Bancroft, and d. 1812, aged 85.

CHILDREN.

i Dorcas, b. May 5, 1749; m. Capt. Eben Perry, who was killed at the battle of Bennington, Vt., 1777; had 6 children, lost 5. The widow m. 2d, Samuel McIntyre, and lived in Nova Scotia some years. Then they went to Upper Canada; and in Southwold, Elgin county, Ont., they lived with their family; and the old folks and part of the family died there. Most of them were pious members of the Baptist Church; two or three were deacons. From records and reports there we find that Samuel and Dorcas McIntyre went to Upper Canada before the American War. They had 13 children, of whom 5 or 6 went with the parents to the then far West. The old gentleman d. July 14, 1827, aged 78; she d. April 16, 1830, aged 81. Those who went were: (1) Deacon James, b. 1779; m. Nancy, daughter of Robert and Mary (Morrill) McDormand, had several children and d. near Chatham, Kent county, 1846; she d. June, 1869, aged 90. (2) Hannah, b. 1780; m. Obadiah Griffin; had 15 children, and d. in Southwold, June 2, 1871, aged 91; he d. Dec. 1, 1870, aged 93. (3) Esther, b. 178–; m. John Philpot, jr., and had 13 children. (4) Deacon Daniel, b. 1789; m. Elizabeth, daughter of Jacob Bodine; she d. Sept. 22, 1839, aged 55; he m. 2d, Mary, daughter of John Lumley and widow of William Lodge; she d. Sept. 21, 1841, aged 45; he m. 3d, Margaret, daughter of John Philpot, sen., and widow of Wm. Roach, and d. Aug. 13, 1857; she d. about 1860, aged 58. His children were Sarah (m. Coaglain Lumley), Catharine (m. James Lodge), Jacob (m. Ann, daughter of Dougald McColl), Abram (m. Margaret Milligan), and Mary (m. Joseph Lodge and Nicol McColl).

ii DANIEL, b. 1750; m. Sarah Kendall (Elisha, Thomas, Thomas, Francis of 1640), 1778, and lived at Rosette, Annapolis county, N. S.; 10 children, d. 1840; she d. 1845, aged 84.

iii HANNAH, b. 1751; m. William E. Tufts, descendant of Rev. John of Newbury, Mass., 1772; 9 children. New Albany, N. S.

5 iv EDWARD, b. 1752.

v JOHN, b. 1753; m. Elizabeth Rice (Phineas, Perez, Thomas, Thomas, Deacon Edmund), from Stow, Mass., 1780, settled at Round Hill, N. S. 11 children and d. 1853, aged 100; she d. 1856, aged 103.

vi SALOME, b. 1755; m. Maj. Ezekiel Cleveland (Lemuel, Isaac, Edward, Moses of Woburn, Mass., 1640), 1772; lived at Nictaux; 2 children; she m. 2d, Maj. Nat Parker, as his 2d wife; had 10 children more. See Parker.

vii ELNATHAN, b. 1756; d. 1765.

viii JACOB, b. 1757; m. Annie Spinney, and d. Sept., 1837; 8 children.

ix ISAAC, b. 1758; d. 1777.

x ABRAM, b. 1761; m. 1793, Hannah Webber, and d. 1854; 9 children.

xi MERCY, b. 1763; m. Nelson Freeman (1764-1819), 1787 (Simeon, Elisha, Samuel, Deacon Samuel, Samuel over to Watertown, 1630), and d. 1828; 9 children.

5. v. Edward Whitman (Deacon John, Deacon John, Rev. Zachariah, Deacon John), b. Stow, Mass., 1752; m. Dorothy, daughter of Capt. Oldham Gates, Annapolis county, N. S., 1775; he weighed 300 lbs., and d. 1829.

CHILDREN.

i OLDHAM, b. 1777; m. Nancy A., daughter of Benjamin Fairn and widow of James Roach, of Rosette; 10 children; d. 1848; she d. about 1850, aged 70.

ii MERCY, m. Andrew Kniffin, a shoemaker, New Albany, N. S., and d. May, 1875; he d. 1870; 8 children.

ALLIED FAMILIES.

 iii JACOB, m. Elizabeth Langley; 11 children; Marshall Mountain; both d. 1850.
 iv LYDIA, b. 1786; m. John Merry, 1809, and d. 1871; he d. 1858; 8 children.
 v SALOME, b. 1790; m. George Armstrong, 1807, and d. 1872; he d. 1876, aged 96; 12 children.
 vi EDWARD, m. Elizabeth Tileston, daughter of Capt. Christopher Prince, about 1808; 5 children. He sailed for Antigua, W. I., 1817, and was never after heard from.
 vii CHARLES, m. Lois Dykeman, New Albany, and d. 1850; she d. 1862; 9 children.
 viii ASA, m. Mary Durland.
 ix DOROTHEA, m. Ferdinand Shafner, 1812, and d. 1874; 8 children.
6 x JAMES, b. 1790 (?).
 xi DIADAMY, b. 1797; m. James Steele, and both d. 1865; he aged 95; 8 children.
 xii MARGARET, b. 1801; m. Henry Kent, 1822, and d. 1887. Lived at Round Hill; he d. 1852; 8 children.

6. vi. James Whitman (Edward, Deacon John, Deacon John, Rev. Zachariah, Deacon John), b. at or near Rosette, about 1790; m. Maria Longley (Isaac, Israel, William, John, William, William, William of Lynn, 1636), 1812, and d. 1832; she d. 1859 aged 65.

CHILDREN.

 i ISRAEL, b. 1813; m. Charlotte daughter of Joseph and Sarah Spinney, Torbrook; 3 children.
 ii MARGARET LOUISA, b. Feb. 12, 1818; m. J. M. Chute. See No. 130.
 iii LUCY A., b. 1823; m. John McGregor, 1840.
 iv ISAAC J., b. 1833; m. Sarah M. Spinney, 1855, Marlboro', Mass.; 5 children. Son, Rev. B. L., President of Colby University, Maine.
 v DAVID E., b. 1838; m. Emma Louisa Rood, daughter of William P. Brown, 1876; Torbrook; 2 children.

1. John Whitman.

2. Sarah, 1st child of Deacon John Whitman, the emigrant; b. about 1627; m. Abram, son of Thomas Jones, tailor of Hingham; had 8 children. They lived at Hull, and both d. 1718.

3. Sarah Jones, the 8th child, m. Mordecai Lincoln (b. in 1657, son of Samuel, who came over in 1637), blacksmith in Hull; had 6 children. They moved to Scituate about 1704 and d. about 1730.

4. Mordecai Lincoln, Jr., b. April 24, 1686; m. Hannah Salter of Freehold, N. J., 1714; 3 or 4 children; m. 2d, Mary ——, and had 2 or 3 more; he d. 1736.

5. **John,** by the first wife, m. —— Moore (?) and owned land in Union, Penn. In 1758 he sold out and went to Augusta county, Va. His sons were John, Thomas, Abram, Isaac, and Jacob, with daughters and perhaps other sons.

6. **Abram,** m. Mary Shipley, in North Carolina, and had Mordecai, Josiah, and Thomas, and about 1782 the family moved to Kentucky, and had Mary and Nancy.

7. **Thomas,** m. Nancy Hanks, near Springfield, Ky., Sept. 23, 1806, and had (8) Abraham, b. July 12, 1809; m. Mary Todd, and had 4 children. He was the 16th President of the United States, shamefully murdered in Washington, April 14, 1865. Thomas, his father, lived in Indiana, and m. a 2d wife, Sarah Bush; d. 1851. It will be seen by examination that Abraham Lincoln was in the 7th generation on the Lincoln, and in the 8th generation on the Whitman.

We here give a parellel of relationship:—

John Whitman,	Zack,	John,	John,	Edward,	James,
Lincoln,	Sarah Jones,	Mordecai, L.,	Mord. L., Jr.,	John,	Abram,
	Bro. & sister.	Cousins.	2d cousins.	3d cousins.	4th cousins.
	Margaret L. Chute,			Israel James Chute.	
	Thomas,			Pres. Abraham.	
	5th cousins.			6th cousins.	

WOODWARD—WOODWORTH.

1. i. **Walter Woodworth,** said to have come over from Kent, Eng., with Gov. John Winthrop (1587-1649), in 1630. He was a resident of Scituate, Mass., in 1633. In Oct., 1664, the Court granted to John Hanmore and Walter Woodward of Scituate, each 60 acres of land, near to Weymouth, provided it entrench not upon former grants, and also that they pay the Indians purchase for it, if any be justly demanded.

In 1635, Mr. Woodward lived on the 3d lot in Kent, south side of the meetinghouse lane in Scituate, where the men of Kent county, Eng., settled. He (living in 1681) left no will or record as to whom he married, but in the town records of Scituate are the following

CHILDREN.

i BENJAMIN, m. Deborah ——, and was killed in King

Philip's war, 1676. Children: Elizabeth, **Deborah**, Abigail, and Robert, b. about 1660; m. Bethiah ——, and had 11 children.

2 ii WALTER, b. 1645.
  iii THOMAS, b. 1647 (?); m. Deborah Damon, 1666, and kept a trader's shop in Scituate, but had lands in Little Compton, R. I. He d. 1718. Children: (1) Deborah, b. 1667; m. Eben. Pincin, 1701. (2) Hezekiah, b. 1670; m. Hannah Clap (Samuel, Thomas), 1697; 6 children. (3) Catharine, b. 1673; m. Thomas Davenport (Jonathan, Thomas); 6 children. (4) Ebenezer, b. 1676; d. 1690. (5) Mary, b. 1678; m. Stephen Vinal, Jr., 1704. (6) John, b. 1683; m. Mary Rose, 1718. (7) Hannah, b. 1685; m. Samuel Jackson, 1713. (8) Jerusha, b. 1688; m. —— Randall. (9) Ebenezer, b. 1690; m. Mary Wade, 1712.
  iv JOSEPH, m. Sarah Stockbridge, 1669, and had (1) Joseph, b. 1670. (2) Mary, b. 1673. (3) Benjamin, b. 1676. (4) Sarah, b. 1678. (5) Elizabeth, b. 1680; m. Thomas Chittenden. (6) Eunice, b. 1682; d. 1709. (7) Abigail, b. 1685; m. Thomas Merritt, 1711. (8) Ruth, b. 1687; m. Benjamin Sylvester, Jr., 1718.
  v MARY, b. March 10, 1650; m. Aaron Symonds, 1677.
  vi MARTHA, m. Lieut. Zachary Damon, son of John, 1679.
  vii ISAAC, b. about 1655; m. Lydia ——; settled in Norwich, Conn. He d. April 1, 1714. Their children were Isaac, Stephen, Joshua, Moses, David, Daniel, Lydia, Joanna, and Grace.
  viii ELIZABETH, single.
  ix MEHITABLE, b. Aug. 15, 1662; single.

2. ii. Walter Woodworth (Walter), b. in Scituate, 1645; m. —— ——, 1669; moved to Little Compton, R. I., east side of Narragansett Bay, about 1676; was a freeman, 1670. His family began to adopt the name Woodworth.

CHILDREN.

  i JOSEPH, b. 1670; m. —— ——, 1694.
3 ii BENJAMIN, b. 1674.
  iii ISAAC, b. 1676; m. —— ——, and had David and Grace.
  iv ELIZABETH, b. 1678; m. Benjamin Southworth, 1701; 4 children, and d. 1713.
  v THOMAS, b. 1680; m.

3. iii. Benjamin Woodworth (Walter, Walter), b. 1674; m. Hannah ——, and lived in Little Compton, R. I. He bought a large tract of land in Lebanon, Conn., of Philip Smith, 1703, and was admitted an inhabitant of that town, 1704; d. April 22, 1729.

ALLIED FAMILIES.

CHILDREN.

    i BENJAMIN, m. Mary Weeks, 1721; 9 children.
4 ii ICHABOD.
5 iii EBENEZER.
    iv AMOS, m. Elie Matthews, Oct. 3, 1722.
    v EZEKIEL, m. Lydia Clark, 1716; son Benjamin b. 1730; went to Nova Scotia, and d. July 25, 1766.
    vi CALEB.
    vii DEBORAH, m. Benjamin Sprague, Dec. 27, 1707.
    viii HANNAH, m. —— Walter.
    ix RUTH, m. —— Owen.
    x JUDITH, m. Thomas Newcomb (Simon, Andrew, Andrew) 1720; 9 children; he m. 1st, Eunice, daughter of Dennis Manning of Nantucket, 1712; she d. 1715; he d. 1761, aged 70.

4. iv. Ichabod Woodworth (Benjamin, Walter, Walter), b. Little Compton, R. I., about 1696; m. Sarah ——, and had in Lebanon, Conn.

CHILDREN.

    i LEBBEUS, b. Jan. 8, 1723; m. Anna Payne, April 23, 1761, and had (1) Anna, b. 1762. (2) Cyrus, b. 1764. (3) Ezra, b. 1765.
6 ii SILAS, b. March 22, 1725.
    iii JEHIEL, b. Sept. 17, 1728; m. Phebe Collins, June 6, 1751. Children: (1) Cyrenius, b. March 6, 1752; d. young. (2) Lucy, b. Jan. 2, 1754. (3) Reuben, b. Dec. 28, 1755. (4) Cyrenius, b. Aug. 27, 1757. (5) Deidamia, b. March 7, 1761.
    iv REUBEN, b. Aug. 22, 1733; m. Elizabeth McGee, Nov. 2, 1757, and had (1) Abel, b. June 6, 1758. (2) Elizabeth, b. Aug. 3, 1760. (3) Olive, b. June 8, 1762. (4) Adah, b. March 11, 1764. (5) Ichabod, b. June 2, 1766. (6) Sarah, b. Nov. 21, 1769. (7) Dorothy, b. Dec. 1, 1772. (8) Joshua, b. Dec. 4, 1774. (9) Josiah, b. Feb. 17, 1777. (10) Clinda, b. June 8, 1781.

5. iv. Ebenezer Woodworth (Benjamin, Walter, Walter), b. at Little Compton, R. I., about 1697; m. Rebecca Smalley, Dec. 27, 1717, Lebanon, Conn.

CHILDREN.

    i EBENEZER, b. Sept. 26, 1718; m. Hopestill Tryon, Sept. 2, 1742; had Phebe, John, Sylvester, and Elijah.
    ii ZERVIAH, b. Nov. 15, 1720.
    iii ELIPHALET, b. Sept. 24, 1722; m. Priscilla ——, and d. about 1777. She d. about 1808, aged 84.
7 iv JOSEPH, b. Oct. 19, 1724.

   v AMASA, b. April 4, 1727; m. Sarah ———, and had a son Israel, who d. June 8, 1761, aged 18 months, in Cornwallis, N. S. It appears that Amasa's wife must have d. soon after or at the time of his son Israel, and then he returned to the "States," for we find Amasa Woodworth in Vermont, m. to Elizabeth Wright, about the time of the Revolution; had a son John m. Eliza Morey; they had a son William S. m. Patience Stephens; they had 8 children; a son John Amasa, b. 1828, m. Sarah M. Sweetser, and two sons, Arthur D., and Elmer C., are in Boston, the last a jeweler.

  vi REBECCA, b. July 25, 1729.
 vii JOHN, b. Jan. 4, 1734.
viii PHEBE, b. Aug. 9, 1737.

6. v. Silas Woodworth (Ichabod, Benjamin, Walter, Walter), b. Lebanon, Conn., March 22, 1725; m. Sarah, daughter of Richard and Mary English, Sept. 22, 1746, and went to Nova Scotia in the ship *Wolfe*, May, 1760, and settled in Lower Cornwallis. He d. Sept. 26, 1790; she d. May 29, 1808, aged 74.

CHILDREN.

     i SILAS, b. March 21, 1747: m. Zerviah Bill (not in the "Bill family"), daughter of Edward and Zerviah, Oct. 5, 1768, and had a daughter Theodory m. Samuel Casey. S. W. d. 1776.
8   ii JOHN, b. Feb. 17, 1749.
9 iii SOLOMON, b. April 16, 1751.
10 iv JOSIAH, b. July 10, 1753.
     v SARAH, b. July 23, 1755; m. Frederick Babcock, had 3 or 4 daughters, and d. May 12, 1826.
    vi EZEKIEL, b. April 11, 1758; d. Sept. 1, 1759.
   vii ELIZABETH SEABORN, b. May 21, 1760, on the ship *Wolfe*, at sea; m. Abram, son of Ezekiel Masters, March 2, 1778, and lived in Cornwallis. He d. May 25, 1846, aged 91; she d. Aug. 9, 1851, aged 91. Children: (1) Silas W., b. Feb. 12, 1779; m. Rebecca Rand (Mayhew, Caleb, John, Thomas, Robert), Nov. 26, 1805, and had (a) Horatia Nelson, b. Dec. 31, 1807; m. Mary A. Boener. (b) Eliza A., b. Jan. 12, 1809; m. Timothy Barnaby. (c) Lydia E., b. March 4, 1811; m. Elijah Phinney. (d) George Edward, b. Jan. 17, 1814; m. ——— Read. (e) Dr. Holmes Chipman, b. Oct. 12, 1815; m. Emeline Morse, and d. 1891. (f) John Freeman, b. Jan. 29, 1818; m. Lottie Masters. (g) Mary Julia, b. June 1, 1821. m. Dr. Tupper. (h) Charles Andrew, b. May 4, 1823; m. Lottie Morse. (i) Rebecca A., b. March 21, 1825; m. ——— Calkins. (10) Eunice Cecelia,

a twin, m. Albert Barnaby. (k) Richard Upham, b. Jan. 2, 1828, off unknown. (2) Enoch Steadman, b. Jan. 26, 1781, off for England, 1802. (3) John, b. Dec. 30, 1782; m. Sarah North (Isaac), 1812, and d. Jan. 10, 1879; she d. Jan. 29, 1850, aged 60. They had Douglass, Abram, James, Angeline, and Isaac. (4) Sarah Knowlton, b. Oct. 6, 1785; m. Wilmot Osborn. (5) Hannah D., b. April 25, 1787; m. Samuel C. Woodworth. (6) James, b. Jan. 27, 1790; m. Nancy Sibly, 1813. (7) Lois, b. Oct. 4, 1891; d. about 1840. (8) Rev. Ezekiel, b. Oct. 19, 1794; m. Fanny, daughter of John and Elizabeth (Durkee) Hayes, 1818. He was a very earnest, resolute, and successful minister in the Baptist church. He moved to Boston about 1850; his wife d. Dec., 1858, aged 57. He returned to Nova Scotia, and m. Harriet, daughter of John Condon, and d. April, 1883. They had (a) Lavinia, b. Jan. 8, 1819; m. William M. Roach (Dea. Zebina, Matthew, Patrick); 3 children. (b) Mary Jane, b. Aug. 31, 1820; m. Wesley Wheelock. See Wheelock. (c) Enoch James, b. Aug. 3, 1825; to Stockton, Cal. (d) Isabella B., b. Aug. 3, 1828; m. William, son of Thomas Moffit, Aug. 28, 1847; 2 children; live in South Boston. (e) Fanny C., b. June 17, 1831; d. aged 6 weeks. (f) Ezekiel W., b. May 14, 1833; m. Sarah C. Johnston, 2 children; Clara Whitten, Boston, 5 children. (g) Frances E., b. Dec. 10, 1836; m. Nicholas C. Cogley; 4 children. (h) John E., b Oct. 5, 1839; m. Lucy A. Kelly; one son in California. (i) Annetta R., b. June 18, 1846; m. George J. Roberts; he d. July, 1883, aged 50, in South Boston. (9) Orinda, b. Aug. 12, 1796; m. Simeon Porter; 8 children. (10) Ann, b. May 29, 1799; m. Isaac W. Newcomb (Andrew, Andrew, Capt. Eddy, John, Simon, Andrew, Andrew, 1635), Oct. 15, 1815; 8 children; John Henry is in Bay City, Mich. (11) William B., b. May 24, 1801; m. Sarah Newcomb, 3 children; d. 1882, aged 27; 2d, Elizabeth Bowles. (12) Sherman, b. Sept. 17, 1805; d. Sept. 19. (13) Shubael B., b. Sept. 17, 1805; m. Pamelia Bowles. (14) Valorious A., b. June 25, 1810; d. July 14.

11 viii RICHARD, b. Cornwallis, N. S., Feb. 8, 1763.
   ix EZEKIEL, b. Jan. 2, 1766; m. Lydia Hayes, and d. Jan. 31, 1812; she m. 2d, Joseph Sibley, Dec., 1812, who fell from a load of hay and d. about 1815; she m. 3d, Jesse Kean, Nov. 2, 1815; he d. 1838 or 9; she d. July, 1851, aged 83.
12 x ELEAZER, b. Nov. 3, 1768.

7. v. **Joseph Woodworth** (Ebenezer, Benjamin, Walter, Walter), b. in Lebanon, Conn., Oct. 19, 1724; m. Rebecca Wright, May

13, 1747 (she b. Sept. 24, 1728; d. in Horton, N. S., May 14, 1816), and moved over to and settled in Horton, N. S., 1760; d. there, March 29, 1794.

CHILDREN.

    i   SAMUEL, b. April 11, 1748, Lebanon.
   ii   ANNIE, b. Nov. 6, 1756, Coventry, Conn.
   iii JOSEPH, b. June 23, 1759; d. in Horton, Oct. 10, 1761.
13 iv JOSEPH, b. April 15, 1764, Horton, N. S.
   v   JAMES, b. March 5, 1768; d. May 2, 1769.
14 vi ELIHU, b. May 17, 1771.

8. vi. John Woodworth (Silas, Ichabod, Benjamin, Walter, Walter), b. in Lebanon, Conn., Feb. 17, 1749; m. Submit Newcomb (Benjamin, Simon, Andrew, Andrew), Feb. 9, 1769, and lived in Cornwallis, Kings county, N. S., a farmer; d. May 29, 1816; she d. May 18, 1831, aged 70.

CHILDREN.

    i   HANNAH, b. Sept. 1, 1769; m. Joseph, son of Samuel and Mary Pearce, April 11, 1793; had Sarah, b. June 11, 1794, in Horton, and d. May 21, 1821. He m. 2d, Lizzie Newcomb, and d. about 1846. She d. before him.
15 ii IRA, b. Feb. 7, 1771.
16 iii ABNER, b. Jan. 19, 1773.
   iv SARAH, b. Oct. 28, 1774; taught school 31 years, and d. March 22, 1841.
   v   ALICE, b. Aug. 9, 1776; m. Stephen, son of Jethro and Dorothy Chase, June 7, 1796; 5 children.
17 vi JOHN, b. April 8, 1779.
   vii BENJAMIN, b. Feb. 2, 1781; m. Phebe Ells, May 19, 1811, and d. Nov. 15, 1856. Children: (1) Enoch Leander, b. Oct. 25, 1812; m. Jane, daughter of Charles Wallis of Halifax, Feb. 13, 1844, and d. Oct. 5, 1867; she d. March 2, 1873; 4 children. (2) Elias Ells, b. May 16, 1814; m. Charlot, daughter of Isaac Jackson, and d. March 25, 1886; 1 daughter. (3) Benjamin, b. and d. Dec., 1815. (4) Charles, b. 1824; d. 1827. (5) Phebe, b. 1826; d. 1827. (6) Benjamin, b. 1828; d. 1851, and buried in Mt. Auburn cemetery. (7) Capt. William Henry, b. April 9, 1830; m. Emma Ealls of Liverpool, Eng., and was drowned at sea, Oct., 1870, leaving 2 daughters. (8) John Samuel, b. June 2, 1832; m. Eliza Corbett; 3 children.
18 viii ELIAS, b. Sept., 1782.
   ix BETTY, b. Sept. 25, 1784; m. Perry B. Ells, 1812; lost at sea about 1820; had John and Willy Ann.
19 x JAMES, b. Aug. 5, 1786.

ALLIED FAMILIES.

20 xi ANDREW, b. Oct. 6, 1788.
21 xii SOLOMON, b. Dec. 16, 1793.
   xiii SUBMIT, b. Jan. 4, 1796; m. Thomas McGee, and d. 1856.
   xiv REBECCA, b. June 4, 1797; d. a good, Christian woman, Jan. 23, 1857.

9. vi. Solomon Woodworth (Silas, etc.), b. in Lebanon, Conn., April 16, 1751; m. Hannah, daughter of Moses and Mary Dewey, July 26, 1772, and lived in Kings county, N. S. She d. March 19, 1863.

CHILDREN.

22 i   DAN, b. Feb. 18, 1778.
   ii LOUISE, b. Aug. 16, 1774.
   iii LYDIA, b. July 22, 1776; m. John Dunn, and had Mary Ann, Sarah Jane, and John.
   iv SARAH, b. Jan. 16, 1780; m. —— Thompson; Michael Wallace.
   v   SILAS, b. Sept. 3, 1784; was lame and somewhat crippled, but a good school-teacher; d. about 1860.
23 vi SAMUEL C., b. Dec. 6, 1787.
24 vii CHARLES, b. Aug. 19, 1792.

10. vi. Josiah Woodworth (Silas, etc.), b. in Lebanon, July 10, 1853; m. Anna Dewey, and moved to West Leyden, Lewis county, N. Y., and d. there 1839. She d. 1837, aged 81.

CHILDREN.

   i   CAROLINE, m. Benjamin Spinning.
   ii SARAH, m. William Belknap; 10 children.
   iii HANNAH, m. Jabez Loomis; 15 children.
   iv ANNA, m. Solomon Stiles (John, Robert, Samuel, Robert, over from England, 1638, to Salem, Mass., and d. July 30, 1690); 5 children. They lived on the River Raisin, in Michigan, and both d. 1842, he aged about 55.
   v   JOSIAH, m. Harriet Hunt; 5 children.

William, son of Daniel Ross, b. in Onondaga county, N. Y., Nov. 30, 1799; m. Sarah (b. June 3, 1880), daughter of William and Sarah Belknap, 1829; 8 children; 2 sons and 2 daughters were living in 1880. They moved from Lewis county, N. Y., and settled in Kenochee, St. Clair county, Mich., June, 1855, as farmers and Baptists. He d. April, 1884.

11. vi. Richard Woodworth (Silas, etc.) b. in Cornwallis, N. S., Feb. 9, 1763; m. Tamer, daughter of John and Phebe Porter Oct. 9, 1783, and d. Sept. 1, 1796; she d. 1802.

CHILDREN.

    i NANCY, b. 1786.
   ii ENEAS EZRA, b. 1788, and two more.

12. vi. Eleazer Woodworth (Silas, etc.), b. in Cornwallis, N. S., Nov. 3, 1768; m. Mary Chute (Samuel, John, Lionel, James, James, Lionel), Sept. 8, 1790, and lived near Berwick, farmers and pious members of the Baptist church. He d. July 5, 1844; she d. in Bayham, Ont., Oct. 7, 1851, aged 81.

CHILDREN.

25   i   WILLIAM, b. April 8, 1792.
     ii CHARLOTTE, b. Nov. 23, 1794; m. John N. Sanford. See Sanford.
    iii OLIVIA, b. July 24, 1796; m. Dea. Andrew Chute. See No. 36.
    iv EUNICE, b. Oct. 1, 1798; m. Dea. Aaron Chute. See No. 60.
26   v   RICHARD, b. May 27, 1801.
    vi ELIZABETH, b. Dec. 23, 1803; m. Samuel Wear. See Wear.
27 vii EZEKIEL, b. July 28, 1806.
28 viii EDWARD, b. March 2, 1809.
    ix MARY J., b. Sept. 6, 1811; m. Benjamin Palmer. See Palmer.
     x SARAH A., b. Aug. 4, 1813; m. David Chute. See No. 65.
29 xi CHARLES, b. Xmas, 1815.

13. vi. Joseph Woodworth (Joseph, Ebenezer, Benjamin, Walter, Walter), b. in Horton, N. S., April 15, 1764; m. and lived in Albert county, N. B.

CHILDREN.

    i ASA, d. single.
   ii JOHN, m. Rhoda Steeves; 10 children.
  iii REBECCA, m. John Steeves, the 4th; 1 child.
  iv ELIZABETH, m. John Farrice; 10 children.
   v NANCY, m. Alex. Smith; 9 children.
  vi JANE, m. Kenneth Presley; 10 children.
 vii JAMES, d. single.
viii ESTHER, m. Aaron Porter; 6 children.
  ix JOSEPH, m. Phebe Dowling; 6 children, of whom Williams is one.
   x MARY, m. John Smith; 5 children.

ALLIED FAMILIES.

14. vi. Dea. Elihu Woodworth (Joseph, Ebenezer, Benjamin, Walter, Walter), b. in Horton, May 17, 1771; was, captain as well as deacon in the Presbyterian church, and a good, useful citizen; m. Dec., 1793, Sabra Davisson (Andrew, Daniel, Daniel, Nicholas, over to Charlestown, 1639); d. on Long Island, Minas Basin, July 7, 1852; she d. about 1846.

CHILDREN.

    i   Clarissa, m. —— Palmeter.
30 ii Joseph, m.
   iii Samuel, b. 1802; m. Mary Ann Moody; both d. 1882.
   iv Amy.
    v Anne.
   vi Capt. Benjamin, m. Charlotte Ells; had Amelia, Elihu, Sabra, and John A.
  vii Sarah, m. Wright, son of Cyrus Davisson; 4 children.
 viii Eunice Rebecca.
   ix John, m. Jane, daughter of Joseph Caldwell.
    x Mary, m. John Duncan.

15. vii. Ira Woodworth (John, Silas, Ichabod, Benjamin, Walter, Walter), b. Cornwallis, N. S., Feb. 7, 1771; m. Deborah Sanford, (see Sanford), 1800, and d. Dec. 30, 1832, she d. Jan 1, 1829.

CHILDREN.

    i James, b. Aug. 6, 1801; m. Catharine Pineo; 5 children; —— Scofield; 3 children. First family, Charles P., Benjamin, Eliza, Catharine, and Eunice. Second family, Henry, William, and Mary.
   ii John, b. Feb. 11, 1803; m. —— McComber; 6 children.
  iii Elias, b. Aug. 18, 1804; d. July 26, 1805.
  iv Benjamin, b. Jan. 2, 1806; m. Eliza, daughter of Patrick Coppill; she d. 1848. Children: (1) Amos, b. 1840; m. Mary Forsyth; 6 children; she d. May, 1880, aged 41; m. 2d, Abbie G. Crowell; 2 children; he a machinist at Boston, live at Braintree. (2) Julia Ann, m. Thomas Briggs; George Simonds. (3) Andrew R., m. Rhoda Berger, off West. By 2d wife, Eliza, daughter of Enoch Huntley: (4) Albert C., b. 1852; m. Orissa Wells. (5) Jane Cordelia, m. —— Woodruff. (6) Eliza Dora, d. aged 10. Mr. B. W. moved from Woburn, Mass., to Saranac, Iona county, Mich., 1857, and d. 1881.
   v Elias, b. Aug. 11, 1808; m. Lavina Huntly, and d. in Cornwallis, N. S., about 1860; she d. about 1880.
  vi George P., b. March 18, 1810; d. March 6, 1872; m. Submit Woodworth, a cousin; she d. May 11, 1854; 2d,

Olive Greenough, Nov., 1855 (Allen and Elizabeth), and had (1) Laura Jane, b. Feb. 14, 1840; d. May 1854. (2) Elias Jefferson, b. Oct. 22, 1842; m. Ellen A. Burke, who d. in South Boston, April 18, 1884, aged 43; m. 2d, Abby Foster Rust (Benjamin, Benjamin, Samuel, Samuel, Samuel, Henry, over to Hingham, 1634, d. in Boston, 1685), daughter of Benjamin and Isabel (Ross) Rust, and widow of Elbridge H., son of Ira and Lucinda Webster, of Sandwich, N. H. Mr. Webster d. Dec. 12, 1884, aged 54, leaving 3 daughters, besides 3 d. in childhood. Mr. E. J. W. is a machinist in Boston. (3) George, b. 1845; d. 1848. (4) Elizabeth, b. 1849; d. 1853.

vii SUBMIT, b. Aug. 30, 1811; m. Silas Lockhart; a daughter, Melissa.

viii IRA BROKE, b. June 21, 1813; m. 1st, Rebecca Ward; one daughter; m. 2nd, Paulina Ward, daughter of Joseph. Children: (1) Judith Ann, b. 1844; m. Fred Baker. (2) Jane, m. James Cochrane. (3) Mary, m. James Allen. (4) Victoria. (5) Amanda.

ix DANIEL, b. Sept. 15, 1816; m. Margaret (Schofield) Ward, and had Philemon, b. 1867. Mr. Ira B. W. d. Jan. 28, 1893, in Nova Scotia.

16. vii. Abner Woodworth (John, Silas, &c.), b in Cornwallis, Jan 19, 1773; m. Hannah, daughter of John Loveless (over to Falmouth, 1760), Feb. 23, 1797. He was a sturdy old farmer, and a pious Presbyterian; d. Sept. 3, 1859; she d. March 19, 1856, aged 80.

CHILDREN.

i JOHN, b. Jan. 30, 1798; d. 1799.
ii ALICE, b. Jan. 14, 1800; m. Isaiah Shaw, 1820, and d. 1825: he d. 1874, aged 76.
iii JANE, b. Aug. 3, 1802; d. 1847.
iv ELIZABETH ANN, b. June 9, 1804; m. Deacon William H. Skinner (Deacon Alfred, Charles), Oct. 27, 1835; children: (1) Hannah, b. and d. 1837. (2) Alice, b. 1839; m. Charles E. Sanford (see Sanford); 6 children. (3) William Albert, b. 1841; m. Mrs. Alpha Dorman. (4) Isabel, b. 1843; d. 1858. (5) John W., b. 1844; m. (6) Rev. Isaac, b. 1846; m. —— Black. (7) Rebecca, b. 1846; m. Parker Spurr. (8) Sophia, b. 1850.
v LYDIA, b. Aug. 4, 1806; m. John Brown; 8 children, and d. 1856.
vi SOLOMON, b. Aug. 28, 1808; m. Sophia Sanford. (See Sanford).
vii HANNAH, b. Sept. 19, 1810; d. 1835.
viii FRANCES SUSAN, b. Jan. 28, 1813; m. Gardner Dodge (Gardner, David); 9 children.

ALLIED FAMILIES. cclv

  ix SUBMIT, b. May 31, 1815; m. John Ells; 4 children, and d. 1870.
  x ISABEL, b. Aug. 22, 1817; m. Rev. John C. Morse; lived at Sandy Cove. See Morse.
  xi JOHN H., b. Feb. 15, 1820; d. 1822.

17. vii. John Woodworth, jr., a brother, b. Aug. 8, 1779; m. Margaret, daughter of Alexander and Elizabeth (Candlish) Bowles, Nov. 14, 1809, and lived in Cornwallis; d. Nov. 1, 1827; she d. Jan. 3, 1864, aged 89.

CHILDREN.

  i WILLIAM, ESQ., b. Oct. 13, 1810; d. at Bridgetown, May 30, 1893.
  ii JOHN BOWLES, b. Sept. 15, 1812; m. Mary Ann, daughter of John W. Caldwell, and d. March, 1859; she m. 2d, Dr. Jonathan Borden, 1862, and had 2 more at Canard. He m. 1st, Mary Frances Brown, and had Frederick William, B.A., M.D., M.P.P., May 14, 1847. Dr. Jonathan d. Jan., 1875, aged 68. Children: (1) Margaret Ann, b. 1842. (2) Thomas Caldwell, b. 1844; m. Julia, daughter of Abner Tilden, Jr.; one son; live in Charlestown, Mass., carpenter and builder. (3) John Candlish, b. 1846; m. Prudence Morton, and twice since. (4) William Somerville, b. 1848; m Minnie Walton. (5) Sarah Adelia, b. 1851; m. Charles Dickey. (6, 7, and 8) Alex Bowles, Agnes, and Maria, all d. of diphtheria, 1859. (9) Maria Frances, and (10) Mary Caldwell, are Bordens.
  iii ELIZABETH CANDLISH, b. Aug. 28, 1814; m. Hanson Chesly (James, Capt. Samuel), and d. 1883; he d. 1888, aged 78. Children: (1) Washington W., b. 1843; m. Hattie A. Porter of Lynn; 5 children. (2) Margaret, m. John W. Ross. (3) Elizabeth, m. Lewis A. Dickie.

18. vii. Elias (John, Silas, etc.), b. Sept. 7, 1782; m. Sarah Jefferson, widow of William Halliday, Oct. 31, 1805, and lived at Stony Beach, below Annapolis; she d. Feb. 12, 1823, aged 43; he m. 2d, Sophia, daughter of James Webber, March 24, 1825, and d Sept. 20, 1879. She d. a month later.

CHILDREN.

  i BENJAMIN, b. 1806; d. in California about 1871; m. Eunice Damon; son, John Edwin.
  ii SUBMIT, b. 1808; m. George P., son of Ira Woodworth.
30 iii JOHN JEFFERSON, b. 1810.
  iv ELIAS, b. 1812, m. Hannah Elizabeth Spencer, and being a bold engineer, he ran his engine into danger, and was killed near Halifax, N. S., about 1857. Children: (1) Hannah Elizabeth. (2) Sarah Elizabeth. (3) Laura

Jane. (4) Edwin F., b. Dec. 27, 1841, shoemaker near School street, Boston; m. Florence Wilson, had a son Harry E., b. 1870, and d. April 22, 1893.
- v SARAH, b. about 1815; m. Henry Hawthorne; 2 children; live at Henniker, N. H.
- vi STEPHEN, m. Frances Blunt, and was killed at ———, on Norwich and Worcester R. R. about 1856; had 2 sons, John B. (d. June, 1892, aged about 46), and William.
- vii ALBERT.
- viii MAY SOPHIA.
- ix JAMES WILLIAM.
- x REBECCA, b. 1832.

The last 4, by the 2d wife, d. young.

Sarah Jefferson (Robert, brother to President Thomas Jefferson, Peter), b. 1780; m. 1st, William Halliday, and lived in Granville; he was drowned in the Annapolis River, spring of 1805, aged 30.

CHILDREN.

- i HENRY, b. 1801; m. Elizabeth, daughter of James Van Blaricom, and d. 1860; she d. Children: (1) William Henry, b. 1834; m. Mary McKenzie (Alex., William, Alex.). (2) Catharine, b. 1836; m. William Milliner. (3) John, b. 1839; m. Agatha, daughter of Sylvester Wade; Eliza A. Anderson. (4) Elias, b. 1842; m. Eleanor E., daughter of Manasseh Litch, Jr. (5) Mary Ann, b. 1844; m. Elias, son of Rev. J. J. Woodworth. (6) Albert, b. 1847; d. 1865.
- ii ELIZABETH, b. 1802; m. John H. Tomlinson; 8 children; some in Chicago.
- iii ROBERT JEFFERSON, b. 1804; m. Fannie Dillon. Children: (1) William Henry, b. 1835; m. Mary Jane Elms; 2 children; live in Boston. (2) George, m. Lucinda Dill; 5 children. (3) Mary E., m. Fred Ferguson; 3 children. (4) Woodworth; uncertain; off West. (5) Rebecca, m. James Smith; Cambridge. (6) Lucy, d. young.

19. vii. **James Woodworth** (John, Silas, etc.), b. in Cornwallis, N. S., Aug. 5, 1786; m. Eunice, daughter of Benjamin and Hannah Fox, Aug. 22, 1809; she d. Feb. 1, 1835, aged 48. He m. 2d, Harriet Newcomb; 2 children, d. in infancy. He m. 3d, Roby (Clark) Hawksworth, and d. 1868; she d. in Digby, N. S., 1891, aged 87.

CHILDREN.

- i HANNAH STARR, b. Aug. 28, 1810; d. June 27, 1858.
- ii ALBINA B., b. April 6, 1812; m. James Carmichael, April 21, 1851; 2 sons.

iii Almira C., b. March 19, 1814; m. William Buchanan, and d. June, 1892.
iv Edgar, b. Jan. 12, 1816; d. Sept. 28, 1817.
v Andrew, b. Nov. 23, 1817; m. Louise, daughter of Timothy Strong; 5 children.
vi Eunice H., b. Oct. 17, 1819; m. John J. McKay, March 5, 1849; 2 children.
vii James E., b. Feb. 1. 1822; d. April 23, 1822.
viii Eliza Jane, b. March 25, 1823; m. Eliakim Tupper (Eliakim, Charles, Capt. Eliakim, Eliakim, Capt. Thomas, Capt. Thomas, of Sandwich, Eng., to Sandwich, Mass., 1635; d. 1676, aged 98), Dec. 16, 1851); 5 children. They came over to Boston, and for many years have lived at Newton Centre.
ix Rebecca Alice, b. April 12, 1825; d. April 18, 1839.
x xi xii James, Sarah A., and John; b. and d. in infancy.

20. vii. Andrew Woodworth (John, Silas), b. Oct. 6, 1788; m. Eunice Davisson (Thomas, Andrew, Andrew, Daniel, Nicholas), and lived in Cornwallis; d. May 23, 1869; she d. Dec. 13, 1869, aged 78.

CHILDREN.

i Sarah, b. March 1, 1821; d. April 15, 1889.
ii Anna, b. May 7, 1823.
iii John E., b. about 1826; d. 1844.
iv Racael A., b. 1829; m. Isaac W., son of Holmes and Christiana (Webster) Morton (Lemuel, Elkanah, Elkanah, Ephraim, George, Ephraim, George, over to America in the *Ann*, 1623); she d. April 22, 1874, aged 45; 10 children; one, Elihu Woodworth, is in the Boston Rubber Works at Malden, Mass., 1892. Mr. J. W. Morton m. again, and they have more family.

21. vii. Solomon Woodworth (John, Silas), b. Dec. 16, 1793; m. Margaret Alice Newcomb (Jonathan, John, John, Simon, Andrew, Andrew), April 26, 1847, and lived in Cornwallis, a blacksmith and a ruling elder in the Presbyterian church; she d. Dec. 11, 1864, aged 53; he d. Dec. 5, 1883.

CHILDREN.

i Edwin, b. March 21, 1848; d. May 7, 1857.
ii John Elihu, b. May 10, 1849; editor *Gazette*, at Berwick, N. S.
iii Mary Clarissa, b. June 3, 1851; in Somerville, Mass.
iv Sarah Somerville, b. Jan. 13, 1854; d. May 13, 1857.

22. vii. Dan Woodworth (Solomon, Silas, Ichabod, Benjamin, Walter, Walter), b. in Cornwallis, N. S., Feb. 18, 1773; was a school-teacher and singing-teacher; m. Deborah Freeman West, 1794, and d. about 1846; she d. about 1860, over 80.

CHILDREN.

    i   MELINDA, b. 1796; m. Jonathan Sanford. See Sanford.
32 ii   JOHN BURTON, b. 1798.
33 iii GUILDFORD DUDLEY, b. 1800.
    iv EBENEZER FOSTER, b. 1802; m. Ann Skinner (Alfred and Ann Bigelow, Charles and Sarah (Osborn) Skinner, the first to Nova Scotia), and went to Boston, a carpenter, 1841, and d. April, 1875; she lives at West Newton, June, 1894, past 90. Children: (1) Rebecca, b. Feb. 10, 1827, Cornwallis; d. Aug. 24, 1845. (2) Melinda, a twin, m. Charles William Smith, Nov. 14, 1844, and d. June 17, 1890. (3) Mary, b. Sept. 27, 1828; m. Freeman G. Briggs, Jan. 11, 1853. (4) Anna Maria, b. Sept. 7, 1830; m. William W. Parsons, June 1, 1852. (5) Robert Newton, b. May 18, 1832; m. Abbie P. Prentiss, June 1, 1852, and d. Jan. 22, 1888. (6) Ellen Amira, b. May 3, 1834; d. June 25, 1835. (7) Alfred Skinner, b. April 24, 1836, Horton, N. S.; m. Anna G. Grafton, April 23, 1857; m. 2d, Elizabeth Tucker, Boston. (8) George Leverett, b. May 5, 1838, Horton; m. Mary J. V. Hugo, Oct. 27, 1864; live at Newtonville; 7 children. (9) Lavenia, b. April 22, 1840, Newport, N. S.; m. Daniel O. Sanger, June 5, 1862; live in Brighton, Mass. (10) Ebenezer Freeman, b. March 14, 1843, Roxbury, Mass.; d. Oct. 5, 1846. (11) Clara, b. Sept. 14, 1846; m. Moses M. Chick, May 22, 1873. (12) Laura B., b. Oct. 29, 1848; m. Frederick L. Felton, Sept. 14, 1870, and live at West Newton.
    v   CAROLINE AMELIA, b. 1809; m. Charles A. Curry; no children.
    vi GEORGE NELSON, b. 1812; m. Mary, daughter of Patrick Wellner; 4 children, and d. 1884.

23. vii. Samuel Casey Woodworth (Solomon, Silas, etc.), b. in Cornwallis, Dec. 6, 1787; m. Hannah D. Masters (Abram, Ezekiel), July 9, 1812; d. Dec., 1862; she d. March, 1863, aged 76.

CHILDREN.

    i   CATHARINE, b. 1813; m. Robert, son of Samuel Bennett; 5 children, and d. Oct., 1891.
    ii SILAS NEWTON, b. Aug. 11, 1817; m. Susan, daughter of William Woodworth, and had, near Kentville (1) William Alfred, b. March 26, 1848; m. Elvira, daughter of

ALLIED FAMILIES. cclix

    John Wilmot, 1870; 4 or 5 children; Chelsea, Mass. (2) Charles Albon, twin, m. Eunice Ann, daughter of John Ells, 1870. (3) Valora Ann, b. July 14, 1851; d. April, 1860. (4) John, b. July 15, 1854; m. Ann, daughter of Denison Davison, 1874, and lives at home.
iii MARY E., b. 1819; m. Matthew Legg, and d. 1889.
iv SAMUEL, b. 1821.
v SHUBAEL, b. 1823; m. Sarah J., daughter of Richard Woodworth, and live near Kentville. Children: (1) Henry Alline, b. 1858, in Ontario; m. Emma, daughter of John Keysor, 1880; Saidie C. Bishop. (2) Julia Armina, b. 1861; m. William Tupper, 1877. (3) Annie Alma, b. 1864; m. David Kiddy, 1880. (4) Alice Love, b. April 6, 1866; m. Harvey, son of John Keysor, son of Peter, Sept. 8, 1883; 4 children live in Beverly, Mass. (5) Burton Alfred, b. 1868; m. Eunice Locker, Dec., 1890. (6) Mary .Catharine, b. 1871; m. Edward Riley, Nov., 1888, and d. April, 1889. (7) George Emerson, b. 1876.

24. vii. Charles Woodworth (Solomon, Silas, etc.), b. Aug. 19, 1792; m. Sarah, daughter of Titus Thornton and Mary Harper, 1814, and lived in Sackville, N. B. He was a blacksmith; d. Jan., 1858, in Sackville; she d. June, 1870, aged 73.

CHILDREN.

i MARY, b. 1816; m. Miles Sears; 10 children; Sackville, N. B.
ii SOLOMON, b. 1818; m. Maria Crawford; 7 children; Hartford, and d. April, 1893.
iii HANNAH, b. 1820; m. Richard Mason; 4 children; Amherst, N. S.
iv LOIS, b. April 7, 1822; m. Nelson, son of William and Susan (Dixon) Chapman, from Hornby, Eng.; 10 children. He d. Feb. 3, 1890, aged 85; she lives in Malden.
v CAROLINE, b. May 17, 1825; m. William Brown; 5 sons; he d. 1873, aged 50.
vi CHARLES, b. 1827; m. Harriet, daughter of John and Mary (Cohoon) Brewster, Sept. 24, 1846; 11 children. He d. Eastport, Me., Jan. 14, 1881; she lives in Malden, Mass.; a son Israel Thornton, b. 1847, m. Susan Jane Martin, 1867; 4 children; to Chelsea, Mass., 1883; lives in Malden.
vii JOHN NELSON, b. 1829; m. Margaret, daughter of Peter Tarney; 6 children; Eastport Me.
viii CYNTHIA, b. 1833; m. Miles, son of Daniel Sears; 5 or 6 children; Sackville, N. B.
ix SARAH A., b. Sept. 28, 1835; m. James Maxwell, 1853; 3 children; m. 2d, Charles King, Nov., 1869; 2 children;

ALLIED FAMILIES.

to Boston, 1886.
- x ALBION, b. Feb. 28, 1838; m. Alice Ridpath; 4 children; She d. 1865, aged 30.

25. vii. William Woodworth (Eleazer, Silas, Ichabod, Benjamin, Walter, Walter), b. in Cornwallis, April 8, 1792; m. Lucy Foster (Benjamin, Isaac, Benjamin, Jacob, Isaac, Reginald), by Rev. Thomas Ansley, 1816; lived in Cornwallis till 1846, when he sold out to his brother-in-law, Benjamin Foster, Jr, and moved to Hampton, where he d. Oct. 27, 1848; she d. April 10, 1855, of dropsy.

CHILDREN.

- 34 i ELEAZER, b. July 21, 1817.
- ii MARY ELIZA, b. Feb. 28, 1819; d. Feb. 7, 1849.
- iii CHARLES MARSDEN, b. April 12, 1821, a dwarf; d. April 9, 1890.
- 35 iv ENOCH HARDING, b. March 3, 1823.
- v LUCY CAROLINE, b. March 2, 1825; m. Job F. See Farnsworth.
- vi SUSANNAH M., b. Dec. 16, 1827; m. Silas N. Woodworth, see page cclviii.
- vii HELEN F., b. Feb. 25, 1830; m. John, son of James Ward, Aug. 29, 1850; lived at Sandy Cove, Digby county. He d. 1860; she m. 2d. Charles T. Crowell, 1864. Children: (1) Charles, b. 1851; m. Mary Ann ——, Meriden, Conn. (2) John Henry, b. 1852; m. Esther Elvira, daughter of Franklin Clough, and live in Lynn, Mass. (3) Reuben, b. 1854; d. 1878.
- viii CATHARINE E., b. June 22, 1833; d. Portsmouth, N. H., Nov. 7, 1849.
- ix PAMELIA, b. Nov. 12, 1834; m. Fitz William, son of Job Puck, July 23, 1855; live in Salem, Mass.; he d. Dec. 1893, aged 77.
- x EMELINE V., b. Oct. 8, 1836; m. Alfred, son of John Ward, Dec. 24, 1857, and d. 1859; he m. 2d, Jane Barr, Trout Cove, Digby county, N. S.
- xi A. LEANDER, b. Feb. 22, 1840; m.
- xii WILLIAM WANFORD, b. Feb. 13, 1843; d. Feb. 25.

26. vii. Richard Woodworth (Eleazer, Elias, etc.), b. in Cornwallis, May 27, 1801; m. Susanna Chute (see No. 21), by Rev. Edward Manning, Dec. 27, 1827, and lived on the south mountain, near Morristown, farmer and carpenter. For a year or two, 1837-8, they lived with Dea. Andrew Chute at Bear River; then in 1858, they went to Elgin county, Ont., and back again. He d. June 23, 1875.

ALLIED FAMILIES. cclxi

CHILDREN.

i Josiah, b. Feb. 21, 1829; d. April 20.
ii Sarah Jane, b. April 4, 1830; m. Shubael Woodworth.
36 iii William Richardson, b. July 15, 1832.
iv Evalina, b. April 30, 1836; m. Benjamin W., son of Alpheus Palmer; he d. March 5, 1886, aged 44, leaving a daughter.
v Elizabeth Ann, b. Jan. 28, 1840; m. Charles E., son of Jonas Ward, May 2, 1865, and d. at Lake Paul, N. S., Dec. 4, 1890; 10 children.
vi Alice Mehitable, b. Feb. 14, 1842; a school-madam; d. Sept. 26, 1865.
vii Richard Burpee, b. March 11, 1846.
viii Mary Loretta, b. Aug. 26, 1848; m. Rufus A., son of Daniel Callahan, and live in Malden, Mass. Children: (1) George M., b. 1875. (2) Fred M., b. 1876. (3) Alalia, b. 1878. (4) Burgess, b. 1879. (5) Harvard R., 1881. (6) Mary R., b. 1887. (7) Lillie E., b. 1890.
ix Susan Matilda, b. Feb. 3, 1851; d. April 15, 1859.
x Hannah Naomi, b. Aug. 6, 1854; m. Thomas S. Birney, Dec. 28, 1881, and live in Tapleyville, West Danvers. Mr. Birney m. 1st, Maggie, daughter of Michael Falvey, and had a daughter Annie Laurie, b. March 19, 1870, in Lynn; m. Eugene Mitchell, 1890, and have a daughter Ethel in Danvers.

27. vii. Ezekiel Woodworth (Eleazer, Silas, etc.), b. July 28, 1806; m. Mary, daughter of Timothy Saunders, 2d Jr., by Rev. Ezekiel Masters, Oct. 27, 1841; lived some years in Cornwallis; moved to Elgin county, Ont., 1846; to Caradoc, Middlesex county, 1852; farmer and mechanic; d. near Strathroy, March, 1874; she lives at Petrolia.

CHILDREN.

i Lucinda, b. July 31, 1842; m. William Garrett, Jr., March, 1864, and live in London township, Ont.; he d. 1892.
ii Josiah, b. Nov. 28, 1843; m. Sarah, daughter of Nicholas Hendy, March 11, 1869; have 3 children, and live in Petrolia, Ont.
iii Elmira, b. April 17, 1845; d. Dec. 23, 1859.
iv Alfred, b. Dec. 31, 1846; in Ontario.
v Albert, b. Oct. 11, 1848.
vi Mary, b. May 20, 1851; m. Thor, son of Lawrence Oak, May 17, 1876
vii Alvin, b. May 22, 1853; m. Mary Ann Dolivar; 3 sons, in Flint, Mich.
viii Amelia, b. Sept. 1, 1855; m. John McGarvey, 1875; live in Genessee county, Mich; 6 children.

ALLIED FAMILIES.

 ix WILLIAM, b. April 22, 1858; m. Mary Ellen, daughter of Jacob Vincent, Oct., 1888.
 x JAMES EDWARD, b. April 27, 1864.

28. vii. James Edward Woodworth, another brother, b. March 2, 1809; m. Sarah Elizabeth Potter (see Potter), Dec. 26, 1839, by Rev. Israel Potter, Jr.; lived at Bear River, farmer and carpenter, till 1862, when he sold out and moved to Bayham, Ont., and bought the north half of the old David Sibly farm, and d. there Jan. 9, 1884; she d. in Nova Scotia, March 12, 1857, aged 42.

CHILDREN.

 i LOUISA, b. April 2, 1841; d. in Bayham, Ont., Jan. 17, 1864.
37 ii EZRA, b. July 7, 1842.
 iii HIRAM, b. Aug. 1, 1846; d. of fits, from a cold, May 15, 1857.
 iv LELALIA L., b. Aug. 17, 1856; m. James, son of Daniel Marr, Oct., 1873, and live in Bayham, Ont.; 3 or 4 children.

29. vii. Charles Woodworth, the youngest, b. Xmas, 1815; m., by Rev. Ezekiel Masters, Eunice, daughter of Thomas Dodge of Granville, Oct. 14, 1840, and lived near Berwick, Kings county, N. S. He was a sober, industrious farmer; d. April 8, 1889; she d. Jan. 4, 1889, aged 86. She m. 1st, Phineas Banks, Jan., 1820; had 3 children; he d. March, 1825; m. 2d, Alex. Stewart, May, 1827; had 3 children again; he d. Dec. 31, 1832.

CHILDREN.

 i DAVID PRIOR, b. April 25, 1841; m. Lavenia, daughter of Thomas Easson, Feb. 26, 1885, and live on the "Post Road," near Berwick.
 ii MARY EUNICE, b. Feb. 22, 1844; m. Walter, son of William Gates, April 3, 1867, and live at Melvern Square.
 iii LINA A., b. Nov. 30, 1846.
 iv EDWARD, b. Sept. 25, 1849; m. Samantha E., daughter of John Hutchinson, Nov. 10, 1885, and live on the old place beside his brother.
 v EMMA JANE, b. April 14, 1851.

30. vii. Joseph Woodworth (Dea. Elihu, Joseph, Ebenezer, Benjamin, Walter, Walter), b. on Long Island, Minas Basin, about 1800; m. Charlotte, daughter of James Neary, 1821, and d. 1841; she d. 1882, aged 82, at Wolfville where they lived.

CHILDREN.

i JAMES WILLIAM, b. Nov. 1, 1822; m. Caroline S. Longard, April 30, 1849; 3 children.
ii JOHN CLARK, b. May 10, 1824; m. Mary Alice, daughter of Stephen Morine, 1856; 8 children.
iii LEANDER, b. Jan. 13, 1827; d. young.
iv HARRIET A., b. April 7, 1828; m. Bayard W. Borden; 12 children.
v CHARLES H., b. Feb. 16, 1830; m. Mary Elizabeth, daughter of Joseph Berry of Danvers, 1851; 9 children; lived in Milton, Mass., a few years; then Wolfville, N. S., and to Milton again since 1880.
vi EDWIN, b. July 21, 1831; d. about 1845.
vii CHARLOTTE, b. July 26, 1833; m. Charles H. Borden, 1854; 13 children.
viii LEWIS, b. March 8, 1835; m. Emeline Harris, July 4, 1855; 5 children; lives at Ashmont, Mass.
ix EMMA L., b. Sept. 3, 1836; m. John Stewart, Jan. 16, 1856; 12 children.
x MARCY, b. March 28, 1838; m. Lysander Freeman; Edwin G., son of John C., a carpenter, Milton.

31. viii. John Jefferson Woodworth (Elias, John, Silas, Ichabod, Benjamin, Walter, Walter), b. in Granville, N. S., 1810; m. Sarah Ann McKenzie (William, Alex.), about 1838, and lived at Litchfield, near Delap's Cove, 4 or 5 miles from Annapolis, about 50 years, an honest, industrious citizen, and a pious, earnest minister of Jesus Christ in the Advent church. His family being all grown up and settled, he moved to Bear River about 1890, and he d. there May, 1893.

CHILDREN.

i WILLIAM CAREY, b. 1840; a singing teacher and dealer in organs; m. Eunice Litch (Dea. John, Manasseh), and had (1) James Arthur, b. 1860. (2) William Ernest, b. 1862. (3) Rebecca Alice, b. 1865. (4) Pythias Damon, b. 1867. (5) Mary Ann, b. 1869. (6) Sarah Jefferson, b. 1871. (7) Eunice L., b. 1873; d. 1892. (8) John Carey, b. 1876, and (9) Corning Litch, b. 1878.
ii ADONIRAM JUDSON, b. 1841; m. Elsie, daughter of Baxter Condon; one son, William.
iii SARAH ANN, b. 1843; d. about 1850.
iv ELIAS, b. 1846; m. Mary Ann, daughter of Henry Halliday; 8 children.
v REV. STEPHEN, m. daughter of Elijah Fitch; Rockland, Me., one son, Campbell, and d. 1894.
vi ALICE, d. at about 25; good singer and Christian.

   vii Rev. James Albert, b. 1854; d. 1877.
  viii Pythias, d. at 16; a good Christian.
   ix John E., m. Bertha, daughter of Thomas Baxter.

In Dec., 1863, 5 British soldiers started from St. John, N. B., in an open boat for Eastport, to join the Union Army, but the wind was contrary, and blew them across the Bay of Fundy, and they came ashore at Delap's Cove, nearly drowned, and nearly frozen to death. Capt. Wm. C. Woodworth took them in, thawed, warmed, fed, and new-clothed them. As soon as they were missed from St. John notice was sent to Annapolis and the police placed on their track. Being a little suspicious they hurried down to Digby Gap, got another boat, slipped away, got over to Eastport, and actually entered the U. S. service. Mr. Woodworth was afraid of censure, but was exonerated.

32. viii. John Burton Woodworth (Dan, Solomon, Silas), b. 1798; m. Eunice A. Calkin (Nathaniel, Jeremiah); she d. May 16, 1828, aged 25; he m. 2d, Martha Knox, May 18, 1831; she d. Nov. 6, 1860, aged 50; he m. 3d, Louise Lugrin; he joined the Baptist church in Halifax in 1841, and was a good and useful member of society through life. He went to Freeport, Ill., and d. 1869; 3d wife d.

CHILDREN.

   i Mary Olivia, b. 1826; m. Silas R. Curry (Jacob B., Richard), 1853; to Boston, 1856; live in Chelsea; 6 children
  ii Martha Louise, b, 1836; m. Robert Rayne; had 2 daughters. She is a popular writer, authoress, reporter, etc., in Detroit, Mich.
 iii Robert Knox, b. 1851; m. Anna ———, La Salle, Ill.
 iv Florence L., b. 1853.
  v Bertie, b. 1866; m. William S. Giles.
 vi Dudley, b. 1868; Dixon, Ill.

33. viii. Guilford Dudley, brother to the above, b. 1800; m. Betsy Condon; had 2 daughters; Betsy d.; he m. 2d. Lucy Grant; she d. 1834; he m. 3d, Selina, daughter of John and Maria (Marshall) Corbit; had 2 children; she d.; he m. 4th, Sarah Nichols; one daughter; he d. since 1870.

CHILDREN.

  i Amanda, m. Gordon Calkins; she d. soon; he m. 2d, Eliza Caldwell, and d. 1869, leaving 4 children.
 ii Ermina, m. John Strong.

ALLIED FAMILIES. cclxv

iii AMANDA, m. George E. Pineo; 7 children.
iv GUILFORD D., m.; off to Oregon; 3 children.
v ERMINA, home with her mother.

34. viii. Eleazer Woodworth (William, Eleazer, Silas, etc.) b. in Cornwallis, N. S., July 21, 1817; taught school and traded some while a young man; m. Susan Adams (James, John), Nov. 16, 1842, and with his father moved to Hampton, 1846; she d. Sept. 19, 1848, aged 27; he m. 2d, Mary Matilda Hall (John, John, William), Feb. 22, 1849; she d. in Lynn, Mass., Nov. 13, 1890, aged 69.

CHILDREN.

i WILLIAM EDWARD, b. Aug. 11, 1843; m. Lois Amanda Miller (James E., James, Michael), Aug. 12, 1873, and had Arche, Maborne, and Mabel; live in Salem, Mass., where Mr. Woodworth is a first rate engineer.
ii LUCY C., b. April 19, 1845; m.
iii CAPT. JAMES E., b. Feb. 27, 1847; m. Alice, daughter of Edmund and Azuba (Foster) Pack, and live in Vancouver; she d. Jan., 1894.
iv JOHN A., b. Sept. 24, 1850; drowned Sept. 7, 1853.
v SYLVESTER W., b. May 31, 1853; m. Sarah Jane, daughter of Gideon and Maria (daughter of Elijah and Abbie (Ash) Taylor) Bent, Dec. 24, 1878, and had a triplet b.
{ Ina
{ Ida } April 16, 1880; the first one d. July 27; the 2d one June, 1889.
{ Isa P.
vi ELLEN, b. April 18, 1856; m. William Black, Lynn, 1881.
vii JOHN H., b. July 9, 1858; d. July 28.
viii EMELINE A., b. Dec. 21, 1860; m. Thomas Knowles, March 20, 1887; live in Lynn.
ix CATHARINE ROSE, b. June 6, 1864; in Lynn.

35. viii. Enoch Harding Woodworth, a brother, b. March 3, 1823; m. Hannah Croscup (Benjamin, John, Ludowick), Aug. 26, 1849, and have lived at Hampton and Upper Granville; farmers.

CHILDREN.

i JAMES WILLIAM, b. May 14, 1851; m. Ruth Loomer, June 19, 1881; live in Revere, Mass. Children: Emma Mary, and Walter Stanley.
ii CHARLES M., b. Nov. 21, 1852, m. Lizzie Elliott, Nov., 1880.
iii BENJAMIN C., b. Feb. 9, 1855; d. Feb., 1874, smallpox.
iv ANN ELIZA, b. March 13, 1858; d. Jan., 1874, smallpox.
v A. SPURGEON, b. June 23, 1860; La Grange, Ohio.
vi HANNAH JANE, b. May 3, 1862; d. May 7, 1866.

vii MARY PRATT, b. Sept. 10, 1863; Chelsea, Mass.
viii ENOCH H., b. March 3, 1868.

36. viii. William R. Woodworth (Richard, Eleazer, Silas, etc.), b. July 15, 1832; m. Matilda Parish (Joel, Joel, Joel), Dec. 3, 1856, and lives in Cornwallis; farmer.

CHILDREN.

i FRED ELMORE, b. Jan. 28, 1858; m. Etta Brown, Sept. 3, 1884.
ii CLARA OLIVIA, b. Feb. 20, 1860; m. Arthur Parish, June 16, 1879.
iii REBECCA AGNES, b. Oct. 31, 1863; m. Neil P. McQuarrie, Oct. 1, 1888.
iv MARGARET ANN, b. Feb. 20, 1866; m.
v LALEAH ALBERTA, b. Dec. 13, 1869; m. Edwin West, 1894.
vi FANNIE AMELIA, b. Dec. 19, 1872; d. Aug. 16, 1873.

37. viii. Ezra Woodworth (James, Edward, Eleazer, Silas), b. July 7, 1842, at Bear River, Annapolis county, N. S.; learned to be a carpenter from his father; went to Bayham, Ont., 1862, and there has the farm his father bought; m. Harriet Raymond (Levi, William), May 18, 1864.

CHILDREN.

i HERCULES, b. Feb. 2, 1865.
ii HIRAM, b. July 23, 1866.
iii LLOYD, b. Jan. 8, 1868; d. Sept. 16, 1869.
iv GEORGE, b. Oct. 8, 1869.
v MINNA GERTRUDE, b. April 3, 1873.

Of the 67 original grantees to the township of Cornwallis, N. S., in 1761, were Amasa, Benjamin, Silas, Thomas, and William Woodworth. The lineage of the first three has been well defined, and now comes the fourth:

38. iv. Elihu Woodworth (Hezekiah, Thomas, Walter), b. July 24, 1700; m. Silence Stoughton, March 6, 1727, and d. Sept., 1780.

CHILDREN.

i MARY, b. 1727. ii HANNAH, b. 1729.
iii SYBIL, b. 1731. iv THOMAS, b. 1734.
v STEPHEN, b. 1736. vi DEBORAH, b. 1738.
vii NAOMI, b. 1741. viii SARAH, b. 1744.

39. v. Thomas (Elihu, Hezekiah, etc.), b. in Little Compton, R. I., Aug. 3, 1734; m. Judith Briggs, Sept. 12, 1755, and settled in

Falmouth, N. S.; she d. April 4, 1762, aged 27. He m. 2d, Margaret McCurdy, June 12, 1762, and d.

CHILDREN.

i Job, b. 1757.
ii Betsey, b. 1759.
iii John, b. 1764.
iv Paul, b. 1765.
v Thomas, b. 1767.
vi Stephen, b. 1769.
vii Benjamin, b. 1770.
viii Joseph, b. 1772.
ix Mary, b. 1774.
x Alexander, b. 1779.
xi Isaac, b. 1781.

Those of Colchester county, N. S., are descendants of these.

40. iv. William Woodworth (Daniel, Isaac, Walter), b. in Norwich, Conn., Oct. 8, 1732; m. Sarah ———; had 3 children in Lebanon, Conn., then went to Nova Scotia; she d. Nov. 10, 1767, aged 31.

CHILDREN.

i Betty, b. Sept. 13, 1753; m. James Smith, Jr., May 14, 1772, Newport, R. I.
41 ii William, b. Aug. 3, 1755.
iii Timothy, b. Aug. 7, 1758.
iv Alexander, b. July 19, 1760.
v Leonard, b. Feb. 4, 1763.
vi Bruneh, b. March 25, 1765.
vii Lemuel, b. Feb. 2, 1767.

41. v. William Woodworth, Jr., b. Lebanon, Conn., Aug. 3, 1755; m. Marcy Pineo (Peter, James), Jan. 8, 1778, in Cornwallis, N. S., and d. about 1838. Aunt Marcy d. about 1814.

CHILDREN.

i Elizabeth, b. Dec. 16, 1779; d. March 16, 1784.
ii Sarah, b. Jan. 27, 1782; m. Henry DeForest, and had (1) Eliza; m. Caleb Hersey. (2) Sarah B., b. 1809; m. William Harned; 6 children, and d. 1868; he d. March, 1890, aged 86; daughter Anna M., b. 1835, m. James Freeman Rogers, Jamaica Plain, Mass. Sarah m. 2d, Benjamin Weaver, and had Jane E., b. 1826; m. John E. Kennedy, and d. Aug. 21, 1882. Mrs. Weaver d. 1838.
iii Peter, b, Dec. 23, 1783; m. Mary, daughter of Robert and Mehitable Kinsman, Dec. 20, 1810, and d. 1877; had (1) Ephraim, d. in Milwaukee, 1893. (2) James, m.; 3 sons, and d. in Milwaukee spring of 1893. (3) Marcy, m. Jehiel Pineo; 2 sons. (4) John M., b. 1822; m. Love E. Margeson (John, Gideon), 1851; 8 children; to Bos-

ton 1864, and d. Oct. 5, 1888. The widow lives with son, John Davenport, b. 1851.

iv JAMES, b. Dec. 23, 1785; m., and lived at Canning, N. S.; d. of lockjaw.

v MATTHEW, b. Jan. 8, 1788; blacksmith at Woodside; d. about 1833.

vi ELIZABETH, b. June 5, 1790; m. Nathan Palmeter, and had James, Oliver, William, Eunice, Waity, Gideon, and Mercy; Cornwallis, N. S.

vii BECCA, b. 1793; m. Dennison Haynes, and had Henry A., James H., Mercy L., Gideon C., Sarah R., Dennison J., Leonard, Gideon C., Mary R., and William J. in Norridgewock, Me. His lineage: Dennison[5], Jonathan[4], Joseph[3], Thomas[2], Jonathan[1], b. in England 1661; over 1634; killed by Indians at Haverhill, 1698.

viii LEONARD, b. 1794 (?); m. Lavinia, dau. of Dr. Jason Mack, and had Maria M., Lucy, William, James, Rebecca, and Lovina; Jay, Me.

ix WILLIAM, b. 1796 (?); m. Mary Hersey, and had Mary, James, Amelia, and Ephraim; Pembroke, Me.

x MARCY, b. May 3, 1798; m. Charles Morton (Lemuel, Elkanah, Elkanah, Ephraim, George, Ephraim, George, from England in the *Ann*, 1623), Nov. 6, 1816, and d. Nov. 15, 1883; he d. Feb. 9, 1868, aged 79. Children; (1) Mary Ann, b. 1817; d. 1820. (2) Mary Ann, b. 1821; m. James Edward Beckwith (Handley, John, James, Matthew, Matthew), 1841; 7 children; Kentville. (3) Lemuel Guy, b. 1823; m. Nancy Foot; 5 children. (4) William Charles, b. 1826; m. Sarah A. Bowles; 2d, Eliza Beggs. (5) Martha Alice, b. 1828; m. William Hen Wood (William, Ephraim, Oliver); 6 children, Danvers, Mass. (6) John Leander, b. 1831; m. Almira Quinn; 6 children. (7) Rebecca Ardelice, b. 1834; m. Leander Crocker; 8 children. (8) Sarah Elizabeth, b. 1836; m. Benjamin Daniels; 2d, John L. Stephens.

xi RUBY, b. 1800 (?); m. Odiorne Lovejoy (Nathaniel, Abial), and d. 1885; he d. 1847, aged 52. They had Mary Ann, Sarah Percy (b. 1828; m. Ezra L. Hersey, in East Boston), Lucretia Maria, William Odiorne, Charles Norman, Leonard Hiram, James Loren, Amanda Elizabeth, Ruby Melvina, Henry Augustus, and 2 daughters d. in infancy; Calais, Me.

xiii AMY, b. 1802 (?); m. Adna Leighton, and had Amy, Leah, Sarah, Ellen, Lorenzo, and ——; Pembroke, Me.

42 xiii OLIVER, b. 1804.

42. vi. Oliver Woodworth (William, William, Daniel, Isaac, Walter), b. Cornwallis, N. S., 1804; m. Isabel, daughter of Robert O'Brien; d. Dec. 10, 1858, aged 55; m. 2d, Eunice, daughter of William Lyons, and d. April 10, 1884, Cornwallis, N. S. Children by first wife:

ALLIED FAMILIES.

i SAMUEL, b. 1827; m. Evaline, daughter of John Balcomb; 7 children, and d. 1885.
ii WILLIAM, b. 1829; d. 1854.
iii JAMES, b. 1830; m. Abbie, daughter of Thomas Johnson, Noel, Hants county, N. S.
iv Sarah, b. 1832; m. Henry Mitchell, and d. Dec., 1857; he m. 2d, —— Weaver.
v ISABEL, b. 1834; m. John B., son of James Best.
vi ROBERT, b. 1836; m. Abbie, daughter of Ralph Russell.
vii LUCY, b. 1838; m. Gordon, son of Andrew Forsyth.
viii THOMAS O., b. Feb. 4, 1841; m. Emma S. J. Hurd (George, Jonathan), 1865; to Malden, 1889; 5 children.
ix RICHARD WATSON, b. Oct., 1842; m. Lydia, daughter of Capt. and Dea. Amos Scott.
x MERCY, b. and d. in infancy.
xi ANNA REBECCA, b. 1850; m. Daniel, son of James Best, 1867 (daughter Eva m. Melbourn Marshall); m. 2d, George Riggs, a soldier, and live in Revere, Mass.

43. iv. Thomas Woodworth (Isaac, Isaac, Walter), b. in Norwich, Conn., July 17, 1726; m. July 9, 1750, Zerviah Fox; went to Nova Scotia, 1760, with many others from Conn. and R. I.; settled at Falmouth, and drew lot 31; she d. June 30, 1767, aged 41. He m. 2d, Jan. 26, 1769, Sarah Shaw; d. He m. 3d, Jan. 15, 1781, Mary Rand; she d. April 28, 1789; he d.

CHILDREN.

i ELIZABETH, b. June 2, 1753; m. Stephen, son of David and Deborah Eaton, Nov. 23, 1775; 10 children, and d. March 28, 1841; he d. April 20, 1838, aged 84.
44 ii OLIVER, b. Jan. 19, 1756.
iii HULDAH, b. Oct. 11, 1758; m. Oct. 25, 1781, Timothy Eaton, brother to Stephen; 7 children, and d. July 14, 1807; he m. 2d, Sarah (Rand) Beckwith.
iv Nathan, b. June 10, 1762; d. Feb. 8, 1784.
v LEVI, b. Feb. 11, 1767; m. Lydia, daughter of Asa and Sarah Clark, Feb. 27, 1794, and had Thomas D., George, Lydia M., Jerusha, and Levi Charles.

44. v. Oliver Woodworth (Thomas, Isaac, Isaac, Walter), b. in Norwich, Conn., June 19, 1756; m. Rube Pineo (Peter, James), April 25, 1782; m. 2d, Ellis, daughter of Asahel and Lucy Bentley, Sept. 7, 1819.

CHILD.

45 i NATHAN, b. June 16, 1785.

45. vi. Nathan Woodworth (Oliver, Thomas, Isaac, Isaac, Walter), b. June 16, 1785; m. Sarah, daughter of Dr. William and

Ruth (Sheffield) Baxter, Feb. 24, 1807; she d. April 16, 1830, aged 45; he m. 2d, Julia Baxter, her sister, and d. July 22, 1866, aged 81.

CHILDREN.

    i   WILLIAM OLIVER, b. July 18, 1808; was deformed, a hunchback; d. about 1850.
    ii   PRUDENCE RUTH, b. June 8, 1810; d. Aug. 31, 1818.
46 iii   BENJAMIN BAXTER, b. May 15, 1812.
    iv   RUTH, b. May 15, 1814; m. John Cox.
    v   DOUGLASS, b. Aug. 5, 1817; d. Jan. 6, 1818.
    vi   RUBY, b. June 1, 1819; m. Newton Cox.
    vii   DOUGLASS N., b. Feb. 19, 1821; m. Assenath, daughter of Nathan Ells, Jan. 30, 1852.
    viii   SARAH ELLIS, b. about 1824; m. Levi W. Eaton, as his 2d wife, July 28, 1851, and had Mary Eliza, b. 1852; Annie Maud, b. 1858, and Nathan Woodworth, b. 1860.

46. vii. Benjamin Baxter Woodworth (Nathan, Oliver, Thomas, Isaac, Isaac, Walter), b. in Cornwallis, N. S., May 15, 1812; m. Eunice L. Pineo (George D., Daniel, Peter, James), March 6, 1834; she d. April 17, 1841, aged 27; he m. 2d, Prudence M. Pineo, her sister; she d. Nov. 10, 1868, aged 52; he m. 3d, Mahala Kinsman, widow of Bishop Fuller. Dea. B. B. W. d.

CHILDREN.

    i   MARIA, b. Jan. 19, 1835; m. Oct. 28, 1862, Ezekiel B. Harris of Canning; 5 children.
    ii   JOSEPH EDWARD, b. April 26, 1837; m. May 3, 1859; Nancy Cox; 2 or 3 children.
    iii   EUNICE ELIZA, b. Feb. 26, 1839; m. Oct. 28, 1868, Joseph Edwin, son of Levi W. Eaton, and moved to Hanson, Mass., 1873; 6 children.
    iv   DOUGLASS BENJAMIN, b. June 1, 1841; m. Elizabeth, daughter of Ezra Churchill of Hantsport, Feb. 28, 1864. He was elected to the Nova Scotia Parliament, from Kings county, in 1871, defeating D. M. Dickie of Canning, and continued a member till 1878, when he opposed Dr. F. W. Borden and was defeated. In June, 1882, he was elected to the Dominion Parliament (Dr. Borden opposing him), and continued a member till the general election of 1887. He has been a barrister 25 years' and Queen's Counsel 5 years, office at Halifax. They have two sons, Percy Churchill, and Joseph Edward.
    v   GEORGE WHITEFIELD, b. Feb. 14, 1846; m. Mary E., daughter of Ezra Churchill; m. 2d, Sarah, daughter of Daniel and Lucinda (Westcoat) Allen, of Long Island, N. S.; 4 children.

ALLIED FAMILIES.   cclxxi

 vi Sarah Rebecca, b. March 24, 1847; m. James N. Wilde, and d. Dec., 1884; one daughter Sarah W.
 vii Mary Louisa, b. Nov. 18, 1849; m. James E., son of Rev. James Hennigar; 5 children.
 viii Prudence, b. May 7, 1852; m. Isaac B. Ells, and d. in Truro, April 3, 1890; 1 child.
 ix Nathan D., b. Dec. 7, 1856; d. Nov. 23, 1858.
 x Effie Clare, b. Jan. 26, 1871.
 xi Alice L. B., b. Feb. 19, 1873.
 xii Benjamin Baxter, b. April 15, 1875.

Samuel C. Woodworth, the poet (Benjamin and Abigail Bryant, Benjamin and Hannah Cudworth, Benjamin and Ann Torrey, Robert and Bethia, Benjamin and Deborah, Walter), b. in Scituate, 1784; learned printing in Boston; d. in New York, 1842. He was a Swedenborgian, and wrote many hymns and poems that were gathered and published in two volumes after his death. Vol. I commences with "The Old Oaken Bucket," written in 1817; Vol. II commences with "The Hunters of Kentucky," written about 1820.

WORCESTER.

1. i. Rev. William Worcester came over from England and settled in Salisbury, Mass, a few miles up the Merrimack river from Newburyport, in 1639. His wife Sarah d. April 23, 1650; he m. 2d, Mrs. Rebecca Hall of Ipswich, July 23, 1650, and d. Oct. 28, 1662, aged 58. She had m. Henry Bylie before; John Hall, 1641; and 4th, Dep. Gov. Samuel Symonds, and d. at Ipswich, Feb. 21, 1695, aged 78. Gov. Symonds d. 1678, aged 83.

CHILDREN.

 2 i Samuel, b. in England.
  ii Susanna, b. in England; m. Thomas Stacy, 1653, and had Thomas, William, Rebecca, Elizabeth, Joseph, and Mary.
  iii William, b. in England; m. Constant ——; had 6 children; 5 b. in Boston; he d. 1683. No descendants left.
  iv Sarah, b. in England; d. in Salisbury, April 1, 1641.
  v Sarah, b. in Salisbury, Mass; d. April 4, 1641.
  vi Timothy, b. Salisbury, May 14, 1642; m. Susanna ——; he was a mariner, left 2 daughters, and d. 1672; she m. 2d, Henry Ambrose.
  vii Moses, b. Nov. 10, 1643; went to Kittery, Me., before 1675, and was living in 1731. He was a famous hunter of Indians, and went by the appelation of "Old Con-

trary." He m. —— ——, and had Thomas, William, and Elizabeth; he m. 2d, Mrs. Sarah Soper.
- viii SARAH, b. June 22, 1646; d. March 9, 1650.
- ix ELIZABETH, b. April 9, 1648; d. 1649.
- x ELIZABETH, b. Jan. 9, 1650.

2. ii. Samuel Worcester (Rev. William), b. in England about 1632, and settled in Salisbury, Mass.; was a partner in a sawmill. He bought land in Newbury bordering on the Merrimack river, etc. He m. Elizabeth (b. in Rowley, May 1, 1640), daughter of Francis Parrott, Nov. 29, 1859; he was a pious man, and was found dead in the road, near Lynn, in the act of kneeling, Feb., 1681.

CHILDREN.

- i WILLIAM, b. July 21, 1661; m. Martha Cheney (Peter, John), 1690; 7 children, and d. 1706; she m. 2d, John Pemberton of Bradford, 1710, and d. 1729.
- ii SAMUEL, b. March 31, 1663; d. July 5, 1686.
- 3 iii FRANCIS, b. about 1665; m. Mary Cheney.
- iv JOSEPH, b. about 1667; m. Sarah ——, 1728; m. 2d, Martha Palmer, 1730, and d.; she m. 2d, Eldad Cheney.
- v TIMOTHY, b. in Rowley, June 4, 1669; m. Huldah Cheney (Peter, John), 1692; 2 children, Samuel and Lydia, and d. 1706; she m. 2d, Simon Daykin of Concord, 1718.
- vi MOSES, b. Jan. 15, 1671; d. Dec. 18, 1689.
- vii ELIZABETH, b. Feb. 16, 1672.
- viii DOROTHY, b. Jan. 21, 1674.
- ix JOHN, b. Aug. 31, 1677; d. 1701.
- x EBER, b. April 29, 1679; in Bradford.
- xi SUSANNAH, b. Feb. 11, 1681.

3. iii. Francis Worcester (Samuel, Rev. William), b. in Rowley about 1665; was an inn-holder and yeoman in Bradford, and was represented as an amiable and pious man; m. Mary Cheney (Peter, John), of Newbury, 1690, and d. Dec. 17, 1717; she m. 2d, Dec. 8, 1726, Joseph Eaton of Salisbury, and d. 1759, aged 88.

CHILDREN.

- i HANNAH, b. Feb. 8, 1692; m. Jacob Hardy, March 3, 1714.
- 4 ii TIMOTHY, b. Dec. 6, 1693.
- iii JEMIMA, b. Jan. 16, 1696; m. John Boynton of Newbury, 1717.
- 5 iv REV. FRANCIS, b. June 7, 1698.
- v JOHN, b. Nov. 5, 1700; m. Mary Carlton, 1727; 5 children; he was selectman, assessor, etc.; d. in Grafton, about 1777.

ALLIED FAMILIES. cclxxiii

vi Daniel, b. Feb. 19, 1703; m. Joanna Pettingall of Salisbury, and lived in Bradford, Newbury, and Haverhill; 3 children.
vii William, b. Nov. 13, 1706; m. Mary Hovey of Bradford, 1733; lived in Bradford, Newbury, and Falmouth, Me.; d. 1788
viii Benjamin, b. Aug. 25, 1709; m. Hannah Simmons of Haverhill, 1732; 9 childern; lived in Haverhill, Methuen, Nottingham West, and Groton; d. 1780.
ix James, b. Sept. 15, 1712; m. Patience Low, 1740; Falmouth, Me.
x Mary, b. Dec. 22, 1714; m. Josiah French of Salisbury, 1736.

4. iv. Timothy Worcester (Francis, Samuel, Rev. William), b. in Bradford, Dec. 6, 1693; m. Mary ——, and lived in Bradford and Newbury till 1728; then to Falmouth — afterward called Portland — Me., where he d. 1751.

CHILDREN.

i Dorothy, b. in Newbury, Oct. 10, 1719.
ii Josiah, b. Jan. 3, 1721; m. Miriam, daughter of John and Elizabeth (?) Carr, Dec. 13, 1748; a daughter Mary b. 1750. He d. about that time, and she went to Portland, Me., and m. Curtis Chute (Thomas, James, James, Lionel), 1754. See No. 9.
iii Rebecca, b. Oct. 8, 1722; d. Aug. 27, 1723.
iv Hannah, b. June 11, 1724.
v Timothy, b. Oct. 26, 1725.

5. iv. Rev. Francis Worcester, brother to Timothy, b. June 8, 1698; m. Abigail Carlton of Rowley, April 18, 1720; lived in Bradford till 1722; lived in Concord and Littleton, some years in both places; a blacksmith; then in Bradford 1728, a selectman; then in Boxford he was licensed to preach; then he went to Sandwich, where he was ordained June 18, 1735, over a Congregational church, where he remained 10 years. Then he moved to Exeter, N. H., Plaistow and Hollis, N. H., 1750. From this time to his death, Oct. 14, 1783, he spent the greater part of his time preaching as an evangelist in destitute parts of New Hampshire and other sections of New England. In 1758-9, he wrote a series of "Meditations all in verse," which was published in Boston, 1760. Joseph Emerson Worcester, LL.D. (1784-1866), author of the dictionary and other works, was a great-grandson as follows: Rev. Francis[4], Noah[5], b. 1735; Jesse[6], b. 1761; Joseph E[7]. Rev. Samuel Worcester, D D. (1770-1821), author of a hymn-book and other works, was a grandson as follows: Noah[5], Samuel[6].

CHILDREN.

i FRANCIS, b. March 30, 1721; m. Hannah Boynton of Newbury, Oct. 28, 1741; 12 children, and d. at Plymouth, N. H., 1800; she d. 1771.

ii JESSE, b. Sept. 5, 1722; m. Patience ———; 4 children. He was at the seige of Oswego, and d. a prisoner in Montreal, 1757, among the French.

iii HANNAH, b. Oct. 7, 1724; m. ——— Churchill and d. 1808.

iv SAMUEL, b. in Boxford, May 3, 1731; drowned in Squam Harbor, 1750.

v NOAH, b. in Sandwich, Oct. 4, 1735; m. Lydia, daughter of Abram Taylor of Hollis (1733–1772), 1757; 7 children; m. 2d, Hepzibah Sherwin (1746–1831); 9 children. He succeeded his father in the homestead at Hollis, and d. Aug. 13, 1817, aged 82.

ADDITIONS AND CORRECTIONS TO THE ALLIED FAMILIES.

Henry Adams,[4] first over to Braintree, son of Wm.,[3] Richard,[2] John.[1]

On page xiii, to Dea. Hall add Joseph.

Near the bottom of page, the words "Balcomb: three children," should follow Reuben, end of the next line.

On page xiv, Win, in a parenthesis, should be William, just below middle of the page, No. 193, should follow James Wm. Chute.

On page xvii, I believe that Nat. Barnes was brother to Seth Barns (John, Jonathan, John of Plymouth, Mass., 1631), who came over to Yarmouth, N. S., 1762.

On page xviii, near the bottom the words "from Ireland," should be after James Ray, not Joseph.

On page xix, Thomas Milbury, m. Phebe, da. of Joseph Saunders (b. in Salem, Mass., 1724, went to Yarmouth, N. S., 1762. A brother of his named Timothy settled in Kings Co., N. S., about the same time.

On page xxvii, Mrs. Hope Chipman, d. 1683, a. 54.

On page xxviii, first line, Hosea Joyce m. 1st, Martha (who d. 1670), and had John and Dorcas; he m. 2d, 1675, had three children and d. 1712. John Huckins d. in 1678, leaving three children. His w. m. 2d, Jonathan, son of Dea. Henry Cobb. John Sargent, son of Wm. d. 1730, a. 76. Shubael Dimock, d. early, and Bethiah m. 2nd Tabitha Lathrop. Mrs. Desire Bourne, d. 1705. Mary Chipman, or Mercy, b. 1692; m. Nathaniel Jackman. Her bro. Joseph, was born 1694, Jacob m. Abigail; m. 2nd, Bethiah Thomas. Hannah d. 1763.

On page xxix, near the top, John Chipman, m. Hannah Fessenden. Of Perez Chipman his descendants are in Del. Carolina, and Miss. Ebenezer, m. Mary ——, and lived at Falmouth (Portland?). After Rebecca, was Benjamin. Dea. Sam. Chipman,[3] m. John Hinckley, jr.,[2] John Hinckley, sen.,[1] was Gov. of Conn.

On page xxxii, Handley Chipman, m. Anne Hoyt,[7] (Jesse,[6] James,[5] James,[4] Zerubbabel,[3] Walter,[2] Simon[1]), 1814, and d. 1858, a. 74. She d. 1856, a. 72.

On page xxxvi, end of Thomas D. Chipman's family should be Agnes Jane, b. April 24, 1854, teacher in Yarmouth.

On page xlvii, middle of the page "James Edward," Manning is one name.

On page l, for Park, read Pack, same on page lvi.

On page lii, for 1838, read 1638.

On page liii, Thompson Wood, was brother to Mary, who m. James Chute jr.

On page liv, near the bottom, for Jacob, b. 1657, read 1757.

On page lviii, Hannah, w. of Edward W. Foster, had six children and d. Taunton, Mass., about 1887.

On page lxv, Ruby Ann Maccaboy, d. 1893. Dudley Foster d. July 1894.

On page lxxii, for Port Buswell, read Port Burwell.

On page lxxviii, the sons of Bart. Hains seems to be about right; but farther on they seem to be rather "mixed."

ALLIED FAMILIES.

On page lxxix, for Hawkinson read Hankinson.

On page lxxxi, Pines read Pineo. At middle of the page Capt. Sam. (son of Thomas) Hains, was run down in the Gulf of Mexico, in 1856 or '57, and lost with two children. Capt. Sam. Y. Hains, at the bottom, d. at home, June 29, '92, a. 85. Tamer Budd, da. of Chas. Hains lived at Marlboro, Mass., instead of Gloucester. Of the family of John Hains, (1), Augustus, was b. 1824; (2), Capt. Sam Young. '27. (3), Lydia, b. 1830; (4), Eliza Ann, 1834, d. 1872; (5), Edward S., b. 1838. (6), Annie S., b. 1844. Capt. John Daniels, d. Oct. 31, '70, a. 28.

On page cix near the top for Felugus read Telugus.

On page cxvii, near the bottom Wm. F. Marshall, m. 2nd, Eliza Shamper, 1892.

On page cxix, under Levi Marshall, instead of she d. ab. 1830, say 1840; he m. 2nd, 1847; she d. 1884. James M. Marshall m. 2nd, Freelove Bruce; Henry Marshall m. 1st, Ann Morton; Edward M. Marshall, m. 2nd, Ruth (Beatty) McGonnagle; 3rd, Ella Bancroft.

On page cxx, after Benj. Ellis, d. ab, 1838. Abba Bell, d. Apr. 6, 1894. Instead of "Mt. Serrat," read son Jabeth at Magnolia, Mass.

On page cxxi, James Marshall, d. in N. Y., Dec. 24, 1892. Alfred lives in Bridgetown, Wm. Marshall, 15, iii, lived at Marshalltown. Farther down, Christiana Marshall, m. 2nd Allen Clark; 3d, Mich. Gilliatt. Joshua Messenger, m. Emma McNeil. Daniel Hall should be David Hall and Capt. Wm. Hall is a blunder. James Moody, d. in N. Y., 1892, a. 80. Shaw Marshall lives at Newburyport.

On page cxxiv, after Enoch Marshall, read son Eben in Beverley.

On page cxxvi, below the middle, for David Waterhouse read Daniel Waterhouse.

On page cxxxii, below the middle, Richard B. Morse, d. in Marblehead, Mar. '94. Fannie, w. of Rev. J. C. Morse, was da. of Edward Dakin.

On page cxxxiii, Capt. E. M. Morse, m. 2nd, Lucretia Croscup, w. of Capt. Isaiah Delap June 1894.

On page cxl, in the family of Theodore Palmer, after John L. (iv), b. 1792, should be (v), Edmund F., b. 1794; (vi), Rachel, b. 1796; (vii), Mary b. 1799.

On page clxiv, for Isaac, William, read Isaac Wm., one name.

On page cxlvi, Lydia Benjamin,[6] (Obed,[5] Obed,[4] Joseph,[3] Joseph,[2] John,[1] over in the ship Lyon 1632, d. 1645).

On page clvii, near the bottom for Mr. Soulice m. 2nd read 3d, for his 1st, wife was Eliza Potter, see page cliii.

On page clviii, Dea. Jas. Purdy,[6] (Anthony,[5] Gabriel,[4] Sam,[3] Francis,[2] Francis,[1] d. at Fairfield, Ct., 1658). For Artemesa Brown read Artamesa. The last two of that family, John and Maggie A., were Rices.

On page clix. John Randall, jr., lived since 1720. Of the six children of his son Ichabod, Green, the 4th m. Lydia Rand, 1779, had eight children; she d. 1857.

On page clxi, Matt. Randall, d. 1736; his w. d. ab. 1735. Peter, m. in 1706. Stephen Randall, m. Abigail, da. of Jos. Sabin, 1697.

On page clxii, at the bottom, after Job, m. 2nd, Mary, da. of William Parker, Esq., read she m. 2nd, Dea Joseph Wade, the centenarian.

On page clxiii, Rev. Henry Saunders, was the son of Timothy jr. Timothy sen., was brother to Joseph, who went to Yarmouth, N. S., from Salem, Mass., 1762.

ALLIED FAMILIES.

On page clxiii, at the middle, after Robert Neily, read he m. 2nd, Sophia Morse, see No. 7; m. 3rd, Elisabeth (Goucher) Gates, see Benj. Gates.

On page clxxviii, Timothy Ruggles,[7] m. Jane Thorne,[6] (Edward,[5] Stephen,[4] Joseph,[3] Joseph,[2] William[1]), 1810; his son Tim. D.,[8] m. 1842, Havilah Jane Thorne,[7] (Stephen S.,[6] James,[5] Stephen,[4] etc.)

On page clxxix, for John Gray, read Hughy Gray, page cxix.

On page clxxxvi, after James Gordon, for d. read b.; in the same paragraph for Eben read Eber.

On page cxcii, Mrs. Althea Sanford d. July 1894.

On page cc, for Stephen, Augustus, read Stephen Augustus.

On page ccii, Maj. Gesner d. 1853, a. 97; Col. Henry, his brother d. ab. 1840. Near the bottom, Elihu Eaton, in the parenthesis, should be Elisha.

On page cciii, John Van Buskirk,[7] must be of Garrett,[6] Lawrence,[5] John,[4] Laurens,[3] Laurens,[2] Laurens A.,[1]

On page ccxix, near the bottom, John Van Buskirk must have m. 2nd, Hannah Steadman (John, John).

On page ccxxvi, near the top, Nicholas and Ann, were the first parents of the Robbins family in America.

On page ccxxviii, to Frances and William White, read Parrsboro, N. S.

On page ccxxxiv, Samuel Felch's, son John, m. Licet, da. of Rev. Tho. Delong; another the (5), Love, m. James Parsons. Mr. Felch, m. 2nd, Elizabeth Parker, da. of Major Nat. and w. of Church Morse, and had a da. Eunice Salome, b. 1824, m. Joseph L. McKennee 1843, see Morse.

INDEX TO THE ALLIED FAMILIES.

WITH A FEW COLLATERAL FAMILIES ATTACHED.

Adams, v. Robert of Ipswich three families. Henry of Braintree, five families.

Banks, ix. Richard of Scituate, Mass., and York, Me., eighteen families.

Barnes, xvii. Nathaniel of Nova Scotia, nine families, which are four families of Milbury.

Cheney, xxi. John of Roxbury and Newbury, eighteen families, including that of Thomas and Hannah Dustin to which is attached the family of William Cheney brother to John.

Chipman, xxvii. John of Plymouth and Barnstable, sixteen families.

Cogswell, xxxvii. John of Chebacco, eleven families.

Crouss, xli. John H. of Bear River, N. S., one family.

Farnsworth, xli. Matthias, of Lynn and Groton, thirteen families, with sketchings and tracings of Longley, Ward and Manning.

Foster, lii. Reginald of Ipswich, twenty families, with sketches of Trumbull, Worthing and Roberts and the families of Isaac Phinney and Job Pack.

Gates, lxvi. Stephen of Hingham, twenty families including an item on Gen. Gates of the Revolution.

Hains, lxxvii. Matthew of Long Island, N. Y., twelve families, including sketches of Godfrey Hanes, family of Maj. Robert Timpany and the tracing of Prof. Thomas A. Edison, the great electrician.

Hale, lxxxii. Thomas of Newbury, nine families, with the descent of Nathan, the patriot, from Dea. Robert Hale, brother to Thomas.

Hankinson, lxxxvii. Robert of New Jersey, five families.

Harris, xc. Arthur of Duxbury, nine families, followed by John C. Heterick, and Capt. Henry Harris one family, and Elijah Purdy of each.

Hicks, xcix. Robert of Plymouth, eight families.

Mullin, cv. Peter of Poughkeepsie, N. Y., one family, followed by Dea. David Shook, one family.

McConnell, cv. Benjamin of Long Island, N. Y., seven families.

McKenzie, cxi. Alexander of Granville, N. S., three families, including the family of Joseph Thomas.

Marshall, cxiv. Four brothers to Nova Scotia, nineteen families.

Mayberry, cxxiv. William of Marblehead, six families, with an extra family attached.

Morse, cxxvii. Samuel of Dedham, eighteen families, with two others added, that include the great "telegraph man."

Noyes, cxxxvi. Rev. James and Dea. Nicholas two families of Newbury, to which is added John Knight, one family.

Palmer, cxxxviii. William of Mamaroneck, N. Y., sixteen families.

Parker, cxliv. William, son of Nat., of Shewsbury, Mass., five families.

Potter, cxlvii. Nicholas of Lynn, twenty families including a sketch of Hayden.

Randall, clx. John of Westerly, R. I., fifteen families.

Rice, clxviii. Dea. Edmund of Sudbury, eleven families.

Ruggles, clxxiv. Thomas of Roxbury, nine families.

Sanford, clxxx. John of Boston and Rhode Island, twenty families.

Saxton, cxciv. William of White Plains, N. Y., two families.

Smith, cxcvi. Richard of Ipswich, eight families.

Spurr, cc. Michael of Annapolis, N. S., two families, with one of Lecain.

Steadman, cci. John of Rhode Island, nine families.

Taylor, ccvi. Rev. Edward, of Westfield, Mass., eight families.

Thurston, ccxiii. Daniel of Newbury, Mass., four families.

Van Buskirk, ccxvii. Laurens A. of New York, fourteen families.

Weare, ccxxii. Peter of York, Me., eleven families.

Wheelock, ccxxx. Rev. Ralph, Medfield, eighteen families.

Whitman, ccxli. Dea. John of Weymouth, Mass., six families, with a sketch and tracing of President Abram Lincoln.

Woodworth, ccxliv. Walter of Scituate, Mass., forty-six families.

Worcester, cclxxi. Rev. William of Salisbury, Mass., five families.

CPSIA information can be obtained
at www.ICGtesting.com
Printed in the USA
BVHW081815270319
543869BV00010B/432/P